MARY BERRY'S
complete COOKBOOK

MARY BERRY'S
complete COOKBOOK

LONDON, NEW YORK, MELBOURNE,
MUNICH AND DELHI

Editorial consultant JENI WRIGHT
Art editor BILL MASON
Design development GRADE DESIGN CONSULTANTS
Managing editor GILLIAN ROBERTS
Managing art editor KAREN SAWYER
Category publisher MARY-CLARE JERRAM
DTP designer (London) SONIA CHARBONNIER
DTP coordinator (India) PANKAJ SHARMA
Production controller LOUISE DALY

Revised edition
Photographer EDWARD ALLWRIGHT
Food stylist VICKI SMALLWOOD
Stylist ROSIE HOPPER

First published in Great Britain in 1995
This revised edition published in 2003
by Dorling Kindersley Limited
80 Strand, London WC2R 0RL
Penguin Group (UK)

A CIP catalogue record for this book is available from
The British Library

ISBN-13: 978-1-4053-2013-9
ISBN-10: 1 4053 2013 3

Colour reproduced by Colourscan, Singapore
Printed by Toppan Printing Co. (Shenzhen) Ltd, China

BEFORE MAKING THE RECIPES IN THIS BOOK, PLEASE REFER
TO COOK'S NOTES ON PAGE 525

DISCOVER MORE AT
www.dk.com

CONTENTS

3

SPECIAL MENU INDEX

The index on pages 8–13 is an easy-to-use reference and visual guide to choosing a special dish, whether you are cooking for a celebration, planning a party, or simply looking to expand your culinary repertoire. Some of the menus present a complete main course – Christmas Roast Turkey, for example. Others – as in Fresh Ways with Salmon Fillets – show how to ring the changes on old favourites. There is inspiration from Italy, India, and Japan as well as indulgent treats to satisfy the sweetest tooth. Whichever dish takes your fancy, I hope you will have as much fun choosing as making and eating it.

TAPAS   68

VEGETABLES WITH GARLIC DIPS Boiled or grilled vegetables with spicy or garlic mayonnaises.
TUNA TOSTADOS Toasted garlic breads topped with tuna, tomato, and melting cheese.
CHICK PEA & RED PEPPER SALAD An earthy salad of contrasting textures.
ANDALUCIAN MUSHROOMS Serrano ham brings the taste of Southern Spain to this dish.

PREPARE-AHEAD FIRST COURSES   78

DOUBLE SALMON TIAN Individual fresh salmon and soft-cheese rounds on peppery salad leaves, topped with luxurious smoked salmon.
ASPARAGUS & QUAILS' EGG SALAD An extremely simple starter that always impresses.
SMOKED SALMON TERRINE The richness of the salmon is tempered by low-fat cheese and the snap of creamed horseradish.

SIMPLE FISH SUSHI   134

NIGIRI SUSHI Bite-size mouthfuls of prawn, delicious sticky rice, and fiery wasabi (Japanese horseradish) paste.
HOSO MAKI Rolls of seaweed with vinegared sushi rice, crabmeat, and cucumber.
SUSHI SQUARES WITH SMOKED SALMON A modern interpretation of sushi, topped with palate-cleansing pickled ginger slices.

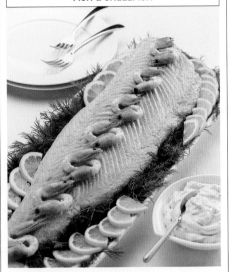

CLASSIC BUFFET PARTY SALMON   144

WHOLE POACHED SALMON A perfect centrepiece for a summer celebration. The fish is poached with black peppercorns, bay leaves, and other aromatics for added flavour, then served cold, with jumbo prawns to garnish, and the traditional accompaniment, fresh dill mayonnaise. Impressive, yet easily made at home.

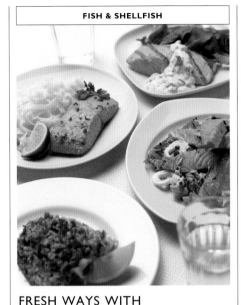

FRESH WAYS WITH SALMON FILLETS 152

GRIDDLED SALMON TRANCHES Served with a crème fraîche and dill sauce.
THAI CHILLI SALMON Spicy salmon fillets with chilli, lime, and a coriander garnish.
WARM HONEYED SALMON SALAD Served with a herbed yogurt dressing.
HERB ROASTED SALMON A breadcrumb, parsley, and cheese topping keeps the fish moist.

CHICKEN & TURKEY SALADS 184

TARRAGON CHICKEN WITH AVOCADO A classic combination enlivened with anchovies, and garnished with peppery watercress.
VIETNAMESE TURKEY SALAD With fish sauce, chilli, mint, and crunchy white cabbage.
RED PEPPER HERBED CHICKEN SALAD A low-fat and colourful salad with a mouthwatering dressing that includes basil and parsley.

MARINATED BARBECUE CHICKEN 196

ORANGE & ROSEMARY CHICKEN Tangy chicken with a colourful and spicy salsa.
FRUITY CORIANDER CHICKEN Aromatic chicken drumsticks with a fresh mango salsa.
YOGURT & MINT CHICKEN A couscous salad with pine nuts complements the Middle Eastern flavours of this dish.

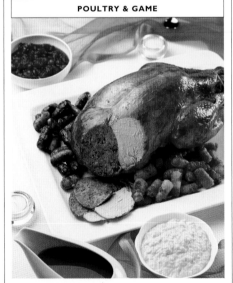

CHRISTMAS ROAST TURKEY 202

GOLDEN ROAST TURKEY A festive feast with all the traditional trimmings – a chestnut, bacon, and pork sausagemeat stuffing, rich gravy, bread sauce flavoured with onion, cloves, bay leaf, and black peppercorns, fruity cranberry sauce, crispy bacon rolls, and chipolata sausages.

CHICKEN & TURKEY STIR FRIES 210

LACQUERED DUCK A new take on a classic dish, sticky, sweet, and satisfying.
CHINESE CHICKEN WITH MANGO Marinated chicken stir-fried with cashew nuts, peppers, pak choi, mushrooms, and mango.
TURKEY TO GO A serve-yourself combination of spiced turkey and red pepper to wrap in warm, soft tortillas – appetizing, and fun to eat as well.

MEXICAN BUFFET PARTY 250

VEGETARIAN ENCHILADAS Crispy tortillas oozing with cheese, beans, and spicy tomato sauce served with guacamole.
MEXICAN BEAN SALAD Nutritious and tasty, this combination of beans in a herby dressing makes an ideal buffet party dish.
CHARGRILLED STEAKS WITH RED VEGETABLES Juicy steaks, onions, and peppers served with the Mexican classic, refried beans.

THE BEST BURGERS 260

LAMB BURGERS Served in warm pitta bread with a cool cucumber and mint yogurt.
THAI BURGERS Top quality beef, lightly spiced and formed into burgers, ideal with a crunchy salad or raw vegetables strips alongside.
VEGGIE BURGERS Meatless but protein-packed, made with beans, cheese, carrots, pine nuts, and dried apricots.

KEBABS ON THE BARBECUE 274

BEEF & RED ONION Classic steak and onions with all the flavour of food cooked on the grill.
ORIENTAL PORK Pork, peppers, and pineapple combine to make this a dish with a difference.
SAUSAGE & SESAME Served with their own side-dish of mushrooms, tomatoes, and courgettes.
CURRIED LAMB Chunks of tender lamb in a spicy yogurt marinade with coriander and mint.

VEGETABLE CASSEROLES 306

SPICY PUMPKIN CASSEROLE Sweet-tasting parsnips, pumpkin, potatoes, and onions, lightly curried. Garnished with chopped fresh coriander.
MUSHROOM STROGANOFF A vegetable twist on the classic (beef) dish – artichoke hearts, peppers, and mushrooms in a creamy wine sauce.
ROAST VEGETABLE MEDLEY Cauliflower, butter beans, carrots, and other tasty vegetables caramelized in a hot oven and dressed with herbs.

VEGETARIAN BAKES 312

TUSCAN CANNELLONI Beans, sun-dried tomatoes, and a creamy blue cheese make up the filling in this Italian pasta dish.
MAJORCAN TUMBET CASSEROLE Layers of vegetables in a tomato sauce flavoured with garlic and rosemary.
KILKERRY PIE Potatoes and leeks in a tangy cheese sauce topped with crisp filo pastry.

VEGETARIAN CURRIES 318

DHAL A hearty and nutritious lentil dish flavoured with cinnamon, coriander seed, and cumin – the perfect accompaniment to any curry.
SAG ALOO Spinach (sag) and potato (aloo) with mustard and cumin seeds, onion, garlic, fresh root ginger, and other spices. Served with a dollop of cooling yogurt.
NIRAMISH Vegetables, including red peppers and green beans, in a rich coconut milk sauce.

ORIENTAL VEGETARIAN SUPPERS 324

THAI CURRY The heat of the curry is tempered by the coconut milk. Served with jasmine rice.
PEKING TOFU WITH PLUM SAUCE Fried tofu replaces the duck in this classic Chinese dish.
FIRECRACKER STIR-FRY Pak choi, sugarsnap peas, peppers, and mushrooms in a fiery stir-fry.
JAPANESE NOODLE SOUP Delicately spiced, with tofu and spring onions – a meal in a bowl.

EASY PASTA SUPPER DISHES 340

RED HOT RAGU A lively pasta dish of pork sausagemeat, chillies, and a spicy tomato sauce.
RIGATONI WITH MUSHROOMS & ROCKET Wilted rocket leaves add pep to this dish of pasta, mushrooms, and a creamy pesto sauce.
FUSILLI WITH DOUBLE TOMATOES Pasta spirals tossed with asparagus, mushrooms, fresh cherry tomatoes, and sun-dried tomatoes.

RAVIOLI 346

CHICKEN & PROSCIUTTO Parcels of Italian cured ham and chicken in a tomato and basil sauce.
RICOTTA & SPINACH A familiar flavour combination, best simply served with butter, Parmesan, and freshly ground black pepper.
CRAB & PRAWN Seafood parcels that melt in the mouth, in a fragrant coriander sauce.

ORIENTAL NOODLE DISHES 352

SINGAPORE NOODLES A simple dish with complex flavours, made with pork and vegetables.
SZECHUAN NOODLES WITH WATER CHESTNUTS Strong contrasts of taste and texture define this favourite Chinese dish.
PAD THAI WITH TIGER PRAWNS Chicken and prawns transform a traditional Thai side-dish into a hearty yet fragrant main course.

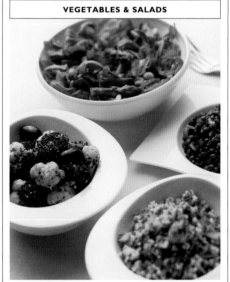

NASI GORENG 358

CHICKEN NASI GORENG A highly-seasoned rice dish with chicken, prawns, bacon, and the crunch of toasted almonds.
VEGETARIAN NASI GORENG Thinly sliced white cabbage, peppers, and tomatoes in a spicy stir-fry with rice, and a garnish of omelette strips.
QUICK NASI GORENG Fried rice with bean sprouts, mushrooms, and succulent prawns.

CHARGRILLED VEGETABLE PLATTER 386

FOR BARBECUE OR GRILL An assortment of fresh vegetables – aubergines, courgettes, red and yellow peppers, red onion, asparagus, pattypan squash, and mushrooms – brushed with good olive oil, then grilled until sweet and tender, and lightly charred. Served hot as a side dish with any meat or firm fish, or cold as an unusual salad.

FRESH & LIGHT SALADS 394

HERB SALAD A tangy orange and mustard dressing is tossed with fine asparagus, sun-dried tomatoes, and leaves including lamb's lettuce.
PUY LENTIL SALAD A simple salad dressed with sharp-sweet balsamic vinegar and olive oil.
TABBOULEH Nutritious, nutty bulgur wheat, lifted by the refreshing taste of mint and lemon.
ITALIAN PESTO SALAD Broccoli, cauliflower, and black olives with the classic Italian basil sauce.

THIN-CRUST PIZZAS 412

MINI PIZZAS Perfect for snacks, with goat's cheese, black olives, artichokes, and Parma ham.
FOUR SEASONS Salami and oregano, mozzarella and mushrooms, anchovies and black olives, and sweet red peppers top each of the four quarters.
TUNA & CAPER An easy, quickly made pizza, using ingredients from the storecupboard.
NAPOLETANA Anchovies are the definitive ingredient in this typical Italian pizza.

DANISH PASTRIES 418

PINWHEELS Filled with almond paste and topped with a cherry.
ENVELOPES Almond paste and apricots, drizzled with a sweet white icing.
CRESCENTS Filled with pure almond paste – the connoisseur's choice for breakfast, or at any time.
KITES A double almond delight, pastry filled with almond paste and topped with toasted almonds.

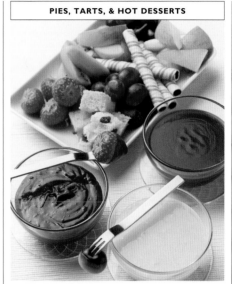

DESSERT FONDUES 438

DARK CHOCOLATE FONDUE A velvety-textured fondue with a subtle hint of orange.
WHITE CHOCOLATE FONDUE Sumptuous and rich, for dipping fresh fruits or crisp biscuits.
CHOCOLATE FUDGE FONDUE A really special treat for those indulgent moments – two favourite flavours blended and enriched with butter, syrup, and cream.

THE APPLE COLLECTION 448

BLACKBERRY & APPLE COBBLER Warming and comforting, with a scone topping.
CLASSIC APPLE CRUMBLE Tart cooking apples, flavoured with sugar and lemon zest, then topped with a sweet crumble and baked until golden brown. Traditionally served with custard.
APPLE TARTE AU CITRON A light lemon and apple filling that is both sweet and sharp, baked in a butter-rich shortcrust pastry shell.

FRUIT TARTLETS 456

RASPBERRY TARTLETS Slightly sharp berries with sweetened mascarpone in a light pastry shell.
BLUEBERRY PUFFS Layers of puff pastry, cream, and blueberries, with additional fruitiness coming from sliced peaches or nectarines.
TROPICAL TARTLETS Delicate almond pastry shells, filled with creamy custard, and topped with mandarin oranges, apricots, and toasted almonds.

RED FRUIT DESSERTS 470

PORT & CLARET JELLY For adults only. Served with seasonal fresh berries or currants.
RASPBERRY PASSION Fresh raspberries topped with a mixture of crème fraîche, yogurt, and passion fruit, and a sprinkling of brown sugar.
CRANBERRY & VODKA SPARKLE Clear and jewel-like, another jelly just for the grown-ups.
JUBILEE TRIFLE Sponge cake, jam, cherries, and pears topped with custard and whipped cream.

MERINGUES 476

MOCHA MERINGUE MILLE-FEUILLES Thin discs of meringue and almonds layered with sweetened coffee cream.
CHOCOLATE MERINGUE SHELLS Crisp, light meringue shells, drizzled with melted plain chocolate, then sandwiched together with a rich chocolate cream.
FRESH FRUIT BASKET Berries of your choice, cream, and meringue served with raspberry sauce.

FRESH FRUIT SALADS 482

SPICED FRUIT A year-round mix of succulent dried fruits, with vanilla and star anise.
FRUITS OF THE FOREST Balsamic vinegar and green peppercorns add zip to juicy fresh berries.
ORANGE PASSION Just fruit: oranges, papaya, passionfruit, and lime juice, with no added sugar.
TROPICAL ISLAND Physalis (cape gooseberries) and Asian pears (nashi) star in this unusual salad.

SORBETS 490

LIME, APRICOT, RASPBERRY, AND PEAR & GINGER So easy to make, from a basic mixture of sugar, water, and egg white, sorbets capture the vivid colours and pure flavours of your favourite fruits in a light, low-fat, refreshing mouthful. The perfect ending to a rich meal or (for a special occasion) try offering a small serving between courses as a palate cleanser.

SMALL CHOCOLATE CAKES 508

DOUBLE-CHOCOLATE MUFFINS Bitter cocoa powder and best-quality dark chocolate chips, enhanced with a little strong coffee, for a deeply chocolatey experience.
BEST-EVER BROWNIES Soft, moist squares of chocolate with the added crunch of walnuts.
CHOCOLATE CUP CAKES Enjoy a whole chocolate cake all to yourself, embellished with smooth chocolate icing.

CHRISTMAS CAKES 514

CANDIED FRUIT CAKE A traditional rich fruit cake with a spectacular topping of apricot jam, nuts, and candied fruit and peel. Finished with a colourful ribbon.
SNOW WHITE CAKE Fairytale icing hides a delicious secret – a moist cake packed with dried fruits, nuts, and candied citrus peel, covered with a layer of home-made marzipan. Decorated with fresh cranberries and silver dragees, or as you wish.

CHOUX PASTRIES 522

COFFEE ECLAIRS Oozing with whipped cream and topped with a silky coffee icing.
RELIGIEUSES Fresh from the patisserie: tiny cream-filled choux buns sitting atop larger ones, crowned with a decadent chocolate icing.
CHOCOLATE PROFITEROLES Golden choux pastry baked until light as air, then split, filled with whipped cream, and drizzled with a creamy warm chocolate sauce. Who could resist?

FOREWORD

MARY BERRY'S COMPLETE COOKBOOK has been the reliable, trusted companion of home cooks for many years. But much has changed since it was first published. We lead busier lives, fulfilling greater dreams. We entertain less formally than in the past, but so much more comfortably, often in the warmth of a cosy kitchen where guests can chat with the cook and enjoy the fun of preparing a meal together. Travel has broadened our horizons, and given us a taste for different foods.

Now, we know what it means to eat well in the modern sense, downplaying butter and sugar and rich sauces, preparing healthier meals using natural ingredients, and letting their flavour and freshness shine through. Fortunately, there's an abundance of good foods available – seasonal fruits and vegetables; fresh fish and lean meat; locally produced cheeses; and interesting breads not mass produced but lovingly formed by hand and baked in the traditional way. Supermarkets as well as small neighbourhood shops have responded to our more adventurous tastes – acquired during holidays to exotic destinations – and provide us with all manner of unusual ingredients, including the herbs, spices, and flavourings that enhance the appeal of simple ingredients.

This new edition of the book takes account of all these changes while retaining the features that made the original one so special – the picture for every dish, the visual indexes at the beginning of each chapter, the ease of use, and the knowledge that each one of the tried-and-tested recipes can be made with absolute confidence of a great result. In preparing the book, I've been enormously helped by my assistant, Lucy Young, who helped to develop and test the new recipes and lent her youthful view to the enterprise, and my editor, Jeni Wright, who carefully reviewed every recipe with me and suggested many good changes. My grateful thanks to them both.

PENN, BUCKINGHAMSHIRE, JANUARY 2003

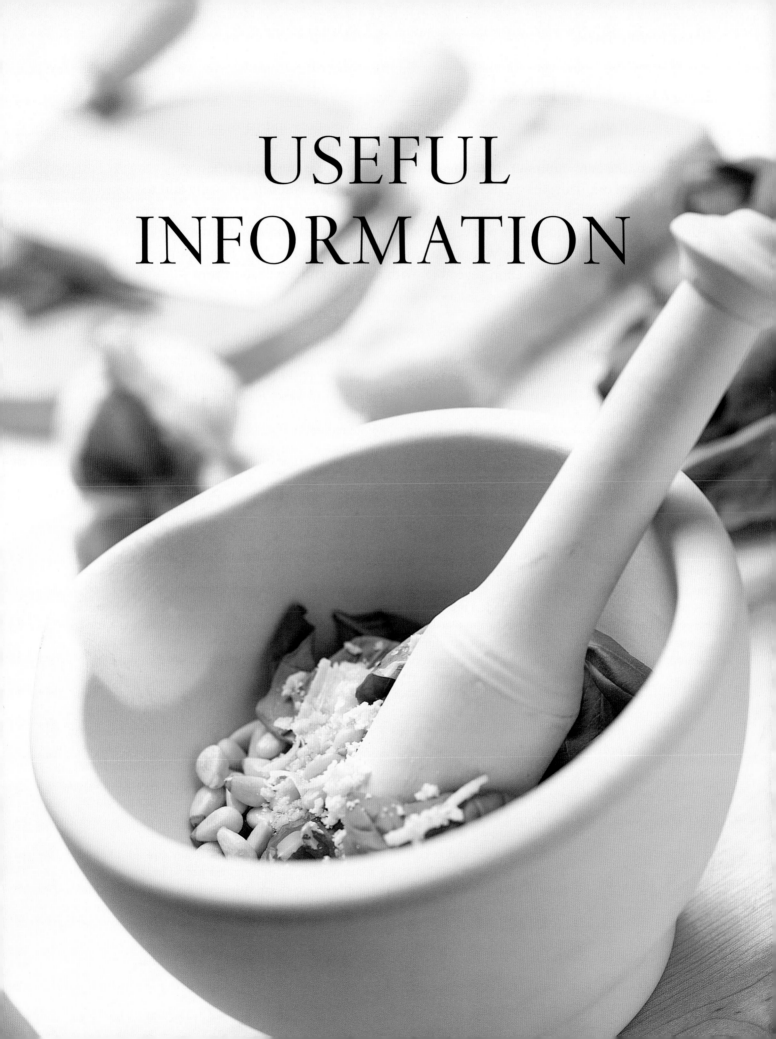

USEFUL
INFORMATION

EQUIPMENT

GOOD EQUIPMENT MAKES cooking easy. With top-quality knives, pots and pans, and other utensils, you will be able to cook efficiently and with pleasure. If you are equipping your first kitchen, the bare minimum is all that is required – there is no need for fancy utensils to turn out delicious meals. As your experience grows, you can gradually add to your collection, buying more specialist and unusual items as your skills increase.

Always buy the best equipment you can afford – it is false economy to save money, because cheap equipment simply will not last. Using a thin pan in which food always sticks and burns, or trying to chop vegetables with a flimsy knife, will soon turn cooking into a chore.

MEASURING EQUIPMENT

Even experienced cooks need accurate measuring tools to ensure ingredients are in correct proportion to one another – vital when baking – or the right size, or at the optimum temperature.

- KITCHEN SCALES may be balance, electronic or spring-operated. Balance scales give the most accurate results, especially for small amounts. Being strong and simple in construction, with no complicated mechanism to wear out, they will last a lifetime. Electronic scales, which run on batteries, are not very accurate with amounts under 30 g (1 oz), but have the advantage that many can be returned to zero when weighing more than one ingredient in the bowl at the same time.

- MEASURING JUGS made of toughened glass are very useful – those made from clear plastic are usually cheaper but will not withstand the heat of boiling liquid. Buy the biggest measuring jug you can store (it can be used for mixing too), and with both metric and imperial calibrations marked on the outside. New and ingenious is an angled measuring jug that allows you to check the accuracy of measurements either from the side or by looking straight down into it.

- MEASURING CUPS, as used in American recipes, are normally sold in sets of four: 1 cup (which holds 250 ml or 8 fl oz), ½ cup, ⅓ cup, and ¼ cup. In the US, and in other countries such as Canada and Australia, both dry ingredients and liquids are measured by volume in standard cups (dry ingredients levelled across the top).

- MEASURING SPOONS, for accurate dispensing of small amounts, usually come in nesting sets of four as follows: 15 ml (1 tablespoon), 5 ml (1 teaspoon), 2.5 ml (½ teaspoon) and 1.25 ml (¼ teaspoon). Unless a recipe specifies a heaped spoon of a dry ingredient, it should be levelled off with a knife.

- A MEAT THERMOMETER, to measure the internal temperature of meat and poultry during cooking, takes the guesswork out of roasting, and ensures thorough, safe cooking. The most common type is inserted into the meat or poultry before cooking begins, whereas instant-read thermometers and thermo forks are used as a spot check during cooking or at the end of the cooking time (these types are very useful when grilling and barbecuing).

- A DEEP-FRYING THERMOMETER checks the temperature of the oil to be sure of the best and crispiest fried results, but the safest way to deep-fry is to use an electric deep-fat fryers that has its own built-in thermometer.

- A SUGAR THERMOMETER performs the same function as a deep-frying thermometer, but for sugar syrups.

- A TAPE MEASURE and/or a ruler will enable you to roll or cut pastry and pasta to the correct dimensions, and also check that pans and tins are the required size.

- AN AUTOMATIC TIMER helps avoid overcooking disasters when you are busy and forget to watch the clock.

POTS & PANS

On the hob, pans need to be heavy enough to sit securely without tipping, yet not so heavy that you have trouble lifting them. A heavy base is important for gentle, even heat distribution. Pots and pans also need to have lids that fit tightly and sturdy handles that stay cool. Ovenproof handles make it easy to transfer pots and pans from the hob to the oven, when necessary.

- SAUCEPANS WITH STRAIGHT SIDES have a multitude of uses, from sauces and vegetables to soups and stews. You need a minimum of three in different sizes, starting with one about 1.5 litres (2½ pints) in capacity. Two handles on larger pans make for easier lifting, and if the handles are short and made of metal the pan can also double up as a casserole in the oven.

- A SMALL MILK PAN, about 1 litre (1¾ pints) in capacity, should have a non-stick coating (milk and cream sauces tend to stick) and pouring lips on both sides.

- A PASTA PAN is tall and fairly narrow, with a perforated inner basket that lifts out for draining; some have an additional insert for steaming. A pasta pan can also be used for steaming puddings, and for making stock and large quantities of soup.

- A STEAMER at its simplest is a collapsible basket that fits inside a large saucepan. Special steamer pans have steamer compartments with perforated bases, which stack on top of each other. Chinese stacking bamboo steamers that fit inside a wok are an alternative.

- A WOK with one long handle is easier to use than a wok with two small handles, and one with a flat base is most stable on both gas and electric hobs. The cheapest Chinese woks are made from unseasoned carbon steel; if pre-seasoned or non-stick, the wok will be easier to clean. A large wok (35 cm/14 in across the top) is the most versatile. Many come complete with lids (very useful) and cooking tools.

- A SAUTE PAN is more versatile than a frying pan because it has deeper sides. Choose from stainless steel or non-stick (the most useful size is 23–28 cm/9–11 in). Non-stick pans with titanium coatings are the best, because they can be used with metal utensils.

- AN OMELETTE PAN, shallow with curved sides, is often made of cast iron or stainless steel; a non-stick finish is easier to use. A 16 cm (5½ in) pan is the right size for a 2-egg French omelette, a 23 cm (9 in) pan for a thick, flat Spanish or Italian omelette. A shallower crêpe or pancake pan is an optional extra.

- THE CHARGRILL PAN is traditionally made of ridged cast iron, but non-stick pans are equally good, especially ones with deep sides that allow for making a sauce in the pan. For low-fat cooking, deep ridges will lift the food out of the fat, and give a "barbecued" finish.

MATERIALS FOR COOKWARE

COPPER (an excellent heat conductor) reacts chemically with food, air, and liquid, so copper pans must be lined. Stainless steel has replaced tin and silver as the most common lining. Lined copper pans are truly the best, preferred by many professional chefs, but they are expensive and heavy.

STAINLESS STEEL is lightweight and durable but not a very good heat conductor, so the bases of stainless steel pans for use on the hob are usually "sandwiched" with aluminium, copper or a copper and silver alloy. Pans with such heavy-gauge bases are expensive but should last a lifetime. Ovenware is usually limited to roasting tins.

CAST IRON can be heated to a high temperature, so cast-iron pans, such as chargrills, are perfect for cooking food quickly and evenly. It also retains and transmits low heat well so is appropriate for long, slow cooking too. Cast-iron pans need to be "seasoned" before use, so food does not stick, and must be thoroughly dried after washing to prevent rusting. Enamelled cast iron will not rust, and is good for flameproof casseroles as it makes very strong, sturdy (though heavy) vessels.

ALUMINIUM (another efficient heat conductor) scratches easily and can react with acidic foods, giving them a metallic taste. It is usually covered with another material, such as stainless steel or a non-stick coating.

GLASS is not as good a conductor of heat as metal, so pastry baked in thick, ovenproof glass will never be as crisp as that baked in a metal tin, but it is very useful for baking dishes, and for taking straight from oven to table.

PORCELAIN, STONEWARE, AND GLAZED EARTHENWARE are quite tough and sturdy materials for ovenware (take care not to chip or crack them), and most can double as serving dishes.

NON-STICK coatings make pans and tins quick and easy to clean. Some coatings are readily scratched and wear off with time; other, newer versions, such as titanium, are more durable and can be used with metal utensils.

OVENWARE

Cooking in the oven requires sturdy vessels that conduct and retain heat efficiently. For convenience, choose oven-to-table dishes that are attractive enough for serving too. The choice of metal or ceramic, non-stick or uncoated, depends largely on the job you want the tins or dishes to do. Whatever you buy, look after it to avoid rusting and scratching.

- A ROASTING TIN needs to be deep, strong, and rigid. If possible, have two in different sizes, one of them as big as your oven will take. Too small a tin makes it difficult to baste the meat or poultry properly; roasting in a tin that is too large will cause juices to evaporate and burn. With a lip or spout on the edge of the tin you can pour off juices; a rack that fits inside the tin enables meat to be roasted free of its fat. Hinged racks can be folded to cradle a bird.

- BAKING SHEETS have many uses – to bake biscuits, meringues, small pastries, pizzas – and to provide a heat-conducting base for pastry cases; you'll need at least two. Buy the largest that will fit comfortably in your oven, and be sure they are heavy-duty, inflexible, and completely flat. Good-quality non-stick coatings are a boon when it comes to cleaning.

- LOAF TINS with deep sides are used for baking breads and cakes, and for pâtés and terrines. Two different sizes are needed: one 500 g (1 lb) and the other 1 kg (2 lb). Some have hinged drop-down sides.

- A DEEP LOOSE-BOTTOMED CAKE TIN, round or square and 20 or 23 cm (8 or 9 in) in diameter, is used mainly for rich fruit cakes.

- A SPRINGFORM CAKE TIN is ideal for delicate cakes, cheesecakes, and layered mousse cakes – it has a clasp on the side to open the tin and release the base, so the cake can be removed easily. Tins with a removable central tube and fluted base can double as a tube tin.

- SANDWICH OR SPONGE TINS are round and shallow. For making layered cakes, you will need two. The most useful size is 20 cm (8 in) in diameter.

- THE SHALLOW SWISS ROLL TIN usually measures 23 x 33 cm (9 x 13 in). It is used for both sweet and savoury sponge mixtures and roulades; a non-stick coating makes unmoulding these very simple. The tin can also double as a small baking tray.

- A TRAYBAKE TIN is similar to a Swiss roll tin in size, but it is deeper. It is used for baking cake mixtures that are cut into squares or rectangles for serving.

- A MUFFIN OR BUN TIN/SHEET will bake American muffins and fruit buns as well as cup cakes and individual Yorkshire puddings. Tins may have 6 or 12 holes or cups, and the width and depth of the holes varies according to what is to be baked.

- A PIE TIN has plain, sloping sides and a lip for the pie edging. A good all-purpose size is 23 cm (9 in) measured across the top.

- AN OVAL PIE DISH with a wide lip is traditional for deep-dish sweet and savoury pies.

- A SHALLOW FLUTED TIN 20 or 23 cm (8 or 9 in) in diameter is best for making quiches and sweet and savoury tarts, as the fluted edge helps to strengthen the fragile pastry case. For easy serving, choose a metal tin with a loose bottom: lift the quiche or tart from the side of the tin and serve it on the tin base. Or bake in a fluted ceramic dish and serve from it.

- A STRAIGHT-SIDED, DEEP SOUFFLE DISH, 1.4 litres (2¼ pints) in capacity, can double as a baking dish for crumbles and other puddings. Small soufflé dishes and ramekins are used for individual soufflés, and baked puddings such as crème caramel, baked eggs, and mousses. Average capacity is 150 ml (¼ pint). Both soufflé dishes and ramekins can be brought straight from the oven to the table.

- GRATIN AND BAKING DISHES come in many different shapes and sizes, and are very versatile. They are used for making vegetable and other gratins, baked pasta dishes, shepherd's pie, and moussaka, and for baking fish and puddings of all kinds; also for roasting. Most gratin and baking dishes will resist very high temperatures, which means they can be put under the grill as well as into a hot oven.

- A RANGE OF CASSEROLES in various sizes, and with tight-fitting lids, is also useful. Choose ones that are described as "flameproof", which means they can be used on the hob as well as in the oven.

- RE-USABLE BAKING MATS or cooking liners spread out in a baking sheet or tin will prevent sticking. These are non-stick, and are good for low-fat cooking as usually no added fat or oil is needed. They are re-usable, and save on washing-up as they can be wiped clean.

ELECTRIC EQUIPMENT

There is an ever-increasing choice of electric appliances to help you in the kitchen. Equipping yourself with the full range is costly and wastes storage space, so when buying, think carefully about what you cook and how often you are likely to use the appliance.

- ELECTRIC MIXERS work much faster than whisking and mixing by hand. They may be compact and hand-held or large and heavy-duty, standing on the worktop. The hand-held mixer is good for whisking egg whites and whipping cream, and can be used in a pan over the heat. Choose a powerful one with at least three speeds, and check that the beaters are easy to remove for cleaning. To mix cake batters and bread doughs efficiently, choose a large mixer with a stand and bowl. Most have a dough hook attachment for kneading and some come with a separate blender, mincer, juice extractor, pasta maker, potato peeler, and a shredder and slicer. Of course, mixers like this are expensive and take up space.

- BLENDERS, also called liquidizers, make smooth soups, sauces, vegetable purées, dips, batters, and drinks. Look for a model with a large container, and blades set low to cope with small quantities. A HAND-HELD BLENDER, a less expensive and more portable version, will purée soup directly in a pan or small quantities in a beaker or deep bowl. It is easier to wash up than the free-standing blender and takes up less storage space.

- A FOOD PROCESSOR almost eliminates the need for a free-standing blender. Different blades chop, grate, slice, or purée all kinds of ingredients, or mix pastry and bread doughs. The more expensive the processor, the more sophisticated the jobs it will do. Some come with a mini bowl for processing small quantities, which is particularly useful for herbs, spices, and nuts.

- ELECTRIC GRINDERS will quickly produce freshly ground coffee or spices, and can also be used for grinding nuts and breadcrumbs.

- AN ICE-CREAM MAKER, BREAD MACHINE, PASTA MACHINE, RICE COOKER, SLOW COOKER, CONTACT GRILL, AND THERMOSTATICALLY CONTROLLED DEEP-FRYER are nice items to have if space and budget permit.

CUTTING TOOLS

A set of sturdy, well-made, and sharpened knives is vital for efficient food preparation. Make sure they are comfortable to hold: the best balanced have the metal of the blade running through the handle, which should be securely riveted, or the knife may be made from a whole piece of metal. Keep knives on a

magnetic strip, or in a knife block, rather than in a drawer where they will not keep so sharp but will be dangerous to fingers.

- A SMALL KNIFE, with a rigid, pointed 7 or 10 cm (3 or 4 in) blade makes trimming fruit and vegetables easy.

- A PARING KNIFE is similar in shape to the small knife but slightly larger – its blade is 12 or 15 cm (5 or 6 in) long. Use it for fine work, such as peeling (paring) and cutting cores from apple quarters and peppers.

- A SMALL SERRATED KNIFE, with a thin, flexible blade, is ideal for slicing lemons, tomatoes, and other fruits and vegetables with tough or slippery skins.

- THE CHEF'S OR COOK'S KNIFE, with a rigid, heavy, wide blade 19 or 20 cm (about 8 in) long that tapers to a pointed tip, is the all-purpose cutting tool, unbeatable for slicing and chopping vegetables and fruit into dice, and for chopping herbs.

- A BREAD KNIFE has a long, thin, firm blade with a serrated edge to cut through bread crusts cleanly. Serrated knifes cannot be sharpened.

- A CARVING KNIFE is long, thin and flexible, with a blade that has a straight, sharp edge curving upwards towards the tip. To hold the meat firmly, use with a two-pronged carving fork that has a safety prong to prevent the knife blade from slipping towards you.

- A CLEAVER with a wide, heavy blade is the tool for tough chopping jobs.

- THE MEZZALUNA has a crescent-shaped single or double blade and two handles. It works by being rocked over the food to be chopped, and is especially efficient for large quanities of tender-leafed herbs.

- KNIFE SHARPENERS are available in manual or electric models, or you can have your knives sharpened professionally once or twice a year. At home, sharpen them every few days – blunt knives cause accidents.

- CUTTING BOARDS are indispensable. Have at least two, either wooden or polypropylene/polyethylene. One should be kept for raw meat and poultry, to ensure that they do not contaminate cooked food or fruits and vegetables to be eaten raw. Always clean boards thoroughly with hot, soapy water, and dry well.

UTENSILS

It is essential to use the right tool for the job – a cliché but a concept that is very important in the kitchen. The wrong tools will only cause frustration and waste valuable time.

- A SET OF MIXING BOWLS in varying sizes is essential. Have at least four, and choose ones that fit inside each other so that they do not take up all your storage space. Toughened glass is heatproof and versatile, and gives you an all-round view of what you are mixing.

- FLEXIBLE RUBBER OR PLASTIC SPATULAS, either flat or spoon-shaped, will scrape bowls clean so nothing is wasted, and they are good for folding mixtures too. Have at least two, one for savoury and the other for sweet mixtures.

- WOODEN SPOONS AND SPATULAS, in varying sizes, are useful for all kinds of tasks, both in preparation and cooking. Wooden spoons will mix and beat; with long handles they are good for stirring mixtures on the hob (they won't scratch a pan). A spoon with a corner will reach right to the edges or the bottom corner of the pan. The flat-sided spatula can be used for folding mixtures together. It doubles up as a lifter and turner too.

- A SLOTTED (OR PERFORATED) SPOON is invaluable when removing food from liquids for serving or testing for doneness, and for skimming fat or scum off the surface of stocks and soups. It is also essential for draining fat or oil from food you have fried, either before further cooking or serving.

- A FISH SLICE is used for any solid food that needs turning in the pan or lifting carefully from pan to plate. It is especially useful for delicate foods like fish (hence its name) that have a tendency to break up.

- TONGS are also useful for turning and moving pieces of hot food, such as when chargrilling, and for moving long pasta like spaghetti and tagliatelle from pan to plate. They grasp the food without piercing it, as a fork would do.

- A PALETTE KNIFE has a flat, blunt, flexible blade. Despite its name, it is used for spreading, not cutting, and for turning and lifting foods. It is useful to have two: one with a blade 23–25 cm (9–10 in) long and the other much shorter, about 13 cm (5 in). An angled or cranked metal spatula (also called an offset spatula) looks like a bent palette knife. Use it to remove slices of tart or cake from rimmed tins.

- A LONG-HANDLED LADLE scoops out hot liquids such as soups, stews, and pasta sauces for serving, so that they don't have to be poured from heavy pans. It can also be used for pouring batter into a pancake pan.

- WHISKS incorporate air into egg whites to produce a snowy foam and into cream to thicken it. To make light work of these tasks, choose a balloon whisk with a comfortable handle and a large balloon of springy wire. A flat coil whisk is ideal for whisking a sauce over the heat or gravy in a roasting tin to produce smooth, well-blended results.

- GRATERS come in many guises. The most familiar are box or conical graters, which have a different grating surface on each face. Flat graters – like the individual faces on box graters – are less convenient to use as they will not stand up on their own. New style FLAT GRATERS with handles come in a variety of ultra-sharp surfaces: fine for rapid zesting, grating, or puréeing; coarse for cheese and chocolate; ribbon graters for hard cheeses; and slicers for shavings of chocolate, Parmesan or root ginger. Also useful are a HAND-OPERATED ROTARY GRATER and a NUTMEG GRATER.

- VEGETABLE PEELERS either have a fixed blade, for peeling potatoes and other round fruits and vegetables, or a swivel blade for straight-sided vegetables such as carrots. Some peelers have a pointed end for digging out "eyes" from potatoes.

- A GARLIC PRESS will crush garlic without fuss, although the aroma and taste will be stronger than if the garlic were chopped by hand. Be sure to choose a press with a detachable grille to make cleaning easy.

- A CITRUS ZESTER has a row of small holes in its wide, flat end that remove the zest (the coloured, oil-rich part of the peel) from citrus fruits in tiny strips. The zest can then be chopped finely if wanted. To take slightly thicker strips of zest, a canelle knife is used.

- SCISSORS (kept solely for kitchen use) are perfect for trimming rind off bacon, snipping herbs, and a myriad other small tasks. Stainless steel ones are easy to keep clean.
- STURDY POULTRY SHEARS work like garden secateurs, making light work of jointing chicken and other birds.
- A LEMON SQUEEZER will juice halved citrus fruits of all kinds very quickly. Choose one with a well-fitting strainer to catch the pips. The traditional reamer is an attrractive alternative, and it extracts a lot of juice, but you will need to strain out the pips afterwards.
- Buy the biggest PESTLE AND MORTAR you can store – apart from grinding herbs, spices, and garlic it is the traditional vessel for making pounded sauces such as pesto. Porcelain is a good choice as it has the weight of marble without the prohibitive cost.
- SIEVES sift dry ingredients and strain wet ones, and can also purée cooked fruit and vegetables. It is handy to have two, large and small, and the best material for a sieve is stainless steel because it will not rust over time.
- A POTATO MASHER needs to be strong and with a comfortable handle so that it can mash and purée cooked potatoes and other root vegetables efficiently. For the lightest, dry, and fluffy results, use a ricer; a dishwasher-proof model is easiest to clean
- A STURDY COLANDER, with legs or a base so it is free-standing, will ensure safe draining of hot cooked vegetables, pasta, and pulses.
- A SALAD SPINNER operated by a handle or pulley uses centrifugal force to remove water from salad leaves without bruising them.
- A GRAVY SEPARATOR enables you to pour fat-free gravies and sauces. The jug either has two spouts, one shallow and one coming up from near the bottom, or just one deep spout. Fat, being light, will float to the surface of the gravy and can be poured off through the shallow spout (or the gravy can just be poured from beneath the fat using the deep spout).
- A LONG, HEAVY ROLLING PIN is needed for pastry, hand-rolled pasta and sweets. One that is 5–7 cm (2–3 in) in diameter is the best choice. Wooden pins are fine, although marble ones stay cooler for rolling pastry and chocolate.

- A PASTRY SCRAPER is a small oblong of flexible plastic that resembles the tool used for smoothing plaster. It is invaluable for scraping up rich doughs that are made directly on the work surface.
- PASTRY CUTTERS are used for stamping out biscuits, scones, and tartlet cases. They may be plain or fluted, as well as in a wide range of shapes and sizes.
- A PASTRY BRUSH is the best tool for glazing and sealing pastry, greasing cake tins, and basting meat. The flat, paintbrush type is easier to use than a round brush.
- A WIRE RACK allows air to circulate around cakes, biscuits and breads as they cool.
- A PIPING BAG AND NOZZLES are handy for piping cream and icings, and for shaping meringues and choux pastry.
- A CHERRY STONER, APPLE CORER, AND CUTLET BEATER are inexpensive but useful items that don't take up space.

AND DON'T FORGET...

- paper towels
- foil
- cling film
- greaseproof paper
- baking parchment
- fine white (undyed) string for trussing and tying
- cocktail sticks
- can opener
- corkscrew and bottle opener (a bottle stopper too for leftovers)
- salt and pepper mills
- small skewers for testing cakes, meat, and poultry; long metal skewers and bamboo ones for kebabs and satay
- ice-cube trays

FREEZING

A freezer offers one of the most natural and economical methods of food preservation, and is invaluable in a busy household: most of the fresh food needed for a week, or even a month, can be bought in just one shopping trip and then frozen until it is needed.

Equipment needs to be airtight and moisture-proof so the food does not spoil or develop "freezer burn" – dry, grey patches on the surface of the food that are not dangerous but spoil the appearance and texture.

- USE RIGID polythene or foil containers with lids, or freezer bags.
- FREEZER-QUALITY cling film, wrap, and foil are good and convenient for interleaving and wrapping.
- FREEZER TAPE will seal packages securely; ordinary sticky tape peels off.

WAYS TO FREEZE

A few simple techniques will keep frozen items at their freshest and best.

Liquids

Pour liquids into rigid containers, leaving 1 cm (½ in) headroom. Freeze until solid, then remove and re-wrap in freezer bags.

Interleaving

Separate individual items like chops and steaks so they do not stick together when frozen, then pack them in a freezer bag.

Tray freezing

Arrange delicate items like berries and meringues on trays so they freeze separately, then pack in freezer bags once solid.

Blanching

Blanch vegetables in boiling water then plunge into iced water and drain well before freezing. This helps retain colour and texture.

WHAT FREEZES WELL?

- FRUIT frozen raw will always be slightly softer after thawing, but is still good. More successful are fruits poached in syrup or juice, puréed or cut in chunks for pies and other puddings. Storage: 12 months
- VEGETABLES – most need to be blanched first (see left), or they can be frozen in cooked dishes such as soups and casseroles. Storage: 12 months
- MEAT, POULTRY, GAME BIRDS, AND FISH must be very fresh; smaller pieces are best. (Shellfish such as crabs, lobsters, and prawns are better bought frozen.) Storage: beef 8 months; lamb, veal, and pork 6 months; bacon and sausages 1 month; game birds 12 months; poultry 8 months; white fish 3 months; oily fish and shellfish 2 months
- FRESH PASTA, both filled and unfilled. Pasta in sauces tends to turn soft when thawed, although made-up pasta dishes work well. Storage: 3 months
- DAIRY PRODUCTS – the higher the fat content the better – full-fat hard cheeses freeze best. Storage: hard cheese 6 months; full-fat soft cheese 6 weeks; butter 3 months; homogenized milk and full-fat yogurt 1 month
- BREADS, PASTRIES, AND CAKES – both cooked and uncooked pastry freezes well; quiche fillings should be made with cream, not milk. Cakes are best frozen before filling or icing. Storage: most bread 6 months; crusty bread: 3 weeks; cakes and pastries 3 months

THAWING & REHEATING

For some foods, thawing before cooking or reheating is not necessary, but others must be thoroughly thawed before cooking. Cook thawed food immediately, to kill any bacteria, and never refreeze foods already thawed unless you cook them first.

- VEGETABLES AND PASTA – add directly to boiling water.
- FISH FILLETS AND SHELLFISH – cook from frozen.
- SAUCES AND SOUPS – heat gently until thawed.
- THICKER PIECES OF MEAT – thaw before cooking.
- POULTRY – unwrap, cover loosely, and thaw completely on a lipped plate in the refrigerator (bacteria multiply at room temperature).

MICROWAVING

The microwave has revolutionized cooking for people with busy lifestyles. It can cook fish and many vegetables and fruit to perfection, retaining vitamins, colour, and texture, and it thaws frozen food quickly and successfully. It also performs myriad other tasks that speed preparation in the kitchen.

Special equipment is not essential for cooking in a microwave, as many containers and implements used for conventional cooking are suitable. For convenience, use the dish you want to eat from.

- ROUND OR OVAL DISHES with straight sides are the most efficient for even heat distribution.
- OVENPROOF GLASS and ceramic dishes are excellent as are plastics specially made for the microwave (other plastic containers may soften and distort, or even melt and collapse). Metal tins should not be used.
- USE LARGE CONTAINERS for liquids, and keep stirring to avoid a build up of hot spots and prevent liquids from boiling over.

TIPS FOR SUCCESS

Arranging food properly (see box, below) will ensure even cooking. Just remember that microwaves penetrate food from the outside towards the middle. Covering food with a lid or cling film (not foil) prevents it from drying out during cooking and traps steam, which helps to heat the food.

- MOST MICROWAVES contain a turntable, which rotates the food and exposes it evenly to the microwaves.
- IF COOKING in a dish that does not have a lid, cover it securely with cling film, or put the food directly in a roasting bag and fasten with a plastic (not metal) tie.
- PAPER TOWELS are useful for soaking up moisture and covering foods loosely to prevent spattering (do not use recycled paper, which may contain tiny fragments of metal). You can also use greaseproof paper.
- FOR THOROUGH, EVEN COOKING, stir foods halfway, or regularly, during microwaving. The microwaves will continue to produce heat inside the food after it has come out of the oven, so food should always stand for a few minutes to finish cooking before serving.

THAWING KNOW-HOW

Thawing must be done slowly and gently, so that the outside does not begin to cook before the inside is thawed. For this reason always use the Defrost setting.

- BREAK UP and stir stews, soups, and sauces as they thaw.
- SET FROZEN BREAD, pastry, and cakes on paper towels so that moisture will be absorbed as they thaw.
- BE SURE meat and poultry are completely thawed before cooking.
- COOK FOOD as soon as possible once it is thawed.

ARRANGING FOODS

Simple, but clever, techniques will help you microwave food as quickly and efficiently as possible.

Arrange unevenly shaped food in a circle with the densest parts – for example, the thick stalks of broccoli or the meaty parts of chicken drumsticks – facing outwards in the dish.

Position foods of the same size and shape, or small individual dishes, in a circle, with space between them, so that the microwaves can penetrate and reach the food from all sides.

USE A MICROWAVE TO ...

- Soften cold butter
- Toast nuts
- Warm bread, rolls, croissants, bagels, and the like
- Cook bacon rashers perfectly crisp (snip rind to prevent curling)
- Make deliciously creamy scrambled eggs
- Soften chopped onions
- Cook rice perfectly
- Make breakfast porridge
- Cook corn on the cob (set it on paper towels)
- Melt chocolate (stir halfway)
- Soften crystallized honey (take lid off jar) and ice cream
- Warm citrus fruit so it yields more juice

THE WELL-PROVISIONED KITCHEN

With a supply of useful ingredients always to hand, you should never be short of ideas for an impromptu meal or interesting flavourings to add zest to your cooking, or the basics for a cake, a loaf of bread, or a favourite pudding. Everyone will have a different list of essential staples, according to what they prefer to cook and eat, but most of our storecupboards, refrigerators, and freezers will contain many of the same basic elements.

THE STORECUPBOARD

Gone are the days when every home had a larder or pantry, a dry, sometimes dark, cold room in which to keep essential ingredients like vegetables and fruit that would otherwise quickly deteriorate in the warmth of the kitchen.

Nowadays most of us have to manage with a cupboard in the kitchens, using the refrigerator for storage more than we used to, if only because it is the only cold place we have. You will find advice on storing different foods in the Know-How pages of individual chapters, but here are some general tips:

- CHOOSE A CUPBOARD in the coolest part of your kitchen – not next to the radiator, boiler, or oven – and make sure it is dry.
- PACK THE SHELVES logically – bags of flour together, alongside packets of sugar or of rice and pasta, for example – with the things that you use most often arranged at the front.
- REGULARLY CHECK use-by dates on packets, bottles, and cans, and on bought chilled and frozen food. Also check if foods need to be refrigerated once opened.

DRY GOODS

Grains, pasta, and pulses form the backbone of the storecupboard – combined with fresh foods they will provide an infinite variety of nutritious meals. Other dry staples to keep on hand are sugars and flours, as well as nuts and seeds, dried fruits (those labelled "ready to eat" are best because they do not need soaking), spices and dried herbs, crispbreads and other savoury biscuits, and breakfast cereals. If you like to bake cakes and biscuits or breads, baking powder, bicarbonate of soda and dried yeast are a must. You might also want to stock cream of tartar, gelatine (leaves and/or powder) and cocoa powder, plus stock cubes or bouillon powder. Not forgetting salt and pepper, and coffee and tea.

Rice is so versatile – it can be served as an accompaniment or used as an ingredient in both savoury and sweet dishes. Many types are available, varying in size and shape of grain, colour, and texture, whether wholegrain or polished (white). Wholegrain rice has had only the outer, inedible husk removed, which makes it more nutritious than white rice. Here is a selection of different rices worth keeping in your storecupboard.

- LONG-GRAIN RICES, which stay in separate grains once cooked, include flavourful basmati, red rice (which is a wholegrain rice), Thai fragrant rice, also called jasmine rice, and long-grain (patna or Carolina) rice. Parboiled or converted rice is a very nutritious white long-grain rice; easy-cook rice has grains that never stick together.
- MEDIUM- AND SHORT-GRAIN RICES have starchy grains that tend to cling together after cooking. Types include risotto rice with plump oval grains (sometimes labelled as arborio or carnaroli rice) and a similar paella rice, the best of which is said to come from Valencia; pudding rice, which looks very like risotto rice but is sweeter; sticky rice (also called glutinous rice – a misnomer because it contains no gluten); and Japanese sushi rice.

- OTHER-GRAINS offer interesting and tasty alternatives to rice, as well as meals or flours, and flakes for muesli and porridge. They include:
- BULGUR, which is part-cooked, cracked, and crushed wheat grains, is very easy to prepare – it needs only soaking or a few minutes cooking. It is popular in the Mediterranean and Middle East. CRACKED or KIBBLED WHEAT is similar but takes longer to cook.
- COUSCOUS is not a true grain but a type of pasta made from semolina flour. It is used much like rice as an accompaniment or as part of a salad or other dish.
- OATMEAL, in varying degrees of coarseness, can be used in bread, biscuits, and oatcakes.
- PEARL BARLEY, and its wholegrain form pot barley, are most often used in soups and casseroles but can also be cooked like rice for side dishes and pilafs.
- POLENTA (sometimes called cornmeal) is a yellow, granular meal ground from maize or corn; cooked with water or stock until it thickens, it makes the northern Italian dish of the same name. Polenta can also be used to make bread, cakes, and biscuits.
- DRIED PASTA is available in very many shapes and sizes – the majority of which are interchangeable in recipes. Italian pasta is made from wheat, sometimes enriched with egg, whereas ORIENTAL AND NON-WHEAT PASTAS can be made from ground mung beans (cellophane or transparent noodles), rice (Chinese vermicelli and rice sticks), buckwheat flour (Japanese soba), corn, barley, and soya beans. SPAGHETTI, TAGLIATELLE, PENNE, AND FUSILLI are the most useful basic pasta shapes to keep in your storecupboard, plus some oriental noodles to partner quick stir-fries or add to soups.
- PULSES – DRIED BEANS, PEAS AND LENTILS – are easy to prepare, although (with the exception of lentils) they need to be soaked before cooking. To save time, use canned pulses, which are just as nutritious as dried.

UNUSUAL GRAINS TO TRY

- KASHA, roasted whole or cracked buckwheat grains, tends to break down when cooked so it is good if used in risotto-type dishes.
- QUINOA (pronounced "keenwa") is a very nutritious and ancient grain from South America. It contains more protein than any other grain, and is also higher in unsaturated fats and lower in carbohydrates than most – all of which make it a useful addition to a healthy diet. Quinoa is quite bland, with a flavour similar to that of couscous. It can be cooked in the same ways as rice.
- WHOLE GRAINS of oat, rye, and wheat, also known as kernels, groats, and berries, make an unusual substitute for brown rice.

PULSES

Dried beans, peas, and lentils make up the family of pulses. All but lentils require soaking for at least 8 hours, and 10 minutes' hard boiling at the beginning of cooking.

Red Kidney Beans
Popular in Mexican cooking, especially in chilli con carne, their bright red skins add colour to many different salads and stews.

Cannellini Beans
These are a good general-purpose bean to use in soups, salads, stews, especially in Italian dishes. French dried white haricots are similar.

Black Beans
Traditional in Caribbean, Mexican, Chinese, and Brazilian dishes, these slightly sweet beans go well with rice and spicy sauces.

Borlotti Beans
Creamy in consistency, borlotti are a favourite with Italians in soups, salads, casseroles, and dips. They are slightly bittersweet in flavour.

Aduki Beans
Tender-textured beans with a strong flavour, aduki are used in Chinese and Japanese rice dishes and soups, and in red bean paste.

Chickpeas
Most famous in hummus, felafel, and other Middle Eastern dishes, chickpeas are also used in Indian and Spanish cooking.

Split Peas
Yellow and green are available, and interchangeable in soups, purées, and bakes. Green split peas are used for "mushy peas".

Lentils
Red and orange lentils cook quickly and become mushy, while green, brown, and Puy lentils retain their shape.

TOMATOES

These three tomato-based products are useful in the storecupboard for boosting the flavour
of fresh tomatoes when they are lacking in taste of their own

Sun-dried Tomatoes in Oil

Sold loose at the delicatessen or in jars and
tubs, these pieces or halves of tomato can be
used as they are or chopped. Sun-blushed
tomatoes are similar, but sweeter and softer.

Tomato Concentrate

Called tomato purée or paste, this is very
strong, useful for adding depth of colour and
flavour to cooked dishes. Sun-dried tomato
versions are milder and sweeter.

Passata

Tomatoes that have been crushed and then
sieved to make a smooth liquid. Sold in bottles
and cans, it is useful in sauces, soups, and stews
that are better without bits.

SAUCES, PRESERVES, SYRUPS, OILS & VINEGARS

For use at the table and as quick-and-easy instant
flavourings.

- TABASCO, HORSERADISH, CHILLI AND MOROCCAN HARISSA
  are hot and spicy sauces that will give a kick to any
  bland food. The green version of Tabasco is less fiery
  than the usual red kind but still packs a punch.
- WORCESTERSHIRE has a piquant salty flavour, good in
  sauces and marinades.
- PESTO, TAPENADE (BLACK OLIVE PASTE) AND SUN-DRIED
  TOMATO PASTE can be stirred into pasta, rice, and dips.
- MAYONNAISE can be used in sandwiches and salad
  dressings as well as dips. Reduced-fat and flavoured
  versions are available.
- TOMATO KETCHUP is good for mixing into sauces,
  dressings, and relishes as well as stews. A spoonful or
  two of TOMATO PUREE OR PASTE will add flavour and
  colour to sauces, soups, and stews, while tomato
  PASSATA (sieved crushed tomatoes) can form the basis
  of a pasta sauce or soup.
- CHINESE AND JAPANESE SAUCES – soy, oyster, chilli,
  hoisin, teriyaki, and bean, plus miso, sesame, and
  wasabi pastes – are traditional in Oriental dishes and
  add exciting flavours to Western ones. For South-east
  Asian cooking, you might want to keep fish sauce
  (also called nam pla), tamarind paste, and creamed
  coconut. Coconut products are high in saturated fat,
  so look also for reduced-fat coconut milk.

- CURRY PASTES come in varying strengths, and are ideal
  for quickly spicing curries as well as soups and
  dressings.
- PRESERVES, such as mango chutney, redcurrant jelly
  and marmalade, add fruity sweetness to a dish, other
  chutneys offer hot and spicy flavours, while pickles
  may be sweet or tangy, according to your preference.
- MUSTARD appears in many different flavours, colours,
  and textures, and all types can be used in cooking or
  as a condiment. It is useful to stock the three basics:
  strong Dijon mustard, coarse-grain mustard, and very
  hot and pungent English mustard.
- OILS are used for frying, brushing, and basting, as well
  as in marinades and dressings. Two types – a neutral-
  flavoured general purpose oil such as sunflower and a
  more flavourful olive oil – are the basics to keep in
  stock. In addition, you might want to add walnut,
  hazelnut, or toasted sesame oils, or an oil or two
  flavoured with your favourite herbs or spices.
- VINEGARS add pep to dressings and sauces as well as
  being essential in pickles and chutneys. Red or white
  wine vinegar is a must, with cider, sherry, and
  balsamic vinegars being optional choices. The cheaper
  balsamics are satisfactory for cooking, the more
  expensive varieties are best kept for drizzling on food
  before serving or at the table.
- SYRUPS – honey, maple and golden – make instant
  sweet sauces for ice-cream and hot puddings.

CANNED GOODS

Storecupboard shelves laden with a variety of canned foods are a boon for a busy cook. If you keep a basic stock of canned fish, vegetables, and fruits, you will be able to whip up a meal at a moment's notice.

- FISH, such as salmon, tuna, sardines, pilchards, herring, and anchovies, are available in many different forms – packed in various oils or in water or brine, or in flavourful sauces. Use your favourites in fish pies, as sandwich fillings, on pizzas, and in salads and pasta sauces.
- TOMATOES come whole or chopped, in natural juice or purée, plain or flavoured with herbs and garlic. Fresh tomatoes are always available, but often lack flavour; canned tomatoes taste good year round. They are also wonderfully convenient, needing no peeling or deseeding before using in soups, sauces, and stews.
- PULSES IN CANS – chickpeas, kidney and haricot beans, and so on – are a quick alternative to their dried form, as they only have to be drained and rinsed well, and just as nutritious. They are excellent in salads and to make dips such as hummus as well as in all kinds of hot dishes, from chilli con carne to pasta with beans.
- ORIENTAL VEGETABLES, such as bamboo shoots and water chestnuts, will add crunch to stir-fries and other Chinese dishes.
- CANNED FRUITS – in natural juice for the best and truest flavour – are great standbys for quick puddings. You can also use them to bulk up a stir-fry or a fresh fruit salad.
- CUSTARD in cans (or refrigerated cartons) is excellent in fools and trifles.

THE COLD STORE

The refrigerator and freezer are natural extensions of the storecupboard, the places where more perishable standbys can be kept safely on hand. Stocking a good selection of chilled and frozen foods means you can have the makings of all kinds of quickly prepared meals.

- DAIRY PRODUCTS – milk and the foods based on it such as butter, cheese, cream, and yogurt – are found in most people's refrigerator. There is such an amazing choice of types of milk and cream, varieties of cheese, and flavours of yogurt, that what you stock is up to you, but two very useful staples are: a piece of Parmesan to grate as needed, and plain or Greek yogurt to serve with and/or in sweet and savoury dishes, or to blend with fruit to make healthy smoothies. In the freezer, you can keep milk, butter, cream, and full-fat yogurt for emergencies, and grated cheese to add frozen to sauces or as a topping. For instant desserts, ice cream and frozen yogurt are a must in the freezer.
- EGGS are another essential standby. They can make simple, nutritious meals by themselves, or be added to countless other dishes, both sweet and savoury.
- VEGETABLES, bought ready-prepared in bags for refrigerator storage or frozen, are a real time-saver. Chilled prepared vegetables range from trimmed whole mangetout, green beans, and baby corn, to shelled fresh peas, cut-up root vegetables for soups and stews, and ready-washed spinach and salad leaves. Frozen vegetables, which are often more nutritious than fresh, are usually best cooked from frozen, which makes them the ultimate convenience food.
- FRUIT such as apples stay deliciously crisp in the refrigerator, ideal for snacks or adding to fruit salads, and citrus fruits also store well in the fridge. Soft fruits – raspberries, red and black currants, loganberries, gooseberries, cranberries, and so on – are very useful to have in the freezer for quick puddings, as are grated citrus zest, apple or other fruit purée or chunks for pie fillings, and fruit juice (decant bought juice into rigid containers).
- BREAD is a top freezer standby. With a sliced loaf, you can take out slices as you need them – they can be toasted from frozen, as can pitta bread. If you prefer unsliced bread, cut loaves into halves or quarters and freeze in separate bags so you can take them out when you need them – this way you will always have fresh bread. Most part-baked bread can be baked from frozen. Also handy are croûtons and breadcrumbs, good ways to use up the last of a staling loaf.
- SEAFOOD such as fish fillets, raw and cooked prawns, crab, and other shellfish bought ready-frozen does not need to be thawed before cooking.
- OTHER FOODS useful in the freezer are chicken fillets and sausages (both must be thoroughly thawed before cooking), fresh pasta (drop it frozen into a big pot of boiling water), herbs, unsalted nuts (they stay fresher in the freezer than in the storecupboard) and coffee.

FLAVOURING FOOD

Herbs, spices, and the essential seasonings, salt and pepper, enhance the flavours of the food we eat, and also often add enticing aromas and vibrant colours. It is hard to imagine cooking without them.

HERBS

With their wonderful flavours, scents, and colours, herbs can transform even the simplest dish into something very special. Most savoury dishes benefit from the inclusion of one or more herbs to add flavour during cooking, or as a garnish to be sprinkled over the top of a dish just before serving. Sweet dishes, too, can be perfumed with herbs such as mint and lemon balm, and decorated with delicate herb flowers such as borage. Herbs are also used to make drinks known as infusions or tisanes.

PRESERVING HERBS

Preserve fresh herbs by freezing them. This is a much better method of preserving most herbs than drying because a fresher flavour is retained. Herbs that freeze well include parsley, tarragon, chives, dill, and fennel. Chop or pull off leaves or small sprigs, then mix with water in ice-cube trays or freeze in small plastic bags.

Herbs that can be dried successfully at home include bay leaves, sage, and rosemary. Hang them in a warm place, such as above the boiler, until dry, then pull or rub off the leaves from the stalks. Pack whole bay leaves into jars; chop or crumble sage and rosemary first.

STORING HERBS

Buy or gather fresh herbs only when they are needed. If you have to store them for a day or so, keep them in a cool place or in the refrigerator. If they have stalks, stand them in a jug of water, like cut flowers, and cover with a plastic bag.

Dried herbs must be stored correctly or they will quickly lose their flavour. Dark glass jars or earthenware pots with airtight lids are the best for storage, but if you only have clear glass jars, keep them in a dark cupboard or drawer because light causes dried herbs to deteriorate. Make sure they are kept in a cool dry place, away from kitchen heat and steam.

Dried herbs will not keep for ever, even if they are stored correctly. Herbs you have dried yourself will keep for 1 year, shop-bought herbs much less, so it is best to buy in small quantities from a shop that has a rapid turnover, checking the label for the best-before date.

USING HERBS

Always try to use fresh herbs, particularly in salads and sauces, as they always taste better than dried or frozen. Bunches and packets of a wide variety of fresh herbs are available now, so there is usually no need to use dried.

Fresh herbs are often chopped or shredded before being added to a dish, and this is best done at the last possible moment. The volatile oils in herbs are released by heat or oxidation, so unless the herbs are used as soon as they are prepared, they will quickly lose their flavour and they may start to discolour (this is especially true of basil). If whole herb sprigs or leaves are used to flavour a dish, lift them out before serving. For easy removal, tie with string or wrap in muslin, as in a bouquet garni (see facing page).

Herbs that dry well include sage, oregano and marjoram, bay, and dill, and these are good used in dishes that require long cooking. When buying dried herbs, look for those that are freeze-dried as they have the best flavour, colour, and aroma.

Another option you might want to try are the preserved herbs packed in squeezy tubes or bottled in oil – they are very convenient, and useful to keep in the refrigerator for those times when you run out of fresh herbs at the last moment and there is no chance of getting any more.

Dried herbs are more pungent than fresh, so a smaller quantity is required. Use ½ teaspoon finely powdered dried herb or 1 teaspoon crumbled dried herb in place of 1 tablespoon chopped fresh herb.

HERB FLAVOURS

The range of herbs in the shops is exciting for adventurous cooks, and even more varieties can be grown at home. These are the most commonly used.

- FRESH-TASTING HERBS: parsley (used both as a flavouring and garnish; flat-leaf has a more pronounced, spicier flavour than curly) and chives (a delicate taste of onion with a crunchy texture).
- SWEET HERBS: basil (spicy and aromatic; many varieties in addition to sweet basil, such as opal or purple basil and anise-flavoured Thai basil), bay leaves (with a pungent, resinous aroma), mint (including cool and mellow spearmint or garden mint, pungent peppermint, spicy Moroccan mint, and fruity apple mint), and oregano and marjoram (marjoram is subtly spicy while oregano has a more peppery or lemony bite; they can be used interchangeably).
- ANISE-FLAVOURED HERBS: chervil (delicate taste and pretty leaves), tarragon (pungent), dill (fragrant and tangy; seeds are used as a spice) and fennel (mild and slightly sweet; seeds are used as a spice).
- PUNGENT HERBS: rosemary (aroma and flavour are not reduced by long cooking), sage (spicy, often slightly musky), thyme (pleasantly strong and slightly peppery), coriander (spicy citrus aroma and taste) and garlic (whole cloves roasted or simmered are mellow, crushed and sautéed much stronger); new "wet" garlic is milder in flavour than dried garlic.

PREPARING HERBS

Rinse the herbs well under cold running water, then dry with paper towels. Then remove the leaves or sprigs from the stalks.

Chopping
Gather the leaves or sprigs into a compact pile on a chopping board. Chop the leaves with a sharp knife, rocking the blade back and forth, until the herbs are as fine as you want them. A mezzaluna (see page 19) is useful for chopping a large quantity.

Snipping
A pair of sharp scissors is best for snipping chives. Hold the stalks in one hand and snip into short lengths, either into a bowl or directly into the dish you are flavouring. This technique is also good for finely shredding large-leaved herbs such as sage.

Making a Bouquet Garni

Hold 2–3 sprigs each of thyme or marjoram and parsley with 1–2 bay leaves. Wrap in two pieces of pared orange zest (or two pieces of celery) if you like, then tie in a bouquet with undyed string. Orange and celery go well in beef and pork casseroles.

HERB MIXTURES

There are classic combinations of herbs, most of them from France, that are often used in cooking, especially in dishes like stews and casseroles that need long, slow simmering or cooking in the oven.

- DRIED MIXED HERBS, which can be used in most savoury dishes, is usually a mixture of marjoram, oregano, rosemary, summer savory, and thyme, but brands vary according to manufacturer.
- A BOUQUET GARNI is used in many long-cooked dishes. For a fresh bouquet garni, the basic combination is parsley, thyme, and bay, but this may be varied according to the dish being flavoured (see box, above). Only tie the string around the stalks of the herbs or you will strangle their flavours. If using dried herbs, wrap them in a muslin bag. Remember to remove the bouquet garni before serving (if you use a long piece of string, this can be tied to the pan handle for easy removal after cooking).
- HERBES DE PROVENCE, an aromatic mixture of sage, basil, savory, thyme, rosemary, and marjoram, is another popular combination. Good in stews, it should be used sparingly. If you do not have any, use dried mixed herbs (above) instead.
- FINES HERBES combines equal quantities of tarragon, chervil, parsley, and chives. It works well in omelettes and with fish and poultry.

GROWING YOUR OWN HERBS

The range of fresh herbs available in shops and supermarkets is extensive, but buying them is much more expensive than using those you grow yourself, especially if you use large amounts. Also, growing your own gives you the chance to try more unusual varieties of herbs. Cultivation, indoors or out, is simple and satisfying. Herbs can be grown in the garden, in pots on a paved terrace or patio, in a hanging basket or in a window box. Indoors, they will flourish in a box or in pots on a sunny windowsill.

SPICES

In the past spices were often used to mask the taste of less-than-perfect food, and at one time were so precious and expensive that they would be locked away in special spice boxes or cupboards. Today, spices are no longer a luxury seasoning, and modern cooks use them to enhance flavours rather than to disguise them.

BUYING AND STORING SPICES

If they are whole, spices do not deteriorate as quickly as herbs (which is why it is best to buy whole spices and grind them as you need them). Store in tightly sealed containers in a cool, dark, dry place. Whole spices will keep for 1 year, ground spices for about 6 months.

USING SPICES

Because spices need time to release their aromas and flavours, they are usually added near the start of cooking. If the cooking process is prolonged, whole, cracked, or bruised spices are normally used rather than ground spices, which may become bitter.

Toasting or warming whole or ground spices before use brings out their flavours, and is a good thing to do if the spices are to be added to a dish that is cooked for only a short time. When toasting, use a heavy frying pan over a low heat because the spices can scorch easily; if toasting ground spices add a little oil to the pan. Warm the spices just until they smell aromatic.

SALT

Salt is the essential seasoning, both for cooking and as a table condiment. It enhances the natural flavours of all savoury foods and some sweet ones, and is important in baking and in the preservation of food. There are two types: rock salt, which is mined from underground, and sea salt which is evaporated from sea water. Both rock and sea salts are available coarse (in large or medium-size crystals) or as table salt (refined to very small grains, with anti-caking agents added to keep it free-flowing).

Monosodium glutamate (MSG) is used in a similar way to salt, to accentuate flavours.

SPICE FLAVOURS

Spices come in many shapes and sizes, with subtly differing flavours and fragrances. They can be as exotic as rosebuds and liquorice root or as familiar as cinnamon and cloves. Here are some of the most commonly used.

• HOT SPICES stimulate the palate and sharpen the appetite as well as encouraging the body to produce perspiration – an excellent means of cooling down in a hot climate. The best known hot spice is chilli, which is available as whole chillies (fresh or dried), crushed dried chillies (also called chilli flakes), and ground into chilli powder (usually a blend of ground chillies and other spices), very hot cayenne pepper and paprika (may be mild or hot). In addition there

PREPARING SPICES

The way in which spices are prepared depends on the recipe in which they are used and the depth of flavour required.

Whole spices
Whole spices (and herbs) that are to be removed before serving are best tied in a piece of muslin, which allows them to be lifted out of the dish all at once.

Toasting spices
Heat a heavy frying pan until hot. Add the spices and cook over a low heat for 1–2 minutes, stirring occasionally, until the aromas are released. Leave to cool, then grind.

Grinding spices
Put the whole spices into a mortar; crush them with a pestle to the required consistency. Or, grind in a small electric mill kept especially for grinding spices.

Soaking saffron
Put threads into a small bowl. Add hot water (usually an amount in the recipe). Soak for 10 minutes. Use the liquid only, or the threads as well, according to the recipe.

are chilli sauces and pastes, oils, and jam. Just as the hundreds of different varieties of chilli vary from pleasantly warm through to burning hot, so do the spices and mixtures derived from them.

- PEPPER is an aromatic hot spice. Black, white, green, and red or pink peppercorns are available, each different in taste and fragrance. Freshly ground black pepper is used in almost every savoury dish plus a few sweet ones and is an essential table condiment. There are also two Asian peppers: fragrant Sichuan pepper and Japanese sansho.

- OTHER HOT SPICES are the familiar mustard, root ginger, and galangal. Mustard is available as whole seeds, powder, or ready-made paste; and in blended mixtures that include herbs, other spices, or even fruit flavours – the French *moutarde au cassis*, for example, contains crème de cassis (blackcurrant) liqueur for a rich taste and vibrant red colour. Root ginger and the less familiar galangal are similar in appearance and in taste; they are actually knobbly rhizomes, not roots. Both are available fresh (try oriental shops or a large supermarket), as powder, and in dried slices which need to be soaked in water before using (they are good to flavour soups and stews, but take care to remove the slices before serving).

- WARM, FRAGRANT SPICES provide a sweet note. They are usually added at the beginning of cooking so that their flavour and aroma can permeate the dish, be it sweet or savoury. Warm spices include allspice (a single spice that is like a peppery mixture of cloves and cinnamon), green cardamom (pods contain tiny, sticky black seeds), cinnamon, cloves, coriander seed, pretty star anise and anise seed (both liquorice-like), nutmeg and mace (nutmeg is the seed and mace – usually available only ground – its wrapping), and vanilla (use pods or pure essence or extract).

- NUTTY SPICES include poppyseeds and sesame seeds.

- PUNGENT SPICES are assertive in taste so should be used judiciously. They include juniper berries (slightly sweet and resinous), cumin (warm and a bit sharp), and caraway.

- FRUITY SPICES may be sweet or refreshingly tart. They range from sourish tamarind (available as dried pulp in a block, paste, or concentrate) to lemon grass stalks and kaffir lime leaves.

- COLOURING SPICES will tint and flavour a dish. Saffron is expensive but only a pinch is needed to colour a dish yellow (and add a warm, musky taste). Turmeric gives a richer, yellow-ochre hue, and is slightly more bitter. The dark red colour of goulash and chorizo sausages comes from paprika (ground chilli).

THE PEPPER FAMILY

The different powders derived from dried chillies can be confusing. Some are much hotter than others, so it is wise to know which is which.

Paprika
The mildest of the pepper family, paprika is available in three forms – sweet (mild), sharp (hot), and smoked (musky).

Cayenne
A searingly hot powder made from one of the hottest varieties of chilli with nothing added. Use with caution.

Chilli Powder
A blend of chillies with herbs and other spices, usually oregano and cumin, plus garlic. Strength varies according to brand.

SPICE MIXTURES

Although there is nothing like the thrill of inventing and grinding your own mixtures from whole spices, ready-made blends of ground spices do save time for the busy cook. Mixtures vary according to individual manufacturers and brands; try different brands to find which you prefer. These are the most common.

- CURRY POWDER may be perfumed and mild or hot, according to the blend of spices (usually turmeric, fenugreek, coriander, cumin, cardamom, chilli, cinnamon, and paprika). It gives curries an authentic flavour, which is often difficult to achieve yourself.

- GARAM MASALA, an aromatic curry spice, is usually a mixture of cumin, coriander, cardamom, cinnamon, pepper, cloves, turmeric, and ginger, sometimes with mace and bay. It is best added to a dish towards the end of the cooking time to preserve its fine aroma.

- MIXED SPICE is a traditional English mixture of six sweet spices: usually allspice, cinnamon, cloves, coriander, mace, and nutmeg.

- FIVE-SPICE POWDER is a Chinese blend of five flavours (salty, sour, bitter, pungent, and sweet) – hence its name. It is a mixture of ground star anise, fennel, cloves, cinnamon and Sichuan pepper. Dried ginger, cardamom, or liquorice can be added to the mixture, although commercial ones rarely include these.

SAFE & HEALTHY COOKING

It is important to handle and store perishable foods with care, so they remain at their best, and to help prevent food poisoning. The common-sense food safety guidelines are easy to follow and will ensure that you can enjoy what you eat without worries.

DAIRY PRODUCTS

Eggs should be stored in the refrigerator. It is best to leave them in their box so you can keep an eye on the date stamp. The "best before" date is a better indicator of age than the packing date, which could be several days after laying.

Even among eggs from free-range hens, it is known that some can harbour the salmonella bacterium, which can cause food poisoning. Health guidelines therefore recommend that it may be safest to avoid eating raw eggs (such as in home-made mayonnaise, mousses, and the like) altogether. Vulnerable groups (pregnant women, babies and young children, the very old, the sick and people with damaged immune systems) should definitely eat only thoroughly cooked eggs (hard boiled rather than soft boiled, for example).

Soft cheeses ripened using moulds (such as Brie and Camembert) and soft blue cheeses (whether made from pasteurized or unpasteurized milk) may harbour the listeria bacterium, which can cause an illness similar to flu. Listeria is of no concern to adults in normal health, but it is recommended that vulnerable groups (as listed above) should avoid these sorts of soft cheeses.

MEAT & POULTRY

Raw meat can contain bacteria that cause food poisoning, so it must be handled safely. Keep it in the refrigerator, in its original wrapping or transferred to fresh wrapping or a covered dish.

Poultry such as chicken and turkey can also harbour food-poisoning bacteria, commonly salmonella and campylobacter. So, as with meat, keep poultry in the fridge (in its original wrapping if you are going to cook it within a few hours, otherwise in fresh, loose wrapping). Thorough cooking will kill any bacteria that might be present. To ensure this, it is recommended that the body cavity not be stuffed (this could pevent heat penetrating to the centre of the bird). If you do want to stuff the body cavity, fill it loosely and only two-thirds full, and stuff no more than 3 hours before cooking. Then at the end of the cooking time test the temperature of the bird and of the stuffing with an instant-read thermometer: the thigh meat and the stuffing should be at least 75°C (170°F) and the breast meat 71°C (160°F).

With leftovers, cool them as quickly as possible (no more than 2 hours at room temperature) and then wrap and store in the refrigerator or freezer.

SEAFOOD

Mussels, clams, and oysters bought live are very perishable. Store, covered with a damp cloth, in the coldest part of the refrigerator, and use the same day. When preparing mussels for cooking, discard any that have broken shells or with open shells that do not close when sharply tapped (these are not safe to eat). After cooking, discard any that have not opened.

Crab, prawns, and lobster, must also be very fresh; they become poisonous when stale. If they smell of ammonia or at all unpleasant, do not buy them.

Fish bought as fresh may previously have been frozen, and this is not always clearly labelled. If it was previously frozen it must not be frozen again (unless it is first used to make a cooked dish such as fish pie).

GRAINS & PULSES

Leftover cooked rice should always be cooled quickly and stored in a covered container in the refrigerator (for no longer than a day or so) or in the freezer – if not kept cool it could develop food-poisoning toxins. Be sure to reheat cooked rice until it is very hot.

Most pulses contain toxic proteins that can cause severe food poisoning symptoms. To destroy the toxins, give all pulses (except chickpeas, lentils, and split peas) a 10–15 minute period of fast boiling at the start of cooking.

A NOTE ABOUT ORGANIC PRODUCE

It is often thought that fruit and vegetables produced organically are free of pesticide and herbicide residues, but this is not always the case as much organic produce is imported from countries where regulations are not strictly followed. If in doubt, wash fruit and vegetables thoroughly under running cold water, scrubbing if necessary, and peel before cooking or eating.

1

HOT & CHILLED
SOUPS

UNDER 30 MINUTES

ORIENTAL CLASSIC

THAI SPICED SOUP

Fresh and chunky: shredded chicken, bean sprouts, and leafy vegetables simmered in coconut milk and stock. Served over noodles.

SERVES 4 238 calories per serving
Takes 25 minutes   Page 55

ECONOMICAL

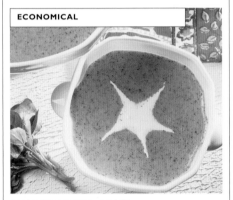

WATERCRESS SOUP

Smooth and creamy: blended onion, potatoes, watercress, stock, and milk, lightly flavoured with a bay leaf. Can be served hot or cold.

SERVES 6 140 calories per serving
Takes 25 minutes   Page 43

SOMERSET MUSHROOM SOUP

Mushrooms, garlic, and onion cooked with stock and white wine, and generously flavoured with thyme and marjoram.

SERVES 4–6 109–73 calories per serving
Takes 25 minutes   Page 41

30–60 MINUTES

LOW FAT

FRENCH PEA SOUP

Smooth and summery: onion blended with frozen or fresh peas (in season) and stock, and flavoured with mint sprigs.

SERVES 4–6 179–119 calories per serving
Takes 35 minutes   Page 40

DINNER PARTY

ASPARAGUS SOUP

Fresh asparagus blended with stock and potatoes, and richly flavoured with garlic. Garnished here with nuggets of butter.

SERVES 6 96 calories per serving
Takes 25 minutes   Page 42

FAMILY CHOICE

TOMATO SOUP

Tomatoes, onions, and garlic blended with stock. Enriched with ready-made pesto and flavoured with a bay leaf.

SERVES 6–8 134–101 calories per serving
Takes 25 minutes   Page 45

CUBAN SWEETCORN & SEAFOOD SOUP

Firm white fish with sweetcorn, pumpkin, potato, stock, and passata, simmered with chilli and garlic.

SERVES 4 379 calories per serving
Takes 40 minutes   Page 50

ORIENTAL CLASSIC

CHINESE CRAB & SWEETCORN SOUP

Blended sweetcorn kernels cooked with crabmeat and stock, and flavoured with soy sauce, spring onions, garlic, and ginger.

SERVES 4 216 calories per serving
Takes 20 minutes   Page 55

HIGH PROTEIN

LENTIL & BACON SOUP

Nourishing and hearty: diced vegetables, bacon, and lentils simmered in stock, and richly flavoured with garlic and herbs.

SERVES 4–6 301–201 calories per serving
Takes 50 minutes   Page 53

30–60 MINUTES

AMERICAN CLASSIC

CLAM CHOWDER

Fresh clams cooked in fish stock, then simmered with milk, onion, and potatoes, and flavoured with bacon and bay leaf.

SERVES 4 497 calories per serving

Takes 50 minutes   Page 48

TRADITIONAL

INDIAN SPICED SMOKED HADDOCK CHOWDER

Vegetables and spices, simmered with smoked haddock and stock, make a rich and piquant soup.

SERVES 4 500 calories per serving

Takes 50 minutes   Page 46

PUMPKIN SOUP

Nourishing and smooth: blended pumpkin, leeks, and stock, enriched with cream, and combined with petits pois and spinach.

SERVES 6 329 calories per serving

Takes 50 minutes   Page 52

GAME SOUP

Rich and aromatic: bacon and mushrooms simmered in game stock, flavoured with a citrus and herb bouquet and redcurrant jelly.

SERVES 4 223 calories per serving

Takes 50 minutes   Page 53

DINNER PARTY

CURRIED PARSNIP SOUP

Smooth and spicy: parsnips blended with mild curry powder, onion, garlic, and stock, and enriched with single cream.

SERVES 6–8 197–147 calories per serving

Takes 35 minutes   Page 44

VEGETARIAN

SPICED AUTUMN SOUP

Potatoes, carrots, dessert apples, orange zest and juice, tomatoes, and stock blended with onion, garlic, curry powder, and dried basil.

SERVES 8 171 calories per serving

Takes 50 minutes   Page 47

HIGH PROTEIN

BLUE STILTON & ONION SOUP

Creamy and rich: finely sliced onions combined with stock, blue Stilton cheese, bay leaves, and nutmeg make a tasty soup.

SERVES 8 255 calories per serving

Takes 50 minutes   Page 47

FAMILY CHOICE

WINTER VEGETABLE SOUP

Assortment of seasonal vegetables simmered with stock, seasoned with dill and turmeric, and coloured with spinach.

SERVES 6 153 calories per serving

Takes 55 minutes   Page 44

HOT & SOUR SOUP

Rich and tangy: dried mushrooms, sliced cabbage, tofu, bamboo shoots, and chicken simmered with stock, and enriched with eggs.

SERVES 4–6 249–166 calories per serving

Takes 50 minutes   Page 54

OVER 60 MINUTES

TZATZIKI SOUP

Cool and refreshing: yogurt, cucumber, and garlic blended with olive oil, white wine vinegar, and mint, and served chilled.

SERVES 4–6 138–92 calories per serving
Takes 15 minutes, plus chilling   Page 56

TRADITIONAL

BORSCHT

Beetroot, cabbage, potatoes, and tomatoes simmered with stock, vinegar, sugar, and dill for a rich sweet-sour flavour.

SERVES 4 244 calories per serving
Takes 1¼ hours   Page 45

BOUILLABAISSE

Mediterranean favourite: assorted white fish and shellfish simmered in stock with vegetables, orange zest, and Provençal herbs.

SERVES 8 337 calories per serving
Takes 1¼ hours   Page 51

GAZPACHO

Tomatoes, pimientos, and garlic blended with stock, olive oil, and red wine vinegar make a rich iced soup. Served with garlic croûtons.

SERVES 4–6 249–166 calories per serving
Takes 15 minutes, plus chilling   Page 57

LOW FAT

RICH FISH SOUP

White fish fillets blended with stock, dry white wine, and mixed vegetables, and richly flavoured with garlic and herbs.

SERVES 4 419 calories per serving
Takes 1¼ hours   Page 48

PRAWN GUMBO

Red pepper and tomatoes cooked with chorizo, stock, and okra make a piquant base for prawns. Served with a rice timbale.

SERVES 4 512 calories per serving
Takes 1¼ hours   Page 50

FRENCH CLASSIC

FRENCH ONION SOUP

Thinly sliced caramelized onions simmered in beef stock and topped with a traditional Gruyère croûte.

SERVES 8 353 calories per serving
Takes 1¼ hours   Page 42

VEGETARIAN

CREAMY CARROT & ORANGE SOUP

Smooth and tangy: carrots and stock mixed with crème fraîche, orange zest and juice, and flavoured with fresh chives.

SERVES 6–8 308–231 calories per serving
Takes 1¼ hours   Page 40

DINNER PARTY

LOBSTER BISQUE

Rich-tasting and luxurious: lobster tails, shallots, brandy, wine, stock, and spices combined with cream (optional) and lemon juice.

SERVES 6 192 calories per serving
Takes 1½ hours   Page 49

OVER 60 MINUTES

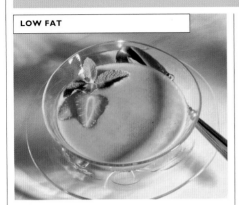

CHILLED STRAWBERRY SOUP

White wine sweetened with caster sugar and blended with strawberries and orange juice, then chilled for a refreshing, sweet soup.

SERVES 4 169 calories per serving
Takes 15 minutes, plus chilling   Page 58

GOULASH SOUP

Rich and wholesome: beef, roasted red peppers, onions, potatoes, and tomatoes cooked in stock, and flavoured with paprika.

SERVES 4–6 544–363 calories per serving
Takes 2¼ hours   Page 52

ROASTED TOMATO & GARLIC SOUP

Light and well flavoured: roasted ripe tomatoes cooked with onion and stock, and richly flavoured with garlic.

SERVES 4 127 calories per serving
Takes 40 minutes, plus standing   Page 41

BLUEBERRY & RED WINE SOUP

Chilled and fruity: cranberry juice, red wine, cinnamon, and sugar simmered with blueberries, and enriched with cream.

SERVES 4 364 calories per serving
Takes 30 minutes, plus chilling   Page 57

VICHYSSOISE

Leeks, onion, and potatoes blended with chicken stock, chilled, then combined with cream, result in this renowned velvety soup.

SERVES 4–6 251–167 calories per serving
Takes 45 minutes, plus chilling   Page 56

VEGETABLE MINESTRONE

Hearty soup: dried beans cooked and added to a tomato sauce with stock, leeks, cabbage, and arborio rice.

SERVES 4–6 250–167 calories per serving
Takes 1¾ hours, plus soaking   Page 43

CHILLED CURRIED APPLE & MINT SOUP

Apples blended with onion, curry powder, stock, mango chutney, lemon juice, yogurt, and mint.

SERVES 6 110 calories per serving
Takes 40 minutes, plus chilling   Page 58

CHICKEN NOODLE SOUP

Rich and warming: simmered chicken, carrots, and stock, flavoured with garlic, parsley, and dill, and served over noodles.

SERVES 6 261 calories per serving
Takes 2½ hours   Page 54

SPLIT PEA & GAMMON SOUP

Green split peas and flavoursome gammon, simmered with onion, celery, potatoes, and leeks, make a substantial meal.

SERVES 6–8 451–338 calories per serving
Takes 3¾ hours, plus soaking   Page 46

SOUPS KNOW-HOW

A BATCH OF SOUP in the fridge is one of the best convenience foods ever, highly nutritious and wonderfully versatile. On a cold day, a bowl of soup is warming and sustaining, and with a sandwich or just some bread it can make a well-balanced lunch or supper. Soup is great for entertaining too, the ideal prepare-ahead starter. And soup is comforting at bedtime or, indeed, at any time of day.

There are all kinds of soups: light and delicate or rich and hearty; simple and quick to prepare or cooked long and slow to extract maximum flavour from the ingredients; velvety smooth in texture or full of delicious pieces of meat, vegetables, pulses or pasta. Soups may be served hot or chilled, in a mug, a bowl or a soup plate, plain or attractively garnished. There are even sweet and fruity soups that can double up as desserts.

Clarifying stock

Skimming will make a stock quite clear, but for crystal-clear results it needs to be clarified. When cold pour into a large pan. For each 600 ml (1 pint) add an egg white and crushed egg shell. Heat slowly, whisking. When frothy and starting to rise up, stop whisking and remove from the heat to subside. The crust that forms will act as a filter, collecting all the impurities. Repeat the rising up and subsiding 2 or 3 times, then simmer gently for 45 minutes. Strain through a muslin-lined sieve, holding back the crust.

STOCKS

A well flavoured stock forms the base of many soups, and nothing tastes as good as home-made stock. Stock is economical to make because it is based on meat, poultry, or fish bones and trimmings, and vegetables. Although it usually takes time to make stock – several hours of gentle simmering for meat and poultry stocks – it is easy to prepare, and can be made well in advance and in large quantities. It can then be frozen until needed. Recipes for stocks can be found on pages 122, 170, 235, and 276. If you don't have any home-made stock, there are fresh stocks available in the chilled cabinets in supermarkets, or you can use stock made from bouillon powder or a cube. Remember, though, that stock cubes are often strong and salty, so go easy on the salt. Another quick alternative is to use canned consommé.

SKIMMING SOUPS

As a soup is brought to the boil, foam or scum may form on the surface. This is most likely with soups that contain meat or poultry, particularly on the bone, or root vegetables and pulses. This foam, which contains impurities, should be removed as it forms.

Use a large metal spoon or skimmer (slotted if there are herbs and whole spices in the soup) to skim off the foam.

If there is a lot of fat on the surface of a soup, skim it off with a large metal spoon, or blot it with paper towels, before serving.

MICROWAVING

For many soups, a microwave cannot give the same results as conventional long, slow cooking, but it can produce light vegetable soups in minutes. And it is useful for thawing frozen stocks and soups, and for reheating soups. The most efficient way of heating soup in the microwave is to transfer the soup to individual bowls or mugs, because soup in larger containers will take longer to heat up than it would in a pan on top of the stove. For cooking soup in the microwave, use a container that is large enough to allow the soup to rise up slightly. Stir once or twice during cooking or heating, and just before serving, as the soup at the edge will be hot and bubbling long before that in the centre. Add single cream, soured cream, or yogurt and any garnish just before serving.

FREEZING

Soups taste best if freshly made, but most can be frozen without impairing flavour or texture. Avoid freezing soups containing ingredients such as pasta, potatoes, and rice as they become mushy. It is always best to underseason, as further seasoning can be added when reheating. Add any cream, eggs, and milk at the reheating stage, as freezing could cause separation or curdling.

To thaw a soup to be served hot, heat from frozen in a heavy saucepan over a low heat, stirring occasionally. If the soup appears to be separating, whisk briskly until smooth or work in a blender or food processor, or with a hand-held blender, for a few seconds. Thaw soup to be served cold in its freezer container, in the refrigerator.

THICKENING SOUPS

Many soups can be slightly thickened simply by being puréed to a smooth consistency. Puréed soups that contain starchy ingredients such as rice, pasta and potatoes will be even thicker.

In some soup recipes, flour is used as a thickener. Normally it is added to the softened vegetables, to bind the fat and juices together. The mixture is then cooked to remove the raw flour taste before the stock is stirred in. Flour can also be added to puréed soups at the end of cooking if they are not thick enough: blend the flour with cold stock, whisk in and simmer until thickened.

GARNISHES

An attractive garnish can lift a soup, adding a contrast in colour, texture, and flavour. Here are some ideas.
• Fresh herbs, either chopped or as whole leaves – mint, chives, thyme, parsley, basil, tarragon, and coriander are all popular. Choose a herb that complements or mirrors any herbs in the soup, and add at the last minute so that it retains its freshness.
• Grated or crumbled cheese
• Chopped hard-boiled egg
• Fine shreds of citrus zest or whole berries
• Crisp pieces of bacon; diced meat or poultry
• Toasted nuts; sunflower seeds
• Croûtons
• Chopped, diced, sliced, or grated vegetables such as spring onions, cucumber, carrots, peppers, and fennel
• A spoonful of a sauce such as pesto
• A blob or decorative swirl of cream or yogurt (see box, below)

Adding cream & yogurt

Double and whipping cream and crème fraîche can be added to a hot soup and heated further, with no danger of curdling.

Single cream, soured cream, and yogurt will curdle if overheated, so add them just before serving and warm through over a low heat. For chilled soups, add cream or yogurt once the soup has been chilled, before serving.

Garnishing with cream

With a teaspoon, quickly swirl single or whipping cream in a spiral on each serving.

PUREEING SOUPS

Soups are often puréed to give them a velvety-smooth texture. This also gives them a thicker texture. Starchy vegetables and a little flour will help to thicken them even more.

Blender or food processor
Either of these can be used to process the cooked ingredients in batches. Scrape the sides of the container once or twice to ensure there are no solid pieces left unprocessed.

Hand-held blender
Use this to purée directly in the saucepan (which should be deep to prevent splashes). It's not useful for large quantities, but is ideal for blending in a final addition of cream or yogurt.

Sieve
To make a puréed soup ultra smooth, and remove any fibres, seeds, or skins, work it through a fine sieve with a wooden spoon. This is much easier to do if the soup is first puréed in a blender or food processor.

FRENCH PEA SOUP

SERVES 4–6

30 g (1 oz) butter

1 large onion, coarsely chopped

1 tbsp plain flour

500 g (1 lb) frozen peas

1.25 litres (2 pints) vegetable chicken or stock

1/2 tsp caster sugar

2 large mint sprigs

salt and black pepper

shredded fresh mint to garnish

1 Melt the butter in a large saucepan, add the chopped onion, and cook very gently, stirring occasionally, for about 10 minutes until soft but not coloured.

2 Sprinkle in the flour and stir for a further 1–2 minutes, then add the frozen peas, stock, caster sugar, and sprigs of mint.

3 Bring to a boil, cover, and simmer gently, stirring occasionally, for 5 minutes or until the peas are soft. Do not simmer any longer than this or the peas will lose their fresh green colour.

4 Remove the mint sprigs and discard. Purée the soup in a food processor or blender until smooth.

5 Return the soup to the rinsed-out pan, reheat, and add salt and pepper to taste. Serve hot, garnished with shredded fresh mint.

Cook's know-how

Use fresh peas when in season. You will need about 1 kg (2 lb) peas in their pods to give you 500 g (1 lb) after shelling, and they will take 20 minutes to cook in step 3.

CREAMY CARROT & ORANGE SOUP

SERVES 6–8

30 g (1 oz) butter

1 onion, coarsely chopped

1 kg (2 lb) carrots, thickly sliced

1.5 litres (2 1/2 pints) vegetable stock

grated zest of 1/2 orange

300 ml (1/2 pint) orange juice (squeezed fresh or from a carton)

salt and black pepper

300 ml (1/2 pint) crème fraîche

3 tbsp snipped fresh chives

1 Melt the butter in a large saucepan, add the onion, and cook gently, stirring occasionally, for a few minutes until soft but not coloured. Add the carrots, cover, and cook gently, stirring from time to time, for 10 minutes.

2 Add the stock and bring to a boil. Cover and simmer, stirring from time to time, for 30–40 minutes until the carrots are soft.

3 Purée the soup in a food processor or blender until smooth. Return the soup to the rinsed-out pan, add the orange zest and juice, and salt and pepper to taste. Stir in the crème fraîche and then gently reheat the soup.

4 Stir in half of the snipped chives, and garnish individual servings with the remaining chives.

Healthy option

The crème fraîche makes this soup rich and creamy for a dinner party first course, but for an everyday soup that is full of zest and vitality, you can easily omit it and increase the stock by 300 ml (1/2 pint) in step 2. Another healthy option is to cook the onion in step 1 in 1 tbsp each olive oil and water rather than using butter.

ROASTED TOMATO & GARLIC SOUP

This soup is light in consistency but full of flavour, making it perfect for late summer when tomatoes are at their ripest and best. Charring the tomatoes in the oven gives the soup a wonderful smoky flavour.

SERVES 4

1 kg (2 lb) ripe tomatoes

2 tbsp olive oil

1 onion, chopped

3 garlic cloves, coarsely chopped

1.5 litres (2½ pints) chicken or vegetable stock

salt and black pepper

ready made pesto to serve

1 Cut the tomatoes in half and arrange them, cut-side down, in a roasting tin. Roast in a preheated oven at 220°C (425°F, Gas 7) for 15 minutes or until the skins are charred.

2 Remove the tomatoes from the oven and leave until they are cool enough to handle, then peel off the skins and discard them. Chop the flesh coarsely, retaining the juice.

3 Heat the oil in a large saucepan, add the onion and garlic, and cook gently, stirring occasionally, for a few minutes until soft but not coloured.

4 Add the stock and the tomato flesh and juices, and bring to a boil. Lower the heat and simmer for 5 minutes, then add salt and pepper to taste.

5 Serve the soup hot, with a bowl of pesto so everyone can stir in a spoonful before they eat.

MEXICAN ROASTED TOMATO SOUP

Add ¼ tsp each ground cumin and crushed dried red chillies (chilli flakes) to the onion and garlic in step 3. Instead of pesto, serve with a relish made with 3–4 tbsp chopped fresh coriander leaves, 1 tbsp chopped raw onion, and 1–2 tbsp lime or lemon juice.

SUN-DRIED TOMATO SOUP

Cook 2–3 chopped sun-dried tomatoes and add them to the saucepan with the onion and garlic in step 3. Serve garnished with finely shredded fresh basil.

SOMERSET MUSHROOM SOUP

SERVES 4–6

30 g (1 oz) butter

1 small onion, finely chopped

1 garlic clove, crushed

500 g (1 lb) mushrooms, sliced

1.25 litres (2 pints) vegetable or chicken stock

150 ml (¼ pint) dry white wine

2 tsp chopped fresh oregano

2 tbsp chopped fresh thyme

salt and black pepper

1 Melt the butter in a large saucepan, add the onion and garlic, and cook gently, stirring occasionally, for a few minutes until soft but not coloured. Add the mushrooms and cook, stirring from time to time, for 10 minutes.

2 Pour in the stock and wine, then add the oregano and half of the thyme, and season with salt and pepper. Bring to a boil, cover, and simmer gently for 10 minutes or until the mushrooms are tender.

3 Taste for seasoning and serve hot, sprinkled with the remaining fresh thyme.

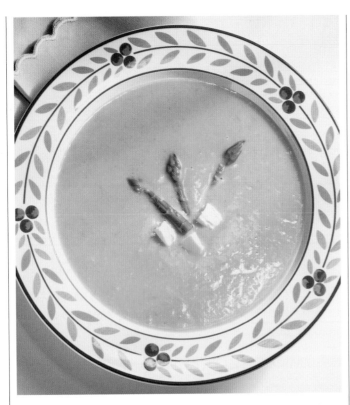

ASPARAGUS SOUP

SERVES 6

250 g (8 oz) potatoes, chopped

1.5 litres (2½ pints) vegetable or chicken stock

500 g (1 lb) asparagus

2 garlic cloves, crushed

2 tbsp chopped fresh basil (optional)

salt and black pepper

30 g (1 oz) butter (optional)

1 Put the potatoes into a large saucepan, add the stock, and bring to a boil. Cover and simmer for 15 minutes or until the potatoes are tender.

2 Meanwhile, cut any woody ends off the asparagus and discard. Cut off the tips and chop the stalks into chunks.

3 Add the asparagus and garlic to the pan and cook for 5 minutes, stirring from time to time, until the asparagus is tender. Remove 9 tips; reserve for the garnish.

4 Purée the soup in a food processor or blender until smooth.

5 Return the soup to the rinsed-out pan and reheat. Add the basil, if using, and salt and pepper to taste. Slice the reserved asparagus tips lengthwise in half. Serve the soup hot, garnished with the asparagus tips and small nuggets of butter, if wished.

ARTICHOKE SOUP

Use 1 x 400 g (13 oz) can artichoke hearts or bottoms, drained and diced, instead of the asparagus, and garnish with basil.

Healthy option

This is a soup for a special occasion and the butter garnish makes it an absolute classic – melted butter is traditional with asparagus. If you are concerned about the fat content, you can garnish with torn basil instead.

FRENCH ONION SOUP

SERVES 8

45 g (1½ oz) butter

1 tbsp sunflower oil

1 kg (2 lb) large onions, thinly sliced

2 tsp caster sugar

30 g (1 oz) plain flour

1.8 litres (3 pints) vegetable, chicken, or beef stock

salt and black pepper

8 Gruyère croûtes (page 49)

1 Melt the butter with the oil in a large saucepan, and caramelize the onions with the sugar (see box, right). Sprinkle the flour into the pan and cook, stirring constantly, for 1–2 minutes.

2 Gradually stir in the stock and bring to a boil. Season with salt and pepper, then cover and simmer, stirring from time to time, for 35 minutes.

3 Taste the soup for seasoning, then ladle into warmed bowls. Float a Gruyère croûte in each bowl and serve at once.

Cook's know-how

Cooking with sugar is the key to developing a rich, golden brown colour and sweet caramel flavour in onions. It is this that produces the characteristic appearance and taste of this classic soup.

Caramelizing onions

Cook the onions in the butter and oil for a few minutes until soft. Add the sugar and continue cooking over a low heat, stirring occasionally, for 20 minutes or until the onions are golden brown.

WATERCRESS SOUP

SERVES 6

30 g (1 oz) butter

1 onion, finely chopped

2 potatoes, coarsely chopped

125 g (4 oz) watercress, tough stalks removed

900 ml (1½ pints) vegetable or chicken stock

300 ml (½ pint) milk

1 bay leaf

salt and black pepper

single cream to garnish (optional)

1 Melt the butter in a large saucepan, add the onion, and cook gently, stirring from time to time, for a few minutes until soft but not coloured.

2 Add the potatoes and the watercress to the saucepan and cook for about 5 minutes until the watercress is wilted.

3 Pour in the chicken or vegetable stock and milk, add the bay leaf, and season with salt and pepper.

4 Bring the mixture to a boil, cover, and simmer very gently for 15 minutes or until the potatoes are tender.

5 Remove the bay leaf and discard. Purée the soup in a food processor or blender until smooth. Return the soup to the rinsed-out pan, reheat, then taste for seasoning.

6 Serve hot, garnishing each bowl with a little single cream if you like.

Cook's know-how

Watercress soup is delicious served chilled in summer. After puréeing, pour the soup into a large bowl, then cover, cool, and chill for at least 3 hours. Taste for seasoning before serving because chilling dulls the flavour slightly. You can also freeze this soup for up to 3 months.

VEGETABLE MINESTRONE

SERVES 4–6

2 tbsp olive oil

1 onion, chopped

2 celery stalks, chopped

2 carrots, diced

1 x 400 g (13 oz) can chopped Italian plum tomatoes

1 tbsp tomato purée

1 garlic clove, crushed

salt and black pepper

1.5 litres (2½ pints) chicken or vegetable stock

1 x 400 g (13 oz) can cannellini or red kidney beans, drained

250 g (8 oz) leeks, trimmed and finely sliced

125 g (4 oz) Savoy cabbage, finely shredded

2 tbsp arborio (risotto) rice

grated Parmesan cheese to serve

1 Heat the oil in a large saucepan, add the onion, celery, and carrots, and cook gently, stirring, for 5 minutes.

2 Add the tomatoes, tomato purée, and garlic, and season with salt and pepper. Stir, then pour in the stock and bring to a boil over a high heat.

3 Cover the pan and lower the heat so the soup is a gently simmering. Cook for 15 minutes, stirring occasionally.

4 Add the beans, leeks, cabbage, and rice, and simmer for for a further 20 minutes. Taste for seasoning.

5 Serve hot, with a bowl of grated Parmesan cheese for everyone to help themselves.

Cook's know-how

If you haven't got arborio or any other type of risotto rice, use broken spaghetti instead. You will need 30 g (1 oz).

CURRIED PARSNIP SOUP

SERVES 6–8

30 g (1 oz) butter

750 g (1½ lb) parsnips, coarsely chopped

1 large onion, chopped

1 large garlic clove, crushed

2 tsp mild curry powder

1.8 litres (3 pints) vegetable or chicken stock

salt and black pepper

200 ml (7 fl oz) single cream

fresh chives to garnish

1 Melt the butter in a large saucepan, add the chopped parsnips, onion, and crushed garlic, and cook gently, stirring occasionally, for 5 minutes or until the onion is softened but not coloured.

2 Stir in the curry powder, and cook for 1 minute, then blend in the stock, and season with salt and pepper. Bring to a boil, stirring, then cover, and simmer gently for 20 minutes or until the parsnips are tender.

3 Purée the soup in a food processor or blender until smooth. Return the soup to the rinsed-out pan, heat gently to warm through, stirring constantly, then taste for seasoning.

4 Stir in the single cream and reheat gently. Serve at once, garnished with fresh chives.

Healthy option

If you are concerned about the fat content, omit the cream and use stock or water instead.

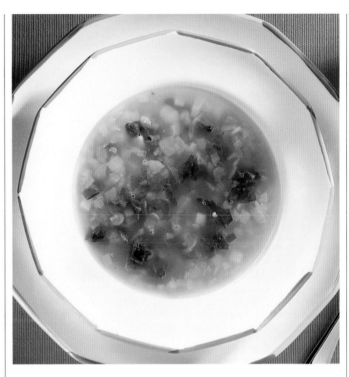

WINTER VEGETABLE SOUP

SERVES 6

45 g (1½ oz) butter

1 leek, trimmed and diced

1 onion, chopped

1 celery stalk, diced

1 small potato, diced

1 turnip, diced

1 small carrot, diced

3 garlic cloves, crushed

1.5 litres (2½ pints) vegetable or chicken stock

250 g (8 oz) spinach, coarsely shredded (see box, right)

3 spring onions, thinly sliced

salt and black pepper

1 Melt the butter in a large saucepan, add the leek, and cook gently, stirring occasionally, for 5 minutes or until softened. Add the onion, celery, potato, turnip, carrot, and garlic, and cook for 8 minutes.

2 Pour in the stock, and bring to a boil. Cover and simmer, stirring occasionally, for 25 minutes or until the vegetables are tender.

3 Add the spinach and spring onions, and cook for just 3 minutes until the spinach is wilted and still bright green. Season well, and serve hot.

Shredding spinach

Remove the stalks and stack several spinach leaves. Roll up tightly, and cut crosswise into shreds.

BORSCHT

SERVES 4

175 g (6 oz) white cabbage, coarsely shredded

200g (7 oz) waxy potatoes, diced

1 x 225 g (8 oz) can chopped tomatoes

1 small carrot, chopped

1 small onion, chopped

1.5 litres (2½ pints) vegetable or chicken stock, more if needed

500 g (1 lb) cooked beetroot, peeled and diced

3–4 dill sprigs, chopped

30 g (1 oz) sugar

2 tbsp wine vinegar

salt and black pepper

soured cream and dill sprigs to garnish

1 Put the cabbage, potatoes, tomatoes, carrot, and onion into a large pan with the stock.

2 Bring to a boil, then simmer for 30–40 minutes until the vegetables are very tender. Add extra stock if necessary.

3 Add the diced beetroot, dill, sugar, and vinegar, and simmer for 10 minutes to let the sweet-sour flavours develop. Add salt and pepper to taste, and more sugar and vinegar if necessary.

4 Serve at once, garnished with spoonfuls of soured cream and sprigs of dill.

TOMATO SOUP

SERVES 6–8

30 g (1 oz) butter

2 onions, coarsely chopped

1 garlic clove, crushed

1 tbsp plain flour

1.25 litres (2 pints) vegetable or chicken stock

2 x 400 g (13 oz) cans tomatoes

1 bay leaf

salt and black pepper

4 tbsp ready made pesto

single cream (optional) and fresh basil leaves to garnish

Healthy option

For a really healthy version of this soup, omit the butter, flour, and pesto and simply simmer the onions and garlic with the stock, tomatoes, and bay leaf. Cook for 30–40 minutes to develop the flavours before puréeing, then serve topped with torn basil.

1 Melt the butter in a large saucepan, add the onions and garlic, and cook gently, stirring from time to time, for a few minutes until soft but not coloured.

2 Add the flour to the pan and cook, stirring constantly, for 1 minute.

3 Pour in the stock, then add the tomatoes and their juice and the bay leaf. Season with salt and pepper. Bring to a boil, cover the pan, and simmer gently for 20 minutes.

4 Remove the bay leaf and discard. Purée the soup in a food processor or blender until smooth.

5 Return the soup to the rinsed-out pan, add the pesto, and heat through. Taste for seasoning.

6 Serve at once, garnished with cream (if you like) and fresh basil leaves.

QUICK TOMATO SOUP

Passata, Italian sieved tomatoes, makes a beautiful deep red soup. Substitute 750 ml (1¼ pints) of bottled or canned passata for the canned tomatoes and then cook as directed.

SPLIT PEA & GAMMON SOUP

SERVES 6–8

500 g (1 lb) green split peas

500 g (1 lb) gammon knuckle

2.5 litres (4 pints) water

1 large onion, finely chopped

4 celery stalks, finely chopped

3 potatoes, diced

3 leeks, trimmed and sliced

3 tbsp chopped parsley (optional)

salt and black pepper

1 Put the green split peas and the gammon knuckle into separate large bowls and cover generously with cold water. Leave to soak overnight.

2 Drain the split peas and gammon knuckle, then put them both into a large saucepan with the measured water. Bring to a boil, then simmer, uncovered, for about 1 hour.

3 Add the onion, celery, potatoes, and leeks to the pan, cover, and simmer gently for 2 1/2 hours until the gammon is tender and the peas are cooked. Add more water, if needed, during cooking.

4 Skim the surface if necessary. Remove the gammon knuckle from the saucepan and let it cool slightly. Pull the meat away from the knuckle bone, discarding any skin and fat.

5 Coarsely chop the meat and return it to the saucepan. Add the parsley, if using, and salt and pepper to taste, then heat gently to warm the meat through. Serve hot.

Cook's know-how

Gammon knuckles are meaty, yet inexpensive. Your butcher will have them, if you can't get one at the supermarket.

INDIAN SPICED SMOKED HADDOCK CHOWDER

SERVES 4

60 g (2 oz) butter

1 small onion, thinly sliced

6 celery stalks, sliced

2 carrots, chopped into 1 cm (½ in) dice

500 g (1 lb) main-crop potatoes, cut into 2 cm (¾ in) chunks

45 g (1½ oz) plain flour

2 tsp curry powder

½ tsp turmeric

½ tsp ground ginger

600 ml (1 pint) fish or vegetable stock

freshly ground black pepper

1 x 400 g (13 oz) can chopped tomatoes

750 g (1½ lb) smoked haddock, skinned and chopped into bite-sized pieces

600 ml (1 pint) full-fat milk

salt (optional)

chopped fresh dill to garnish

1 Melt the butter in a large saucepan, and add the onion, celery, and carrots. Stir to coat the vegetables in the butter, cover, and cook gently until they begin to soften. Add the potatoes and cook for a further 1–2 minutes.

2 Add the flour and spices to the vegetables and stir to mix together, then add the stock and season with pepper (do not add salt at this stage as smoked fish is salty). Bring to a boil, and simmer until the vegetables are tender, about 10–15 minutes.

3 Add the tomatoes, smoked haddock, and milk to the vegetable mixture in the pan, and simmer gently for 10–15 minutes until the fish is cooked.

4 Taste the soup for seasoning. Serve hot in warmed bowls, garnished with chopped fresh dill.

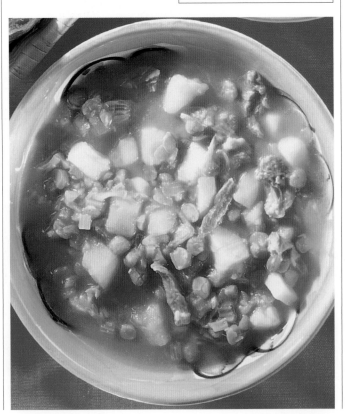

SPICED AUTUMN SOUP

SERVES 8

60 g (2 oz) butter
2 large onions, coarsely chopped
2 potatoes, coarsely chopped
2 carrots, coarsely chopped
3 garlic cloves, crushed
pared zest and juice of 1 orange
2 tsp mild curry powder
1.8 litres (3 pints) vegetable or chicken stock
2 x 400 g (13 oz) cans chopped tomatoes
2 eating apples, peeled and chopped
salt and black pepper
herb croûtes (page 49) to serve

1 Melt the butter in a large saucepan, add the onions, potatoes, carrots, garlic, and orange zest, and cook gently, stirring from time to time, for about 5 minutes.

2 Add the curry powder, and cook, stirring constantly, for 1–2 minutes.

3 Add the stock, orange juice, tomatoes, and apples, and season with salt and pepper. Bring to a boil, cover, and simmer gently for 30 minutes or until the vegetables are tender. Discard the orange zest.

4 Purée the soup in a food processor or blender until smooth. Return to the rinsed-out pan, reheat, and taste for seasoning. Serve hot, with herb croûtes.

Paring orange zest

With a vegetable peeler, remove strips of zest, excluding the bitter white pith.

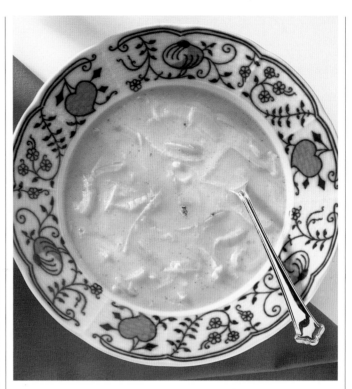

BLUE STILTON & ONION SOUP

SERVES 8

600 ml (1 pint) milk
2 bay leaves
1/4 tsp grated nutmeg
90 g (3 oz) butter
2 large onions, finely sliced
75 g (2 1/2 oz) plain flour
1.5 litres (2 1/2 pints) vegetable or chicken stock
salt and black pepper
150 g (5 oz) blue Stilton cheese, crumbled
single cream to serve (optional)

1 Pour the milk into a saucepan, add the bay leaves and nutmeg, and bring almost to a boil. Remove from the heat, cover, and leave to infuse for 20 minutes.

2 Meanwhile, melt the butter in a large pan, add the onions, and cook very gently, stirring occasionally, for about 10 minutes or until they are soft but not coloured.

3 Add the flour, and cook, stirring, for 2 minutes. Strain the milk and gradually blend it into the onion and flour. Add the stock, and season with salt and pepper. Bring to a boil and simmer, half covered, for 10 minutes.

4 Add the cheese and stir over a very low heat until it melts (do not boil or the cheese will be stringy). Taste for seasoning, and stir in a little cream if you wish. Serve hot.

Healthy option

There are ways of making this soup lighter if you are concerned about the fat content. Use semi-skimmed milk in step 1, only 30 g (1 oz) butter in step 2, and omit the flour in step 3. At the end, whisk the flour to a paste with a little cold stock or water, then whisk into the soup and boil, whisking, until thickened. Add only 60–90 g (2–3 oz) cheese in step 4.

CLAM CHOWDER

SERVES 4

500 g (1 lb) fresh clams in their
shells, cleaned (page 124)

250 ml (8 fl oz) fish stock

45 g (1 1/2 oz) butter

1 onion, chopped

3 unsmoked bacon rashers, rinds
removed, diced

2 tbsp plain flour

2 potatoes, diced

750 ml (1 1/4 pints) milk

1 bay leaf

salt and black pepper

1 Put the clams into a large
saucepan, add the fish stock,
and bring to a boil. Lower the
heat, cover, and cook over a
medium heat for 5–8 minutes
until the clam shells open.

2 Discard any clams that have
not opened. Set aside 12
clams in their shells for garnish
and keep warm. Remove the
remaining clams from their
shells. Discard the shells and
strain the cooking juices.

3 Melt the butter in a large
pan, add the onion, and
cook gently for a few minutes
until soft but not coloured.
Add the bacon and the flour,
and cook, stirring, for
1–2 minutes.

4 Add the potatoes, milk,
strained clam juices, and
bay leaf to the pan. Bring to a
boil, then lower the heat and
simmer for 15 minutes. Add
the shelled clams, and heat
gently for about 5 minutes.
Remove the bay leaf and discard.

5 Add salt and pepper to taste.
Serve hot, garnished with the
reserved clams in their shells.

Cook's know-how

If fresh clams are not in
season or you want to save
time, use 1 × 200 g (7 oz) jar
or can clams in brine, drained.
Omit steps 1 and 2 and
increase the fish stock to
300 ml (1/4 pint), then heat
the clams through in step 4.

RICH FISH SOUP

SERVES 4

4 tbsp olive oil

2 leeks, trimmed and chopped

1 celery stalk, chopped

1 potato, chopped

1 carrot, chopped

1 small red pepper, halved, seeded,
and chopped

3 garlic cloves, roughly chopped

375 g (12 oz) ripe tomatoes,
quartered, seeded, and chopped,
or 1 × 400 g (13 oz) can chopped
tomatoes

500 g (1 lb) mixed white fish fillets,
chopped (see box, right)

1 litre (1 3/4 pints) fish stock

500 ml (16 fl oz) dry white wine

1/4 tsp cayenne pepper

salt and black pepper

Gruyère croûtes (opposite) and
basil sprigs to garnish

Cook's know-how

This fine puréed soup is
based on the French soupe
de poisson. For an
interesting flavour, ask your
fishmonger for a mixture of
different fish – whatever is
cheapest and best on the
day. Bony fish, small pieces,
and scraps will all do very
well, because the fish is
sieved after puréeing.

1 Heat the oil in a large
saucepan, add the leeks,
celery, potato, carrot, red
pepper, and garlic, and cook
gently, stirring occasionally, for
5 minutes or until the
vegetables are just soft.

2 Add the tomatoes and
fish, and cook for 3
minutes. Add the stock, wine,
and cayenne pepper, and
bring to a boil. Simmer for
35 minutes.

3 Purée the soup in a food
processor or blender, then
work it through a sieve to make
it velvety smooth.

4 Return the soup to the
rinsed-out pan and reheat
gently, stirring occasionally.
Add salt and pepper to taste.

5 Serve hot, each bowl
garnished with a Gruyère
croûte and a sprig of basil.

LOBSTER BISQUE

A bisque is a purée flavoured with brandy, white wine, and cream, prepared by a complex process which brings out the maximum flavour. When made with lobster, it is perfect for a special occasion. This lighter and healthier version of the traditional recipe is just as delicious.

SERVES 6

30 g (1 oz) butter
6 shallots, coarsely chopped
1/2 carrot, finely chopped
1 cooked large lobster
pinch of cayenne pepper
1/2 tsp paprika
juice of 1 small lemon
4 tbsp brandy
300 ml (1/2 pint) dry white wine
1.5 litre (2 1/2 pints) fish stock
60 g (2 oz) long-grain rice
about 3 tbsp single cream (optional)

1 Melt the butter in a large saucepan, add the shallots and carrot, and cook gently for about 5 minutes until softened.

2 Using a mallet or wooden rolling pin, crack the lobster shells, remove the cooked meat (page 125), and set aside. Reserve a single large piece of the shell to add to the bisque, and discard the rest.

3 Slice the meat from the large claws and tail of the lobster, reserving a few pieces for garnish.

4 Add the cayenne, paprika, lemon juice, and brandy to the shallots and carrot in the pan, and reduce over a high heat to about 2 tablespoons.

5 Add the wine, fish stock, rice, and reserved lobster shell to the pan, and cook for about 15 minutes until the rice is tender. Remove the lobster shell, and discard.

6 Add the lobster meat (except the garnish) to the pan, and season lightly with salt and pepper. Cook the soup over a low heat just until the lobster is heated through, about 5 minutes.

7 Purée the soup in a food processor or blender until smooth. Pour the purée through a sieve to remove any tiny pieces of lobster shell.

8 Return the purée to the pan, and add the cream if using. Taste for seasoning, and adjust if necessary.

9 Serve the soup at once, garnished with the reserved lobster slices.

Cook's know-how

Most fishmongers sell cooked lobsters, or you can order one specially and ask for it to be supplied ready cooked. Buy only from a reputable fishmonger or supermarket with a quick turnover. The lobster should feel heavy for its size, and smell fresh. Keep it as cool as possible until you get home, then unwrap it, cover with a clean cloth or paper towels, and store in the coldest part of the refrigerator. Use the lobster the same day, or within 24 hours.

CROUTES & CROUTONS

These need not be reserved for special occasions. They can turn the most basic of everyday soups into a complete meal.

HERB CROUTES

Trim the crusts from slices of bread. Cut each slice into a square or decorative shape. Heat a very thin film of oil in a non-stick frying pan, add the bread, and brown on both sides. Finely chop some parsley or separate into small sprigs. Drain the croûtes on paper towels. Roll the edges of the croûtes in the parsley or put a leaf on top of each one.

GARLIC CROUTONS

Trim the crusts from slices of bread and cut into 1 cm (1/2 in) cubes. Heat a very thin film of oil in a non-stick frying pan. Peel and crush 1 garlic clove and cook for 1 minute. Add the bread cubes and cook, stirring occasionally, until brown all over. Remove, and drain on paper towels.

GRUYERE CROUTES

Cut slices from a baguette and toast on one side under a hot grill. Remove from the heat and turn the slices over. Grate Gruyère cheese evenly over the untoasted sides of the bread slices. Return to the grill and cook until the cheese has melted and is gently bubbling.

CUBAN SWEETCORN & SEAFOOD SOUP

SERVES 4

30 g (1 oz) butter

1 small onion, chopped

2 garlic cloves, crushed

500 g (1 lb) frozen sweetcorn kernels

200 g (7 oz) pumpkin or sweet potato, peeled and cut into chunks

1 mild fresh red chilli, halved, seeded, and chopped, or 1/4 tsp crushed dried red chillies

1.25 litres (2 pints) fish, chicken, or vegetable stock

250 ml (8 fl oz) tomato passata

1 bay leaf

1/2 tsp dried thyme

salt and black pepper

250 g (8 oz) any firm white fish fillets, cut into large chunks

lime wedges to serve

1 Melt the butter in a large pan, add the onion and garlic, and cook gently for a few minutes until soft but not coloured. Add the pumpkin or sweet potato and the chilli, and cook, stirring occasionally, for 5 minutes.

2 Add the stock, passata, bay leaf, and thyme, and season with salt and pepper. Bring to a boil, cover, and simmer, stirring occasionally, for 15 minutes or until the pumpkin or sweet potato pieces are just tender.

3 Add the fish to the soup, and cook very gently for 3–5 minutes, just until the chunks become opaque.

4 Discard the bay leaf and taste for seasoning. Serve hot, with lime wedges.

Cook's know-how

Monkfish is the firmest white fish, but it is expensive. You could use hoki, coley, cod, or haddock, but take care not to let the fish break up – they are not as firm as monkfish.

PRAWN GUMBO

SERVES 4

3 tbsp sunflower oil

1 small onion, diced

1 red pepper, halved, seeded, and diced

1 celery stalk, diced

3 garlic cloves, crushed

2 tbsp chopped parsley

30 g (1 oz) plain flour

1 tsp each ground cumin and dried oregano

750 g (1 1/2 lb) ripe tomatoes, chopped, or 2 x 400 g (13 oz) cans chopped tomatoes

175 g (6 oz) chorizo, sliced

1.25 litres (2 pints) fish stock

250 g (8 oz) okra, sliced

250–375 g (8–12 oz) cooked peeled prawns

pinch of cayenne pepper

salt and black pepper

rice timbales (see box, right) to serve

4 large cooked prawns and 4 spring onions to garnish

1 Heat the oil, add the onion, red pepper, celery, garlic, and parsley, and cook for 8 minutes or until softened. Add the flour, and cook, stirring all the time, for 1 minute.

2 Sprinkle in the cumin and oregano, and cook, stirring, for 1 minute, then add the tomatoes, chorizo, and stock. Bring to a boil, then simmer, stirring occasionally, for about 30 minutes or until the soup has thickened slightly.

3 Add the okra, and cook for 5–7 minutes until tender, then add the prawns and heat through. Add the cayenne, and season with salt and pepper.

4 Serve the gumbo hot, with rice timbales. Garnish each serving with a large cooked prawn and a spring onion.

Making a rice timbale

Oil a small bowl or ramekin, fill with cooked rice, and press down lightly. Turn upside down on to a warmed soup plate and lift off the bowl.

BOUILLABAISSE

Bouillabaisse, the classic fish soup-stew with the authentic flavours of Provence, is one of the most satisfying and delectable dishes you can bring to your table. In France it is traditionally served with thick slices of toasted bread spread with rouille, a chilli-flavoured mayonnaise.

SERVES 8

- 2 tbsp olive oil
- 1 large onion, chopped
- 1 small fennel bulb, sliced
- 4 garlic cloves, crushed
- 1 tbsp chopped parsley
- 1 bay leaf
- 1 litre (1¾ pints) water
- 600 ml (1 pint) fish stock
- 500 g (1 lb) ripe tomatoes, finely chopped
- ½ tsp dried herbes de Provence or mixed herbs
- a strip of orange zest
- ¼ tsp fennel seeds (optional)
- 2–3 potatoes, cut into chunks
- 500 g (1 lb) assorted fish, cut into bite-sized pieces
- 500 g (1 lb) assorted shellfish, shelled
- pinch of saffron threads
- salt and black pepper
- 8 toasted baguette slices, to serve

ROUILLE

- 3 garlic cloves
- 125 ml (4 fl oz) mayonnaise
- 2 tsp paprika
- 1 tsp mild chilli powder
- 3 tbsp olive oil
- 1 small fresh red chilli, halved, seeded, and finely chopped
- 1 tbsp lemon juice
- salt

1 Heat the olive oil in a large, heavy saucepan. Add the onion, fennel, garlic, parsley, and bay leaf, and cook, stirring occasionally, for 5 minutes.

2 Add the water, stock, tomatoes, herbs, orange zest, and fennel seeds (if using). Bring to a boil, cover, and simmer for 30 minutes.

3 Meanwhile, make the rouille (see box, right). Chill until needed.

4 Add the potatoes to the soup, cover, and simmer for 10 minutes. Do not stir or the potatoes will break up.

5 Add the fish, shellfish, and saffron, and season with salt and pepper. Cover and cook for a few minutes, just until the fish turns opaque.

6 Remove the bay leaf and orange zest and discard. Serve the bouillabaisse with slices of toasted baguette spread with the rouille.

Cook's know-how

Ask your fishmonger to recommend a variety of white fish and shellfish. Ideally, you should have a combination of pieces of chunky white fish with small whole fish, plus two or three different shellfish such as clams, mussels, and prawns.

Making rouille

Use a knife blade to crush the garlic to a paste. Mix in a bowl with the mayonnaise, paprika, and chilli powder.

Pour in the olive oil, drop by drop, whisking constantly as the oil is absorbed into the spicy mayonnaise.

Add the red chilli and lemon juice to the sauce; add salt to taste, and stir well to combine.

Cook's know-how

Controversy surrounds the ingredients that should be included in bouillabaisse, with some cooks insisting that saffron, orange zest, and fennel seeds are essential.

GOULASH SOUP

SERVES 4–6

2 red peppers

2 tbsp sunflower oil

500 g (1 lb) stewing beef, trimmed and cut into 3.5 cm (1 1/2 in) pieces

2 large onions, thickly sliced

1 tbsp plain flour

2 tsp paprika

1.5 litres (2 1/2 pints) beef stock

1 x 400 g (13 oz) can chopped tomatoes

2 tbsp tomato purée

1 tbsp red wine vinegar

1 garlic clove, crushed

1 bay leaf

salt and black pepper

750 g (1 1/2 lb) potatoes, coarsely chopped

dash of Tabasco sauce

soured cream and snipped fresh chives to garnish (optional)

1 Roast and peel the red peppers (page 388). Cut the flesh into chunks.

2 Heat the oil in a large pan. Add the beef and brown all over. Add the onions, peppers, flour, and paprika, and stir over a high heat for 1–2 minutes.

3 Add the stock, tomatoes, tomato purée, vinegar, garlic, and bay leaf, and season with salt and pepper. Bring to a boil, cover tightly, and simmer for 1 1/2 hours.

4 Add the potatoes and cook for 30 minutes or until the beef and potatoes are tender. Remove the bay leaf and discard.

5 Add a little Tabasco sauce and taste for seasoning. Serve hot, garnished with soured cream and snipped chives if you like.

Cook's know-how

To save time, use about 4 pieces of bottled roasted red pepper instead of roasting your own. They can be preserved in oil or brine, whichever you prefer.

PUMPKIN SOUP

SERVES 6

1.5 kg (3 lb) pumpkin

150 g (5 oz) butter

2 leeks, trimmed and sliced

1 litre (1 3/4 pints) chicken or vegetable stock

1/4 tsp grated nutmeg

salt and black pepper

30 g (1 oz) petits pois

250 g (8 oz) spinach leaves, finely chopped

300 ml (1/2 pint) single cream

1 Cut out the flesh from the pumpkin, discarding the seeds and fibres. Cut the flesh into 2 cm (3/4 in) chunks.

2 Melt 100 g (3 1/2 oz) of the butter in a large saucepan. Add the leeks, and cook very gently, covered, for 10 minutes or until soft.

3 Add the stock, pumpkin chunks, and nutmeg, and season with salt and pepper. Bring to a boil, cover, and simmer for 30 minutes or until the vegetables are very soft.

4 Meanwhile, cook the petits pois in boiling salted water for 5 minutes. Drain thoroughly.

5 Melt the remaining butter in a saucepan. Add the spinach, cover, and cook gently for 3 minutes until wilted.

6 Purée the soup in a food processor or blender until smooth, in batches if necessary. Return to the pan and stir in the cream. Stir the petits pois and spinach into the soup, heat through, and serve hot.

Cook's know-how

You can serve the soup in small hollowed-out pumpkins, scalloping the edges as illustrated above. Other possibilities include leaving the soup chunky rather than puréeing it, using double the amount of spinach and omitting the peas, and halving the butter and cream to reduce the fat content.

GAME SOUP

Orange-herb bouquet

Tie the parsley, orange zest, bay leaf, and thyme or marjoram with a piece of white string. Leave a length of string to tie to the saucepan handle, so that the orange and herb bouquet can be easily lifted from the pan at the end of cooking.

SERVES 4

30 g (1 oz) butter

125 g (4 oz) smoked streaky bacon rashers, rinds removed, diced

1 onion, sliced

125 g (4 oz) chestnut mushrooms, sliced

1 tbsp plain flour

1.25 litres (2 pints) game stock (page 170)

salt and black pepper

1 tbsp redcurrant jelly

ORANGE-HERB BOUQUET

6 parsley stalks

pared zest of 1 orange

1 bay leaf

1 large thyme or marjoram sprig

1 Make the orange-herb bouquet (see box, above right) and set aside.

2 Melt the butter in a large saucepan, add the bacon, and cook over a high heat, stirring occasionally, for 5–7 minutes until crisp.

3 Lower the heat, add the onion to the pan, and cook gently, stirring from time to time, for a few minutes until softened but not coloured.

4 Add the mushrooms to the pan, and cook for about 5 minutes, then add the flour and cook, stirring constantly, for 1 minute. Add the stock and the orange-herb bouquet, season with salt and pepper, and bring to a boil. Cover and simmer for 30 minutes.

5 Discard the bouquet, then stir in the redcurrant jelly. Taste for seasoning before serving.

LENTIL & BACON SOUP

SERVES 4–6

30 g (1 oz) butter

1 onion, chopped

1 carrot, diced

1 celery stalk, diced

3 garlic cloves, crushed

2–3 lean back bacon rashers, rinds removed, diced

175 g (6 oz) red lentils

about 125 g (4 oz) potatoes, swede or turnip, peeled and diced

2 bay leaves

1/2 tsp dried sage (optional)

2 litres (3 1/2 pints) vegetable or chicken stock

salt and black pepper

chopped parsley to garnish

1 Melt the butter in a large saucepan, add the onion, carrot, celery, and garlic, and cook, stirring, for 5–6 minutes until soft and lightly coloured.

2 Add the bacon, lentils, potato, swede or turnip, bay leaves, and sage (if using). Cook for 15 minutes.

3 Pour in the stock and bring to a boil, then simmer gently, uncovered, for about 20 minutes or until the lentils and vegetables are tender. Add salt and pepper to taste.

4 Remove the bay leaves and discard. Serve hot, sprinkled with chopped parsley.

LENTIL & FRANKFURTER SOUP

For a hearty main meal soup, add 250 g (8 oz) frankfurters. Chop them into 1 cm (1/2 in) pieces and add to the soup about 5 minutes before the end of the cooking time, so that they warm through but do not overcook. Smoked sausages can also be used.

CHICKEN NOODLE SOUP

SERVES 6

1 kg (2 lb) chicken thighs
500 g (1 lb) carrots, sliced
1/2 head celery, chopped
1 small onion, peeled but left whole
2–3 garlic cloves, coarsely chopped
a few parsley sprigs
3 litres (5 pints) water
2–3 chicken stock cubes
salt and black pepper
125 g (4 oz) thin noodles
chopped fresh dill to garnish

1 Put the chicken pieces into a large saucepan with the carrots, celery, onion, garlic, and parsley. Pour in the measured water and bring to a boil. Using a slotted spoon, skim off the foam that rises to the top of the pan.

2 Lower the heat, crumble in the stock cubes, and season with salt and pepper. Cover and simmer gently for 1 hour.

3 Skim any fat from the surface of the soup. With a slotted spoon, lift out the parsley, onion, and chicken. Discard the parsley. Chop the onion, and shred the chicken meat, discarding the skin and bones. Set aside.

4 Break the noodles into 5 cm (2 in) pieces and drop them into the soup. Bring to a boil, cover, and simmer for about 10 minutes or until tender.

5 Return the onion and chicken to the soup, heat through, and taste for seasoning. Serve hot, garnished with dill.

Healthy option

To reduce the fat content of the soup, strip the skin off the chicken thighs before cooking. Chicken meat is low in fat and calories; the fatty part is in the skin and just underneath it.

HOT & SOUR SOUP

SERVES 4–6

2 dried Chinese mushrooms
1/4 head Chinese leaves, sliced
1.5 litres (2 1/2 pints) chicken or vegetable stock
60 g (2 oz) Chinese noodles, such as rice sticks
salt
125 g (4 oz) firm tofu, diced
90 g (3 oz) drained canned bamboo shoots, sliced
90 g (3 oz) cooked lean boneless and skinless chicken, diced
30 g (1 oz) bean sprouts
3 tbsp cornflour mixed with 3 tbsp cold water
2 eggs, lightly beaten
2 tbsp white wine vinegar
1 tbsp dark soy sauce
1/4 tsp cayenne pepper

TO SERVE

2 tsp sesame oil
2 spring onions, thinly sliced
coriander sprigs

1 Put the mushrooms into a bowl, cover with hot water, and leave to soak for about 30 minutes.

2 Meanwhile, put the sliced Chinese leaves into a large saucepan, add the stock, and bring to a boil. Simmer for 15 minutes. Set aside.

3 Break the noodles into pieces. Simmer in boiling salted water for 3–4 minutes until just tender. Drain.

4 Drain the mushrooms, reserving the soaking liquid. Squeeze the mushrooms dry, then cut them into thin strips.

5 Add the tofu, bamboo shoots, chicken, bean sprouts, noodles, and the mushrooms and their liquid to the Chinese leaves and stock. Heat until almost boiling, then stir in the cornflour mixture. Simmer until the soup thickens slightly, then drizzle in the beaten eggs to form strands.

6 Combine the vinegar, soy sauce, and cayenne pepper, and pour into the soup. Taste for seasoning. Drizzle a little sesame oil over each serving, and garnish with spring onion slices and coriander sprigs.

CHINESE CRAB & SWEETCORN SOUP

SERVES 4

375 g (12 oz) frozen sweetcorn kernels

1 litre (1³/₄ pints) hot chicken stock

3 spring onions, thinly sliced

1 cm (¹/₂ in) piece of fresh root ginger, peeled and grated

1 garlic clove, crushed

1 tbsp light soy sauce

250 g (8 oz) cooked crabmeat

1 tbsp cornflour mixed with 2 tbsp cold water

salt and black pepper

sesame oil and coriander sprigs to serve

1 Purée the sweetcorn with one-quarter of the hot stock in a food processor or blender until smooth.

2 Pour the remaining stock into a pan, and add the spring onions, ginger, garlic, and soy sauce. Heat until bubbles form at the edge.

3 Add the crabmeat and the sweetcorn purée, and continue to heat until bubbles form again. Blend the cornflour mixture into the soup, and cook, stirring occasionally, for 10 minutes or until it thickens slightly. Season to taste with salt and pepper.

4 Pour the soup into bowls, drizzle a little sesame oil over each serving, and garnish with coriander. Serve hot.

THAI SPICED SOUP

SERVES 4

90 g (3 oz) thin egg noodles

salt and black pepper

500 ml (16 fl oz) chicken stock

1 x 400 g (13 oz) can coconut milk

1 small carrot, coarsely chopped

30 g (1 oz) French beans, cut into 1 cm (¹/₂ in) pieces

3 spring onions, thinly sliced

250 g (8 oz) cooked lean boneless and skinless chicken, shredded

125 g (4 oz) mixed green leaves, such as spinach and pak choi, shredded

30 g (1 oz) bean sprouts

2 tbsp fish sauce

2 tsp Thai curry paste (green or red)

¹/₄ cucumber, cut into matchstick-thin strips, and coriander sprigs to garnish

1 Cook the noodles in boiling salted water for 2–3 minutes, or according to package instructions, until just tender. Drain and rinse in cold water. Set aside while preparing the soup.

2 Put the stock, coconut milk, carrot, French beans, and spring onions into a large saucepan, and bring to a boil.

3 Lower the heat, add the chicken, green leaves, bean sprouts, fish sauce, and spice paste, and cook for 2 minutes or until the green leaves are just wilted. Season to taste with salt and pepper.

4 To serve, divide the cooked noodles among warmed bowls. Ladle the hot soup over the noodles, and garnish with cucumber strips and coriander sprigs.

Cook's know-how

For a vegetarian version, omit the cooked chicken and use a vegetable stock instead of the chicken stock. You can also vary the vegetables, but their cooking times may be different. Try shredded white cabbage instead of the green leaves and mangetout instead of French beans. Shredded Swiss chard would also be good in this soup, as would a small quantity of sweetcorn kernels or peas, and even a little diced aubergine.

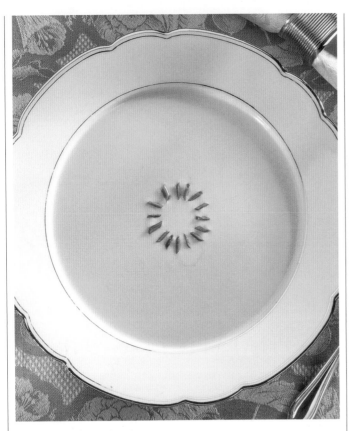

TZATZIKI SOUP

SERVES 4–6

600 g (1 lb 3 oz) plain yogurt

250 ml (8 fl oz) water

1 cucumber, seeded (see box, right) and diced

4 garlic cloves, coarsely chopped

1 tbsp olive oil

1 tsp white wine vinegar

1 tsp dried mint

salt and black pepper

2–3 tbsp chopped fresh mint and 3 spring onions, thinly sliced, to garnish

1 Purée the yogurt, measured water, one-quarter of the diced cucumber, the garlic, oil, vinegar, and dried mint in a food processor or blender until smooth. Season well with salt and add pepper to taste.

2 Transfer the soup to a large bowl and stir in the remaining cucumber. Cover and chill for at least 1 hour.

3 Taste for seasoning. Sprinkle the soup with chopped fresh mint and spring onions before serving.

Seeding a cucumber

Trim the cucumber with a small knife, then cut it in half lengthwise. With a teaspoon, scoop out and discard the seeds from each cucumber half.

Cook's know-how

Don't be surprised to find dried mint in this recipe. Although fresh mint is generally far superior to dried, here the mint is left to steep in the yogurt for a minimum of an hour, and this brings the dried mint to life, giving it a more intense flavour than fresh, which would discolour in this time. Once chopped, fresh mint is best used as soon as possible.

VICHYSSOISE

SERVES 4–6

60 g (2 oz) butter

3 large leeks, trimmed and sliced

1 small onion, chopped

2 potatoes, coarsely chopped

1.25 litres (2 pints) chicken stock

salt and black pepper

TO SERVE

150 ml (¼ pint) single cream

milk (optional)

2 tbsp fresh snipped chives

1 Melt the butter in a large saucepan, add the leeks and onion, and cook very gently, stirring occasionally, for 10–15 minutes until soft but not coloured.

2 Add the potatoes, stock, and salt and pepper to taste, and bring to a boil. Cover and simmer gently for 15–20 minutes until the potatoes are tender.

3 Purée the soup in a food processor or blender until smooth. Pour into a large bowl or pass through a sieve for a smoother finish. Cover and chill for at least 3 hours.

4 To serve, stir in the cream. If the soup is too thick, add a little milk. Taste for seasoning. Garnish with snipped chives before serving.

Cook's know-how

For an elegant, pale coloured soup, trim off the dark green parts of the leeks (both the ends and the outside leaves) and only use the white and pale green parts. After you have sliced them, swish them in lots of cold water in the sink and change the water several times to get rid of all traces of grit. Finally, rinse the leeks thoroughly in a colander.

GAZPACHO

SERVES 4–6

1 kg (2 lb) tomatoes, peeled (see box, right), quartered, and seeded

1 large Spanish onion

1 x 200 g (7 oz) jar roasted peppers (in oil or brine), drained

2 large garlic cloves

600 ml (1 pint) cold vegetable or chicken stock

75 ml (2½ fl oz) olive oil

4 tbsp red wine vinegar

juice of ½ lemon

salt and black pepper

TO GARNISH

½ cucumber, diced

1 small green pepper, halved, seeded, and diced

garlic croûtons (page 49)

1 Coarsely chop the tomatoes, onion, peppers, and garlic. Purée in a food processor or blender with the stock, oil, and vinegar until smooth.

2 Turn the mixture into a bowl and add the lemon juice, and salt and pepper to taste. Cover and chill for at least 1 hour.

Peeling tomatoes

Cut the cores from the tomatoes and score an "x" on the base. Immerse the tomatoes in boiling water for 8–15 seconds until their skins start to split. Transfer at once to cold water. When the tomatoes are cool enough to handle, peel off the skin with a small knife.

3 Serve the soup well chilled in bowls, each one garnished with spoonfuls of diced cucumber, green pepper, and garlic croûtons.

BLUEBERRY & RED WINE SOUP

SERVES 4

350 ml (12 fl oz) cranberry juice

250 ml (8 fl oz) red wine

1 cinnamon stick

about 125 g (4 oz) caster sugar

250 g (8 oz) blueberries

1 tbsp cornflour mixed with 2 tbsp cold water

125 ml (4 fl oz) soured cream

125 ml (4 fl oz) single cream

1 Put the cranberry juice, wine, and cinnamon stick into a large saucepan, and add the sugar (the amount depends on the sweetness of the fruit). Bring to a boil and simmer for 15 minutes.

2 Stir most of the blueberries into the pan, reserving a few for garnish, and cook for 5 minutes. Taste and add more sugar, if you think it needs it.

3 Gradually blend the cornflour mixture into the soup, and return to a boil. Cook for 3 minutes or until the soup thickens slightly. Remove the pan from the heat, discard the cinnamon stick, then pour the soup into a bowl. Leave to cool for about 30 minutes.

4 Stir the soured cream and the single cream into the soup until evenly blended. Cover and chill for at least 3 hours. Serve well chilled, garnished with the reserved blueberries.

Cook's know-how

Served chilled, this American-style soup makes a cooling and refreshing summer first course. To prevent it from tasting too sweet, use a robust red wine, such as a Californian Zinfandel or a Bulgarian Cabernet Sauvignon. When in season, dark sweet cherries can be used instead of blueberries.

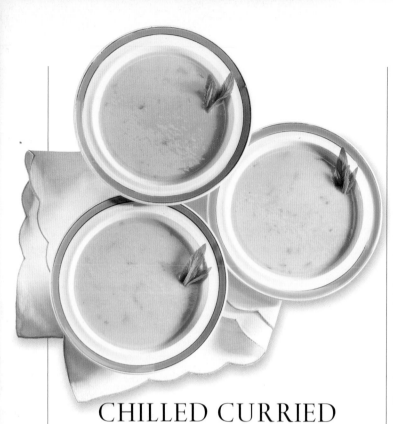

CHILLED CURRIED APPLE & MINT SOUP

SERVES 6

30 g (1 oz) butter

1 onion, coarsely chopped

1 tbsp mild curry powder

900 ml (1½ pints) vegetable stock

750 g (1½ lb) cooking apples, peeled, cored, and coarsely chopped

2 tbsp mango chutney

juice of ½ lemon

7–8 sprigs of fresh mint

salt and black pepper

100 g (3½ oz) plain yogurt

a little milk, if needed

1 Melt the butter in a large saucepan, add the onion, and cook gently, stirring occasionally, for a few minutes until soft but not coloured. Add the curry powder and cook, stirring constantly, for 1–2 minutes.

2 Add the stock and chopped apples and bring to a boil, stirring. Cover and simmer for 15 minutes or until the apples are tender.

3 Purée the apple mixture, mango chutney, and lemon juice in a food processor or blender until very smooth.

4 Strip the mint leaves from the stalks, reserving 6 small sprigs for garnish. Finely chop the mint leaves.

5 Pour the soup into a large bowl, stir in the chopped mint, and add salt and pepper to taste. Cover and chill in the refrigerator for at least 3 hours.

6 Whisk in the yogurt, then taste for seasoning. If the soup is too thick, add a little milk. Garnish with the reserved mint before serving.

Cook's know-how

This soup is equally delicious served hot. After puréeing, return the soup to the rinsed-out pan and reheat it gently, stirring occasionally. Stir in the chopped mint, then remove from the heat and swirl in the yogurt. Serve at once.

CHILLED STRAWBERRY SOUP

SERVES 4

250 ml (8 fl oz) dry white wine

90 g (3 oz) caster sugar

1 very small piece of pared lime zest (optional)

250 g (8 oz) strawberries

250 ml (8 fl oz) orange juice (squeezed fresh or from a carton)

4 mint sprigs to garnish

1 Put the wine and sugar into a saucepan and bring to a boil. Continue boiling for 5 minutes, then remove the pan from the heat and add the lime zest, if using. Leave to cool.

2 Remove and discard the lime zest, if used. Hull and chop the strawberries, reserving 4 for garnish.

3 Purée the wine syrup and strawberries in a food processor or blender until very smooth.

4 Turn the purée into a large bowl and stir in the orange juice. Cover and chill for at least 3 hours.

5 Serve well chilled and garnished with the reserved strawberries and mint sprigs.

STRAWBERRY & CHAMPAGNE SOUP

Omit the white wine and lime zest. Purée the strawberries, reserving a few for garnish, with the sugar and orange juice. Divide the mixture between chilled glass serving bowls, and top with chilled Champagne or dry sparkling wine. Garnish and serve.

STRAWBERRY & WATERMELON SOUP

Remove the seeds from a 1 kg (2 lb) piece of watermelon. Cut up the flesh and purée until smooth, then combine with the wine syrup, strawberries, and a little lime juice. Omit the orange juice.

2

FIRST COURSES

UNDER 30 MINUTES

QUICK & EASY

MIMOSA FISH SALAD
Rich creamy salad of white fish fillets, soured cream, hard-boiled egg, mayonnaise, and parsley. Served on tomatoes.

SERVES 4 213 calories per serving
Takes 10 minutes   Page 84

QUICK & EASY

HUMMUS
Smooth and summery: cannellini beans blended with rosemary, olive oil, and lemon juice, and richly flavoured with garlic.

SERVES 6 150 calories per serving
Takes 10 minutes   Page 75

PRAWN COCKTAIL
Prawns in a dressing of mayonnaise, creamed horseradish, and tomato purée, spiked with lemon juice and Tabasco sauce.

SERVES 4 338 calories per serving
Takes 10 minutes   Page 83

AVOCADO WITH TOMATOES & MINT
Light and refreshing: chopped tomatoes combined with mint and vinaigrette dressing, and piled into avocado halves.

SERVES 4 232 calories per serving
Takes 15 minutes   Page 88

CHEVRE CROUTES
Goat's cheese and pesto, on toasted baguette slices and sprinkled with olive oil, give a tangy flavour to this inviting appetizer.

SERVES 4 450 calories per serving
Takes 20 minutes   Page 66

JUMBO PRAWNS WITH AIOLI
Stir-fried jumbo prawns served with a Provençal mayonnaise combining garlic, egg yolks, mustard, olive oil, and lemon juice.

SERVES 4 482 calories per serving
Takes 20 minutes   Page 82

FRENCH CLASSIC

SCALLOPS WITH CHEESE SAUCE
Rich and luxurious: scallops poached with white wine and bay leaf, then stirred into a Mornay sauce flavoured with Gruyère cheese.

SERVES 4 297 calories per serving
Takes 25 minutes   Page 80

SARDINES WITH CORIANDER
Lightly grilled sardines, flavoured with a butter combining coriander and shallot with lime juice, make a refreshing starter.

SERVES 4 511 calories per serving
Takes 25 minutes   Page 82

DINNER PARTY

ASPARAGUS WITH QUICK HOLLANDAISE
Tender fresh asparagus served with an easy version of hollandaise sauce, garnished with lemon twists.

SERVES 4 384 calories per serving
Takes 20 minutes   Page 86

UNDER 30 MINUTES

VEGETARIAN

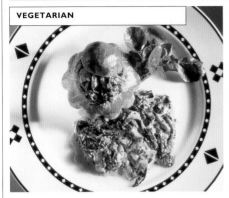

BRIOCHES WITH WILD MUSHROOMS & WATERCRESS
Light-textured, rich bread filled with a mixture of mushrooms, watercress, and cream.

SERVES 6 295 calories per serving

Takes 20 minutes   Page 86

WARM SALAD WITH BACON & SCALLOPS
Crisp bacon, scallops, salad leaves tossed in walnut oil, and a hot wine vinegar and shallot dressing.

SERVES 4 276 calories per serving

Takes 20 minutes   Page 85

SPICY MEATBALLS
Tiny warm meatballs seasoned with garlic, onion, paprika, fresh coriander, and tomato purée. Served with a sesame dip.

SERVES 6 481 calories per serving

Takes 25 minutes   Page 65

SMOKED CHICKEN SALAD WITH WALNUTS
Sliced smoked chicken in an orange dressing, on a bed of salad leaves, orange segments, and walnuts.

SERVES 6 472 calories per serving

Takes 15 minutes   Page 85

MOULES MARINIERE
Traditional French dish: mussels cooked with dry white wine, onion, garlic, parsley, thyme, and a bay leaf. Served in a light sauce.

SERVES 6 302 calories per serving

Takes 25 minutes   Page 80

DINNER PARTY

CHEESE AIGRETTES
Warm nuggets of choux pastry, flavoured with mature Cheddar cheese, then deep-fried and served warm.

SERVES 10–12 238–198 calories per serving

Takes 25 minutes   Page 67

30–60 MINUTES

PREPARE AHEAD

SALMON & PRAWN FILO PURSES
Bite-sized pieces of salmon combined with prawns in light-textured filo pastry purses. Served with a wine, cream, and dill sauce.

SERVES 8 448 calories per serving

Takes 55 minutes   Page 71

CANAPES
Lightly toasted bread served with a selection of toppings: anchovy and prawn, cheese and spring onion, salami, and asparagus.

SERVES 4 251 calories per serving

Takes 40 minutes   Page 65

CHEESE & OLIVE BITES
Pimiento-stuffed olives wrapped in cheese pastry flavoured with paprika and mustard. Baked, then served warm or cold.

SERVES 4 317 calories per serving

Takes 40 minutes   Page 66

30–60 MINUTES

WARM SALAD WITH PEARS & STILTON

Toast topped with Stilton cheese on a bed of watercress and pears. Served with a warm red onion and balsamic vinegar dressing.

SERVES 4   563 calories per serving

Takes 35 minutes   Page 90

MEXICAN CLASSIC

NACHOS GRANDE

Spicy and nourishing: refried beans, tomatoes, chilli, onion, garlic, and green pepper, enclosed by tortilla chips. Topped with cheese.

SERVES 4–6   594–396 calories per serving

Takes 45 minutes   Page 70

OVER 60 MINUTES

PAN-FRIED PATES

Blended chicken livers with bacon, spinach, shallots, parsley, garlic, and sage. Moulded into ovals and wrapped in bacon.

SERVES 4   392 calories per serving

Takes 60 minutes   Page 75

SARDINE PATE

Individual pâtés of sardines blended with butter, low-fat soft cheese, and lemon juice, seasoned with black pepper, then chilled.

SERVES 8   197 calories per serving

Takes 10 minutes, plus chilling   Page 72

LEEK PARCELS WITH PROVENÇAL VEGETABLES

Layers of aubergine, pesto, red pepper, courgette, and tomato, wrapped in leek strips.

SERVES 4   283 calories per serving

Takes 40 minutes   Page 77

LOW CALORIE

SUMMER MELONS

Contrastingly coloured melon balls, mixed with tomato strips, and dressed in vinaigrette. Chilled and served with mint.

SERVES 4   282 calories per serving

Takes 15 minutes, plus chilling   Page 88

ITALIAN CLASSIC

ANTIPASTI

Two popular Italian starters: crostini, made from thin slices of baguette brushed with garlic and olive oil and baked until crispy, then topped with sun-dried tomato purée; mozzarella, tomato, and basil salad, dressed with olive oil and balsamic vinegar.

SERVES 8   311 calories per crostini serving 180 calories per salad serving

Takes 45 minutes   Page 89

EGG PATE

Hard-boiled eggs mixed with crème fraîche, consommé, and whipped double cream, and garnished with large prawns.

SERVES 8   243 calories per serving

Takes 45 minutes, plus chilling   Page 77

OVER 60 MINUTES

PREPARE AHEAD

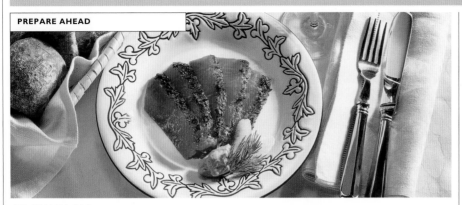

GRAVADLAX

Scandinavian speciality: fresh salmon fillets pickled in sugar, sea salt, dill, and black pepper, sandwiched together, and chilled. Served in slices, with a rich sauce combining mustard, sugar, white wine vinegar, egg yolk, sunflower oil, and dill.

SERVES 16 395 calories per serving
Takes 30 minutes, plus chilling   Page 83

CAPONATA

Aubergine cooked with celery, onions, tomato purée, sugar, and vinegar, then mixed with olives, garlic, and parsley.

SERVES 4–6 297–198 calories per serving
Takes 35 minutes, plus standing   Page 90

SALMON QUENELLES

Little dumplings of salmon, egg whites, and cream, shaped and poached, and served with a luxurious asparagus sauce.

SERVES 4–6 766–511 calories per serving
Takes 30 minutes, plus chilling   Page 81

PICNIC FARE

SMOKED CHICKEN TART

Strips of smoked chicken mixed with onion, mushrooms, and spinach, in a light pastry shell, and baked with an egg and crème fraîche topping.

SERVES 6 290 calories per serving
Takes 1¼ hours, plus chilling   Page 74

SMOKED HADDOCK MOUSSE

Tender smoked fish blended with soft cheese, mayonnaise, and vibrant turmeric for a rich colour and flavour.

SERVES 6 217 calories per serving
Takes 45 minutes, plus chilling   Page 76

RUSSIAN CLASSIC

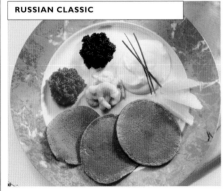

PRAWN BLINI

Russian pancakes made with yeast and buckwheat flour. Served with red and black lumpfish roe, prawns, and crème fraîche.

SERVES 6–8 369–277 calories per serving
Takes 35 minutes, plus standing   Page 84

PREPARE AHEAD

THREE FISH TERRINE

Layers of smoked fish pâtés – trout with cream cheese and lemon juice; salmon with lemon juice, tomato purée, cream cheese, and dill; mackerel with cream cheese and lemon juice – wrapped in smoked salmon slices. Served here on a bed of watercress.

SERVES 10 424 calories per serving
Takes 40 minutes, plus chilling   Page 73

OVER 60 MINUTES

SMOKED SALMON ROULADE
Savoury spinach roulade layered with smoked salmon, a mixture of soft cheese, yogurt, spring onions, and tomatoes.

SERVES 4–6 407–271 calories per serving
Takes 45 minutes, plus chilling   Page 87

INDIVIDUAL FISH PATES
Rich and delicate: haddock blended with smoked salmon, white sauce, mayonnaise, and cream, and flavoured with white wine.

SERVES 8 217 calories per serving
Takes 50 minutes, plus chilling   Page 72

DINNER PARTY

SAVOURY DIPS WITH CRUDITES
Three popular dips: bagna cauda, a warm anchovy and garlic dip; taramasalata, a chilled mixture of smoked cod's roe, lemon juice, garlic, and oil and an aubergine dip, in which aubergines, shallots, and garlic are mixed with parsley and tahini paste.

SERVES 12 120 calories per serving
Takes 1¹/2 hours, plus chilling `   Page 67

AMERICAN CLASSIC

SPICY CHICKEN WINGS
Authentic American recipe: chicken wings marinated in oil, lemon juice, and spices, then baked. Served with blue cheese dressing.

SERVES 4–6 206–137 calories per serving
Takes 60 minutes, plus marinating   Page 70

BROCCOLI TERRINE
Broccoli florets blended with milk and egg yolk, flavoured with grated nutmeg, and set with gelatine and double cream.

SERVES 4–6 236–157 calories per serving
Takes 50 minutes, plus chilling   Page 76

PREPARE AHEAD

BRANDIED CHICKEN LIVER PATE
Chicken livers blended with bread, bacon, thyme, egg, and nutmeg, and flavoured with brandy. Baked, then chilled.

SERVES 8 268 calories per serving
Takes 1¹/4 hours, plus chilling   Page 74

CANAPES

Home-made canapés are an excellent accompaniment for drinks, or they can be served as an appetizer before dinner. These use toasted bread as a base, but if you prefer, fry the bread in a mixture of oil and butter instead.

SERVES 4

4 slices of white bread, crusts removed

ANCHOVY TOPPING

1 tbsp mayonnaise

1 or 2 spring onion tops

8 anchovy fillets, drained

4 cooked peeled prawns

CHEESE TOPPING

30 g (1 oz) full-fat soft cheese

2 spring onion tops, very finely sliced

4 capers

SALAMI TOPPING

15 g (½ oz) butter

2 slices of salami

4 slices of gherkin

ASPARAGUS TOPPING

1 tbsp mayonnaise

6 asparagus tips, cooked and drained

2 slices of radish

a few parsley leaves to garnish

1 Make the canapé bases: toast the white bread lightly on both sides. Leave to cool.

2 Make the anchovy topping: spread 1 piece of toast with mayonnaise and cut into 4 squares. Cut the spring onion tops into 4 pieces, then make vertical cuts to separate each piece into strands. Cut the anchovies in half and arrange in a lattice pattern on each square. Place a prawn on top, and garnish with the spring onions.

3 Make the cheese : spread 1 piece of toast with soft cheese and cut into 4 squares. Arrange the spring onion slices diagonally across the cream cheese. Place a caper on each square.

4 Make the salami topping: butter 1 piece of toast and cut into 4 rounds with a pastry cutter.

5 Cut each slice of salami in half to make 2 half-moon-shaped pieces. Roll each piece to form a point at the straight end so that a cornet shape is made. Put 1 cornet and 1 piece of gherkin on each canapé.

6 Make the asparagus topping: spread 1 piece of toast with mayonnaise and cut into 4 squares. Halve the asparagus tips lengthwise. Halve the radish slices and cut away the centres to form 4 crescents. Put 3 halved asparagus tips on each square, arrange the radish on top, and garnish.

Cook's know-how

Ring the changes with different types of salami. The Danish salami used here is mild in flavour, but you may prefer spicier Italian salami, such as salame di Milano or salame di Napoli.

SPICY MEATBALLS

SERVES 8

1 kg (2 lb) lean minced beef

1 small onion, grated

2 garlic cloves, crushed

1 egg, beaten

90 g (3 oz) fresh breadcrumbs

2 tbsp tomato purée

2 tbsp paprika

2 tbsp chopped fresh coriander

salt and black pepper

3 tbsp olive oil for frying

chopped parsley to garnish

crudités to serve

SESAME DIP

2 tbsp soy sauce

2 tbsp sesame oil

1 tbsp rice wine or sherry

1 spring onion, thinly sliced

1 tbsp sesame seeds, toasted

1 Make the sesame dip: whisk all the ingredients together and set aside.

2 Combine the meatball ingredients in a bowl. Using your hands, roll the mixture into little balls.

3 Heat the oil in a frying pan, and cook the meatballs, in batches, over a medium heat for 5 minutes or until browned, firm, and cooked through. Garnish, and serve warm with the sesame dip and crudités.

CHEVRE CROUTES

SERVES 4

1/2 baguette

about 2 tbsp ready-made pesto

I log-shaped goat's cheese

olive oil for sprinkling

black pepper

radicchio and frisée leaves to serve

chervil sprigs to garnish

1 Cut the baguette into 8 slices, 1 cm (1/2 in) thick, and toast under a hot grill on one side only. Lightly spread the untoasted sides of the baguette slices with the ready-made pesto.

2 Cut the goat's cheese into 8 slices, 1 cm (1/2 in) thick, and arrange on top of the pesto. Toast the topped croûtes under the hot grill, 7 cm (3 in) from the heat, for 3 minutes or until the cheese just begins to soften. Remove the grill pan from the heat.

3 Lightly sprinkle a little olive oil and grind a little pepper over each cheese croûte. Return the croûtes to the hot grill, close to the heat, for 3 minutes or until the cheese begins to bubble and is just tinged golden brown.

4 Line a serving platter with radicchio and frisée leaves, arrange the croûtes on top, and garnish with chervil sprigs. Serve at once.

ITALIAN BRUSCHETTA WITH GOAT'S CHEESE

Substitute 8 slices of Italian ciabatta for the baguette. After toasting the topped croûtes in step 3, sprinkle chopped pitted black olives over them and drizzle with extra virgin olive oil. Serve sprinkled with fresh basil leaves.

CHEESE & OLIVE BITES

SERVES 4

175 g (6 oz) mature Cheddar cheese, grated

90 g (3 oz) plain flour

15 g (1/2 oz) butter, plus extra for greasing

1 tsp paprika

1/2 tsp mustard powder

20 pimiento-stuffed green olives

cayenne pepper and parsley sprigs to garnish

1 Work the cheese, flour, butter, paprika, and mustard powder in a food processor until the mixture resembles fine breadcrumbs.

2 Flatten the dough mixture, and wrap around the olives (see box, right).

3 Butter a baking tray. Add the wrapped olives and bake in a preheated oven at 200°C (400°F, Gas 6) for 15 minutes until the pastry is golden.

4 Remove the cheese and olive bites from the baking tray and leave to cool slightly.

5 Serve warm or cold, sprinkled with cayenne pepper and garnished with parsley sprigs.

Wrapping the olives in the dough

Take a thumb-sized piece of the dough mixture and flatten on a work surface.

Place an olive in the middle of the dough. Wrap the dough around the olive, pressing to make it stick. If the pastry is too crumbly and will not stick, add a little water. Repeat with the remaining dough and olives.

SAVOURY DIPS WITH CRUDITES

For an informal start to a meal, a selection of dips served with fresh, crisp vegetables and some good bread is hard to beat. Bagna cauda, meaning "hot bath", is a rustic Italian dip which should be put over a gentle heat to keep it warm.

POOR MAN'S CAVIAR

SERVES 4

750 g (1 1/2 lb) aubergines

salt and black pepper

2 shallots, halved

1–2 garlic cloves

4 tbsp lemon juice

4 tbsp olive oil

4 tbsp chopped parsley

2 tbsp tahini paste

1 Cut the aubergines in half lengthwise. Score the flesh in a lattice pattern, sprinkle with salt, and leave to stand for 30 minutes.

2 Rinse the aubergine halves with cold water, and pat dry with paper towels. Place on a baking tray and bake in a preheated oven at 200°C (400°F, Gas 6) for 20 minutes.

3 Add the shallots and garlic to the baking tray, and bake for 15 minutes.

4 Purée the aubergines, shallots, and garlic with the lemon juice, oil, parsley, tahini paste, and salt and pepper to taste in a food processor until smooth.

5 Turn the dip into a bowl. Cover and chill for at least 1 hour before serving.

TARAMASALATA

SERVES 4

500 g (1 lb) smoked cod's roe, skinned and coarsely chopped

4 small slices of white bread, crusts removed

4 tbsp lemon juice

1 large garlic clove, coarsely chopped

250 ml (8 fl oz) olive oil

salt and black pepper

1 Purée the cod's roe in a food processor or blender until smooth. Break the bread into a bowl, add the lemon juice, and let the bread soak for 1 minute. Add to the cod's roe with the garlic, and purée until smooth.

2 Pour the oil into the mixture, a little at a time, and purée until all the oil has been absorbed. Add salt and pepper to taste. Turn the taramasalata into a bowl. Cover and chill for at least 1 hour before serving.

BAGNA CAUDA

SERVES 4

150 ml (1/4 pint) good-quality olive oil

2 garlic cloves, crushed

1 x 60 g (2 oz) can anchovy fillets, drained and chopped

black pepper

1 Heat the oil in a frying pan, add the garlic, and cook gently, stirring occasionally, for a few minutes until soft but not coloured. Add the anchovies and cook over a very low heat until they dissolve in the oil. Season with black pepper.

2 To serve, carefully pour the bagna cauda into an earthenware pot (or a fondue pot) and place over a candle heater to keep warm.

CHEESE AIGRETTES

SERVES 10–12

300 ml (1/2 pint) water

60 g (2 oz) butter

125 g (4 oz) self-raising flour

2 egg yolks

2 eggs

125 g (4 oz) mature Cheddar cheese, grated

salt and black pepper

vegetable oil for deep-frying

1 Put the water and butter into a saucepan and bring to a boil. Remove from the heat, and add the flour. Beat well until the mixture is smooth and glossy and leaves the side of the pan clean. Leave to cool slightly.

2 In a bowl, lightly mix the yolks and eggs, then beat into the flour mixture a little at a time. Stir in the cheese. Add salt and pepper to taste.

3 Heat the oil to 190°C (375°F). Lower the mixture a teaspoonful at a time into the oil, and cook very gently until golden brown. Lift out and drain on paper towels. Serve warm.

Cook's know-how

These little deep-fried French savouries made from choux pastry are traditionally cheese-flavoured, but chopped anchovies are sometimes added for extra piquancy.

TAPAS

Tapas are Spanish appetizers: little plates of savoury foods traditionally served in bars, and accompanied by drinks (often chilled dry sherry) and good conversation. All sorts of hot and cold dishes make excellent tapas: just make sure they can easily be eaten with the fingers or a fork.

VEGETABLES WITH GARLIC DIPS

SERVES 4

750 g (1½ lb) small new potatoes

2 aubergines, cut into chunky wedges

olive oil for brushing

2 red peppers, roasted and peeled (page 388)

small bunch of watercress to serve

rouille and aïoli (pages 51 and 82) to serve

1 Boil the potatoes for 10–15 minutes until just tender. Drain and leave to cool, or keep warm, as desired.

2 Arrange the aubergine wedges in a grill pan and brush with olive oil. Cook under a hot grill, 10 cm (4 in) from the heat, for 10 minutes or until tender and lightly browned, turning occasionally. Cut the roasted peppers into chunks.

3 Arrange the vegetables on a serving plate, garnish with the watercress, and serve with rouille and aïoli.

CHICK PEA & RED PEPPER SALAD

SERVES 4

1 x 400 g (13 oz) can chick peas, drained

½ red onion or 3 spring onions, chopped

3 garlic cloves, crushed

3 tbsp olive oil

2 tbsp white wine vinegar

salt and black pepper

a bunch of flat-leaf parsley

1 red pepper, roasted and peeled (page 388)

about 12 pimiento-stuffed olives

1 Combine the chick peas with the onion, garlic, oil, vinegar, and salt and pepper to taste. Remove the parsley leaves from the stems, chop them roughly and stir in.

2 Cut the red pepper into small chunks and chop the olives if you like. Stir into the chick pea mixture until evenly mixed.

TUNA TOSTADOS

SERVES 4

½ baguette, sliced on the diagonal

1 garlic clove, crushed

3 tbsp olive oil

2 ripe tomatoes, thinly sliced

100 g (4 oz) can tuna, drained

100 g (4 oz) manchego or Cheddar cheese, grated or thinly sliced

1 Lightly toast the bread on both sides under a hot grill. Meanwhile, combine the garlic with the olive oil.

2 Brush each slice of toasted bread with a little of the garlic oil, then top with a thin slice of tomato. Place a little tuna on each, then top with cheese.

3 Return to the grill and cook, about 10 cm (4 in) from the heat, for 2–3 minutes, until the cheese has melted. Serve piping hot.

TRADITIONAL TAPAS

An appetizing selection of tapas does not have to involve a lot of work. In addition to the dishes on this page, serve some of the following – they require little or no preparation.

- pan-fried and salted almonds
- black or green olives
- slices or chunks of manchego cheese
- squares of Spanish omelette (page 101)
- slices of chorizo (spicy sausage)
- chunks of crusty bread
- jumbo prawns (good with aïoli)

ANDALUCIAN MUSHROOMS

SERVES 4

250 g (8 oz) button mushrooms

2 tbsp olive oil

6 shallots, chopped

3 garlic cloves, crushed

30 g (1 oz) serrano ham, cut into strips

¼ tsp mild chilli powder

¼ tsp paprika (preferably sweet smoked)

1 tsp lemon juice

90 ml (3 fl oz) dry red wine

4 tbsp chopped flat-leaf parsley to garnish

1 Pull the mushroom stems from the caps. Heat the olive oil in a frying pan until hot, add the shallots and half of the garlic, and cook, stirring, for about 5 minutes until soft but not coloured. Add the mushroom caps and stems, and cook, stirring, for 3 minutes until lightly browned.

2 Add the serrano ham, chilli powder, and paprika, and cook, stirring constantly, for 1 minute.

3 Add the lemon juice, and cook over a high heat for a few minutes until the liquid has almost evaporated and the mushrooms are just tender.

4 Add the red wine and continue to cook over a high heat until the liquid is reduced and flavourful. Stir in the remaining garlic, sprinkle with the chopped parsley, and serve at once.

CLOCKWISE FROM TOP: Vegetables with Garlic Dips (Rouille and Aïoli), Chick Pea & Red Pepper Salad, Andalucian Mushrooms, Tuna Tostados.

SPICY CHICKEN WINGS

SERVES 4–6

500 g (1 lb) chicken wings

2 tbsp sunflower oil

1 tsp lemon juice

1 tbsp paprika

1 tsp ground cumin

1/2 tsp dried oregano

1/2 tsp mild chilli powder

black pepper

parsley sprigs and cress to garnish

TO SERVE

1/2 red pepper, cut into strips

1/2 head celery, cut into sticks, plus leaves

blue cheese dressing (page 372)

1 Cut the chicken wings in half and put the pieces in a shallow dish.

2 In a large bowl, combine the oil, lemon juice, paprika, cumin, oregano, chilli powder, and black pepper. Brush the mixture over the chicken, cover, and leave to marinate at room temperature for at least 1 hour.

3 Line a large baking tray with foil and place a rack on top. Lay the chicken wings in a single layer on the rack, and cook in a preheated oven at 200°C (400°F, Gas 6) for 40 minutes, or until browned, sizzling, and crispy.

4 Remove the chicken from the rack and drain on paper towels. Serve with red pepper strips, celery sticks, and blue cheese dressing, and garnish with parsley and cress.

Healthy option

The skin is the crispiest part of the chicken but it is also the fattiest. If you strip it off before marinating the chicken will still taste good but it will not be crisp and crunchy.

NACHOS GRANDE

SERVES 4–6

2 tbsp sunflower oil

1 onion, finely chopped

1/2 green pepper, chopped

3 garlic cloves, crushed

1 x 225 g (8 oz) can chopped tomatoes

1/2–1 fresh green chilli, halved, seeded, and finely chopped

1/2 tsp chilli powder

1/2 tsp paprika

1 x 400 g (13 oz) can refried beans

75 ml (2 1/2 fl oz) water

75 g (2 1/2 oz) packet tortilla chips

1/4 tsp ground cumin

175 g (6 oz) Cheddar cheese, grated

paprika to garnish

1 Heat the oil in a frying pan, add the onion, green pepper, and garlic, and cook gently, stirring occasionally, for 5 minutes or until softened.

2 Add the tomatoes and chilli and cook over a medium heat for a further 5 minutes, or until most of the liquid has evaporated.

3 Stir in the chilli powder and paprika and cook for 3 minutes, then add the refried beans, breaking them up with a fork. Add the measured water and cook, stirring from time to time, for 8–10 minutes, until the mixture thickens.

4 Spoon the beans into a baking dish, arrange the tortilla chips around the edge, and sprinkle with cumin. Sprinkle the cheese over the beans and tortilla chips.

5 Bake in a preheated oven at 200°C (400°F, Gas 6) for 15–20 minutes until the cheese has melted. Sprinkle paprika in a lattice pattern on top.

Cook's know-how

The spicy bean mixture makes a tasty filling for soft tortilla wraps. Make it up to the end of step 3 and serve it in a bowl for everyone to help themselves, with a bowl of soured cream or plain yogurt to spoon on top. There is enough to fill 8 tortillas.

SALMON & PRAWN FILO PURSES

These crisp, golden purses and their creamy sauce are ideal for a party as they can be prepared up to
24 hours ahead, kept covered with a damp tea towel in the refrigerator, and cooked at the last minute.
For a really special occasion, use scallops instead of prawns.

MAKES 8 PURSES

500 g (1 lb) tail end of salmon, boned, skinned, and cut into bite-sized pieces

250 g (8 oz) cooked peeled prawns

lemon juice for sprinkling

250 g (8 oz) packet filo pastry

60 g (2 oz) butter, melted

butter for greasing

salt and black pepper

lemon slices and dill sprigs to garnish

WHITE WINE SAUCE

100 ml (3½ fl oz) dry white wine

300 ml (½ pint) double cream

1 tsp chopped fresh dill

1 Combine the salmon pieces and prawns. Sprinkle with lemon juice and add salt and pepper to taste. Set aside.

2 Cut the filo into sixteen 18 cm (7 in) squares. Brush 2 squares with the melted butter, covering the remaining squares with a damp tea towel. Make a filo purse (see box, right). Repeat to make 8 purses.

Healthy option

You can use about 2 tbsp olive oil to brush the filo rather than melted butter, and serve the purses with lemon halves for squeezing rather than the creamy sauce.

3 Butter a baking tray. Add the filo purses, lightly brush with the remaining melted butter, and bake in a preheated oven at 190°C (375°F, Gas 5) for 15–20 minutes, until crisp and golden.

4 Meanwhile, make the sauce: pour the wine into a saucepan and boil rapidly until it has reduced to about 3 tbsp. Add the cream and simmer until it reaches a light coating consistency. Remove from the heat and add the dill and salt and pepper to taste.

5 Pour the sauce into a bowl and garnish with a dill sprig. Garnish the purses with the lemon slices and dill sprigs and serve with the warm sauce.

Making a filo purse

Place one-eighth of the salmon and prawn mixture in the middle of one buttered filo pastry square.

Fold 2 sides of filo pastry over the mixture to form a rectangle. Take the 2 open ends and fold one over the filling and the other underneath.

Place this parcel on the second buttered pastry square and draw up the edges. Squeeze the pastry together at the neck to seal the purse.

INDIVIDUAL FISH PATES

Rich in flavour, these little pâté parcels make an ideal starter for a special occasion. With the gelatine, they are firm enough to be sliced. For softer pâtés, omit the gelatine and wine and serve in ramekin dishes.

SERVES 8

250 g (8 oz) haddock fillets

150 ml (1/4 pint) milk

20 g (3/4 oz) butter

20 g (3/4 oz) plain flour

1 tsp powdered gelatine

4 tbsp dry white wine

250 g (8 oz) smoked salmon pieces

2 tbsp mayonnaise

4 tbsp double cream

dash of lemon juice

black pepper

oil for greasing

smoked salmon and lemon slices, and dill sprigs to garnish

1 Put the haddock into a saucepan, and add the milk. Bring almost to a boil, then simmer gently for 10 minutes or until the fish is opaque and flakes easily.

2 Lift the haddock out of the pan, remove the skin and bones, and discard. Flake the fish and leave to cool. Reserve the cooking liquid.

3 Melt the butter in a small pan, add the flour, and cook, stirring, for 1 minute. Gradually blend in the reserved cooking liquid, and bring to a boil, stirring constantly, until the mixture thickens. Place a piece of damp greaseproof paper over the surface of the sauce to prevent a skin forming, and leave to stand until cold.

4 Sprinkle the gelatine evenly over the wine in a small bowl. Leave to stand for about 3 minutes or until the gelatine becomes spongy.

5 Put the bowl into a saucepan of gently simmering water for about 3 minutes or until the gelatine has dissolved. Leave to cool slightly.

6 Purée the haddock, cold white sauce, smoked salmon, and mayonnaise in a food processor or blender until almost smooth. Gradually add the gelatine mixture, pulsing between each addition. Add the cream and lemon juice, season with pepper, and pulse again.

7 Grease 8 small moulds. Spoon the pâté into the moulds, cover, and chill for at least 2 hours.

8 To serve, unmould each pâté and garnish with smoked salmon and lemon slices, and dill sprigs.

SARDINE PATE

SERVES 8

2 x 125 g (4 oz) cans sardines in oil, drained, bones removed

125 g (4 oz) butter, softened

125 g (4 oz) low-fat soft cheese

3 tbsp lemon juice

black pepper

lemon twists and parsley sprigs to garnish

1 Purée the sardines, butter, cheese, and lemon juice in a food processor until almost smooth. Add pepper and more lemon juice to taste.

2 Divide the sardine mixture between 8 small ramekins (or put into 1 large bowl) and level the surface. Cover and chill in the refrigerator for at least 30 minutes.

3 Serve chilled, garnished with lemon twists and parsley sprigs.

PRAWN PATE

Substitute 250 g (8 oz) cooked peeled prawns for the sardines.

Healthy note

Sardines are an oily fish, rich in omega-3 fatty acids, which can help to discourage heart disease and blood clots. They also provide vitamin D and, if you eat the bones as you do in this pâté, they are an important source of calcium.

THREE FISH TERRINE

Three kinds of smoked fish – trout, salmon, and mackerel – are blended with soft cheese, arranged in layers, then wrapped in smoked salmon for a subtle variety of flavours. The finished terrine can be frozen for up to 1 month.

SERVES 10

sunflower oil for greasing

175–250 g (6–8 oz) smoked salmon slices

salt and black pepper

watercress to serve

TROUT PATE

175 g (6 oz) smoked trout

90 g (3 oz) butter

90 g (3 oz) full-fat soft cheese

1 1/2 tbsp lemon juice

SALMON PATE

125 g (4 oz) smoked salmon pieces

60 g (2 oz) butter

60 g (2 oz) full-fat soft cheese

1 1/2 tbsp lemon juice

1 tbsp tomato purée

1 tbsp chopped fresh dill

MACKEREL PATE

175 g (6 oz) smoked mackerel

90 g (3 oz) butter

90 g (3 oz) full-fat soft cheese

1 1/2 tbsp lemon juice

1.25 LITRE (2 PINT) LOAF TIN OR TERRINE

1 Make the trout pâté: remove the skin and bones from the trout and purée with the butter, cheese, lemon juice, and salt and pepper to taste in a food processor until smooth and well blended. Turn into a bowl, cover, and chill.

2 Make the salmon pâté: purée the smoked salmon pieces, butter, cheese, lemon juice, tomato purée, dill, and salt and pepper to taste in a food processor until smooth and well blended. Turn into a bowl, cover, and chill.

3 Make the mackerel pâté: remove the skin and bones from the mackerel and purée with the butter, cheese, lemon juice, and salt and pepper to taste in a food processor until smooth and well blended. Turn into a bowl, cover, and chill.

4 Assemble the terrine (see box, right). Cover and chill overnight.

5 To serve, carefully turn out the terrine, cut into thick slices, and arrange on beds of watercress on individual serving plates.

Assembling the terrine

Oil the loaf tin and line with overlapping slices of smoked salmon. Arrange them crosswise and allow 3.5–5 cm (1 1/2–2 in) to overhang the sides of the tin.

Turn the trout pâté into the loaf tin and spread it evenly with a palette knife, levelling the surface. If necessary, wet the knife to prevent sticking. Add the salmon pâté in the same way, and then top with the mackerel pâté.

Fold the smoked salmon over the mackerel pâté, tucking in the ends.

SMOKED CHICKEN TART

SERVES 6

250 g (8 oz) ready made shortcrust pastry

15 g (1/2 oz) butter

1/2 small onion, finely chopped

60 g (2 oz) mushrooms, thinly sliced

60 g (2 oz) baby spinach, washed

salt and black pepper

200 ml (7 fl oz) half-fat crème fraîche

2 large eggs

2 tbsp chopped parsley

90 g (3 oz) cooked smoked chicken, sliced into thin strips

30 g (1 oz) Cheddar cheese, grated

18 CM (7 IN) FLAN DISH OR TIN

1 Roll out the pastry, and use to line the flan dish or tin. Prick the bottom of the patsry with a fork. Line the pastry shell with foil or greaseproof paper, and fill with baking beans, rice, or pasta.

2 Place the dish or tin on a heated baking tray, and bake in a preheated oven at 220°C (425°F, Gas 7) for about 15 minutes, removing the foil and beans for the final 5 minutes. Remove from the oven and turn the temperature down to 180°C (350°F, Gas 4).

3 Melt the butter in a frying pan, add the onion, cover, and cook gently for 10–15 minutes until soft. Remove the lid, increase the heat, add the mushrooms, and cook for 1–2 minutes. Add the spinach and cook until just wilted, then season and leave to cool.

4 Mix the crème fraîche, eggs, and parsley in a bowl, and season with salt and pepper. Mix the chicken with the cold spinach, spread over the pastry base, and top with the grated cheese. Pour the egg mixture over the top and bake for 25–30 minutes until golden brown and set. Serve warm.

BRANDIED CHICKEN LIVER PATE

SERVES 8

125 g (4 oz) bread, crusts removed

1 garlic clove, coarsely chopped

125 g (4 oz) streaky bacon rashers, rinds removed, coarsely chopped

2 tsp chopped fresh thyme

500 g (1 lb) chicken livers, trimmed

1 egg

4 tbsp brandy

1/2 tsp grated nutmeg

salt and black pepper

60 g (2 oz) butter, melted

1 KG (2 LB) LOAF TIN OR TERRINE

1 Line the loaf tin with foil, leaving 5 cm (2 in) foil overhanging on each side.

2 Cut the bread into thick chunks, and work them with the garlic in a food processor to form fine breadcrumbs. Add the bacon and thyme, and work until finely chopped.

3 Add the chicken livers, egg, brandy, and nutmeg, season with salt and pepper, and purée until smooth. Add the butter and purée again.

4 Put the pâté mixture into the prepared loaf tin, level the surface, and fold the foil over the top. Place in a roasting tin, pour in boiling water to come about halfway up the side of the loaf tin, and bake in a preheated oven at 160°C (325°F, Gas 3) for 1 hour.

5 Test the pâté for doneness (see box, below). Leave the pâté to cool completely, then cover, and leave to chill in the refrigerator overnight.

6 To serve, cut the pâté into slices.

Is it cooked?

Insert a skewer into the middle of the pâté. If it comes out hot and clean, the pâté is cooked.

PAN-FRIED PATES

These little bacon-wrapped chicken liver and spinach pâtés are easy to make, and they are at their most delicious when served with a tangy salad of sliced tomatoes and chopped onions in a herb vinaigrette dressing.

SERVES 4

30 g (1 oz) butter

125 g (4 oz) chicken livers, trimmed

5 shallots, coarsely chopped

125 g (4 oz) lean bacon rashers, rinds removed, coarsely chopped

60 g (2 oz) spinach leaves, shredded

2 tbsp chopped parsley

1 tsp chopped fresh thyme leaves

1 garlic clove, crushed

salt and black pepper

8 streaky bacon rashers, rinds removed

1 Melt half of the butter in a frying pan, add the chicken livers, and cook gently, stirring occasionally, for 3 minutes or until they are browned on the outside but still pink inside.

2 Purée the chicken livers in a food processor until smooth. Turn into a large bowl and set aside.

3 Melt the remaining butter in the frying pan, add the shallots, and cook gently, stirring occasionally, for a few minutes until soft but not coloured.

4 Add the shallots to the chicken livers with the chopped bacon, spinach, parsley, garlic, and thyme. Season with salt and pepper. Purée half of this mixture until smooth, then stir it into the remaining mixture in the bowl.

5 Shape and wrap the chicken liver pâtés (see box, right).

6 Heat a frying pan, add the pâtés, and cook them gently until browned all over. Lower the heat, cover, and cook over a very gentle heat for 35–40 minutes.

7 Serve the pan-fried pâtés either warm or at room temperature.

Cook's know-how

To trim the chicken livers, use kitchen scissors to cut away any membranes.

Shaping and wrapping the pâtés

Mould the pâté mixture into 8 equal-sized oval shapes, using your hands.

Lay a bacon rasher flat, put a pâté oval at one end and roll the bacon round it.

Twist the rasher round the ends to enclose the pâté, then tuck it in underneath to secure. Repeat with the remaining bacon rashers and pâté.

HUMMUS

SERVES 6

2 x 400 g (13 oz) cans chick peas, drained

2–3 garlic cloves, coarsely chopped

1 tbsp tahini paste, or to taste

3 tbsp olive oil, or to taste

juice of 1 lemon, or to taste

salt and black pepper

TO GARNISH (OPTIONAL)

6 rosemary sprigs

1 red pepper, halved, seeded, and cut into strips

12 small black olives

1 Purée the chick peas, garlic, tahini paste, oil, and lemon juice in a food processor or blender until smooth.

2 Add salt and pepper to taste, and more oil, tahini, and lemon juice if you think it needs it, then purée again.

3 Spoon into dishes and level the surface. If you like, garnish with rosemary, red pepper, and olives.

Cook's know-how

There are no hard-and-fast rules about the amounts of oil, tahini paste, and lemon juice when making hummus. The best method is to purée the amount suggested, then taste it and see before adding more. Serve chilled if you like.

SMOKED HADDOCK MOUSSE

SERVES 6

250 g (8 oz) smoked haddock, skinned

juice of 1/2 lemon

salt and black pepper

250 g (8 oz) full-fat soft cheese

2 tbsp reduced-calorie mayonnaise

1 tbsp turmeric

6 SMALL RAMEKINS

1 Line a baking sheet with a long, wide piece of foil, and place the haddock on it. Sprinkle the fish with the lemon juice, and season with pepper. Bring the long edges of the foil together, and fold to seal. Bring each of the short edges together, and fold to seal, forming a parcel.

2 Bake the fish in a preheated oven at 160°C (350°F, Gas 3) for 7–10 minutes, or until the fish is just cooked and flakes easily with a fork. Set aside in the foil parcel until cold.

3 Flake the fish, removing any bones. Place in a food processor or blender, adding any juices that are left on the foil. Add the cheese, mayonnaise, and turmeric. Season lightly with salt.

4 Process or blend the mixture until smooth, then check and adjust the seasoning if necessary.

5 Lightly oil the ramekins and spoon in the fish mixture. Cover and chill for at least 3 hours, when the mixture will be set to a soft mousse.

6 Serve with thin slices of plain wholemeal toast (the cheese adds richness to the mousse, so no butter is needed).

Cook's know-how

Turmeric comes from the same family as ginger, but the root is rarely used in cooking and it is only seen in its powdered form in recipes. It is often used to add warm colour and flavour to Asian dishes, especially curries (it is the spice that makes curry powder the colour it is), and is known to be an important source of curcumin, a phytochemical with anti-cancer and anti-inflammatory effects.

BROCCOLI TERRINE

SERVES 4–6

500 g (1 lb) broccoli florets

salt and black pepper

15 g (1/2 oz) gelatine powder

125 ml (4 fl oz) milk

1 egg yolk

pinch of grated nutmeg

125 ml (4 fl oz) double cream

oil for greasing

carrot julienne salad (page 391) to serve

1 KG (2 LB) LOAF TIN

1 Cook the broccoli in boiling salted water for 3–4 minutes or until just tender. Drain well, pouring 75 ml (2 1/2 fl oz) of the cooking water into a small bowl.

2 Leave the reserved cooking water to cool slightly, then sprinkle the gelatine evenly over the top. Leave to stand for 3 minutes or until the gelatine becomes spongy. Put the bowl into a pan of gently simmering water for 3 minutes or until the gelatine has dissolved.

3 Put the milk and egg yolk into a small saucepan and beat together. Heat gently, stirring, until the mixture thickens enough to coat the back of the spoon. Leave to cool slightly.

4 Reserve a few broccoli florets for garnish. Roughly chop half of the broccoli, and purée the remainder with the milk and egg mixture in a food processor until smooth. Pour the puréed broccoli mixture into a large bowl, and add the chopped broccoli, gelatine mixture, and nutmeg. Season with salt and pepper, and mix together.

5 Whip the cream until it forms firm peaks, then fold into the broccoli mixture. Oil the loaf tin and pour in the broccoli mixture. Cover and chill for at least 3 hours.

6 Turn out the terrine and cut into slices. Garnish with the reserved broccoli florets, and serve with the carrot julienne salad.

LEEK PARCELS WITH PROVENÇAL VEGETABLES

Punchy pesto features twice in this stunning first course – inside the parcels and in the dressing. The flavours of basil, pine nuts, garlic, and Parmesan complement the leeks, courgettes, and aubergines, three vegetables that go together surprisingly well.

SERVES 4

1 large leek, green part only, trimmed and cut in half lengthwise

1 aubergine, cut into 8 slices

1 courgette, sliced

olive oil for brushing

1/2 tsp herbes de Provence or dried mixed herbs

salt and black pepper

3 tbsp ready made pesto

1 red pepper, halved, seeded, roasted, and peeled (page 388), or 1 large piece of bottled roasted red pepper, chopped

1 x 225 g (8 oz) can tomatoes, drained and chopped

carrot julienne to garnish

PESTO DRESSING

3 tbsp olive oil

3 tbsp white wine vinegar

1 tsp ready made pesto

1 Blanch the leek in boiling water for 1 minute. Drain and rinse. Separate the green layers to give 13 strips.

2 Brush the aubergine and courgette with the oil, and sprinkle with the herbs and salt and pepper. Cook under a hot grill for 5 minutes, about 10 cm (4 in) from the heat. Brush the aubergine with pesto.

3 Cut one of the strips of leek into 4 long strands and set aside. Take 3 strips of leek and lay on top of one another in a star formation. Assemble the leek parcels (see box, right).

4 Put the parcels on to a baking tray and bake in a preheated oven at 180°C (350°F, Gas 4) for 10 minutes.

5 Whisk the dressing ingredients together, and spoon on to 4 serving plates. Place a parcel on top, garnish, and serve.

Assembling the leek parcels

Place a slice of aubergine where the strips of leek cross. Place a piece of red pepper on top, then 1–2 slices of courgette, a piece of tomato, and finally another slice of aubergine.

Fold the leek strips over the filling so they meet on top in the middle and enclose the filling completely.

Tie the parcel with one of the long strands of leek or with a length of string. Repeat with the remaining leek strips, vegetables and leek strands.

EGG PATE

SERVES 8

15 g (1/2 oz) gelatine powder

2 tbsp water

1 x 400 g (13 oz) can consommé

150 ml (1/4 pint) double cream

6 hard-boiled eggs, peeled and chopped

150 ml (1/4 pint) crème fraîche

salt and black pepper

8 large cooked prawns in their shells, lemon slices, and dill sprigs to garnish

1 Sprinkle the gelatine over the water in a bowl. Leave to stand for 3 minutes or until the gelatine becomes spongy. Put the bowl into a saucepan of simmering water for 3 minutes or until the gelatine has dissolved.

2 Pour the consommé into a jug and stir in the gelatine liquid.

3 Whip the cream in a large bowl until it forms soft peaks. Fold in the eggs, crème fraîche, and three-quarters of the consommé. Season with salt and pepper.

4 Divide the mixture between 8 ramekins and level the surface. Leave to stand for about 30 minutes until set. If it has already set, reheat the remaining consommé gently. Spoon it over the pâté. Chill for at least 3 hours.

5 To serve, turn out the pâté, and garnish with the prawns, lemon slices, and fresh dill sprigs.

PREPARE-AHEAD FIRST COURSES

If you are having friends in for a party it is always best to try and get the first course made ahead of time. Then, before you sit down to eat, you can concentrate on the main course and vegetables, which almost always need last-minute attention. These three dishes can all be made several hours ahead of serving.

ASPARAGUS & QUAILS' EGG SALAD

SERVES 6

12 quails' eggs

18 asparagus spears

1 x 340 g (12 oz) jar roasted artichokes hearts in oil

TO SERVE

1 tbsp balsamic vinegar

salt and black pepper

about 30 g (1 oz) Parmesan shavings

1 Put the eggs in a pan of cold water, bring to a boil, and boil for 3 minutes (start timing as soon as the water comes to a boil). Drain and rinse under cold running water, then peel immediately. The shells come off very easily when the eggs are just cooked.

2 Peel the asparagus stems with a potato or vegetable peeler if they are woody, then cut the asparagus into 5 cm (2 in) lengths. Cook in boiling salted water for about 2 minutes until only just tender. Drain into a sieve and rinse thoroughly under cold running water, then pat dry with kitchen paper.

3 Drain the artichoke hearts, reserving the oil. Cut the artichokes and eggs lengthwise in half. Divide the artichokes and asparagus between 6 plates, and top each serving with four egg halves.

4 Make a dressing by mixing 3 tbsp of the reserved oil from the artichoke jar with the balsamic vinegar, and season with salt and pepper.

5 To serve, drizzle the dressing over the salad, top with Parmesan shavings, and serve with crusty rolls.

DOUBLE SALMON TIAN

SERVES 6

650 g (1 lb 5 oz) fresh salmon fillet, skinned

200 g (7 oz) low-fat soft cheese

4 tbsp chopped fresh dill

salt and black pepper

TO SERVE

50-60 g (1½-2 oz) fresh mizuna leaves, or any other peppery leaves such as rocket

6 small slices of smoked salmon, total weight about 200 g (7 oz)

6 lemon wedges to serve

6 x 7.5 CM (3 IN) METAL RINGS OR 150 ML (5 FL OZ) RAMEKIN DISHES

1 Wrap the fresh salmon tightly in foil and bake in a preheated oven at 190°C (375°F, Gas 5) for 15–20 minutes or until just cooked. Leave to cool in the foil.

2 Mix the cheese and dill in a large bowl until smooth. Flake the cooled salmon into the bowl, including any fish juices and jelly, but discarding any bones. Season well with salt and pepper, and fold gently together.

3 Put the metal rings on a flat plate or baking tray (if using ramekins, line them with cling film). Divide the salmon and cheese mixture between them, smoothing the surface with the back of a metal spoon. Cover and refrigerate for at least 2 hours, overnight if possible.

4 To serve, divide the salad leaves between 6 plates. Lift a ring filled with salmon on to the leaves using a fish slice, then carefully ease off the ring. (If using ramekins, invert the salmon on to the leaves and gently remove the cling film.) Top each tian with a loosely curled piece of smoked salmon and serve with wedges of lemon for squeezing.

SMOKED SALMON TERRINE

SERVES 8

275 g (9 oz) thinly sliced smoked salmon

black pepper

250 g (8 oz) low-fat soft cheese

125 g (4 oz) unsalted butter, softened

2 tbsp creamed horseradish

4 canned anchovy fillets (more if you wish)

1–2 tbsp chopped fresh parsley or dill, or a mixture of the two

TO SERVE

salad leaves, tossed in your favourite dressing

lime or lemon wedges

500 G (1 LB) LOAF TIN

1 Dampen the loaf tin and line with cling film, letting it overhang the sides. Divide the smoked salmon into four equal piles. Cover the base of the tin with a quarter of the salmon and sprinkle with black pepper.

2 Put the soft cheese, butter, horseradish, anchovies, and parsley or dill into a blender or food processor, season with black pepper, and work to a very smooth paste. Do not add salt. (If you haven't got a blender or food processor, beat the mixture vigorously with a wooden spoon.)

3 Spread a third of the paste over the salmon in the tin and cover with a second layer of salmon. Continue alternating the layers, finishing with salmon. Tightly pull the cling film over the top and press down firmly. Refrigerate for at least 6 hours, preferably overnight.

4 To serve, put the terrine in the freezer for 30 minutes (this will make it easy to slice). Turn it out of its tin and discard the cling film, then cut into 16 thin slices. Serve 2 slices on each plate, on a bed of dressed salad leaves, with lime or lemon wedges for squeezing.

CLOCKWISE FROM TOP: Smoked Salmon Terrine, Asparagus & Quails' Egg Salad, Double Salmon Tian.

SCALLOPS WITH CHEESE SAUCE

SERVES 4

8 scallops, with 4 shells if possible

150 ml (1/4 pint) water

4 tbsp medium dry white wine

1 bay leaf

salt and black pepper

lemon wedges and bay leaves to garnish

MORNAY SAUCE

45 g (1 1/2 oz) butter

3 tbsp plain flour

4 tbsp single cream

60 g (2 oz) Gruyère cheese, grated

1 Cut each scallop into 2–3 pieces. Put the measured water, wine, and bay leaf into a small pan, and season with salt and pepper. Bring to a boil, then lower the heat and add the scallops.

2 Poach for 1 minute or until the scallops are just tender when tested with the tip of a knife. Lift out the scallops with a slotted spoon, strain the cooking liquid, and reserve.

3 Make the Mornay sauce: melt the butter in a saucepan, add the flour, and cook, stirring, for 1 minute. Gradually stir in the reserved cooking liquid, and bring to a boil, stirring constantly, until the mixture thickens. Simmer gently for about 5 minutes. Lower the heat, and stir in the cream and half of the grated cheese. Taste for seasoning.

4 Stir the scallops into the sauce, divide among the shells, and sprinkle with the remaining cheese.

5 Place the filled shells under a hot grill, 7 cm (3 in) from the heat, for 5 minutes or until the cheese has melted and the sauce is golden and bubbling. Garnish with lemon wedges and bay leaves.

Cook's know-how

If you can't get scallop shells for serving, use individual baking dishes or gratin dishes. The French type with two small handles or "ears" are traditional for this dish.

MOULES MARINIERE

SERVES 6

90 g (3 oz) butter

1 small onion, finely chopped

1 garlic clove, crushed

3 kg (6 lb) mussels, cleaned (page 124)

450 ml (3/4 pint) dry white wine

6 parsley sprigs

3 thyme sprigs

1 bay leaf

salt and black pepper

1 tbsp plain flour

3 tbsp chopped parsley to garnish

1 Melt two-thirds of the butter in a large saucepan, add the onion and garlic, and cook gently, stirring occasionally, for a few minutes until soft but not coloured.

2 Add the mussels, wine, parsley, thyme, and bay leaf, and season with salt and pepper. Cover the saucepan tightly and bring to a boil.

3 Cook, shaking the saucepan frequently, for 5–6 minutes or until the mussels open.

4 Throw away any mussels that are not open. Transfer the open mussels to a warmed tureen or large serving bowl.

5 Strain the cooking juices into a small pan and boil until reduced by one-third.

6 Mix the remaining butter and the flour on a plate to make a paste (beurre manié).

7 Whisk the beurre manié into the cooking liquid, and bring to a boil, stirring constantly. Taste for seasoning, and pour over the mussels. Garnish and serve at once.

Healthy option

This classic recipe is made with a butter-and-flour beurre manié, which thickens the sauce. For a healthier option, cook the onion and garlic in 2 tbsp olive oil and omit the flour. To compensate for the lack of thickening, boil the cooking liquid in step 5 until reduced by about half.

SALMON QUENELLES

Quenelles are delicate little dumplings, traditionally oval but sometimes round, which can be made with fish, meat, or chicken. The name comes from Knödel, the German word for dumpling. They are simple to make, and yet they look elegant and impressive, as if they require professional skills.

SERVES 4–6

500 g (1 lb) salmon fillet, skinned, boned, and cut into chunks

2 egg whites

salt and white pepper

150 ml (1/4 pint) double cream

lemon slices and flat-leaf parsley sprigs to garnish

ASPARAGUS SAUCE

90 ml (3 fl oz) dry white wine

250 g (8 oz) young asparagus, trimmed, woody parts removed

300 ml (1/2 pint) double cream

1 Make the quenelles: purée the salmon, egg whites, and salt and pepper to taste in a food processor until completely smooth.

2 With the machine still running, pour in the cream in a steady stream until it is thoroughly blended. Turn the mixture into a large bowl, cover, and chill for about 2 hours.

3 Bring a saucepan of salted water to a simmer. Shape and cook the quenelles (see box, right). Keep the quenelles warm while you make the sauce.

4 Make the asparagus sauce: pour the wine into a saucepan and boil rapidly for about 2 minutes until it is reduced to a thin syrup.

5 Cook the asparagus in a pan of boiling salted water for 3–5 minutes until tender. Drain, then cut off the asparagus tips, and reserve them for garnish.

6 Purée the reduced wine and the asparagus stalks until very smooth.

7 Boil the cream in a saucepan for 4 minutes or until it is thick enough to coat the back of a metal spoon. Stir in the purée, and taste for seasoning.

8 Pour the sauce on to warmed plates, arrange the quenelles on top, and garnish with the reserved asparagus tips, lemon slices, and parsley sprigs.

Cook's know-how

Take care not to overprocess the purée when blending the quenelle mixture. If you work it too hard, this could cause the cream to curdle.

Shaping and cooking the quenelles

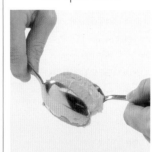

Dip a dessertspoon into the simmering water, then take a spoonful of the chilled quenelle mixture. Using a second warm wetted dessertspoon or your fingers, mould into an oval. Repeat with the remaining mixture.

Lower some quenelles into the simmering water and cook for 6–10 minutes until they are firm when pressed with a finger. Do not put too many into the pan at one time.

Remove the quenelles with a slotted spoon, drain well, and keep them warm while you cook the remainder.

SARDINES WITH CORIANDER

SERVES 4

12–16 large sardines

olive oil for brushing

salt and black pepper

lime wedges and flat-leaf parsley
  sprigs to garnish

CORIANDER LIME BUTTER

1 tsp ground coriander

60 g (2 oz) unsalted butter, at
  room temperature

1 1/2 tsp lime juice

1 shallot, finely chopped

1/4 tsp finely grated lime zest

1 Scale the sardines with the back of a kitchen knife. With a sharp knife, cut the stomachs open, and scrape out the contents, particularly any dark blood.

2 Rinse the sardines inside and out, and pat dry. Brush all over with oil, and sprinkle with salt and pepper.

3 Prepare the coriander lime butter: heat a heavy pan, add the coriander and toast lightly. Transfer the coriander to a bowl and leave to cool slightly.

4 Add the butter and lime juice to the coriander and whisk until thick. Stir in the shallot and lime zest, and salt and pepper to taste.

5 Place the sardines under a hot grill, 10 cm (4 in) from the heat, and grill for 1 1/2–2 minutes on each side until they begin to feel firm.

6 Transfer the sardines to a platter, and spread a little coriander lime butter on each one. Garnish with lime wedges and flat-leaf parsley sprigs, and serve at once.

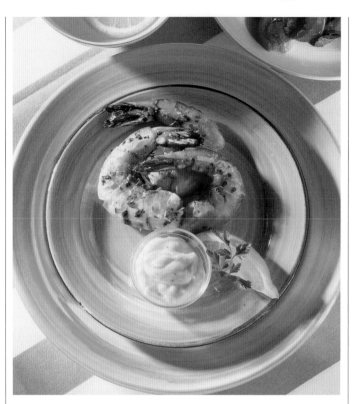

JUMBO PRAWNS WITH AIOLI

SERVES 4

2 tbsp olive oil

12 uncooked jumbo prawns in their
  shells

1 tbsp chopped parsley

lemon wedges and flat-leaf parsley
  sprigs to garnish

AÏOLI

2 garlic cloves, coarsely chopped

salt and black pepper

1 egg yolk

1 tsp mustard powder

150 ml (1/4 pint) olive oil

1 tbsp lemon juice

1 Make the aïoli: in a small bowl, crush the garlic with a pinch of salt until it forms a smooth paste. Add the egg yolk and mustard powder, and beat well. Beat in the oil, drop by drop, whisking constantly until the mixture is thick and smooth, and all the oil has been absorbed. Beat in the lemon juice, and add pepper to taste.

2 Heat the oil in a large frying pan, add the prawns, and toss over a high heat for 3–4 minutes, just until the shells turn bright pink. Remove the prawns from the frying pan and drain on paper towels.

3 To serve, arrange the prawns on warmed plates, sprinkle with chopped parsley, and garnish with lemon wedges and parsley sprigs. Serve with individual bowls of aïoli.

Cook's know-how

Uncooked, or raw, prawns are usually grey in colour – it is only when they are cooked that they turn into the pink prawns we are more familiar with. The golden rule when cooking prawns is never to overcook them, so remove them from the heat as soon as they turn pink. Overcooked prawns are rubbery, chewy, and tasteless.

GRAVADLAX

You can buy this Scandinavian "pickled" salmon, but it is easy (and less expensive) to make it yourself – and your guests will be very impressed. Serve it with thin slices of dark rye bread. You will find the gravadlax easier to slice if it has been frozen for about 4 hours beforehand.

SERVES 16

2.25 kg (4¹/2 lb) whole fresh salmon, boned and cut lengthwise in half into 2 fillets (ask your fishmonger)

dill sprigs and lemon segments to garnish

PICKLING MIXTURE

75 g (2¹/2 oz) granulated sugar

4 tbsp coarse sea salt

4 tbsp chopped fresh dill

MUSTARD DILL SAUCE

3 tbsp Dijon mustard

2 tbsp caster sugar

1 tbsp white wine vinegar

1 egg yolk

150 ml (¹/4 pint) sunflower oil

salt and black pepper

2 tbsp chopped fresh dill

1 Make the pickling mixture: put the granulated sugar, sea salt, and chopped fresh dill into a small bowl, season generously with black pepper, and stir well to mix.

2 Sandwich the salmon fillets together (see box, right).

3 Wrap the fillets in a double thickness of foil and place in a large dish. Weigh down with kitchen weights or heavy cans, and keep in the refrigerator for 24 hours. Halfway through this time, turn the salmon over.

4 Make the mustard dill sauce: in a medium bowl, whisk together the mustard, sugar, vinegar, and egg yolk, then whisk in the oil a little at a time. The sauce should have the consistency of mayonnaise. Add salt and pepper to taste, and stir in the chopped dill.

5 Unwrap the gravadlax. A lot of sticky, salty liquid will drain from the fish when it has been pickled: this is quite normal. Remove the fish from the pickling liquid, and dry well. Separate the 2 salmon fillets.

6 To serve, slice each fillet on the slant, cutting the flesh away from the skin. The slices should be a little thicker than for smoked salmon and each one should have a fringe of dill. Garnish with dill sprigs and lemon segments, and serve with the mustard dill sauce.

Sandwiching the salmon

Put 1 salmon fillet skin-side down on a board, cover the surface with the pickling mixture, and place the second fillet on top, skin-side up.

PRAWN COCKTAIL

SERVES 4

150 ml (¹/4 pint) mayonnaise

2 tbsp creamed horseradish

1 tbsp lemon juice

1 tsp Worcestershire sauce

1 tsp tomato purée

¹/4 tsp caster sugar

few drops of Tabasco sauce

black pepper

250 g (8 oz) cooked peeled prawns

salad leaves to serve

thin lemon wedges, parsley sprigs, and 4 large cooked prawns in their shells to garnish

1 Make the dressing: in a medium bowl, combine the mayonnaise, creamed horseradish, lemon juice, Worcestershire sauce, tomato purée, caster sugar, and Tabasco sauce, and season well with a little black pepper.

2 Add the peeled cooked prawns and stir to coat with the dressing.

3 Line 4 individual glass serving bowls with the salad leaves and top with the prawn mixture. Garnish each serving with a thin lemon wedge, a parsley sprig, and a large prawn.

PRAWN BLINI

Blini are small Russian pancakes made with yeast and buckwheat flour. Buckwheat flour is available from health food shops but if you cannot find any, use wholemeal flour instead. This mixture makes about 24 blini.

SERVES 6–8

BLINI

125 g (4 oz) plain flour
125 g (4 oz) buckwheat flour
1/2 tsp salt
1/2 tsp fast-action dried yeast
450 ml (3/4 pint) milk, warmed
1 egg, separated
sunflower oil for frying

TO SERVE

2 x 75 g (2 1/2 oz) jars lumpfish roe (1 red, 1 black)
125 g (4 oz) cooked peeled prawns
125 ml (4 fl oz) crème fraîche
lemon segments and fresh chives to garnish

1 Put both types of flour into a large bowl. Add the salt and yeast, then stir together until evenly mixed.

2 Gradually beat in the warm milk to make a smooth batter. Cover the bowl and leave in a warm place for about 40 minutes until the mixture is frothy and has doubled in volume.

3 Beat the egg yolk into the flour and yeast mixture. Put the egg white into a clean bowl and whisk until stiff but not dry, then fold into the mixture.

4 Heat a large non-stick frying pan or griddle, brush with oil, and heat until the oil is hot. Spoon about 2 tbsp batter into the pan for each blini (you should be able to cook 3 or 4 at a time), and cover a moderate heat for 2–3 minutes, or until bubbles rise to the surface and burst.

5 Turn the blini over with a palette knife and cook for a further 2–3 minutes until golden on the other side. Wrap the cooked blini in a tea towel and keep them warm.

6 Cook the remaining batter in batches until all the batter is used up, lightly oiling the pan between each batch.

7 To serve, arrange the blini on warmed plates, with spoonfuls of red and black lumpfish roe, prawns, and crème fraîche. Garnish with lemon segments and chives.

Cook's know-how

If you buy ready made blini, they will need to be gently warmed through.

MIMOSA FISH SALAD

SERVES 4

2 hard-boiled eggs
300 g (10 oz) firm white fish fillets, cooked, skinned, and flaked
3 tbsp soured cream
3 tbsp mayonnaise
1 tbsp chopped parsley
1 tsp chopped fresh dill
a few drops of Tabasco sauce
salt and black pepper
4 large tomatoes, halved
lemon twists, flat-leaf parsley sprigs, and celery leaves to garnish

1 Remove the yolk from one egg and reserve. Chop the white and the remaining egg.

2 Mix the fish with the chopped egg, soured cream, mayonnaise, parsley, dill, and Tabasco. Add salt and pepper.

3 Top the tomatoes with the fish mixture. Sieve the egg yolk, sprinkle it over the mixture, and garnish with lemon, parsley, and celery.

SMOKED CHICKEN SALAD WITH WALNUTS

SERVES 6

1 smoked chicken, weighing about 1.25 kg (2½ lb)
100 ml (3½ fl oz) sunflower oil
2 tbsp walnut oil
75 ml (2½ fl oz) orange juice
¼ tsp ground coriander
¼ tsp caster sugar
salt and black pepper
375 g (12 oz) mixed salad leaves
4 oranges, peeled and segmented
60 g (2 oz) walnut pieces

1 Remove the meat from the chicken carcass, and discard all of the skin and any gristle. Cut the meat into thin, neat slices. Put the chicken into a shallow non-metallic dish.

2 In a small bowl, combine the sunflower and walnut oils, orange juice, ground coriander, and sugar. Season with salt and pepper. Pour the mixture over the chicken slices and toss them gently until evenly coated.

3 Arrange the salad leaves, orange segments, and chicken slices on individual serving plates, scatter the walnut pieces over the top, and serve immediately.

WARM DUCK SALAD

Substitute 375 g (12 oz) smoked duck or turkey breast for the chicken. Gently heat the poultry slices in the dressing, and add warm garlic croûtons (page 49) to the salad.

WARM SALAD WITH BACON & SCALLOPS

SERVES 4

375 g (12 oz) mixed salad leaves, such as radicchio, lamb's lettuce, frisée, and rocket
8 shallots, finely chopped
1 tbsp sunflower oil
250 g (8 oz) lean unsmoked bacon rashers, rinds removed, diced
12 scallops, halved
3 tbsp white wine vinegar
2 tbsp walnut oil
salt and black pepper

1 Put the salad leaves into a large bowl and sprinkle with half of the shallots.

2 Heat the oil in a frying pan, add the bacon, and cook quickly, stirring occasionally, for 5 minutes or until crisp. Add the scallops and cook quickly for 1–2 minutes until just opaque. Remove from the pan and keep warm.

3 Add the remaining shallots and cook for 1 minute. Add the vinegar and boil rapidly, stirring to incorporate the pan juices.

4 Sprinkle the walnut oil over the salad leaves and toss together until the leaves are evenly coated and shiny. Add the bacon and scallops, hot vinegar and shallots, and season to taste.

Cook's know-how

Stirring vinegar into the frying pan loosens and dissolves the flavoursome juices on the bottom of the pan so they are not wasted. This is called deglazing.

ASPARAGUS WITH QUICK HOLLANDAISE

SERVES 4

625 g (1 1/4 lb) asparagus

salt and black pepper

lemon twists to garnish

QUICK HOLLANDAISE

1 tbsp lemon juice

1 tbsp white wine vinegar

4 egg yolks, at room temperature

150 g (5 oz) unsalted butter, melted

1 Cut any woody ends off the asparagus and discard. Lay the spears flat in salted boiling water in a shallow pan (a sauté pan or frying pan is ideal), and simmer gently for 3–4 minutes until the asparagus is tender but still firm.

2 Meanwhile, make the quick hollandaise: three-quarters fill a food processor or blender with hot water from the kettle and pulse or process briefly, to warm the bowl. Pour the water away and dry the bowl.

3 Put the lemon juice and vinegar into the warm bowl of food processor or blender, add the egg yolks and pulse or process briefly.

4 With the machine running, gradually pour in the melted butter, and work until thick and creamy. Season to taste.

5 To serve, drain the asparagus. Ladle the hollandaise sauce on to warmed plates, arrange the asparagus on top, and garnish with lemon twists.

Healthy option

An alternative way to cook asparagus, and one that gives it lots of flavour, is to chargrill it. Heat a ridged non-stick or cast iron chargrill pan until very hot. While it is heating up, roll the asparagus spears in a little olive oil, sea salt, and freshly ground black pepper. As soon as the pan is hot but not smoking, lay the spears across the ridges and cook for 3–4 minutes, turning them with tongs so they become evenly charred on all sides. Instead of serving with a buttery Hollandaise, sprinkle with a little extra-virgin olive oil and grated Parmesan cheese.

BRIOCHES WITH WILD MUSHROOMS & WATERCRESS

SERVES 6

30 g (1 oz) butter

250 g (8 oz) wild mushrooms, trimmed and sliced

60 g (2 oz) watercress, finely chopped

4 tbsp double cream

squeeze of lemon juice

salt and black pepper

6 brioches (page 416)

watercress sprigs to garnish

1 Melt the butter in a large frying pan, add the mushrooms, and cook over a high heat, stirring from time to time, for 3 minutes or until all the liquid has evaporated. Add the watercress, cream, lemon juice, and salt and pepper to taste, and cook until the watercress is just wilted.

2 Hollow out the brioches (see box, right). Spoon in some of the mixture.

Preparing brioches

Remove brioche top and set aside. Using your fingers, pull out the soft inside, leaving a 5 mm (1/4 in) crust. Repeat with the remaining brioches.

3 To serve, transfer the brioches to warmed serving plates and replace the brioche tops. Spoon the remaining mushroom and watercress mixture on to the plates beside the brioches, and garnish with watercress sprigs.

SMOKED SALMON ROULADE

The richness of the cheese and smoked salmon layers is offset by a thin layer of tomatoes that provides a fresh and tangy contrast. Here the roulade is served in slices, but you could serve it whole, with just a few slices cut at one end.

SERVES 4–6

15 g (½ oz) butter

1 garlic clove, crushed

150 g (5 oz) spinach, cooked, squeezed dry, and chopped

4 eggs, separated

1 tsp chopped fresh rosemary

pinch of grated nutmeg

salt and black pepper

salad leaves and lemon slices to garnish

FILLING

200 g (7 oz) full-fat soft cheese

3 tbsp Greek yogurt or 2 tbsp milk

4 spring onions, thinly sliced

125 g (4 oz) smoked salmon

2 ripe tomatoes, thinly sliced

33 × 23 CM (13 × 9 IN) SWISS ROLL TIN

1 Make the roulade: line the Swiss roll tin with a sheet of baking parchment, cutting the corners of the paper so that it fits snugly into the tin.

2 Put the butter into a saucepan, add the garlic, and cook gently until the butter melts. Remove from the heat. Stir in the spinach.

3 Add the egg yolks, rosemary, and nutmeg, season to taste, and beat into the spinach mixture.

4 In another bowl, whisk the egg whites until firm but not dry. Fold 2–3 spoonfuls into the spinach mixture, then fold in the remainder.

5 Spread the mixture in the Swiss roll tin, and bake in a preheated oven at 190°C (375°F, Gas 5) for 10–12 minutes until the mixture feels firm. Remove from the oven, cover with a damp tea towel, and leave to cool.

6 Meanwhile, make the filling: beat the cheese and yogurt or milk together until smooth, then stir in the onions.

7 Turn out the cooled roulade and peel off the paper. Fill and roll the roulade (see box, right).

8 Wrap the roulade in foil, then overwrap with a damp tea towel, and chill overnight.

9 To serve, trim off the hard edges of the roulade, cut into thick slices, and arrange on a serving platter. Garnish with salad leaves and lemon slices.

PARMA HAM ROULADE

Substitute 125 g (4 oz) thinly sliced Parma ham for the smoked salmon.

Cook's know-how

This roulade can be prepared up to the end of step 8 up to 2 days ahead, making it ideal for a dinner party or other special occasion.

Filling and rolling the roulade

Arrange the slices of smoked salmon on top of the roulade, leaving a 2.5 cm (1 in) border on each side.

Spread the cheese filling over the salmon, using a palette knife. Arrange the tomato slices over half of the cheese filling, looking at it widthways.

Roll up the roulade, starting from the end where the tomato slices have been placed.

AVOCADO WITH TOMATOES & MINT

SERVES 4

4 small firm tomatoes

2 ripe avocados

1 tbsp chopped fresh mint

mint sprigs to garnish

DRESSING

2 tsp white wine vinegar

1 tsp Dijon mustard

2 tbsp olive oil

1/4 tsp caster sugar

salt and black pepper

1 Peel the tomatoes: cut out the cores and score an "x" on the base of each one, then immerse in a bowl of boiling hot water until the skins start to split. Transfer at once to a bowl of cold water. Peel, seed, and then coarsely chop the tomato flesh.

2 Make the dressing: in a small bowl, whisk together the vinegar and mustard. Gradually whisk in the oil, then add the caster sugar, and salt and pepper to taste.

3 Halve and stone the avocados. Brush the flesh with a little dressing to prevent discoloration.

4 Combine the tomatoes, chopped mint, and dressing. Pile the tomato mixture into the avocado halves, garnish with mint sprigs, and serve at once.

SUMMER MELONS

SERVES 4

2 x 750 g (1 1/2 lb) ripe melons with different coloured flesh (see box, right)

500 g (1 lb) tomatoes

1 tbsp chopped fresh mint

mint sprigs to garnish

DRESSING

90 ml (3 fl oz) sunflower oil

2 tbsp white wine vinegar

1/4 tsp caster sugar

salt and black pepper

1 Cut the melons in half, and remove and discard the seeds. Using a melon baller or a knife, cut balls or neat cubes of flesh into a bowl.

2 Peel the tomatoes: cut out the cores and score an "x" on the base of each one, then immerse in a bowl of boiling water until the skins start to split. Transfer at once to a bowl of cold water. Peel and seed the tomatoes, then cut the flesh into long strips. Add the strips to the melon.

3 Make the dressing: in a small bowl, whisk together the sunflower oil and vinegar, then add the caster sugar, and salt and pepper to taste. Pour the dressing over the melon and tomato mixture. Cover and chill for at least 1 hour.

4 To serve, stir the chopped mint into the melon and tomato mixture, spoon the salad into chilled bowls, and garnish each serving with a mint sprig.

Cook's know-how

Choose two or three varieties of melon to make an attractive colour combination. Honeydew has pale greenish yellow flesh, cantaloupe has either pale green or orange flesh, Ogen and Galia have pale yellow or green flesh, while Charentais melons have deep orange flesh.

ANTIPASTI

This is the Italian version of the French hors d'oeuvre or Spanish tapas – a selection
of appetizers offered to guests with drinks before a meal, or just for snacking
on informally at any time of day.

MOZZARELLA, TOMATO, & BASIL SALAD

SERVES 8

4 slicing or beefsteak tomatoes

250 g (8 oz) mozzarella cheese

4 tbsp shredded fresh basil

4 tbsp olive oil

1 tbsp balsamic vinegar or wine vinegar

salt and black pepper

basil sprig to garnish

1 Peel the tomatoes: cut out the cores and score an "x" on the base of each one, then immerse in boiling water until the skins start to split. Transfer at once to cold water; when cool, peel off the skin. Thinly slice the tomatoes.

2 Slice the mozzarella and arrange with the tomato slices alternately on a plate, overlapping one another.

3 Just before serving, sprinkle with the basil, olive oil and vinegar, and salt and pepper to taste. Garnish with a basil sprig.

Cook's know-how

As well as the salad and crostini, make up a platter of sliced Parma ham, mortadella, bresaola, and salami. Another good choice for antipasti is a seafood salad of prawns, mussels, and squid, which you can buy at supermarkets and delicatessens.

SUN-DRIED TOMATO CROSTINI

SERVES 8

1 baguette

2 garlic cloves, crushed

about 3 tbsp olive oil

4 sun-dried tomatoes in oil

30 g (1 oz) butter

salt and black pepper

12 pitted black olives, chopped

¼ tsp dried rosemary

1 Cut the baguette into 24 thin slices and arrange them on 2 baking trays. Add the garlic to the olive oil, then brush about half of the mixture on to the slices of bread. Bake in a preheated oven at 180°C (350°F, Gas 4) for 10 minutes.

2 Remove the baking trays from the oven, turn the slices of bread over, brush with a little more garlic oil, and bake for a further 10 minutes or until crisp and golden. Leave to cool.

3 Dry the sun-dried tomatoes with a paper towel and cut them into pieces. Put the tomato and butter in the small bowl of a food processor and work until finely chopped (or pound them with a mortar and pestle). Season with salt and pepper to taste.

4 Spread the sun-dried tomato purée over the crostini, arrange the chopped olives on top, and sprinkle with rosemary.

CAPONATA

SERVES 4–6

| about 4 tbsp olive oil |
| 1 large aubergine, cut into 1 cm (¹/₂ in) chunks |
| ¹/₂ head celery, diced |
| 2 onions, thinly sliced |
| 125 g (4 oz) tomato purée |
| 60 g (2 oz) sugar |
| 125–175 ml (4–6 fl oz) red wine vinegar |
| 125 g (4 oz) pitted green olives |
| 30 g (1 oz) capers (optional) |
| 1–2 garlic cloves, crushed |
| 30 g (1 oz) parsley, chopped |
| salt and black pepper |

1 Heat 3 tbsp of the oil in a large saucepan, add the aubergine, and cook gently, stirring, for 8 minutes or until tender. Remove the aubergine from the pan with a slotted spoon.

2 Heat the remaining oil in the pan, add the celery, and cook gently, stirring occasionally, for 7 minutes or until browned.

3 Return the aubergine to the pan with the onions, tomato purée, sugar, and vinegar. Cook over a medium heat for 10 minutes to reduce the harshness of the vinegar. Add a little water if the mixture becomes too thick and starts sticking to the pan.

4 Remove from the heat, and add the green olives, capers, if using, garlic, and half of the parsley. Add salt and pepper to taste. Cover and leave to cool. To serve, transfer to serving plates and sprinkle with the remaining parsley.

WARM SALAD WITH PEARS & STILTON

SERVES 4

| 8 thin slices of white bread (crusts removed), cut into small rounds |
| 2 garlic cloves, halved |
| 250 g (8 oz) blue Stilton cheese, sliced |
| 2 bunches of watercress, trimmed and chopped |
| 2 pears, peeled and cut into thin wedges |
| 4 tbsp sunflower oil |
| 1 small red onion, finely chopped |
| 2 tbsp balsamic vinegar |

1 Toast the bread shapes on both sides under a hot grill. Rub both sides of the bread with the garlic cloves and arrange the slices of Stilton cheese on top of each piece.

2 Arrange the chopped watercress and pear wedges on 4 individual serving plates, then set aside.

3 Heat the sunflower oil in a frying pan, add the onion, and cook gently for 5 minutes or until soft but not coloured.

4 Meanwhile, put the Stilton-topped toasts under the hot grill, close to the heat, for 1–2 minutes until the cheese is melted and warmed through. Cut the toasts in half.

5 Add the vinegar to the onion in the frying pan, and let it heat through, stirring occasionally. Pour the onion mixture over the watercress and pears. Arrange the toasts on the plates and serve at once.

WARM SALAD WITH PEARS & BRIE

For a milder flavour, substitute 250 g (8 oz) French Brie or Italian Dolcelatte for the Stilton. As they are softer in texture, slice them thickly.

3

EGGS & CHEESE

UNDER 30 MINUTES

SPINACH & MUSHROOM FRITTATA
Firm and chunky Italian omelette enclosing bacon, mushrooms, and spinach, sprinkled with Parmesan, and browned under the grill.

SERVES 2–3 673–449 calories per serving
Takes 25 minutes   Page 100

SPANISH OMELETTE
Traditional Spanish dish: diced potatoes, onions, and eggs cooked slowly make a nourishing and simple meal.

SERVES 4 389 calories per serving
Takes 25 minutes   Page 101

RACLETTE
Boiled new potatoes topped with Swiss raclette cheese, and heated in the oven until sizzling. Served with gherkins and onions.

SERVES 4 446 calories per serving
Takes 25 minutes   Page 111

OEUFS EN COCOTTE
Warm creamy snack: whole eggs in ramekins, topped with double cream and parsley, and steamed or baked.

SERVES 4 176 calories per serving
Takes 25 minutes   Page 114

PICNIC FARE

COURGETTE & PARMA HAM FRITTATA
Light and easy to make: thinly sliced courgettes and diced Parma ham cooked with beaten eggs make a

SERVES 4 270 calories per serving
Takes 25 minutes   Page 101

colourful Italian omelette. Browned under the grill, cut into wedges, and garnished with shredded fresh basil. Served hot or cold.

MEXICAN CLASSIC

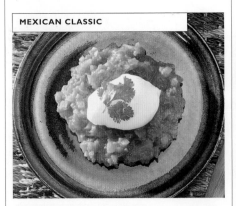

HUEVOS RANCHEROS
Classic Mexican dish of tomatoes simmered with onion, garlic, green pepper, fresh chilli, and cumin. Topped with a poached egg.

SERVES 4 196 calories per serving
Takes 25 minutes   Page 114

MUSHROOM OMELETTE WITH CIABATTA
Italian ciabatta bread, filled with an omelette brimming with sliced shiitake mushrooms.

SERVES 2 673 calories per serving
Takes 25 minutes   Page 100

TRADITIONAL

EGGS BENEDICT
Hearty snack: poached eggs and bacon rashers on toasted muffins, topped with lemon-flavoured hollandaise sauce.

SERVES 4 602 calories per serving
Takes 25 minutes   Page 113

30–60 MINUTES

SWISS CLASSIC

CHEESE FONDUE
Gruyère and Emmental cheeses melted in a fondue pot with wine, garlic, and kirsch. Served with bread and apple for dipping.

SERVES 6 813 calories per serving

Takes 30 minutes   Page 111

SAVOURY SOUFFLE OMELETTE
Light and summery: courgette, red pepper, and tomatoes combined with soufflé mixture. Flavoured with garlic, onion, and thyme.

MAKES 2 479 calories per serving

Takes 35 minutes   Page 99

HIGH PROTEIN

MEDITERRANEAN COURGETTE PIE
Wholesome and rich: courgettes mixed with Parmesan and mozzarella cheeses, eggs, pesto, garlic, and mint. Topped with puff pastry.

SERVES 4 545 calories per serving

Takes 50 minutes   Page 104

CROQUE SENOR
Sandwich of Cheddar cheese and ham given a Mexican flavour with salsa of tomatoes, chilli, and red pepper. Cooked until golden.

SERVES 4 413 calories per serving

Takes 30 minutes   Page 112

VEGETARIAN

MEXICAN OMELETTE
Classic omelette with a substantial filling of onion and garlic cooked with green pepper, tomatoes, mushrooms, and Tabasco.

MAKES 2 547 calories per serving

Takes 50 minutes   Page 99

BROCCOLI SOUFFLES
Broccoli, shallots, and blue cheese combined with soufflé mixture and flavoured with nutmeg and cayenne pepper.

SERVES 4 499 calories per serving

Takes 45 minutes   Page 110

EGGS FLORENTINE
Nutritious and creamy: spinach mixed with spring onions and double cream, topped with a poached egg and Parmesan cheese sauce.

SERVES 4 475 calories per serving

Takes 30 minutes   Page 113

PREPARE AHEAD

PIZZA TARTLETS
Rich and tangy: tomatoes, black olives, and Fontina or mozzarella cheese, complemented by the robust Mediterranean flavours of garlic and oregano, set in shortcrust pastry tartlet shells spread with pesto. Sprinkled with Parmesan cheese to give a tasty, crispy finish.

MAKES 12 198 calories each

Takes 55 minutes   Page 105

30–60 MINUTES

VEGETARIAN

SWISS CHEESE TOMATO RAREBIT

Variation of Welsh rarebit: tomatoes and wine cooked with Gruyère cheese and mushrooms. Served on buttered toast.

SERVES 4 640 calories per serving

Takes 30 minutes   Page 112

FAMILY CHOICE

STRATA WITH CHEESE & PESTO

Savoury custard of eggs, crème fraîche, and milk, poured over slices of bread and pesto. Sprinkled with Italian cheeses.

SERVES 4 600 calories per serving

Takes 50 minutes   Page 106

DINNER PARTY

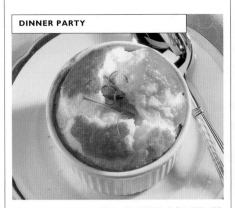

GARLIC & GOAT'S CHEESE SOUFFLES

Tangy soufflés combining garlic-flavoured milk with butter, flour, goat's cheese, egg yolks, and whisked egg whites.

SERVES 6 267 calories per serving

Takes 55 minutes   Page 110

OVER 60 MINUTES

SOUFFLE PANCAKES WITH BROCCOLI & CHEESE

Pancakes with a soufflé filling combining tiny broccoli florets, Cheddar cheese, and mustard.

MAKES 8 300 calories per serving

Takes 45 minutes, plus standing   Page 108

BROCCOLI & RICOTTA GRATIN

Ricotta, Cheddar, and Parmesan cheeses mixed with broccoli, eggs, garlic, and thyme, baked in a buttered breadcrumb crust.

SERVES 4–6 689–460 calories per serving

Takes 1 hour 5 minutes   Page 106

FRENCH CLASSIC

QUICHE LORRAINE

Classic savoury tart: shortcrust pastry shell spread with lightly cooked onion and crispy pieces of streaky bacon. Sprinkled with grated Gruyère cheese, then filled with an egg and cream mixture, and baked until golden brown. Served warm or cold.

SERVES 4–6 756–504 calories per serving.

Takes 60 minutes, plus chilling   Page 102

DINNER PARTY

CREAMY SEAFOOD CREPES

Pieces of cod fillet cooked with onion, garlic, tomatoes, fresh dill, cream, and prawns, and flavoured with fresh basil. The creamy filling is spread over pancakes, which are then folded into triangles, and garnished with prawns, sprigs of basil, and lemon coronets.

SERVES 6 308 calories per serving
Takes 50 minutes, plus standing   Page 107

FAMILY CHOICE

CHICKEN PANCAKES FLORENTINE

Pancakes filled with chicken, mushrooms, and thyme, served on a bed of spinach. Sprinkled with Gruyère cheese and baked.

SERVES 4 721 calories per serving
Takes 50 minutes, plus standing   Page 108

SPINACH, LEEK, & GRUYERE TART

Nourishing and creamy: leek and spinach in a shortcrust pastry shell with a mixture of eggs, milk, cream, and Gruyère cheese.

SERVES 4–6 721–480 calories per serving
Takes 60 minutes, plus chilling   Page 104

SMOKED SALMON & ASPARAGUS QUICHE

Salmon and asparagus set in a shortcrust pastry shell with a savoury custard of Greek yogurt, eggs, and dill.

SERVES 6–8 321–241 calories per serving
Takes 1¼ hours, plus chilling   Page 103

TRADITIONAL

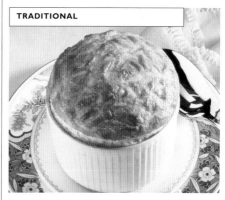

CLASSIC CHEESE SOUFFLE

Delicate and light: milk flavoured with bay leaf, parsley, and onion, combined with butter, flour, eggs, and Cheddar cheese.

SERVES 4 363 calories per serving
Takes 1¼ hours   Page 109

VEGETARIAN

SWISS DOUBLE CHEESE SOUFFLES

Rich and very creamy: individual soufflés flavoured with Gruyère cheese and chives. Baked until golden and firm, then unmoulded and topped with double cream and Parmesan cheese. Baked again until golden, and garnished with snipped fresh chives.

SERVES 6 465 calories per serving
Takes 1 hour 5 minutes   Page 110

ROQUEFORT QUICHE

Roquefort and low-fat soft cheese combined with eggs, crème fraîche, and chives, set in a shortcrust pastry shell, and baked.

SERVES 4–6 504–336 calories per serving
Takes 1 hour 5 minutes   Page 103

EGGS & CHEESE KNOW-HOW

EGGS ARE ONE of the most useful foods in a cook's repertoire. They can be cooked in many delicious ways, from simple boiling, poaching, and scrambling to omelettes and soufflés that require a little more skill. Eggs are also used to enrich pastries and doughs, give volume and moistness to cakes and many puddings, thicken sauces and custards, bind mixtures ranging from burgers to pâtés, and provide a coating for foods to be fried.

Cheese has countless culinary uses. Apart from its everyday use as a sandwich filling, it is found in sauces, fondues, and pizza toppings; it flavours savoury pastries, doughs, and quiche fillings; it is essential in many pasta dishes; and it is popular in puddings such as cheesecake and tiramisu.

BUYING & STORING

Most of the eggs we eat are hen's eggs, although there are also tiny quail's eggs, large duck eggs, and even larger goose eggs. Hen's eggs are usually described according to the farming method used – for example, "free-range", "barn", "from caged hens" (ie the battery system), and "organic" – and these descriptions guarantee that the eggs have been produced according to certain rules. Labels such as "farm fresh" and "country" are meaningless. Whichever you buy, choose the ones with the longest "use-by" date, and check that none is damaged or cracked. Store eggs in their box in the refrigerator (away from strong foods so that they do not absorb flavours and odours through their shells). If you place them pointed end down, the yolk will remain centred in the white. Always use them by their use-by date.

Cheese deteriorates once cut, so do not buy it in a large piece unless you know it will be used up quickly. Keep all cheeses well wrapped in the refrigerator or in a cool larder (soft cheeses must be stored in the refrigerator and used within a few days).

SEPARATING EGGS

For best results, take eggs straight from the fridge so they are well chilled.

1 Holding an egg over a bowl, break open the shell. Carefully transfer the yolk from one half shell to the other, letting the egg white run into the bowl. Repeat several times.

2 Put the yolk in another bowl. Remove any yolk from the white with the tip of a spoon (the white will not whisk if there is any trace of yolk).

COOKING WITH CHEESE

Cheese needs to be cooked with care as heat can spoil its texture, making it rubbery or stringy. Hard and firm cheeses can withstand heat best, melting and blending smoothly. When adding cheese to a sauce, do this at the end of cooking and melt gently; do not boil. If grilling a cheese topping, cook as briefly as possible.

MICROWAVING

Never microwave an egg that is still in its shell as it will burst. Even out of its shell, a whole egg may burst, so always pierce the membrane on the yolk with a toothpick before cooking. The yolk cooks more quickly than the white, so standing time should be allowed to let the white continue cooking. Where yolks and whites are combined, as for scrambled eggs, the mixture will appear undercooked but will firm up during standing time.

Cheeses melt quickly in the microwave, so take care not to overcook or burn them. Hard or firm mature cheeses and processed cheeses are the best. Frozen soft ripened cheeses can be softened and brought to room temperature in the microwave before serving.

FREEZING

Shelled raw eggs freeze very successfully, and can be stored for up to 6 months. If whole, whisk gently to mix the yolk and white; add a little salt to whole eggs and egg yolks for use in savoury foods or sugar for use in sweet dishes (nothing needs to be added to whites). Thaw at room temperature. Egg-based dishes such as quiches, custards, and mousses can also be frozen.

Hard and firm cheeses freeze well, as do soft ripened cheeses such as Brie. Store them for up to 1 month. Thaw in the refrigerator before use. Note that the texture of hard cheeses may change after freezing, becoming more crumbly, making the cheeses suitable only for cooking. Soft fresh cheeses and soft blue-veined cheeses do not freeze well.

COOKING EGGS

Eggs are one of the cheapest sources of protein and could not be easier to cook. Once you have mastered the basic techniques you will be able to produce a wide range of nutritious meals in minutes.

BOILING

Use eggs at room temperature (the shells are less likely to crack). Put the eggs into a pan of simmering water. Bring back to a boil, then simmer gently. Cooking times are calculated from the time the water comes back to a boil, and can vary according to individual taste and on the size and freshness of the eggs. For soft-boiled eggs, simmer gently for 4–5 minutes; for hard-boiled eggs, allow 8–10 minutes. After cooking hard-boiled eggs, lift them out of the water and crack the shell to allow steam to escape, then plunge the eggs into iced water. Peel when cool enough to handle. (An unsightly black line may form round the yolk if you cook them too long, or keep them in the shell.) Use straight away or keep in a bowl of cold water in the refrigerator for up to 24 hours.

ALL ABOUT EGGS

Hen's eggs are graded by weight. Those weighing 73 g and over are classified as "very large"; eggs weighing 63–73 g are "large"; eggs weighing 53–63 g are "medium"; and eggs below 53 g are "small". The shell – usually brown or white, but now also blue, green, pink, or speckled – is a result of the breed of hen. The colour of the yolk depends on the hen's diet and added natural or artificial colourants.

SCRAMBLING

Scrambled eggs can be served plain, or flavoured with herbs, cheese, ham, or smoked salmon. Allow 2 eggs per person.

1 Lightly beat the eggs with salt and pepper to taste and a little milk, if you like. Melt a knob of butter in a pan. Add the eggs.

2 Cook over a medium heat, stirring constantly with a wooden spatula or spoon, until almost set – they will continue to cook after they have been removed from the heat. Serve at once.

FRYING

Fresh eggs are essential for successful frying because they keep their shape during cooking. Fry the eggs in your favourite oil, adding a knob of butter for extra flavour if you like.

1 Heat a thin layer of oil in a non-stick frying pan. When the oil is very hot and starting to sizzle, slip in an egg and cook over a medium heat.

2 Spoon the oil over once or twice to give a white top. Remove and serve, or turn over and cook for a few seconds, to set the yolk a little more.

POACHING

The classic method for poaching eggs is in a pan of simmering water. Use the freshest eggs possible, as they will keep a neat shape.

1 Bring a wide pan of water to the boil. Lower the heat so that the water is simmering, and slide in an egg. Swirl the water round the egg to give it a neat shape. Simmer for 3–4 minutes until the egg is cooked to your taste.

2 Lift out the egg with a slotted spoon and drain briefly on paper towels. To keep them warm, or to reheat them if they have been prepared ahead, immerse them in a bowl of hot water (they will take 1 minute to reheat).

MAKING AN OMELETTE

Omelettes are best made in a special pan kept solely for the purpose, then they are less likely to stick. If you do not have one, use a small frying pan, no more than 20 cm (8 in) in diameter.

1 Beat 2–3 eggs with salt and pepper, plus chopped fresh herbs if you like. Heat the pan, then add a knob of butter. When the butter is foaming, tilt the pan to coat the bottom. Pour in the eggs.

2 Cook over a medium heat. As the eggs begin to set, lift and pull back the edge of the omelette towards the middle, and tilt the pan so the liquid egg runs underneath.

3 Continue cooking until the omelette is just set and the underside is golden. Tilt the pan, loosen the edge of the omelette and flip over in half, to fold it. Slide on to a plate to serve.

Omelette know-how

Gently stir to combine the yolks with the whites: vigorous beating will make the omelette rubbery.

Make sure the pan is hot and the butter foaming when you add the eggs.

The omelette will continue to cook after you remove it from the heat, so the middle should still be a little moist.

MAKING PANCAKES

The quantities given here will make enough batter for about 12 thin pancakes (the kind that the French call crêpes), using an 18–20 cm (7–8 in) pan. Do not worry if the first pancake or two is a failure: it acts as a test for the consistency of the batter and the heat of the pan, and if you are new to pancake making you may prefer to make them slightly thicker, to be on the safe side, in which case you may only make 8 pancakes. Any uneaten pancakes will keep in a stack for 24 hours, or they can be frozen.

1 Sift 125 g (4 oz) plain flour into a bowl and make a well in the middle. Whisk together 1 egg, 1 egg yolk, and a little milk taken from 300 ml (½ pint), then pour into the well. Whisk with a little of the flour.

2 Gradually whisk in half of the remaining milk, drawing in the rest of the flour a little at a time, to make a smooth batter. Stir in the remaining milk. Cover and leave to stand for about 30 minutes.

3 Heat the frying pan and brush with a little oil. Ladle 2–3 tbsp batter into the pan and tilt the pan so that the batter spreads out evenly over the bottom.

4 Cook the pancake over a medium-high heat for 45–60 seconds until small holes appear on the surface, the underside is lightly browned, and the edge has started to curl. Loosen the pancake and turn it over by tossing or flipping it with a palette knife. Cook the other side for about 30 seconds until golden.

5 Slide the pancake out of the pan. Heat and lightly grease the pan again before making the next pancake. Serve the pancakes as they are made, or stack them on a plate and reheat before serving. (If the pancakes are hot when you stack them they will not stick together; there is no need to interleave them with greaseproof paper.)

MEXICAN OMELETTE

An omelette is one of the most useful of all egg dishes, quick and easy to make, and nutritious either plain or with a filling. This recipe combines a classic French omelette with a piquant filling, but you can add whatever filling you like.

MAKES 2

6 eggs

30 g (1 oz) butter

chopped parsley to garnish

FILLING

2 tbsp olive oil

1 onion, finely chopped

1 garlic clove, crushed

1 green pepper, halved, seeded, and finely chopped

2 ripe tomatoes, finely chopped

125 g (4 oz) button mushrooms, thinly sliced

1/4 tsp Worcestershire sauce

a few drops of Tabasco sauce

salt and black pepper

1 Make the filling: heat the oil in a frying pan, add the onion and garlic, and cook for 5 minutes or until softened. Add the pepper, and cook, stirring, for 5 minutes.

2 Add the tomatoes and mushrooms, and cook, stirring, for 10 minutes. Add the Worcestershire and Tabasco sauces, season with salt and pepper, and simmer for about 5 minutes. Keep warm.

3 Beat 3 of the eggs in a bowl with salt and pepper. Heat an omelette pan or small frying pan and add half of the butter.

4 When the butter is foaming, add the eggs, and cook over a medium heat, pulling back the edge as the eggs set, and tilting the pan so the liquid egg runs underneath. Continue until lightly set and golden.

5 Spoon half of the filling on to the half of the omelette farthest from the pan handle. With a palette knife, lift the uncovered half of the omelette and flip it over the filling.

6 Slide the omelette on to a warmed plate, and garnish with chopped parsley. Make the second omelette in the same way, reheating the pan before adding the butter.

MUSHROOM OMELETTE

Substitute 175 g (6 oz) sliced button mushrooms for the filling. Cook in a little melted butter, and season with salt and pepper.

SMOKED CHICKEN OMELETTE

Substitute 125 g (4 oz) diced smoked chicken and 1 tbsp snipped fresh chives for the filling.

TOMATO OMELETTE

Substitute 5 finely chopped ripe tomatoes for the filling. Cook the tomatoes in a little butter for 2–3 minutes. Season well, and stir in a few snipped fresh chives.

SAVOURY SOUFFLE OMELETTE

MAKES 2

4 eggs, separated

30 g (1 oz) butter

FILLING

2 tbsp olive oil

1/2 onion, thinly sliced

1 garlic clove, crushed

1 courgette, sliced

1 red pepper, halved, seeded, and sliced

1 x 200 g (7 oz) can chopped tomatoes

1 tbsp chopped fresh thyme leaves

salt and black pepper

1 Make the filling: heat the oil in a frying pan, add the onion and garlic, and cook gently for 5 minutes or until softened. Add the courgette and red pepper, and cook for about 2 minutes. Add the tomatoes and thyme, season with salt and pepper, and simmer for about 20 minutes.

2 Whisk together the egg yolks and salt and pepper. Whisk the egg whites until stiff, then fold into the yolks.

3 Melt half of the butter in an omelette pan. When it foams, add half of the egg mixture, and cook over a gentle heat for 3 minutes. Add half of the filling, fold the omelette in half, and serve. Repeat with the remaining eggs and filling.

MUSHROOM OMELETTE WITH CIABATTA

SERVES 2

4 eggs

salt and black pepper

30 g (1 oz) butter

60 g (2 oz) shiitake mushrooms, sliced

1 tbsp snipped fresh chives

1 loaf of ciabatta bread, warmed and split lengthwise

1 Break the eggs into a small bowl, season with salt and black pepper, and beat with a fork.

2 Melt half of the butter in a small frying pan, add the mushrooms, and cook over a high heat for 3–5 minutes until all the liquid has evaporated. Remove from the heat, stir in the chives, season with salt and pepper, and keep hot.

3 Heat an omelette pan or small frying pan until very hot. Add the remaining butter and swirl the pan to evenly coat the base and sides. When the butter is foaming, pour in the seasoned egg mixture.

4 Cook the omelette over a medium heat, pulling back the edge as the eggs set, and tilting the pan to allow the uncooked egg to run to the side of the pan. Continue until the omelette is lightly set and the underside is golden brown. Remove from the heat.

5 Scatter the mushrooms over half of the omelette, then flip the uncovered half over them. Fill the warmed split ciabatta with the omelette, cut the ciabatta in half crosswise, and serve at once.

SPINACH & MUSHROOM FRITTATA

SERVES 2–3

3 tbsp olive oil

60 g (2 oz) thick-cut smoked bacon rashers, rinds removed, diced

250 g (8 oz) chestnut mushrooms, quartered

125 g (4 oz) spinach leaves, coarsely chopped

6 eggs

salt and black pepper

2 tbsp grated Parmesan cheese

1 Heat the oil in a large frying pan. Add the bacon and mushrooms and cook over a high heat, stirring, for about 7 minutes or until the bacon is crisp. Add the spinach and turn it in the oil for 1–2 minutes. Do not allow the spinach to wilt. Lower the heat.

2 Break the eggs into a bowl, season with salt and pepper, and beat with a fork.

3 Pour the eggs over the mushrooms and spinach and cook over a medium heat for 10 minutes. As the eggs set, lift the frittata with a spatula and tilt the pan so the uncooked egg runs underneath.

4 When the eggs are set, sprinkle with grated Parmesan, and place the pan under a hot grill, 10 cm (4 in) from the heat, for 1–2 minutes or until the top is golden brown and firm when pressed. Serve at once, cut in half.

Healthy option

You can omit the bacon to lower the fat content of this frittata (and make it vegetarian too). To compensate for the lack of flavour, add a splash of soy sauce in step 2. Always add soy sauce sparingly, because it has a high salt content.

SPANISH OMELETTE

SERVES 4

3 tbsp olive oil

2 large potatoes, diced

2 large onions, chopped

6 eggs

salt and black pepper

1 tbsp chopped parsley

1 Heat the oil in a frying pan, add the potatoes and onions, and stir until coated with the oil. Cook gently for about 10 minutes until golden brown. Pour the excess oil from the pan.

2 Break the eggs into a bowl, season with salt and pepper, and beat with a fork.

3 Pour the eggs into the pan, and mix with the vegetables. Cook for about 10 minutes until the eggs are almost set, then brown the top of the omelette under a hot grill for 1–2 minutes.

4 Slide the omelette on to a warmed plate, and cut into quarters. Sprinkle with chopped parsley and serve warm or cold.

MIXED BEAN OMELETTE

Lightly cook 60 g (2 oz) French beans and 125 g (4 oz) shelled broad beans. Add to the pan in step 3, when mixing the potatoes and onions with the eggs.

COURGETTE & PARMA HAM FRITTATA

SERVES 4

2 tbsp olive oil

625 g (1 1/4 lb) small courgettes, thinly sliced on the diagonal

6 eggs

salt and black pepper

60 g (2 oz) Parma ham, diced

shredded fresh basil or chopped flat-leaf parsley to garnish

1 Heat the olive oil in a large frying pan. Add the courgettes and cook gently for 5 minutes or until just tender.

2 Break the eggs into a bowl, season with salt and pepper, and beat with a fork.

3 Add the ham to the courgettes in the frying pan, then pour in the eggs.

4 Cook over a medium heat for about 10 minutes. As the eggs set, lift the frittata with a spatula and tilt the pan to allow the uncooked egg to run underneath. Continue until almost set and the underside is golden brown.

5 Place the frying pan under a hot grill, 10 cm (4 in) from the heat, for 1–2 minutes until the top is a light golden brown colour and the egg is cooked through and quite firm when pressed.

6 Cut the frittata into wedges, and lightly garnish with shredded fresh basil or parsley. Serve hot or cold.

Cook's know-how

Genuine Parma ham (prosciutto di Parma) comes from a very small area in and around the town of Parma in northern Italy. It is perfect in this frittata, but you could use a honey roast ham if you prefer.

QUICHE LORRAINE

This most famous of all quiches is named after the area it comes from – Alsace Lorraine in north-eastern France – where it was traditionally served on May Day, following a dish of roast suckling pig.

SERVES 4–6

30 g (1 oz) butter
1 onion, chopped
175 g (6 oz) unsmoked streaky bacon rashers, rinds removed, diced
125 g (4 oz) Gruyère cheese, grated
250 ml (8 fl oz) single cream or milk
2 eggs, beaten
salt and black pepper

SHORTCRUST PASTRY

125 g (4 oz) plain flour
60 g (2 oz) butter
about 1 tbsp cold water
20 CM (8 IN) FLAN DISH OR TIN
BAKING BEANS

1 Make the pastry with the flour, butter, and water (see box, right). Wrap in cling film and chill for 30 minutes.

2 Roll out the pastry on a lightly floured work surface, and use to line the flan dish or tin. Prick the bottom of the pastry shell with a fork.

3 Line the pastry shell with a sheet of foil or greaseproof paper, and fill with baking beans (or rice or pasta if you have no beans). Place the flan dish on a heated baking tray and bake the shell in a preheated oven at 220°C (425°F, Gas 7) for 15–20 minutes, removing the foil and beans for the final 10 minutes.

4 Meanwhile, make the filling: melt the butter in a frying pan, add the onion and bacon, and cook gently, stirring occasionally, for 10 minutes or until the onion is golden brown and the bacon is crisp.

5 Spoon the onion and bacon into the pastry shell, and sprinkle the cheese on top. Mix the cream and eggs in a jug, season with salt and pepper, and pour into the pastry shell.

6 Reduce the oven temperature to 180°C (350°F, Gas 4), and bake the quiche for 25–30 minutes until the filling is golden and set. Serve warm or cold.

Making shortcrust pastry

Tip the flour into a bowl and rub in the butter lightly with your fingertips until the mixture looks like fine breadcrumbs. **Add** the water and mix with a round-bladed knife to form a soft but not sticky dough.

SMOKED SALMON & ASPARAGUS QUICHE

SERVES 6–8

125 g (4 oz) fine asparagus, cooked, drained, and cut into 3.5 cm (1½ in) lengths

90 g (3 oz) smoked salmon, cut into strips

300 g (10 oz) Greek yogurt or low-fat crème fraîche

2 eggs

1 tbsp chopped fresh dill

black pepper

SHORTCRUST PASTRY

175 g (6 oz) plain flour

90 g (3 oz) butter

about 2 tbsp cold water

23 CM (9 IN) FLAN DISH OR TIN

BAKING BEANS

1 Make the pastry: tip the flour into a bowl, rub in the butter with your fingertips, then add enough water to bind to a soft dough. Wrap in cling film and chill for 30 minutes.

2 Roll out the pastry, and use to line the dish or tin. Prick the pastry with a fork.

3 Line the pastry shell with foil or greaseproof paper, and fill with baking beans (or rice or pasta if you have no beans). Place the dish or tin on a heated baking tray and bake in a preheated oven at 220°C (425°F, Gas 7) for 15–20 minutes, removing the foil and beans for the final 10 minutes.

4 Arrange the asparagus and half of the salmon in the pastry shell. Mix the yogurt or crème fraîche, eggs, dill, and plenty of pepper, and pour into the shell. Arrange the remaining salmon on top.

5 Reduce the oven temperature to 180°C (350°F, Gas 4), and bake for 35 minutes or until golden and set. Serve warm or cold.

ROQUEFORT QUICHE

SERVES 4–6

90 g (3 oz) Roquefort or other blue cheese, crumbled

175 g (6 oz) low-fat soft cheese

2 eggs, beaten

150 ml (¼ pint) crème fraîche

1 tbsp snipped fresh chives

salt and black pepper

SHORTCRUST PASTRY

125 g (4 oz) plain flour

60 g (2 oz) butter

about 1 tbsp cold water

20 CM (8 IN) FLAN DISH OR TIN

BAKING BEANS

1 Make the pastry: tip the flour into a bowl and rub in the butter with your fingertips. Add enough water to bind to a soft dough. Wrap in cling film and chill for 30 minutes.

2 Roll out the shortcrust pastry, and use to line the flan dish or tin. Prick the bottom of the pastry shell with a fork.

3 Line the pastry shell with foil or greaseproof paper, and fill with baking beans (or rice or pasta if you have no beans). Place the dish or tin on a heated baking tray, and bake in a preheated oven at 220°C (425°F, Gas 7) for 15–20 minutes, removing the foil and beans for the final 10 minutes.

4 Meanwhile, make the filling: mix the Roquefort and low-fat cheese in a bowl, then beat in the eggs, crème fraîche, and chives, and season with salt and pepper. Take care not to add too much salt as blue cheese is quite salty.

5 Pour the mixture into the pastry shell, reduce the oven temperature to 180°C (350°F, Gas 4), and bake the quiche for about 30 minutes until golden and set. Serve warm or cold.

SPINACH, LEEK, & GRUYERE TART

SERVES 4–6

30 g (1 oz) butter

175 g (6 oz) leeks, trimmed and finely sliced

250 g (8 oz) young spinach leaves, coarsely chopped

2 eggs, beaten

150 ml (¼ pint) each double cream and milk, or 300 ml (½ pint) milk

90 g (3 oz) Gruyère cheese, grated

salt and black pepper

SHORTCRUST PASTRY

175 g (6 oz) plain flour

90 g (3 oz) butter

about 2 tbsp cold water

23 CM (9 IN) FLAN DISH OR TIN

BAKING BEANS

1 Make the pastry: tip the flour into a bowl and rub in the butter with your fingertips. Add enough water to bind to a soft dough. Wrap in cling film and chill for 30 minutes.

2 Roll out the pastry on a lightly floured work surface, and use to line the flan dish or tin. Prick the bottom of the pastry shell with a fork.

3 Line the pastry shell with foil or greaseproof paper, and fill with baking beans (or rice or pasta if you have no beans). Put the dish or tin on a heated baking tray, and bake in a preheated oven at 220°C (425°F, Gas 7) for 15–20 minutes, removing the foil and beans for the final 10 minutes.

4 Make the filling: melt the butter in a frying pan, add the leeks, and cook over a high heat for 5 minutes or until just beginning to turn golden brown. Add the spinach and cook for about 2 minutes until it just begins to wilt. Spoon the filling into the pastry shell.

5 Mix together the eggs, milk, cream, and Gruyère cheese in a jug, season with salt and pepper, and pour into the pastry shell.

6 Reduce the oven temperature to 180°C (350°F, Gas 4), and bake for 25 minutes or until the filling is golden and set. Serve warm or cold.

MEDITERRANEAN COURGETTE PIE

SERVES 4

500 g (1 lb) courgettes

90 g (3 oz) Parmesan cheese, grated

90 g (3 oz) mozzarella or Fontina cheese, grated

2 eggs, lightly beaten

2–3 tbsp ready made pesto

2–3 garlic cloves, crushed

1 tsp dried mint

salt and black pepper

250 g (8 oz) puff pastry

beaten egg for glazing

23 CM (9 IN) SQUARE BAKING DISH OR TIN

1 Grate the courgettes into a large bowl, then blot off any excess moisture with paper towels. Add the Parmesan and mozzarella, eggs, pesto, garlic, and mint, and season with salt and pepper. Stir well to mix, then spoon into the dish or tin.

2 Roll out the pastry into a rough square, about 2.5 cm (1 in) larger than the dish or tin and 3–5 mm (⅛–¼ in) thick. Cover the dish or tin with the pastry, trimming the edges. Cut slits in the top with a knife.

3 Cut out shapes from the pastry trimmings, using a shaped pastry cutter if you like. Brush the top of the pie with beaten egg, arrange the pastry shapes on top, and glaze them with the beaten egg.

4 Bake the pie in a preheated oven at 200°C (400°F, Gas 6) for 15–20 minutes until lightly browned on top and puffy. Serve hot.

PIZZA TARTLETS

These tartlets, with their traditional pizza flavours, will serve 4 people as a light lunch or supper dish, accompanied by a crisp, green salad. They also make a tasty appetizer to serve with pre-dinner drinks. They taste just as good cold as hot, so they can be prepared well in advance.

MAKES 12

90 g (3 oz) ready made red or green pesto
250 g (8 oz) ripe tomatoes, finely chopped
9 black olives, pitted and quartered
125 g (4 oz) Fontina or mozzarella cheese, grated
2–3 garlic cloves, crushed
2–3 tbsp grated Parmesan cheese
1 tsp dried oregano

SHORTCRUST PASTRY

175 g (6 oz) plain flour
90 g (3 oz) butter
about 2 tbsp cold water

1 Make the pastry: tip the flour into a bowl and rub in the butter with your fingertips. Add enough water to bind to a soft dough. Wrap in cling film and chill for 30 minutes.

2 Make the tartlet shells (see box, right).

3 Spread the pesto in the tartlet shells, then fill the shells with the tomatoes, garlic, black olives, and Fontina cheese.

4 Sprinkle the grated Parmesan cheese over the tartlets, covering the pastry edges as well as the filling. Sprinkle the dried oregano on top.

5 Bake the tartlets in a preheated oven at 200°C (400°F, Gas 6) for 20–30 minutes until the edges are a golden brown colour and the cheese topping has melted and become crispy.

6 Serve the tartlets warm or cold.

GOAT'S CHEESE TARTLETS

Cut a log of goat's cheese into 12 slices and use instead of the grated Fontina or mozzarella.

Making tartlet shells

Sprinkle the work surface with flour, then roll out the shortcrust pastry until 3–5 mm (1/8–1/4 in) thick

Cut out 12 rounds from the pastry, using a 10 cm (4 in) pastry cutter or the rim of a glass or saucer.

Fold up the edges of the rounds to form rims; put the rounds on a baking tray.

BROCCOLI & RICOTTA GRATIN

SERVES 4–6

250 g (8 oz) broccoli

salt and black pepper

375 g (12 oz) ricotta or cottage cheese, lightly mashed

125 g (4 oz) mature Cheddar cheese, grated

60 g (2 oz) Parmesan cheese, grated

2 eggs, lightly beaten

2–3 garlic cloves, crushed

1 tsp chopped fresh thyme

75 g (2¹/₂ oz) butter

175 g (6 oz) fresh breadcrumbs

23 CM (9 IN) FLAN DISH

1 Trim the broccoli and cut the stalks from the heads. Peel and dice the stalks, and break the heads into small florets. Plunge the florets and stalks into a pan of boiling salted water for 1 minute. Drain, rinse under cold running water, and drain again.

2 Put the ricotta into a large bowl with the Cheddar and Parmesan, the eggs, garlic, and thyme. Season with salt and pepper, mix until smooth, then add the broccoli stalks.

3 Melt the butter in a saucepan, remove it from the heat, and stir in the breadcrumbs.

4 Line the baking dish with about three-quarters of the buttered breadcrumbs, pushing them up the side of the dish to form a loose crust. Spoon in the cheese mixture, and then sprinkle with the remaining breadcrumbs. Arrange the broccoli florets on top.

5 Bake in a preheated oven at 180°C (350°F, Gas 4) for about 40 minutes or until quite firm. Serve warm or cold.

STRATA WITH CHEESE & PESTO

SERVES 4

4–6 thick slices of stale bread

60–90 g (2–3 oz) ready made pesto

4 eggs, lightly beaten

125 ml (4 fl oz) crème fraîche

125 ml (4 fl oz) milk

175 g (6 oz) Fontina or mature Cheddar cheese, grated

60 g (2 oz) mozzarella cheese, grated

30 g (1 oz) Parmesan cheese, grated

1 Cut off and discard the crusts from the bread. Spread the slices with pesto, then arrange them in a single layer in a baking dish.

2 In a bowl, combine the eggs with the crème fraîche and milk, then pour over the bread. Sprinkle with the grated cheeses.

3 Bake the strata in a preheated oven at 200°C (400°F, Gas 6) for 35–40 minutes until golden brown. It will puff up slightly as it bakes but, unlike a soufflé, it can be safely left to stand for about 5 minutes before serving.

Cook's know-how

You need stale bread to make a good, moist strata (a Californian recipe for using up leftover bread). If the bread is fresh, the strata will be soggy.

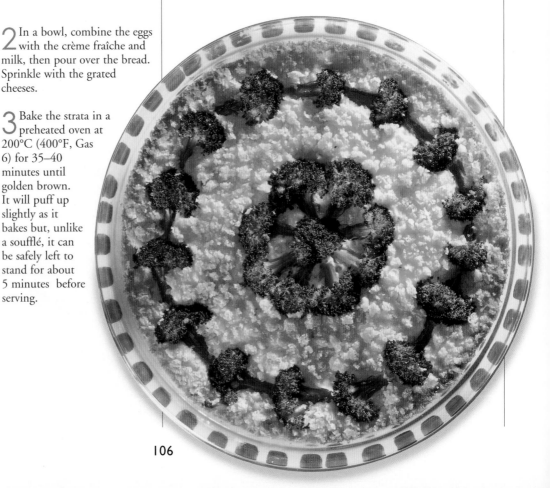

CREAMY SEAFOOD CREPES

The succulent filling of prawns and white fish in a herby cream sauce makes these crêpes really rich and special – ideal for a weekend lunch served with a crisp green salad. You could also serve them as a dinner party first course, allowing just one per person The unfilled crêpes can be made in advance and stored in the freezer for up to 1 month.

SERVES 6

FILLING

250 g (8 oz) cod fillet, skinned
375 g (12 oz) cooked prawns in their shells
2 tbsp olive oil
1 small onion, finely chopped
1 garlic clove, crushed
4 tomatoes, finely chopped
1 tbsp chopped fresh dill
salt and black pepper
3 tbsp single cream
2 tbsp chopped fresh basil
basil and lemon to garnish

PANCAKES

125 g (4 oz) plain flour
1 egg, plus 1 egg yolk
300 ml (1/2 pint) milk
sunflower oil for frying

1 Make the pancake batter: sift the flour into a large bowl, and make a well in the middle. Add the egg, extra egg yolk, and a little of the milk.

2 Gradually blend in the flour, beating until smooth. Add the remaining milk to make a thin, creamy batter. Leave to stand while you make the filling.

3 Cut the cod fillet into 1 cm (1/2 in) pieces. Reserve 12 prawns for the garnish, and peel the remainder.

4 Heat the oil in a medium saucepan, add the onion and garlic, and cook over very gently, stirring occasionally, for about 10 minutes until soft but not coloured.

5 Add the cod, tomatoes, and dill, and season with salt and pepper. Cook over a medium heat, stirring, for 10 minutes or until thick.

6 Stir in the cream and prawns and heat gently. Remove from the heat and stir in the basil. Keep warm.

7 Make the pancakes. Heat a small frying pan, and brush with a little oil. Stir the batter, ladle about 3 tbsp into the pan, and cook for 1 minute until the underside is golden. Turn and cook the second side, then slide out of the pan and keep hot. Repeat to make 12 pancakes.

8 Fill the pancakes with the seafood mixture, and fold (see box, right). Garnish with basil and lemon, and the reserved prawns.

Filling and folding the crêpes

Put a pancake on a serving plate. Put 2–3 spoonfuls of the seafood filling on to one half and spread it to within 5 mm (1/4 in) of the edge.

Fold the unfilled half of the pancake over the seafood filling to enclose it.

Fold the pancake in half again, to form a triangle. Transfer to a serving plate and keep warm. Repeat with the remaining pancakes and filling.

SOUFFLE PANCAKES WITH BROCCOLI & CHEESE

MAKES 8

8 pancakes (page 107)
butter for greasing
2 tbsp grated Parmesan cheese

FILLING

125 g (4 oz) tiny broccoli florets
salt and black pepper
45 g (1 1/2 oz) butter
45 g (1 1/2 oz) plain flour
300 ml (1/2 pint) milk
1/2 tsp Dijon mustard
125 g (4 oz) mature Cheddar cheese, grated
4 eggs, separated

1 Make the filling: blanch the broccoli florets in boiling salted water for 1 minute. Drain, rinse under cold running water, and drain again.

2 Melt the butter in a small saucepan, add the flour, and cook, stirring occasionally, for about 1 minute.

3 Remove the pan from the heat, and gradually blend in the milk. Bring to a boil, stirring until thickened. Remove from the heat, add the mustard and cheese, and season with salt and pepper. Stir, then leave to cool slightly.

4 Beat the egg yolks into the sauce. In a large bowl, whisk the egg whites until soft peaks form, then fold into the cheese sauce with the broccoli.

5 Lay the pancakes on two lightly buttered baking trays. Divide the soufflé mixture among the pancakes, arranging it down the middle of each one. Fold the sides of each pancake loosely over the top of the filling, and sprinkle with grated Parmesan cheese.

6 Bake in a preheated oven at 200°C (400°F, Gas 6) for 15–20 minutes, until the soufflé mixture has risen and the pancakes are crisp.

CHICKEN PANCAKES FLORENTINE

SERVES 4

500 g (1 lb) spinach leaves, coarsely chopped
30 g (1 oz) butter
pinch of grated nutmeg
8 pancakes (page 107)
125 g (4 oz) Gruyère cheese, grated

FILLING

60 g (2 oz) butter
375 g (12 oz) chestnut mushrooms, quartered
45 g (1 1/2 oz) plain flour
300 ml (1/2 pint) chicken stock
375 g (12 oz) boneless and skinless cooked chicken, cut into bite-sized pieces
1 tbsp chopped fresh tarragon
salt and black pepper

1 Make the filling: melt the butter in a heavy pan, add the mushrooms, and cook, stirring often, for 2–3 minutes.

2 Add the flour, and cook, stirring, for 1 minute. Remove the pan from the heat, and gradually blend in the stock. Bring to a boil, stirring, and simmer for 2–3 minutes. Add the chicken and tarragon, and season with salt and pepper.

3 Rinse the spinach and put into a saucepan with only the water that clings to the leaves. Cook for 2 minutes or until tender. Drain well, squeezing to extract any excess water, then stir in the butter and nutmeg. Spoon into a shallow ovenproof dish.

4 Divide the chicken and mushroom mixture between the 8 pancakes. Roll up the pancakes, and place them in a single layer on top of the spinach.

5 Sprinkle with the cheese, and bake in a preheated oven at 190°C (375°F, Gas 5) for about 25 minutes until golden. Serve hot.

Healthy option

There are several ways in which you can cut the amount of fat and calories in this dish. For the filling, halve the butter and cook the mushrooms in a non-stick pan, then halve the amount of chicken and shred it finely. The Gruyère cheese can also be halved, or you could use a reduced-fat Cheddar instead.

CLASSIC CHEESE SOUFFLE

SERVES 4

300 ml (½ pint) milk
1 bay leaf
a few parsley stalks
½ onion, peeled
pinch of cayenne pepper
salt and black pepper
45 g (1½ oz) butter, plus extra for greasing
45 g (1½ oz) plain flour
3 eggs, separated
1 tbsp Dijon mustard
125 g (4 oz) mature Cheddar cheese, grated
1.25 LITRE (2 PINT) SOUFFLE DISH

1 Bring the milk to a boil in a saucepan with the bay leaf, parsley stalks, and onion half. Remove from the heat, cover, and leave to infuse for about 20 minutes. Strain, then add the cayenne and season with salt and pepper.

2 Melt the butter in a large pan, add the flour, and cook, stirring, for 1 minute. Remove from the heat, slowly blend in the milk, then bring to a boil. Simmer for 2–3 minutes, stirring, until thickened, then remove from the heat. Leave to cool for about 10 minutes.

3 Beat the egg yolks in a bowl. Stir them into the cooled white sauce, then stir in the mustard and all but 15 g (½ oz) of the Cheddar.

4 Whisk the egg whites until they form firm but not dry peaks. Fold 1–2 tbsp egg whites into the cheese mixture until evenly combined, then fold in the remaining egg whites.

5 Lightly butter the soufflé dish, pour in the soufflé mixture, and sprinkle with the remaining cheese.

6 Bake on a preheated baking sheet in the top half of a preheated oven at 180°C (350°F, Gas 4) for about 25 minutes, or until just set in the middle. Serve at once.

BROCCOLI SOUFFLES

SERVES 4

45 g (1½ oz) butter, plus extra for greasing
45 g (1½ oz) plain flour
250 ml (8 fl oz) milk
pinch of grated nutmeg
salt and cayenne pepper
375 g (12 oz) broccoli florets
3–4 shallots, finely chopped
2 tbsp grated Parmesan cheese
4 egg yolks
175 g (6 oz) blue cheese, crumbled
6 egg whites
4 × 250 ML (8 FL OZ) SOUFFLE DISHES

1 Melt 30 g (1 oz) butter in a large pan, add the flour, and cook, stirring, for 1 minute. Remove from the heat, gradually blend in the milk, then bring to a boil, stirring, until thickened. Add the nutmeg, season with salt, and stir in a pinch of cayenne pepper. Cool for 10 minutes.

2 Steam the broccoli for 2–3 minutes until just tender. Rinse under cold running water, then chop coarsely.

3 Heat the remaining butter in a pan, add the shallots, and cook gently for 3 minutes or until soft.

4 Prepare the soufflé dishes (see box, below).

5 Beat the egg yolks and add to the cooled sauce with the broccoli, shallots, and blue cheese.

6 Whisk the egg whites until they form firm but not dry peaks. Fold 1–2 tbsp of the egg whites into the broccoli mixture, then fold in the remaining egg whites.

7 Pour the mixture into the soufflé dishes. Bake the soufflés in the top half of a preheated oven at 180°C (350°F, Gas 4) for 30 minutes. Serve at once.

Preparing the soufflé dishes

Butter the bottoms and sides of the soufflé dishes. Sprinkle with a thin layer of grated Parmesan cheese.

SWISS DOUBLE CHEESE SOUFFLES

SERVES 6

45 g (1½ oz) butter, plus extra for greasing

45 g (1½ oz) plain flour

300 ml (½ pint) milk

60 g (2 oz) Gruyère cheese, grated

2 tbsp snipped fresh chives

salt and black pepper

3 eggs, separated

60 g (2 oz) Parmesan cheese, grated

300 ml (½ pint) double cream

snipped fresh chives to garnish

1 Melt the butter in a large saucepan, add the flour, and cook, stirring, for 1 minute. Remove from the heat and gradually blend in the milk. Return to the heat and bring to a boil, stirring until the mixture thickens.

2 Remove the pan from the heat and beat in the Gruyère cheese and chives. Season with salt and pepper, and stir in the egg yolks.

3 Whisk the egg whites until stiff but not dry. Stir 1 tbsp into the mixture, then fold in the rest.

4 Generously butter 6 small ramekins, and divide the mixture equally among them. Place the ramekins in a small roasting tin, and pour boiling water into the tin to come halfway up the sides of the ramekins.

5 Bake the soufflés in a preheated oven at 220°C (425°F, Gas 7) for 15–20 minutes until golden and springy to the touch. Leave the soufflés to stand for 5–10 minutes; they will shrink by about one-third.

6 Butter a large shallow gratin dish. Sprinkle half of the Parmesan cheese over the bottom. Run a palette knife around the edge of each soufflé, unmould carefully, and arrange on top of the Parmesan in the gratin dish.

7 Season the cream with salt and pepper, and pour over the soufflés. Sprinkle the remaining Parmesan over the top, and return to the oven for 15–20 minutes until golden. Garnish with snipped chives.

GARLIC & GOAT'S CHEESE SOUFFLES

SERVES 6

1 head of garlic

250 ml (8 fl oz) milk

125 ml (4 fl oz) water

45 g (1½ oz) butter, plus extra for greasing

45 g (1½ oz) plain flour

150 g (5 oz) goat's cheese, diced

6 eggs, separated

salt and black pepper

fresh chives to garnish

6 × 150 ML (¼ PINT) SOUFFLE DISHES

1 Separate and peel the garlic cloves. Put the milk, measured water, and all but one of the garlic cloves into a saucepan. Bring to a boil, then simmer for 15–20 minutes until the garlic is tender and the liquid has reduced to 250 ml (8 fl oz). Leave to cool. Lightly mash the garlic in the milk.

2 Melt the butter in a saucepan, add the flour, and cook, stirring, for 1 minute. Remove from the heat, and gradually blend in the garlic milk.

3 Return to the heat and bring to a boil, stirring constantly, until the mixture thickens. Simmer for 2–3 minutes. Transfer to a large bowl and leave to cool for about 10 minutes. Chop the remaining garlic clove.

4 Add the chopped garlic, diced goat's cheese, and egg yolks to the cooled sauce. Season with salt and pepper.

5 In a large bowl, whisk the egg whites until stiff but not dry. Stir 1 tbsp of the egg whites into the garlic and cheese mixture, then fold in the remaining egg whites.

6 Lightly butter the soufflé dishes, pour in the soufflé mixture, and bake in a preheated oven at 180°C (350°F, Gas 4) for 15–20 minutes. Serve at once, garnished with chives.

RACLETTE

SERVES 4

1 kg (2 lb) new potatoes, halved

salt

250 g (8 oz) Swiss raclette cheese, cut into 16 thin slices

1 red onion, thinly sliced

12 small gherkins

12 cocktail pickled onions

1 Cook the potatoes in boiling salted water for 12–15 minutes until just tender. Drain, and keep the potatoes warm.

2 Put 4 heavy, ovenproof serving plates into a preheated oven at 240°C (475°F, Gas 9) to warm for 3–5 minutes.

3 Divide the potatoes among the plates, and arrange 4 slices of raclette cheese on top of each serving. Return the plates to the oven for 1–2 minutes until the cheese is melted and sizzling.

4 Divide the red onion slices, gherkins, and pickled onions among the plates, and serve at once.

Cook's know-how

Gruyère or Emmental cheese can be used instead of raclette.

CHEESE FONDUE

SERVES 6

1 large loaf of crusty bread, crusts left on, cut into 2.5 cm (1 in) triangles

250 g (8 oz) Gruyère cheese, coarsely grated

250 g (8 oz) Emmental cheese, coarsely grated

30 g (1 oz) cornflour

500 ml (16 fl oz) dry white wine

1 garlic clove, lightly crushed

2 tbsp kirsch

pinch of grated nutmeg

salt and black pepper

TO SERVE (OPTIONAL)

2 eating apples, quartered and sliced

60 g (2 oz) sesame seeds, toasted

30 g (1 oz) cumin seeds, toasted

1 FONDUE SET

1 Place the pieces of bread on a large baking tray and put into a preheated oven at 160°C (325°F, Gas 3) for 3–5 minutes until dried out slightly.

2 Put the Gruyère and Emmental cheeses into a medium bowl, and toss with the flour.

3 Put the wine and garlic into a fondue pot and boil for 2 minutes, then lower the heat so that the mixture is barely simmering. Add the cheese mixture, a spoonful at a time, stirring constantly with a fork and letting each spoonful melt before adding the next.

4 When the fondue is creamy and smooth, stir in the kirsch, nutmeg, and salt and pepper to taste.

5 Stand the fondue pot over the burner, with the heat low so the mixture barely simmers. Offer the baked bread round for dipping into the fondue, with apple slices, and sesame seeds and cumin seeds if you like.

CROQUE SENOR

SERVES 4

8 slices of white bread

4 slices of mature Cheddar cheese

4 slices of ham

30 g (1 oz) butter, softened

lemon wedges and coriander sprigs
to serve

SPICY TOMATO SALSA

3 ripe but firm tomatoes, finely
chopped

1 red pepper, halved, seeded,
roasted, and peeled (page 388),
finely chopped

1 garlic clove, crushed

2 spring onions, thinly sliced

1 fresh green chilli, halved, seeded,
and chopped

1 tbsp red wine vinegar

salt

1 Make the salsa: combine the
tomatoes, red pepper, garlic,
spring onions, chilli, and
vinegar in a bowl. Season with
salt and set aside.

2 Put 4 slices of bread on to a
board, and arrange the
cheese slices, then the ham
slices, on top. Spoon the salsa
over the ham.

3 Lightly spread the butter
over one side of the
remaining slices of bread and
put them, butter-side up, on
top of the salsa.

4 Heat a heavy frying pan,
and cook each sandwich,
butter-side down, over a
medium-high heat until the
cheese begins to melt and the
bread becomes golden. Lightly
spread the second side of each
sandwich with butter. Turn
over and cook the other side
until golden.

5 Garnish with lemon
wedges, coriander sprigs,
and any remaining spicy
tomato salsa. Serve hot.

SWISS CHEESE & TOMATO RAREBIT

SERVES 4

3 garlic cloves

30 g (1 oz) butter, plus extra for
spreading

30 g (1 oz) plain flour

250 g (8 oz) ripe tomatoes, finely
chopped

125 ml (4 fl oz) dry white wine

375 g (12 oz) Gruyère cheese,
grated

125 g (4 oz) mushrooms, chopped

1 tbsp chopped fresh tarragon

salt and black pepper

4 slices of bread, crusts removed

chopped parsley to garnish

1 Crush 2 of the garlic cloves.
Melt the butter in a
saucepan, add the crushed
garlic, and cook gently, stirring,
for 1–2 minutes. Add the flour,
and cook, stirring, for 1 minute.
Add the chopped tomatoes and
cook for 2 minutes.

2 Pour in the wine, and cook,
stirring, for 5 minutes or
until the mixture thickens. Add
the Gruyère cheese, a little at a
time, and stir until it has
melted. Add the chopped
mushrooms and tarragon,
season with salt and pepper,
and cook for 3 minutes or until
the mushrooms are tender.

3 Cut the remaining garlic
clove in half. Toast the
bread on both sides under a hot
grill. Rub one side of the toast
with the cut sides of the garlic.

4 Spread the garlic side of the
toast with butter, place on
warmed plates, and top with the
cheese mixture. Serve at once,
sprinkled with chopped parsley.

EGGS BENEDICT

SERVES 4

8 lean back bacon rashers, rinds removed

2 muffins, halved

4 eggs

butter for spreading

fresh flat-leaf parsley to garnish

HOLLANDAISE SAUCE

2 tsp lemon juice

2 tsp white wine vinegar

3 egg yolks, at room temperature

125 g (4 oz) unsalted butter, melted

salt and black pepper

1 Cook the bacon under a hot grill, 7 cm (3 in) from the heat, for 5–7 minutes until crisp. Keep the bacon warm.

2 Toast the cut sides of the muffin halves under the grill. Keep warm.

3 Make the hollandaise sauce: put the lemon juice and wine vinegar into a small bowl, add the egg yolks, and whisk with a balloon whisk until light and frothy.

4 Place the bowl over a pan of simmering water and whisk until the mixture thickens. Gradually add the melted butter, whisking constantly until thick. Season. Keep warm.

5 Poach the eggs: bring a large pan of water to the boil. Lower the heat so that the water is simmering, and slide in the eggs. Swirl the water round the eggs to make neat shapes. Simmer for about 4 minutes. Lift out with a slotted spoon.

6 Butter the muffin halves and put on to warmed plates. Put 2 bacon rashers and an egg on each one, and top with the sauce. Serve at once, garnished with parsley.

SPICY LIME HOLLANDAISE

Substitute 2 tsp lime juice for the lemon juice in the hollandaise sauce, and add ½ tsp each of paprika and mild chilli powder.

EGGS FLORENTINE

SERVES 4

250 g (8 oz) spinach leaves

3 spring onions, thinly sliced

2 tbsp double cream

4 eggs

3 tbsp grated Parmesan cheese

CHEESE SAUCE

30 g (1 oz) butter

30 g (1 oz) plain flour

250 ml (8 fl oz) milk

175 g (6 oz) mature Cheddar cheese, grated

pinch each of cayenne pepper and grated nutmeg

salt and black pepper

1 Rinse the spinach, and put into a saucepan with only the water that clings to the leaves. Cook for about 2 minutes until tender. Drain, and set aside.

2 Make the cheese sauce: melt the butter in a saucepan, add the flour, and cook, stirring, for 1 minute. Remove from the heat and gradually blend in the milk. Bring to a boil, stirring constantly until the mixture thickens. Simmer for 2–3 minutes.

3 Stir in the Cheddar cheese, add the cayenne pepper and nutmeg, and season with salt and pepper. Keep warm.

4 Combine the spinach in a bowl with the spring onions and cream, and season with salt and pepper. Set aside.

5 Poach the eggs: bring a large pan of water to a boil. Lower the heat so that the water is simmering, and slide in the eggs, one at a time. Swirl the water round the eggs to make neat shapes. Lift out with a slotted spoon.

6 Divide the spinach and spring onion mixture among 4 warmed flameproof dishes. Arrange the poached eggs on the spinach, and spoon the cheese sauce over the eggs.

7 Sprinkle the grated Parmesan cheese over the sauce, then place the dishes under a hot grill, 7 cm (3 in) from the heat, until the cheese has melted and is lightly browned, and the whole dish is heated through. Serve hot.

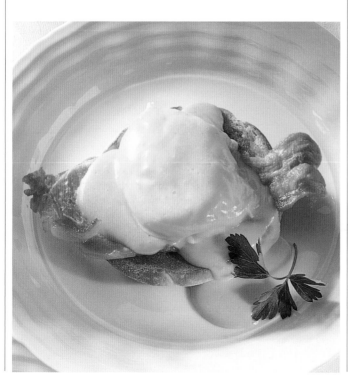

OEUFS EN COCOTTE

SERVES 4

15 g (½ oz) butter

4 eggs

salt and black pepper

4 tbsp double cream

1 tbsp chopped parsley

4 SMALL RAMEKINS

1 Melt the butter, and pour a little into each ramekin.

2 Break each egg into a saucer, then slide into a prepared ramekin. Sprinkle with salt and pepper, and top each egg with 1 tbsp cream.

3 Place the ramekins in a roasting tin and pour in boiling water to come halfway up the sides of the ramekins. Cover with foil.

4 Bake in a preheated oven at 200°C (400°F, Gas 6) for 10 minutes or until the whites are opaque and firm but the yolks still soft. Or, put the ramekins into a large frying pan, add boiling water to come halfway up the sides, cover, and cook over a medium heat for 10 minutes, letting the water boil and gently steam the eggs.

5 Sprinkle a little parsley over each baked egg 1–2 minutes before the end of cooking time.

FETA CHEESE COCOTTES

After pouring the butter into the ramekins, divide 125 g (4 oz) diced feta cheese, marinated in chopped fresh herbs and diced fresh red chilli, among the ramekins. Proceed as directed, substituting 2–3 thinly sliced spring onions for the parsley.

HUEVOS RANCHEROS

SERVES 4

2 tbsp sunflower oil

1 onion, finely chopped

3 garlic cloves, crushed

1 green pepper, halved, seeded, and chopped

1–2 fresh green chillies, halved, seeded, and chopped

500 g (1 lb) ripe tomatoes, finely chopped, or 1 x 400 g (13 oz) can chopped tomatoes

1 tsp ground cumin

¼ tsp sugar

salt

4 eggs

coriander sprigs to garnish

1 Heat the oil in a frying pan, add the onion, garlic, green pepper, and chillies, and cook gently, stirring occasionally, for about 5 minutes until the onion is soft.

2 Add the tomatoes, cumin, and sugar, season with salt, and simmer, stirring occasionally, for 10 minutes or until the mixture is thick.

3 Meanwhile, poach the eggs: bring a large pan of water to a boil. Lower the heat so that the water is simmering, and slide in the eggs, one at a time. Swirl the water round the eggs to make neat shapes. Simmer for 4 minutes. Lift out with a slotted spoon.

4 Taste the tomato sauce for seasoning, and ladle on to serving plates. Top each of the servings with a poached egg, and garnish with a coriander sprig.

HUEVOS RANCHEROS WITH CHEESE

Fry the eggs instead of poaching them. Transfer the eggs to serving plates, top with the sauce, and sprinkle with 60 g (2 oz) grated mature Cheddar cheese.

4

FISH & SHELLFISH

UNDER 30 MINUTES

THAI PRAWN STIR-FRY

Spicy oriental dish: prawns, red pepper, ginger, chilli, and lemon grass, stir-fried with rice noodles, soy sauce, and lime juice.

SERVES 4 522 calories per serving

Takes 15 minutes   Page 127

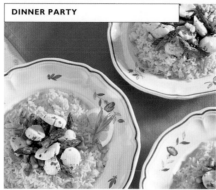

DINNER PARTY

SCALLOPS WITH ASPARAGUS & LEMON

Fresh and aromatic: scallops cooked with asparagus and garlic, with a parsley, lemon, and tarragon sauce.

SERVES 6 159 calories per serving

Takes 20 minutes   Page 130

DEVILLED CRAB

Crabmeat in a sauce flavoured with nutmeg, sherry, spring onion, and Tabasco sauce. Topped with breadcrumbs and baked.

SERVES 4 502 calories per serving

Takes 25 minutes   Page 128

TIGER PRAWNS WITH TARRAGON SAUCE

Prawns simmered with wine, garlic, and parsley. Served with a tarragon sauce.

SERVES 4 252 calories per serving

Takes 20 minutes   Page 126

HERRINGS WITH OATMEAL

Crispy and wholesome: herrings coated in oatmeal and mustard, then grilled. Served with deep-fried parsley.

SERVES 4 461 calories per serving

Takes 15 minutes   Page 137

OYSTER STEW WITH PERNOD & SAFFRON

An unusual Mediterranean-style dish: fresh oysters simmered with Pernod, single cream, white wine, fish stock, leek, carrot, watercress, saffron, and lemon juice. Lightly seasoned with cayenne pepper, and garnished with fresh chervil.

SERVES 4 251 calories per serving

Takes 25 minutes   Page 133

UNDER 30 MINUTES

SEVERN SALMON

Baked salmon flavoured with pepper, in a pool of sauce made from cream, watercress, lemon juice, butter, and egg yolk.

SERVES 6 414 calories per serving

Takes 25 minutes   Page 142

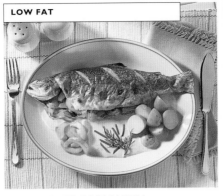
LOW FAT

GRILLED TROUT WITH CUCUMBER & DILL

Trout with a stuffing of lightly cooked cucumber, dill, and lemon juice.

SERVES 4 435 calories per serving

Takes 25 minutes   Page 138

HIGH PROTEIN

SCALLOPS WITH SPICY CASHEW SAUCE

Scallops stir-fried with mustard seeds and garlic, served in a cashew and chilli sauce.

SERVES 6 276 calories per serving

Takes 25 minutes   Page 130

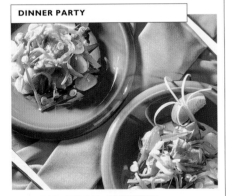
DINNER PARTY

CHINESE-STYLE OYSTERS

Oysters wrapped in bacon and stir-fried with green pepper, garlic, and water chestnuts, then sprinkled with spring onion slices.

SERVES 4 248 calories per serving

Takes 25 minutes   page 133

LOW CALORIE

SALMON WITH SPINACH

Grilled salmon served with a salsa of lightly cooked spring onions mixed with spinach, lemon juice, and mustard.

SERVES 4 454 calories per serving

Takes 25 minutes   Page 142

FAMILY FARE

BEST-EVER FRIED FISH

Crispy and nourishing: plaice fillets coated in flour, beaten egg, and fresh breadcrumbs. Cooked until golden and served with lemon.

SERVES 4 298 calories per serving

Takes 25 minutes   Page 148

HERRINGS WITH MUSTARD SAUCE

Baked herrings served with a classic sauce made from mustard powder, sugar, and white wine vinegar.

SERVES 4 479 calories per serving

Takes 25 minutes   Page 137

FILLETS OF SOLE MEUNIERE

Fresh and summery: lemon sole fillets lightly floured and cooked in butter, then served with parsley and lemon-flavoured butter.

SERVES 4 274 calories per serving

Takes 20 minutes   Page 146

PRAWN TACOS

Crispy and hot: taco shells with a spicy filling of prawns, coriander, tomatoes, onion, garlic, green pepper, and paprika.

SERVES 4 414 calories per serving

Takes 25 minutes   Page 126

30–60 MINUTES

CAJUN-SPICED RED SNAPPER

Red snapper fillets marinated in a piquant mixture of garlic, paprika, cumin, and chilli powder. Topped with coriander butter.

SERVES 4 258 calories per serving

Takes 15 minutes, plus marinating　　Page 154

HOT & SOUR MACKEREL

Red pepper, fresh chilli, carrots, and spring onions stir-fried, then grilled with mackerel fillets. Served with a hot and sour sauce.

SERVES 4 539 calories per serving

Takes 35 minutes　　Page 136

MUSSEL GRATIN

Mussels simmered with wine, shallot, and garlic, topped with cream and parsley sauce, and breadcrumbs, then grilled.

SERVES 4 448 calories per serving

Takes 35 minutes　　Page 131

FAMILY CHOICE

GOLDEN FISH CAKES

Cod or haddock simmered in milk flavoured with bay leaf and peppercorns. Mixed with potato and coated in fresh breadcrumbs.

SERVES 4 613 calories per serving

Takes 50 minutes　　Page 158

LOBSTER WITH BLACK BEAN SALSA

Lobster tails spread with garlic and oregano-flavoured butter and grilled. Served with black bean salsa.

SERVES 4 531 calories per serving

Takes 35 minutes　　Page 129

CHEESE-TOPPED BAKED BREAM

Bream fillets baked with finely grated lemon zest and juice. Covered in a white sauce and sprinkled with Cheddar cheese, then grilled.

SERVES 4 401 calories per serving

Takes 40 minutes　　Page 155

MACKEREL WITH GOOSEBERRY SAUCE

Grilled mackerel served with a tangy gooseberry sauce enriched with butter, sugar, and ginger.

SERVES 4 489 calories per serving

Takes 35 minutes　　Page 136

SALMON WITH AVOCADO

Succulent salmon steaks baked with tarragon, and served with a rich sauce of avocado, yogurt, and lime zest and juice.

SERVES 4 543 calories per serving

Takes 35 minutes　　Page 143

MUSHROOM-STUFFED SOLE FILLETS

Sole fillets rolled and stuffed with onion and mushrooms. Baked with tarragon and wine, which form the base for a cream sauce.

SERVES 4 568 calories per serving

Takes 35 minutes　　Page 146

30–60 MINUTES

CLASSIC STEAMED CLAMS WITH PARSLEY

Clams cooked in a delicious sauce made of white wine, onion, garlic, and parsley.

SERVES 4 207 calories per serving

Takes 40 minutes   Page 132

SPICED FISH WITH COCONUT

Sweet and spicy: monkfish pieces lightly coated in flour, cooked with coconut milk, onion, coriander, cumin, and turmeric.

SERVES 4 389 calories per serving

Takes 45 minutes   Page 151

SPICY CLAMS WITH CORIANDER PESTO

Clams richly flavoured with tomatoes, stock, garlic, and chilli. Served with coriander pesto.

SERVES 4–6 349–233 calories per serving

Takes 45 minutes   Page 132

MONKFISH WITH GINGER-ORANGE SAUCE

Monkfish fillets cooked with orange, ginger, onion, and stock; served with a sauce spiked with lime.

SERVES 4 221 calories per serving

Takes 40 minutes   Page 150

DINNER PARTY

COD STEAKS WITH ANCHOVY & FENNEL

Cod steaks baked with a topping of anchovies, fennel, parsley, and breadcrumbs.

SERVES 4 429 calories per serving

Takes 40 minutes   Page 154

SEA BASS WITH LEMON BUTTER SAUCE

Whole sea bass baked in foil with tarragon, lemon, and wine. Served with a creamy sauce.

SERVES 4 363 calories per serving

Takes 40 minutes   Page 157

LOW FAT

ORIENTAL FISH PARCELS

An aromatic oriental dish: white fish fillets sprinkled with ginger, spring onion, soy sauce, and rice wine, baked in a parcel.

SERVES 4 312 calories per serving

Takes 35 minutes   Page 157

BLACK BREAM NIÇOISE

Baked black bream on a bed of fennel, onion, and garlic, sprinkled with lemon juice, olives, and chopped parsley.

SERVES 4 356 calories per serving

Takes 50 minutes   Page 155

CRISPY-TOPPED SEAFOOD PIE

Cod poached in milk, then baked with prawns, leeks, and broccoli. Topped with white sauce, Gruyère, and crispy pastry.

SERVES 4 575 calories per serving

Takes 55 minutes   Page 158

GINGERED PLAICE

Light and tangy: plaice fillets marinated in sunflower and sesame oils, fresh root ginger, garlic, sherry, and vinegar, then grilled.

SERVES 4 247 calories per serving

Takes 15 minutes, plus marinating Page 147

DINNER PARTY

LOBSTER TAILS WITH MANGO & LIME

Lobster tail meat coated in a sauce of wine, cream, mango, and grated lime zest and juice. Sprinkled with Parmesan cheese and baked.

SERVES 4 442 calories per serving

Takes 40 minutes Page 128

SEAFOOD & AVOCADO SALAD

Poached monkfish with crabmeat and prawns on a bed of salad leaves, avocado, and tomatoes, dressed with crème fraîche.

SERVES 4 396 calories per serving

Takes 35 minutes, plus cooling Page 129

MEDITERRANEAN STUFFED SQUID

Tender squid pouches filled with breadcrumbs, onion, garlic, chopped squid, parsley, and dill, and pan-fried in butter.

SERVES 4 224 calories per serving

Takes 40 minutes Page 127

ROAST MONKFISH NIÇOISE

Richly flavoured monkfish cooked with roasted garlic, lemon, wine, artichoke hearts, herbs, olives, and sun-dried tomatoes.

SERVES 4 448 calories per serving

Takes 50 minutes Page 150

LEMON SOLE FLORENTINE

Lemon sole fillets baked on a bed of white sauce and spinach and topped with Parmesan. Served with hot lemon bread.

SERVES 4 422 calories per serving

Takes 1 hour 5 minutes Page 147

MUSSELS WITH POTATOES & CHORIZO

Mussels cooked with potatoes, spicy chorizo sausage, garlic, stock, sherry, and cumin seeds.

SERVES 6 523 calories per serving

Takes 40 minutes Page 131

HADDOCK WITH MUSHROOMS & CREAM

Baked haddock topped with mushrooms, a creamy sauce, breadcrumbs, and Parmesan.

SERVES 4–6 429–286 calories per serving

Takes 55 minutes Page 149

HALIBUT IN FILO PARCELS

Delicate and moist: leek and carrot strips cooked with wine, stock, and saffron, form a bed for halibut wrapped in filo pastry.

SERVES 4 564 calories per serving

Takes 1 hour 5 minutes Page 156

OVER 60 MINUTES

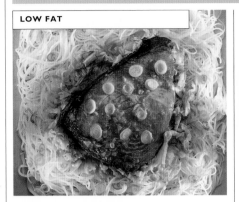

LOW FAT

TUNA TERIYAKI

Light and simple: tuna steaks marinated in garlic, ginger, soy sauce, and sesame oil. Grilled, and sprinkled with spring onion.

SERVES 4   339 calories per serving

Takes 15 minutes, plus marinating   Page 139

TUNA WITH FENNEL & TOMATO RELISH

Tuna marinated in oil, lemon juice, garlic, and herbs, grilled, and topped with relish.

SERVES 4   467 calories per serving

Takes 25 minutes, plus marinating   Page 139

MONKFISH KEBABS

Pieces of monkfish marinated in oil, lemon zest and juice, and dill, threaded with lightly cooked cucumber, lemon, and bay leaves.

SERVES 4   286 calories per serving

Takes 30 minutes, plus marinating   Page 151

KOULIBIAC

Flaked salmon mixed with rice, onion, tomatoes, parsley, and lemon. Wrapped in puff pastry and decorated with a pastry plait.

SERVES 8–10   518–414 calories per serving

Takes 1¼ hours   Page 141

INDIAN SPICED HADDOCK

Pieces of haddock marinated in a mixture of coriander, cayenne, and turmeric. Simmered with ginger, chilli, and potato.

SERVES 4   365 calories per serving

Takes 40 minutes, plus marinating   Page 149

DINNER PARTY

SALMON EN CROUTE

Salmon fillets marinated in dill and lemon zest and juice, baked in puff pastry with spinach, spring onions, and soft cheese.

SERVES 8   745 calories per serving

Takes 1½ hours, plus marinating   Page 143

SWORDFISH WITH ORANGE RELISH

Swordfish steaks marinated in orange and lemon juices, olive oil, and garlic. Grilled, then served with an orange relish.

SERVES 4   429 calories per serving

Takes 20 minutes, plus marinating   Page 140

BARBECUE

SHARK WITH TROPICAL SALSA

Shark steaks marinated in cumin, garlic, lemon juice, and coriander. Served with a salsa of pineapple, papaya, and chilli.

SERVES 4   534 calories per serving

Takes 25 minutes, plus marinating   Page 140

BAKED TROUT WITH ORANGE

Fresh and hearty dish: trout stuffed with mushrooms, shallots, orange zest and juice, white wine vinegar, thyme, and parsley.

SERVES 4   378 calories per serving

Takes 45 minutes, plus chilling   Page 138

FISH & SHELLFISH KNOW-HOW

SEAFOOD IS DELICIOUS, versatile, and quick to cook. Compared with other protein foods it is excellent value for money as there is usually little wastage. In addition, it is very nutritious: all fish and shellfish are good sources of essential vitamins and minerals, but oily fish are particularly rich in vitamins A and D and also provide beneficial omega-3 fatty acids.

Seafood is divided into two broad categories: fish and shellfish. Fish may be white (its oil is found mainly in the liver) or oily (the oil is distributed in the flesh); white fish are further sub-divided according to body shape (round or flat). Of the shellfish, crustaceans (crab, prawns) have shells and legs; molluscs (mussels, scallops) just have shells. Squid is a mollusc with an internal "shell".

CLEANING & BONING ROUND FISH

Round fish such as trout, mackerel, herring, and salmon are often cooked whole, and boning makes them easier to serve and eat. When boned they can also be stuffed. Fishmongers will prepare the fish for you, but if you want to do it yourself, here's how.

1 To clean the fish, first snip off the fins. Cut along the belly, from the vent end to just below the head. Remove the innards, scraping away any dark blood. Lift the gill covering and remove the concertina-shaped gills. Rinse well.

2 To bone, extend the belly opening so that it goes all the way to the tail. Hold the belly open and carefully run the knife between the flesh and the bones along one side, from tail to head, to cut the flesh from the ribcage.

3 Turn the fish around and cut the flesh from the ribcage on the other side. Snip through the backbone at each end and gently pull it away from the flesh, removing it with the ribcage in one piece.

4 If the head and tail have been cut off, open out the fish and lay it skin-side up. Press along the backbone to loosen the bones. Turn over and lift or cut out the ribcage and backbone. The fish is now "butterflied".

FISH STOCK

Ask your fishmonger for heads, bones, and trimmings from lean white fish (not oily fish, which make a bitter-tasting stock).

1 Rinse 750 g (1 1/2 lb) bones and trimmings and put them into a large pan. Add 1 litre (1 3/4 pints) water and 250 ml (8 fl oz) dry white wine. Bring to a boil, skimming the surface.

2 Add 1 sliced onion, 1 sliced carrot, 1 chopped celery stalk, 1 bay leaf, a few parsley sprigs, and a few black peppercorns. Simmer for 20–25 minutes. Strain. Use immediately, or cool, cover, and refrigerate to use within 2 days. It can also be frozen for up to 3 months.

SCALING

Unless skinning a fish before cooking, the scales should be removed. Dip your fingers in salt to ensure a firm grip and grasp the fish tail. Using the blunt side of a knife, with firm strokes scrape off the scales, from tail to head. Rinse well. Or ask your fishmonger to do this.

MICROWAVING

One of the best uses for a microwave is for cooking fish and shellfish: they retain their texture and all of their flavourful juices. However, care must be taken not to overcook the delicate flesh. Whether cooking or thawing, arrange pieces of fish so that the thicker areas are at the outside of the dish; overlap thin areas or fold them under. With whole fish, shield delicate areas, such as the tail and head, with smooth strips of foil. If thawing seafood, again protect thin, delicate areas by shielding them with smooth strips of foil. Except when doing this never put metal or metal containers in microwave ovens (see also page 23.)

FREEZING

It's best to buy fish ready-frozen, as it will have been processed and frozen at very low temperatures immediately after being caught – while still at sea – to prevent there being any deterioration.

If you have fish to freeze yourself, clean it and wrap tightly. For the best flavour, store white fish for no longer than 3 months, oily fish and shellfish for 2 months. (When buying, be aware that some seafood sold as "fresh" may have been frozen and then thawed, so it should not be frozen again at home.)

Fish fillets and some shellfish can be cooked very successfully from frozen, but if you need to thaw seafood before cooking, do so slowly in the refrigerator or quickly in the microwave.

BUYING & STORING

When buying fish and shellfish, aroma and appearance are your guides. Seafood should have the clean smell of the sea. If it has an unpleasantly "fishy" or ammonia-like odour, it is not fresh.

Whole fresh fish should have clean, red gills, the scales should be firmly attached, and it should be covered in a clear slime; the flesh should feel firm and springy. The flesh of fillets and steaks should be firm, moist and lustrous. If at all possible ask for steaks to be cut while you wait. If buying pre-packaged fish, check the colour of any liquid that has accumulated in the pack: it should not be cloudy or off-white.

Shellfish is sold both in the shell and shelled, raw and cooked. The shells of crabs, lobsters, and prawns become pink or red when cooked. Live shellfish, such as mussels, clams, and oysters, should have tightly closed shells. If any shells are open they should close if lightly tapped; if they do not, the shellfish is dead and should be discarded. Shelled oysters, scallops, and clams should be plump; scallops should smell slightly sweet. Prawns should also smell faintly sweet, and feel firm.

Keep the fish or shellfish cool until you get home, then unwrap it, cover with a wet cloth or wet paper towels, and store in the coldest part of the refrigerator. Use oily fish and shellfish the same day; keep white fish no more than 24 hours.

FILLETING FLAT FISH

Either 2 wide or 4 narrow fillets can be cut from a small flat fish. Larger flat fish will yield 4 good-sized fillets. Keep the bones for making stock.

1 Make a shallow cut through the skin around the edge of the fish, where the fin bones meet the body. Cut across the tail and make a curved cut around the head. Then cut down the centre of the fish, cutting through the flesh to the bone.

2 Insert the knife between the flesh and the bones on one side at the head end. Keeping the knife almost parallel to the fish, cut close to the bones, loosening the flesh to detach the fillet in one piece.

3 Repeat to remove the second fillet on the same side. Then turn the fish over and remove both of the fillets from the other side. Check the fillets for any stray bones, pulling them out with tweezers.

4 To skin, lay each fillet skin-side down and hold the tail with salted fingers to ensure a firm grip. Cut through the flesh at the tail end, then holding the knife at an angle and cut the flesh from the skin.

PREPARING PRAWNS

Both raw and cooked prawns can be used successfully in a variety of tasty dishes. When buying, take into account that prawns lose at least half of their weight when the heads and shells are removed.

1 Gently pull off the head and then the legs. Peel the shell from the body, leaving on the last tail section of shell if you like.

2 Make a shallow cut along the centre of the back of the prawn. Lift out the black intestinal vein and rinse the prawn under cold running water.

PREPARING MUSSELS & CLAMS

Most mussels and clams are sold live and are cooked by steaming in their shells. They must be scrubbed before cooking. The anchoring threads found on mussels, known as beards, must also be removed.

1 To clean the shells of mussels and clams, hold under cold running water and scrub with a small stiff brush. Use a small knife to scrape off any barnacles.

2 To remove the beard from a mussel, hold the beard firmly between your thumb and the blade of a small knife and pull the beard away from the shell.

PREPARING A COOKED CRAB

The meat inside a crab is of two types – a soft, rich, brown meat and a flaky, sweet, white meat. When a crab is "dressed", the meat is removed from the shell, with the two types being kept separate, and then arranged back in the shell for serving.

1 Put the crab on its back and twist off the legs and claws, close to the body.

2 Using nutcrackers, a small hammer, or a rolling pin, crack the shells of the claws without crushing them. Break open the shells and carefully remove the meat, using a small fork or skewer.

3 Press your thumbs along the "perforation" to crack the central section of the shell and prise it apart. Remove and discard the "apron" flap from the underside of the body.

4 Pull the central body section up and away from the shell. Scoop the creamy-textured brown meat out of the shell and put it into a bowl (keeping it entirely separate from the white claw and leg meat). Scoop out any roe. Discard the stomach sac, which is located between the eyes.

5 Pull the spongy gills (known as "dead man's fingers") from the body and discard them.

6 Cut the body in half with a large knife and pick out all the white meat from the crevices. Add to the white meat from the claws.

PREPARING A COOKED LOBSTER

Ready-cooked lobster meat can be added to cooked dishes for a brief heating, or it can be served cold with mayonnaise (most attractively in the shell) or in a salad. For instructions on cooking a live lobster, see page 31.

To remove the meat

1 Twist off the large claws. Using a sturdy nutcracker, small hammer, or rolling pin, crack the shells of the claws without crushing them. Pick out the meat, in 1 or 2 large pieces. If the shell is not to be used for serving, pull apart the body and tail. Twist off the small legs, crack them, and remove the meat with a skewer or lobster pick.

2 Lift off the top of the body shell. Scoop out the grey-green liver (tomalley) and any coral-coloured roe, both of which are edible, and reserve. Discard the stomach and spongy gills ("dead man's fingers").

To serve in the shell

1 Use a sharp, heavy knife to split the lobster in half lengthwise, cutting from the head to the tail. Pull the halves apart.

4 Bend back the flaps and carefully remove the tail meat, keeping it in 1 piece. Remove and discard the intestinal tract that runs through the centre of the tail meat. Slice the tail meat, or prepare as required, and serve with the claw and leg meat.

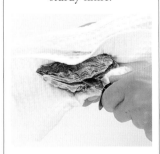

3 With scissors or a sharp knife, cut along the soft underside of the tail.

2 Scoop out the liver and roe, and discard the intestine. Twist off the legs and claws (remove the meat). Loosen the meat in the shell.

PREPARING OYSTERS

To shuck oysters, use an oyster knife or small, sturdy knife.

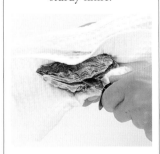

Hold oyster round-side down, and insert the knife near the hinge. Lever the shells apart. Slide in the knife to sever the top muscle. Lift off the shell. Run the knife under the oyster to loosen it.

PREPARING A SQUID

Once cleaned, fresh squid yields a tube-like body, which can be stuffed or sliced, and separate tentacles. You can buy it already cleaned or do this yourself as shown here.

1 Pull the head and tentacles away from the body (the innards will come away with the head as will the long, narrow ink sac if it is present). Cut off the tentacles, just in front of the eyes.

2 Squeeze the tentacles near the cut end so that the hard beak can be removed. Discard it. Rinse the tentacles well and set aside. Discard the head and innards (and the ink sac unless using it in a sauce).

3 Peel the skin from the body. Pull the long piece of cartilage (quill) out of the body and discard. Rinse the body thoroughly, inside and out, and pull off the two flaps (slice these for cooking).

PRAWN TACOS

SERVES 4

2 tbsp sunflower oil

2 onions, chopped

3 garlic cloves, crushed

1 green pepper, halved, seeded, and diced

1 tbsp paprika

2 tsp mild chilli powder

1/2 tsp ground cumin

4 ripe firm tomatoes, chopped

500 g (1 lb) cooked peeled prawns

2 tbsp chopped fresh coriander

salt and black pepper

12 taco shells

1 round lettuce, shredded

sliced pickled chillies, large cooked peeled prawns, and coriander leaves to garnish

1 Heat the oil in a large frying pan, add the onions, and cook gently, stirring occasionally, for 3–5 minutes until softened but not coloured. Add the garlic and diced green pepper, and cook, stirring occasionally, for 3 minutes or until the pepper is soft.

2 Stir in the paprika, chilli powder, and cumin, and cook, stirring, for 1 minute. Add the tomatoes and cook for 3–5 minutes until soft.

3 Lower the heat and stir in the prawns and chopped coriander, and season with salt and pepper.

4 Meanwhile, heat the taco shells in a preheated oven at 180°C (350°F, Gas 4) for 3 minutes or according to packet instructions.

5 Spoon the prawn mixture into the taco shells, top with the shredded lettuce, and garnish with chillies, prawns, and coriander. Serve at once.

Healthy note

Prawns, like most shellfish, are a healthy food low in calories and fat. They are rich in the antioxidant selenium, which is linked to a healthy heart and circulation, and they are also a good source of iodine, zinc, and calcium.

TIGER PRAWNS WITH TARRAGON SAUCE

SERVES 4

12 uncooked tiger prawns in their shells

olive oil for brushing

300 ml (1/2 pint) dry white wine

1 garlic clove, crushed

4 tbsp chopped parsley

lemon and tarragon to garnish

TARRAGON SAUCE

150 ml (1/4 pint) soured cream

4 tbsp chopped fresh tarragon

1 tsp Dijon mustard

squeeze of lemon juice

salt and black pepper

1 Make the tarragon sauce: combine the soured cream, tarragon, mustard, and lemon juice, and season with salt and pepper.

2 Heat a heavy frying pan. Brush the prawns with oil, add to the pan, and cook the prawns over a high heat for 2 minutes or until pink.

3 Keeping the heat high, add 150 ml (1/4 pint) of the wine and the garlic. Boil rapidly for 2–3 minutes, then stir in 2 tbsp of the parsley.

4 When the wine has reduced slightly, lower the heat, and add the remaining wine, and season with salt and pepper. Simmer for 5 minutes or until the prawns have released their juices into the wine.

5 Spoon the cooking juices over the prawns, sprinkle with the remaining parsley, and garnish with lemon and sprigs of fresh tarragon. Serve hot, with the tarragon sauce.

MEDITERRANEAN STUFFED SQUID

SERVES 4

8 small whole squid, cleaned (page 125)

30 g (1 oz) butter, plus a little extra for frying

1 large onion, finely chopped

2 garlic cloves, crushed

60 g (2 oz) fine fresh breadcrumbs

1 tbsp chopped fresh dill

1 tbsp chopped parsley

salt and black pepper

lemon slices and chopped parsley to serve

1 Chop the squid tentacles roughly and set aside.

2 Make the stuffing: melt the butter in a frying pan, add the onion and garlic, cover and sauté over a low heat for about 15–20 minutes until very soft.

3 Add the chopped squid tentacles, breadcrumbs, dill, and parsley to the onion and garlic, and fry over a high heat for 2–3 minutes. Season with salt and pepper, and leave to cool.

4 Fill the squid bodies with the cold stuffing, and secure the tops (see box, below).

5 Heat a little butter in a clean frying pan, and fry the stuffed squid for about 4–5 minutes until golden brown all over and firm to the touch, and the filling is heated through.

6 Garnish the squid with the lemon slices and parsley, and serve at once.

Securing the squid

Thread a cocktail stick through the top of each stuffed squid to secure the opening.

THAI PRAWN STIR-FRY

SERVES 4

250 g (8 oz) rice noodles

salt

3 tbsp sunflower oil

1 red pepper, halved, seeded, and cut into thin strips

1 carrot, cut into thin strips

1 fresh green chilli, halved, seeded, and cut into thin strips

2.5 cm (1 in) piece of fresh root ginger, peeled and cut into thin strips

1 garlic clove, crushed

8 spring onions, sliced

2 lemon grass stalks, trimmed and sliced

500 g (1 lb) cooked peeled tiger prawns

2 tbsp white wine vinegar

2 tbsp soy sauce

juice of 1/2 lime

1 tbsp sesame oil

3 tbsp chopped fresh coriander to garnish

1 Put the rice noodles into a large saucepan of boiling salted water and stir to separate the noodles. Turn off the heat, cover, and leave to stand for 4 minutes. Drain well and set aside.

2 Heat 1 tbsp of the sunflower oil in a wok or large frying pan. Add the red pepper, carrot, chilli, ginger, garlic, spring onions, and lemon grass, and stir-fry over a high heat for 2 minutes.

3 Add the prawns, and stir-fry for 1 minute, then stir in the noodles.

4 Add the remaining sunflower oil, the vinegar, soy sauce, lime juice, and sesame oil, and stir-fry for 1 minute.

5 Sprinkle with the chopped fresh coriander, and serve at once.

SCALLOP STIR-FRY

Substitute 500 g (1 lb) shelled scallops for the tiger prawns, cutting each scallop into two or three pieces if they are large. Stir-fry for about 2 minutes, then add the red pepper, carrot, chilli, fresh root ginger, garlic, spring onions, and lemon grass, and stir-fry for a further 2 minutes. Add the soaked and drained noodles, then continue with the recipe from the beginning of step 4.

DEVILLED CRAB

SERVES 4

75 g (2¹/2 oz) butter
1¹/2 tbsp plain flour
175 ml (6 fl oz) milk
¹/4 tsp mustard powder
¹/4 tsp grated nutmeg
1 egg yolk
1¹/2 tbsp dry sherry
1 tsp Worcestershire sauce
2–3 dashes of Tabasco sauce
4 small dressed crabs with their claws (page 106), or 500 g (1 lb) white and dark crabmeat
1 spring onion, thinly sliced
salt and black pepper
125 g (4 oz) fresh breadcrumbs
paprika and finely chopped spring onions to garnish

1 Melt 45 g (1¹/2 oz) of the butter in a saucepan, add the flour, and cook, stirring, for 1 minute. Remove from the heat, and gradually blend in the milk. Bring to a boil, stirring constantly until the mixture thickens. Simmer for 2–3 minutes. Remove from the heat, and stir in the mustard and nutmeg.

2 Put the egg yolk into a small bowl, and whisk in a little of the sauce. Stir this mixture back into the sauce.

3 Add the dry sherry, Worcestershire sauce, Tabasco sauce, crabmeat, spring onion, and salt and pepper to taste, and stir to mix. Spoon the mixture into the crab shells, or into ramekins, and stand them on a baking sheet.

4 Melt the remaining butter in a saucepan, add the breadcrumbs, and cook, stirring, for 5 minutes or until golden brown.

5 Spoon the breadcrumbs over the crabmeat mixture, replace the claws if you have them, and bake in a preheated oven at 200°C (400°F, Gas 6) for 10 minutes or until the tops are browned and bubbling. Sprinkle with paprika and chopped spring onions before serving.

LOBSTER TAILS WITH MANGO & LIME

SERVES 4

4 cooked lobster tails
90 ml (3 fl oz) dry white wine
250 ml (8 fl oz) double cream
1 small mango, peeled, stoned, and cut into cubes (page 430)
grated zest and juice of 1 lime
30 g (1 oz) Parmesan cheese, grated

1 Remove the flesh from the lobster tails (see box, below), then cut each piece of lobster flesh in half lengthwise. Arrange the pieces of lobster flesh, cut side-side up, in a large shallow ovenproof dish.

2 Pour the white wine into a small saucepan and boil rapidly until it has reduced to about 2 tbsp.

3 Add the cream to the saucepan and boil until the mixture has reduced to a coating consistency. Stir in the mango cubes and grated lime zest and juice.

4 Spoon the mixture over the lobster in the dish. Sprinkle with the Parmesan cheese and bake in a preheated oven at 220°C (425°F, Gas 7) for about 20 minutes, until hot and bubbling. Serve hot.

Removing the flesh from a lobster tail

Hold the tail in 1 hand. With a pair of scissors, cut along both sides of the underside of the shell, towards the end, without damaging the flesh.

Pull back the underside of the shell, and lift out the lobster flesh, making sure it is all in 1 piece.

LOBSTER TAILS WITH BLACK BEAN SALSA

SERVES 4

4 cooked lobster tails

lime twists and coriander sprigs to garnish

BLACK BEAN SALSA

4 ripe but firm tomatoes, finely chopped

I small onion, chopped

I garlic clove, crushed

2 tbsp chopped fresh coriander

I mild fresh green chilli, halved, seeded, and chopped

I x 375 g (12 oz) can black beans, drained

salt and black pepper

GARLIC BUTTER

150 g (5 oz) butter

5 garlic cloves, crushed

2 tsp finely chopped fresh oregano

1 Make the black bean salsa: in a bowl, combine the tomatoes, onion, garlic, coriander, and chilli. Add the beans, and salt and pepper to taste.

2 With a sharp knife, cut each lobster tail in half lengthwise and loosen the flesh, keeping it in the shell.

3 Make the garlic butter: cream the butter in a bowl, add the garlic, oregano, and salt and pepper to taste, and mix well. Spread half of the butter mixture over the lobster flesh.

4 Place the lobster under a hot grill, 10 cm (4 in) from the heat, and grill for 5 minutes or until slightly browned in patches and heated through.

5 Spread the lobster with the remaining garlic butter, and then garnish with lime twists and coriander sprigs. Serve hot, with the black bean salsa.

Healthy option

Instead of garlic butter, drizzle the lobster with a little olive oil, either plain or flavoured with garlic and herbs. Or use a chilli-flavoured oil, which would go well in this recipe.

SEAFOOD & AVOCADO SALAD

SERVES 4

500 g (1 lb) monkfish, trimmed and skinned

150 ml (1/4 pint) fish stock

I slice of onion

6 black peppercorns

squeeze of lemon juice

I bay leaf

mixed salad leaves, such as frisée, radicchio, and rocket

2 avocados

lemon juice for brushing

2 large tomatoes, peeled (page 57), seeded, and cut into strips

125 g (4 oz) cooked peeled prawns

90 g (3 oz) white crabmeat

flat-leaf parsley to garnish

CREME FRAICHE DRESSING

125 ml (4 fl oz) crème fraîche

3 tbsp lemon juice

salt and black pepper

1 Put the monkfish into a saucepan with the stock, onion, peppercorns, lemon juice, and bay leaf. Bring to a gentle simmer, cover, and poach very gently, turning once, for 10 minutes until opaque throughout and firm.

2 Remove the pan from the heat and leave the fish to cool in the liquid, then lift it out and cut into bite-sized pieces.

3 Make the crème fraîche dressing: put the crème fraîche and lemon juice into a bowl, add salt and pepper to taste, and stir to mix.

4 To serve, arrange the salad leaves on individual plates. Halve, stone (page 88), and peel the avocados, and brush with lemon juice. Slice lengthwise and arrange in a fan shape on the leaves. Add the strips of tomato, the monkfish, prawns, and crabmeat. Spoon the crème fraîche dressing over the salad, garnish with the parsley, and serve at once.

Healthy option

You can use low-fat crème fraîche for the cold dressing because it holds its shape well. It is only when you heat crème fraîche that it becomes runny and thin.

SCALLOPS WITH ASPARAGUS & LEMON

SERVES 6

500 g (1 lb) fresh asparagus tips, chopped into 2 cm (1 in) lengths

60 g (2 oz) butter

500 g (1 lb) queen scallops

3 garlic cloves, crushed

juice of 1 lemon

2 tbsp finely chopped parsley

1 tbsp chopped fresh tarragon

salt and black pepper

1 Blanch the asparagus in boling salted water for about 2 minutes, then drain and refresh in cold water to stop the cooking and set the bright green colour.

2 Melt half the butter in a frying pan, and fry the scallops for about 30 seconds on each side until just opaque and firm to the touch (you may need to do this in batches). Remove the scallops with a slotted spoon, and keep warm.

3 Heat the remaining butter in the frying pan. Add the garlic, lemon juice, parsley, and tarragon, and season with salt and pepper.

4 Return the scallops and asparagus to the pan and heat them through very gently, shaking the pan to coat them in the sauce. Serve hot.

Cook's know-how

If queen scallops are not available, use the larger king scallops instead. Slice each one in half horizontally, and they will then cook in the same amount of time. If scallops are not available at all, or if you prefer, you can substitute an equal quantity of raw tiger prawns. Peel them, but leave the tails on for a decorative touch.

SCALLOPS WITH SPICY CASHEW SAUCE

SERVES 6

100 g (3 1/2 oz) toasted, salted cashew nuts

3 tbsp sunflower oil

3 garlic cloves, crushed

500 g (1 lb) scallops

1 onion, chopped

1 green pepper, halved, seeded, and cut into thin strips

1 fresh red chilli, halved, seeded, and finely chopped

1/2 tsp turmeric

250 ml (8 fl oz) fish stock

1 tsp coarse-grain mustard

salt and black pepper

1 Grind the cashew nuts in a food processor or nut grinder until smooth.

2 Heat the oil in a large frying pan, add the garlic and scallops, and stir-fry for 2 minutes or just until the scallops turn opaque. Remove with a slotted spoon

3 Add the onion, green pepper, and chilli to the frying pan, and cook gently, stirring occasionally, for 3–5 minutes until the onion is soft but not coloured. Add the turmeric and cook, stirring, for 1 minute.

4 Add the ground cashew nuts and stock to the mixture in the frying pan, bring to a boil, and simmer for 5–10 minutes until the sauce thickens.

5 Stir the scallops into the sauce, add the mustard and salt and pepper to taste, and gently warm through. Serve hot.

Cook's know-how

If you are short of time, use 2 heaped tablespoons of cashew nut butter or peanut butter (smooth or crunchy) instead of grinding the cashews in step 1.

MUSSEL GRATIN

SERVES 4

150 ml (¼ pint) dry white wine
1 shallot, finely chopped
1 garlic clove, crushed
3 kg (6 lb) large mussels, cleaned (page 124)
300 ml (½ pint) single cream
3 tbsp chopped parsley
salt and black pepper
30 g (1 oz) fresh white breadcrumbs
30 g (1 oz) butter, melted

1 Pour the wine into a large saucepan, add the chopped shallot and crushed garlic, and bring to a boil. Simmer for 2 minutes.

2 Add the mussels, cover tightly, and return to a boil. Cook, shaking the pan frequently, for 5–6 minutes until the mussels open.

3 Using a slotted spoon, transfer the mussels to a large bowl. Discard any that have not opened; do not try to force them open.

4 Strain the cooking liquid into a saucepan, bring to a boil, and simmer until reduced to about 3 tbsp. Add the cream and heat through. Stir in half of the parsley, and season with salt and pepper.

5 Remove the top shell of each mussel and discard. Arrange the mussels, in their bottom shells, on a large flameproof serving dish.

6 Spoon the sauce over the mussels, and sprinkle with the breadcrumbs and melted butter. Cook under a hot grill, 10 cm (4 in) from the heat, for 3–5 minutes until golden. Garnish with the remaining parsley and serve at once.

Cook's know-how

Mussels are often sold by volume: 900 ml (1½ pints) is equivalent to 750 g (1½ lb), which will yield about 375 g (12 oz) shelled mussels.

MUSSELS WITH POTATOES & CHORIZO

SERVES 6

2 tbsp olive oil
2 large potatoes, diced
375 g (12 oz) chorizo sausage, diced
3 garlic cloves, crushed
125 ml (4 fl oz) fish stock
4 tbsp dry sherry or white wine
about 2 dozen large mussels, cleaned (page 124)
salt and black pepper
chopped flat-leaf parsley to garnish

1 Heat the olive oil in a large saucepan, add the potatoes, and cook gently, stirring from time to time, for 12–15 minutes until golden and softened. Add the chorizo sausage and garlic, and cook, stirring constantly, for about 2 minutes.

2 Add the fish stock, sherry or wine, and mussels, and season with salt and pepper. Cover the pan tightly, and bring to a boil. Cook, shaking the pan frequently, for 5–8 minutes or until the mussels have opened.

3 Discard any mussels that have not opened; do not try to force them open.

4 Transfer the mussel, potato, and chorizo mixture to a large serving dish, and pour over the cooking juices. Serve hot, garnished with parsley.

Healthy option

Mussels, potatoes, and chorizo make a delicious combination, popular in traditional Spanish cooking. Chorizo gives this dish its characteristic russet colour, but it is a fatty sausage so you may prefer to use less – just 125 g (4 oz) will give some colour, and you could make up the remaining weight by adding frozen broad beans in step 2.

SPICY CLAMS WITH CORIANDER PESTO

SERVES 4–6

4 tbsp olive oil

6 ripe firm tomatoes, diced

4 garlic cloves, crushed

1 tbsp mild chilli powder

about 4 dozen baby clams, cleaned (page 106)

600 ml (1 pint) fish stock, or 300 ml (1/2 pint) each dry white wine and fish stock

juice of 1/2 lime

CORIANDER PESTO

12 coriander sprigs

2 tbsp olive oil

1 large garlic clove, roughly chopped

1 mild fresh green chilli, halved, seeded, and roughly chopped

salt and black pepper

1 Make the coriander pesto: strip the coriander leaves from the stalks. Purée the coriander leaves, olive oil, garlic, and green chilli in a food processor or blender until smooth. Season with salt and pepper, and set aside.

2 Heat the oil in a large saucepan, add the tomatoes, garlic, and chilli powder, and cook gently, stirring occasionally, for 8 minutes or until slightly thickened.

3 Add the clams and stir for about 1 minute, then pour in the stock. Cover the pan tightly, and cook the clams over a medium heat, shaking the pan frequently, for about 5–8 minutes until the clams open. Discard any that have not opened; do not try to force them open.

4 Using a slotted spoon, transfer the clams to a warmed bowl.

5 Pour the cooking juices into a small pan, and boil until reduced by about half. Add the lime juice, and season to taste, then pour the sauce over the clams.

6 Serve the clams at once, topped with the coriander pesto.

CLASSIC STEAMED CLAMS WITH PARSLEY

SERVES 4

about 3 dozen clams, cleaned (page 124)

15 g (1/2 oz) butter

2 onions, coarsely chopped

2 garlic cloves, crushed

300 ml (1/2 pint) dry white wine

150 ml (1/4 pint) water

30 g (1 oz) butter

about 6 tbsp chopped parsley

1 Melt the butter in a large, deep saucepan. Add the onions and garlic, and fry for 2–3 minutes.

2 Pour in the wine and water, and add 2 tbsp of the parsley. Add the clams, cover the pan, and bring to a boil. Cook, shaking the pan, for about 12 minutes until the clams open. Discard any that have not opened; do not try to force them open.

3 Using a slotted spoon, transfer the clams to a warmed bowl or serving dish.

4 Bring the sauce to a boil, and whisk in the remaining butter and parsley.

5 Pour the sauce over the clams, and serve immediately.

Cook's know-how

Hard-shell clams come in different sizes. The smallest are called littlenecks, the next size up are known as cherrystones, and the largest are chowder clams, although they may not be given these names at the fishmonger. Buy whatever you can get for this recipe, bearing in mind that the smaller they are the more fiddly they will be to prepare and eat. If clams are not available, you can use mussels instead.

OYSTER STEW WITH PERNOD & SAFFRON

SERVES 4

| 12 oysters in their shells |
| 375 ml (12 fl oz) single cream |
| 250 ml (8 fl oz) dry white wine |
| 250 ml (8 fl oz) fish stock |
| 1 small head of fennel, trimmed and finely chopped |
| 1 small carrot, diced |
| 30 g (1 oz) watercress, tough stalks removed, coarsely chopped |
| 2 tbsp Pernod or vermouth |
| 1 tbsp lemon juice |
| pinch of saffron threads (optional) |
| pinch of cayenne pepper (optional) |
| salt |
| chervil sprigs to garnish |

1 Remove the oysters from their shells (page 125), and strain their liquid into a jug. Set aside.

2 Put the cream, wine, stock, leek, and carrot into a saucepan, and bring to a boil. Simmer for 7–10 minutes until the vegetables are just tender.

3 Add the oyster liquid to the pan with the watercress, Pernod or vermouth, lemon juice, saffron and cayenne pepper (if using). Season with salt. Bring to a boil, add the oysters, and simmer until the oysters heat through and curl slightly at the edges. Serve at once, garnished with chervil sprigs.

CHINESE-STYLE OYSTERS

SERVES 4

| 8 streaky bacon rashers, rinds removed, cut in half |
| 1 x 100 g (3 1/2 oz) can smoked oysters, drained |
| 1 small green pepper, halved, seeded, and cut into bite-sized pieces |
| 1 garlic clove, crushed |
| 250 g (8 oz) canned water chestnuts, drained |
| 1 spring onion, thinly sliced |
| lemon wedges and Tabasco sauce to serve |

Healthy note

Oysters are rich in zinc and iron, two minerals that are essential in a healthy diet.

1 Wrap half a bacon rasher around each oyster, and fasten securely with wooden cocktail sticks.

2 Heat a frying pan, add the bacon-wrapped oysters, and cook gently for 6–8 minutes until browned and crisp. Add the green pepper, garlic, and water chestnuts, and stir-fry over a high heat for 2 minutes.

3 Sprinkle with the spring onion slices, and serve with lemon wedges and Tabasco.

SIMPLE FISH SUSHI

Making your own sushi is easy as long as you keep it simple, as here. The three different
types of sushi shown are made from one batch of rice and just a few ingredients in addition to the fish.
Presented in a stylish way, the finished result is stunning.

HOSO MAKI

MAKES 20

2 sheets of nori (dried Japanese seaweed)

a bowl of vinegar water (see box, in third column)

prepared Simple Sushi Rice (see recipe, bottom of next column)

a little wasabi (Japanese horseradish paste)

175 g (6 oz) canned white crabmeat, drained and flaked

½ cucumber, halved lengthwise, seeded, and cut into long thin strips

BAMBOO ROLLING MAT

1 Lay the rolling mat on a flat surface with one of the longest edges facing towards you. Lay one sheet of nori shiny side down on the mat.

2 Dip your hand in vinegar water, take a handful of the sushi rice, and spread it over the nori, leaving a 2.5 cm (1 in) gap along the edge furthest away from you.

3 Spread a thin layer of wasabi – about 1 cm (½ in) wide – lengthwise along the middle of the rice (from left to right). Cover the wasabi with half the crab, then put a strip of cucumber on either side of the crab.

4 Moisten the uncovered edge of the nori with a little cold water. Using the mat and starting from the edge nearest to you, roll the rice in the nori, squeezing it to make a tight roll. Seal the moistened edge around the roll, then wrap in cling film. Now make a second roll in the same way.

5 To serve, unwrap the rolls and cut each one into 10 pieces with a very sharp knife that has been dipped in cold water (trim off the ends first so you get neat slices).

SUSHI SQUARES WITH SMOKED SALMON

MAKES 40

a bowl of vinegar water (see box, next column)

prepared Simple Sushi Rice (see recipe, below)

4 thin slices of smoked salmon

a few strips of sushi pickled ginger (gari), from a jar

32.5 × 23 CM (13 × 9 IN) SWISS ROLL TIN

1 Line the Swiss roll tin with cling film (if you don't have a tin, cover a chopping board with cling film). Dip your hand in vinegar water, take a handful of the sushi rice, and press it into the tin, patting it level with your hand. Repeat with more handfuls of rice until the tin is full. Refrigerate for about 15 minutes until firm.

2 Turn the tin upside down on to a board and remove the cling film. Cut into about 40 small squares with a very sharp, wet knife. Cut the smoked salmon into little strips to fit on each square and top with a little pickled ginger.

SIMPLE SUSHI RICE

500 g (1 lb) sushi rice

4 tbsp rice wine vinegar

50 ml (2 fl oz) Japanese rice wine (mirin or sake)

¼ tsp salt

1 Put the rice into a sieve and rinse under cold running water, then tip it into a saucepan and pour in 750 ml (1¼ pints) cold water. Bring to a boil, lower the heat, and simmer, covered, for 15 minutes or until all the water has been absorbed.

2 Remove the pan from the heat and cover it immediately with a tea towel and lid (this is to make sure no steam can escape). Leave for about 10 minutes.

3 Mix together the vinegar, rice wine, and salt in a small bowl and fold gently into the rice. Continue to cut and fold through the rice while cooling with a fan or a firm piece of card (it is important to cool the rice down quickly so that it remains sticky).

NIGIRI SUSHI

MAKES 10

10 raw tiger prawns, shells and tails on

salt

a little wasabi

a bowl of vinegar water (see box, below)

prepared Simple Sushi Rice (see recipe, previous column)

10 SMALL METAL SKEWERS

1 Push a skewer lengthwise through each prawn so the prawn becomes straight. Boil for 1–2 minutes in salted water until pink and cooked, drain, and cool. Remove the skewers and gently shell the prawns, leaving the tails intact.

2 Make a slit down the length of the belly of each prawn (without cutting right through), and gently open the prawn out. Remove the black vein from the back.

3 Using your finger, spread a little wasabi along the middle of the slit in the belly. Dip your hand in vinegar water and take a small amount of rice, about the size of a small walnut. Shape the rice with your hand (it will be very sticky) so that it fills the slit on top of the wasabi, then reshape the prawn around the rice by squeezing. Turn the right way up to serve.

Cook's know-how

The secret of good sushi is to make a good sticky rice, which is very simple. Instructions are usually on the packet, but the recipe here includes a little rice wine for sweetness, and a little salt.

To stop the rice sticking to your hand you will need a bowl of vinegar water (water with a little vinegar added).

Always use sushi rice on the day it is made. After you have made all the sushi, you can refrigerate them for up to 24 hours until ready to serve.

CLOCKWISE FROM TOP: Nigiri Sushi, Hoso Maki, Sushi Squares with Smoked Salmon.

HOT & SOUR MACKEREL

SERVES 4

2 carrots

1 red pepper, cored and seeded

1 fresh green chilli, halved and seeded

6 garlic cloves

8 spring onions

1 lemon grass stalk, slit lengthwise and bruised

2 tbsp sunflower oil

4 x 175 g (6 oz) mackerel fillets

coriander sprigs to garnish

HOT AND SOUR SAUCE

4 tbsp Thai fish sauce or light soy sauce

4 tbsp cider vinegar, white wine vinegar, or rice vinegar

2 tbsp lime juice

2 tbsp sugar

1 Make the hot and sour sauce: in a small bowl, combine the fish sauce, vinegar, lime juice, and sugar.

2 Cut the carrots, red pepper, green chilli, and garlic into matchstick-thin strips. Slice the spring onions.

3 Line a grill pan with foil. Arrange the mackerel on the foil, and cook under a hot grill, 10 cm (4 in) from the heat, for 3 minutes on each side. Continue to grill until the fish is opaque and the flesh flakes easily. Meanwhile, stir-fry the vegetables.

4 Heat the sunflower oil in a wok or large frying pan. Add the carrots, red pepper, chilli, garlic, spring onions, and lemon grass, and stir-fry over a high heat for 3 minutes or until the vegetables are just tender.

5 Remove and discard the lemon grass. Arrange the vegetable mixture on top of the fish, pour the sauce over, garnish with the coriander sprigs, and serve at once.

MACKEREL WITH GOOSEBERRY SAUCE

SERVES 4

4 x 250 g (8 oz) mackerel, cleaned, with heads removed (page 123)

salt and black pepper

GOOSEBERRY SAUCE

375 g (12 oz) gooseberries

2 tbsp water

30 g (1 oz) caster sugar, more if needed

30 g (1 oz) butter

1/2 tsp ground ginger

1 Cut the fins off the mackerel, and make 3–4 diagonal cuts on both sides of each fish. Season the mackerel inside and out with salt and pepper.

2 Make the gooseberry sauce: top and tail the gooseberries, and put them into a pan with the water and sugar. Cover tightly and simmer very gently, shaking the pan occasionally, for 5 minutes or until tender.

3 Reserve 12 of the cooked gooseberries for garnish, then work the remainder through a nylon sieve. Beat in the butter and ginger and add more sugar if necessary. Return the sauce to the pan and keep warm.

4 Cook the mackerel under a hot grill, 10 cm (4 in) from the heat, for 7–8 minutes on each side until the fish is opaque and the flesh flakes easily.

5 Serve the mackerel hot, garnished with the reserved gooseberries. Hand the sauce separately.

MACKEREL WITH CRANBERRY SAUCE

Substitute 375 g (12 oz) cranberries for the gooseberries. You can use frozen cranberries, but they will take slightly longer to cook – simmer them until they pop open.

HERRINGS WITH OATMEAL

SERVES 4

125 g (4 oz) medium oatmeal

2 tsp mustard powder

salt and black pepper

4 x 175–250 g (6–8 oz) herrings, cleaned (page 123), heads removed, and filleted

8 parsley sprigs

parsley and lemon wedges to garnish

1 In a shallow dish, combine the oatmeal and mustard powder, and season with salt and pepper.

2 Open out the herrings and press them into the oatmeal mixture to coat well on both sides.

3 Grill the herrings under a hot grill, 10 cm (4 in) from the heat, for about 4 minutes on each side or until the fish is opaque and the flesh flakes easily.

4 Arrange the grilled herrings on a warmed serving platter, and garnish with parsley and lemon wedges.

Healthy note

Herrings are an inexpensive oily fish, and eating oily fish regularly (once a week) is one of the best ways to eat for good health. This is because they contain omega-3 fatty acids, which help discourage heart disease and blood clots. Herrings also provide vitamin D, which is good for healthy bones, teeth, nerves and muscles.

HERRINGS WITH MUSTARD SAUCE

SERVES 4

4 x 175–250 g (6–8 oz) herrings, cleaned (page 123), heads removed, and filleted

salt and black pepper

butter for greasing

lemon wedges and parsley sprigs to garnish

MUSTARD SAUCE

30 g (1 oz) butter

30 g (1 oz) plain flour

300 ml (1/2 pint) milk

2 tsp mustard powder

1 tsp caster sugar

2 tsp white wine vinegar

1 Season the herrings inside and out with salt and black pepper, fold the fish over, and place in a single layer in a buttered ovenproof dish.

2 Cover and bake in a preheated oven at 200°C (400°F, Gas 6) for 12 minutes or until the fish is opaque and the flesh flakes easily.

3 Meanwhile, make the mustard sauce: melt the butter in a saucepan, add the flour, and cook, stirring, for 1 minute. Remove from the heat and gradually blend in the milk. Bring to a boil, stirring constantly until the mixture thickens. Simmer for 2–3 minutes. Add the mustard powder, sugar, and vinegar, season with salt and pepper, and cook for a further minute.

4 To serve, garnish the herrings with lemon wedges and parsley sprigs, and hand the mustard sauce separately.

Healthy option

Instead of the mustard sauce, make a quick "dip" by mixing a teaspoonful or two of Dijon mustard and a squeeze of lemon juice into your favourite reduced-calorie mayonnaise or low-fat crème fraîche.

GRILLED TROUT WITH CUCUMBER & DILL

SERVES 4

1 cucumber, peeled
30 g (1 oz) butter
small bunch of fresh dill, chopped
salt and black pepper
juice of 1 lemon
4 x 375–425 g (12–14 oz) trout, cleaned (page 123)
dill sprigs and fresh chives to garnish
dill cream sauce (page 148) to serve

1 Cut the cucumber in half lengthwise and scoop out the seeds, then cut the flesh across into 5 mm (1/4 in) slices. Melt the butter in a saucepan, add the cucumber, and cook gently for 2 minutes.

2 In a bowl, combine two-thirds of the cooked cucumber with the chopped dill, season with salt and pepper, and sprinkle with the lemon juice. Stuff the trout with the mixture.

3 Line a grill pan with foil. Arrange the trout on the foil, and put the remaining cucumber around them.

4 Grill the trout under a hot grill, 10 cm (4 in) from the heat, for 4–7 minutes on each side until the flesh flakes easily.

5 Garnish the trout with dill sprigs and fresh chives, and serve at once, with dill cream sauce handed separately.

TROUT WITH ALMONDS

Dip the trout in seasoned flour. Melt 60 g (2 oz) butter in a large frying pan, and cook the trout, in batches if necessary, for 6–8 minutes on each side until the fish is opaque and the flesh flakes easily. Drain on paper towels, and keep warm. Wipe the pan, melt 15 g (1/2 oz) butter, and fry 60 g (2 oz) flaked almonds until lightly browned. Add a squeeze of lemon juice, then pour the lemon and almond mixture over the trout. Serve at once.

BAKED TROUT WITH ORANGE

SERVES 4

4 x 375–425 g (12–14 oz) trout, cleaned (page 123)
4 large thyme sprigs
4 large parsley sprigs
125 g (4 oz) button mushrooms, sliced
2 shallots, chopped
4 tbsp white wine vinegar
grated zest and juice of 1 orange
salt and black pepper
orange and thyme to garnish

1 With a sharp knife, make 2 diagonal cuts through the skin and into the flesh on both sides of each trout.

2 Strip the thyme and parsley leaves from their stalks. In a bowl, combine the mushrooms, shallots, white wine vinegar, orange zest and juice, thyme and parsley leaves, and salt and pepper to taste.

3 Reserve one-quarter of the mushroom and herb mixture to spoon over the stuffed trout.

4 Stuff the trout with the remaining mushroom and herb mixture (see box, below).

5 Arrange the trout in a non-metallic baking dish and spoon over the reserved mushroom mixture. Cover and marinate in the refrigerator for up to 4 hours.

6 Bake in a preheated oven at 180°C (350°F, Gas 4) for 20–25 minutes until the fish is opaque and the flesh flakes easily. Garnish with orange and thyme before serving.

Stuffing the trout

Hold the fish open, spoon in one-quarter of the mushroom and herb mixture, then press firmly closed.

TUNA WITH FENNEL & TOMATO RELISH

SERVES 4

4 tbsp olive oil

juice of 1/2 lemon

3 garlic cloves, crushed

4 x 175 g (6 oz) tuna steaks, about 2.5 cm (1 in) thick

salt and black pepper

lime wedges and fennel tops to garnish

FENNEL AND TOMATO RELISH

1 small fennel bulb, chopped

2 ripe but firm tomatoes, finely chopped

2 tbsp olive oil

1 tbsp lemon juice

1 tbsp tapenade (see box, right)

1 garlic clove, chopped

1 Combine the olive oil, lemon juice, and garlic in a large non-metallic dish. Add the tuna steaks and turn to coat. Cover dish and leave to marinate in the refrigerator, turning occasionally, for about 1 hour.

2 Meanwhile, make the relish: put the fennel, tomatoes, olive oil, lemon juice, tapenade, and garlic into a bowl, and stir well to combine.

3 Remove the tuna from the marinade, reserving the marinade. Cook the tuna under a hot grill, 7 cm (3 in) from the heat, basting once or twice with the reserved marinade, for 3–4 minutes on each side.

4 Season the tuna with salt and pepper, and top with the fennel and tomato relish. Garnish with lime wedges and fennel tops before serving.

Cook's know-how

Tapenade comes from Provence in the south of France. It is a tangy paste made of typical Provençal ingredients – black olives, anchovies, capers, and fruity olive oil. It is sold in tubes, jars and tubs at supermarkets.

TUNA TERIYAKI

SERVES 4

4 x 175 g (6 oz) tuna steaks, about 2.5 cm (1 in) thick

2 spring onions, thinly sliced, to garnish

MARINADE

3 tbsp dark soy sauce

2 tbsp sesame oil

1 tbsp Japanese rice wine or sweet sherry

3 garlic cloves, chopped

1 tbsp caster sugar

1 cm (1/2 in) piece of fresh root ginger, peeled and grated

1 Make the marinade: put the soy sauce, sesame oil, rice wine, garlic, sugar, and ginger into a non-metallic dish. Add the tuna steaks to the marinade and turn to coat. Cover dish and marinate in the refrigerator for up to 4 hours.

2 Reserve the marinade. Cook the steaks under a hot grill, 7 cm (3 in) from the heat, brushing with the marinade, for 3–4 minutes on each side. Serve at once, garnished with spring onions.

BARBECUED SALMON TERIYAKI

Cut 4 salmon fillets into 2.5 cm (1 in) cubes and marinate in the refrigerator for up to 4 hours, as in step 1, then thread on to kebab skewers. Cook over a hot barbecue, turning and brushing frequently with the marinade, for 6–8 minutes.

Healthy note

Fresh root ginger, a key ingredient in Asian cooking, is known to have healing properties. It helps stimulate the circulation, fights coughs and colds, and relieves indigestion. It may also relieve rheumatism.

SWORDFISH WITH ORANGE RELISH

SERVES 4

4 x 175 g (6 oz) swordfish steaks

MARINADE

3 tbsp olive oil

juice of 1 orange

juice of 1 lemon

3 garlic cloves, crushed

salt and black pepper

ORANGE RELISH

2 oranges, peeled, separated into segments, and diced

3 tbsp olive oil

2 tbsp chopped fresh basil

1 Make the marinade: in a shallow non-metallic dish, combine the olive oil, orange and lemon juices, and garlic, and season with salt and pepper. Turn the swordfish steaks in the marinade, cover, and leave to marinate in the refrigerator for about 1 hour.

2 Make the orange relish: in a bowl, combine the oranges, olive oil, basil, and season with salt and pepper to taste.

3 Remove the swordfish from the marinade, reserving the marinade. Place the steaks under a hot grill, 7 cm (3 in) from the heat, and grill, basting once or twice with the marinade, for 5 minutes on each side or until the flesh is opaque and flakes easily. Serve hot, with the relish.

TUNA WITH ORANGE RELISH

Substitute tuna steaks for the swordfish steaks, and fresh coriander for the basil.

Cook's know-how

When marinating fish, leave it for no more than 4 hours. After this time the acid in the marinade will start to seep deep into the fish, which will make it dry when it is cooked.

SHARK WITH TROPICAL SALSA

SERVES 4

4 x 175 g (6 oz) shark steaks

MARINADE

125 ml (4 fl oz) olive oil

juice of 1/2 lemon

3 garlic cloves, crushed

1 tbsp chopped fresh coriander

1 tsp ground cumin

pinch of cayenne pepper

salt and black pepper

TROPICAL SALSA

1 x 275 g (9 oz) can pineapple pieces in natural juices, drained

1 small ripe papaya or mango, peeled, seeded or stoned, and diced

1 small red pepper, halved, seeded, and diced

1 mild fresh red or green chilli, halved, seeded, and diced

2 tbsp chopped fresh coriander

1 tbsp white wine vinegar

sugar (optional)

1 Make the marinade: in a non-metallic dish, combine the oil, lemon juice, garlic, coriander, cumin, and cayenne. Season with salt and pepper.

2 Turn the shark steaks in the marinade, cover, and marinate in the refrigerator for about 1 hour.

3 Make the tropical salsa: in a large bowl, combine the pineapple, papaya or mango, red pepper, chilli, coriander, and vinegar. Season with salt and pepper. If the fruit is sour, add a little sugar.

4 Remove the steaks from the marinade, reserving the marinade. Place the steaks under a hot grill, 7 cm (3 in) from the heat, basting once or twice with the marinade, for 3–4 minutes on each side until the flesh is opaque and flakes easily. Serve hot, with the salsa.

Cook's know-how

Try this cranberry and orange salsa instead of the tropical salsa. Peel, segment, and finely chop 1 orange. Mix with 250 g (8 oz) chopped cranberries and 125 g (4 oz) sugar. Serve chilled, with the hot fish.

KOULIBIAC

This is a type of salmon kedgeree enclosed in crisp puff pastry, which makes an impressive dish for a dinner party or other special occasion. In Russia, its country of origin, there is a saying, "Houses make a fine street, pies make a fine table".

SERVES 8–10

75 g (2½ oz) long grain rice

salt and black pepper

60 g (2 oz) butter, plus extra for greasing

1 large onion, chopped

1 x 400 g (13 oz) can chopped tomatoes, drained

500 g (1 lb) fresh salmon fillets, cooked and flaked

2 tbsp chopped parsley

grated zest and juice of 1 lemon

500 g (1 lb) puff pastry

1 egg, beaten

60 g (2 oz) butter, melted, and juice of ½ lemon to serve

lemon twists and watercress sprigs to garnish

1 Cook the rice in boiling salted water for 12 minutes or until just tender.

2 Meanwhile, melt the butter in a saucepan, add the onion, and cook very gently for about 10 minutes until soft but not coloured. Add the tomatoes and cook for 15 minutes. Leave to cool.

3 Drain the rice thoroughly, and combine with the onion and tomato mixture, the flaked salmon, parsley, and lemon zest and juice. Season with salt and pepper.

4 Roll out 425 g (14 oz) of the puff pastry into a 28 x 40 cm (11 x 16 in) rectangle.

5 Arrange the salmon mixture down the middle of the rectangle, leaving a 7 cm (3 in) border on each side. Brush the border with a little of the beaten egg, and wrap and decorate the koulibiac (see box, right).

6 Bake the koulibiac in a preheated oven at 220°C (425°F, Gas 7) for 30–45 minutes until golden.

7 Transfer to a warmed serving dish, and pour the melted butter and lemon juice into the cuts. Serve in thick slices, garnished with lemon twists and watercress.

Wrapping and decorating the koulibiac

Fold the shortest ends of pastry over the salmon filling and brush the top of the folded pastry with beaten egg.

Fold the longest sides over the filling to make a long parcel. Turn the parcel over and place on a lightly buttered baking tray. Brush all over with beaten egg.

Make 2 decorative cuts in the top of the pastry. Roll the remaining pastry into a 5 x 30 cm (2 x 12 in) piece, trim, then cut into 3 equal strips. Press the ends together and plait the strips. Lay the plait down the middle of the parcel, and glaze with beaten egg.

SEVERN SALMON

SERVES 6

6 x 175 g (6 oz) salmon steaks

butter for greasing

salt and black pepper

watercress sprigs to garnish

WATERCRESS SAUCE

300 ml (1/2 pint) single cream

60 g (2 oz) watercress, trimmed

90 g (3 oz) butter, melted

1 tsp plain flour

juice of 1 lemon

1 egg yolk

Cook's know-how

You can vary this recipe by using boneless salmon fillets instead of steaks. They usually weigh about 150 g (5 oz), and can be chargrilled or pan-fried with a little oil – they will take 10 minutes at the most. Instead of watercress, you can use a small bunch of fresh dill or tarragon.

---

1 Arrange the salmon steaks in a single layer in a buttered roasting tin, and sprinkle with black pepper.

2 Cover tightly with foil, and bake in a preheated oven at 180°C (350°F, Gas 4) for 15 minutes or until the fish is opaque and flakes easily.

3 Meanwhile, make the watercress sauce: put the cream, watercress, butter, flour, lemon juice, and egg yolk into a food processor, season with salt and pepper, and purée until smooth.

4 Transfer the cream and watercress mixture to a small saucepan, and cook over a gentle heat, stirring, until the sauce thickens. Taste for seasoning.

5 Serve the salmon hot on a pool of watercress sauce, garnished with fresh sprigs of watercress.

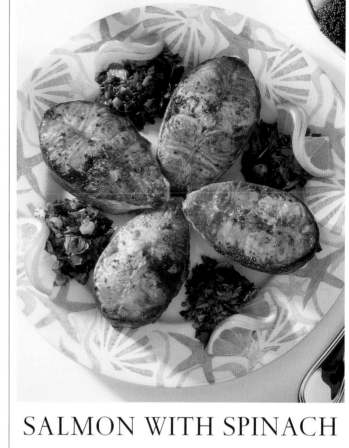

SALMON WITH SPINACH

SERVES 4

4 x 175 g (6 oz) salmon steaks

salt and black pepper

15 g (1/2 oz) butter

lemon twists to garnish

SPINACH SALSA

2 tbsp olive oil

8 spring onions, finely sliced

1 garlic clove, crushed

4 tbsp lemon juice

1 tsp wholegrain mustard

500 g (1 lb) spinach, finely chopped

Healthy note

Spinach is not as rich in iron as was previously thought, although it does contain a useful source. One of its main benefits to good health is that it contains a phytochemical called lutein, an antioxidant that can help protect against age-related degeneration of eyesight.

---

1 Season the salmon steaks with black pepper and dot with the butter.

2 Cook the salmon steaks under a hot grill, 7 cm (3 in) from the heat, for 2–3 minutes on each side until the fish is opaque and the flesh flakes easily. Leave to rest.

3 Make the spinach salsa: heat the oil in a frying pan, add the spring onions and garlic, and cook, stirring, for about 1 minute. Stir in the lemon juice, mustard, and spinach, and cook, stirring, for about 2 minutes. Transfer to a bowl, and season with salt and pepper.

4 Garnish the salmon with lemon twists and serve at once, with the salsa.

SALMON EN CROUTE

SERVES 8

1.7–2 kg (3½–4 lb) salmon, cleaned and filleted (page 123), then cut lengthwise in half and skinned

1 tbsp chopped fresh dill

grated zest and juice of 1 lemon

salt and black pepper

30 g (1 oz) butter

8 spring onions, sliced

250 g (8 oz) spinach, coarsely shredded

250 g (8 oz) low-fat soft cheese

plain flour for dusting

750 g (1½ lb) puff pastry

1 egg, beaten

lemon slices, cherry tomatoes, and parsley sprigs to garnish

1 Put the 2 pieces of salmon into a shallow non-metallic dish and sprinkle with the dill, lemon zest and juice, and salt and pepper. Cover and leave to marinate in the refrigerator for about 1 hour.

2 Melt the butter in a small pan, add the onions, and cook gently for 2–3 minutes until soft but not coloured. Remove from the heat.

3 Add the spinach, toss in the butter, then leave to cool. Stir in the cheese, and season with salt and pepper.

4 Roll out half of the pastry on a lightly floured surface to a 20 x 38 cm (8 x 15 in) rectangle. Put the pastry on a baking tray, and place 1 salmon fillet, skinned side down, on top. Spread with the spinach mixture, then put the second salmon fillet on top, skinned side up. Brush the pastry border with a little beaten egg.

5 Roll out the remaining pastry to a slightly larger rectangle, cover the salmon completely, then trim and seal the edges. Make "scales" on the top with the edge of a spoon, then make 2 small holes to let steam escape during baking.

6 Brush with beaten egg and bake in a preheated oven at 200°C (400°F, Gas 6) for 40–45 minutes until the pastry is risen and golden brown. Serve hot, garnished with lemon, tomatoes, and parsley.

SALMON WITH AVOCADO

SERVES 4

30 g (1 oz) butter, melted

4 x 175 g (6 oz) salmon steaks

salt and black pepper

4 tarragon sprigs

4 slices of lime

AVOCADO SAUCE

2 avocados, halved, stoned (page 88), and peeled

150 ml (¼ pint) plain yogurt

grated zest and juice of 1 lime

1 Brush 4 large squares of foil with melted butter. Put a salmon steak on each square, season, and top with a tarragon sprig and a slice of lime. Wrap the foil around the salmon. Put on a baking tray, and bake in a preheated oven at 150°C (300°F, Gas 2) for 25 minutes or until the fish is opaque and the flesh flakes easily.

2 Meanwhile, make the avocado sauce: put the flesh of 1 avocado into a food processor with the yogurt, and lime zest and juice. Season with salt and pepper and purée until smooth. Transfer to a serving bowl. Dice the remaining avocado, and stir into the sauce.

3 Unwrap the salmon, transfer to warmed serving plates, and serve with the avocado sauce.

CLASSIC BUFFET PARTY SALMON

This is the perfect dish for a buffet party. The salmon is gently poached, with the skin and head for added flavour, and left to cool in the cooking liquid to keep it moist. Fish kettles can be hired from some fishmongers or the fish counters of some supermarkets,

SERVES 10

2.75 kg (5½ lb) salmon, cleaned (page 123)

salt and black peppercorns

4 bay leaves

1 onion, sliced

4 tbsp white wine vinegar

3 tbsp chopped fresh dill

about 200 ml (7 fl oz) mayonnaise (page 372)

TO GARNISH

about 14 cooked jumbo prawns, tail shells taken off but heads left on

1–2 bunches of fresh dill

lemon wedges or slices

FISH KETTLE

1 Lift out the rack from the fish kettle and set aside. Half fill the kettle with cold water and add 2 tbsp salt, 12 black peppercorns, the bay leaves, onion, and vinegar.

2 Put the salmon on to the rack, and lower into the kettle. Bring to a boil, then simmer for 1 minute only. Remove from the heat, cover, and leave to stand for about 2 hours, until the fish is just warm.

3 Lift the rack and salmon out of the fish kettle. Strain the cooking liquid and reserve. Cover the salmon with a large piece of cling film and flip the fish over on to the cling film. Bone and skin the salmon (see box, below). Cover and chill in the refrigerator for at least 1 hour.

4 Mix the dill into the mayonnaise, then taste for seasoning. Spoon into a serving bowl, and chill until ready to serve.

5 Arrange the prawns in a line along the middle of the salmon so that the heads are facing in opposite directions (this will hide the line where the backbone was). The number of prawns will depend on the length of your salmon, so buy extra just in case – you can always use any leftover prawns around the edge of the plate as an extra garnish.

6 Arrange dill sprigs around the edge of the salmon and on the plate, together with lemon slices or wedges. Serve with the dill mayonnaise.

Boning and skinning a salmon

1 Using a chef's knife, neatly remove the head from the salmon.

2 Run the knife along the backbone of the fish to loosen the top fillet.

3 Flip the top fillet over and remove the bones from the fish.

4 Use the cling film to flip the bottom fillet back on to the top and remove the skin and any dark flesh.

5 Use the cling film to flip the fish on to a large serving plate, and remove the remaining skin.

6 With a small knife, gently scrape away the brownish flesh, leaving behind only the pink flesh.

FILLETS OF SOLE MENUIERE

SERVES 4

60 g (2 oz) plain flour

salt and black pepper

4 small lemon sole, each cut into 4 fillets and skinned (see box, right)

60 g (2 oz) butter

1 tbsp chopped parsley

juice of 1/2 lemon

lemon slices and parsley sprigs to garnish

1 Sprinkle the flour on to a plate and season with salt and pepper. Dip the 16 fillets into the seasoned flour and shake off any excess.

2 Melt half of the butter in a large frying pan. When it is foaming, add the fillets, and cook for 2 minutes on each side or until the flesh is opaque and flakes easily. Transfer to warmed serving plates and keep warm.

3 Wipe the pan with paper towels. Melt the remaining butter and heat quickly until golden. Stir in the parsley and lemon juice, then pour over the fillets. Serve hot, garnished with lemon and parsley.

Cook's know-how

You can fillet and skin the sole yourself (page 123), but your fishmonger will do it for free, and this will save a lot of time. Explain that you need "quarter" fillets from each sole, that is two slim fillets from each side of the fish. For a special occasion you can use Dover sole, sometimes described as the king of sole. It is less widely available than lemon sole, and more expensive, but the flavour is superb.

MUSHROOM-STUFFED SOLE FILLETS

SERVES 4

60 g (2 oz) butter

1 onion, finely chopped

375 g (12 oz) mushrooms, finely chopped

2 large lemon sole, each cut into 4 fillets and skinned (see box, below left)

250 ml (8 fl oz) dry white wine

2 tsp chopped fresh tarragon

salt and black pepper

250 ml (8 fl oz) double cream

squeeze of lemon juice

1 Melt half of the butter in a saucepan, add the onion and mushrooms, and cook gently for 5 minutes.

2 Roll the fillets (see box, right), with the skinned sides facing inwards. Stand them in a shallow baking dish, and fill with the mushrooms.

3 Add the wine, tarragon, and salt and pepper to taste. Cover and bake in a preheated oven at 180°C (350°F, Gas 4) for 15 minutes or until the fish is opaque and flakes easily.

4 Remove the fish from the dish and keep warm. Pour the juices into a saucepan and boil for 3 minutes or until reduced by half. Stir in the cream and lemon juice, heat through gently, and taste for seasoning before serving.

Rolling the fillets

Bring round the 2 ends of each fillet to form a circle, with the smaller tail end on the outside.

Thread a wooden cocktail stick through both ends of each fillet, to secure.

LEMON SOLE FLORENTINE

Fillets of lemon sole are topped with a cheese sauce and baked on a bed of spinach, so they stay moist while cooking. Slices of hot lemon bread – an interesting variation of garlic bread – make an unusual accompaniment.

SERVES 4

4 large lemon sole, each cut into 4 fillets and skinned (see box, opposite page)

juice of 1/2 lemon

salt and black pepper

45 g (1 1/2 oz) butter

45 g (1 1/2 oz) plain flour

450 ml (3/4 pint) milk

750 g (1 1/2 lb) spinach

30 g (1 oz) Parmesan cheese, grated

hot lemon bread to serve (see box, below)

1 Sprinkle the lemon sole fillets with the lemon juice and salt and pepper. Fold the fillets in half widthways, and set aside.

2 Melt the butter in a saucepan, add the flour, and cook, stirring, for 1 minute. Remove from the heat and gradually blend in the milk. Bring to a boil, stirring constantly until the white sauce mixture thickens. Simmer for 2–3 minutes, then add salt and pepper to taste.

3 Wash the spinach and put into a pan with only the water remaining on the leaves. Cook for 2 minutes or until wilted. Drain well.

4 Stir half of the sauce into the cooked spinach and spoon into a shallow ovenproof dish. Arrange the sole on top. Pour the remaining sauce over the top and sprinkle with the cheese. Bake in a preheated oven at 200°C (400°F, Gas 6) for 30 minutes. Serve hot, with hot lemon bread.

Hot lemon bread

Beat the grated zest of 1/2 lemon into 125 g (4 oz) softened butter, using a fork. Work in the juice of 1/2 lemon, and salt and pepper to taste.

Cut 1 baguette into 1 cm (1/2 in) slices, leaving the slices attached underneath.

Spread the butter in between the slices, and a little on top. Wrap in foil and bake in a preheated oven at 200°C (400°F, Gas 6) for 20 minutes, opening the foil for the last 5 minutes to crisp the top.

GINGERED PLAICE

SERVES 4

4 large plaice fillets

spring onions to garnish (optional)

GINGER MARINADE

2.5 cm (1 in) piece of fresh root ginger, peeled and finely sliced

1 large garlic clove, sliced

2 tbsp sunflower oil

1 tbsp sesame oil

1 tbsp dry sherry

1 tbsp sherry vinegar

2 tsp light soy sauce

1 Put the plaice fillets into a shallow non-metallic dish.

2 Make the marinade: combine the ginger, garlic, sunflower and sesame oils, sherry, sherry vinegar, and soy sauce, and pour over the fish.

3 Cover the fish and leave to marinate in the refrigerator, turning once, for 30 minutes.

4 Grill the fillets, skin-side down, under a hot grill, 7 cm (3 in) from the heat, for 4–5 minutes, until the fish is opaque and flakes easily. Serve hot, garnished with spring onions if you like.

BEST-EVER FRIED FISH

These plaice fillets are shallow-fried in a crisp coating of fresh breadcrumbs. This is far superior to a batter coating in both flavour and texture, and it protects the fish from the heat of the fat and keeps it moist, in the same way as batter.

SERVES 4

3 tbsp plain flour

salt and black pepper

I large egg, beaten

30 g (I oz) fresh white breadcrumbs

4 large plaice fillets, skinned

2 tbsp sunflower oil

lemon wedges to garnish

1 Sprinkle the flour into a shallow dish and season with salt and pepper. Pour the beaten egg into another dish, and sprinkle the breadcrumbs into a third.

2 Lightly coat the fish fillets with breadcrumbs (see box, below).

3 Heat the oil in a large frying pan, add the coated fillets, in 2 batches if necessary, and fry over a high heat for 2–3 minutes on each side until they are crisp, golden, and juicy inside.

4 Lift the fillets out of the frying pan with a fish slice and then leave to drain briefly on paper towels. Serve the fish at once, garnished with the lemon wedges.

SAUCES FOR FISH

DILL CREAM SAUCE

Purée 300 ml (1/2 pint) single cream, 90 g (3 oz) butter, I egg yolk, the juice of I lemon, and I tsp plain flour in a food processor until smooth. Transfer the mixture to a small saucepan and heat very gently, stirring constantly, until the sauce has thickened and will coat the back of a spoon. Add salt and pepper to taste, then stir in 2 tbsp chopped fresh dill and I tbsp snipped fresh chives.

TARTARE SAUCE

Purée I egg, 1 1/2 tsp sugar, 1/2 tsp mustard powder, and salt and pepper to taste in a food processor or blender until smooth. Add 300 ml (1/2 pint) sunflower oil, pouring in a steady stream, and purée until the mixture is very thick and all of the oil has been incorporated. Add the juice of I lemon, and purée. Transfer to a bowl, and stir in I tbsp each chopped gherkins, capers, and parsley, and 2 tbsp chopped fresh tarragon. Cover and leave to stand for at least I hour to allow the flavours to blend.

Coating a fish fillet

Dip the fillet into the seasoned flour, to coat. Shake off any excess.

Dip the floured fillet into the beaten egg, letting any excess drain off.

Dip the fillet into the breadcrumbs, making sure it is evenly coated.

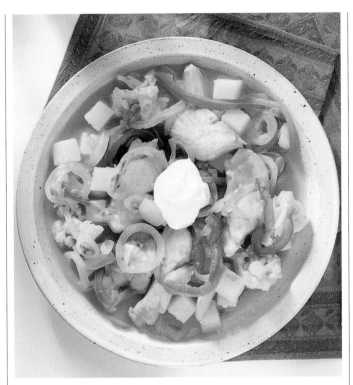

INDIAN SPICED HADDOCK

SERVES 4

750 g (1 1/2 lb) thick pieces of haddock fillet, skinned

1 tsp ground cumin

1 tsp ground coriander

pinch of cayenne pepper

1/4 tsp turmeric

1 tsp salt

2 tbsp sunflower oil

1 small onion, sliced

2.5 cm (1 in) piece of fresh root ginger, peeled and grated

1 fresh green chilli, halved, seeded, and finely chopped

1 small cauliflower, cut into small florets

2 potatoes, diced

1 large green pepper, halved, seeded, and cut into strips

150 ml (1/4 pint) water

black pepper

low-fat plain yogurt to serve

1 Cut the haddock into 5 cm (2 in) squares and put them into a bowl.

2 Mix the spices and salt together, sprinkle over the haddock, and stir to coat evenly. Cover, and chill in the refrigerator for about 1 hour.

3 Heat half of the oil in a frying pan, add the onion, and cook over a high heat for 5 minutes. Stir in the ginger and chilli and cook for 2 minutes. Add the cauliflower, potatoes, and green pepper and cook for 5–7 minutes. Remove the vegetables with a slotted spoon and set aside.

4 Heat the remaining oil, add the haddock and brown lightly all over. Add the cooked vegetables and measured water, and simmer for 10 minutes or until the fish is cooked and the vegetables are tender. Taste for seasoning. Serve hot, with yogurt.

HADDOCK WITH MUSHROOMS & CREAM

SERVES 4–6

300 ml (1/2 pint) milk

1 slice of onion

6 black peppercorns

1 bay leaf

60 g (2 oz) butter, plus extra for greasing

750 g (1 1/2 lb) haddock fillet, skinned

salt and black pepper

squeeze of lemon juice

250 g (8 oz) button mushrooms, sliced

30 g (1 oz) plain flour

3 tbsp single cream (optional)

30 g (1 oz) fresh white breadcrumbs

30 g (1 oz) Parmesan cheese, grated

chopped parsley to garnish

1 Put the milk into a small saucepan with the onion, peppercorns, and bay leaf, and bring just to a boil. Remove from the heat, cover, and leave to infuse for 10 minutes. Lightly butter a shallow ovenproof dish.

2 Cut the haddock into 7 cm (3 in) pieces, and place in a single layer in the dish. Sprinkle with salt and pepper.

3 Melt half of the butter in a saucepan, add the lemon juice and mushrooms, and season with salt and pepper. Cook gently, stirring occasionally, for 3 minutes or until just tender. Remove the mushrooms with a slotted spoon and put them on top of the fish.

4 Strain the infused milk and set aside. Melt the remaining butter in a saucepan, add the flour, and cook, stirring, for 1 minute. Remove from the heat and gradually blend in the infused milk. Bring to a boil, stirring until the mixture thickens. Simmer for 2–3 minutes. Stir in the cream, if using, and season with salt and pepper.

5 Pour the sauce over the fish and mushrooms, then sprinkle with the breadcrumbs and Parmesan. Bake in a preheated oven at 190°C (375°F, Gas 5) for 25–30 minutes until the fish is cooked and the top is golden and bubbling. Garnish with parsley, and serve at once.

ROAST MONKFISH NIÇOISE

SERVES 4

3 tbsp olive oil

1 head of garlic, separated

1 lemon, thickly sliced

500 g (1 lb) monkfish fillets, skinned and cut into chunky pieces

1 tsp dried herbes de Provence or mixed herbs

250 ml (8 fl oz) dry white wine

125 ml (4 fl oz) fish stock

1 x 400 g (13 oz) can artichoke hearts, drained and rinsed

15 pitted black olives

10 sun-dried tomatoes in oil, drained

squeeze of lemon juice

salt and black pepper

lemon wedges and thyme sprigs to garnish

1 Put 1 tbsp of the oil into an ovenproof dish, add the garlic cloves, and roast in a preheated oven at 190°C (375°F, Gas 5) for about 10 minutes until softened.

2 Arrange the lemon slices in the dish, and put the garlic and monkfish on top.

3 Sprinkle with the remaining oil and the herbs, and pour in the wine and stock. Return to the oven for 10 minutes.

4 Add the artichoke hearts, olives, and sun-dried tomatoes, and cook for 5 minutes to heat through.

5 Transfer the fish and vegetables to a serving dish, discarding the lemon slices. Keep warm.

6 Pour the cooking juices into a small saucepan, and boil for about 8 minutes until reduced to about 125 ml (4 fl oz). Add the lemon juice, season with salt and pepper, and pour over the fish. Garnish with lemon and thyme, and serve at once.

ROAST MONKFISH BASQUAISE

Instead of the artichokes, use 2 peppers (1 red and 1 yellow), halved, seeded, and cut into strips, and roast with the garlic cloves.

MONKFISH WITH GINGER-ORANGE SAUCE

SERVES 4

1 orange, washed and thinly sliced

1 onion, chopped

1 cm (1/2 in) piece of fresh root ginger, peeled and grated

500 g (1 lb) monkfish fillets, skinned

250 ml (8 fl oz) fish stock

grated zest of 1/2 lime

75 ml (2 1/2 fl oz) lime juice

salt and cayenne pepper

60 g (2 oz) unsalted butter, chilled and cubed

sugar or honey to taste (optional)

orange and snipped chives to garnish

1 Put the orange slices, onion, and ginger into a pan. Add the monkfish, spring onions, and stock. Bring to a boil, and simmer, without stirring, for 10 minutes or until the fish is firm. With a slotted spoon, transfer the fish to a serving dish. Keep hot.

2 Put a sieve over a bowl, tip in the remaining contents of the pan and press hard with the back of a spoon to extract all the juices.

3 Pour the juices into a small saucepan and boil rapidly, uncovered, for about 12 minutes until the liquid has reduced to about 2 tbsp.

4 Add the lime zest and juice, season with salt and cayenne, and heat gently, stirring, until warm. Remove from the heat and finish the sauce (see box, below).

5 Pour the sauce over the fish, garnish, and serve at once.

Finishing the sauce

Add the cubes of butter one at a time, whisking between each addition until the butter melts. The sauce will become glossy at the end. Taste, and add a little sugar or honey if you like.

MONKFISH KEBABS

SERVES 4

500 g (1 lb) monkfish fillets, skinned

4 tbsp olive oil

grated zest and juice of 1 large lemon

1 tbsp chopped fresh dill

salt and black pepper

1/2 cucumber

30 g (1 oz) butter

12 fresh bay leaves

2 lemons, sliced

dill sprigs to garnish

1 Cut the monkfish fillets into 2.5 cm (1 in) pieces and put them into a bowl. Whisk together the olive oil, lemon zest and juice, and dill. Season with salt and pepper, then pour over the fish. Cover and leave to marinate in the refrigerator for up to 4 hours.

2 Peel the cucumber, and cut it in half lengthwise. Scoop out the seeds from each half, and cut the flesh across into 2 cm (3/4 in) slices. Melt the butter in a small saucepan, add the cucumber slices, and cook gently for 1 minute or until they begin to soften.

3 Lift the monkfish out of the marinade with a slotted spoon, reserving the marinade. Thread the kebabs (see box, below).

4 Brush the kebabs with marinade, and put under a hot grill, 7 cm (3 in) from the heat. Cook the kebabs, brushing them occasionally with the marinade, for 5–6 minutes on each side until the fish is cooked through. Serve at once, garnished with dill sprigs.

Threading the kebabs

Push a piece of fish and a fresh bay leaf on to a kebab skewer. Fold a lemon slice around a cucumber slice and push on to the skewer. Keep threading the fish, bay leaves, and lemon and cucumber in turn until 4 skewers are evenly filled.

SPICED FISH WITH COCONUT

SERVES 4

750 g (1 1/2 lb) monkfish fillets, skinned

30 g (1 oz) plain flour

salt and black pepper

2 tbsp sunflower oil

1 onion, finely sliced

1 garlic clove, crushed

1 tsp ground coriander

1 tsp ground cumin

1/2 tsp turmeric

150 ml (1/4 pint) canned coconut milk

1 x 400 g (13 oz) can chopped tomatoes

3 tbsp chopped fresh coriander

coriander sprigs to garnish

1 Cut the monkfish into 5 cm (2 in) pieces. Season the flour with salt and pepper. Lightly coat the monkfish with the flour.

2 Heat the oil in a large frying pan, add the onion, garlic, coriander, cumin, and turmeric, and cook gently, stirring from time to time, for 3 minutes or until the onion begins to soften.

3 Pour in the coconut milk and tomatoes, stir well, and bring to a boil. Simmer for about 5 minutes.

4 Add the monkfish, cover, and cook gently, stirring occasionally, for 10 minutes or until the fish is opaque and the flesh flakes easily. Add the chopped coriander, and taste for seasoning. Serve hot, garnished with coriander sprigs.

FRESH WAYS WITH SALMON FILLETS

Fresh salmon is inexpensive and available all year round, either wild or farmed. Quick, easy and light, these four recipes using salmon fillets can all be prepared in advance, making them perfect stress-free main courses for dinner parties.

HERB ROASTED SALMON

SERVES 4

4 x 150 g (5 oz) salmon tail fillets, skinned

salt and black pepper

a little vegetable oil

125 g (4 oz) low-fat garlic and herb soft cheese

TOPPING

30 g (1 oz) fresh white breadcrumbs

30 g (1 oz) mature Cheddar cheese, grated

2 tbsp chopped fresh flat-leaf parsley

finely grated zest of 1 lime

TO SERVE

lemon wedges

flat-leaf parsley sprigs

1 Season the salmon on both sides with salt and pepper. Place on lightly oiled foil on a baking sheet and spread with the soft cheese, not going quite to the edges.

2 Mix the topping ingredients together, adding seasoning to taste, then sprinkle over the salmon. (You can prepare ahead to this stage, cover the salmon, and keep it in the refrigerator for up to 12 hours.)

3 Cook in a preheated oven at 220°C (425°F, Gas 7) for 15 minutes or until the salmon is opaque and the flesh flakes easily. Garnish with lemon and parsley.

THAI CHILLI SALMON

SERVES 4

4 x 150–175 g (5–6 oz) middle-cut salmon fillets, skinned

MARINADE

2 tbsp fish sauce (nam pla)

finely grated zest and juice of 1 lime

1 large fresh red chilli, halved, seeded, and finely chopped

2.5 cm (1 in) piece of fresh root ginger, peeled and finely grated

a few fresh coriander stems, finely chopped

TO SERVE

fresh coriander leaves

1 lime, cut into wedges

1 Put the salmon fillets in a single layer in a shallow non-metallic dish, add the marinade ingredients and turn to coat. Cover and marinate in the refrigerator for 2–3 hours, turning the salmon once.

2 Lift the salmon from the marinade and cook under a preheated hot grill, 7.5 cm (3 in) away from the heat, for 5–6 minutes on each side until the salmon is opaque and the flesh flakes easily. Serve hot, with coriander and lime.

GRIDDLED SALMON TRANCHES

SERVES 4

a little olive oil

4 x 150–175 g (5–6 oz) middle-cut salmon fillets, skinned

salt and black pepper

SAUCE

200 ml (7 fl oz) low-fat crème fraîche

about 5 cm (2 in) cucumber, peeled, seeded, and finely diced

4 tbsp chopped fresh dill

pinch of caster sugar

1 tbsp capers

a good squeeze of lemon juice

1 Heat a griddle pan until piping hot, and lightly oil a sheet of foil on a baking sheet. Lightly oil and season the salmon.

2 Cook the salmon in the hot pan on one side only for 1½ minutes until golden underneath. Transfer, cooked side up, to the foil and finish cooking in a preheated oven at 190°C (375°F, Gas 5) for about 10 minutes or until the salmon is opaque and the flesh flakes easily. Leave to cool.

3 Mix the sauce ingredients in a bowl with salt and pepper to taste. Cover and refrigerate. When the salmon is cold, cover and refrigerate too – for up to 12 hours.

4 To serve, let the salmon come to room temperature and serve with the chilled sauce spooned alongside.

WARM HONEYED SALMON SALAD

SERVES 4

4 x 150–175 g (5–6 oz) middle-cut salmon fillets, skinned

3 tbsp clear honey

1 tbsp olive oil

juice of 1 lemon

about 2 tbsp chopped fresh thyme

new potatoes, to serve

FOR THE SALAD

1 fennel bulb, thinly sliced

6 spring onions, thinly sliced

3 tbsp extra virgin olive oil

1 tbsp lemon juice

1 tbsp clear honey

4 tbsp Greek yogurt

salt and black pepper

1 Romaine lettuce, shredded

2 tbsp chopped parsley

2 tbsp snipped fresh chives

1 Make the salad. Mix the fennel and spring onions in a bowl with the olive oil, lemon juice, honey, yogurt and seasoning. Toss the lettuce in a separate large salad bowl with the chopped fresh herbs and seasoning. Cover both bowls and refrigerate for about 1 hour.

2 Cut each salmon fillet into four lengthways – they will look like flat sausages. Toss in the honey and season well. Heat the oil in a large non-stick frying pan and pan-fry the salmon over a high heat for 2–3 minutes on each side or until just opaque. Take care when turning the salmon as it breaks up quite easily. Add the lemon juice and thyme to the pan and heat until bubbling.

3 Toss the fennel salad through the lettuce, then spoon the honeyed salmon on top. Serve warm.

CLOCKWISE FROM TOP: Griddled Salmon Tranches, Warm Honeyed Salmon Salad, Herb Roasted Salmon, Thai Chilli Salmon.

CAJUN-SPICED RED SNAPPER

SERVES 4

4 x 150–175 g (5–6 oz) red snapper
   fillets

30 g (1 oz) butter

coriander butter (page 247) and
   watercress sprigs to serve

CAJUN SPICE MIXTURE

30 g (1 oz) plain flour

1 garlic clove, crushed

1 tbsp paprika

1 tsp ground cumin

1 tsp hot chilli powder

1 Make the Cajun spice
mixture: combine the flour,
garlic, paprika, cumin, and
chilli powder.

2 Rub over the red snapper
fillets, cover, and leave to
marinate in the refrigerator for
about 30 minutes.

3 Melt the butter in a large
frying pan, add the fillets,
and cook gently for 2–3
minutes on each side until the
fish is opaque and the flesh
flakes easily.

4 Top the fillets with pats of
coriander butter, garnish
with watercress, and serve hot.

Cook's know-how

You can buy ready mixed
Cajun seasoning, but it tends
to include dried garlic and
onion salt, both of which
overpower the spices in the
mix. This simple version uses
chilli powder, which is not just
ground dried chillies as its
name suggests, but a special
fiery mixture of chilli with
herbs and spices. Check the
label before buying.

COD STEAKS WITH ANCHOVY & FENNEL

SERVES 4

1 x 60 g (2 oz) can anchovy fillets

30 g (1 oz) butter, plus extra for
   greasing

1 small onion, finely chopped

1 small fennel bulb, finely chopped

30 g (1 oz) parsley, chopped

125 g (4 oz) fresh white
   breadcrumbs

salt and black pepper

4 x 250 g (8 oz) cod steaks

dill sprigs, lemon wedges, and
   watercress sprigs to garnish

1 Drain the anchovy fillets,
reserving the oil. Cut the
anchovies into small pieces and
set aside.

2 Melt the butter in a pan,
add the onion and fennel,
and cook over a medium heat,
stirring, for 5 minutes or until
soft but not browned. Remove
from the heat, stir in the
anchovies, parsley, and
breadcrumbs. Season with salt
and pepper.

3 Put the cod steaks into a
buttered ovenproof dish and
top each one with the anchovy
and fennel mixture, pressing it
down firmly with your hand.

4 Drizzle a little of the
reserved anchovy oil over
each steak. Bake the steaks in a
preheated oven at 200°C
(400°F, Gas 6) for 10–15
minutes until the cod is opaque
and the flesh flakes easily from
the bone.

5 Transfer to a warmed
serving plate. Garnish the
cod steaks with dill sprigs,
lemon wedges, and watercress
sprigs, and serve at once.

COD STEAKS WITH SUN-DRIED TOMATOES

Omit the anchovies, fennel,
parsley, and breadcrumbs. Chop
4 ripe but firm tomatoes. Drain
30 g (1 oz) sun-dried tomatoes in
oil, and snip them into small
pieces. Add both types of tomato
to the softened onion in step 2,
with 12 pitted and chopped black
olives. Season with salt and pepper.
Drizzle the cod steaks with 1 tbsp
olive oil, top with the tomato
mixture, and bake as in step 4.

CHEESE-TOPPED BAKED BREAM

SERVES 4

2 x 560 g (1 lb 2 oz) black bream, filleted and skinned

grated zest and juice of 1/2 lemon

salt and black pepper

150 ml (1/4 pint) water

butter for greasing

30 g (1 oz) mature Cheddar cheese, grated

lemon zest and parsley sprigs to garnish

WHITE SAUCE

30 g (1 oz) butter

1 tbsp plain flour

150 ml (1/4 pint) milk

1 Cut the black bream fillets in half lengthwise, and arrange them in a single layer in a large ovenproof dish.

2 Sprinkle the fish evenly with the grated lemon zest and season with salt and pepper. Pour the lemon juice and measured water over the fish fillets. Cover the dish with buttered greaseproof paper.

3 Bake in a preheated oven at 160°C (325°F, Gas 3) for about 20 minutes until the flesh flakes easily.

4 Transfer the bream to a warmed flameproof platter, cover, and keep hot. Strain the cooking liquid and reserve. Increase the oven temperature to 220°C (425°F, Gas 7).

5 Make the white sauce: melt the butter in a small saucepan, add the flour, and cook, stirring, for 1 minute. Remove from the heat, and gradually blend in the milk and the reserved cooking liquid. Bring to a boil, stirring constantly until the mixture thickens. Simmer for 2–3 minutes. Taste for seasoning.

6 Pour the white sauce over the fish, sprinkle with the cheese, and bake in the oven for 3–5 minutes until bubbling and golden. Serve hot, garnished with lemon zest and parsley sprigs.

BLACK BREAM NIÇOISE

SERVES 4

2 x 560 g (1 lb 2 oz) black bream, cleaned (page 122), with heads removed

salt and black pepper

3 tbsp olive oil

1 large onion, sliced

1 small fennel bulb, sliced

1 garlic clove, crushed

12 pitted black olives

2 tbsp chopped parsley

juice of 1 lemon

lemon segments and parsley sprigs to garnish

1 Prepare the bream (see box, below).

2 Heat 2 tbsp of the oil in a frying pan, add the onion, fennel, and garlic, and cook gently, stirring occasionally, for 5–8 minutes until the vegetables are soft but not coloured.

3 Spoon the vegetables into an ovenproof dish, and place the bream on top. Scatter the olives and parsley over the fish, sprinkle with the lemon juice, and drizzle with the remaining olive oil.

4 Cover the fish loosely with foil, and bake in a preheated oven at 200°C (400°F, Gas 6) for 15 minutes.

5 Remove the foil and bake for 10 minutes or until the fish is cooked. Garnish with lemon segments and parsley sprigs before serving.

Healthy note

Slashing whole fish through the skin deep into the flesh is not just to make it look more attractive. It allows the fish to cook quicker, which helps retain juices and nutrients.

Preparing the bream

Make 2 deep diagonal cuts in the flesh on both sides of each bream, using a sharp knife.

Put salt and pepper into a bowl and combine. Sprinkle on the inside and outside of the bream.

HALIBUT IN FILO PARCELS

Halibut is a very fine fish with a delicate flavour and firm texture. Enclosing the halibut steaks in filo parcels with matchstick-thin vegetables keeps the fish moist and seals in all the flavours, while the pastry trimmings on top provide an attractive, crunchy finish.

SERVES 4

2 x 375 g (12 oz) halibut steaks, skinned and boned

1 carrot

1 leek, trimmed

150 ml (1/4 pint) fish stock

2 tbsp dry white wine

2 tsp lemon juice

3 strands of saffron or 1/4 tsp turmeric

salt and black pepper

8 large sheets of filo pastry

60 g (2 oz) butter, melted

lemon slices and dill sprigs to garnish

1 Cut the halibut steaks crosswise so you have 4 equal-sized pieces. Cut the carrot and leek into matchstick-thin strips.

2 Put the vegetables into a pan with the stock, wine, lemon juice, and saffron.

3 Bring to a boil, and cook, uncovered, for 5 minutes or until the vegetables are just tender. Drain, and then season with salt and pepper.

4 Cut the filo pastry into eight 25 cm (10 in) squares, and reserve the trimmings. Brush 1 square with a little melted butter, put a second square on top, and brush with more melted butter. Make a filo parcel (see box, far right). Repeat to make 4 filo parcels.

5 Place the filo parcels on a baking tray, and bake in a preheated oven at 200°C (400°F, Gas 6) for 20 minutes or until golden and crispy. Garnish with lemon slices and dill sprigs, and serve at once.

Cook's know-how

Sheets of filo pastry are usually sold in a roll, fresh or frozen. The size of the sheets may vary with different brands, so don't worry if they are slightly smaller than 25 cm (10 in) wide – just be sure there is sufficient pastry to cover the filling.

SALMON IN FILO PARCELS

Substitute skinned salmon fillets for the halibut, and 1 courgette and 4 spring onions, both cut into matchstick-thin strips, for the carrot and leek.

Making a filo parcel

Spoon one-quarter of the vegetable mixture into the middle of the pastry square. Put 1 piece of halibut on top of the vegetable mixture.

Fold 2 sides of the filo pastry over the halibut and vegetables, and tuck the remaining 2 ends underneath to form a neat parcel. Brush the top of the parcel with a little melted butter.

Crumple some of the reserved filo trimmings, and arrange them on top of the filo parcel. Brush with melted butter.

SEA BASS WITH LEMON BUTTER SAUCE

SERVES 4

sunflower oil for greasing

1.1 kg (2¼ lb) sea bass, cleaned and filleted (page 122)

4 tarragon sprigs

1 lemon, sliced

salt and black pepper

2 tbsp dry white wine

LEMON BUTTER SAUCE

150 ml (¼ pint) single cream

juice of ½ lemon

45 g (1½ oz) butter, melted

1 egg yolk

1 tsp plain flour

white pepper

1 tsp chopped fresh tarragon

1 Put a large piece of foil on to a baking tray and brush lightly with oil. Put the sea bass on to the foil, tuck 3 of the tarragon sprigs and all but 1–2 of the lemon slices inside the cavity, and sprinkle with salt and black pepper.

2 Season the outside of the fish, and lift up the sides of the foil. Pour the wine over the fish, then seal the foil into a loose parcel. Bake in a preheated oven at 200°C (400°F, Gas 6) for 30 minutes or until the flesh is opaque and flakes easily.

3 Meanwhile, make the sauce: whisk the cream in a pan with the lemon juice, butter, egg yolk, and flour until mixed. Heat very gently, stirring constantly, until the mixture is thick enough to coat the back of a spoon. Season with salt and white pepper, and stir in the tarragon. Keep warm.

4 Remove the sea bass from the foil and arrange on a warmed serving dish. Pour over the cooking juices. Garnish with the remaining lemon slices and tarragon sprig, and serve at once. Serve the warm lemon butter sauce separately.

ORIENTAL FISH PARCELS

SERVES 4

45 g (1½ oz) butter

4 x 250 g (8 oz) white fish fillets, such as sole or plaice, skinned

2 cm (¾ in) piece of fresh root ginger, peeled and thinly sliced

3 spring onions, thinly sliced

2–3 garlic cloves, crushed

2 tbsp light soy sauce

1 tbsp rice wine or dry sherry

½ tsp sugar

NON-STICK BAKING PARCHMENT

1 Cut 8 sheets of baking parchment into oval shapes, each one measuring about 30 x 37 cm (12 x 15 in). Put the ovals together in pairs to make a double thickness.

2 Melt 30 g (1 oz) of the butter. Brush the butter over the top oval of each pair, and over 2 large baking trays.

3 Place a fish fillet on the buttered side of one of the oval pairs, positioning it on one side. Top with ginger, spring onions, and garlic, and dot with one-quarter of the remaining butter.

4 Whisk together the soy sauce, rice wine, and sugar, and drizzle one-quarter of this mixture over the fish. Fold the paper over the fish, and fold and pleat the edges together like a Cornish pasty to seal in the fish and juices. Repeat to make 4 parcels altogether.

5 Put the paper cases on to the prepared baking trays and bake the fish in a preheated oven at 230°C (450°F, Gas 8) for 8–10 minutes until the paper has turned brown and the cases have puffed up. Serve at once, on individual plates.

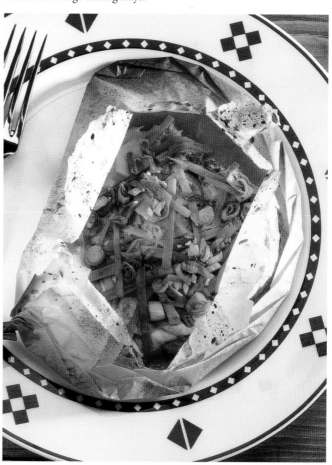

GOLDEN FISH CAKES

SERVES 4

500 g (1 lb) potatoes, cut into chunks

salt and black pepper

500 g (1 lb) cod, haddock or salmon fillets (or a mixture of white fish and salmon)

300 ml (1/2 pint) milk

1 bay leaf

9 black peppercorns

60 g (2 oz) butter

4 tbsp chopped parsley

finely grated zest of 1 lemon

dash of Tabasco (optional)

1 egg, beaten

175 g (6 oz) fresh breadcrumbs

sunflower oil for frying

tartare sauce (page 148) to serve

1 Cook the potatoes in boiling salted water for 15–20 minutes until tender.

2 Meanwhile, put the fish into a pan with the milk, bay leaf, and peppercorns. Bring slowly to a boil, and simmer for 10 minutes or until the fish is just opaque.

3 Drain the fish, reserving the liquid. Cool the fish, then flake the flesh, discarding the skin and bones.

4 Drain the potatoes, put them in a bowl, and mash with the butter and 3 tbsp of the fish cooking liquid. Add the fish, parsley, lemon zest, Tabasco if using, and salt and pepper to taste, and mix well.

5 Shape the mixture into 8 flat cakes, 7 cm (3 in) in diameter. Coat with beaten egg, then with breadcrumbs.

6 Heat a little oil in a frying pan and fry the fish cakes, a few at a time, for 5 minutes on each side or until golden. Serve hot, with the tartare sauce.

CRISPY-TOPPED SEAFOOD PIE

SERVES 4

500 g (1 lb) cod fillet

300 ml (1/2 pint) milk

1 bay leaf

2 leeks, trimmed and sliced

175 g (6 oz) broccoli, cut into florets

175 g (6 oz) cooked peeled prawns

15 g (1/2 oz) butter

15 g (1/2 oz) plain flour

salt and black pepper

250 g (8 oz) ready-made shortcrust pastry, well chilled

30 g (1 oz) Gruyère cheese, grated

1 Put the cod into a saucepan with the milk and bay leaf, bring slowly to a boil, and poach gently for about 10 minutes until the fish flakes easily.

2 Meanwhile, blanch the leeks and broccoli for 3 minutes in a saucepan of boiling salted water. Drain.

3 Lift out the fish, remove and discard the skin and bones, and flake the fish. Strain and reserve the milk.

4 Put the leeks and broccoli into a pie dish, and add the cod and prawns.

5 Melt the butter in a small saucepan, add the flour, and cook, stirring, for 1 minute. Remove from the heat and gradually blend in the reserved milk. Bring to a boil, stirring constantly until thickened. Simmer for 2–3 minutes. Season to taste and pour over the pie filling.

6 Grate the pastry (see box, below), and sprinkle over the sauce. Sprinkle with the grated cheese. Bake in a preheated oven at 200°C (400°F, Gas 6) for 25–30 minutes. Serve at once.

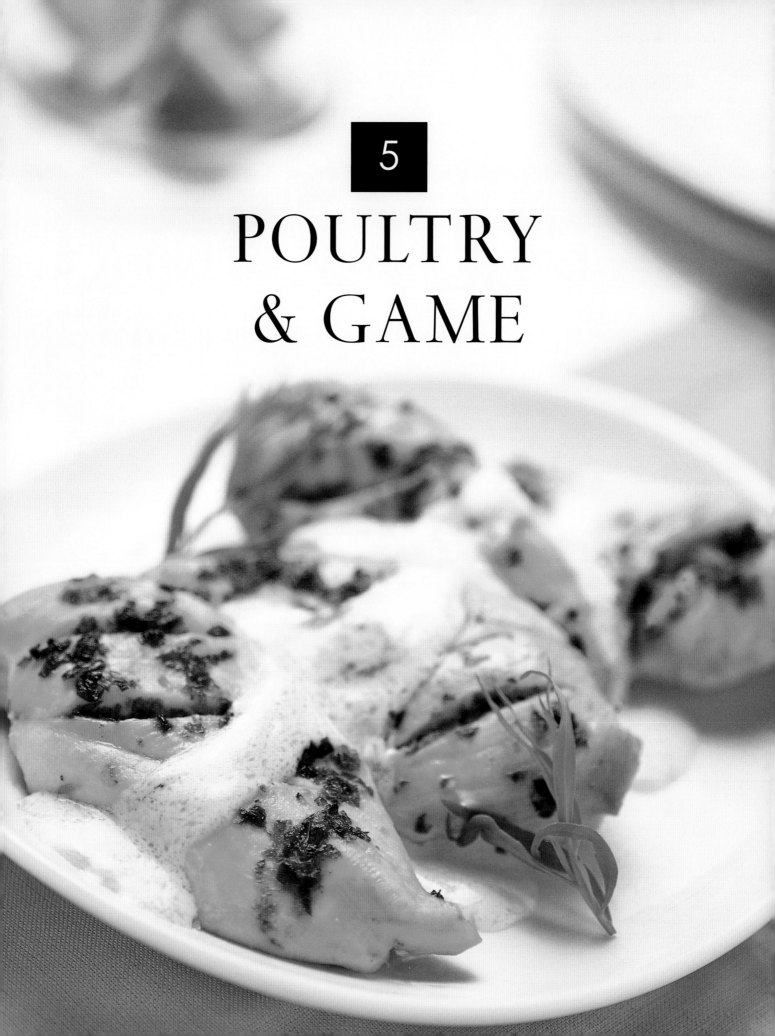

5
POULTRY & GAME

UNDER 30 MINUTES

BARBECUE

HERB GRILLED CHICKEN

Fresh and summery: chicken quarters brushed with parsley, chives, and garlic in melted butter, then barbecued or grilled.

SERVES 8   297 calories per serving
Takes 25 minutes   Page 182

CHICKEN KEBABS

Pieces of chicken marinated in soy sauce, vinegar, oil, and thyme. Grilled with green pepper, mushrooms, and cherry tomatoes.

SERVES 6   441 calories per serving
Takes 25 minutes   Page 190

DINNER PARTY

WARM CHICKEN SALAD WITH MANGO & AVOCADO

Marinated chicken with mango and avocado, and rum-flavoured cooking juices.

SERVES 4   411 calories per serving
Takes 25 minutes   Page 200

MUSTARD CHICKEN

Hot and creamy: strips of chicken coated with garlic, in a cream sauce piquantly flavoured with mustard.

SERVES 4   380 calories per serving
Takes 25 minutes   Page 189

DINNER PARTY

TURKEY WITH SOURED CREAM & CHIVES

Strips of turkey breast in a bacon, mushroom, and soured cream sauce.

SERVES 4   542 calories per serving
Takes 25 minutes   Page 204

LOW FAT

STIR-FRIED CHICKEN WITH CRISP VEGETABLES

Strips of chicken dry marinated in spices including ginger and turmeric. Stir-fried with vegetables.

SERVES 4   405 calories per serving
Takes 25 minutes   Page 188

GREEK CHICKEN SALAD

Creamy and intensely flavoured with herbs: pieces of cooked chicken coated in yogurt, crème fraîche, spring onions, and herbs.

SERVES 6   264 calories per serving
Takes 15 minutes   Page 200

QUICK & EASY

CHICKEN STIR-FRY

Light oriental dish: strips of chicken stir-fried with spring onions, ginger, carrots, and peppers. Flavoured with soy sauce and sherry.

SERVES 4   381 calories per serving
Takes 15 minutes   Page 191

HOT & SPICY STIR-FRIED DUCK

Strips of duck marinated in soy sauce, vinegar, ginger, chilli, and orange. Stir-fried with vegetables and water chestnuts.

SERVES 4   453 calories per serving
Takes 25 minutes   Page 215

30–60 MINUTES

CORONATION CHICKEN

Bite-sized pieces of chicken in a sauce made from spring onions, curry paste, wine, lemon, apricot jam, mayonnaise, and yogurt.

SERVES 6 580 calories per serving
Takes 15 minutes, plus cooling   Page 199

HERB-MARINATED CHICKEN BREASTS

Chicken breasts marinated in lemon juice, herbs, and garlic. Cooked until crispy, and served with a hot stock sauce.

SERVES 4 641 calories per serving
Takes 30 minutes, plus marinating   Page 194

ORIENTAL CLASSIC

THAI CHICKEN WITH WATER CHESTNUTS

Aromatic stir-fry: chicken with water chestnuts, lemon grass, garlic, ginger, coriander, chilli, and tofu.

SERVES 4 272 calories per serving
Takes 30 minutes   Page 188

DINNER PARTY

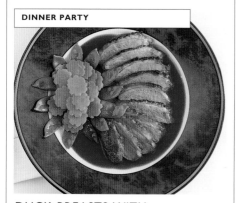

DUCK BREASTS WITH RASPBERRY SAUCE

Rich and fruity: slices of grilled duck breast served with a sauce of raspberries, port, and orange juice.

SERVES 4 975 calories per serving
Takes 45 minutes   Page 214

STIR-FRIED TURKEY MEATBALLS

Mixture of minced turkey, garlic, soy sauce, and ginger, stir-fried with onion, pepper, courgette, mushrooms, and bean sprouts.

SERVES 4 232 calories per serving
Takes 30 minutes   Page 207

TARRAGON CHICKEN WITH LIME

Chicken breasts coated with lime butter and sprinkled with lime juice and tarragon. Baked, and served with a crème fraîche sauce.

SERVES 4 428 calories per serving
Takes 45 minutes   Page 192

TURKEY SCHNITZEL

Golden and tender: turkey breast escalopes coated in seasoned flour, beaten egg, and fresh breadcrumbs, and decorated with a criss-cross pattern. Chilled in the refrigerator, then cooked until golden. Garnished with lemon slices and chopped parsley.

SERVES 4 394 calories per serving
Takes 25 minutes, plus chilling   Page 205

CHEESE & GARLIC STUFFED CHICKEN

Chicken breasts stuffed with soft cheese, onion, garlic, fresh tarragon, egg yolk, and nutmeg, then baked. Served cut into slices.

SERVES 6 628 calories per serving
Takes 45 minutes   Page 192

30–60 MINUTES

DEVILLED CHICKEN DRUMSTICKS

Crispy and piquant: chicken drumsticks covered with a mixture of wine vinegar, ketchup, mustard, and sugar, then baked.

MAKES 12 138 calories each

Takes 45 minutes Page 198

TURKEY WITH CHEESE & PINEAPPLE

Bite-sized pieces of turkey with a cheese and pineapple sauce, sprinkled with fresh brown breadcrumbs, then baked.

SERVES 6 450 calories per serving

Takes 40 minutes Page 208

CHICKEN SATAY

Pieces of chicken marinated in soy sauce, lemon juice, garlic, and spring onions. Served with a peanut and coconut sauce.

SERVES 4 815 calories per serving

Takes 25 minutes, plus marinating Page 190

HIGH PROTEIN

CHICKEN THIGHS NORMANDE

Chicken thighs baked with leeks, bacon, cider, and thyme, richly flavoured with garlic. Served with a crème fraîche sauce.

SERVES 4 599 calories per serving

Takes 55 minutes Page 195

BACON-WRAPPED CHICKEN BREASTS

Tender and tangy: boneless chicken breasts spread with coarse-grain mustard, and wrapped in bacon rashers.

SERVES 6 528 calories per serving

Takes 50 minutes Page 193

LOW FAT

TURKEY & LEMON STIR-FRY

Turkey breast strips marinated in white wine and lemon zest and juice, stir-fried with courgettes, green pepper, and baby sweetcorn.

SERVES 4 342 calories per serving

Takes 20 minutes, plus marinating Page 205

CHICKEN PINWHEELS

Pounded chicken breasts spread with a cheese and basil mixture, rolled up, simmered, then sliced. Served with a tomato and herb sauce.

SERVES 4 423 calories per serving

Takes 50 minutes Page 191

FRAGRANT CHICKEN CURRY WITH ALMONDS

Chicken breasts cooked in an authentic blend of Indian spices, including cinnamon, cardamom seeds, cloves, cumin seeds, ginger, and garam masala, with a creamy yogurt sauce. Served with a sprinkling of sultanas and toasted almonds.

SERVES 4 527 calories per serving

Takes 45 minutes Page 186

30-60 MINUTES

ORIENTAL POUSSINS

Tangy and succulent: poussins brushed with soy and hoisin sauces, sherry, garlic, and ginger, and baked.

SERVES 4 395 calories per serving

Takes 50 minutes   Page 179

CHICKEN THIGHS WITH CHESTNUT STUFFING

Delicious and filling: boneless chicken thighs stuffed with diced bacon, chestnuts, onion, fresh brown breadcrumbs, chopped parsley, and egg yolk, and then roasted until a golden brown colour. Served with a fruity cranberry jelly sauce.

SERVES 4 598 calories per serving

Takes 55 minutes   Page 195

FAMILY CHOICE

BARBEQUE

PICNIC FARE

TURKEY BURGERS HOLSTEIN

Golden and tasty: minced turkey combined with chopped ham, parsley, and onion, then shaped into burgers. Served with a fried egg.

SERVES 4 429 calories per serving

Takes 30 minutes, plus chilling   Page 207

JERK CHICKEN

Crispy and spicy: chicken pieces spread with blended lime juice, rum, spring onions, chilli, garlic, and spices, then barbecued.

SERVES 4 304 calories per serving

Takes 30 minutes, plus marinating   Page 183

LEMON & HERB DRUMSTICKS

Fresh and easy to make: chicken drumsticks marinated in olive oil, lemon juice and zest, onion, garlic, and parsley, then grilled.

MAKES 12 200 calories each

Takes 25 minutes, plus marinating   Page 198

ORIENTAL CLASSIC

TEX-MEX CHICKEN

Chicken breasts marinated in oil, orange juice, and cumin, then grilled. Served with sliced avocado, and a tomato and lime salsa.

SERVES 4 659 calories per serving

Takes 30 minutes, plus marinating   Page 183

ORIENTAL DUCK WITH GINGER

Duck marinated in orange, soy sauce, sesame oil, rice wine, honey, and ginger. Served with baby sweetcorn and toasted sesame seeds.

SERVES 4 445 calories per serving

Takes 30 minutes, plus marinating   Page 215

TURKEY MOLE

Hot and spicy: turkey pieces cooked with a blended sauce of tomatoes, almonds, chocolate, chilli, cinnamon, and cloves.

SERVES 6 334 calories per serving

Takes 55 minutes   Page 206

30–60 MINUTES

SWEET & SOUR CHINESE CHICKEN
Pieces of chicken marinated in soy sauce and rice wine. Stir-fried with peppers, celery, onion, ketchup, pineapple, and lychees.

SERVES 4–6 458–305 calories per serving

Takes 30 minutes, plus marinating Page 189

SAFFRON CHICKEN
Chicken breasts marinated in saffron, ginger, lemon, cardamom, coriander, and cinnamon, then roasted. Served with crème fraîche sauce.

SERVES 6 527 calories per serving

Takes 40 minutes, plus marinating Page 187

CHICKEN WITH SAGE & ORANGE
Fresh and tangy: chicken breasts marinated in orange juice, soy sauce, sage, and ginger. Served with a sage and orange sauce.

SERVES 6 435 calories per serving

Takes 40 minutes, plus marinating Page 193

OVER 60 MINUTES

DUCK BREASTS WITH RED WINE SAUCE
Duck marinated in garlic, balsamic, and rosemary, then cooked, sliced, and served with a wine sauce.

SERVES 4 906 calories per serving

Takes 40 minutes, plus chilling Page 214

POUSSINS WITH ROMESCO SAUCE
Spatchcocked poussins and spring onions marinated in oil, vinegar, and cinnamon. Served with sauce of tomatoes and almonds.

SERVES 2 845 calories per serving

Takes 60 minutes, plus marinating Page 179

MOROCCAN POUSSINS
Spatchcocked poussins marinated in lime, garlic, coriander, paprika, curry powder, cumin, and saffron, then grilled.

SERVES 2 467 calories per serving

Takes 45 minutes, plus marinating Page 178

FAMILY CHOICE

AMERICAN FRIED CHICKEN
Pieces of buttermilk-soaked chicken coated in flour seasoned with paprika. Cooked until golden, and served with bacon.

SERVES 4 683 calories per serving

Takes 40 minutes, plus standing Page 182

CHICKEN TIKKA
Chicken marinated in yogurt, tomato purée, garlic, tamarind paste, paprika, and ginger. Served with cucumber raita.

SERVES 4–6 266–177 calories per serving

Takes 20 minutes, plus marinating Page 187

DINNER PARTY

CHICKEN CORDON BLEU
Golden and tender: pounded chicken breasts filled with ham and Gruyère cheese, and folded. Coated with egg and breadcrumbs.

SERVES 4 602 calories per serving

Takes 45 minutes, plus chilling Page 194

OVER 60 MINUTES

LEMON POUSSINS WITH ARTICHOKE HEARTS

Roasted poussins served with artichokes marinated in lemon, garlic, and parsley.

SERVES 4 555 calories per serving

Takes 1¼ hours   Page 178

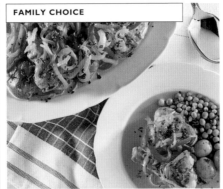

TURKEY CASSEROLE WITH PEPPERS & CIDER

Turkey pieces cooked with cider, red and yellow peppers, onion, and garlic.

SERVES 6 234 calories per serving

Takes 1½ hours   Page 206

PROVENÇAL-STYLE ROAST CHICKEN

Chicken cooked on a bed of vegetables which form the basis of a delicious sauce.

SERVES 6 547 calories per serving

Takes 1½ hours   Page 176

COQ AU VIN

Rich and nourishing: chicken pieces cooked with bacon, shallots, mushrooms, red wine, stock, and a medley of fresh herbs.

SERVES 4 531 calories per serving

Takes 1½ hours   Page 181

TRADITIONAL ROAST PHEASANT

Two pheasants, buttered and covered with bacon rashers, then roasted and served with redcurrant-flavoured gravy, and the traditional accompaniments of game chips, fried breadcrumbs, and bread sauce. Garnished with watercress sprigs.

SERVES 4 660 calories per serving

Takes 1½ hours   Page 217

MUSHROOM-STUFFED QUAIL

Whole boned quail stuffed with shallots, mushrooms, and breadcrumbs, and served with a lime and crème fraîche sauce.

SERVES 6 651 calories per serving

Takes 1¼ hours   Page 216

TURKEY SALAD WITH MANGO & GRAPES

Turkey breast poached with peppercorns, coated in lemon mayonnaise. Served with walnuts and fruits.

SERVES 4 734 calories per serving

Takes 1½ hours, plus cooling   Page 208

CHICKEN MARENGO

Chicken pieces cooked with shallots, wine, stock, tomatoes, mushrooms, garlic, parsley, thyme, bay leaf, and prawns.

SERVES 4 479 calories per serving

Takes 1¾ hours   Page 181

OVER 60 MINUTES

NORMANDY PHEASANT
Rich and tangy: pheasant cooked with apples, celery, onion, stock, and wine. Served with a creamy sauce and apple rings.

SERVES 6–8 751–563 calories per serving

Takes 1¾ hours   Page 218

BRAISED RABBIT WITH MUSHROOMS & CIDER
Rabbit cooked with shallots, mushrooms, cider, herbs, and enriched with cream.

SERVES 4 506 calories per serving

Takes 2 hours   Page 220

FRENCH ROAST CHICKEN
Tender and succulent: a whole chicken spread with softened butter, seasoned with black pepper, and roasted with chicken stock and a sprig of tarragon.

SERVES 4 433 calories per serving

Takes 2 hours   Page 175

Served with gravy made from the cooking juices, and garlic flowers, drizzled with olive oil, then roasted.

FAMILY CHICKEN CASSEROLE
Popular wholesome meal: chicken quarters cooked with bacon, carrots, celery, onion, stock, bay leaf, thyme, and parsley.

SERVES 4 659 calories per serving

Takes 1¾ hours   Page 180

ROAST CHICKEN WITH ORANGE & PEPPERS
Chicken with red pepper and garlic, flambéed with brandy, and served with orange sauce.

SERVES 4 411 calories per serving

Takes 1¾ hours   Page 176

SUNDAY ROAST CHICKEN
Traditional English Sunday lunch: chicken flavoured with parsley and thyme, and cooked with an apple, lemon, and herb stuffing.

SERVES 4 534 calories per serving

Takes 2 hours, plus cooling   Page 174

OVER 60 MINUTES

ROAST TURKEY WITH GARLIC & TARRAGON

Turkey joint marinated in lemon, tarragon, thyme, and garlic, roasted with the marinade.

SERVES 4 296 calories per serving

Takes 1¾ hours, plus marinating Page 204

MARINATED CHICKEN WITH PEPPERS

Chicken roasted with strips of red and yellow peppers, cooled, then tossed with a honey and herb marinade. Served with black olives.

SERVES 6 376 calories per serving

Takes 1¾ hours, plus cooling Page 199

RABBIT WITH MUSTARD & MARJORAM

Pieces of rabbit marinated in mustard and marjoram, and cooked with garlic, bacon, and stock. Served with a mustard sauce.

SERVES 4 548 calories per serving

Takes 2 hours, plus marinating Page 220

PHEASANT STEW

Pieces of pheasant simmered with red wine, game stock, bacon, celery, mushrooms, shallots, and garlic.

SERVES 6–8 633–475 calories per serving

Takes 2 hours Page 218

GAME PIE WITH FENNEL & CARROTS

Richly flavoured with fennel, carrots, onion, stock, and wine, and baked with a puff pastry lid.

SERVES 6 672 calories per serving

Takes 2 hours Page 219

CHICKEN CACCIATORE

Pieces of chicken sprinkled with thyme, and cooked with bacon, onion, green pepper, garlic, mushrooms, wine, tomatoes, and sage.

SERVES 4 540 calories per serving

Takes 1¾ hours Page 180

CHICKEN POT PIE

Hearty meal: chicken simmered with stock, garlic, carrots, and potatoes. Flavoured with nutmeg and parsley, and baked with pastry.

SERVES 6 508 calories per serving

Takes 2 hours, plus cooling Page 177

GUINEA FOWL MADEIRA

Pieces of guinea fowl cooked with shallots, stock, wine, and Madeira, enriched with double cream and green grapes.

SERVES 6 613 calories per serving

Takes 1¾ hours Page 216

RUBY HARE CASSEROLE

Rich and full of flavour: hare marinated in port, and cooked with shallots, bacon, chestnut mushrooms, and herbs.

SERVES 4 1068 calories per serving

Takes 2½ hours, plus marinating Page 219

OVER 60 MINUTES

ORIENTAL CLASSIC

PEKING DUCK

Oriental speciality: whole duck brushed before cooking with sherry, honey, and soy sauce. Served with Chinese pancakes.

SERVES 6 848 calories per serving

Takes 2¹/2 hours, plus drying   Page 212

POT ROAST VENISON

Rolled shoulder of venison marinated in red wine, orange and lemon zests, and juniper berries, and slowly braised in the marinade with chopped carrots, celery, and onions. Redcurrant jelly is added to the sauce just before serving.

SERVES 6 454 calories per serving

Takes 3¹/2 hours, plus marinating   Page 221

PREPARE AHEAD

ROAST DUCK WITH CRANBERRIES

Duck with a stuffing of onion, fresh brown breadcrumbs, and cranberries, roasted until crisp-skinned. Served with cranberry sauce.

SERVES 4 580 calories per serving

Takes 2¹/2 hours, plus cooling   Page 213

VENISON CASSEROLE

Rich stew: cubes of venison marinated in wine, parsley, and allspice, and cooked with celery, mushrooms, and carrots.

SERVES 6 466 calories per serving

Takes 2¹/4 hours, plus marinating   Page 221

RATHER SPECIAL GAME PIE

A selection of meats marinated in port. Baked in a pastry case filled with jellied stock, then chilled.

SERVES 20 507 calories per serving

Takes 6 hours, plus marinating   Page 222

TRADITIONAL

BALLOTINE OF CHICKEN

Boned chicken pounded and stuffed with pork, liver, bacon, brandy, ham, and pistachio nuts. Rolled, cooked, chilled, and sliced.

SERVES 8–10 617–494 calories per serving

Takes 2³/4 hours, plus chilling   Page 201

CHRISTMAS ROAST GOOSE

Succulent and fruity: goose stuffed with pork sausagemeat, sage, and apple, and roasted. Served with wine-flavoured gravy, enriched with goose stock, and baked apples with a stuffing of Calvados, ground cinnamon, ground allspice, and prunes.

SERVES 6–8 1228–921 calories per serving

Takes 5¹/4 hours, plus cooling   Page 209

POULTRY & GAME KNOW-HOW

POULTRY IS THE TERM FOR all domesticated birds reared for the table – the most familiar being chicken, turkey, goose, and duck – but the classification "poultry" can also be applied to game birds that once lived in the wild and are now farmed, such as guinea fowl, pigeon, and quail. Pheasant and partridge are also often intensively reared, to be released into the so-called "wild" for the shooting season. Truly wild game birds taste quite different from their farmed or semi-wild counterparts; they are left to hang to enhance their "gamey" flavour and tenderize their flesh.

BUYING & STORING

There is a great variety of poultry available, produced by different farming methods. Free-range birds, which have been allowed access to the open air, cost more than intensively reared birds but they tend to have a superior flavour as they are slaughtered when they are older. Corn-fed chickens, which may or may not be free-range, are another option. Their diet does include maize (corn), but it is an artificial dye in their food that gives their flesh its yellow colour. The more expensive organically reared birds are not routinely given antibiotics nor artificial growth-promoting hormones in their feed.

Poultry can be bought fresh or frozen as whole birds – ranging in size from tiny quail and poussins to huge turkeys – as well as in pieces. Game birds are generally sold whole. Poultry and game birds should have a plump breast and moist, unblemished skin, and poultry should smell fresh and sweet, never "off".

All poultry and game birds are very perishable so they must be kept cool. As soon as you can, remove any tight plastic wrapping and giblets, then put the bird on a plate to collect any drips, cover it loosely, and store in the refrigerator. Check the use-by date – most poultry should be cooked within 2 days of purchase:

MICROWAVING

Casseroles and stews made with poultry and game can be cooked quite easily in the microwave oven. They are quick to prepare and the meat stays tender and juicy. You may choose to brown the poultry or game and any vegetables on the hob first, then transfer to a dish to finish cooking in the microwave. Be sure to transfer the flavoursome pan drippings to the microwave dish as well.

The microwave is also really good for reheating cooked poultry and game dishes, particularly when the meat is off the bone.

For roasting poultry and game, a conventional oven gives better results than the microwave.

FREEZING

Frozen poultry and game, particularly "fresh-frozen" (quickly air-cooled before freezing), is very good and a useful standby. When buying frozen poultry and game, check it is completely frozen and get it home as quickly as possible. Chicken, turkey, and wild game birds can be stored for up to 6 months; duck, goose, and guinea fowl for 4 months.

Poultry and game must be thoroughly thawed before cooking. This can take time – a 4.5 kg (10 lb) turkey needs 22–24 hours. Unwrap the bird, cover loosely with fresh wrapping, and set on a plate to thaw in the refrigerator. Remove any giblets as soon as possible. Raw poultry or game should never be re-frozen once thawed.

TYPES OF BIRDS

Poussins are small single-serving-size chickens; spring chickens or poulets are a little bigger. Roasters are the most widely available, either whole or in joints. The largest chickens are boiling fowl, which are old laying hens, and capons, which are neutered male birds. Turkey is sold whole as well as in escalopes, breast steaks and large thigh, leg or breast joints, boned or on the bone. Duck is sold whole and in legs or boneless breasts. Other poultry (eg goose, guinea fowl, pigeon and quail) and game birds (eg wild duck such as mallard, widgeon and teal, grouse, partridge and pheasant) are sold whole, sometimes boned.

THOROUGH COOKING

Cook poultry thoroughly to kill any bacteria.

To test a whole roasted bird, lift it on a long fork – the juices that run out should be clear. For joints, insert a skewer into the thickest part of the meat and check the colour of the juices. Alternatively, use an instant-read thermometer: the thigh meat should register 75°C (170°F), breast 70°C (160°F).

POULTRY OR GAME STOCK

To make 2.5 litres (4 pints) stock, use 1.5 kg (3 lb) raw poultry or game pieces or bones, or the carcass and trimmings from a roast bird. Don't mix raw and cooked bones.

1 Crush or break up bones and carcasses. Put the bones (or pieces) into a stockpot or large pan. Add 2 or 3 halved, unpeeled onions and cook until browned.

2 Add 4 litres (7 pints) water. Bring to a boil, skimming off any scum from the surface. Add 3 chopped carrots, 3 chopped celery stalks, 1 large bouquet garni, and a few black peppercorns.

3 Half cover the pan and simmer for 2¹/₂–3 hours. Strain the stock into a bowl. Leave to cool, then remove the solidified fat from the surface and discard. Cover and keep in the refrigerator for up to 3 days, or freeze for 3 months. (You can keep raw or cooked bones in the freezer too, for making stock at a later date.)

GIBLET STOCK

Giblets are not often found in birds, but they make a really good stock.

1 Put the giblets (the neck, heart, and gizzard but not the liver) in a stockpot or large saucepan and cook until lightly browned. Stir in 1 litre (1³/4 pints) water (or previously made stock). Bring to a boil, skimming off any scum that forms on the surface.

2 Add 1–2 quartered, unpeeled onions, 1 chopped celery stalk, 1 chopped carrot, 1 bouquet garni, and a few black peppercorns. Simmer for about 1 hour. Strain, then cool, cover, and keep in the refrigerator for up to 3 days, or freeze for 3 months.

JELLIED STOCK

This stock is used in cold dishes such as Rather Special Game Pie (page 222), where it forms a jelly around the meat. Make it in the same way as other stocks, but use bones only, because they contain a high level of gelatine. Crack the bones before adding them to the pot. The stock will set when cool.

Stock know-how

If you do not have a carcass from a whole bird, chicken wings make a good base for a stock.

•

Peppercorns, instead of ground black pepper, are used in stock: prolonged cooking can turn ground black pepper bitter.

•

Skim off fat with a large spoon, soak it up with paper towels, or cool and lift it off.

JOINTING A BIRD

Chicken portions are widely available, but cutting a bird into 4 or 8 serving pieces is not at all difficult to do yourself, and it can be done before or after cooking. A pair of special poultry shears makes the job particularly easy, otherwise use good, strong scissors or a sharp chef's knife.

Drumstick   Thigh

Breast   Wing

1 Cut through to the joint between one of the legs and the body. Twist the leg out and away from the body to pop the ball and socket joint, then cut through the joint to remove the leg. Remove the other leg.

2 To remove the breasts, cut through the skin and flesh along both sides of the breastbone. Cut through the bones of the ribcage where it joins the sides of the breastbone, then remove the breastbone.

3 Turn over and cut along the backbone, to give 2 breasts with wings attached. For 8 pieces, cut each breast diagonally in two: the wing half should be slightly smaller. Cut each leg through the joint into thigh and drumstick.

BONING A WHOLE CHICKEN

Although boning a chicken requires a little time and effort, the result is impressive. Stuffed and rolled into a ballotine, it is ideal for entertaining because it is so easy to carve. Other birds can be boned in the same way.

1 Set the bird breast-side down and slit the skin along the backbone. Remove the wishbone (page 172). Slide the knife into the cut and gently pull and scrape the flesh away from the ribcage. Continue cutting away the flesh until you reach the leg and wing joints. Repeat on the other side.

2 Scrape away the flesh from the ribcage, working on one side at a time. Take care not to make any holes in the skin as you are doing this. Cut through the ball and socket joints connecting the legs to the carcass (they will still be attached to the skin).

3 Keep cutting the flesh from the bone on both sides until you reach the ridge of the breastbone in the middle. Cut the breastbone free, without cutting through the skin, and lift it away with the carcass.

4 Cut through the tendons in the legs that join the flesh to the bone. Scrape back the flesh until the bones of each leg have been exposed, then pull out the bones, cutting them free of the skin.

5 Bone the wings in the same way as the legs. Push the legs and wings skin-side out. The chicken is now ready for stuffing and rolling. Keep the carcass and bones for making chicken stock.

BONING A QUAIL

For a special occasion, tiny quail can be boned but left whole. It is then quite simple to fill them with a savoury stuffing and secure with a cocktail stick ready for roasting. Make sure you use a very small knife and be careful not to pierce the skin.

1 With your fingers, carefully loosen the skin at the neck of the quail, and push it back to reveal the wishbone. With a small, sharp knife, cut the flesh from around the wishbone and remove it.

2 Loosen 1 wing by carefully cutting through the tendon at the base. Repeat with the other wing.

3 Insert the knife between the ribcage and the flesh and, working all around the bird, scrape the flesh from the bones, pushing it back as you go. Remove the ribcage. The bird is now ready to stuff.

SPATCHCOCKING

This method of splitting and flattening a bird makes it quicker to cook and suitable for grilling or cooking over a barbecue. Poussins, chickens, guinea fowl, and game birds can all be spatchcocked.

1 With poultry shears or a knife, cut along both sides of the backbone and discard. Cut off the wing tips and the ends of the legs. Remove the wishbone.

2 Turn the bird over. Put your hands on top of the breast and press down firmly with the heels of your hands to break the breastbone and flatten the bird.

3 Thread a long metal skewer through the bird at the neck end, passing through the wings. Thread another skewer below the breast, passing through the legs. If small birds are spatchcocked, 2 or 3 can be threaded on the same skewers.

PREPARING POULTRY FOR ROASTING

Tying or skewering a bird before roasting holds it together so that it keeps a neat shape during cooking. It will also prevent any stuffing from falling out. To be sure that heat can penetrate into the centre of the bird and cook it thoroughly, it is best to put stuffing into the neck end and not into the large body cavity.

Trussing with string
1 Thread a trussing needle with string. Put the bird breast-side up. Push the legs back and down. Insert the needle into a knee joint. Pass through the bird and then out through the other knee.

2 Pull the neck skin over the end of the bird and tuck the wing tips over it. Push the needle through both sections of one wing, through the neck skin and beneath the backbone, and out the other wing.

3 With the bird on its side, pull the string tightly, tie the ends together, and trim. Tuck the tail into the cavity and fold the top skin over it.

4 Push the needle through the top skin. Loop the string around one of the drumsticks, under the breastbone, and then around the other drumstick. Pull the string tight and tie the ends.

Simple trussing
1 Put the bird breast-side up and push the legs back and down. Holding the legs with one hand, insert a skewer below the knee joint and push it through the bird.

2 Turn the bird over. Pull the neck skin over the end and tuck the wing tips over it. Push a skewer through 1 wing, the neck skin, and out through the other wing.

REMOVING THE WISHBONE

A bird is easier to carve if the wishbone is removed before cooking.

With your fingers, loosen the skin from the flesh at the neck end. Fold back the skin to expose the breastbone. Use a small, sharp knife to cut the wishbone free, taking any fat with it.

CARVING DUCKS & GEESE

Once cooked, small ducks need simply to be cut into quarters or even halves for serving.
Larger ducks and geese can be carved as for other poultry (below).

3 Carve the breast meat in diagonal slices. For a larger bird, carve the breast meat without removing it first, as for a chicken (below).

1 Remove trussing. Cut through the joints between legs and body to remove the legs. (Cook them further if necessary.) Cut off the wings in the same way.

2 Slit the skin along both sides of the breastbone. Slide the knife blade into the cut on one side to free the breast meat in a single piece. Repeat on the other side.

CARVING POULTRY

After roasting, wrap bird in foil and leave to rest before carving – at least 15 minutes and up to 45 minutes for a large bird – to allow the juices to settle. Remove any trussing first.

1 Put the bird breast-side up on a carving board (ideally one with a well to catch all the juices). Insert a carving fork into one breast to keep the bird steady, then cut into the joint between the far leg and body.

2 Turn the bird on its side and cut away the meat close to the backbone, cutting around the "oyster" meat on the back so that it remains attached to the thigh. Turn the bird over.

3 Twist the leg outwards to break the joint, then cut it to remove the leg. If preferred, divide into thigh and drumstick, cutting through the ball and socket joint. Remove the other leg.

4 Make a horizontal cut into the breast above the wing joint on one side, cutting all the way to the bone. Carve neat slices from the breast, holding the knife blade parallel to the ribcage. Repeat on the other side.

ROASTING TIMES

These times are a guide only; always test a bird to make sure it is thoroughly cooked (page 169).

Bird	Oven temperature	Time
Poussin	190°C (375°F, Gas 5)	40–45 minutes total cooking, depending on size
Chicken	190°C (375°F, Gas 5)	20 minutes per 500 g (1 lb) plus 20 minutes
Duck	200°C (400°F, Gas 6)	25 minutes per 500 g (1 lb) for "just cooked"
Goose	180°C (350°F, Gas 4)	20 minutes per 500 g (1 lb) plus 20 minutes
Pheasant	200°C (400°F, Gas 6)	50 minutes total cooking
Turkey		
3.5–4.5 kg (7–9 lb)	190°C (375°F, Gas 5)	2½–3 hours total cooking
5–6 kg (10–12 lb)	190°C (375°F, Gas 5)	3½–4 hours total cooking
6.5–8.5 kg (13–17 lb)	190°C (375°F, Gas 5)	4½–5 hours total cooking

Roasting know-how

To calculate roasting time, weigh the bird after you have added any stuffing.

•

Cover large birds loosely with foil if the skin is becoming too browned.

•

Place fatty birds, such as duck and goose, on a rack, to allow the fat to drain away and keep the skin crisp.

SUNDAY ROAST CHICKEN

Traditional roast chicken is very much a family favourite at weekends. With its crisp skin, light, juicy stuffing of onion, apple, herbs, and lemon zest, and accompaniment of rich gravy, it is hard to beat.

SERVES 4

a few parsley and thyme sprigs
1.7–2 kg (3½–4 lb) chicken
½ lemon, sliced
½ onion, sliced
60 g (2 oz) butter, softened

APPLE & HERB STUFFING

30 g (1 oz) butter
1 small onion, finely chopped
1 cooking apple, peeled, cored, and grated
60 g (2 oz) fresh white breadcrumbs
1 small egg, beaten
1 tbsp chopped parsley
1 tbsp chopped fresh thyme
grated zest of 1 lemon
salt and black pepper

GRAVY

2 tsp plain flour
300 ml (½ pint) chicken stock or giblet stock (page 170)
splash of red wine or sherry and a spoonful of redcurrant jelly or cranberry sauce (optional)

1 Make the apple and herb stuffing: melt the butter in a saucepan, add the onion, and cook gently for a few minutes until softened. Remove from the heat, cool slightly, then stir in the apple, breadcrumbs, egg, parsley, thyme, and lemon zest. Season with salt and pepper, then leave until cold.

2 Put the parsley and thyme sprigs into the cavity of the chicken, add the lemon and onion, and season well with black pepper. Tie the legs together with string.

3 Spoon the stuffing into the neck end of the chicken, secure the skin flap over the stuffing with a small skewer, and pat into a rounded shape. Put any remaining stuffing into a baking dish.

4 Weigh the stuffed chicken, and calculate the roasting time at 20 minutes per 500 g (1 lb), plus an extra 20 minutes. Rub the butter over the breast, and season with salt and pepper.

5 Place the chicken, breast-side down, in a roasting tin. Roast in a preheated oven at 190°C (375°F, Gas 5) for the calculated time, turning the bird over when lightly browned and basting it every 20 minutes. Put any stuffing in the oven for the last 40 minutes.

6 Check that the chicken is done (page 170), then transfer to a warmed serving platter, and cover with foil. Make the gravy (see box, right).

7 Carve the chicken (page 173). Remove the stuffing from the neck cavity and transfer to a serving dish with any other stuffing. Serve hot, with the gravy.

Making gravy

Tilt the roasting tin, and spoon off all but 1 tbsp of the fat that is on the surface, leaving behind the cooking juices and sediment. Put the roasting tin on the hob.

Add the flour, and cook over a medium heat for 1–2 minutes, stirring constantly with a whisk or metal spoon to dissolve any sediment from the bottom of the tin.

Pour in the stock, and bring to a boil, stirring. Simmer for 2 minutes, then add wine or sherry, redcurrant jelly or cranberry sauce, and salt and pepper to taste. Strain.

FRENCH ROAST CHICKEN

Chicken roasted in the traditional French style is particularly moist and succulent because of the stock added to the roasting tin. In France, the chicken liver is often cooked in a little butter, then sliced and added to the gravy, but this is optional.

SERVES 4

a small bunch of tarragon or rosemary

90 g (3 oz) butter, softened, plus extra for greasing

1.7–2 kg (3¹/₂–4 lb) chicken

salt and black pepper

300 ml (¹/₂ pint) chicken stock or giblet stock (page 170)

4 heads of roast garlic (see box, right) to serve

a good splash of red or white wine

1 Put the bunch of herbs and 30 g (1 oz) of the butter into the cavity of the chicken. Tie the legs together with string. Weigh the chicken and calculate the roasting time at 20 minutes per 500 g (1 lb), plus an extra 20 minutes.

2 Rub the remaining butter all over the chicken and sprinkle with salt and pepper.

3 Put the chicken, breast-side down, into a small roasting tin. Pour the stock into the bottom of the tin, and cover the chicken with buttered greaseproof paper or foil. Roast in a preheated oven at 190°C (375°F, Gas 5) for the calculated time. At regular intervals, baste the chicken and turn it first on to one side, then on to the other, and finally on to its back.

4 Check that the chicken is done (page 169), then transfer to a warmed serving platter, and cover with foil.

5 Leave the chicken to rest for about 15 minutes, then carve and serve with the cooking juices, boiled in the roasting tin with some red or white wine.

ITALIAN ROAST CHICKEN

Roast the chicken in a large roasting tin. Forty minutes before the end of the roasting time, add 1 trimmed and thinly sliced fennel bulb and 2 red onions, peeled and quartered lengthwise, to the tin.

Roast garlic

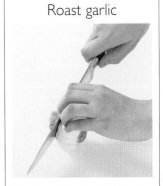

Cut the stalk ends off 4 heads of garlic, arrange in an oiled baking dish, and drizzle a little olive oil over the tops. Cook in a preheated oven at 190°C (375°F, Gas 5) for 45–60 minutes. To eat, squeeze the soft cloves of garlic from the papery skins.

ROAST CHICKEN WITH ORANGE & PEPPERS

SERVES 4

3 oranges

a few parsley sprigs

I head of garlic, separated into cloves

1.7–2 kg (3½–4 lb) chicken

salt and black pepper

I tsp paprika

pinch of cayenne pepper

15 g (½ oz) butter, softened

I red pepper, halved, seeded, and diced

90 ml (3 fl oz) orange juice

75 ml (2½ fl oz) brandy

chopped fresh basil to garnish

1 Cut 2 of the oranges lengthwise into quarters, leaving them unpeeled. Peel the remaining orange, and separate into segments, without the tough membranes.

2 Put the parsley, orange quarters, and half of the garlic cloves into the cavity of the chicken.

3 Weigh the chicken, and calculate the roasting time at 20 minutes per 500 g (1 lb), plus an extra 20 minutes.

4 Rub the chicken with salt and pepper, and the paprika, cayenne, and butter. Place the chicken, breast-side down, in a roasting tin. Add the red pepper and the remaining garlic cloves.

5 Roast in a preheated oven at 190°C (375°F, Gas 5) for the calculated time, turning the chicken breast-side up halfway through cooking.

6 Check that the chicken is done (page 169), then remove it from the tin with the red pepper and garlic. Carve the chicken, and arrange on a warmed serving platter with the red pepper and garlic. Keep hot.

7 Spoon off all but 1 tbsp fat from the roasting tin, leaving behind the cooking juices. Add the orange juice and brandy and boil on the hob until reduced. Add the orange segments and heat through.

8 Spoon the orange segments and sauce over the chicken, sprinkle with the basil, and serve at once.

PROVENÇAL-STYLE ROAST CHICKEN

SERVES 6

I large onion, cut into wedges

2 large carrots, peeled and sliced

125 g (4 oz) whole button mushrooms

3 garlic cloves, peeled

250 ml (8 fl oz) dry white wine

375 ml (12 fl oz) chicken stock

1.7 kg (3½ lb) chicken, with any giblets removed

I x 400 g (13 oz) can chopped tomatoes

I tbsp tomato purée

salt and black pepper

chopped parsley to garnish

1 Arrange the onion wedges, carrot slices, whole mushrooms and garlic cloves in a single layer in a roasting tin, and pour over the wine and stock.

2 Place the chicken breast-side up on a small roasting rack, and place in the middle of the roasting tin on top of the vegetables. Roast in a preheated oven at 200°C (400°F, Gas 6) for 1½ hours or until the chicken is tender and done (page 169).

3 Remove the chicken from the tin, transfer to a large warmed serving dish, and keep warm.

4 Make the sauce: add the chopped tomatoes and tomato purée to the vegetables in the tin, stir well, and return to the oven for 5 minutes or until hot.

5 Carefully pour the contents of the tin into a food processor or blender, and purée until smooth. Season with salt and pepper.

6 Pour the sauce over the roast chicken, garnish with chopped parsley, and serve at once.

CHICKEN POT PIE

This recipe makes a great family dish, packed with tender chicken and colourful vegetables.
You can vary the vegetables according to season and availability.
The pie will be a great success any time of the year.

SERVES 6

| 1 kg (2 lb) chicken |
| 1.25 litres (2 pints) chicken stock |
| 1 onion, quartered |
| 1 celery stalk, thickly sliced |
| pared zest and juice of 1 lemon |
| 2 carrots |
| 2 waxy potatoes |
| 45 g (1 1/2 oz) butter |
| 45 g (1 1/2 oz) plain flour, plus extra for dusting |
| salt and black pepper |
| 125 g (4 oz) frozen peas |
| 175 g (6 oz) shortcrust pastry |
| beaten egg yolk for glazing |
| 2 LITRE (3 1/2 PINT) PIE DISH |

1 Put the chicken, stock, onion, celery, and lemon zest into a large saucepan. Bring to a boil, cover, and simmer for 30 minutes.

2 Add the carrots and potatoes, cover, and simmer for about 20 minutes or until the vegetables are cooked and the chicken is just tender. Remove the vegetables from the liquid and set aside. Leave the chicken to cool in the liquid.

3 Remove the meat from the chicken, and cut into bite-sized pieces, discarding the skin and bones. Dice the vegetables.

4 Skim the fat from the cooking liquid, then bring 600 ml (1 pint) to a boil. Melt the butter in another pan, add the flour, and cook, stirring occasionally, for 1 minute. Stir in the hot stock, whisking until it comes to a boil and thickens. Add the lemon juice and season with salt and pepper.

5 Stir the chicken, diced vegetables, and peas into the sauce, then leave to cool.

6 On a lightly floured work surface, roll out the pastry, then cut out the lid, and fill, cover, and decorate the pie (see box, right).

7 Bake in a preheated oven at 190°C (375°F, Gas 5) for 30 minutes or until the top is crisp and golden brown. Serve hot.

Cook's know-how

The chicken, vegetables, and sauce need to be cold before covering with pastry or the pastry will become soggy. This is a good dish to make ahead up to the end of step 5, then all you have to do is assemble the pie and bake it for half an hour. You can make the filling up to 24 hours ahead and keep it covered in the refrigerator.

Filling, covering, and decorating the pie

Invert the pie dish on to the pastry, and use a small knife to cut around the edge, keeping the blade close to the dish. Reserve all trimmings. Transfer the cold filling to the pie dish, and top with the pastry.

Press the pastry with your fingertips on to the rim of the pie dish. Crimp the edge of the pastry with a fork. Brush the pastry with the beaten egg yolk, making a lattice pattern.

Cut decorative shapes from the reserved pastry trimmings with a pastry cutter. Arrange on top of the pie, and glaze the shapes with the beaten egg yolk.

MOROCCAN POUSSINS

SERVES 2

2 x 375 g (12 oz) poussins,
  spatchcocked (page 172)

MARINADE

3 tbsp olive oil

grated zest of 1 lime and juice
  of 2 limes

1 small onion, finely chopped

2–3 garlic cloves, crushed

2 tbsp chopped fresh coriander

1 tbsp paprika

2 tsp curry powder

pinch of cayenne pepper

salt

1 Mix all the marinade
  ingredients, except salt, in a
non-metallic dish. Turn the
poussins in the marinade,
cover, and marinate in the
refrigerator for at least 3 hours
(or overnight), turning
occasionally.

2 When ready to cook,
  preheat the grill to hot, and
sprinkle the poussins with a
little salt.

3 Put the poussins, skin-side
  down, on a rack under the
grill, 15 cm (6 in) from the
heat, and grill for 15–20
minutes on each side, turning
once and brushing with the
marinade. Check the poussins
are done by pricking with a
fork – the juices should run
clear, not pink or red. Serve hot
or cold.

Cook's know-how

It is quick and easy to
spatchcock poussins, but you
can buy them ready
spatchcocked at most
supermarkets, especially
during the barbecue season.

LEMON POUSSINS WITH ARTICHOKE HEARTS

SERVES 4

4 x 375 g (12 oz) poussins

salt and black pepper

4 garlic cloves

1 lemon, cut into quarters
  lengthwise

4 rosemary sprigs

60 g (2 oz) butter, softened

1 x 300 g (10 oz) jar artichoke
  hearts in oil

175 ml (6 fl oz) dry white wine

fresh rosemary and lemon wedges
  to garnish

1 Season the poussins inside
  and out, and put a garlic
clove, lemon quarter, and
rosemary sprig into each one.
Tie the legs together with
string, then rub the birds with
the softened butter.

2 Put the poussins upside
  down on a rack in a
roasting tin. Roast in a
preheated oven at 190°C
(375°F, Gas 5) for 40–45
minutes, turning them the right
way up halfway through.

3 While the poussins are
  roasting, drain the artichoke
hearts, reserving 2–3 tbsp of the
oil, and cut each artichoke
heart in half.

4 Check the poussins are
  done by pricking with a
fork – the juices should run
clear, not pink or red. Remove
them from the tin, and keep
warm. Spoon off all but 1 tbsp
fat from the tin, leaving behind
the cooking juices.

5 Add the wine to the tin,
  mix with the juices, then
boil on the hob until reduced
to about 90 ml (3 fl oz).

6 Stir in the artichokes and
  the reserved oil, and heat
through gently. Serve the
poussins with the artichokes
and sauce, garnished with
rosemary and lemon wedges.

POUSSINS WITH ROMESCO SAUCE

SERVES 2

2 x 375 g (12 oz) poussins, spatchcocked (page 172)

8 spring onions, trimmed (optional)

coriander sprigs to garnish

MARINADE

2 tbsp olive oil

1 tbsp balsamic vinegar

4 garlic cloves, crushed

1/2 tsp ground cinnamon

salt and black pepper

ROMESCO SAUCE

1 x 225 g (8 oz) can chopped tomatoes

90 g (3 oz) blanched almonds

1 slice of stale bread, broken into pieces

2 tbsp olive oil

1 tbsp balsamic vinegar

1 garlic clove

1 small dried red chilli, crumbled

a few sprigs of parsley

1/2 tsp ground cinnamon

1 Make the marinade: combine the oil, vinegar, garlic, and cinnamon, and season with salt and pepper. Brush over the poussins and spring onions (if using), cover, and marinate in the refrigerator for 1 hour, or overnight.

2 Place the poussins skin-side down under a hot grill, 15 cm (6 in) from the heat, and grill for 15–20 minutes on each side. Grill the spring onions close to the heat for 5–8 minutes on each side until the onions are slightly charred.

3 Meanwhile, make the romesco sauce: put all the ingredients in a food processor with a pinch of salt and purée until smooth.

4 Check the poussins are done by pricking with a fork – the juices should run clear, not pink or red. Serve hot, with the romesco sauce and the spring onions (if used). Garnish each serving with a coriander sprig.

ORIENTAL POUSSINS

SERVES 4

2 x 625 g (1 1/4 lb) poussins

4 tbsp dark soy sauce

3 tbsp dry sherry

3 tbsp hoisin sauce

3 tbsp sunflower oil

3 garlic cloves, crushed

2 tbsp brown sugar

1 tsp five-spice powder

2.5 cm (1 in) piece of fresh root ginger, peeled and grated

spring onions to garnish

1 Halve the poussins, and remove the backbones (see box, right).

2 Combine the soy sauce, sherry, hoisin sauce, oil, garlic, sugar, five-spice powder, and ginger. Brush this mixture on both sides of the poussins.

3 Put the poussins, skin-side up, into a roasting tin, and roast in a preheated oven at 190°C (375°F, Gas 5) for 30 minutes. Check the poussins are done by pricking with a fork – the juices should run clear, not pink or red.

4 With a sharp knife, finely shred the green tops of the spring onions, working on the diagonal. Serve the poussins hot, garnished with the spring onion slices.

Halving a poussin

Cut along the middle of the breast with poultry shears or sturdy kitchen scissors. Take the 2 sides and open out slightly.

Turn the poussin over and cut in half, along one side of the backbone. Remove and discard the backbone.

CHICKEN CACCIATORE

SERVES 4

8 small chicken portions (4 legs and 4 breasts or 8 thighs)

plain flour for dusting

salt and black pepper

3–4 tbsp olive oil

90 g (3 oz) streaky bacon or pancetta, cut into strips

1 large onion, chopped

1 small green pepper, halved, seeded, and diced

2 garlic cloves, crushed

250 g (8 oz) mushrooms, quartered

125 ml (4 fl oz) red or white wine

1 x 400 g (13 oz) can chopped tomatoes

75 ml (2½ fl oz) tomato purée

2 tsp chopped fresh sage

4 tbsp chopped parsley

grated zest of 1 lemon

2 tbsp capers, chopped

fresh sage sprigs to garnish

1 Lightly dust the chicken pieces with flour seasoned with salt and pepper, and shake off any excess.

2 Heat half of the oil in a large frying pan, add the bacon and chicken, and cook for 10–12 minutes until browned all over. Transfer to a casserole with a slotted spoon, then pour off the fat from the frying pan.

3 Heat the remaining oil in the frying pan, add the onion, green pepper, and half of the garlic, and cook gently, stirring, for 5 minutes until soft but not coloured. Transfer to the casserole with a slotted spoon. Add the mushrooms, and cook for 2 minutes. Add to the casserole.

4 Pour the wine into the frying pan, and boil until reduced to about 4 tbsp. Add to the casserole with the tomatoes, tomato purée, and the sage. Cover and cook in a preheated oven at 180°C (350°F, Gas 4) for 45 minutes or until the chicken is tender when pierced with a fork.

5 Combine the remaining garlic with the chopped parsley, lemon zest, and capers. Stir into the casserole, and taste for seasoning. Serve hot, garnished with sage sprigs.

FAMILY CHICKEN CASSEROLE

SERVES 4

2 tbsp sunflower oil

4 chicken portions (legs or thighs)

125 g (4 oz) streaky bacon rashers, cut into strips

250 g (8 oz) carrots, thickly sliced

2 celery stalks, thickly sliced

1 large onion, sliced

30 g (1 oz) plain flour

600 ml (1 pint) chicken stock

1 bouquet garni

salt and black pepper

4 potatoes, cut into large chunks

chopped parsley to garnish

1 Heat the oil in a large flameproof casserole. Add the chicken, skin-side down, and cook for 10–12 minutes until browned all over. Lift out and drain on paper towels. Add the bacon, carrots, celery, and onion, and cook over a high heat, stirring, until golden. Lift out with a slotted spoon, and drain on paper towels.

2 Spoon off all but 1 tbsp fat from the casserole. Add the flour, and cook, stirring constantly, for 3–5 minutes until lightly browned. Gradually pour in the chicken stock, stirring until smooth. Add the bouquet garni, and season with salt and pepper.

3 Return the chicken, bacon, carrots, celery, and onion to the casserole, add the potatoes, and bring to a boil. Cover and cook in a preheated oven at 160°C (325°F, Gas 3) for 1–1¼ hours or until the chicken is tender when pierced with a fork. Serve hot, garnished with parsley.

ITALIAN CHICKEN CASSEROLE

Substitute 250 g (8 oz) sliced courgettes for the carrots, and 1 x 400 g (13 oz) can chopped tomatoes and 1 tbsp tomato purée for the chicken stock. If the mixture is too thick, add a splash of water, chicken stock, or wine.

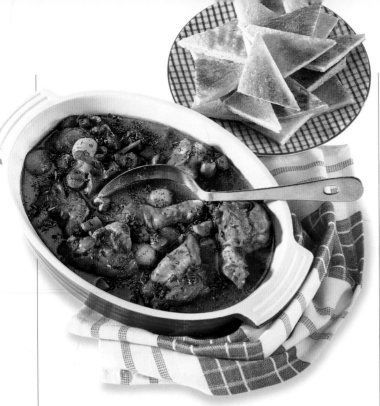

CHICKEN MARENGO

SERVES 4

- 30 g (1 oz) butter
- 1 tbsp sunflower oil
- 1.5 kg (3 lb) chicken, cut into 8 serving pieces (page 170)
- 8 small shallots or pickling onions
- 30 g (1 oz) plain flour
- 300 ml (½ pint) dry white wine
- 150 ml (¼ pint) chicken stock
- 1 x 400 g (13 oz) can chopped tomatoes
- 250 g (8 oz) button mushrooms
- 1 tbsp tomato purée
- 2 garlic cloves, crushed
- 1 bouquet garni
- salt and black pepper
- 250 g (8 oz) cooked peeled prawns
- chopped parsley to garnish

1 Melt the butter with the oil in a large flameproof casserole. Add the chicken pieces, and cook for 10–12 minutes until browned all over. Lift out and leave to drain on paper towels.

2 Add the shallots or onions, and cook over a high heat for about 8 minutes or until golden brown.

3 Lift out the shallots or onions and leave to drain on paper towels. Spoon off all but 1 tbsp of the fat from the casserole, add the flour, and cook, stirring, for 3–5 minutes until lightly browned.

4 Lower the heat, and stir in the wine and stock until combined. Add the tomatoes, mushrooms, tomato purée, garlic, and bouquet garni. Season with salt and pepper.

5 Return the shallots or onions and the chicken to the casserole, and bring to a boil. Cover and cook in a preheated oven at 180°C (350°F, Gas 4) for 35 minutes or until the chicken is almost tender. Stir in the prawns, and return to the oven for another 10 minutes or until the chicken is tender when pierced with a fork. Garnish each serving with chopped parsley before serving.

COQ AU VIN

SERVES 4

- 30 g (1 oz) butter
- 1 tbsp sunflower oil
- 1.5 kg (3 lb) chicken, cut into 8 serving pieces (page 170)
- 125 g (4 oz) streaky bacon rashers, cut into strips
- 8 small shallots or pickling onions
- 250 g (8 oz) button mushrooms
- 30 g (1 oz) plain flour
- 300 ml (½ pint) chicken stock
- 300 ml (½ pint) red wine
- 1 bouquet garni
- 1 large garlic clove, crushed
- salt and black pepper
- 2 tbsp chopped parsley to garnish
- croûtes (page 49) to serve

1 Melt the butter with the oil in a large flameproof casserole. Add the chicken, and cook for 10–12 minutes until browned all over. Lift out and leave to drain on paper towels.

2 Spoon off any excess fat, then add the bacon, shallots or onions, and mushrooms, and cook over a high heat, stirring, until golden brown.

3 Lift the mixture out of the pan with a slotted spoon and leave to drain thoroughly on paper towels.

4 Add the flour to the pan, and cook for 3–5 minutes, stirring constantly until lightly browned. Gradually pour in the stock, then the wine, stirring until smooth.

5 Return the chicken, bacon, shallots, and mushrooms to the casserole, and add the bouquet garni, and garlic. Season with salt and pepper. Bring to a boil, cover, and cook in a preheated oven at 180°C (350°F, Gas 4) for 45 minutes or until the chicken is tender when pierced with a fork.

6 Sprinkle the chicken with the chopped parsley, and serve hot, with croûtes.

Healthy option

To reduce the fat content of this classic dish, skin the chicken before cooking, use 2 tbsp oil and no butter, and half the amount of bacon (or omit it altogether).

AMERICAN FRIED CHICKEN

SERVES 4

350 ml (12 fl oz) buttermilk

8 chicken thighs

125 g (4 oz) plain flour

1 1/2 tsp salt

1 tsp paprika

1/2 tsp black pepper

1/2 tsp garlic granules (optional)

large pinch of grated nutmeg

sunflower oil for deep-frying

TO SERVE (OPTIONAL)

4 streaky bacon rashers, grilled

parsley sprigs

1 Pour the buttermilk into a large non-metallic bowl. Add the chicken, and turn to coat. Cover and chill, turning occasionally, for 2–3 hours.

2 In a large bowl, combine the flour with the salt, paprika, pepper, garlic granules (if using), and nutmeg.

3 Lift the chicken pieces out of the buttermilk and shake off any excess liquid. Coat with the seasoned flour.

4 Pour 2 cm (3/4 in) oil into a deep frying pan, and heat to 180°C (350°F), or until a cube of bread browns in 1 minute.

5 Fry the chicken in the oil, in 2–3 batches if necessary. Cook each batch for 10–15 minutes or until the pieces are tender when pierced with a fork, turning them several times so they cook evenly.

6 Remove the chicken from the oil with a slotted spoon, and drain on paper towels. Serve hot, with grilled bacon rashers and parsley if you like.

HERB GRILLED CHICKEN

SERVES 8

8 chicken portions (legs or breasts)

HERB BUTTER

90 g (3 oz) butter, softened

3 tbsp chopped parsley

3 tbsp snipped fresh chives

2 garlic cloves, crushed (optional)

salt and black pepper

1 Mix the butter with the parsley, chives, and garlic, if using, and a good pinch each of salt and pepper.

2 Spread the chicken with the butter, and put, skin-side down over a hot barbecue, or skin-side up under a hot grill, 10 cm (4 in) from the heat. Cook for 10 minutes on each side or until the juices run clear when the chicken is pierced.

JAMAICAN CHICKEN

Substitute 1/2 tsp crushed peppercorns (red, green, and black), 1 tsp chopped fresh thyme, and 3 chopped spring onions for the parsley and chives.

HOT PAPRIKA CHICKEN

Substitute 2 tsp paprika and 2 tsp mustard powder for the parsley and chives.

THAI CORIANDER CHICKEN

Substitute 1–2 tbsp chopped fresh coriander and 2 tbsp Thai green curry paste for the parsley and chives.

Healthy option

Butter makes the chicken luscious and golden brown, but it is high in saturated fat and calories. You can reduce this by using half the amount of butter or 2 tbsp olive oil. Skinning the chicken before cooking is another option.

JERK CHICKEN

SERVES 4

4 chicken legs or drumsticks

JERK PASTE

3 tbsp lime juice

2 tbsp dark rum

2 tbsp sunflower oil

4 spring onions, roughly chopped

1–2 fresh green chillies, halved, seeded, and roughly chopped

2 garlic cloves, roughly chopped

1 tbsp ground allspice

2 tsp fresh thyme leaves

salt and black pepper

TO SERVE

chopped fresh thyme

grilled pineapple rings (optional)

1 Make the jerk paste: purée the ingredients in a food processor with a pinch each of salt and pepper.

2 Put the chicken pieces in a non-metallic dish and brush them all over with the jerk paste. Cover and marinate in the refrigerator for at least 30 minutes, or overnight.

3 Put the chicken over a hot barbecue, or under a hot grill, 10 cm (4 in) from the heat. Cook for 10 minutes on each side or until the juices run clear when the chicken is pierced.

4 Serve the chicken hot or cold, sprinkled with thyme and accompanied by grilled pineapple rings, if you like.

TEX-MEX CHICKEN

SERVES 4

4 skinless, boneless chicken breasts

2 avocados

2 tbsp lime juice

1 red onion, finely chopped

MARINADE

4 tbsp olive oil

4 tbsp orange juice

1 tsp ground cumin

SALSA

500 g (1 lb) tomatoes, chopped

1 small red onion, finely chopped

3 tbsp olive oil

2 tbsp lime juice

3 tbsp chopped fresh coriander

2 garlic cloves, crushed

1 fresh green chilli, halved, seeded, and chopped

salt

1 Make several diagonal slashes in each chicken breast, then put the chicken in a non-metallic dish. Mix the marinade ingredients together, and pour over the chicken. Cover and marinate in the refrigerator for at least 30 minutes, or overnight.

2 Make the salsa: combine the tomatoes, onion, oil, lime juice, coriander, garlic, chilli, and salt to taste. Cover and chill until ready to serve.

3 Remove the chicken from the marinade, and put under a hot grill, 10 cm (4 in) from the heat. Grill for 3–5 minutes on each side, depending on the size of the chicken, until the juices run clear when the chicken is pierced.

4 Meanwhile, halve, stone (page 88), and peel the avocados. Slice lengthwise, and brush with lime juice.

5 Thinly slice the chicken breasts, following the slashes made before marinating. Arrange the avocado and chicken slices on plates, and sprinkle the chopped red onion around the edges. Spoon a little of the salsa into the middle of each serving, and hand the remainder separately.

CHICKEN AND TURKEY SALADS

Lean, low-fat chicken and turkey teamed with fresh seasonal salad ingredients and vegetables make healthy meals for every day and special occasions, and if you buy ready cooked meat they are very quick to put together. These salads are good for buffets too, as most of the preparation can be done well in advance.

TARRAGON CHICKEN WITH AVOCADO

SERVES 6

500 g (1 lb) skinless, boneless cooked chicken

3 spring onions, finely sliced

SAUCE

5 tbsp sunflower oil

3 tbsp white wine vinegar

2 tsp Dijon mustard

2–3 tsp caster sugar, to taste

2 canned anchovy fillets, finely chopped

200 ml (7 fl oz) half-fat crème fraîche

1 tbsp chopped fresh tarragon

1 tbsp chopped parsley

salt and black pepper

TO SERVE

2 perfectly ripe avocados

juice of ½ lemon

1 bunch of watercress

2 spring onions, trimmed and cut lengthwise into fine slices

1 Cut the chicken into bite-sized pieces and mix with the spring onions in a bowl. Whisk all the sauce ingredients together in another bowl, adding salt and pepper to taste. Mix the sauce with the chicken, cover, and marinate in the refrigerator for at least 2 hours, overnight if possible.

2 Just before serving, halve, stone, and peel the avocados, slice the flesh into 1 cm (½ in) strips, and toss in the lemon juice. Gently mix the avocado into the salad, and spoon into a serving dish. Garnish with watercress and spring onions, and serve.

VIETNAMESE TURKEY SALAD

SERVES 4

4 tbsp fish sauce (nam pla)

500 g (1 lb) turkey breast steaks

4 tbsp lime juice

1 tbsp sugar, or more to taste

¼ tsp ground black pepper

1 small fresh red chilli, halved, seeded, and finely chopped

250 g (8 oz) hard white cabbage, finely shredded

2 medium carrots, finely shredded

1 small onion, finely sliced

1 large bunch of fresh mint

1 Half fill a medium wok or deep frying pan with water, sprinkle in half the fish sauce and bring to a boil. Turn the heat down to a simmer, lower in the turkey breast steaks, and cover the pan with a lid. Simmer for 10 minutes or until the turkey is cooked through. Lift the turkey out of the water, and leave until cool enough to handle.

2 Meanwhile, mix the remaining fish sauce in a large bowl with the lime juice, 1 tbsp sugar, the black pepper and chilli. Add the cabbage, carrots, and onion, and mix well.

3 Cut the turkey into bite-sized strips and roughly chop 2 tbsp mint. Toss the turkey and chopped mint into the salad, and mix again. Cover and marinate in the refrigerator for 2–4 hours.

4 To serve, toss the salad again, then taste for seasoning and add more sugar if you like. Serve on a bed of the remaining mint leaves.

RED PEPPER HERBED CHICKEN SALAD

SERVES 6

500 g (1 lb) skinless, boneless cooked chicken

SAUCE

1 bunch of fresh parsley

1 bunch of fresh basil

60 g (2 oz) red pepper in oil or brine (from a jar), drained

juice of 1 small lemon

2 tsp caster sugar

90 g (3 oz) low-fat Greek yogurt

4 tbsp low-fat mayonnaise

90 g (3 oz) half-fat soft cheese

salt and black pepper

TO SERVE

fresh basil

strips of red pepper

tossed salad leaves

1 Make the sauce. Put the parsley, basil, red pepper, lemon juice, and 2 tsp sugar in a food processor and pulse for about 30 seconds until quite coarsely chopped. Add the yogurt, mayonnaise, soft cheese, and seasonings and pulse again for about 30 seconds. The sauce should be mixed but not finely chopped – it should have texture and flecks of herbs. Taste and add more sugar and seasoning if you like. (If you haven't got a food processor, coarsely chop the parsley, basil and red pepper. Mix the other ingredients together, then mix in the chopped herbs and red pepper.)

2 Cut the chicken into strips, mix into the sauce, and turn into a shallow serving dish. Cover and leave in the refrigerator for at least 4 hours, or overnight, for the flavours to infuse.

3 Before serving, check the seasoning, and garnish with basil and strips of red pepper. Serve on a bed of tossed salad.

CLOCKWISE FROM TOP: Tarragon Chicken with Avocado, Red Pepper Herbed Chicken Salad, Vietnamese Turkey Salad.

Blanch the almonds and loosen the skins: immerse in a bowl of boiling water. When cool enough to handle, squeeze the almonds between your fingers to slide and pull off the skins.

Slice the almonds in half lengthwise. Cut the halves into shreds.

FRAGRANT CHICKEN CURRY WITH ALMONDS

The spices in this recipe are among those used in ready-made curry powders, but using your own individual blend of spices gives a truly authentic flavour to a curry. This is a creamy, mild dish – not too hot or spicy.

SERVES 4

2 cloves

2 tsp cumin seeds

seeds of 4 cardamom pods

1 tsp garam masala

pinch of cayenne pepper

2 tbsp sunflower oil

4 skinless, boneless chicken breasts

1 large onion, finely chopped

2 garlic cloves, crushed

2.5 cm (1 in) piece of fresh root ginger, peeled and grated

salt and black pepper

300 ml (1/2 pint) chicken stock

150 ml (1/4 pint) single cream

1 x 150 g (5 oz) carton plain yogurt

sultanas and whole almonds, blanched, shredded, and toasted (see box, right) to garnish

1 Crush the cloves in a mortar and pestle with the cumin and cardamom seeds. Mix in the garam masala and cayenne.

2 Heat the oil in a flameproof casserole. Add the chicken breasts, and cook for 2–3 minutes on each side until golden. Remove with a slotted spoon and leave to drain on paper towels.

3 Add the onion, garlic, and ginger to the pan, and cook gently, stirring occasionally, for a few minutes until just beginning to soften. Add the spice mixture and season with salt and pepper, then stir over a high heat for 1 minute.

4 Return the chicken to the casserole. Pour in the stock, and bring to a boil. Cover and simmer gently for 15 minutes or until the chicken is tender.

5 Stir in the cream and yogurt, heat through very gently, then taste for seasoning.

6 Spoon the curry into a serving dish, and sprinkle with the sultanas and toasted shredded almonds. Serve hot.

Cook's know-how

Cardamom comes in 3 forms: as pods, whole seeds, and ground seeds. As the seeds lose their flavour quickly, it is best to buy whole cardamom pods and remove the seeds when you need them.

If you like, use 1 x 400 g (13 oz) can coconut milk (either full-fat or reduced-fat) instead of the stock in step 4, and omit the single cream in step 5. You can then finish the curry with just a swirl of yogurt and a scattering of chopped fresh coriander.

Place the shredded almonds on a baking tray, and toast in a preheated oven at 180°C (350°F, Gas 4), stirring the almonds occasionally to ensure that they colour evenly, for 8–10 minutes until lightly browned.

SAFFRON CHICKEN

SERVES 6

6 boneless chicken breasts, with the skin left on

1 tbsp vegetable oil

200 ml (7 fl oz) crème fraîche

salt and black pepper

chopped coriander to garnish

MARINADE

2 pinches of saffron threads

2.5 cm (1 in) piece of fresh root ginger, peeled and grated

juice of 1 lemon

1 tsp ground cardamom

1 tsp ground coriander

1 tsp ground cinnamon

1 Make the marinade: put the saffron and the ginger into a mortar and grind with a pestle. Add the lemon juice, cardamom, coriander, and cinnamon, and mix well.

2 Put the chicken into a non-metallic dish, and brush the marinade over it. Cover and marinate in the refrigerator for at least 20 minutes.

3 Pour the oil into a small roasting tin. Turn the chicken breasts in the oil, and put them, skin-side up, in the roasting tin. Cook in a preheated oven at 190°C (375°F, Gas 5) for 15–20 minutes or until the juices run clear when the chicken is pierced with a fork. Remove from the tin and keep warm.

4 Put the tin on the hob, pour in the crème fraîche, and stir to combine with the juices. Season with salt and pepper, and heat through.

5 Divide the sauce among 6 warmed plates. Place the chicken breasts on top, and sprinkle with chopped coriander before serving.

CHICKEN TIKKA

SERVES 4–6

750 g (1½ lb) skinless, boneless chicken breasts, cut into 2.5 cm (1 in) cubes

cucumber raita (see box, right) to serve

MARINADE

2 tbsp plain yogurt

2 tbsp tomato purée

1 small onion, finely chopped

2.5 cm (1 in) piece of fresh root ginger, peeled and grated

3 garlic cloves, crushed

1 tbsp tamarind paste (optional)

1 tbsp paprika

1 tsp ground cumin

large pinch of cayenne pepper

4–6 METAL SKEWERS

1 Make the marinade: in a large bowl, combine the yogurt, tomato purée, onion, ginger, garlic, tamarind paste (if using), paprika, cumin, and cayenne pepper.

2 Toss the chicken in the marinade. Cover and marinate in the refrigerator for at least 2 hours (or overnight), stirring occasionally.

3 Thread the chicken on to skewers, put under a hot grill, 10 cm (4 in) from the heat, and grill for 3–5 minutes on each side or until cooked through. Serve hot, with raita.

Cucumber raita

Cut half a cucumber in half lengthwise. Scoop out the seeds, then coarsely grate the flesh into a sieve set over a bowl. Sprinkle with salt, and leave to drain for 10 minutes. Press hard to extract the juices.

Tip the cucumber into a bowl and add 1 x 150 g (5 oz) carton plain yogurt, 3 thinly sliced spring onions, 3 heaped tbsp chopped fresh mint, and pepper to taste. Stir well to combine. Serve chilled.

STIR-FRIED CHICKEN WITH CRISP VEGETABLES

SERVES 4

4 skinless, boneless chicken breasts, cut diagonally into 5 mm (1/4 in) strips

2 tbsp mild curry powder

black pepper

8 spring onions

250 g (8 oz) carrots

3 tbsp sunflower oil

175 g (6 oz) baby sweetcorn

175 g (6 oz) sugar snap peas

2–3 tbsp lemon juice

2 tbsp clear honey

2.5 cm (1 in) piece of fresh root ginger, peeled and grated

salt

125 g (4 oz) bean sprouts

noodles to serve

1 Put the chicken strips in a bowl with the curry powder and season with black pepper. Toss until the chicken is coated, then set aside while you prepare the vegetables.

2 Finely slice the white parts of the spring onions, reserving the green tops to garnish the finished dish.

3 Peel the carrots and cut them into matchstick-thin strips.

4 Heat 2 tbsp of the oil in a wok or large frying pan. Add the chicken strips and stir-fry over a high heat for 3–4 minutes until golden brown.

5 Add the sliced spring onions, the carrot matchsticks, the whole baby sweetcorn, and the sugar snap peas, then add the lemon juice, honey, ginger, and a pinch of salt. Stir-fry over a high heat for 4 minutes or until the vegetables are tender-crisp and the chicken is cooked through.

6 Toss in the bean sprouts, and stir-fry over a high heat for 1–2 minutes until heated through. Taste for seasoning. Serve on a bed of noodles, and garnish with the reserved green spring onions.

THAI CHICKEN WITH WATER CHESTNUTS

SERVES 4

4 skinless, boneless chicken breasts, cut into 2.5 cm (1 in) pieces

3 tbsp sunflower oil

2 garlic cloves, crushed

2.5 cm (1 in) piece of fresh root ginger, peeled and grated

1/2 –1 fresh green chilli, halved, seeded, and chopped

1 tsp light soy sauce, or more to taste

1/2 tsp sugar

salt and black pepper

600 ml (1 pint) chicken stock

1 stem of lemon grass, bruised

grated zest of 1 lime

1 x 200 g (7 oz) can water chestnuts, drained, rinsed, and sliced

1 small bunch of fresh coriander, coarsely chopped

lime wedges, sliced spring onions, and peanuts to garnish

1 Put the chicken into a dish, and add the oil, garlic, ginger, chilli, soy sauce, and sugar. Season with black pepper, stir well, then leave to stand for a few minutes.

2 Heat a non-stick wok or frying pan, add the chicken mixture, in batches if necessary, and stir-fry for 2–3 minutes or until lightly browned.

3 Pour in the stock, add any marinade left in the dish, then add the lemon grass, lime zest, water chestnuts, and coriander. Continue stir-frying for a few minutes more until the chicken is tender.

4 Taste the stir-fry and add more soy sauce, if you like. Serve at once, garnished with lime wedges, spring onion slices, and peanuts.

SWEET & SOUR CHINESE CHICKEN

SERVES 4–6

500 g (1 lb) skinless, boneless chicken breasts, cut into 2.5 cm (1 in) pieces

2 tbsp dark soy sauce

1 tbsp Chinese rice wine or dry sherry

1 x 250 g (8 oz) can pineapple chunks in natural juice, drained and juice reserved

2 tbsp cornflour

3 tbsp sunflower oil

1 green pepper, halved, seeded, and cut into bite-sized pieces

1 red pepper, halved, seeded, and cut into bite-sized pieces

1 celery stalk, thickly sliced

1 onion, cut into bite-sized chunks

4 tbsp tomato ketchup

250 g (8 oz) canned lychees, drained and juice reserved

salt and black pepper

chopped fresh coriander to garnish

1 Toss the chicken pieces in a large bowl with the soy sauce and rice wine. Cover, and marinate in the refrigerator for at least 30 minutes.

2 Meanwhile, make the reserved pineapple juice up to 250 ml (8 fl oz) with water and blend with the cornflour. Set aside.

3 Heat the oil in a wok or large frying pan, add the chicken, in batches if necessary, and stir-fry for 3–4 minutes until golden all over. Lift out with a slotted spoon.

4 Add the green and red peppers, celery, and onion to the wok, and stir-fry for about 5 minutes.

5 Add the cornflour and pineapple juice mixture, ketchup, and reserved lychee juice to the wok, and cook for 3–5 minutes until thickened.

6 Return the chicken to the wok with the lychees and pineapple chunks, and heat through. Season with salt and pepper, and serve at once, garnished with chopped fresh coriander.

MUSTARD CHICKEN

SERVES 4

1 tbsp olive oil

4 skinless, boneless chicken breasts, cut diagonally into 2.5 cm (1 in) strips

1 garlic clove, crushed

250 ml (8 fl oz) single cream

1 tbsp plain flour

1 tbsp coarse-grain mustard

salt and black pepper

flat-leaf parsley sprigs to garnish

1 Heat the oil in a frying pan until hot. Add the chicken strips and garlic, in batches if necessary, and cook over a moderate heat, stirring frequently, for 3–4 minutes.

2 With a slotted spoon, lift the chicken and garlic out of the frying pan, and keep them warm.

3 In a small bowl, mix a little of the cream with the flour to make a smooth paste, then mix in the remaining cream.

4 Lower the heat and pour the cream into the pan. Cook gently for 2 minutes, stirring constantly until the sauce has thickened. Stir in the mustard and heat through gently, then season with salt and pepper.

5 Return the chicken to the pan, coat with the sauce, and cook gently for a few minutes more until the chicken is tender when pierced with a fork. Serve hot, garnished with parsley sprigs.

Cook's know-how

Do not let the sauce boil once you have added the mustard or it may taste bitter. Coarse-grain mustard gives an interesting texture to this dish, but if you prefer a smooth sauce, use Dijon mustard.

CHICKEN SATAY

In this traditional Indonesian speciality, the rich satay sauce made from peanuts and coconut complements the pieces of chicken tenderized by a tangy marinade. Serve as a starter or a buffet party dish.

SERVES 4

4 skinless, boneless chicken breasts, cut into 2 cm (3/4 in) pieces

flat-leaf parsley sprigs and coarsely chopped peanuts to garnish

MARINADE

90 ml (3 fl oz) dark soy sauce

juice of 1 lemon

3 tbsp sunflower oil

2 tbsp dark brown sugar

3 garlic cloves, crushed

3 spring onions, thinly sliced

Healthy option

Peanut butter is high in fat and calories, so you may wish to reduce the amount used here. Make the sauce with half the amount of ingredients, except for the lemon juice and ginger, and simmer it for longer in step 4 until it becomes thick.

SATAY SAUCE

250 g (8 oz) peanut butter

2 garlic cloves, crushed

175 ml (6 fl oz) water

30 g (1 oz) creamed coconut, coarsely chopped

1 tbsp dark soy sauce

1 tbsp dark brown sugar

1 cm (1/2 in) piece of fresh root ginger, peeled and grated

1 tbsp lemon juice

cayenne pepper

salt and black pepper

12 BAMBOO SKEWERS

1 Make the marinade: in a bowl, combine the soy sauce, lemon juice, oil, sugar, garlic, and spring onions.

2 Toss the chicken in the marinade. Cover and leave to marinate in the refrigerator for 30 minutes.

3 Soak the skewers in warm water for 30 minutes.

4 Make the satay sauce: heat the peanut butter with half of the garlic for 2 minutes. Add the water, creamed coconut, soy sauce, sugar, and ginger, and cook, stirring, for about 2 minutes or until the sauce is smooth.

5 Add the lemon juice and remaining garlic, and season with cayenne pepper, salt, and black pepper. Keep warm.

6 Thread the chicken pieces on to the skewers. Place under a hot grill, 10 cm (4 in) from the heat, and grill for 2–3 minutes on each side until cooked through.

7 Serve the chicken satay at once, garnishing the sauce with parsley sprigs and peanuts.

CHICKEN KEBABS

SERVES 6

4 skinless, boneless chicken breasts, cut into 2.5 cm (1 in) pieces

2 green peppers, halved, seeded, and cut into 2.5 cm (1 in) pieces

500 g (1 lb) cherry tomatoes

375 g (12 oz) button mushrooms

MARINADE

175 ml (6 fl oz) olive oil

125 ml (4 fl oz) light soy sauce

4 tbsp red wine vinegar

freshly ground black pepper

12 SKEWERS

1 Make the marinade: in a large bowl, combine the oil, soy sauce, and wine vinegar. Season with pepper, add the chicken, and mix well. Cover and marinate for 5–10 minutes.

2 Lift the chicken out of the marinade, reserving the marinade. Thread the skewers, alternating green peppers, tomatoes, chicken, and mushrooms.

3 Place the kebabs under a hot grill, 10 cm (4 in) from the heat. Grill the kebabs, basting with the marinade, for 3–5 minutes on each side or until the chicken is tender and cooked through. Serve hot.

CHICKEN PINWHEELS

This is an elegant dinner party dish that is simple and economical to make, yet it looks stunning. An accompaniment of fresh tagliatelle goes well with the tomato and herb sauce.

SERVES 4

4 skinless, boneless chicken breasts

melted butter for greasing

basil sprigs to garnish

FILLING

125 g (4 oz) full-fat soft cheese with garlic and herbs

2 tbsp sun-dried tomatoes in oil, drained and chopped

4 tbsp shredded fresh basil

salt and black pepper

TOMATO & HERB SAUCE

1 tbsp olive oil

1 small onion, chopped

1 x 400 g (13 oz) can chopped tomatoes

1 tbsp chopped fresh herbs, such as parsley, chives, and thyme

1 Make the filling: combine the cheese, sun-dried tomatoes, and basil. Season with salt and pepper, and mix well to combine.

2 Put the chicken breasts between sheets of cling film, and pound with a rolling pin until 5 mm (1/4 in) thick. Spread one-quarter of the filling over each breast, and tightly roll up each one.

3 Brush 4 squares of foil with melted butter, and wrap each chicken roll in a square, twisting the ends to seal them tightly. Put the rolls into a shallow pan of gently simmering water, cover, and poach for 15 minutes.

4 Meanwhile, make the tomato and herb sauce: heat the oil in a pan, add the onion, and cook, stirring often, for a few minutes until soft. Stir in the tomatoes with half of their juice, bring to a boil, and simmer for 3 minutes.

5 Purée the tomato mixture in a food processor until smooth. Work the purée through a sieve, and add more tomato juice if the sauce is too thick. Stir in the chopped fresh herbs, and season with salt and pepper.

6 Unwrap the chicken, and slice on the diagonal. Serve with the tomato and herb sauce, and garnish with basil.

CHICKEN STIR-FRY

SERVES 4

3 tbsp sunflower oil

4 spring onions, sliced

2.5 cm (1 in) piece of fresh root ginger, peeled and grated

1 tsp Chinese five-spice powder

1/2 tsp crushed dried red chillies

3 carrots, thinly sliced

2 peppers (red and yellow), halved, seeded, and cut into thin strips

4 tbsp dark soy sauce

2 tbsp dry sherry mixed with 2 tsp cornflour

4 skinless, boneless chicken breasts, cut into 1 cm (1/2 in) strips

1 Heat 1 tbsp of the oil in a wok or large frying pan, add the spring onions, ginger, five-spice powder, and chillies, and stir-fry for 1 minute.

2 Add the remaining oil, then add the carrots and peppers, and stir-fry over a high heat for 2–3 minutes. Add the soy sauce, sherry mixture, and chicken strips, and stir-fry for 3–4 minutes.

3 Add 125 ml (4 fl oz) water and stir-fry for 1–2 minutes until the liquid boils and thickens slightly. Serve at once.

CHEESE & GARLIC STUFFED CHICKEN

SERVES 6

6 boneless chicken breasts, with the skin on

melted butter for brushing

STUFFING

30 g (1 oz) butter

1 onion, finely chopped

2 large garlic cloves, crushed

250 g (8 oz) full-fat soft cheese

1 tbsp chopped fresh tarragon

1 egg yolk

pinch of grated nutmeg

salt and black pepper

1 Make the stuffing: melt the butter in a small saucepan, add the onion and garlic, and cook gently, stirring occasionally, for a few minutes until soft but not coloured. Turn the onion mixture into a bowl, and leave to cool slightly.

2 Add the soft cheese to the onion mixture with the tarragon, egg yolk, and nutmeg. Season with salt and pepper and mix well.

3 Stuff the chicken breasts: lift up the skin along one side of each breast, spread the cheese mixture over the chicken and then gently press the skin back on top. Put the chicken breasts into an ovenproof dish and brush with the melted butter.

4 Roast the chicken in a preheated oven at 190°C (375°F, Gas 5) for 25–30 minutes until the chicken is cooked through. Cut each breast into diagonal slices, and serve hot.

Cook's know-how

Full-fat soft cheese is used here because it holds its shape well during cooking. Do not substitute a low-fat cheese because this will melt too quickly and make the chicken watery and soggy.

TARRAGON CHICKEN WITH LIME

SERVES 4

60 g (2 oz) butter, softened

grated zest of 1 lime and juice of 2 limes

4 skinless, boneless chicken breasts

1 tbsp chopped fresh tarragon

salt and black pepper

150 ml (1/4 pint) low-fat crème fraîche

lime segments and fresh tarragon to garnish

1 Put the butter into a bowl, and beat in the lime zest. Prepare the chicken breasts (see box, right).

2 Put the chicken breasts into a roasting tin. Sprinkle with the lime juice, tarragon, and salt and pepper, and roast in a preheated oven at 200°C (400°F, Gas 6) for 20 minutes or until the chicken is cooked through.

3 Transfer the chicken breasts to warmed serving plates and keep warm.

4 Put the tin on the hob, add 1 tbsp water to the cooking juices, stirring to dissolve the sediment, and bring to a boil, stirring. Cook, stirring, for 1–2 minutes. Stir in the crème fraîche and heat gently until warmed through.

5 Serve the chicken with the sauce, and garnish each serving with the lime segments and fresh tarragon.

Preparing the chicken

Make 3–4 deep diagonal cuts in each chicken breast with a sharp knife. Spread the top of each breast with one-quarter of the lime butter.

BACON-WRAPPED CHICKEN BREASTS

SERVES 6

6 skinless, boneless chicken breasts

4 tbsp coarse-grain mustard

black pepper

18 streaky bacon rashers, rinds removed

snipped fresh chives to garnish

1 Spread both sides of the chicken breasts with the mustard, and season with pepper.

2 Take 3 bacon rashers, stretch them with the back of a knife, and arrange them side by side and slightly overlapping. Wrap a chicken breast with the bacon (see box, right). Repeat with the remaining bacon and chicken.

3 Place the chicken breasts with the bacon seam-side down in a roasting tin, and roast in a preheated oven at 190°C (375°F, Gas 5) for 25–30 minutes until the bacon is crisp and brown and the chicken cooked through. Serve at once, garnished with snipped chives.

Wrapping a chicken breast in bacon

Place a chicken breast at one end of the overlapped bacon rashers, and then wrap the rashers diagonally (working from side to side) around the chicken to make a neat parcel.

Healthy option

Use the leanest bacon you can and trim off all the fat along the top edge of each rasher. Allow 12 rashers rather than 18 – it does not matter if some of the chicken peeps through.

CHICKEN WITH SAGE & ORANGE

SERVES 6

6 boneless chicken breasts, with the skin on

1 tbsp plain flour

orange segments and fresh sage leaves to garnish

MARINADE

300 ml (1/2 pint) orange juice

1 tbsp light soy sauce

2 garlic cloves, crushed

2 tbsp chopped fresh sage

1 cm (1/2 in) piece of fresh root ginger, peeled and grated

salt and black pepper

1 Make the marinade: combine the orange juice, soy sauce, garlic, sage, ginger, and salt and pepper. Toss the chicken in the marinade, cover, and leave to marinate in the refrigerator for 20–30 minutes.

2 Reserve the marinade, and arrange the chicken breasts, skin-side up, in a large roasting tin.

3 Roast the chicken in a preheated oven at 190°C (375°F, Gas 5) for 10 minutes. Pour the reserved marinade over the chicken, and continue roasting for 10 minutes or until the chicken is cooked through.

4 Remove the chicken with a slotted spoon, and arrange on a warmed platter. Cover and keep warm.

5 Pour all but 2 tbsp of the marinade into a jug, and reserve. Add the flour to the marinade remaining in the roasting tin, and mix to a smooth paste.

6 Put the roasting tin on the hob, and cook, stirring, for 1 minute. Gradually stir in the reserved marinade. Bring to a boil, simmer for 2 minutes, and taste for seasoning. Strain, pour a little around the chicken breasts, and garnish with the orange segments and fresh sage. Serve the remaining sauce separately.

CHICKEN CORDON BLEU

SERVES 4

4 skinless, boneless chicken breasts

4 thin slices of Gruyère cheese

4 thin slices of cooked ham

salt and black pepper

1 egg, beaten

125 g (4 oz) fresh white breadcrumbs

30 g (1 oz) butter

3 tbsp sunflower oil

1 With a sharp knife, cut each chicken breast horizontally, leaving it attached at one side.

2 Open out each chicken breast, place between 2 sheets of greaseproof paper, and pound to a 3 mm (1/8 in) thickness with a rolling pin. Fill and fold the chicken breasts (see box, right).

3 Dip each folded chicken breast into the beaten egg, then dip each breast into the breadcrumbs, making sure each one is evenly coated. Cover and chill for 15 minutes.

4 Melt the butter with the sunflower oil in a large frying pan. When the butter is foaming, add the chicken breasts, and cook for 10 minutes on each side or until the breadcrumb coating is crisp and golden and the chicken is cooked through. Remove the chicken breasts with a slotted spoon and drain thoroughly on paper towels. Cut into 1 cm (1/2 in) slices, and serve at once.

Folding the chicken

Place 1 slice of cheese and 1 slice of ham on half of each chicken breast, season with salt and pepper, and fold the breast over to cover the filling.

HERB-MARINATED CHICKEN BREASTS

SERVES 4

4 boneless chicken breasts, with the skin left on

30 g (1 oz) butter

2 tbsp sunflower oil

150 ml (1/4 pint) chicken stock

1 bunch of watercress, tough stalks removed, to serve

chopped parsley to garnish

MARINADE

2 tbsp olive oil

1 tbsp lemon juice

3 garlic cloves, crushed

3 tbsp chopped parsley

1/2 tsp dried herbes de Provence or mixed herbs

salt and black pepper

1 Make the marinade: combine the oil, lemon juice, garlic, parsley, and dried herbs, and season with salt and pepper. Turn the chicken in the marinade, cover, and marinate in the refrigerator for at least 30 minutes.

2 Remove the chicken from the marinade, and dry on paper towels.

3 Melt the butter with the oil in a large frying pan. When the butter is foaming, add the chicken breasts, skin-side down, and cook for 10 minutes. Turn the chicken, and cook for a further 5 minutes or until golden and cooked through.

4 Using a slotted spoon, remove the chicken breasts, and keep hot.

5 Pour the chicken stock into the pan, and boil until reduced to about 8 tbsp.

6 Arrange the chicken breasts on beds of watercress, and strain over the hot sauce. Serve hot, garnished with chopped parsley.

SPICY CHICKEN BREASTS

Substitute 1 tsp paprika and 1/4 tsp crushed dried red chillies (chilli flakes) for the dried herbs in the marinade.

CHICKEN THIGHS WITH CHESTNUT STUFFING

You do not need to roast a whole bird to enjoy the classic combination of chicken with a savoury stuffing. In this recipe, chicken thighs are wrapped around a nutty filling of chestnuts and bacon, and served with cranberry sauce.

SERVES 4

8 boneless chicken thighs, with the skin left on

150 ml (¼ pint) chicken stock

1 tbsp cranberry or redcurrant jelly

STUFFING

15 g (½ oz) butter

2 streaky bacon rashers, rinds removed, diced

1 small onion, finely chopped

125 g (4 oz) frozen chestnuts, thawed and finely chopped

30 g (1 oz) fresh brown breadcrumbs

1 tbsp chopped parsley

salt and black pepper

1 egg yolk

1 Make the stuffing: melt the butter in a frying pan, add the bacon and onion, and cook over a medium heat for 3–5 minutes until the bacon is crisp and the onion soft but not coloured.

2 Add the chestnuts, and cook, stirring occasionally, for 5 minutes. Remove from the heat, add the breadcrumbs, and parsley, and season with salt and pepper, then bind with the egg yolk.

3 Place the chicken thighs, skin-side down, on a chopping board, and divide the stuffing among them. Roll up each thigh to enclose the stuffing.

4 Arrange the chicken thighs in a single layer in a roasting tin, and cook in a preheated oven at 190°C (375°F, Gas 5) for 20–25 minutes until the chicken is lightly browned and cooked through. Lift the chicken thighs out of the roasting tin, and keep hot.

5 Spoon off any excess fat, put the tin on the hob, and pour in the stock. Bring to a boil, and boil for 3–5 minutes until syrupy, stirring to dissolve any sediment and cooking juices.

6 Stir in the cranberry or redcurrant jelly, and cook for 1 minute to melt the jelly. Taste for seasoning. Strain the sauce, and serve at once, with the chicken thighs.

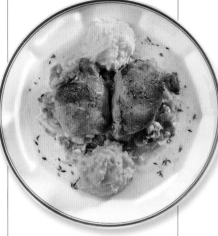

CHICKEN THIGHS NORMANDE

SERVES 4

3 leeks, trimmed and thinly sliced

4 lean back bacon rashers, rinds removed, diced

2 garlic cloves, crushed

350 ml (12 fl oz) strong dry cider

8 chicken thighs, with the bone in and skin left on

½ tsp chopped fresh thyme

salt and black pepper

125 ml (4 fl oz) crème fraîche

1 Put the leeks, bacon, and garlic into a roasting tin. Pour in the cider, and put the chicken on top. Sprinkle with the thyme, and season.

2 Roast in a preheated oven at 190°C (375°F, Gas 5) for 20–25 minutes until the chicken is tender and cooked through. Remove the chicken thighs, bacon, and vegetables, and keep warm.

3 Spoon off any excess fat from the roasting tin. Put the tin on the hob, and boil the cooking juices until reduced by half. Stir in the crème fraîche, and heat gently. Pour the sauce on to serving plates, arrange the bacon, vegetables, and chicken on top, and serve hot.

195

MARINATED BARBECUED CHICKEN

Smoke-scented, crisp-skinned, and with tender flesh, marinated chicken is full of delicious flavour when cooked on the barbecue. These three recipes use different parts of the bird, all cooked with the skin on for the juiciest results.

ORANGE & ROSEMARY

SERVES 4

4 chicken breasts, with the skin left on

a few rosemary sprigs

MARINADE

75 ml (2¹/2 fl oz) olive oil

75 ml (2¹/2 fl oz) white wine vinegar

juice of 1 orange

2 tbsp clear honey

4 garlic cloves, crushed

salt and black pepper

ORANGE SALSA

2 oranges, peeled, segmented, and diced

1 red pepper, halved, seeded, and diced

¹/4 tsp crushed dried red chillies (chilli flakes)

1 tbsp clear honey

1 Combine the marinade ingredients in a shallow non-metallic dish. Add the chicken and turn to coat, then cover and leave to marinate in the refrigerator for up to 24 hours.

2 Lay the rosemary sprigs on the barbecue rack, put the chicken on top, and barbecue for 15–20 minutes until the juices run clear. Turn the chicken over several times during cooking, and baste or brush with the marinade.

3 Mix together the ingredients for the salsa. Serve the chicken breasts sliced diagonally, with the salsa alongside.

FRUITY CORIANDER

SERVES 4

8 chicken drumsticks, with the skin left on

MARINADE

75 ml (2¹/2 fl oz) olive oil

juice of 1 lime

2 tbsp mango chutney

2.5 cm (1 in) piece of fresh root ginger, peeled and grated

30 g (1 oz) fresh coriander, chopped

salt and black pepper

MANGO SALSA

1 ripe large mango, diced (page 466)

1 cm (¹/2 in) piece of fresh root ginger, peeled and grated

3 spring onions, finely chopped

1 tbsp mango chutney

1 tbsp lime juice

1 Combine the marinade ingredients in a shallow non-metallic dish. Slash the drumsticks, add to the marinade, and turn to coat. Cover and leave to marinate in the refrigerator for up to 24 hours.

2 Barbecue the drumsticks, turning and basting or brushing with the marinade, for 15–20 minutes or until the juices run clear.

3 Mix together the ingredients for the salsa. Serve the drumsticks hot, with the mango salsa alongside.

YOGURT & MINT

SERVES 4

8 chicken thighs on the bone, with the skin left on

couscous salad (made with chopped fresh mint, spring onions, red pepper, cherry tomatoes, and pine nuts tossed in vinaigrette dressing) to serve

MARINADE

4 tbsp olive oil

juice of ¹/2 lemon

3 garlic cloves, crushed

30 g (1 oz) fresh mint, chopped

150 g (5 oz) plain yogurt

¹/4 tsp each ground cumin and turmeric

salt and black pepper

1 Combine the marinade ingredients in a shallow non-metallic dish. Add the chicken and turn to coat, then cover and leave to marinate in the refrigerator for up to 24 hours.

2 Barbecue the chicken, turning and basting or brushing with the marinade, for 15–20 minutes or until the juices run clear.

3 Serve the chicken thighs hot or cold, on a bed of couscous salad, or with couscous salad served separately in a bowl.

SUCCESSFUL MARINATING

A marinade will give poultry or meat extra flavour before it is cooked over a barbecue, and it may help tenderize it at the same time.

A marinade is a mixture of liquids and seasonings. There is always an acid such as lemon juice, wine, or vinegar, which helps make poultry or meat more tender. An oil, such as olive, sesame, or sunflower, keeps the meat or poultry moist and carries the flavours of the seasonings into the food. Seasonings usually include salt and pepper, but all kinds of spices and herbs can be used as well. Marinades often include garlic, onions, and fresh root ginger, which also add flavour. Allow enough time for large pieces of poultry or meat to pick up the flavour of the marinade. Smaller pieces will pick up the flavour more quickly.

Turn the food in the marinade occasionally to ensure an even coating, and baste or brush with the marinade when barbecuing.

CLOCKWISE FROM TOP: Orange & Rosemary, Fruity Coriander, Yogurt & Mint.

LEMON & HERB DRUMSTICKS

MAKES 12

12 chicken drumsticks

MARINADE

150 ml (¼ pint) olive oil

grated zest and juice of 1 lemon

6 large parsley sprigs, chopped

1 onion, thinly sliced

2 large garlic cloves, crushed

salt and black pepper

1 Make the marinade: in a bowl, combine the olive oil, lemon zest and juice, parsley sprigs, onion, and garlic. Season with salt and pepper.

2 Turn the drumsticks in the marinade. Cover and leave to marinate in the refrigerator for at least 30 minutes.

3 Place the drumsticks under a hot grill, 10 cm (4 in) from the heat, and grill, turning frequently and basting with the marinade, for 20 minutes until crisp, brown, and cooked through. Serve the drumsticks hot or cold.

STICKY HONEYED DRUMSTICKS

Use a different marinade: combine 250 g (8 oz) plain yogurt, 2 tbsp clear honey, and 1 tsp ground coriander, and season with salt and black pepper.

DEVILLED CHICKEN DRUMSTICKS

MAKES 12

12 chicken drumsticks

2 tbsp sesame seeds

SPICY COATING

2 tbsp olive oil

2 tbsp white wine vinegar

2 tbsp tomato ketchup

1 tbsp Dijon mustard

1 small onion, quartered

2 tbsp dark muscovado sugar

1 large garlic clove, coarsely crushed

¼ tsp chilli powder

salt and black pepper

tortilla chips to serve

1 Make the spicy coating: put the oil, vinegar, ketchup, mustard, onion, sugar, garlic, and chilli powder in a food processor. Season with salt and pepper, and purée until fairly smooth.

2 Make 3 deep cuts in each chicken drumstick, arrange in a single layer in a shallow ovenproof dish, and spoon the coating over them. Sprinkle with half of the sesame seeds.

3 Roast in a preheated oven at 190°C (375°F, Gas 5 for 30 minutes or until the drumsticks are cooked through. Turn and baste halfway through cooking, and sprinkle with the remaining sesame seeds. Serve hot or cold, with tortilla chips.

CHILLI-ROASTED DRUMSTICKS WITH BACON

Use a different spicy coating: combine 3 tbsp lemon juice, 4 crushed garlic cloves, 1½ tbsp paprika, 1 tbsp mild chilli powder, 1 tsp ground cumin, and ¼ tsp oregano. Coat the drumsticks with the mixture, then wrap each one in a streaky bacon rasher.

Healthy note

Chicken is a very lean meat, but the skin is high in fat. If you want to reduce the fat content of these drumsticks, strip the skin off before marinating. The marinade will compensate for the lack of skin, and will keep the chicken moist during cooking.

CORONATION CHICKEN

SERVES 6

1 tbsp sunflower oil

125 g (4 oz) spring onions, chopped

4 tsp mild curry paste

150 ml (¼ pint) red wine

pared zest and juice of 1 lemon

1 tbsp tomato purée

2 tbsp apricot jam

300 ml (½ pint) mayonnaise

150 g (5 oz) plain yogurt

salt and pepper

500 g (1 lb) cooked chicken, cut into bite-sized pieces

watercress sprigs to garnish

1 Heat the oil in a small saucepan, add the spring onions, and cook for about 2 minutes until beginning to soften but not colour. Stir in the curry paste, and cook, stirring, for 1 minute.

2 Add the red wine, lemon zest and juice, and tomato purée. Simmer, uncovered, stirring, for 5 minutes or until reduced to 4 tbsp. Strain into a bowl, cover, and leave to cool.

3 Work the apricot jam through the sieve, then stir it into the curry paste and wine mixture. Add the mayonnaise and yogurt, season with salt and pepper, then stir well to blend evenly. The mixture should have a coating consistency, and be the colour of pale straw.

4 Add the chicken pieces to the mayonnaise mixture, and stir to coat evenly. Garnish with watercress sprigs before serving.

MARINATED CHICKEN WITH PEPPERS

SERVES 6

1.7 kg (3½ lb) chicken

2 tbsp olive oil

1 large red pepper, halved, seeded, and cut into thin strips

1 large yellow pepper, halved, seeded, and cut into thin strips

125 g (4 oz) pitted black olives

MARINADE

4 tbsp olive oil

2 tbsp clear honey

juice of ½ lemon

1 tbsp chopped mixed fresh herbs, such as parsley, thyme, and basil

salt and black pepper

1 Put the chicken into a roasting tin, rub the breast with oil, and roast in a preheated oven at 190°C (375°F, Gas 5) for 20 minutes per 500 g (1 lb). Twenty minutes before the end of the roasting time, remove from the oven, and spoon off the fat. Add the peppers and return to the oven for 20 minutes.

2 Remove the chicken and peppers from the tin, and leave to stand until cool.

3 Meanwhile, make the marinade: in a large bowl, combine the olive oil, honey, lemon juice, and herbs, and season with salt and pepper.

4 Strip the chicken flesh from the carcass, and cut it into small bite-sized strips. Toss the strips in the marinade, cover, and leave to cool completely.

5 Spoon the chicken on to a platter, arrange the peppers and olives around the edge, and serve at room temperature.

Cook's know-how

If time is short, use a ready-cooked chicken and toss with roasted peppers from a jar. If the peppers are packed in oil they will be very moist, so you will only need half the amount of marinade.

GREEK CHICKEN SALAD

SERVES 6

500 g (1 lb) cooked chicken, cut into bite-sized pieces

pitta bread to serve

1 spring onion, cut into strips, to garnish

SAUCE

150 g (5 oz) Greek yogurt

150 ml (¼ pint) crème fraîche

8 spring onions, thinly sliced

2 tbsp chopped fresh mint

1 tbsp chopped flat-leaf parsley

2 tbsp lemon juice

a pinch of sugar

salt and black pepper

1 Make the sauce: in a large bowl, combine the yogurt, crème fraîche, spring onions, mint, parsley, lemon juice, and sugar, and season with salt and pepper.

2 Toss the chicken pieces in the sauce.

3 Sprinkle the bread with a little water and cook under a hot grill for 1 minute on each side. Garnish the chicken with the spring onion strips, and serve with the pitta bread.

WARM CHICKEN SALAD WITH MANGO & AVOCADO

This unusual salad combines refreshing slices of mango and avocado with spicy chicken breast and a warm, rum-flavoured dressing. The combination of flavours makes a truly tropical dish.

SERVES 4

3 skinless, boneless chicken breasts, cut into 2.5 cm (1 in) strips

1 round lettuce, leaves separated

1 bunch of watercress, trimmed

1 avocado, peeled, stoned (page 88), and sliced lengthwise

1 mango, peeled, stoned (page 430), and sliced lengthwise

4 tbsp dark rum

paprika to garnish

MARINADE

2 tbsp olive oil

2 tbsp lemon juice

2 tsp balsamic vinegar

2 garlic cloves, crushed

1 tbsp paprika

1 mild fresh red chilli, halved, seeded, and finely chopped

½ tsp ground cumin

salt

1 Make the marinade: combine the oil, lemon juice, vinegar, garlic, paprika, chilli, and cumin, and season with salt. Toss in the chicken strips, cover, and leave to marinate for a few minutes.

2 Arrange beds of lettuce and watercress on 4 serving plates. Arrange the avocado and mango slices on top.

3 Heat a large frying pan, and add the chicken strips with the marinade. Cook over a high heat, stirring, for 5–6 minutes until golden on all sides and cooked through.

4 Using a slotted spoon, remove the chicken strips from the pan, and arrange on top of the avocado and mango.

5 Return the frying pan to the heat, and pour in the rum. Let it bubble, stirring constantly to dissolve any sediment in the frying pan and incorporate the cooking juices, for about 1 minute. Pour the hot rum mixture over the salads, sprinkle with a little paprika, and serve at once.

BALLOTINE OF CHICKEN

A ballotine is a bird or cut of meat which has been boned, stuffed, and rolled. It is slowly cooked in the oven, allowed to cool, then chilled for several hours or overnight until firm. With its colourful, pistachio-studded filling, this ballotine makes an excellent centrepiece for a buffet party, and is easy to slice and serve.

SERVES 8–10

2 kg (4 lb) chicken, boned (page 171)

4 thin slices of cooked ham

125 g (4 oz) pistachio nuts, shelled

60 g (2 oz) butter, softened

600 ml (1 pint) chicken stock

STUFFING

500 g (1 lb) belly pork

375 g (12 oz) chicken livers, trimmed

250 g (8 oz) streaky bacon rashers, rinds removed, coarsely chopped

2 shallots, quartered

2 garlic cloves

4 tbsp brandy

2 tsp chopped fresh thyme

1 tsp chopped fresh sage

1/2 tsp ground ginger

1/2 tsp ground cinnamon

salt and black pepper

1 Make the stuffing: chop the pork into 5 mm (1/4 in) pieces, and place in a bowl.

2 Purée the chicken livers, bacon, shallots, garlic, and brandy in a food processor until smooth. Add to the pork in the bowl with the thyme, sage, ginger, and cinnamon, and season generously with salt and pepper. Stir well to combine.

3 Place the boned chicken, skin-side down, between 2 pieces of cling film and pound to an even thickness with a rolling pin.

4 Remove the cling film from the chicken, and assemble the ballotine (see box, right). Tie several pieces of string around the chicken to keep it in shape.

5 Spread the softened butter over the chicken skin, and season generously with salt and pepper. Place the chicken roll on a wire rack in a roasting tin.

6 Bring the stock to a boil, and pour over the chicken in the roasting tin. Cook in a preheated oven at 160°C (325°F, Gas 3), basting occasionally and adding more stock if necessary, for 2 hours or until the juices run clear when the chicken is pierced.

7 Transfer the ballotine to a plate, and leave to cool. Cover and chill overnight. Cut into thin slices to serve.

Assembling the ballotine

Spread half of the stuffing over the chicken, to within 2.5 cm (1 in) of the edges. Arrange the ham slices on top. Scatter the pistachio nuts on top of the ham.

Spoon on and spread the remaining stuffing over the pistachio nuts.

Fold the chicken over the stuffing to form a sausage shape, and sew the edges together with thin string or fasten them with small metal skewers.

Cook's know-how

Classic French ballotine recipes wrap the chicken roll in muslin before cooking, but this is not necessary.

201

CHRISTMAS ROAST TURKEY

If you have a large number to cater for at Christmas, be sure to order a fresh turkey well in advance from your butcher. You can collect it on Christmas Eve or store it for up to 2 days in the refrigerator. If you buy a frozen turkey, make sure that it is thoroughly thawed before cooking – see page 169 for thawing times.

SERVES 12

pared zest of 1 lemon

a few parsley stalks

a few thyme sprigs

2 celery stalks, roughly sliced

5 kg (10 lb) oven-ready turkey, with giblets

75 g (3 oz) butter, softened

salt and black pepper

250 g (8 oz) streaky bacon rashers (optional)

CHESTNUT STUFFING

30 g (1 oz) butter

1 onion, finely chopped

90 g (3 oz) streaky bacon, finely chopped

375 g (12 oz) frozen chestnuts, thawed, or 175 g (6 oz) dried chestnuts, soaked, finely chopped

175 g (6 oz) pork sausagemeat

3 tbsp chopped parsley

1 tbsp chopped fresh thyme

salt and black pepper

1 small egg, beaten

GRAVY

30 g (1 oz) plain flour

600 ml (1 pint) giblet stock (page 170) or chicken stock

about 2 tbsp port, Madeira or sherry

redcurrant jelly to taste (optional)

TO SERVE

bread sauce

cranberry sauce

bacon rolls

chipolatas

1 Prepare the stuffing: melt the butter in a frying pan, add the onion and bacon, and cook until the onion is soft and both the onion and bacon are golden. Transfer to a large bowl, mix in the remaining stuffing ingredients, and leave until cold.

2 Place the lemon zest, parsley stalks, thyme, and celery into the cavity of the turkey. Fill the neck end with stuffing. Put the leftover stuffing into an ovenproof dish and set aside.

3 Shape the stuffed end of the turkey into a neat round and secure the loose skin with fine skewers. Tie the legs with string to give a neat shape.

4 Weigh the turkey and calculate the cooking time, allowing 20 minutes per 500 g (1 lb). Arrange 2 large sheets of foil across a large roasting tin. Place the turkey on top and spread the butter over the bird, concentrating on the breast in particular.

5 Season with a little salt and plenty of pepper. If you are using the bacon rashers, overlap them across the turkey, again concentrating on the breast.

6 Fold the sheets of foil loosely over the turkey, leaving a large air gap between the turkey and the foil. Cook the turkey in a preheated oven at 220°C (425°F, Gas 7) for 30 minutes.

7 Reduce the oven temperature to 160°C (325°F, Gas 3) and cook for the remainder of the calculated cooking time.

8 Thirty minutes before the end of the cooking time, fold back the foil and remove the bacon (if used), to allow the breast to brown, then baste with the cooking juices. To check if the turkey is thoroughly cooked, pierce the thickest part of the thigh with a fine skewer: the juices should run clear, not pink or red.

9 Lift the turkey on to a warmed serving platter, cover with fresh foil, and leave to stand in a warm place for 30 minutes before carving.

10 Meanwhile, put the dish of stuffing in the oven and cook for 25–30 minutes. Now make the gravy: spoon all but 2 tbsp of fat from the roasting tin, leaving behind the cooking juices. Place the tin over a low heat on the hob, add the flour, and cook, stirring, for 1 minute. Add the stock and port, Madeira or sherry to taste, then cook, stirring, until thickened. Season to taste, and add some redcurrant jelly if you think the gravy is too sharp.

11 Carve the turkey and serve with the extra stuffing, gravy, bread sauce, cranberry sauce, bacon rolls, and chipolatas.

BREAD SAUCE

Insert 8 whole cloves into 1 onion. Put it into a pan with 900 ml (1½ pints) milk, 1 bay leaf, and 6 whole black peppercorns. Bring to a boil, remove from the heat, cover, and leave to infuse for 1 hour. Strain the milk and return to the pan. Gradually add about 175 g (6 oz) fresh white breadcrumbs, then bring to a boil, stirring. Simmer for 2–3 minutes. Season with salt and black pepper, and stir in 60 g (2 oz) butter. If liked, stir in 4 tbsp double cream before serving. Serve hot.

CRANBERRY SAUCE

Put 500 g (1 lb) fresh cranberries into a saucepan with 125 ml (4 fl oz) water. Bring to a boil and simmer for about 5 minutes, until the cranberries have begun to break down. Stir in 125 g (4 oz) caster sugar and simmer until the sugar has dissolved. Stir in 2 tbsp port before serving. Serve hot or cold.

BACON ROLLS

With the back of a knife, stretch 6 streaky bacon rashers until twice their original size. Cut in half and roll up loosely. Thread on to skewers and cook under a hot grill, turning, for 6 minutes or until browned.

CHIPOLATAS

Twist 6 chipolata sausages in the centre and cut in half, to make 12 small sausages. Cook under a hot grill for 10–15 minutes until cooked through and browned all over.

ROAST TURKEY WITH GARLIC & TARRAGON

SERVES 4

1.25 kg (2½ lb) turkey breast joint

1 tsp plain flour

300 ml (½ pint) chicken stock

salt and black pepper

watercress sprigs to garnish

MARINADE

3 tbsp sunflower oil

grated zest and juice of 1 lemon

1 small onion, sliced

1 garlic clove, crushed

1 large tarragon sprig

1 large lemon thyme sprig

1 Make the marinade: combine the oil, lemon zest and juice, onion, garlic, tarragon, and thyme. Spoon the marinade over the turkey, cover, and leave to marinate in the refrigerator, turning occasionally, for 8 hours.

2 Put the turkey into a roasting tin. Strain the marinade, and pour around the turkey. Cover with foil, and cook in a preheated oven at 190°C (375°F, Gas 5) for 20 minutes per 500 g (1 lb). Remove the foil after 20 minutes of cooking to brown the turkey.

3 Test whether the turkey is done by inserting a fine skewer into the thickest part: the juices will run clear when it is cooked. Remove the turkey from the roasting tin, and keep warm while you make the gravy.

4 Put the tin on the hob, add the flour to the juices in the tin, and cook, stirring, for 1 minute until lightly browned. Add the stock, and bring to a boil, stirring constantly until thickened slightly. Simmer for 2–3 minutes, season with salt and pepper, and strain into a warmed gravy boat.

5 Garnish the turkey with watercress, and serve the gravy separately.

Cook's know-how

Turkey breast joints are now widely available from supermarkets. They are excellent if you like roast turkey but don't want to buy a whole bird, or if you find carving a whole turkey difficult. They either come with the breastbone (and sometimes the wings) attached, or as a boned and rolled joint.

TURKEY WITH SOURED CREAM & CHIVES

SERVES 4

30 g (1 oz) butter

2 tbsp sunflower oil

600 g (1¼ lb) turkey breast fillets, cut diagonally into 1 cm (½ in) strips

4 streaky bacon rashers, rinds removed, diced

1 large onion, sliced

250 g (8 oz) button mushrooms, halved

30 g (1 oz) plain flour

150 ml (¼ pint) turkey or chicken stock

salt and black pepper

150 g (5 oz) soured cream

2 tbsp snipped fresh chives

1 Melt the butter with the oil in a large frying pan until foaming. Add the turkey, and cook over a high heat, stirring, for 8 minutes. Remove the turkey from the pan with a slotted spoon, and keep warm.

2 Lower the heat and add the bacon, onion, and mushrooms. Cook gently, stirring occasionally, for 3–5 minutes until the onion is soft but not coloured. Sprinkle in the flour and cook, stirring, for about 1 minute.

3 Pour in the stock, and bring to a boil, stirring until thickened. Add the turkey, and season with salt and pepper. Cover and simmer for about 5 minutes or until the turkey is tender.

4 Stir in the soured cream, and heat gently without boiling. Serve at once, sprinkled with the chives.

Healthy option

To lower the fat content of this dish, omit the butter and bacon and use just 4 tbsp low-fat plain yogurt instead of the soured cream.

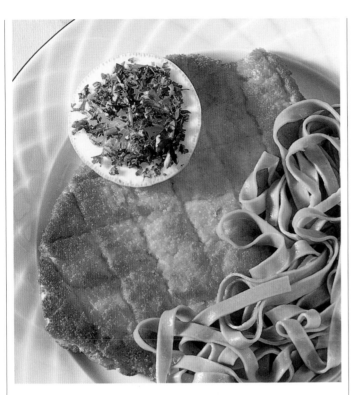

TURKEY SCHNITZEL

SERVES 4

3 tbsp plain flour

salt and black pepper

1 large egg, beaten

60 g (2 oz) fresh breadcrumbs

4 x 175 g (6 oz) turkey breast escalopes

2 tbsp sunflower oil

15 g (1/2 oz) butter

lemon slices and chopped parsley to garnish

1 Sprinkle the flour on to a plate, and season generously with salt and pepper. Pour the beaten egg on to another plate, and sprinkle the breadcrumbs on to a third plate.

2 Coat each escalope with the seasoned flour, shaking off any excess. Dip each floured escalope into the beaten egg, then dip into the breadcrumbs.

3 With a sharp knife, score the escalopes in a criss-cross pattern. Cover and chill in the refrigerator for 30 minutes.

4 Heat the oil with the butter in a large frying pan. When the butter is foaming, add the escalopes, and cook over a high heat until golden on both sides.

5 Lower the heat and cook for 10 minutes or until the escalopes are tender. Test the escalopes by piercing with a fine skewer: the juices should run clear.

6 Lift the escalopes out of the pan, and drain on paper towels. Garnish with lemon slices and chopped parsley, and serve at once.

Cook's know-how

If you can't find turkey breast escalopes, buy breast fillets. Put them between 2 sheets of cling film, and pound with the bottom of a saucepan until they are about 5 mm (1/4 in) thick.

TURKEY & LEMON STIR-FRY

SERVES 4

600 g (1 1/4 lb) turkey breast fillets, cut diagonally into 2.5 cm (1 in) strips

375 g (12 oz) courgettes

1 large green pepper

1 tbsp olive oil

250 g (8 oz) baby sweetcorn

salt

chopped parsley and lemon twists to garnish

MARINADE

125 ml (4 fl oz) dry white wine

grated zest and juice of 1 large lemon

2 tbsp olive oil

black pepper

1 Make the marinade: combine the wine, lemon zest and juice, oil, and season with pepper. Toss the turkey strips in the marinade, cover, and marinate in the refrigerator for at least 30 minutes.

2 Slice the courgettes thickly on the diagonal. Halve the green pepper and remove the seeds, then cut the pepper halves into long thin strips.

3 Heat the oil in a wok, add the courgettes, sweetcorn, and green pepper, and stir-fry over a high heat for 2 minutes. Remove with a slotted spoon, and keep warm.

4 Remove the turkey strips from the marinade, reserving the marinade. Add the turkey to the wok, and stir-fry over a high heat for 5 minutes or until golden.

5 Pour the reserved marinade over the turkey and cook for 3 minutes or until tender. Return the vegetables to the wok, and heat through. Taste for seasoning. Serve at once, garnished with parsley and lemon twists.

TURKEY MOLE

SERVES 6

2 tbsp sunflower oil

750 g (1 1/2 lb) turkey pieces

300 ml (1/2 pint) turkey or chicken stock

salt and black pepper

MOLE SAUCE

1 x 400 g (13 oz) can chopped tomatoes

1 small onion, coarsely chopped

90 g (3 oz) blanched almonds

30 g (1 oz) raisins (optional)

20 g (3/4 oz) plain chocolate, coarsely chopped

1 garlic clove

1 tbsp sesame seeds

1 tbsp hot chilli powder

1 tsp ground cinnamon

1/2 tsp ground cloves

1/2 tsp ground coriander

1/2 tsp ground cumin

1/4 tsp ground aniseed (optional)

1 Make the mole sauce: put the tomatoes, onion, almonds, raisins (if using), chocolate, garlic, sesame seeds, chilli powder, cinnamon, cloves, coriander, cumin, aniseed (if using), and 4 tbsp water into a food processor and process briefly.

2 Heat the sunflower oil in a large saucepan, add the turkey pieces, and cook over a high heat for about 5 minutes until golden on all sides.

3 Add the mole sauce mixture, and cook, stirring, for 2 minutes. Pour in the stock, and bring to a boil. Cover and simmer very gently for 40 minutes or until the turkey is tender. Season with salt and pepper before serving.

Cook's know-how

If you would rather not use the almonds, you can use 15 g (1/2 oz) plain flour to thicken the sauce instead.

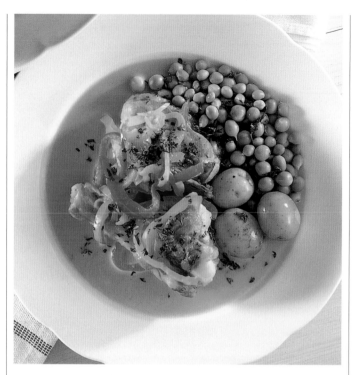

TURKEY CASSEROLE WITH PEPPERS & CIDER

SERVES 6

30 g (1 oz) butter

1 tbsp sunflower oil

750 g (1 1/2 lb) turkey pieces

1 onion, sliced

1 garlic clove, crushed

1 red pepper, halved, seeded, and thinly sliced

1 yellow pepper, halved, seeded, and thinly sliced

300 ml (1/2 pint) dry cider

salt and black pepper

chopped parsley to garnish

1 Melt the butter with the oil in a flameproof casserole. When the butter is foaming, add the turkey pieces, and cook over a high heat for 5 minutes or until golden on all sides. Lift out with a slotted spoon, and drain on paper towels.

2 Lower the heat, add the onion, garlic, and red and yellow pepper slices to the casserole, and cook for 5 minutes or until the vegetables are just beginning to soften.

3 Return the turkey to the casserole, pour in the cider, and bring to a boil. Season with salt and pepper, cover, and cook in a preheated oven at 160°C (325°F, Gas 3) for 1 hour or until the turkey is tender.

4 Using a slotted spoon, transfer the turkey and vegetables to a warmed platter. Put the casserole on the hob and boil, stirring, until the cooking juices are thickened slightly. Taste for seasoning.

5 Spoon the sauce over the turkey and vegetables, garnish with chopped parsley, and serve at once.

TURKEY & APPLE CASSEROLE

Substitute 2 cored, halved, and sliced eating apples for the red and yellow peppers, and add them 20 minutes before the end of the cooking time.

STIR-FRIED TURKEY MEATBALLS

SERVES 4

3 tsp sunflower oil

I onion, thinly sliced

I green pepper, halved, seeded, and cut into bite-sized pieces

I courgette, sliced

4–6 mushrooms, thinly sliced

125 g (4 oz) bean sprouts

MEATBALLS

375 g (12 oz) minced turkey

45 g (1½ oz) parsley stuffing mix or breadcrumbs

I onion, finely chopped

4 garlic cloves, crushed

3 tbsp soy sauce

I cm (½ in) piece of fresh root ginger, peeled and grated

salt and black pepper

1 Make the meatballs: in a bowl, combine the turkey, stuffing or breadcrumbs, onion, garlic, 1 tbsp of the soy sauce, and the ginger. Season with salt and pepper, then shape into meatballs (see box, right).

2 Heat 1 tsp of the oil in a wok, add the onion, green pepper, and courgette, and stir-fry for 2–3 minutes.

3 Remove the vegetables with a slotted spoon. Heat another 1 tsp of the oil, add the mushrooms, and stir-fry for 2–3 minutes. Remove with a slotted spoon.

4 Heat the remaining oil in the wok, add the meatballs, and cook gently, turning, for 6–7 minutes or until cooked through. Return the vegetables to the wok, add the bean sprouts and the remaining soy sauce, and heat through for 1 minute. Serve hot.

Shaping meatballs

Break off pieces of the turkey mixture and, with dampened hands to prevent the mixture sticking, roll into 5 cm (2 in) meatballs.

TURKEY BURGERS HOLSTEIN

SERVES 4

60 g (2 oz) butter

I small onion, very finely chopped

500 g (1 lb) minced turkey

90 g (3 oz) sliced cooked ham, finely chopped

I tbsp chopped parsley

salt and black pepper

2 tbsp sunflower oil

4 eggs to serve

1 Melt half of the butter in a small saucepan, add the onion, and cook gently, stirring occasionally, for 3–5 minutes until soft but not coloured. Leave to cool.

2 Put the onion into a large bowl, add the turkey, ham, and parsley, and season with salt and pepper. Mix well, then shape into 4 burgers. Cover and chill for 30 minutes.

3 Melt the remaining butter with the oil in a frying pan. When the butter is foaming, add the burgers, and cook over a high heat for 2–3 minutes on each side until golden.

4 Lower the heat, and cook, turning once, for about 10 minutes until the burgers are cooked through.

5 Lift the burgers out of the frying pan with a slotted spoon and drain on paper towels.

6 Break the eggs into the frying pan, and fry over a medium heat until the whites are firm and the yolks are still soft. Divide the turkey burgers among serving plates, top each burger with an egg, and serve at once.

BLUE CHEESE TURKEY BURGERS

Make the burgers as directed. Omit the eggs. Crumble 125 g (4 oz) blue cheese, such as Roquefort, Stilton, or Danish Blue, over the burgers 5 minutes before the end of the cooking time.

207

TURKEY WITH CHEESE & PINEAPPLE

SERVES 6

60 g (2 oz) butter

1 onion, sliced

60 g (2 oz) plain flour

450 ml (3/4 pint) turkey or chicken stock

1 x 250 g (8 oz) can pineapple pieces in natural juice, drained and juice reserved

250 g (8 oz) mature Cheddar cheese, grated

salt and black pepper

500 g (1 lb) cooked turkey, cut into bite-sized pieces

3 tbsp fresh brown breadcrumbs

chopped parsley to garnish

1 Melt the butter in a saucepan, add the onion, and cook gently, stirring occasionally, for 3–5 minutes until soft but not coloured. Add the flour, and cook, stirring, for 1 minute.

2 Gradually blend in the stock and the pineapple juice, and bring to a boil, stirring until thickened.

3 Add the pineapple pieces, reserving 6 for garnish. Stir in three-quarters of the cheese, and season with salt and pepper.

4 Divide the turkey pieces among 6 individual gratin dishes, or put into 1 large ovenproof dish. Pour the sauce over the turkey, and sprinkle with the remaining cheese and then the breadcrumbs.

5 Bake in a preheated oven at 200°C (400°F, Gas 6) for 15–20 minutes until the turkey has heated through and the topping is golden. Garnish with chopped parsley and the reserved pineapple pieces, and serve at once.

TURKEY SALAD WITH MANGO & GRAPES

SERVES 4

1.25 kg (2 1/2 lb) turkey breast joint

1 onion, quartered

1 carrot, sliced

a few parsley sprigs

pared zest of 1 lemon

6 black peppercorns

1 bay leaf

200 ml (7 fl oz) lemon mayonnaise

1 bunch of watercress, tough stalks removed

1 ripe mango, peeled, stoned, and cut into cubes (page 466)

125 g (4 oz) seedless green grapes

90 g (3 oz) walnut pieces

1 Put the turkey joint into a large saucepan, and cover with cold water. Add the onion, carrot, parsley, lemon zest, peppercorns, and bay leaf, and bring to a boil. Cover and simmer very gently for 1 hour or until the turkey is tender. Remove from the heat, and leave the turkey to cool completely in the poaching liquid.

2 Lift the turkey out of the poaching liquid, and remove the flesh from the carcass. Discard the skin and bones, then cut the meat into bite-sized pieces.

3 Put the turkey pieces into a large bowl, and add the lemon mayonnaise. Stir well to coat the turkey pieces thoroughly and evenly.

4 Arrange the watercress on individual serving plates, and pile the turkey mixture on top. Arrange the mango cubes and grapes around the edge, sprinkle with the walnut pieces, and serve at room temperature.

Healthy option

To reduce the fat content of this salad, use equal quantities of low-fat plain yogurt and reduced-calorie mayonnaise instead of the lemon mayonnaise, and omit the walnuts.

WALDORF TURKEY SALAD

Substitute 2 cored and cubed red eating apples, and 2 sliced celery stalks for the mango and grapes, and then add to the turkey and lemon mayonnaise mixture.

CHRISTMAS ROAST GOOSE

Goose is a traditional Christmas bird in Britain and northern Europe, and it is a favourite festive alternative to turkey when a small group of people is to be served. It is simple to cook and tastes delicious with a fruit stuffing and spicy accompaniments.

SERVES 6–8

5–6 kg (10–12 lb) goose, with giblets reserved for stock

1 onion, quartered

1 cooking apple, quartered

a few sage sprigs

salt and black pepper

30 g (1 oz) plain flour

450 ml (3/4 pint) goose giblet stock (page 170)

150 ml (1/4 pint) dry white wine

spiced stuffed apples (see box, right) to serve

watercress sprigs to garnish

PORK & APPLE STUFFING

300 g (10 oz) pork sausagemeat

60 g (2 oz) fresh breadcrumbs

2 tsp dried sage

30 g (1 oz) butter

1 onion, finely chopped

1 large cooking apple, peeled, cored, and finely chopped

1 Make the pork and apple stuffing: in a bowl, combine the sausagemeat, breadcrumbs, and sage.

2 Melt the butter in a pan, add the onion, and cook gently, stirring occasionally, for 3–5 minutes until soft but not coloured.

3 Add the cooking apple, and cook for 5 minutes. Stir the onion and apple into the sausagemeat mixture, season with salt and pepper, and leave to cool.

4 Remove any fat from the cavity of the goose. Put the onion and apple quarters into the cavity together with the sage. Spoon the stuffing into the neck end of the goose, pat it into a rounded shape, and secure the skin flap with a small skewer. Weigh the goose.

5 Prick the skin of the goose all over with a fork, and rub with salt and pepper. Place the goose, breast-side down, on a wire rack in a large roasting tin, and cook in a preheated oven at 220°C (425°F, Gas 7) for 30 minutes.

6 Turn the goose breast-side up, and cook for 20 minutes. Reduce the oven temperature to 180°C (350°F, Gas 4) and cook for 20 minutes per 500 g (1 lb).

7 Test the goose by inserting a fine skewer into the thickest part of a thigh: the juices should run clear when the meat is thoroughly cooked.

8 Lift the goose on to a warmed serving platter, and then leave to rest, covered with foil, for about 20 minutes.

9 Make the gravy while the goose is resting: pour off all but 2 tbsp of the fat from the roasting tin. Put the tin on the hob, add the flour, and cook, stirring, for 1 minute. Add the stock and wine, and bring to a boil, stirring constantly. Simmer for 2–3 minutes, then taste for seasoning. Strain into a warmed gravy boat.

10 To serve, arrange the spiced stuffed apples around the goose, and garnish with watercress. Hand the gravy separately.

Spiced stuffed apples

Core 8 eating apples, keeping them whole. For the stuffing, combine 2 tbsp Calvados in a small bowl with 1 tsp ground cinnamon, 1/2 tsp ground allspice, and 8 finely chopped ready-to-eat prunes.

Place the apples in a buttered ovenproof dish, and spoon the stuffing into the centres. Melt 60 g (2 oz) butter, pour over the apples, and cover with foil. Bake in a preheated oven at 180°C (350°F, Gas 4) for 1 hour or until tender.

Cook's know-how

Goose is even richer and fattier than duck. Putting it on a wire rack in the roasting tin ensures it does not sit in the fat during cooking and this gives it a good, crisp skin.

CHICKEN AND TURKEY STIR-FRIES

Fresh and colourful, these light, healthy stir-fries cook in minutes. If time is short, just marinate the meat while you prepare the other ingredients. Another alternative, for a more intense flavour, is to prepare ahead and marinate overnight.

CHINESE CHICKEN WITH MANGO

SERVES 6

3 skinless, boneless chicken breasts (about 125 g/4 oz each), cut into thin strips

about 2 tbsp sunflower oil

1 large red pepper, halved, seeded, and cut into strips

250 g (8 oz) button chestnut mushrooms, halved

2 tsp cornflour blended with 5 tbsp cold chicken stock or water

salt and black pepper

250 g (8 oz) bean sprouts

about 200 g (7 oz) pak choi, coarsely sliced

60 g (2 oz) roasted cashew nuts, salted or unsalted

1 large ripe mango, peeled and sliced lengthwise (see page 466)

chopped fresh coriander to serve (optional)

MARINADE

1 tbsp soy sauce

3 tbsp rice wine vinegar or white wine vinegar

3 tbsp clear honey

1 Put the chicken in a bowl with the marinade ingredients and mix well. Cover and marinate in the refrigerator for about 2 hours, more if time allows.

2 Heat 1 tbsp oil over a high heat in a wok or large frying pan. Lift half the chicken from the marinade (reserving it), and stir-fry for 1–2 minutes until golden all over and nearly cooked. Remove the chicken and set aside, then repeat with the remainder.

3 Heat the remaining oil in the pan, add the red pepper and mushrooms, and stir-fry for 1–2 minutes.

4 Return the chicken to the wok. Stir the cornflour mixture and pour it into the wok, then add the reserved marinade. Season with salt and pepper and bring to a boil. Add the bean sprouts and pak choi, and stir-fry until the pak choi has just wilted, about 2 minutes. Stir in the cashew nuts and mango slices, and serve at once, sprinkled with chopped coriander if you like.

TURKEY TO GO

SERVES 6

about 750 g (1½ lb) turkey breast fillets, cut into thin strips

1 tsp ground coriander

1 tsp ground cumin

salt and black pepper

12 soft tortilla wraps

about 2 tbsp sunflower oil

1 large red pepper, halved, seeded, and thinly sliced

TO SERVE

soured cream

tomato salsa or mango chutney

shredded Romaine lettuce

1 Put the turkey strips in a bowl with the coriander and cumin. Season with salt and pepper, then mix well to coat the turkey in the spices. Cover and marinate in the refrigerator for about 30 minutes, more if time allows.

2 When you are ready to cook the turkey, warm the tortillas (see page 226). Heat the oil in a wok or large frying pan and fry the turkey in batches with the red pepper strips until golden brown and cooked through, about 4 minutes. You may need to add more oil with each batch.

3 Transfer the warm tortillas to a basket and spoon the turkey and peppers into a serving dish. Let each person spread their tortillas with soured cream and salsa or chutney, top this with some shredded lettuce and turkey, then roll into a fat cigar shape. The filled tortillas are easy to eat with your hands if they are sliced in half on the diagonal.

Cook's know-how

Soft tortillas are flat Mexican breads that can be made from wheat or corn (both are suitable for this recipe). They are widely available at supermarkets, and some are flavoured with tomato, garlic, or herbs.

LACQUERED DUCK

SERVES 4

4 skinless duck breasts, 150–175 g (5–6 oz) each, cut diagonally into 1 cm (½ in) strips

2 tbsp sunflower oil

8 spring onions, trimmed and cut into 2.5 cm (1 in) lengths

salt and black pepper

1 tbsp sesame seeds, toasted

MARINADE

2 large garlic cloves, crushed

1 tbsp soy sauce

1 tbsp olive oil

2 tbsp clear honey

1 Put the duck in a bowl with the marinade ingredients and mix well. Cover and marinate in the refrigerator for about 2 hours, or overnight if time allows.

2 Heat the sunflower oil in a wok or large frying pan. Lift the duck from the marinade (reserving it), and stir-fry over a high heat for about 3–4 minutes or until browned all over. Add the spring onions, and stir-fry for a further 2–3 minutes or until the duck is cooked.

3 Pour the marinade and 5 tbsp water into the pan, bring quickly to a boil, and simmer for a few moments until the sauce has a syrupy consistency – take care not to overcook or the marinade may burn. Season with salt and pepper, scatter over the sesame seeds, and serve immediately.

CLOCKWISE FROM TOP: Lacquered Duck, Chinese Chicken with Mango, Turkey to Go.

PEKING DUCK

This Chinese dish is great fun to make, but you can buy the pancakes if you are short of time – they are sold at most large supermarkets. Let everyone help themselves to some crisp-skinned duck, spring onions, cucumber, and hoisin sauce, so they can assemble their own pancakes.

SERVES 6

2.5 kg (5 lb) duck, with any giblets removed

3 tbsp dry sherry

3 tbsp clear honey

3 tbsp soy sauce

CHINESE PANCAKES

275 g (9 oz) plain flour

200 ml (7 fl oz) boiling water

2 tbsp sesame oil

TO SERVE

6 spring onions, cut into matchstick-thin strips

1/2 cucumber, peeled and cut into matchstick-thin strips

90 ml (3 fl oz) hoisin sauce, sprinkled with sesame seeds

spring onions to garnish

1 Remove any fat from the cavity of the duck. Put the duck into a bowl, pour boiling water over it, then remove and dry inside and out.

2 Mix together the sherry, honey, and soy sauce, and brush over the duck. Leave to stand, uncovered and at room temperature, for 4 hours or until the skin is dry.

3 Put the duck, breast-side down, on a wire rack in a roasting tin, and roast in a preheated oven at 200°C (400°F, Gas 6) for 25 minutes or until browned. Turn over and roast for a further 1–1 1/4 hours or until tender.

4 Meanwhile, make the pancake dough: sift the flour into a large bowl, add the boiling water, and mix to form a soft dough. Knead until smooth. Cover and leave to stand for about 30 minutes.

5 Knead the dough for 5 minutes. Shape into a roll about 2.5 cm (1 in) in diameter. Cut into 18 pieces, then roll into balls. Shape and cook the pancakes (see box, right).

6 When the duck is cooked, leave it to stand for about 15 minutes. Meanwhile, stack the pancakes on a plate in a steamer, cover, and steam for 10 minutes. Cut the duck into small pieces. Serve with the pancakes, spring onions, cucumber, and hoisin sauce, and garnish with spring onions.

Shaping and cooking Chinese pancakes

Pour the sesame oil into a bowl. Take 2 balls of dough, dip half of 1 ball into the oil, then press the oiled half on to the second ball.

Flatten the dough balls with the palms of your hands and roll out to a pancake about 15 cm (6 in) in diameter. Heat a frying pan. Put the double pancake into the pan and cook for 1 minute. Flip over and cook the other side for 1 minute.

Remove from the pan, and peel the 2 pancakes apart. Repeat with the remaining dough, to make 18 pancakes in all. Cover the pancakes with a damp tea towel to stop them drying out.

ROAST DUCK WITH CRANBERRIES

Many people like the flesh of roast duck breast a little pink, but the legs need to be well cooked, or they may be tough. To accommodate the difference, serve the breast meat first, and return the duck to the oven for 15 minutes to finish cooking the legs.

SERVES 4

2.5 kg (5 lb) duck, with any giblets reserved for stock

cranberry sauce to serve (page 202)

watercress sprigs to garnish

CRANBERRY STUFFING

30 g (1 oz) butter

1 small onion, finely chopped

175 g (6 oz) fresh brown breadcrumbs

125 g (4 oz) cranberries

1 tbsp chopped parsley

1/4 tsp ground mixed spice

salt and black pepper

1 egg, beaten

GRAVY

1 tsp plain flour

300 ml (1/2 pint) duck giblet stock (page 170)

1 Make the cranberry stuffing: melt the butter in a pan, add the onion, and cook gently for 3–5 minutes until softened.

2 Stir in the breadcrumbs, cranberries, parsley, and mixed spice, and season with salt and pepper. Bind with the egg, and leave to cool.

3 Remove any fat from the cavity of the duck. Spoon the stuffing into the neck end of the duck, secure the skin flap over the stuffing with a small skewer, and pat into a rounded shape. Put any leftover stuffing into an ovenproof dish and set aside.

4 Prick the skin of the duck all over with a fork, and rub salt and pepper into the skin. Place the duck, breast-side down, on a wire rack in a deep roasting tin, and roast in a preheated oven at 200°C (400°F, Gas 6) for 25 minutes or until golden brown.

5 Pour off some of the fat from the tin to reduce splashing. Turn the duck breast-side up, and roast for another 20 minutes or until brown.

6 Reduce the oven temperature to 180°C (350°F, Gas 4), and roast the duck, without basting, for 1–1 1/4 hours. Cook any leftover stuffing with the duck for the last 40 minutes.

7 Test the duck by inserting a fine skewer into the thickest part of a thigh: the juices will run clear when it is cooked. Keep warm, uncovered, while you make the gravy.

8 Pour off all but 1 tbsp of the fat from the roasting tin. Set the tin on the hob, add the flour, and cook, stirring, for 2 minutes. Pour in the stock, and bring to a boil, stirring until lightly thickened. Taste for seasoning, and strain into a warmed gravy boat.

9 Put the stuffing into a serving dish, carve the duck (page 173), and garnish with watercress. Serve with the gravy and cranberry sauce.

Cook's know-how

If there are no giblets in the duck, use chicken stock and add a splash of port or sherry and some grated orange zest to the gravy.

SAUCES FOR DUCK

ORANGE SAUCE

Put 2 finely chopped shallots, 300 ml (1/2 pint) chicken stock, and the juice of 2 oranges into a pan, and bring to a boil. Simmer until reduced by half, then season with salt and pepper. Push through a sieve, add the pared zest of 1 large orange, cut into fine strips, and reheat gently. Serve hot.

HONEY SAUCE

Cook 2 finely chopped shallots in 30 g (1 oz) butter until soft. Add 1 tbsp plain flour, and cook, stirring, for 1 minute. Blend in 300 ml (1/2 pint) chicken stock and 75 ml (2 1/2 fl oz) dry white wine. Boil, stirring, until thick. Add 3 tbsp clear honey, 1 tbsp white wine vinegar, and a pinch each of salt and pepper, and cook for 1 minute. Push through a sieve, and add 3 tbsp finely chopped parsley. Serve hot.

BLACKCURRANT SAUCE

Put 250 g (8 oz) blackcurrants and 300 ml (1/2 pint) water into a saucepan, and bring slowly to a boil. Simmer for 10 minutes until tender. Add 250 g (8 oz) caster sugar and 1 tbsp port, and cook gently until the sugar has dissolved. Serve hot or cold.

DUCK BREASTS WITH RASPBERRY SAUCE

SERVES 4

4 x 250–300 g (8–10 oz) duck breasts, with the skin left on

salt and black pepper

RASPBERRY SAUCE

150 ml (¼ pint) port

75 ml (2½ fl oz) water

45 g (1½ oz) caster sugar

250 g (8 oz) raspberries

1 tsp cornflour

juice of 2 oranges

salt and black pepper

1 Make the raspberry sauce: pour the port and measured water into a small saucepan. Add the sugar, and bring to a boil, stirring until the sugar has dissolved. Add the raspberries, bring back to a boil, then cover and simmer very gently for 5 minutes.

2 With a wooden spoon, push the raspberry mixture through a sieve to extract the seeds. Return the raspberry purée to the saucepan, and bring back to a boil.

3 Mix the cornflour with the orange juice. Add a little of the raspberry purée to the cornflour mixture, and blend together. Return to the saucepan, and bring back to a boil, stirring constantly until thickened. Season with salt and pepper, and set aside.

4 Score and season each duck breast (see box, below right).

5 Place the duck breasts under a hot grill, 10 cm (4 in) from the heat, and cook for 8 minutes on each side or until the skin is crisp and the duck is tender but still slightly pink inside.

6 Slice the duck breasts, skin-side up, and arrange in a fan shape on warmed plates. Spoon raspberry sauce around each of the servings, and serve at once.

DUCK BREASTS WITH RED WINE SAUCE

SERVES 4

4 x 250–300 g (8–10 oz) duck breasts, with the skin left on

125 ml (4 fl oz) beef stock

125 ml (4 fl oz) red wine

1 tsp tomato purée

1 tsp lemon juice

15 g (½ oz) butter

salt and black pepper

1 tbsp chopped fresh rosemary to garnish

MARINADE

5 garlic cloves, sliced

2 tbsp balsamic vinegar

1 tbsp chopped fresh rosemary

1 Make the marinade: in a bowl, combine the garlic, vinegar, and rosemary. Score the duck breasts (see box, right), and put them, skin-side down, in a shallow dish. Spoon the marinade over the top. Chill for 30 minutes.

2 Put the duck breasts, skin-side down, with the marinade, in a frying pan and cook for 5–7 minutes. Turn, and cook for a further 5 minutes. Remove from the pan, and keep warm.

3 Spoon any excess fat from the frying pan. Add the stock and wine, and boil over a high heat until reduced to a dark glaze, then add the tomato purée and lemon juice.

4 Remove from heat, and whisk in the butter, letting it thicken the sauce as it melts. Taste for seasoning.

5 Slice the duck, and arrange on warmed plates. Spoon the sauce around the duck, sprinkle with the chopped rosemary, and serve hot.

Scoring and seasoning the duck

With a sharp knife, score the skin of each duck breast with criss-cross lines. Season both sides with salt and pepper.

HOT & SPICY STIR-FRIED DUCK

SERVES 4

4 x 250–300 g (8–10 oz) skinless duck breasts, cut diagonally into 1 cm (½ in) strips

2 tbsp sunflower oil

8 spring onions, cut into 2.5 cm (1 in) lengths

125 g (4 oz) carrots, cut into matchstick-thin strips

250 g (8 oz) mangetout

1 x 200 g (7 oz) can water chestnuts, drained, rinsed, and sliced

MARINADE

2 tsp dark soy sauce

2 tsp red wine vinegar

2.5 cm (1 in) piece of fresh root ginger, peeled and grated

2 fresh red chillies, halved, seeded, and coarsely chopped

grated zest and juice of 1 orange

1 tsp sesame oil

1 tsp cornflour

1 tsp caster sugar

salt and black pepper

1 Make the marinade: in a large bowl, combine the soy sauce, vinegar, ginger, chillies, orange zest and juice, sesame oil, cornflour, and sugar, then season with salt and pepper.

2 Toss the duck strips in the marinade, cover, and leave to stand for 10 minutes.

3 Lift the duck strips out of the marinade, reserve the marinade, and drain the duck on paper towels.

4 Heat the oil in a wok or large frying pan, add the duck, and stir-fry over a high heat for 5 minutes or until browned all over. Add the spring onions and carrots, and stir-fry for 2–3 minutes. Add the mangetout, and stir-fry for 1 minute.

5 Pour the marinade into the wok, and stir-fry for about 2 minutes or until the duck is just tender. Stir in the water chestnuts, heat through, and taste for seasoning. Serve hot.

ORIENTAL DUCK WITH GINGER

SERVES 4

4 x 250–300 g (8–10 oz) skinless duck breasts

1 tbsp sunflower oil

8 baby sweetcorn

bean sprouts and 1 tbsp toasted sesame seeds to garnish

MARINADE

200 ml (7 fl oz) orange juice

3 tbsp dark soy sauce

1 tbsp sesame oil

1 tbsp Chinese rice wine or dry sherry

1 tbsp clear honey

5 cm (2 in) piece of fresh root ginger, peeled and grated

1 garlic clove, crushed

salt and black pepper

1 Make the marinade: in a large bowl, combine the orange juice, soy sauce, sesame oil, rice wine, honey, fresh root ginger, and garlic, then season with salt and pepper.

2 With a sharp knife, make several diagonal slashes in each duck breast. Pour the marinade over the duck breasts, turn them over, then cover and marinate in the refrigerator for about 30 minutes.

3 Lift the duck breasts out of the marinade, reserving the marinade. Heat the oil in a large frying pan, add the duck breasts, and cook over a high heat, turning frequently, for 10–12 minutes until tender. Add the marinade and simmer for 2–3 minutes until slightly reduced.

4 Meanwhile, blanch the baby sweetcorn in boiling salted water for 1 minute. Drain, then make lengthwise cuts in each one, leaving them attached at the stem.

5 To serve, slice each duck breast, and arrange on 4 individual plates. Spoon the hot sauce over the duck, add the sweetcorn, then garnish with bean sprouts and the toasted sesame seeds. Serve hot.

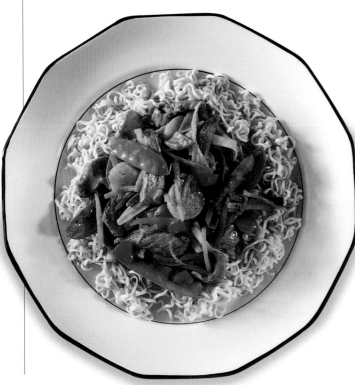

GUINEA FOWL MADEIRA

SERVES 6

2 tbsp sunflower oil
2 x 1.25 kg (2½ lb) guinea fowl, cut into serving pieces (page 170)
4 shallots, halved
1 tbsp plain flour
600 ml (1 pint) chicken stock
150 ml (¼ pint) dry white wine
4 tbsp Madeira
salt and black pepper
375 g (12 oz) seedless green grapes
150 ml (¼ pint) double cream
chopped parsley to garnish

1 Heat the oil in a flameproof casserole, and cook the guinea fowl pieces in batches for a few minutes until browned all over. Lift out and drain. Lower the heat, add the shallots, and cook, stirring, for 5 minutes or until softened. Lift out and drain.

2 Add the flour, and cook, stirring, for 1 minute. Pour in the stock, and bring to a boil, stirring. Add the wine and Madeira, and season with salt and pepper. Add the guinea fowl and shallots, and bring to a boil. Cook in a preheated oven at 160°C (325°F, Gas 3) for 1 hour or until just tender.

3 Transfer the casserole to the hob, add the grapes, and cook for 15 minutes. Add the cream, and heat gently. Garnish with parsley and serve hot.

MUSHROOM-STUFFED QUAIL

Whole quail make an impressive dinner party dish. They can be quite fiddly to eat, so boning and stuffing them makes it much easier for your guests. If you are short of time to bone the birds yourself, you can buy them ready boned at supermarkets, or ask the butcher to do it.

SERVES 6

12 quail, boned (page 171)
30 g (1 oz) butter, plus extra for greasing
1 tbsp lime marmalade

MUSHROOM STUFFING

60 g (2 oz) butter
3 shallots, finely chopped
375 g (12 oz) button mushrooms, coarsely chopped
60 g (2 oz) fresh white breadcrumbs
salt and black pepper
1 egg, beaten

LIME SAUCE

150 ml (¼ pint) chicken stock
juice of 1 lime
200 ml (7 fl oz) crème fraîche
4 tbsp chopped parsley

1 Make the mushroom stuffing: melt the butter in a saucepan, add the shallots, and cook gently, stirring occasionally, for 3–5 minutes until soft but not coloured.

2 Add the mushrooms and cook for 2 minutes, then remove from the heat. Stir in the breadcrumbs, season with salt and pepper, then stir in the egg and leave to cool. Stuff the quail (see box, right).

3 Put the quail into a buttered roasting tin. Melt the butter gently in a saucepan, add the lime marmalade, and heat gently, stirring, until combined. Brush over the quail, and cook in a preheated oven at 200°C (400°F, Gas 6) for 15–20 minutes until golden brown and tender. Remove from the tin and keep warm.

4 Make the lime sauce: put the roasting tin on the hob. Add the stock, and bring to a boil, then stir for 5 minutes or until reduced a little.

5 Stir in the lime juice and crème fraîche, and heat gently, stirring constantly, until the sauce has a smooth, creamy consistency.

6 Add half of the parsley and season with salt and pepper. Serve the quail with the lime sauce, and garnish with the remaining parsley.

Stuffing the quail

Spoon some of the stuffing into the cavity of each quail; secure the skin with a wooden cocktail stick.

STUFFED PHEASANT BREASTS

Use 6 pheasant breasts, with their skin on, and put the stuffing between the skin and the meat. Cook in the oven for 35 minutes.

TRADITIONAL ROAST PHEASANT

Pheasants are often sold in pairs (called a brace) – a cock and a hen. Make sure you get young pheasants for this recipe; old ones are not suitable for roasting and can be very tough unless they are cooked slowly in a casserole.

SERVES 4

2 pheasants, any giblets reserved

90 g (3 oz) butter, softened

salt and black pepper

4 streaky bacon rashers

1 tsp plain flour

300 ml (½ pint) pheasant giblet stock or chicken stock (page 170)

1 tsp redcurrant jelly

watercress sprigs to garnish

TO SERVE

fried breadcrumbs (far right)

game chips (far right)

bread sauce (page 202)

1 Spread the pheasants with the butter, and season. Lay two bacon rashers crosswise over each breast.

2 Put the pheasants into a roasting tin, and cook in a preheated oven at 200°C (400°F, Gas 6), basting once, for 1 hour or until tender.

3 Test the pheasants by inserting a fine skewer in the thickest part of a thigh: the juices should run clear when they are cooked.

4 Lift the pheasants on to a warmed serving platter, cover with foil, and keep warm. Pour off all but 1 tbsp of the fat from the roasting tin, reserving any juices. Put the tin on the hob, add the flour, and cook, stirring, for 1 minute.

5 Add the stock and redcurrant jelly, and bring to a boil, stirring until lightly thickened. Simmer for 2–3 minutes, then taste for seasoning. Strain into a warmed gravy boat.

6 To serve, garnish the pheasants with the watercress sprigs, and serve with fried breadcrumbs, game chips, bread sauce, and the gravy.

Healthy option

The breast meat of pheasant is lean, which means it dries out easily. Covering it liberally with butter is the traditional way to help keep the meat moist, but you can use a drizzle of olive oil instead.

EXTRAS FOR GAME

These traditional accompaniments can be served with roast pheasant and many other game dishes, including grouse and partridge.

FRIED BREADCRUMBS

Melt 30 g (1 oz) butter with 1 tbsp sunflower oil. When the butter is foaming, add 90 g (3 oz) fresh white breadcrumbs and cook, stirring, for 3–5 minutes until golden.

GAME CHIPS

Using a mandoline or the finest blade on a food processor, slice 500 g (1 lb) old potatoes finely, then dry them. Heat some sunflower oil in a deep-fat fryer, add the potato slices, and deep-fry for 3 minutes or until crisp and golden. Drain, then sprinkle with salt.

STUFFING BALLS

Combine 125 g (4 oz) fresh white breadcrumbs, 60 g (2 oz) grated cold butter, 1 beaten egg, 2 tbsp chopped parsley, and the finely grated zest of 1 lemon. Season with salt and pepper, stir to mix well, then roll into 12 small balls. Melt 30 g (1 oz) butter with 1 tbsp olive oil in a frying pan. When the butter is foaming, add the stuffing balls, and cook for 5 minutes or until golden all over. Drain thoroughly.

PHEASANT STEW

SERVES 6–8

2 tbsp sunflower oil

2 pheasants, cut into serving pieces (page 170)

375 g (12 oz) shallots, chopped

125 g (4 oz) piece of smoked streaky bacon, cut into strips

3 garlic cloves, crushed

1 tbsp plain flour

600 ml (1 pint) game stock or chicken stock (page 170)

300 ml (1/2 pint) red wine

1 head of celery, separated into stalks, sliced

250 g (8 oz) button mushrooms

1 tbsp tomato purée

salt and black pepper

chopped parsley to garnish

1 Heat the oil in a large flameproof casserole. Add the pheasant pieces and cook over a high heat until browned. Lift out and drain.

2 Add the shallots and bacon and cook for 5 minutes. Add the garlic and flour and cook, stirring, for 1 minute. Add the stock and wine and bring to a boil. Add the celery, mushrooms, tomato purée, and season. Simmer for 5 minutes.

3 Add the pheasant, bring back to a boil, cover, and cook in a preheated oven at 160°C (325°F, Gas 3) for 2 hours. Garnish with parsley.

NORMANDY PHEASANT

Apples and cream are traditional ingredients in the cuisine of Normandy. Here, apples and a rich sauce perfectly complement the pheasant, which is cooked slowly and gently in wine and stock to keep it moist and tender.

SERVES 6–8

30 g (1 oz) butter

1 tbsp sunflower oil

2 pheasants, cut into serving pieces (page 170)

2 cooking apples, quartered, cored, and sliced

4 celery stalks, sliced

1 onion, sliced

1 tbsp plain flour

300 ml (1/2 pint) chicken or game stock (page 170)

150 ml (1/4 pint) dry white wine

salt and black pepper

150 ml (1/4 pint) double cream

apple rings to serve (see box, right)

chopped parsley to garnish

1 Melt the butter with the oil in a flameproof casserole. When the butter is foaming, add the pheasant pieces, and cook for about 5 minutes until browned. Lift out and drain.

2 Lower the heat, add the apples, celery, and onion, and cook for 5–6 minutes until soft.

3 Add the flour and cook, stirring, for 1 minute. Pour in the stock and wine, season with salt and pepper, and bring to a boil, stirring until lightly thickened.

4 Return the pheasant to the casserole and spoon the sauce over the top. Bring back to a boil, cover with greaseproof paper and the casserole lid, and cook in a preheated oven at 180°C (350°F, Gas 4) for 1–1 1/2 hours until tender. Remove the pheasant from the casserole with a slotted spoon and keep warm.

5 Strain the sauce into a saucepan. Whisk in the cream, taste for seasoning, then reheat gently. Arrange the pheasant on serving plates with the apple rings. Spoon the sauce over the pheasant and serve at once, garnished with parsley.

Apple rings

Core 2 cooking apples, leaving them whole, and slice crosswise into 5 mm (1/4 in) rings. Melt 30 g (1 oz) butter in a frying pan, add the apple rings, and sprinkle with a little caster sugar. Cook over a high heat for 3 minutes, turning once, until caramelized and golden.

Healthy option

Instead of cream, use low-fat crème fraîche and only 150 ml (1/4 pint) stock. Crème fraîche is runnier than double cream, so less liquid is needed.

RUBY HARE CASSEROLE

SERVES 4

1 hare, cut into serving pieces
30 g (1 oz) butter
2 tbsp olive oil
125 g (4 oz) piece of streaky bacon, cut into strips
16 small shallots
250 g (8 oz) chestnut mushrooms, halved
30 g (1 oz) plain flour
900 ml (1½ pints) game stock or chicken stock (page 170)
2 large thyme sprigs
2 large parsley sprigs
salt and black pepper
stuffing balls (page 217)
fresh thyme to garnish

MARINADE

300 ml (½ pint) ruby port
4 tbsp olive oil
1 large onion, sliced
2 bay leaves

1 Make the marinade: in a large bowl, combine the port, oil, onion, and bay leaves. Add the hare pieces, turn in the marinade, cover, and leave to marinate in the refrigerator for 8 hours.

2 Remove the hare from the marinade, reserving the marinade. Melt the butter with the oil in a large flameproof casserole. When the butter is foaming, add the hare pieces and cook over a high heat until browned all over. Lift out and drain on paper towels.

3 Lower the heat, add the bacon and shallots, and cook for 5 minutes or until lightly browned. Add the mushrooms and cook for 2–3 minutes. Remove and drain on paper towels. Add the flour and cook, stirring, for 1 minute. Gradually add the stock and bring to a boil, stirring until thickened.

4 Return the hare, bacon, shallots, and mushrooms to the casserole with the strained marinade. Add the thyme and parsley, season with salt and pepper, and bring to a boil. Cover and cook in a preheated oven at 160°C (325°F, Gas 3) for 2 hours.

5 Taste for seasoning. Place the stuffing balls on top, garnish with fresh thyme, and serve hot.

GAME PIE WITH FENNEL & CARROTS

SERVES 6

2 tbsp sunflower oil
750 g (1½ lb) boneless game meat, cut into strips or dice
2 large carrots, sliced
1 fennel bulb, sliced
1 large onion, chopped
2 tsp plain flour
300 ml (½ pint) game stock or chicken stock (page 170)
150 ml (¼ pint) red wine
1 tbsp redcurrant jelly
salt and black pepper
plain flour for dusting
250 g (8 oz) ready made puff pastry
beaten egg for glazing
chopped parsley to garnish
2 LITRE (3½ PINT) PIE DISH

1 Heat the oil in a large flameproof casserole. Add the game in batches and cook over a high heat until browned all over. Lift out and drain on paper towels.

2 Lower the heat, add the carrots, fennel, and onion, and cook, stirring occasionally, for 5 minutes or until softened. Add the flour and cook, stirring, for about 1 minute.

3 Gradually pour in the stock and bring to a boil, stirring until thickened slightly. Add the game, wine, and redcurrant jelly, and season with salt and pepper. Cover tightly and simmer very gently for 1 hour. Leave to cool.

4 Lightly flour a work surface. Roll out the puff pastry until 2.5 cm (1 in) larger than the pie dish. Invert the dish on to the dough and cut around the edge. Cut a long strip of pastry from the trimmings and press on to the rim of the pie dish. Reserve the remaining trimmings. Spoon in the game and vegetable mixture. Brush the pastry strip with water, top with the pastry lid, and crimp the edge with a fork.

5 Make a hole in the top of the pie to let the steam escape. Roll out the reserved pastry and cut decorative shapes with a pastry cutter. Brush the bottoms of the shapes with beaten egg, and arrange on the pie. Glaze with beaten egg.

6 Bake the pie in a preheated oven at 200°C (400°F, Gas 6) for 25–30 minutes until the pastry is well risen and golden. Garnish with parsley.

RABBIT WITH MUSTARD & MARJORAM

SERVES 4

4 tbsp Dijon mustard

1 tsp chopped fresh marjoram

4 rabbit portions

30 g (1 oz) butter

2 tbsp olive oil

1 large onion, chopped

2 garlic cloves, crushed

90 g (3 oz) piece of smoked streaky bacon, cut into pieces

1 tsp plain flour

450 ml (3/4 pint) chicken stock

salt and black pepper

150 ml (1/4 pint) single cream

2 tbsp chopped parsley to garnish

1 Mix the mustard and marjoram and spread over the rabbit pieces. Place in a shallow dish, cover, and leave to marinate in the refrigerator for 8 hours.

2 Melt the butter with the oil in a large flameproof casserole. When the butter is foaming, add the rabbit, and cook for about 5 minutes until browned all over. Lift out and drain on paper towels.

3 Add the onion, garlic, and bacon to the casserole and cook for 3–5 minutes. Add the flour and cook, stirring, for 1 minute. Gradually blend in the stock and bring to a boil, stirring until thickened.

4 Return the rabbit to the casserole, season with salt and pepper, and bring back to a boil. Cover and cook in a preheated oven at 160°C (325°F, Gas 3) for 1 1/2 hours or until the rabbit is tender.

5 Transfer the rabbit to a warmed platter and keep hot. Boil the sauce for 2 minutes until reduced. Stir in the cream, taste for seasoning, and spoon over the rabbit. Garnish with parsley.

Healthy option

To decrease the amount of saturated fat, omit the bacon and use low-fat crème fraîche instead of cream. Crème fraîche is runnier than cream, so reduce the amount of chicken stock to 300 ml (1/2 pint) to compensate.

BRAISED RABBIT WITH MUSHROOMS & CIDER

SERVES 4

30 g (1 oz) butter

1 tbsp sunflower oil

4 rabbit portions

8 small shallots

375 g (12 oz) mushrooms, quartered

300 ml (1/2 pint) dry cider

a few parsley sprigs

3–4 tarragon sprigs

salt and black pepper

300 ml (1/2 pint) single cream

2 tbsp chopped parsley to garnish

1 Melt the butter with the oil in a flameproof casserole. When the butter is foaming, add the rabbit, and cook for about 5 minutes until browned all over. Lift out the rabbit with a slotted spoon and drain on paper towels.

2 Add the shallots to the casserole and cook over a high heat, stirring, for about 3 minutes until golden. Add the mushrooms, and cook, stirring occasionally, for 3–4 minutes until softened.

3 Return the rabbit to the casserole, and add the cider, parsley sprigs, and tarragon. Season with salt and pepper, and bring to a boil. Cover and cook in a preheated oven at 160°C (325°F, Gas 3) for 1 1/2 hours or until the rabbit is tender.

4 Transfer the rabbit to a warmed platter and keep warm. Remove and discard the parsley and tarragon. Bring the sauce in the casserole to a boil on the hob, then boil until slightly reduced. Stir in the cream, taste for seasoning, and reheat gently.

5 Pour the sauce over the rabbit, and serve at once, garnished with parsley.

BRAISED RABBIT WITH PRUNES

Substitute 125 g (4 oz) ready-to-eat pitted prunes for the mushrooms. Add to the casserole 30 minutes before the end of the cooking time.

POT ROAST VENISON

SERVES 6

1.25–1.5 kg (2½–3 lb) boned
    venison shoulder, rolled and tied

30 g (1 oz) butter

2 tbsp sunflower oil

1 large onion, chopped

2 large carrots, sliced

2 celery stalks, sliced

300 ml (½ pint) beef stock

salt and black pepper

1 tbsp redcurrant jelly

MARINADE

300 ml (½ pint) red wine

2 tbsp olive oil

pared zest of 1 orange

pared zest of 1 lemon

2 tsp crushed juniper berries

6 black peppercorns

1 garlic clove, crushed

1 large thyme sprig

1 large parsley sprig

1 Make the marinade: in a large bowl, combine the wine, oil, orange and lemon zests, juniper berries, black peppercorns, garlic, thyme, and parsley. Turn the venison in the marinade, cover, and marinate in the refrigerator, turning occasionally, for 2–3 days.

2 Lift the venison out of the marinade, straining and reserving the marinade, and pat dry. Melt the butter with the oil in a large flameproof casserole. When the butter is foaming, add the venison and cook over a high heat for 5 minutes or until well browned all over. Remove the venison from the casserole.

3 Lower the heat and add the onion, carrots, and celery to the casserole. Cover and cook very gently for 10 minutes. Place the venison on top of the vegetables, add the stock and the strained marinade, then season with salt and pepper and bring to a boil. Cover with a piece of greaseproof paper and the casserole lid, and cook in a preheated oven at 160°C (325°F, Gas 3) for 2½–3 hours until tender.

4 Lift out the venison and keep warm. Strain the liquid in the casserole, spoon off the fat, then return the liquid to the casserole. Add the redcurrant jelly, and boil for a few minutes until syrupy. Slice the venison, and arrange on a warmed platter. Pour over the sauce, and serve hot.

VENISON CASSEROLE

SERVES 6

1 kg (2 lb) stewing venison, cut into
    2.5 cm (1 in) cubes

2 tbsp olive oil

6 celery stalks, thickly sliced on the
    diagonal

150 g (5 oz) chestnut mushrooms,
    quartered

30 g (1 oz) plain flour

salt and black pepper

125 g (4 oz) small carrots

chopped parsley to garnish

MARINADE

450 ml (¾ pint) red wine

3 tbsp sunflower oil

1 onion, sliced

1 tsp ground allspice

a few parsley sprigs

1 bay leaf

1 Make the marinade: in a large bowl, combine the red wine, oil, onion, allspice, parsley sprigs, and bay leaf. Toss the venison cubes in the marinade to coat them thoroughly, cover, and leave to marinate in the refrigerator, turning occasionally, for 2 days.

2 Lift the venison and onion out of the marinade and pat dry. Strain and reserve the marinade.

3 Heat the oil in a large flameproof casserole, add the venison and onion, and cook for 3–5 minutes until well browned. Lift out and drain on paper towels.

4 Lower the heat, add the celery and mushrooms, and cook for 2–3 minutes until softened. Remove with a slotted spoon. Add the flour and cook, stirring, for 1 minute. Gradually blend in the marinade and bring to a boil, stirring until thickened.

5 Return the venison, onion, celery, and mushrooms to the casserole, and season with salt and pepper. Bring to a boil, cover, and cook in a preheated oven at 160°C (325°F, Gas 3) for 1½ hours.

6 Add the carrots, and return to the oven for 30 minutes or until the venison is tender. Serve hot, garnished with parsley.

RATHER SPECIAL GAME PIE

This raised game pie follows a classic recipe which takes about 6 hours to make, over 3 days, but it is well worth the effort. Boned mixed game meats – usually pheasant, hare, and venison – are available in large supermarkets and food halls. There is chicken in the pie too, which goes very well with game, but you could use turkey.

SERVES 20

2 kg (4 lb) chicken, boned and skinned (page 171)

1 kg (2 lb) boneless mixed game meats, cut into 1 cm (1/2 in) pieces

375 g (12 oz) belly pork, coarsely chopped

500 g (1 lb) piece of streaky bacon, cut into small pieces

butter for greasing

hot-water crust pastry (see box, right)

about 2 tsp salt

black pepper

1 egg, beaten

450 ml (3/4 pint) jellied stock (page 170)

MARINADE

150 ml (1/4 pint) port

1 small onion, finely chopped

3 garlic cloves, crushed

leaves of 4 thyme sprigs, chopped

1 tsp grated nutmeg

29 CM (11 1/2 IN) SPRINGFORM OR LOOSE-BOTTOMED CAKE TIN

1 Make the marinade: in a bowl, combine the port, onion, garlic, thyme, and grated nutmeg.

2 Cut the chicken breast into long strips, about 1 cm (1/2 in) wide, and set aside. Cut the rest of the chicken into 1 cm (1/2 in) chunks. Add the chunks to the marinade with the game meats, belly pork, and bacon. Cover and leave to marinate in the refrigerator for 8 hours.

3 Lightly butter the tin. Take two-thirds of the hot-water crust pastry, pat it out over the bottom of the tin, and push it up the side, until it stands 1 cm (1/2 in) above the rim.

4 Season the meat mixture with plenty of salt and pepper and spoon half into the pastry shell. Smooth the surface evenly.

5 Arrange the reserved chicken breast strips on top of the meat, radiating from the middle. Season with salt and pepper.

6 Top with the remaining meat mixture. Brush the top edge of the pastry with beaten egg. Roll out the remaining pastry, and cover the pie, reserving the trimmings. Pinch around the edge to seal, then crimp.

7 Decorate the pie with the pastry trimmings, attaching them with beaten egg. Make 3 steam holes in the pastry lid, and glaze the pie with beaten egg.

8 Bake in a preheated oven at 220°C (425°F, Gas 7) for 1 hour. If the pastry browns too quickly, cover with foil. Reduce the heat to 160°C (325°F, Gas 3) and cook for 2–2 1/4 hours.

9 Test the pie by piercing the centre with a skewer: the juices will run clear and the meat will feel tender when it is done. Leave the pie to cool in the tin for 8 hours.

10 Put the jellied stock into a saucepan and heat until melted. Using a funnel, slowly pour the stock through the holes in the pie. Cover and chill for 6 hours or until the stock has set. Unmould the pie and cut into wedges to serve.

Hot-water crust

Sift 750 g (1 1/2 lb) plain flour and 1 tsp salt into a large bowl. Put 400 ml (14 fl oz) water and 300 g (10 oz) white vegetable fat into a saucepan and heat until the water is boiling and the fat has melted.

Pour on to the flour and mix quickly with a wooden spoon until the mixture holds together.

Turn the dough on to a floured surface, invert the bowl over the top to keep the dough moist, and leave to cool until lukewarm.

6

MEAT DISHES

UNDER 30 MINUTES

BEEF STROGANOFF

Classic Russian dish: strips of rump steak cooked with shallots and button mushrooms, and mixed with soured cream.

SERVES 6 329 calories per serving

Takes 20 minutes   Page 249

HIGH PROTEIN

LAMB CHOPS WITH MINTED HOLLANDAISE SAUCE

Grilled chops served with hollandaise sauce, flavoured with lemon juice and fresh mint.

SERVES 4 611 calories per serving

Takes 20 minutes   Page 278

STEAK DIANE

Flambéed rump steaks served with a light sauce combining onion, beef stock, lemon juice, Worcestershire sauce, and parsley.

SERVES 4 373 calories per serving

Takes 25 minutes   Page 248

BARBECUE

STEAKS WITH SMOKED OYSTER RELISH

Steaks rubbed with garlic, and sprinkled with smoked oyster relish flavoured with parsley.

SERVES 4 278 calories per serving

Takes 15–20 minutes   Page 247

HERBED BUTTERFLY CHOPS

Lamb chops brushed with olive oil, sprinkled with pepper, and flavoured with rosemary, mint, and thyme sprigs, then grilled.

SERVES 4 320 calories per serving

Takes 15 minutes   Page 278

FAMILY CHOICE

LIVER & BACON WITH ONION SAUCE

Strips of liver simmered with onion, bacon, beef stock, tomato ketchup, and Worcestershire sauce.

SERVES 4 441 calories per serving

Takes 15 minutes   Page 269

FRENCH CLASSIC

TOURNEDOS ROQUEFORT

Crunchy and nutritious: grilled tournedos steaks topped with a mixture of melted Roquefort cheese, butter, and chopped walnuts.

SERVES 4 430 calories per serving

Takes 20 minutes   Page 248

PEPPER STEAKS

Piquant and creamy: fillet steak encrusted with black peppercorns. Served in a pool of cream and brandy sauce.

SERVES 4 489 calories per serving

Takes 25 minutes   Page 246

CALF'S LIVER WITH SAGE

Slices of calf's liver, coated with seasoned flour, and cooked quickly. Served with pan juices flavoured with sage and lemon juice.

SERVES 4 364 calories per serving

Takes 10 minutes   Page 270

UNDER 30 MINUTES

30–60 MINUTES

SALTIMBOCCA

Veal escalopes topped with sage leaves and Parma ham, and cooked with garlic. Served with a wine and cream sauce.

SERVES 4 342 calories per serving

Takes 25 minutes   Page 267

VEAL MARSALA

Veal escalopes lightly coated in seasoned flour and cooked until golden. Served in a Marsala sauce, and garnished with parsley.

SERVES 4 239 calories per serving

Takes 30 minutes   Page 268

HIGH PROTEIN

GRILLED PORK CHOPS WITH MANGO SAUCE

Sweet and tender: chops served with a sauce combining fresh mango and mango chutney.

SERVES 4 347 calories per serving

Takes 35 minutes   Page 288

MEXICAN CLASSIC

BEEF TACOS

Minced beef and tomatoes richly seasoned with garlic, chilli, and coriander. Served in taco shells with lettuce and soured cream.

SERVES 4 407 calories per serving

Takes 25 minutes   Page 263

ECONOMICAL

CORNED BEEF HASH

Quick and nourishing: chunks of corned beef cooked with onion, pieces of potato, and stock, and grilled until crispy and brown.

SERVES 4 444 calories per serving

Takes 30 minutes   Page 258

PORK CHOPS WITH ORANGES

Fresh and tangy: pork chops spread with wholegrain mustard, topped with orange slices and sugar, and baked.

SERVES 6 361 calories per serving

Takes 55 minutes   Page 289

DINNER PARTY

CHATEAUBRIAND WITH BEARNAISE SAUCE

Grilled steak basted with butter, served with a béarnaise sauce flavoured with tarragon.

SERVES 2 761 calories per serving

Takes 25 minutes   Page 246

BEEF & BEAN BURRITOS

Popular and piquant: strips of rump steak cooked with garlic, chilli, tomatoes, and pinto beans. Wrapped in tortillas.

SERVES 4 471 calories per serving

Takes 35 minutes   Page 249

HIGH PROTEIN

PORK STEAKS WITH MIXED PEPPERCORNS

Lean meat encrusted with peppercorns, served with a white wine, beef stock, and cream sauce.

SERVES 4 567 calories per serving

Takes 30 minutes, plus standing   Page 290

30–60 MINUTES

LAMB WITH MINT GLAZE

Best end lamb chops glazed with white wine, vinegar, mint sprigs, honey, and Dijon mustard, then barbecued or grilled.

SERVES 4 304 calories per serving
Takes 15 minutes, plus marinating   Page 277

MADEIRA PORK WITH PAPRIKA

Rich and creamy: pork fillet simmered with Madeira, stock, onion, mushrooms, red pepper, and paprika, then mixed with cream.

SERVES 4 560 calories per serving
Takes 50 minutes   Page 287

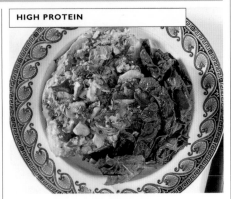

VEAL CHOPS WITH MUSHROOMS & CREAM

Veal chops cooked with mushrooms, cream, shallots, garlic, wine, and tarragon.

SERVES 4 604 calories per serving
Takes 30 minutes, plus soaking   Page 266

MEATBALLS IN CIDER

Balls of minced beef and pork in a sauce of cider and tomato purée, with onion, garlic, celery, red pepper, and mushrooms.

SERVES 4 416 calories per serving
Takes 40 minutes   Page 259

KIDNEYS TURBIGO

Lamb's kidneys cooked with chipolata sausages, then simmered with stock, sherry, onions, mushrooms, and bay leaf.

SERVES 4 455 calories per serving
Takes 50 minutes   Page 284

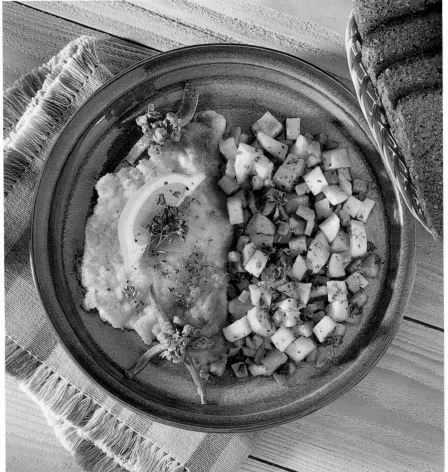

VEAL SCHNITZELS

A classic Viennese dish: veal escalopes coated in beaten egg and fresh white breadcrumbs, chilled, then cooked until light golden brown.

SERVES 4 373 calories per serving
Takes 20 minutes, plus chilling   Page 267

Traditionally served with piquant anchovy fillets, chopped capers, lemon wedges, and a few parsley sprigs.

OVER 60 MINUTES

JAPANESE CLASSIC

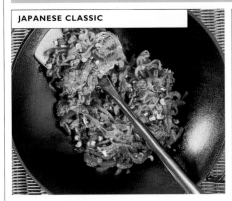

TERIYAKI BEEF

Strips of tender rump steak marinated in soy sauce, Japanese rice wine, and sugar. Stir-fried with onion and red pepper.

SERVES 4 329 calories per serving

Takes 15 minutes, plus marinating   Page 252

LAMB NOISETTES WITH ORANGE & HONEY

Grilled noisettes served with a sauce made from the marinade of orange, honey, olive oil, and herbs.

SERVES 4 457 calories per serving

Takes 20 minutes, plus marinating   Page 279

HIGH PROTEIN

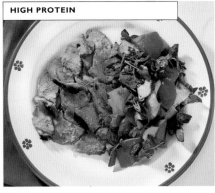

LEMON-GRILLED LAMB

Butterflied leg of lamb marinated in a tangy mixture of lemon juice, honey, garlic, and mustard, and grilled.

SERVES 6–8 425–318 calories per serving

Takes 45 minutes, plus marinating   Page 273

DINNER PARTY

BACON-WRAPPED PORK IN VERMOUTH SAUCE

Pork fillets wrapped in bacon and served with a vermouth and mushroom sauce.

SERVES 6 547 calories per serving

Takes 1¼ hours   Page 287

FAJITAS

Chuck steak marinated in orange and lime juices, tequila, garlic, coriander, and chilli, and grilled. Served with relish and tortillas.

SERVES 4 543 calories per serving

Takes 40 minutes, plus marinating   Page 252

MEAT LOAF

Minced beef mixed with tomatoes, stuffing, onion, carrot, parsley, and garlic, wrapped in bacon and baked.

SERVES 6 478 calories per serving

Takes 1½ hours   Page 262

ORIENTAL CLASSIC

PORK WITH CHILLI & COCONUT

Strips of pork in a dry marinade of ginger, chilli, and curry powder. Cooked with coconut, spring onions, and red pepper.

SERVES 6 332 calories per serving

Takes 40 minutes, plus marinating   Page 288

CREAMED SWEETBREADS

Calf's sweetbreads simmered with onion, parsley, and bay leaf. Served with a lemon-flavoured sauce.

SERVES 6 230 calories per serving

Takes 40 minutes, plus soaking   Page 270

HIGH PROTEIN

PORK CHOPS WITH SPINACH & MUSHROOM STUFFING

Loin chops with a savoury mixture of spinach and mushrooms, and topped with Gruyère cheese.

SERVES 6 345 calories per serving

Takes 40 minutes   Page 289

OVER 60 MINUTES

AFRICAN CLASSIC

TRADITIONAL

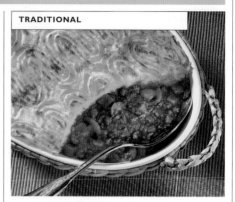

BOBOTIE

Minced beef baked with garlic, apricots, almonds, chutney, lemon, and milk-soaked bread. Topped with eggs and almonds.

SERVES 6–8 656–492 calories per serving

Takes 1 hour 5 minutes   Page 263

DANISH MEATBALLS

Minced pork seasoned with onion, thyme, and paprika and shaped into ovals. Cooked in a tomato sauce, and topped with Greek yogurt.

SERVES 4–6 586–391 calories per serving

Takes 1¹/₂ hours   Page 292

SHEPHERD'S PIE

Minced lamb baked with mushrooms, carrot, onion, garlic, stock, and mushroom ketchup. Topped with mashed potato.

SERVES 6 383 calories per serving

Takes 1¹/₂ hours   Page 283

ORIENTAL CLASSIC

FAMILY CHOICE

SPICED LAMB WITH COCONUT

Cubes of lamb, dry marinated in ginger and spices, are cooked with tomato, lime, mango chutney, and coconut, then mixed with yogurt.

SERVES 6 496 calories per serving

Takes 1¹/₄ hours   Page 282

PASTICCIO

Minced pork simmered with red wine, tomatoes, garlic, herbs, and cinnamon. Baked with macaroni and cheese custard.

SERVES 6 679 calories per serving

Takes 1¹/₄ hours   Page 292

BEEF WITH ROAST VEGETABLE SALAD

Roast beef served with a salad of roasted aubergine, courgettes, fennel, and peppers.

SERVES 4–6 522–348 calories per serving

Takes 1³/₄ hours, plus cooling   Page 244

SPANISH CLASSIC

MERGUEZ WITH POTATOES & PEPPERS

Bite-sized pieces of spicy merguez sausage in a casserole with potatoes, red and green peppers, and garlic.

SERVES 4 381 calories per serving

Takes 1¹/₄ hours, plus cooling   Page 284

MARINATED LOIN OF PORK WITH PINEAPPLE

Pork marinated in pineapple juice, maple syrup, soy sauce, and herbs, then roasted.

SERVES 8 320 calories per serving

Takes 2¹/₂ hours, plus marinating   Page 286

BEEF FLORENTINE

Layer of minced beef, tomato, and garlic, topped with spinach and three types of cheese. Covered with filo pastry.

SERVES 8 576 calories per serving

Takes 1¹/₂ hours   Page 259

OVER 60 MINUTES

HIGH FIBRE

SAUSAGE & LENTIL CASSEROLE

Herby pork sausages baked with lentils, stock, and vegetables. Flavoured with bay leaves, parsley, and sage.

SERVES 6   522 calories per serving
Takes 1 3/4 hours   Page 296

RACK OF LAMB WITH A WALNUT & HERB CRUST

Rack of lamb coated with a walnut and parsley crust, and roasted.

SERVES 4–6   626–417 calories per serving
Takes 1 3/4 hours, plus chilling   Page 277

FRENCH CLASSIC

BLANQUETTE OF LAMB

Chunks of lamb simmered with onion, carrot, bay leaves, lemon juice, and mushrooms. Served with a cream and egg sauce.

SERVES 6   439 calories per serving
Takes 2 hours   Page 281

GREEK CLASSIC

LIGHT MOUSSAKA WITH FRESH MINT

Minced lamb in a tomato-mint sauce, layered with aubergines, and topped with yogurt, egg, and cheese.

SERVES 8   351 calories per serving
Takes 1 3/4 hours   Page 283

ECONOMICAL

TOAD IN THE HOLE WITH ONION SAUCE

Pork sausagemeat combined with leek, sage, and parsley, and baked in a batter.

SERVES 4   802 calories per serving
Takes 45 minutes, plus standing   Page 296

FAMILY CHOICE

COTTAGE PIES WITH CHEESY POTATO TOPPING

Minced beef cooked with vegetables and stock. Topped with mashed potato and cheese.

SERVES 6   567 calories per serving
Takes 1 1/2 hours   Page 262

LEMON ROAST VEAL WITH SPINACH STUFFING

Veal marinated in lemon and thyme, with a stuffing of spinach, shallot, and bacon.

SERVES 6–8   444–333 calories per serving
Takes 1 3/4 hours, plus marinating   Page 265

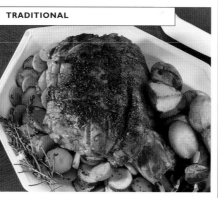

TRADITIONAL

ROAST LEG OF LAMB WITH RED WINE GRAVY

Lamb flavoured with herbs, roasted and served with red wine gravy and mint sauce.

SERVES 4–6   517–344 calories per serving
Takes 2 hours   Page 271

LAMB TAGINE

Cubes of lamb cooked with apricots, fennel, green peppers, and stock. Flavoured with saffron, ginger, and orange.

SERVES 8   412 calories per serving
Takes 1 3/4 hours   Page 282

OVER 60 MINUTES

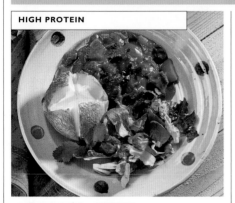

CHILLI CON CARNE

Tex-Mex speciality: cubes of chuck steak cooked with red kidney beans, chilli, onion, garlic, stock, tomato purée, and red pepper.

SERVES 6 362 calories per serving

Takes 3¼ hours, plus soaking   Page 257

SPINACH-STUFFED LAMB

Succulent and nutritious: boned leg of lamb stuffed with spinach and garlic, and roasted with wine and anchovies.

SERVES 6–8 459–344 calories per serving

Takes 2½ hours, plus cooling   Page 272

SHOULDER OF LAMB WITH GARLIC & HERBS

Lamb flavoured with garlic, rosemary, mint, and thyme. Served with haricot beans.

SERVES 6 464 calories per serving

Takes 1¾ hours   Page 276

FARMER'S BACON BAKE

Joint of bacon simmered with vegetables, parsley, and peppercorns, cut into pieces, and baked with a cheese sauce.

SERVES 6–8 510–383 calories per serving

Takes 2¼ hours   Page 294

AFELIA

Cubes of pork marinated in red wine, coriander seeds, and cinnamon, cooked with wine, and sprinkled with cumin seeds.

SERVES 4 582 calories per serving

Takes 2 hours, plus marinating   Page 291

WINTER BEEF CASSEROLE

Cubes of chuck steak and strips of bacon cooked with stock, celery, and carrots, and flavoured with wine and passata.

SERVES 4–6 680–454 calories per serving

Takes 2¾ hours   Page 253

SWEET & SOUR CHINESE SPARE RIBS

Spare ribs baked until tender, and coated in a sauce combining ginger, garlic, soy and hoisin sauces, tomato purée, and sherry.

SERVES 4 491 calories per serving

Takes 2 hours   Page 290

FRAGRANT LAMB KORMA

Rich and creamy: chunks of lamb cooked with an aromatic blend of ginger, chillies, cardamom, and other spices, in a creamy yogurt sauce.

SERVES 6 508 calories per serving

Takes 2½ hours   Page 280

BEEF OLIVES WITH VEGETABLE JULIENNE

Slices of topside wrapped around stir-fried vegetables, and cooked with beef stock.

SERVES 6 257 calories per serving

Takes 2¼ hours   Page 257

OVER 60 MINUTES

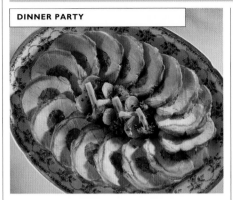

BONED LOIN OF PORK WITH APRICOT STUFFING

Pork filled with an apricot and herb stuffing, then rolled and roasted.

SERVES 8 428 calories per serving

Takes 2¼ hours, plus cooling   Page 285

LATIMER BEEF WITH HORSERADISH

Chuck steak cooked with stock, shallots, curry powder, sugar, ginger, and horseradish cream, and garnished with parsley.

SERVES 6 298 calories per serving

Takes 3 hours   Page 255

AROMATIC LAMB WITH LENTILS

Chunks of lamb marinated in orange juice, garlic, ginger, and coriander. Cooked with apricots, stock, onion, and lentils.

SERVES 8 475 calories per serving

Takes 2½ hours, plus marinating   Page 281

SALT BEEF WITH MUSTARD SAUCE

Boned salt beef cooked with carrots, celery, potatoes, turnips, and leeks. Served with a mustard sauce flavoured with wine vinegar.

SERVES 6–8 575–431 calories per serving

Takes 2¼ hours, plus soaking   Page 243

HUNGARIAN GOULASH

Cubes of chuck steak cooked with stock, onion, tomatoes, red pepper, potatoes, paprika, and soured cream.

SERVES 6 474 calories per serving

Takes 2½ hours   Page 254

CHIANTI BEEF CASSEROLE

Cubes of steak cooked until meltingly tender with Chianti, garlic, thyme, artichoke hearts, sun-dried tomatoes, and olives.

SERVES 4–6 512–342 calories per serving

Takes 2½ hours   Page 255

THAI RED BEEF CURRY

Cubes of chuck steak cooked with cardamom, cinnamon, bay leaves, cloves, ginger, garlic, paprika, tomatoes, yogurt, and red pepper.

SERVES 6 327 calories per serving

Takes 2½ hours   Page 256

BEEF WELLINGTON

Roasted fillet of beef coated with mushrooms, onion, and liver pâté, and encased in puff pastry. Served with a mushroom gravy.

SERVES 8 580 calories per serving

Takes 2¼ hours, plus cooling   Page 245

FRENCH-STYLE BRAISED BEEF

Beef marinated in wine, vinegar, garlic, orange, and herbs, and cooked with bacon, carrots, mushrooms, tomatoes, and olives.

SERVES 4–6 604–402 calories per serving

Takes 2½ hours, plus marinating   Page 243

OVER 60 MINUTES

FRENCH CLASSIC

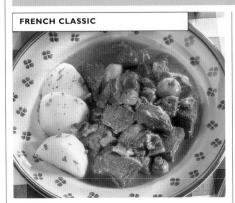

BOEUF BOURGUIGNON

Rich casserole: cubes of chuck steak cooked with shallots, bacon, red Burgundy, beef stock, mushrooms, and herbs.

SERVES 6   490 calories per serving

Takes 2³/4 hours   Page 253

OSSO BUCO

Slices of veal shin cooked with onion, tomato, carrots, celery, garlic, white wine, and stock. Sprinkled with gremolata.

SERVES 6   354 calories per serving

Takes 2³/4 hours   Page 268

FAMILY CHOICE

COUNTRY BEEF CASSEROLE

Chunky and nourishing: cubes of chuck steak cooked in a casserole with stock and vegetables. Served with herb dumplings.

SERVES 8   405 calories per serving

Takes 3 hours   Page 256

DINNER PARTY

VEAL STEW WITH OLIVES & PEPPERS

Cubes of veal cooked in a casserole of peppers, wine, tomatoes, and olives, and flavoured with garlic and rosemary.

SERVES 8   355 calories per serving

Takes 2 hours   Page 269

TRADITIONAL

SHOULDER OF LAMB WITH LEMON & OLIVES

Lamb rolled with an olive, lemon, and herb stuffing, and roasted in wine and stock.

SERVES 6–8   460–345 calories per serving

Takes 2³/4 hours   Page 273

ENGLISH ROAST BEEF

Traditional succulent family roast: rolled beef sirloin basted and cooked until deliciously tender. Served with a variety of vegetables, traditional Yorkshire puddings, a rich red wine gravy, and creamy horseradish sauce.

SERVES 8   394 calories per serving

Takes 3¹/4 hours   Page 241

OVER 60 MINUTES

ROAST LEG OF PORK
Tender and nourishing: pork roasted with carrot and onion until crackling is crisp. Served with gravy and apple sauce.

SERVES 6–8 338–254 calories per serving
Takes 2¹/4 hours   Page 286

TRADITIONAL

IRISH STEW
Traditional Irish family meal: lamb chops cooked in layers of potato and onion, and flavoured with bay leaf, thyme, and parsley.

SERVES 4 539 calories per serving
Takes 3¹/4 hours   Page 280

WILTSHIRE PORK CASSEROLE
Shoulder of pork cut into cubes, cooked in a casserole with stock, white wine vinegar, honey, soy sauce, mushrooms, and prunes.

SERVES 8 402 calories per serving
Takes 3¹/4 hours   Page 291

LANCASHIRE HOT POT
Lamb chops and kidneys cooked with potatoes, carrots, and onions, and flavoured with thyme, parsley, and bay leaf.

SERVES 4 689 calories per serving
Takes 3 hours   Page 279

FAMILY CHOICE

TEXAS BARBECUE BEEF BRISKET
Spicy and rich: beef baked in a marinade of barbecue sauce, pale ale, lemon juice, onions, garlic, and Worcestershire sauce.

SERVES 6 693 calories per serving
Takes 3¹/2 hours, plus marinating   Page 242

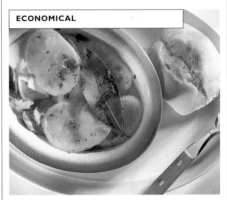

ECONOMICAL

SAUSAGE BAKE
Slices of pork sausage with layers of vegetables, lentils, and potatoes, cooked in a casserole with stock, bay leaves, and cloves.

SERVES 6 712 calories per serving
Takes 3¹/4 hours   Page 295

TRADITIONAL STEAK & KIDNEY PIE
Rich and satisfying: cubes of beef and kidney cooked with stock, Worcestershire sauce, and mushrooms. Topped with shortcrust pastry.

SERVES 6 577 calories per serving
Takes 3¹/4 hours, plus cooling   Page 258

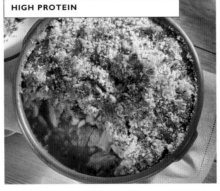

HIGH PROTEIN

SAUSAGE CASSOULET
Garlic sausage, pork sausages, and bacon baked with beans, tomatoes, wine, onion, and herbs. Topped with breadcrumbs.

SERVES 8 619 calories per serving
Takes 3 hours, plus soaking   Page 295

TRINIDAD PEPPERPOT BEEF
Boneless beef simmered with stock, vinegar, Worcestershire sauce, chillies, sugar, parsley, peppercorns, cinnamon, and thyme.

SERVES 4–6 697–465 calories per serving
Takes 3³/4 hours   Page 244

OVER 60 MINUTES

TRADITIONAL

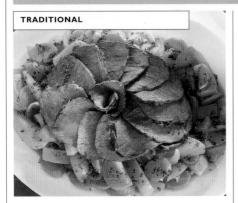

BEEF POT ROAST WITH WINTER VEGETABLES

Topside of beef in a casserole with onions, swede, celery, carrot, wine, and herbs.

SERVES 6 360 calories per serving

Takes 3½ hours   Page 242

CARBONNADE OF BEEF

Cubes of chuck steak cooked with onion, garlic, fresh herbs, brown ale, and stock, and topped with mustard croûtes.

SERVES 6 465 calories per serving

Takes 3½ hours   Page 254

VEAL WITH TUNA MAYONNAISE

Veal flavoured with garlic and rosemary, and roasted in white wine. Served cold with a tuna mayonnaise.

SERVES 8 636 calories per serving

Takes 3½ hours, plus cooling   Page 266

GREEK ROAST LAMB

Traditional Greek dish: leg of lamb richly flavoured with garlic, rosemary, and lemon juice, and cooked until tender.

SERVES 6 328 calories per serving

Takes 4¼ hours   Page 272

DINNER PARTY

INDIAN SPICED LAMB

Lamb coated in a mixture of spices, honey, yogurt, and saffron, roasted, and garnished with cashew nuts and chopped coriander.

SERVES 6 379 calories per serving

Takes 4¼ hours, plus marinating   Page 276

DINNER PARTY

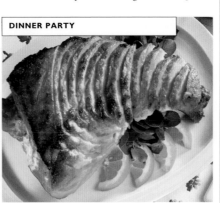

MUSTARD-GLAZED HAM

Smoked gammon cooked with cider, glazed with sugar and mustard, roasted, and served with a lemon mustard sauce.

SERVES 16–20 477–382 calories per serving

Takes 4 hours, plus soaking   Page 293

FAMILY CHOICE

OXTAIL STEW

Tender thick stew: slices of oxtail simmered slowly with beef stock, onions, tomato purée, celery, and herbs.

SERVES 6 337 calories per serving

Takes 4½ hours   Page 264

AMERICAN CLASSIC

BOSTON BAKED BEANS

Haricot beans, bacon, and onions cooked with muscovado sugar, tomato purée, treacle, golden syrup, and mustard powder.

SERVES 6–8 433–325 calories per serving

Takes 5¾ hours, plus soaking   Page 294

PRESSED TONGUE

Salted ox tongue simmered with bay leaf and onion, then covered with gelatine, pressed, and chilled until set.

SERVES 10 392 calories per serving

Takes 4¼ hours, plus chilling   Page 264

MEAT KNOW-HOW

FOR CENTURIES, MEAT HAS BEEN the protein food around which the majority of meals have been planned. Today that tradition has been turned on its head, with healthy eating advice to make meat and other protein foods just one part of a healthy diet, not the major part. Nevertheless, meat is enjoyed by most families several times a week, and it still forms the traditional centrepiece for many celebration meals. By making sure the cooking method suits the cut of meat you are preparing – quick cooking for lean meats, long, slow cooking for tougher cuts – you will always have perfectly moist and tender results.

BUYING & STORING

If possible, buy your meat from a good local butcher, or the butcher in a supermarket, because he's most likely to have just the cut you want (or will be prepared to cut it for you), and he will also advise you how to cook it. Wherever you shop, choose meat that looks fresh and moist (not wet), with a good colour and no greyish tinge. Check that pieces are neatly trimmed, without excess fat and splinters of bone. If the meat is packaged, check the use-by date. Appetites vary, but as a general guide, allow 125–175 g (4–6 oz) of lean boneless meat per person, and about 250 g (8 oz) each if the meat has a reasonable amount of bone.

Store all meat in the refrigerator, with raw kept separate from cooked and on a lower shelf (also below any food that will not be cooked before eating). Mince and offal are more perishable than other kinds of meat, so cook them within 1 day of purchase. Chops, steaks, and joints can be kept for about 3 days: remove the wrapping and replace with fresh. Eat cooked meat within 2–3 days.

PREPARING MEAT FOR COOKING

Trim off excess fat before cooking and remove any visible gristle, sinew, and tough connective tissue. If grilling or frying steaks, chops, or bacon rashers, slash or snip any fat at intervals to prevent the meat from curling up during cooking.

Marinate very lean joints to be roasted or lean cuts to be grilled or barbecued to keep them moist during cooking.

MICROWAVING

Because microwave cooking is so fast, meat does not have time to brown and become crisp. This can be overcome by using a special browning dish, which sears meat in the way a frying pan does.

The microwave is very useful for thawing frozen meat. This must be done evenly at the manufacturer's recommended setting to prevent some parts of the meat beginning to cook before others are totally thawed. All wrapping should be removed from the meat before thawing to ensure that the meat does not start to cook.

FREEZING

Meat to be frozen must be very fresh. Wrap it tightly and thoroughly so that all the air is excluded. Pad any sharp bones so that they don't pierce the wrapping. If packing chops, cutlets, steaks, or hamburgers, separate them with cling film or freezer wrap. The larger the piece of meat the longer it will keep. Mince and sausages can be stored in a freezer for 3 months; offal, chops, and cutlets for 4 months; joints and steaks for 6 months. Thaw frozen meat, in its wrapping and on a plate to catch any juices, at the bottom of the refrigerator.

MEAT STOCK

Ask your butcher to saw 2 kg (4 lb) bones into 6 cm (2½ in) pieces. Beef and veal bones are best.

1 Roast the bones in a preheated oven at 230°C (450°F, Gas 8) for 30 minutes. If you have time, add 2–3 roughly chopped onions, carrots, and celery stalks and roast for another 30 minutes.

2 Transfer the bones and vegetables to a large stockpot. Add 4 litres (7 pints) water, a bouquet garni made of 1–2 bay leaves, a few parsley stalks, and 1–2 sprigs of thyme, and a few black peppercorns.

3 Bring to a boil. Skim off scum, then cover and simmer for 4–6 hours. Ladle into a sieve to strain. Skim off fat, or let cool and lift off solidified fat.

BASIC COOKING TECHNIQUES

Tougher pieces of meat should be cooked slowly by stewing or braising to make them beautifully tender.
Those cuts that are naturally tender can be cooked quickly by frying or grilling or by roasting.

Frying and sautéing

1 Dry the meat with paper towels (if too moist it will not brown quickly and evenly). Heat oil or a mixture of oil and butter in a heavy frying pan until it is very hot, then add the meat, taking care not to crowd the pan.

2 Cook until well browned on both sides. Reduce the heat and continue cooking until the meat is done to your taste. When turning meat, use tongs rather than a fork, as a fork pierces the meat and allows the juices to run out.

Grilling and barbecuing

1 Preheat the grill to hot, or light the barbecue (it will take 20–30 minutes to reach cooking temperature unless it is gas, which will heat up immediately).

2 Put the meat on the grill rack and put under the hot grill, or arrange on the grid over charcoal. Brush with oil or a marinade, and cook the meat until it is browned on both sides, turning and re-brushing as necessary.

3 For sausages or thicker pieces of meat that need to be well cooked, reduce the heat or move the meat further away from the heat, and complete cooking.

Stir-frying

1 Cut the meat into uniform pieces for even cooking. Heat a wok or heavy frying pan, then add a little oil.

2 When the oil is hot, start adding the meat, a little at a time – adding too much at once will lower the temperature of the oil. Using a slotted spoon or a spatula, stir and toss the meat constantly until it is evenly browned.

3 If some of the pieces of meat are cooked before others, they can be pushed up the side of the wok or to the side of the pan where they will keep warm but not overcook.

Roasting

1 Take the joint from the refrigerator and allow it to come to room temperature.

2 Preheat the oven. Rub the meat with fat or oil and seasonings, or make incisions all over and insert herbs or slivers of garlic. Insert a meat thermometer, if using.

3 Put the joint and any vegetables in a roasting tin. Roast, basting with the fat and juices in the tin, until

cooked to your taste (page 240). If not using a meat thermometer (or an instant-read thermometer), test whether the meat is cooked by inserting a skewer into the centre. If the juices that run out are bloody, the meat is rare; if pink, medium; if clear, well-done.

4 Transfer the joint to a carving board and leave to rest for 10–15 minutes while making gravy. Carve the joint (page 213) and serve.

Stewing

Cut the meat into even cubes. Put into a flameproof casserole with any vegetables and liquid to cover plus any flavourings. Bring to a boil, then cover and simmer on the hob, or cook in the oven. Alternatively, heat some oil in the casserole and brown the cubes of meat, then brown the vegetables. Add the liquid and any flavourings. Bring to a boil, cover, and simmer as above.

Braising

1 Brown the meat on all sides in a flameproof casserole, to add flavour and a rich colour. Remove the meat from the casserole.

2 Add chopped vegetables and cook until they are beginning to brown. Return the meat and add liquid and any flavourings. Bring to a boil, then cover and cook gently on the hob or in the oven, as instructed in the recipe.

BONING & BUTTERFLYING A LEG OF LAMB

A boned leg of lamb is much easier to carve than meat still on the bone. Tunnel boning leaves a pocket that can be filled with a savoury stuffing. If the leg is cut open to lie flat, this is known as butterflying.

1 To tunnel bone, trim the skin and most or all of the fat from the lamb. Cut around the pelvic bone, at the wide end of the leg, to separate it from the meat. Sever the tendons that connect it to the leg bone. Remove the pelvic bone.

2 At the narrow end of the leg, cut around the shank bone and then scrape the meat away from the whole length of the bone using short strokes.

3 Cut away the meat to expose the joint that joins the shank bone to the leg bone. Sever the tendons and then remove the shank bone.

6 Open out the boned leg into a "butterfly" shape. Cut through any thick portions of meat so that the whole leg can be opened out flat and is roughly even in thickness. Trim off excess fat and any remaining tendons.

4 Cut around each end of the leg bone. Ease the leg bone out, cutting and scraping away the meat as you twist and pull the bone out. Trim off the tendons.

5 If you want to butterfly the boned leg, carefully insert a large chef's knife into the cavity left by the leg bone and cut to one side to slit open the meat.

BONING A SHOULDER OF LAMB

A special boning knife, with a narrow, pointed blade, is useful for preparing shoulders of lamb, pork, and veal. If you don't have such a knife, a small, sharp chef's knife can be used instead.

1 Remove the skin and fat. Set the shoulder meat-side up. Cut through the meat to the blade bone, and then cut away the meat on either side, keeping the knife as close to the bone as possible, until the bone is revealed.

2 Cut through the ball and socket joint that lies between the blade bone and the central shoulder bone. This will separate the 2 bones.

3 Cut beneath the ball and socket joint to free the end. Hold it firmly in one hand and pull the blade bone away from the meat

4 Cut around the central shoulder bone, severing the tendons, and cutting and scraping away the meat. Pull out the bone. If necessary, enlarge the pocket left by the bone so that it will accommodate a stuffing.

PREPARING A BEST END OF NECK OR RACK OF LAMB

Best end of neck, or rack of lamb, is a tender joint for roasting or grilling. A single rack, which is one side of the upper ribcage, comprises 6–9 cutlets and serves 2–3 people. Two racks can be used to make impressive joints such as a guard of honour or crown roast.

Rack of lamb

1 If the butcher hasn't done so, remove the backbone (chine) from the meaty end. Pull off the skin. Score through the fat and meat 5 cm (2 in) from the ends of the rib bones.

2 Turn the rack over and set it at the edge of the chopping board, so the ends of the rib bones are suspended. Score the meat along the rack, about 5 cm (2 in) from the ends of the rib bones, cutting through the meat to the bones.

3 Cut out the meat from between the bones, cutting from the crosswise cuts to the ends. Turn the rack over and scrape the ends of the bones clean.

4 Trim away most of the fat from the meat.

GUARD OF HONOUR

Hold 1 rack in each hand, meat-side out, and push them together, interlocking the rib bones. Cover the exposed bones with foil, if desired, to prevent them from charring during cooking, then cook as directed in the recipe.

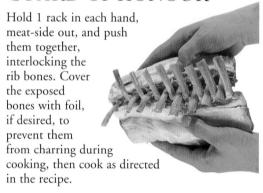

CROWN ROAST

Two racks of lamb are tied together in the shape of a crown

1 Prepare 2 racks as above. Slit the membrane between the rib bones at the meaty end so that the racks can be bent.

2 Stand the racks, meat-side in, on a work surface and curve to form a crown shape. Bend the bones so that the crown will stand upright.

3 Tie string around the middle of the 2 racks, to hold them in place.

4 Fill the centre of the roast with a stuffing, then roast (or add a filling just before serving). Carve the roast by cutting down between the rib bones.

STUFFING, ROLLING, & TYING A JOINT

Joints that have been boned and opened out can be rolled around a savoury stuffing, which adds moisture and flavour to the meat during cooking.

1 Open out the meat and spread with an even layer of stuffing, leaving a small border clear around the edge.

2 Roll up or fold the joint around the stuffing, to make a compact bolster shape. Turn it so that the join is underneath.

3 Tie string around the meat at regular intervals, to hold it in shape during cooking. Remove the string before carving.

CARVING A JOINT ON THE BONE

Once a joint of meat has finished cooking, transfer it to a carving board, cover with foil, and let it "rest" in a warm place for 10–15 minutes. During this time, the temperature of the joint will even out, and the flesh will reabsorb most of the juices. To carve, use a very sharp, long carving knife and a 2-pronged carving fork.

Shoulder of lamb

1 Insert the fork into the shank end. Cut a narrow, wedge-shaped piece from the centre, in the meatiest part between the angle formed by the blade bone and the shoulder bone.

2 Carve neat slices from either side of this wedge-shaped cut until the blade and central shoulder bones are reached. Turn the shoulder over and cut horizontal slices lengthwise.

Rib of beef

1 Set the roast upright on a carving board, insert the carving fork into the meaty side, to steady the joint, and cut close to the large rib bones at the base of the meat, to remove them.

2 Hold the now boneless roast upright on the board. With the knife at a slight angle, carve the meat into slices that are about 2 cm (3/4 in) thick.

Leg of lamb

1 Set the joint with the meaty side up, and insert the carving fork firmly into the meat at the knuckle end. Cut a narrow, wedge-shaped piece from the centre of the meaty portion, cutting all the way to the bone.

2 Carve neat slices from either side of this wedge-shaped cut, gradually changing the angle of the knife to make the slices larger. Turn the leg over. Trim off the fat, then carve off horizontal slices.

Whole ham

1 Cut a few horizontal slices from one side of the ham, to make a flat surface. Turn the ham over on to this surface. Insert the carving fork into the meat at the shank end. Make 3 or 4 cuts through to the bone at the shank end.

2 Insert the knife into the last cut and slide it along the bone, to detach the slices. Make a few more cuts in the ham and continue to remove the slices in the same way. Turn over and carve off horizontal slices.

MAKING GRAVY

A delicious gravy can be made from the richly flavoured sediment and juices from roasting meat. Boost flavour with a splash of red or fortified wine, redcurrant jelly, Worcestershire sauce, or lemon juice, to taste.

1 Pour all but about 2 tbsp fat from the roasting tin, leaving the juices and sediments. Set the tin on the hob and heat until sizzling. Stir in 2 tbsp plain flour.

2 Whisk briskly to mix the flour with the juices, and scrape the bottom and sides of the tin to dislodge any sediment and make a well-browned paste.

3 Gradually add 1 litre (1 3/4 pints) stock or vegetable cooking water, whisking constantly to combine with the flour paste. Whisk until smooth. Simmer, stirring frequently, until the gravy reaches the desired consistency. Season and flavour to taste, then strain if wished. Serve piping hot, in a warmed gravy boat.

ROASTING MEAT

As all ovens are different, these times are intended as a general guide only. When calculating timings, add an extra 500 g (1 lb) on the weight of your joint if it weighs less than 1.5 kg (3 lb). Be sure to preheat the oven before putting the meat in to cook.

Meat		Oven temperature	Time	Internal temperature
Beef	Rare	180°C (350°F, Gas 4)	15 mins per 500 g (1 lb)	60°C (140°F)
	Medium	180°C (350°F, Gas 4)	20 mins per 500 g (1 lb)	70°C (160°F)
	Well-done	180°C (350°F, Gas 4)	25 mins per 500 g (1 lb)	80°C (175°F)
Veal	Well-done	180°C (350°F, Gas 4)	25 mins per 500 g (1 lb)	80°C (175°F)
Lamb	Medium rare	180°C (350°F, Gas 4)	20 mins per 500 g (1 lb)	75°C (170°F)
	Well-done	180°C (350°F, Gas 4)	25 mins per 500 g (1 lb)	80°C (175°F)
Pork	Medium	180°C (350°F, Gas 4)	25 mins per 500 g (1 lb)	80°C (175°F)
	Well-done	180°C (350°F, Gas 4)	30 mins per 500 g (1 lb)	85°C (180°F)

USING A MEAT THERMOMETER

The most accurate way to test if a large piece of meat is cooked is to use a meat thermometer, which registers the internal temperature. Before cooking, insert the spike of the thermometer into the middle or thickest part of the joint. Make sure that the thermometer does not touch a bone as bones become hotter than meat and will therefore give a false reading. Start checking the temperature reading towards the end of the suggested cooking time. Alternatively, use an instant-read thermometer, which is inserted near the end of the calculated cooking time. A joint will continue to cook by retained heat for 5–10 minutes after it is removed from the oven.

PREPARING OFFAL

Although not as popular as it used to be, offal, which includes liver, kidneys, sweetbreads, and tongue, is both nutritious and delicious. Flavour and texture vary according to the animal from which the offal comes – offal from veal has the most delicate flavour and texture; offal from pork has the strongest and toughest.

Sweetbreads

1 Soak the sweetbreads in cold water with 1 tbsp lemon juice for 2–3 hours to clean them. Drain, and rinse well. Cut away any discoloured parts. Use your fingers to carefully peel off the thin membrane surrounding the sweetbreads.

2 Cut away the ducts and any fat and discard. Don't remove too much or the sweetbreads will break up. Put into a saucepan of cold water and bring to a boil. Blanch calf's sweetbreads for 5 minutes, and lamb's sweetbreads for 3 minutes.

Lamb's kidneys

1 (If using beef or veal kidneys, first separate them.) Carefully cut through any fine membrane around each kidney and use your fingers to peel it off (cut the ducts from beef or veal kidneys).

2 Set each kidney round-side up and slice lengthwise in half (or leave attached at the base, according to recipe directions). With a sharp pair of scissors, snip out the small fatty, white core and the tubes.

Sift 125 g (4 oz) plain flour and a pinch of salt into a bowl. Make a well, and add 3 beaten eggs and a little milk taken from 200 ml (7 fl oz).

Whisk the milk and egg together in the well with a little of the flour from the sides, then whisk in the remaining milk, gradually drawing in all of the flour to make a smooth batter.

Put some white vegetable fat into each cup of a 12-hole bun tin and heat in a preheated oven at 220°C (425°F, Gas 7) until very hot. Remove the tin from the oven. Whisk the batter and pour into the cups in the tin. Bake the Yorkshire puddings in the oven for 15 minutes or until well risen, golden, and crisp. Serve immediately.

ENGLISH ROAST BEEF

SERVES 8

3.25 kg (6 1/2 lb) prime rib of beef on the bone

vegetable oil for brushing

salt and black pepper

1 onion, quartered

TO SERVE

Yorkshire puddings (see box, right)

gravy of your choice (page 265)

horseradish sauce (see box, below)

1 Insert a meat thermometer, if using, into the middle of the meat. Put the beef into a roasting tin, brush all over the meat with oil, and season with salt and pepper. Add the onion quarters to the tin and roast with the beef in a preheated oven at 200°C (400°F, Gas 6) for 20 minutes.

2 Meanwhile, make the Yorkshire pudding batter and set aside.

3 After the beef has been roasting for 20 minutes, baste it with the juices from the tin, and lower the oven temperature to 180°C (350°F, Gas 4).

4 Roast, basting frequently, for a further 1 1/2 hours for rare beef, 1 3/4 hours for medium, and 2 hours for well-done, or until the meat thermometer registers 60°C (140°F), 70°C (160°F), or 80°C (175°F).

5 Transfer the beef to a carving board, cover with foil, and leave to stand in a warm place. Increase the oven temperature to 220°C (425°F, Gas 7) and bake the Yorkshire puddings.

6 While the puddings are in the oven and the meat is resting, make the gravy in the roasting tin according to the instructions on page 265.

7 Serve the beef with the Yorkshire puddings, gravy, and horseradish sauce.

Horseradish sauce

Mix 2–3 tbsp grated fresh horseradish with 1 tbsp white wine vinegar in a bowl. In another bowl, whisk 150 ml (1/4 pint) whipping cream until thick.

Fold the cream into the horseradish mixture, and add salt, black pepper, and caster sugar to taste. Cover and leave to chill until ready to serve.

BEEF POT ROAST WITH WINTER VEGETABLES

SERVES 6

2 tbsp sunflower oil

1.15 kg (2¹/₂ lb) beef topside or silverside

4 onions, quartered

1 large swede, cut into thick chunks

2 celery stalks, thickly sliced

2 large carrots, thickly sliced

150 ml (¹/₄ pint) dry white wine

150 ml (¹/₄ pint) hot water

1 bouquet garni

salt and black pepper

chopped parsley to garnish

1 Heat the sunflower oil in a large flameproof casserole. Add the beef and cook over a high heat, turning occasionally, for about 10 minutes until browned all over.

2 Lift the beef out of the casserole and put in the onions, swede, celery, and carrots. Stir well to coat the vegetables in the oil, then cook, stirring occasionally, for about 5 minutes.

3 Push the vegetables to the side of the casserole, and place the meat in the middle, with the vegetables around it.

4 Add the wine, measured water, and bouquet garni, and season with salt and pepper. Bring to a boil, then cover tightly, and cook in a preheated oven at 150°C (300°F, Gas 2) for 2¹/₂–3 hours until the meat is tender.

5 Transfer the meat and vegetables to a warmed platter, cover, and keep warm.

6 Spoon the fat from the surface of the cooking liquid, then boil over a high heat until the liquid is reduced by half. Taste for seasoning, and strain into a warmed gravy boat. Carve the meat into thin slices, garnish with parsley, and serve with the gravy.

TEXAS BARBECUE BEEF BRISKET

SERVES 6

1.15–1.5 kg (2¹/₂–3 lb) beef brisket

2 tbsp sunflower oil

cayenne pepper

MARINADE

750 ml (1¹/₄ pints) ready made spicy barbecue sauce

250 ml (8 fl oz) pale ale or lager

juice of 1 lemon

2 tbsp Worcestershire sauce

3 onions, chopped

5 garlic cloves, crushed

3 tbsp brown sugar

2 tsp ground cumin

¹/₂ tsp ground ginger

1 Make the marinade: in a large bowl, combine the barbecue sauce, pale ale, lemon juice, Worcestershire sauce, onions, garlic, brown sugar, cumin, and ginger. Turn the brisket in the marinade, cover, and leave to marinate in the refrigerator, turning occasionally, for 1–2 days.

2 Remove the beef from the marinade, reserving the marinade, and pat dry with paper towels.

3 Heat the vegetable oil in a flameproof casserole, add the brisket, and brown.

4 Pour over the marinade, cover, and cook in a preheated oven at 160°C (325°F, Gas 3) for 2¹/₂–3 hours until tender, adding a little water if the sauce becomes too thick.

5 Remove the casserole from the oven and leave to stand for 15–20 minutes. Remove the meat and slice. Season the sauce with cayenne pepper to taste, then heat through. Arrange the meat on a serving platter, and pour over the sauce.

Healthy note

If you cook this dish a day ahead of serving, the fat will rise to the surface as it cools. When it is completely cold, put it in the refrigerator overnight. The next day, spoon off the solidified fat from the surface before reheating – this will make the dish less fatty.

FRENCH-STYLE BRAISED BEEF

SERVES 4–6

1 kg (2 lb) piece of lean braising steak (eg chuck steak)
2 tbsp olive oil
125 g (4 oz) piece of lean bacon, cut into strips
1 onion, sliced
250 g (8 oz) carrots, thickly sliced
250 g (8 oz) mushrooms, quartered
500 g (1 lb) tomatoes, chopped
125 g (4 oz) pitted black olives
600 ml (1 pint) beef stock
salt and black pepper
chopped parsley to garnish

MARINADE

500 ml (16 fl oz) red wine
3 tbsp red wine vinegar
2 large garlic cloves
1 strip of orange zest
1 bouquet garni

1 Make the marinade: combine the wine, vinegar, garlic, orange zest, and bouquet garni. Add the beef, cover, and leave to marinate in the refrigerator overnight.

2 Remove the beef from the marinade and pat dry with paper towels. Strain the marinade and reserve. Heat the oil in a large flameproof casserole, add the beef and bacon, and brown all over. Lift out and drain on paper towels.

3 Add the onion, carrots, and mushrooms and cook, stirring, for 5 minutes or until lightly browned.

4 Add the beef, bacon, tomatoes, olives, and reserved marinade. Pour in sufficient stock to cover the meat and season with salt and pepper.

5 Bring to a boil, cover tightly, and cook in a preheated oven at 180°C (350°F, Gas 4) for 1 1/2–2 hours or until the meat is very tender.

6 Slice the meat and arrange on a warmed platter with the vegetables. Skim the sauce and pour over the meat. Garnish with parsley before serving.

SALT BEEF WITH MUSTARD SAUCE

SERVES 6–8

1 kg (2 lb) salted silverside
500 g (1 lb) baby carrots
8 potatoes, halved
8 celery stalks, cut into chunks
250 g (8 oz) turnips, cut into chunks
chopped parsley to garnish

MUSTARD SAUCE

30 g (1 oz) butter
30 g (1 oz) plain flour
150 ml (1/4 pint) milk
4 tsp white wine vinegar
2 tsp mustard powder
2 heaped tsp caster sugar
salt and black pepper

1 Put the salt beef into a large bowl. Cover with cold water and leave to soak overnight to remove any excess salt.

2 Rinse the beef under cold running water, place in a large saucepan, and cover with cold water. Cover the pan with its lid, bring to a boil, and simmer very gently, topping up the water in the pan when necessary, for about 1 hour.

3 Add the carrots, potatoes, celery, and turnips and cook for 40 minutes or until the beef and vegetables are tender.

4 Transfer the meat to a warmed platter. Lift out the vegetables with a slotted spoon, reserving the liquid, and arrange around the meat. Cover and keep warm.

5 Make the sauce: melt the butter in a saucepan, add the flour, and cook, stirring, for 1 minute. Remove from the heat and gradually blend in the milk and 150 ml (1/4 pint) of the cooking liquid from the beef. Bring to a boil, stirring constantly, until the sauce thickens. Simmer for 2 minutes.

6 In a jug, combine the vinegar, mustard powder, and sugar, and stir into the sauce. Cook for 1 minute, then season with salt and pepper. (Be careful not to add too much salt because the liquid from the beef is salty.)

7 Slice the beef and arrange on warmed serving plates with the vegetables. Pour the mustard sauce over the beef, and sprinkle with parsley.

TRINIDAD PEPPERPOT BEEF

SERVES 4–6

1 kg (2 lb) boneless beef, such as brisket, trimmed
2–3 litres (3½–5 pints) beef stock
2 large onions, coarsely chopped
2–4 fresh red chillies, halved, seeded, and chopped
2 tbsp chopped parsley
4 tbsp vinegar, plus extra if necessary
2 tbsp dark brown sugar
1 tbsp Worcestershire sauce
1 tbsp tropical peppercorns (see box, right), coarsely crushed, plus extra if necessary
1 tsp ground cinnamon
1 tsp dried thyme
large pinch of ground allspice
salt

1 Put the beef into a large pan, add enough stock to cover, and bring to a boil, skimming off any scum that rises to the surface. Lower the heat, cover, and simmer for 1½ hours or until the meat feels just tender when pierced with a skewer.

2 Add the onions, chillies, and half of the parsley, then add the vinegar, sugar, Worcestershire sauce, peppercorns, cinnamon, thyme, allspice, and salt to taste. Cover and simmer for 2 hours or until the beef is very tender.

3 Transfer the beef to a carving board, cover, and keep warm.

4 Skim any fat from the cooking liquid, and boil for about 10 minutes until reduced to 300 ml (½ pint). Season, adding more vinegar and peppercorns if needed. Slice the beef thickly, discarding the fat. Pour the sauce over the beef, and sprinkle with the parsley.

Cook's know-how

Tropical peppercorns come as a mix of black, green, pink, and white peppercorns. They look pretty, and have an intense, complex taste. If you cannot get them, use as many colours as you have.

BEEF WITH ROAST VEGETABLE SALAD

SERVES 4–6

1 kg (2 lb) beef fillet cut from the centre, trimmed
2 tbsp tapenade (black olive paste)
1 tbsp black peppercorns, coarsely crushed
2 tbsp olive oil
chopped parsley to garnish

ROAST VEGETABLE SALAD

1 tbsp olive oil
1 aubergine, cut into 5 mm (¼ in) slices
3 courgettes, cut into 5 mm (¼ in) slices
1 fennel bulb, cut lengthwise into 5 mm (¼ in) pieces
1 red pepper, halved, seeded, and cut into 5 mm (¼ in) strips
1 yellow pepper, halved, seeded, and cut into 5 mm (¼ in) strips
salt and black pepper
2 tsp balsamic vinegar

1 Tie the beef to retain its shape, if necessary. Spread the black olive paste all over the beef, then press on the peppercorns.

2 Pour the oil into a roasting tin and heat in a preheated oven at 220°C (425°F, Gas 7).

3 Insert a meat thermometer, if using, into the middle of the beef.

4 Put the beef into the hot oil, and roast for 25 minutes for rare beef, 35 minutes for medium, or 40 minutes for well-done, or until the meat thermometer registers 60°C (140°F), 70°C (160°F), or 75°C (170°F).

5 Meanwhile, put the olive oil for the roast vegetable salad into a large bowl. Add the aubergine, courgettes, fennel, and red and yellow peppers, and toss in the oil.

6 When the beef is cooked to your liking, remove it from the roasting tin and leave until cold. Meanwhile, put the vegetables into the hot tin and sprinkle with salt and pepper. Cook in the oven, turning the vegetables once, for 30 minutes or until tender. Leave to cool, then sprinkle with the balsamic vinegar and toss to coat.

7 When the beef is cold, slice very thinly and serve with the roast vegetable salad. Garnish with parsley.

Roll out 300 g (10 oz) of the pastry to a 30 x 40 cm (12 x 16 in) rectangle. Spread half of the pâté mixture down the middle, leaving a 10 cm (4 in) border on each side.

Remove the string from the beef and place on the pâté mixture. Cover with remaining pâté mixture.

Brush the pastry border with beaten egg. Fold the short sides of the pastry over the beef.

Fold over the long ends and turn the parcel over. Brush with beaten egg. Roll out the remaining pastry, and cut into strips, 5 mm (1/4 in) wide. Arrange in a lattice pattern on top of the pastry, then glaze the strips with beaten egg.

BEEF WELLINGTON

Inside a puff pastry case is a succulent piece of prime beef and a rich stuffing of liver pâté and mushrooms. The pastry locks in all the juices and ensures none of the wonderful flavours are lost. Serve with a mushroom and red wine gravy.

SERVES 8

1.5 kg (3 lb) beef fillet, trimmed and tied

salt and black pepper

2 tbsp sunflower oil

45 g (1 1/2 oz) butter

1 small onion, finely chopped

250 g (8 oz) flat mushrooms, finely chopped

175 g (6 oz) smooth liver pâté

400 g (13 oz) ready made puff pastry

1 egg, beaten

thin mushroom gravy to serve (page 265)

1 Season the beef with black pepper. Heat the oil in a large frying pan, add the beef, and cook over a high heat until browned all over.

2 Put the beef fillet in a roasting tin and cook in a preheated oven at 220°C (425°F, Gas 7) for 25 minutes for rare beef, 35 minutes for medium, or 40 minutes for well-done. Leave to cool completely.

3 Meanwhile, melt the butter in the frying pan, add the onion and mushrooms, and cook, stirring, for 3 minutes or until softened. Increase the heat to high, and cook until the excess moisture has evaporated. Turn into a bowl and leave to cool completely.

4 Add the liver pâté to the mushroom and onion mixture, season with salt and pepper, and stir well to combine.

5 Wrap the beef in the pastry (see box, right).

6 Bake at 220°C (425°F, Gas 7) for 45 minutes or until the pastry is crisp and golden. Cover with foil after 30 minutes to prevent the pastry becoming too brown. Leave to stand for about 10 minutes, then slice and serve with the gravy.

INDIVIDUAL BEEF WELLINGTONS

Cut the raw beef into 8 slices. Brown the slices in a frying pan, cool, then wrap each one in pastry with a little of the pâté mixture. Bake for 25–30 minutes.

PEPPER STEAKS

SERVES 4

4 x 150–175 g (5–6 oz) fillet steaks, about 2.5 cm (1 in) thick, trimmed

salt and black pepper

2 tbsp black peppercorns

30 g (1 oz) butter

1 tbsp sunflower oil

2 tbsp brandy

150 ml (¼ pint) double cream

chopped parsley to garnish

1 Season the steaks on both sides with salt. Crush the peppercorns and spread them on a plate. Coat the steaks with the peppercorns (see box, right).

2 Melt the butter with the oil in a frying pan. When the butter is foaming, add the steaks, and cook over a high heat for 2 minutes on each side.

3 Lower the heat and continue cooking until the steaks are to your liking: rare steaks need 1–2 minutes on each side, medium steaks 3 minutes on each side, and well-done steaks 4–5 minutes on each side. Lift out of the pan and keep warm.

4 Pour the brandy into the frying pan, and boil rapidly to drive off the alcohol. When the brandy has almost disappeared, stir in the cream, and add salt and pepper to taste. Gently reheat the sauce, pour it over the steaks, and garnish with parsley. Serve hot.

Coating steaks

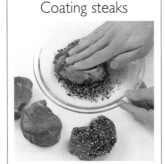

Press each steak firmly on to the peppercorns, until both sides are well coated.

Healthy option

Instead of the classic brandy-creamy sauce, deglaze the pan with 2 tbsp Madeira, port, or sherry, and make a gravy with 75 ml (2½ fl oz) each red wine and stock. Season well.

CHATEAUBRIAND WITH BEARNAISE SAUCE

SERVES 2

400 g (13 oz) Chateaubriand steak (a thick piece of fillet from the middle of the tenderloin)

30 g (1 oz) butter, melted

black pepper

béarnaise sauce (see box, right)

1 Cut the steak crosswise in half. Brush one side of each half with melted butter and season with pepper.

2 Put the steaks, buttered-side up, under a hot grill, 7 cm (3 in) from the heat, and cook for 2 minutes or until browned. Turn the steaks over, brush with melted butter, and season with pepper. Grill for about 2 minutes until browned.

3 Lower the heat and cook, turning once and brushing with the butter, for 4–5 minutes. Cover and leave to stand for 5 minutes. Slice the steaks, and serve with the béarnaise sauce.

Béarnaise sauce

Put 4 tbsp tarragon vinegar, 1 finely chopped shallot, and 1 tbsp chopped tarragon into a pan and boil for a few minutes until reduced by one-third. Leave to cool. Pour 2 egg yolks into a bowl over a saucepan of simmering water, add the vinegar mixture, and whisk over a gentle heat until thick and fluffy.

Melt 90 g (3 oz) butter and gradually add to the sauce, whisking constantly until thick. Season with salt and white pepper.

STEAKS WITH SMOKED OYSTER RELISH

SERVES 4

4 x 175 g (6 oz) rump steaks

salt and black pepper

2 garlic cloves, crushed

1 tbsp olive oil

smoked oyster relish (see box, below) and lemon wedges to serve

1 Season the steaks with salt and pepper, rub with the garlic, and brush with the oil.

2 Heat a frying pan over a high heat, add the steaks, and cook for 3–4 minutes on each side for rare steaks, 4–5 minutes for medium steaks, or 7–8 minutes for well-done steaks. Transfer the steaks to warmed serving plates.

3 Generously spoon the smoked oyster relish over the steaks, and serve at once, accompanied by lemon wedges.

CLASSIC CARPETBAG STEAKS

Melt 15 g (½ oz) butter and cook 2 chopped shallots until softened. Remove from the heat and add 6 chopped fresh oysters, 125 g (4 oz) fresh breadcrumbs, 1 tbsp chopped parsley, and salt and pepper. Cut a pocket in each steak and fill with the stuffing.

Smoked oyster relish

Drain 1 x 100 g (3½ oz) can smoked oysters. Finely chop 1 small onion and 1 handful of parsley sprigs.

Chop the drained smoked oysters with a large, sharp chef's knife.

Put the oysters, onion, and parsley into a small bowl and mix well. Chill until needed.

SAVOURY BUTTERS

These simple butters are quickly made, and ideal for adding an elegant touch to plain grilled meats such as steaks, chops, and noisettes.

CORIANDER BUTTER

Soften 125 g (4 oz) butter and blend in 2 tbsp chopped fresh coriander, 1 tbsp lemon juice, 1 tsp ground coriander, and season with salt and black pepper. Chill. Garnish with a coriander sprig and a sprinkling of ground coriander.

ANCHOVY BUTTER

Soften 125 g (4 oz) butter and blend in 2 tbsp finely chopped anchovies, 1 tbsp lemon juice, 1 tsp ground coriander, and season with black pepper. Chill. Garnish with anchovy fillets.

PARSLEY BUTTER

Soften 125 g (4 oz) butter and blend in 2 tbsp chopped parsley, 1 tbsp lemon juice, and seson with salt and black pepper. Chill. Garnish with a lemon twist and a parsley sprig.

MUSTARD BUTTER

Soften 125 g (4 oz) butter and blend in 2 tbsp Dijon mustard, 2 tbsp chopped fresh tarragon, and season with salt and black pepper. Chill. Garnish with a tarragon sprig.

STEAK DIANE

SERVES 4

4 x 150–175 g (5–6 oz) rump steaks, trimmed

30 g (1 oz) butter

2 tbsp sunflower oil

3 tbsp brandy

1 small onion, finely chopped

300 ml (½ pint) beef stock

2 tbsp Worcestershire sauce

1 tbsp lemon juice

1 tbsp chopped parsley

salt and black pepper

1 Place the steaks between 2 sheets of greaseproof paper and pound with a rolling pin until 5 mm (¼ in) thick.

Cook's know-how

In the classic Steak Diane the brandy is flambéed at the table and poured over the steaks at the last minute. This version is more practical.

2 Melt the butter with the sunflower oil in a large frying pan. When the butter is foaming, add the pounded steaks and cook over a high heat for about 3 minutes on each side until browned. Lift the steaks out of the frying pan and cover with foil to keep warm.

3 Pour the brandy into the pan, and add the onion. Cook over a high heat, stirring occasionally, for a few minutes until the onion has softened and absorbed most of the brandy. Stir in the stock, Worcestershire sauce, lemon juice, and parsley, season with salt and pepper, and cook for about 2 minutes.

4 Return the steaks to the pan and spoon over the sauce. Reheat quickly and briefly, and serve hot.

TOURNEDOS ROQUEFORT

SERVES 4

125 g (4 oz) Roquefort cheese, crumbled

60 g (2 oz) walnut pieces, roughly chopped

30 g (1 oz) butter, softened

salt and black pepper

4 x 125 g (4 oz) tournedos (small fillet steaks), 2.5 cm (1 in) thick

chopped parsley to garnish

1 In a small bowl, combine the Roquefort, walnuts, butter, and pepper to taste.

2 Season the tournedos steaks on both sides with salt and pepper, and place them under a hot grill, 7–10 cm (3–4 ins) from the heat. Grill for 3–4 minutes on each side for rare steaks, 4–5 minutes for medium steaks, or 7–8 minutes for well-done steaks.

3 Two minutes before the steaks are ready, sprinkle with the Roquefort mixture, and return to the hot grill until the cheese has melted. Serve hot, garnished with chopped parsley.

Healthy option

Roquefort cheese and walnuts are a classic French topping for steak, but they are both high in fat and calories. If you prefer to keep these down, try this tasty mushroom topping instead.
Finely chop 250 g (8 oz) chestnut mushrooms in a food processor, then finely chop 1 shallot with a sharp knife, and crush 1 garlic clove. Cook the shallot and garlic with a few tablespoons of water, stock, or wine in a non-stick frying pan for 2–3 minutes until softened. Add the mushrooms, stir well, and cook for 15 minutes until softened and quite dry. Stir in 2 tbsp chopped parsley and 1 tsp finely grated lemon zest, and season with salt and pepper. Spoon the mixture on top of the steaks, and serve at once.

Cook's know-how

Roquefort is a superb blue-veined cheese that melts beautifully under the grill. A blue Stilton will melt equally well – and taste just as good.

BEEF & BEAN BURRITOS

SERVES 4

375 g (12 oz) rump steak, trimmed of fat and cut into thin strips

salt and black pepper

2 tbsp olive oil

1 garlic clove, crushed

1/2–1 fresh red chilli, halved, seeded, and chopped

1/2 tsp cumin seeds

1 x 400 g (13 oz) can tomatoes, drained, juice reserved

1 x 400 g (13 oz) can pinto or black beans, drained

8 flour tortillas

4 tbsp soured cream or crème fraîche

chopped fresh coriander to garnish

1 Season the steak strips with salt and pepper. Heat the olive oil in a large frying pan, add the steak, crushed garlic, chopped chilli, and cumin seeds, and cook, stirring, for 5 minutes or until lightly browned.

2 Add the tomatoes to the pan and cook for about 3 minutes. Pour in the reserved tomato juice and boil for 8–10 minutes until the liquid is reduced.

3 Add the beans and cook until heated through. Taste for seasoning, cover, and keep hot. Warm the tortillas (page 252).

4 Divide the steak and tomato mixture among the tortillas and roll them up. Serve topped with soured cream and garnished with coriander.

BEEF STROGANOFF

SERVES 6

30 g (1 oz) butter

1 tbsp sunflower oil

750 g (1 1/2 lb) rump steak, trimmed and cut into strips (see box, right)

8 shallots, quartered

300 g (10 oz) button mushrooms, halved

salt and black pepper

300 ml (1/2 pint) soured cream

chopped parsley to garnish

1 Melt the butter with the oil in a large frying pan. When the butter is foaming, add the steak strips, in batches if necessary, and cook over a high heat for 5 minutes or until browned all over. Remove from the pan with a slotted spoon.

2 Add the shallots and mushrooms and cook for about 5 minutes until soft and browned.

3 Return the steak strips to the pan, and season with salt and pepper. Stir in the soured cream and heat gently. Garnish with parsley, and serve at once.

Cutting the beef

Slice the beef at an angle into thin strips, 5 mm (1/4 in) wide and 5 cm (2 in) long, using a sharp chef's knife.

Healthy option

Stroganoff is a classic dish of steak pan-fried in butter and oil with mushrooms and soured cream, but there are ways of cutting down on the fat without compromising the flavours in the dish. Use a non-stick pan and omit the butter, then use just 150 ml (1/4 pint) low-fat crème fraîche instead of the soured cream. Crème fraîche becomes very runny when heated, which is why you do not need as much.

MEXICAN BUFFET PARTY

Mexican food is ideal for an informal party where everyone helps themselves because it is the tradition
in Mexico to put lots of different dishes on the table together rather than serving separate courses.
In this hearty menu for 6 people there is something for everyone – meat eaters and vegetarians alike.

CHARGRILLED STEAKS WITH RED VEGETABLES

SERVES 6

6 x 150 g (5 oz) fillet steaks

2 roasted red peppers in olive oil (from a jar), cut into strips, with oil reserved

salt and black pepper

2 red onions, cut into chunky wedges

2 garlic cloves, coarsely chopped

2 tbsp lime juice

fresh coriander to garnish

1 Heat a ridged cast iron chargrill pan over a medium heat until very hot. Brush the fillet steaks with a little of the reserved oil from the peppers, and season with salt and pepper. When the pan is hot, chargrill the steaks for about 3–4 minutes on each side for rare meat, 4–5 minutes on each side for medium, and 7–8 minutes on each side for well-done. Remove the steaks from the pan and leave to rest.

2 Turn down the heat under the pan to low, add the red onion wedges, and cook for about 5–8 minutes, turning them occasionally, until they are charred and softened. Add the red pepper strips, the garlic and lime juice, and stir-fry for 1–2 minutes until hot and sizzling. Season with salt and pepper.

3 Serve the steaks whole or sliced thickly on the diagonal, with a garnish of fresh coriander and the red peppers and onions spooned alongside.

GUACAMOLE

Roughly mash the flesh of 1 large ripe avocado in a bowl with a fork. Add ½ finely chopped onion, 1 tbsp chopped fresh coriander, and the juice of 1 lime, Mix well, and season to taste. Chill for no more than 30 minutes before serving, or the avocado will discolour.

VEGETARIAN ENCHILADAS

SERVES 6

4 large tortilla wraps, about 23 cm (9 ins) in diameter

1 x 175 g (6 oz) can red kidney beans, drained

60 g (2 oz) feta cheese, grated

60 g (2 oz) Cheddar cheese, grated

1 tbsp olive oil

MEXICAN TOMATO SAUCE

1 tbsp olive oil

½ small onion, finely chopped

1 green chilli, halved, seeded, and finely chopped

1 garlic clove, crushed

1 x 400 g (13 oz) can chopped tomatoes

grated zest of ½ lime

2 tbsp chopped fresh coriander

salt and black pepper

1 Make the tomato sauce. Heat the oil in a pan, add the onion, chilli and garlic, and fry over a high heat for a few minutes. Add the tomatoes and simmer without a lid over a low heat, stirring from time to time, for about 10 minutes until the mixture is fairly thick (the consistency of chutney). If it is still a little runny, reduce it by boiling over a high heat, stirring continuously. Add the lime zest and coriander, and season with salt and pepper.

2 Take one tortilla and spread half of the tomato sauce over it to within 2.5 cm (1 in) of the edge. Top with half of the red kidney beans, and sprinkle over half of both the cheeses. Put another tortilla on top and press down a little with your hand so the two tortillas are sandwiched together. Make a separate tortilla sandwich (enchilada) with the remaining ingredients.

3 Heat the oil in a frying pan with a wide base, so the tortillas can fit in flat. Fry each enchilada for 3-4 minutes on each side or until the tortillas are golden brown and crisp, the filling is hot, and the cheese melted. Slice each enchilada into 6 wedges to serve.

MEXICAN BEAN SALAD

SERVES 6

350 g (12 oz) mixed dried beans, eg red kidney, haricot, black eye, and aduki, soaked in cold water overnight, or 2 x 400 g (13 oz) cans beans

3 celery stalks, finely chopped

1 red onion, finely chopped

2 garlic cloves, crushed

DRESSING

4 tbsp olive oil

2 tbsp lime juice

2 tbsp chopped fresh coriander

1 tsp Dijon mustard

1 tsp clear honey

salt and black pepper

1 Drain the soaked dried beans into a colander and rinse well under cold running water. Tip them into a large saucepan, cover with cold water, and bring to a boil. Half cover the pan and simmer for 1 hour or until all the beans are tender.

2 Drain the beans, rinse under hot water, and tip into a large bowl. If using canned beans, drain and rinse them before putting them in the bowl.

3 Whisk together all the dressing ingredients with plenty of salt and pepper, pour over the beans, and add the celery, red onion, and garlic. Toss well, cover the bowl, and leave to marinate until cold, or overnight.

REFRIED BEANS

Heat 1–2 tbsp sunflower oil in a frying pan. Add ½ finely chopped onion, and cook for 8 minutes, until lightly browned. Add 1 crushed garlic clove, and cook for 2 minutes. Drain and rinse 1 x 400 g (13 oz) can red kidney beans, and add to the pan. Cook over a gentle heat until warmed through, mashing the beans with a potato masher or fork and adding 1–2 tbsp water if necessary, to prevent sticking.

CLOCKWISE FROM TOP RIGHT: Vegetarian Enchiladas with guacamole, Refried Beans, Chargrilled Steaks with Red Vegetables, Mexican Bean Salad.

TERIYAKI BEEF

SERVES 4

500 g (1 lb) rump steak, trimmed and cut into thin strips

2 tbsp sunflower oil

1 large onion, thinly sliced

1 red pepper, halved, seeded, and cut into strips

2 spring onions, sliced, to garnish

MARINADE

125 ml (4 fl oz) dark soy sauce

90 ml (3 fl oz) Japanese rice wine or dry sherry

2 tbsp caster sugar

1 Make the marinade: in a bowl, combine the soy sauce, rice wine, and sugar. Toss the steak strips in the marinade, cover, and leave in the refrigerator overnight.

2 Remove the steak strips from the marinade, reserving the marinade. Heat 1 tbsp of the oil in a wok, add the onion and red pepper, and stir-fry for about 2 minutes. Remove from the wok with a slotted spoon and set aside. Heat the remaining oil, and stir-fry the steak strips for 5 minutes or until just cooked through.

3 Return the onion and red pepper to the wok with the marinade and cook for 2 minutes or until heated through. Garnish with the spring onions before serving.

FAJITAS

This Mexican speciality features slices of steak marinated in spices and fruit juice. Serve with tortillas, avocado, soured cream, and *pico de gallo* relish.

SERVES 4

500 g (1 lb) piece of rump steak

8 tortilla wraps

chopped coriander to garnish

1 avocado, stoned, peeled (page 370), and diced

soured cream

MARINADE

juice of 1 orange and 1 lime

3 garlic cloves, crushed

2 tbsp chopped fresh coriander

a few drops of Tabasco sauce

salt and black pepper

PICO DE GALLO RELISH

6 tomatoes, diced

10 radishes, coarsely chopped

5 spring onions, thinly sliced

1–2 green chillies, halved, seeded, and chopped

4 tbsp chopped fresh coriander

juice of 1/2 lime

1 Make the marinade: in a large bowl, combine the orange and lime juice, garlic, coriander, and Tabasco, and season with salt and pepper. Turn the steak in the marinade, cover, and leave to marinate in the refrigerator overnight.

2 Make the pico de gallo relish: in a bowl, combine the tomatoes, radishes, spring onions, chillies, coriander, lime juice, and salt to taste. Cover and chill until ready to serve.

3 Remove the steak from the marinade and pat dry. Put the steak under a hot grill, 7–10 cm (3–4 in) from the heat, and grill for 3 minutes on each side for rare steak, 4 minutes for medium steak, or 5–6 minutes for well-done steak. Cover with foil and leave to stand for 5 minutes.

4 Meanwhile, warm the tortillas (see box, right).

5 Slice the steak, arrange on serving plates, and sprinkle with coriander. Serve with the tortillas, pico de gallo relish, diced avocado, and soured cream.

Warming tortillas

Sprinkle each tortilla with a little water, and stack the tortillas in a pile.

Wrap the tortillas in foil and warm in a preheated oven at 140°C (275°F, Gas 1) for 10 minutes.

WINTER BEEF CASSEROLE

SERVES 4–6

2 tbsp sunflower oil

1 kg (2 lb) braising steak, trimmed and cut into 2.5 cm (1 in) cubes

3 streaky bacon rashers, rinds removed, cut into strips

1 large onion, chopped

45 g (1 1/2 oz) plain flour

500 g (1 lb) passata (sieved tomatoes)

450 ml (3/4 pint) beef stock

150 ml (1/4 pint) red wine

6 celery stalks, sliced

250 g (8 oz) carrots, cut into thin strips

1 garlic clove, crushed

1 tsp chopped fresh marjoram or 1/2 tsp dried marjoram or oregano

salt and black pepper

chopped parsley to garnish

1 Heat the oil in a large flameproof casserole, add the beef and bacon, and cook over a moderately high heat for 2–3 minutes until browned. Remove with a slotted spoon, and drain on paper towels.

2 Add the onion and cook, stirring occasionally, for a few minutes until soft but not coloured.

3 Add the flour and cook, stirring, for 1 minute. Add the passata, stock, and wine and bring to a boil, stirring until smooth and thickened. Return the meat to the pan, add the celery, carrots, garlic, and marjoram, and season with salt and pepper.

4 Bring to a boil, cover and cook in a preheated oven at 160°C (325°F, Gas 3) for 2 hours or until the beef is tender. Taste for seasoning and garnish with chopped parsley before serving.

BOEUF BOURGUIGNON

SERVES 6

2 tbsp sunflower oil

1 kg (2 lb) braising steak, trimmed and cut into 5 cm (2 in) cubes

250 g (8 oz) thickly sliced smoked bacon, rinds removed, cut into strips

12 shallots

30 g (1 oz) plain flour

300 ml (1/2 pint) red Burgundy

150 ml (1/4 pint) beef stock

1 bouquet garni

1 garlic clove, crushed

salt and black pepper

250 g (8 oz) button mushrooms

1 Heat the oil in a large flameproof casserole. Add the beef in batches, and cook over a high heat, turning occasionally, until browned on all sides. Remove with a slotted spoon and set aside to drain on paper towels.

2 Add the bacon and shallots and cook gently, stirring occasionally, for 3 minutes or until the bacon is crisp and the shallots are softened. Lift out and drain on paper towels.

3 Add the flour and cook, stirring, for 1 minute. Gradually blend in the wine and stock and bring to a boil, stirring until thickened.

4 Return the beef and bacon to the casserole, add the bouquet garni and garlic, and season with salt and pepper. Cover and cook in a preheated oven at 160°C (325°F, Gas 3) for 1 1/2 hours.

5 Return the shallots to the casserole, add the whole button mushrooms, and cook for 1 hour or until the beef is very tender.

6 Remove the bouquet garni and discard. Taste the sauce for seasoning before serving.

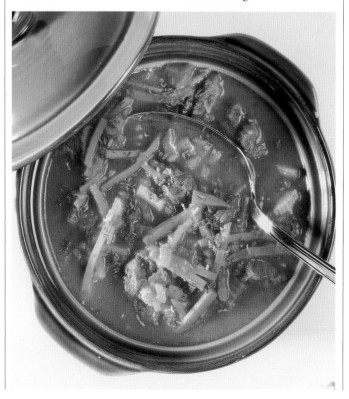

CARBONNADE OF BEEF

SERVES 6

2 tbsp sunflower oil

1 kg (2 lb) braising steak, trimmed and cut into 5 cm (2 in) cubes

2 large onions, sliced

1 garlic clove, crushed

2 tsp light muscovado sugar

1 tbsp plain flour

450 ml (³/4 pint) beer or lager

150 ml (¹/4 pint) beef stock

1 tbsp red wine vinegar

1 bouquet garni

salt and black pepper

thyme sprigs to garnish

¹/2 baguette, cut into 1.25 cm (¹/2 in) slices,

Dijon mustard for spreading

1 Heat the oil in a large flameproof casserole, add the beef in batches, and cook over a high heat for a few minutes until browned. Lift out with a slotted spoon.

2 Lower the heat and add the onions, garlic, and sugar. Cook, stirring, for 4 minutes or until browned. Add the flour and cook, stirring, for 1 minute. Add the beer and stock, and bring to a boil, stirring until thickened.

3 Return the meat to the casserole, add the vinegar and bouquet garni, and season with salt and pepper. Bring back to a boil, cover, and cook in a preheated oven at 150°C (300°F, Gas 2) for 2¹/2 hours or until the meat is really tender. Remove from the oven, lift out the bouquet garni, and discard. Taste for seasoning.

4 Increase the oven temperature to 190°C (375°F, Gas 5). Toast the baguette slices, and spread with mustard on one side. Put them, mustard-side up, in the casserole, and baste with sauce.

5 Return the casserole to the oven, uncovered, for 10 minutes or until the croûtes are just crisp. Garnish with thyme sprigs before serving.

HUNGARIAN GOULASH

SERVES 6

2 tbsp sunflower oil

1 kg (2 lb) braising steak, trimmed and cut into 5 cm (2 in) cubes

2 large onions, sliced

1 garlic clove, crushed

1 tbsp plain flour

1 tbsp paprika

600 ml (1 pint) beef stock

1 x 400 g (13 oz) can tomatoes

2 tbsp tomato purée

salt and black pepper

2 large red peppers, halved, seeded, and cut into 2.5 cm (1 in) pieces

4 potatoes, peeled and quartered

150 ml (¹/4 pint) soured cream

paprika to garnish

1 Heat the sunflower oil in a large flameproof casserole, add the beef in batches, and cook over a high heat until browned.

2 Lift out the beef with a slotted spoon. Lower the heat slightly, add the onions and garlic, and cook gently, stirring occasionally, for a few minutes until soft but not coloured.

3 Add the flour and paprika and cook, stirring, for 1 minute. Pour in the stock and bring to a boil, stirring.

4 Return the meat to the casserole, add the tomatoes and tomato purée, and season with salt and pepper. Bring back to a boil, cover, and cook in a preheated oven at 160°C (325°F, Gas 3) for 1 hour.

5 Add the red peppers and potatoes and continue cooking for 1 hour or until the potatoes and meat are tender.

6 Taste for seasoning, and stir in the soured cream. Sprinkle with a little paprika before serving.

Healthy option

Soured cream is the classic finish for goulash, but to reduce the fat content of this dish you can omit it. To compensate for its richness, add 250 g (8 oz) chestnut mushrooms, sliced, in step 5, and stir in a good handful of chopped flat-leaf parsley with the soured cream in step 6.

CHIANTI BEEF CASSEROLE

SERVES 4–6

1 kg (2 lb) braising steak, trimmed and cut into 5 cm (2 in) cubes

2 large onions, roughly chopped

2 large garlic cloves, crushed

45 g (1½ oz) plain flour

150 ml (¼ pint) Chianti

300 ml (½ pint) beef stock

60 g (2 oz) sun-dried tomatoes in oil, roughly chopped, with oil reserved

a few fresh thyme sprigs

salt and black pepper

1 x 400 g (13 oz) can artichoke hearts, drained and halved

12 pitted black olives

1 heaped tbsp mango chutney

1 Heat 2 tbsp of the reserved oil from the sun-dried tomatoes in a large frying pan, and brown the beef on all sides (you may need to do this in batches). Remove with a slotted spoon and keep warm.

2 Heat another 2 tbsp sun-dried tomato oil in a large flameproof casserole, add the onions and garlic, and cook for 2–3 minutes.

3 Add the flour and cook, stirring, for 1 minute. Blend in the wine and stock, bring to a boil, and add the tomatoes and thyme (reserving a sprig for garnish). Season with salt and pepper.

4 Return the beef to the casserole, cover, and reduce the heat. Simmer for 1½–2 hours or until the meat is tender.

5 Add the artichokes, olives, and mango chutney, and simmer for 10 minutes. Taste for seasoning and garnish with thyme before serving.

LATIMER BEEF WITH HORSERADISH

SERVES 6

2 tbsp sunflower oil

1 kg (2 lb) braising steak, trimmed and cut into strips

12 shallots or button onions

30 g (1 oz) plain flour

2 tsp mild curry powder

2 tsp light muscovado sugar

1 tsp ground ginger

600 ml (1 pint) beef stock

2 tbsp Worcestershire sauce

salt and black pepper

3 tbsp chopped parsley

2 tbsp creamed horseradish

extra chopped parsley to garnish

1 Heat the sunflower oil in a large flameproof casserole, and cook the beef strips over a high heat until browned all over. Lift out with a slotted spoon and drain on paper towels.

2 Lower the heat, add the shallots, and cook gently, stirring occasionally, for a few minutes until softened. Lift out with a slotted spoon and drain on paper towels.

3 Add the flour, curry powder, sugar, and ginger to the casserole and cook, stirring, for 1 minute. Pour in the stock and bring to a boil, stirring until smooth and thickened. Add the Worcestershire sauce, season with salt and pepper, and return to a boil.

4 Return the beef and shallots to the casserole and stir in the parsley. Bring back to a boil, cover, and cook in a preheated oven at 160°C (325°F, Gas 3) for 2–2½ hours until the meat is tender.

5 Stir in the horseradish cream, taste for seasoning, and garnish with parsley.

Healthy option

Creamed horseradish is a mixture of grated horeradish with vinegar, seasonings, and cream. For a less rich finish, use just 1 tbsp botttled grated horseradish.

THAI RED BEEF CURRY

SERVES 6

3 tbsp sunflower oil

8 cardamom pods, split

2.5 cm (1 in) piece of cinnamon stick

6 cloves

8 black peppercorns

1 kg (2 lb) braising steak, trimmed and cut into 2.5 cm (1 in) cubes

1 large onion, chopped

5 cm (2 in) piece of fresh root ginger, peeled and grated

4 garlic cloves, crushed

4 tsp paprika

2 tsp ground cumin

1 tsp ground coriander

1 tsp salt

1/4 tsp cayenne pepper or 1/2 tsp chilli powder

600 ml (1 pint) water

90 g (3 oz) full-fat plain yogurt

1 x 400 g (13 oz) can chopped tomatoes

1 large red pepper, halved, seeded, and cut into chunks

1 Heat the oil in a large flameproof casserole, add the cardamom pods, cinnamon stick, cloves, and peppercorns, and cook over a moderate heat, stirring, for 1 minute. Lift out with a slotted spoon and set aside on a plate.

2 Add the beef in batches, and cook over a high heat until browned all over. Lift out the beef with a slotted spoon and drain on paper towels.

3 Add the onion to the pan and cook over a high heat, stirring, for about 3 minutes until beginning to brown. Add the ginger, garlic, paprika, cumin, coriander, salt, cayenne or chilli, and 4 tbsp of the measured water. Cook, stirring, for about 1 minute.

4 Return the beef and spices to the casserole, then gradually add the yogurt, stirring. Stir in the remaining water. Add the tomatoes and red pepper, and bring to a boil. Cover and cook in a preheated oven at 160°C (325°F, Gas 3) for 2 hours or until the beef is tender. Taste for seasoning before serving.

Cook's know-how

If you are short of time, use 3–4 tbsp ready made Thai red curry paste instead of the whole and ground spices in this recipe. If you prefer, you can use coconut milk instead of the yogurt.

COUNTRY BEEF CASSEROLE

SERVES 8

3 tbsp sunflower oil

1 kg (2 lb) braising steak, trimmed and cut into 5 cm (2 in) cubes

500 g (1 lb) carrots, thickly sliced

250 g (8 oz) turnips, cut into large chunks

250 g (8 oz) parsnips, thickly sliced

2 onions, sliced

1 large leek, sliced

1 tbsp plain flour

600 ml (1 pint) beef stock

1 x 400 g (13 oz) can chopped tomatoes

2 tbsp chopped fresh herbs, such as parsley and thyme

1 large bay leaf

salt and black pepper

herb dumplings (see box, right)

1 Heat the oil in a large flameproof casserole, add the beef in batches, and cook over a high heat until browned. Lift out the beef with a slotted spoon.

2 Add the carrots, turnips, parsnips, onions, and leek, and cook over a high heat, stirring occasionally, for 5 minutes or until the vegetables are softened.

3 Add the flour and cook, stirring, for 1 minute. Add the stock and tomatoes, and 1 tbsp of the herbs, and season with salt and pepper. Bring to a boil, then return the meat to the casserole. Cover and cook in a preheated oven at 160°C (325°F, Gas 3) for 2 hours.

4 Place the dumplings on top of the meat. Increase the oven temperature to 190°C (375°F, Gas 5) and cook for 20–25 minutes until the dumplings are firm. Serve hot, sprinkled with the remaining chopped herbs.

Herb dumplings

Sift 125 g (4 oz) self-raising flour into a bowl, and add 60 g (2 oz) shredded vegetable suet, 1 tbsp chopped fresh thyme or parsley, and salt and pepper. Add 4–5 tbsp water to make a soft dough. Shape into 12–16 balls with your hands.

CHILLI CON CARNE

SERVES 6

250 g (8 oz) dried red
   kidney beans

2 tbsp sunflower oil

750 g (1 1/2 lb) braising steak,
   trimmed and cut into large cubes

2 onions, chopped

2 fresh red chillies, halved, seeded,
   and finely chopped

1 garlic clove, crushed

1 tbsp plain flour

900 ml (1 1/2 pints) beef stock

2 tbsp tomato purée

1 square of plain chocolate, grated

salt and black pepper

1 large red pepper, halved, seeded,
   and cut into chunks

chopped coriander to garnish

1 Put the red kidney beans into a large bowl, cover generously with cold water, and leave to soak overnight.

2 Drain the beans, rinse under cold running water, and drain again. Put the beans into a large saucepan. Cover with cold water, bring to a boil, and boil rapidly for 10 minutes. Lower the heat and simmer, partially covered, for 50 minutes or until the beans are just tender. Drain.

3 Heat the oil in a large flameproof casserole. Add the beef and cook in batches over a high heat for 5–7 minutes until browned. Lift out with a slotted spoon.

4 Lower the heat, add the onions, chillies, and garlic, and cook, stirring occasionally, for a few minutes until softened.

5 Add the flour and cook, stirring, for 1 minute. Add the stock, tomato purée, and chocolate, and season with salt and pepper. Return the beef to the casserole, add the beans, and bring to a boil. Cover and cook in a preheated oven at 150°C (300°F, Gas 2) for 1 1/2 hours.

6 Add the red pepper and cook for 30 minutes. Taste for seasoning, and garnish with coriander.

QUICK CHILLI CON CARNE

Substitute 1 x 400 g (13 oz) can red kidney beans for the dried beans, and minced beef for the chuck steak. Simmer gently on the hob for 45 minutes.

BEEF OLIVES WITH VEGETABLE JULIENNE

SERVES 6

8 thin slices of beef topside, total
   weight about 750 g (1 1/2 lb)

2 tbsp sunflower oil

375 g (12 oz) piece of celeriac,
   peeled and cut into matchstick-
   thin strips

250 g (8 oz) carrots, cut into
   matchstick-thin strips

2 small leeks, cut into matchstick-
   thin strips

salt and black pepper

30 g (1 oz) plain flour

1 onion, sliced

1 garlic clove, sliced

450 ml (3/4 pint) beef stock

1 Pound each slice of topside between 2 sheets of cling film with a rolling pin until 3 mm (1/8 in) thick

2 Heat 1 tbsp of the oil in a large frying pan, add the celeriac, carrots, and leeks, and stir-fry over a high heat for 1 minute. Season with salt and pepper, then lift out and drain. Leave to cool.

3 Divide the vegetables among the beef slices. Roll up and secure with wooden cocktail sticks.

4 Lightly coat the beef olives in half of the flour, shaking off any excess. Heat the remaining oil in a flameproof casserole, add the beef olives, and cook over a high heat for 5–7 minutes until browned. Lift out with a slotted spoon.

5 Add the onion and garlic and cook gently until softened. Add the remaining flour and cook, stirring, for 1 minute. Gradually blend in the stock, season with salt and pepper, and bring to a boil, stirring until thick.

6 Return the beef olives to the casserole, bring to a boil, cover, and cook in a preheated oven at 180°C (350°F, Gas 4) for 1 1/2 hours. Lift out the beef and set aside. Sieve the sauce, then reheat. Thinly slice the beef, removing the cocktail sticks. Serve hot, with the sauce.

CORNED BEEF HASH

SERVES 4

60 g (2 oz) butter

1 large onion, chopped

750 g (1¹/₂ lb) potatoes, cut into small chunks

300 ml (¹/₂ pint) beef stock

salt and black pepper

1 x 325 g (11 oz) can corned beef, cut into chunks

chopped parsley to garnish

1 Melt the butter in a large frying pan, add the onion, and cook gently, stirring occasionally, for a few minutes until softened.

2 Add the potatoes and stir to coat in the butter. Pour in the stock, and season with salt and pepper. Simmer for 10–15 minutes until the potatoes are tender and the stock absorbed.

3 Stir in the corned beef and heat to warm through. Put the pan under a hot grill, 7 cm (3 in) from the heat, to brown the top. Garnish with parsley

Cook's know-how

Corned beef hash can be made up to the grilling stage several hours ahead and then grilled until hot all the way through just before serving. You can add other vegetables, or a splash of Worcestershire or Tabasco sauce, and top each portion with a poached or fried egg.

TRADITIONAL STEAK & KIDNEY PIE

This pie is a classic, but for those who do not like kidneys you can omit them and use double the amount of mushrooms. For convenience, the meat can be cooked a day in advance, then all you have to do on the day of serving is make the pastry and bake the pie in the oven.

SERVES 6

2 tbsp sunflower oil

1 large onion, chopped

750 g (1¹/₂ lb) stewing steak, cut into 2.5 cm (1 in) cubes

250 g (8 oz) beef or lamb's kidney, trimmed (page 240), and cut into 2.5 cm (1 in) cubes

30 g (1 oz) plain flour

300 ml (¹/₂ pint) beef stock

2 tbsp Worcestershire sauce

salt and black pepper

250 g (8 oz) button mushrooms

beaten egg for glazing

SHORTCRUST PASTRY

250 g (8 oz) plain flour

125 g (4 oz) butter

about 3 tbsp cold water

1 Heat the oil in a large saucepan, add the onion, and cook, stirring from time to time, for a few minutes until soft but not coloured.

2 Add the beef and kidney and cook until browned. Add the flour and cook, stirring, for 1 minute. Add the stock and Worcestershire sauce, season with salt and pepper, and bring to a boil, stirring. Partially cover, and simmer gently for 2 hours.

3 Add the mushrooms and cook for 30 minutes or until the meat is tender. Taste for seasoning, then leave to cool completely.

4 Make the pastry: sift the flour into a bowl. Add the butter and rub in lightly with your fingertips until the mixture looks like fine breadcrumbs. Add the water and mix with a flat-bladed knife until the dough comes together to form a ball.

5 Roll out the pastry on a floured work surface until 2.5 cm (1 in) larger than the pie dish. Invert the dish over the pastry and cut around the dish. Brush the rim of the dish with water and press on a strip of pastry cut from the trimmings.

6 Put a pie funnel into the middle of the dish, then spoon in the meat mixture.

7 Lightly brush the pastry strip with water and top with the pastry lid, making a hole in the middle so the steam can escape through the pie funnel. Seal the pastry edges and crimp with a fork, then decorate the top of the pie with pastry trimmings, attaching them with beaten egg.

8 Brush the pastry all over with beaten egg, and bake in a preheated oven at 200°C (400°F, Gas 6) for 25–30 minutes until the pastry is crisp and golden. Serve hot.

STEAK & KIDNEY PUDDING

Mix 300 g (10 oz) self-raising flour, 150 g (5 oz) shredded suet, salt and pepper, and 200 ml (7 fl oz) water. Use ³/₄ pastry to line a 1.7 litre (3 pint) bowl. Add the uncooked filling, top with pastry, and steam for 5 hours.

BEEF FLORENTINE

Filo provides a quick and easy way to cover a pie, and it gives a lovely crisp topping. If you prefer not to use butter you can use olive oil instead and, to make a lighter dish, you can use reduced-fat Cheddar cheese and low-fat soft cheese, and omit the Gruyère or Emmental.

SERVES 8

11 sheets of filo pastry
60 g (2 oz) butter, melted

BEEF LAYER

30 g (1 oz) butter
1 kg (2 lb) lean minced beef
1 tbsp plain flour
1 x 400 g (13 oz) can chopped tomatoes
2 tbsp tomato purée
2 garlic cloves, crushed
1 tsp caster sugar
salt and black pepper

SPINACH & CHEESE LAYER

625 g (1¼ lb) spinach, tough stalks removed, roughly chopped
90 g (3 oz) mature Cheddar cheese, grated
90 g (3 oz) Gruyère or Emmental cheese, grated
125 g (4 oz) full-fat soft cheese
2 eggs, lightly beaten

1 Prepare the beef layer: melt the butter in a large saucepan, add the minced beef, and cook, stirring, for 10–15 minutes or until the meat is browned all over.

2 Add the flour and cook, stirring, for 1 minute. Add the tomatoes, tomato purée, garlic, and sugar, season with salt and pepper, and bring to a boil. Cover and simmer, stirring occasionally, for 35 minutes. Taste for seasoning.

3 Meanwhile, prepare the spinach and cheese layer: wash the spinach and put it into a large saucepan. Cook over a gentle heat until the spinach wilts. Drain thoroughly, squeezing to remove excess water. Mix the spinach with the Cheddar, Gruyère, soft cheese, and eggs, and season with salt and pepper.

4 Spoon the beef mixture into a shallow ovenproof dish, then spoon the spinach mixture over the top.

5 Prepare the filo topping (see box, right).

6 Bake in a preheated oven at 200°C (400°F, Gas 6) for 20–25 minutes until the filo pastry is crisp and golden. Serve hot.

Preparing the filo topping

Brush 3 of the filo pastry sheets with a little of the melted butter and layer them on top of the spinach mixture, trimming to fit the dish if necessary.

Arrange the remaining 8 filo pastry sheets over the dish, lightly brushing with a little butter and scrunching each one up, in order to completely cover the lower layer of filo pastry.

MEATBALLS IN CIDER

SERVES 4

250 g (8 oz) minced beef
125 g (4 oz) minced pork
salt and black pepper
plain flour for dusting
2 tbsp sunflower oil
2 large onions, sliced
1 garlic clove, crushed
300 ml (½ pint) dry cider
3 tbsp tomato purée
4 celery stalks, thickly sliced
1 large red pepper, halved, seeded, and cut into strips
125 g (4 oz) mushrooms, sliced
2 tsp caster sugar

1 Mix together the beef and pork, and season with salt and pepper. On a floured work surface, shape the mixture into 16 even-sized balls.

2 Heat the oil in a flameproof casserole, add the meatballs, and cook over a high heat until browned. Remove and drain on paper towels. Lower the heat, add the onions and garlic, and cook, stirring occasionally, for a few minutes until softened.

3 Return the meatballs to the casserole and add the cider, tomato purée, celery, red pepper, mushrooms, and sugar. Season with salt and pepper, and bring to a boil. Cover and simmer for 20 minutes or until the meatballs are cooked through. Serve hot.

THE BEST BURGERS

Burgers don't have to be made with plain minced beef, as these three recipes illustrate. They are very quick and easy to make, and will keep in the freezer for up to three months. If you want to be sure that the burgers are seasoned enough, take a teaspoonful of the raw mixture and flatten it into a mini burger shape. Fry it for a minute, turning once, then taste it to see if it needs more seasoning or flavourings. If it does, add more to the raw mixture.

THAI BURGERS

SERVES 6

500 g (1 lb) best-quality minced beef
1 tbsp red Thai curry paste
2 tbsp chopped fresh coriander
2.5 cm (1 in) piece of fresh root ginger, peeled and finely grated
salt and black pepper
1 tbsp olive oil

1 Put the beef in a bowl with the curry paste, fresh coriander, grated ginger and salt and pepper. Mix together thoroughly.

2 Shape the mixture into six even-sized burgers. Put on a large plate, cover and refrigerate for about 30 minutes (they will keep for up to 24 hours).

3 Heat the oil in a large non-stick frying pan or lightly coat a preheated ridged griddle pan with a little oil. Cook the burgers over a medium heat for about 3-4 minutes on each side until they are brown. They are best served just pink in the middle, but they can be cooked another minute or two on each side if you prefer them more done than this.

LAMB BURGERS

SERVES 4-8

1–2 tbsp olive oil
1 small onion, finely chopped
1 garlic clove, crushed
500 g (1 lb) best-quality minced lamb
1 tsp ground cumin
2 tbsp chopped fresh mint
salt and black pepper

TO SERVE

4 warm pitta breads, halved
about 8 tbsp tzatziki (ready made or see page 271)

1 Heat 1 tbsp oil in a frying pan and cook the onion and garlic until completely softened – this can take up to 10 minutes. Allow to cool completely.

2 Mix the cooled onion and garlic with the remaining ingredients, then shape into 8 small burgers. Put on a large plate, cover and refrigerate for about 30 minutes (they will keep for up to 24 hours).

3 Heat a large non-stick frying pan or lightly coat a preheated ridged griddle pan with a little oil. Cook the burgers over a medium heat until browned and cooked through, about 3–4 minutes on each side. Serve in warm pitta pockets, with tzatziki.

VEGGIE BURGERS

SERVES 6

1 small red onion, finely chopped
3 tbsp chopped parsley
1 x 400 g (13 oz) can cannellini beans, drained
1 x 300 g (10 oz) can red kidney beans, drained
60 g (2 oz) no-need-to-soak dried apricots, snipped into pieces
175 g (6 oz) carrots, grated
60 g (2 oz) Cheddar cheese, grated
salt and black pepper
30 g (1 oz) pine nuts, toasted
about 2–3 tbsp olive oil

1 Purée the onion and parsley in a food processor until fairly smooth. Add the remaining ingredients, except the pine nuts and oil, and blitz until smooth. (If you haven't got a processor, mash the beans and mix the other ingredients except the pine nuts and oil.) Season really well.

2 Add the toasted pine nuts and pulse the machine to mix them in. Shape the mixture into 12 small burgers. Put on a large plate, cover, and refrigerate for about 1 hour (they will keep for up to 24 hours).

3 Place the burgers on a grill tray lined with foil, under a hot grill 7 cm (3 in) from the heat. Brush the burgers frequently with oil, for 4 minutes each side until until they are hot right through.

TOPPINGS FOR BURGERS

CHILLI AIOLI

In a small bowl, combine 2 egg yolks, 1 tbsp lemon juice, 1 tsp Dijon mustard, and salt and pepper to taste, and whisk until thick. Gradually add 250 ml (8 fl oz) olive oil, whisking constantly until the mixture is very thick. Stir in 1 crushed garlic clove, 1/2 tsp chilli powder, and 1/4 tsp ground cumin. Taste for seasoning. Cover and refrigerate until ready to serve. Use on the day of making.

BARBECUE SAUCE

Heat 1 tbsp sunflower oil in a saucepan and cook 1 finely chopped onion and 1 crushed garlic clove until soft but not coloured. Add 1 x 400 g (13 oz) can chopped tomatoes, 2 tbsp water, 2 tbsp lemon juice, 1 tbsp brown sugar, 1 tbsp Worcestershire sauce, 2 tsp Dijon mustard, 1/2 tsp each paprika and chilli powder, and salt and pepper. Bring to a boil, and simmer for 20 minutes. Serve warm. or cold.

CLOCKWISE FROM TOP: Lamb Burgers in pitta pockets with tzatziki, Veggie Burgers with a fresh tomato salsa, Thai Burgers with cucumber and carrot sticks, and a coconut milk, coriander, and chilli dip.

MEAT LOAF

SERVES 6

750 g (1½ lb) minced beef

1 x 400 g (13 oz) can chopped
    tomatoes

90 g (3 oz) herby stuffing mix

1 onion, chopped

1 carrot, coarsely shredded

3 garlic cloves, crushed

2 tbsp chopped parsley

1 egg, beaten

1 tbsp Worcestershire sauce

salt and black pepper

4–5 streaky bacon rashers, rinds
    removed

1 KG (2 LB) LOAF TIN

1 Combine the minced beef,
tomatoes, stuffing mix,
onion, carrot, garlic, parsley,
beaten egg, and Worcestershire
sauce, and season with salt and
pepper.

2 Arrange bacon rashers
crosswise in the loaf tin,
letting them hang over the
sides. Put the beef mixture into
the tin and fold over the bacon.
Turn the loaf out into a
roasting tin and bake in a
preheated oven at 190°C
(375°F, Gas 5), basting once or
twice, for 1 hour.

3 Increase the heat to 230°C
(450°F, Gas 8) and bake for
15 minutes or until the meat
loaf is firm. Spoon off any fat,
slice the loaf, and serve hot (or
leave whole and serve cold).

COTTAGE PIES WITH CHEESY POTATO TOPPING

The minced beef mixture can be made a day ahead of serving, and kept in the refrigerator overnight.
If you prefer you can omit the cheese in the potato topping, and use olive oil instead of butter.

SERVES 6

2 tbsp sunflower oil

1 large onion, finely chopped

1 celery stalk, finely chopped

1 large carrot, finely chopped

750 g (1½ lb) minced beef

2 tsp plain flour

300 ml (½ pint) beef stock

1 tbsp tomato purée

2 tbsp Worcestershire sauce

salt and black pepper

TOPPING

750 g (1½ lb) potatoes, cut into
    chunks

30 g (1 oz) butter

2–3 tbsp hot milk

125 g (4 oz) mature Cheddar
    cheese, grated

1 Heat the oil in a large
saucepan, add the onion,
celery, and carrot, and cook for
3 minutes. Add the minced
beef, and cook for 5 minutes or
until browned.

2 Add the flour and cook,
stirring, for 1 minute. Add
the stock, tomato purée, and
Worcestershire sauce, season
with salt and pepper, and bring
to a boil. Cover and simmer,
stirring occasionally, for
45 minutes. Remove from the
heat and spoon into 6
individual ovenproof dishes, or
1 large dish. Leave to cool.

3 Prepare the potato topping:
cook the potatoes in boiling
salted water for 20 minutes or
until tender. Drain. Add the
butter and hot milk to the
potatoes and mash until soft,
then stir in the cheese and
season with salt and pepper.

4 Cover the minced beef
mixture with the mashed
potato (see box, right). Cook
in a preheated oven at 200°C
(400°F, Gas 6), allowing 20–25
minutes for small pies, 35–40
minutes for a large one, until
the potato topping is golden
brown and the meat mixture is
bubbling. Serve hot.

Covering the pies

Spoon the mashed potato on to
the beef mixture, and spread
over the top to cover
completely.

Score the surface of the
mashed potato, using a fork, to
make a decorative topping.

BEEF TACOS

SERVES 4

1 tbsp sunflower oil
375 g (12 oz) minced beef
1 onion, chopped
3 garlic cloves, crushed
1/2 tsp chilli powder
1 tsp paprika
1/2 tsp ground cumin (optional)
1 x 225 g (8 oz) can chopped tomatoes
salt and black pepper
1 fresh green chilli, halved, seeded, and thinly sliced
2 tbsp chopped fresh coriander
8 taco shells
8 lettuce leaves, finely shredded
4 tbsp soured cream
chopped coriander to garnish

1 Heat the oil in a large frying pan, add the minced beef, onion, and garlic, and cook, stirring, for 5 minutes or until the beef is browned and the onion and garlic are softened.

2 Add the chilli powder, paprika, and cumin (if using), and cook, stirring, for 2 minutes.

3 Stir in the tomatoes, cover, and cook over a medium heat for 5 minutes. Add salt and pepper to taste, remove from the heat, and stir in the chilli and coriander.

4 Warm the taco shells in a preheated oven at 180°C (350°F, Gas 4) for 2–3 minutes, or according to packet instructions. Fill the taco shells (see box, below), and serve hot.

Filling taco shells

Holding each shell in one hand, put a layer of shredded lettuce into the bottom. Add a generous spoonful of the meat mixture and top with soured cream and a sprinkling of chopped coriander.

BOBOTIE

SERVES 6–8

1 slice of white bread, crusts removed
300 ml (1/2 pint) milk
30 g (1 oz) butter
1 large onion, chopped
2 garlic cloves, crushed
1 kg (2 lb) minced beef
1 tbsp medium-hot curry powder
90 g (3 oz) ready-to-eat dried apricots, coarsely chopped
90 g (3 oz) blanched almonds, coarsely chopped
2 tbsp fruit chutney
1 tbsp lemon juice
salt and black pepper
2 eggs
30 g (1 oz) flaked almonds

1 Put the bread into a shallow dish. Sprinkle over 2 tbsp of the milk and leave to soak for 5 minutes.

2 Meanwhile, melt the butter in a large frying pan, add the onion and garlic, and cook gently, stirring occasionally, for a few minutes until soft.

3 Increase the heat, add the beef, and cook, stirring, for 5 minutes or until browned. Spoon off any excess fat.

4 Add the curry powder and cook, stirring, for 2 minutes. Add the chopped apricots and almonds, the chutney, lemon juice, and salt and pepper to taste.

5 Mash the bread and milk in the dish, then stir into the minced beef. Turn into an ovenproof dish and bake in a preheated oven at 180°C (350°F, Gas 4) for 35 minutes.

6 Break the eggs into a bowl, and whisk in the remaining milk, and salt and pepper to taste. Pour over the minced beef mixture, sprinkle with the almonds, and bake for 25–30 minutes until the topping is set.

Healthy option

Almonds are the traditional topping for this South African recipe, but they can be omitted if you want to reduce the fat content of the dish.

OXTAIL STEW

SERVES 6

1 tbsp sunflower oil
1.25 kg (2¹/2 lb) oxtail, cut into 5 cm (2 in) slices and trimmed
30 g (1 oz) plain flour
900 ml (1¹/2 pints) beef stock
2 large onions, sliced
1 tbsp tomato purée
1 tbsp chopped parsley
1 tbsp chopped fresh thyme
1 bay leaf
salt and black pepper
8 celery stalks, thickly sliced
chopped parsley to garnish

1 Heat the oil in a large flameproof casserole, add the oxtail, and cook over a high heat for 10 minutes or until browned all over. Remove the oxtail and drain on paper towels.

2 Add the flour and cook, stirring occasionally, for about 1 minute. Blend in the beef stock and bring to a boil, stirring until the sauce has thickened.

3 Return the oxtail to the casserole, and add the onions, tomato purée, parsley, thyme, and bay leaf. Season with salt and pepper, and bring to a boil. Cover and simmer gently for 2 hours.

4 Add the celery and cook for a further 1¹/2–2 hours or until the meat can be removed from the bones easily. Skim off any fat, then taste the sauce for seasoning. Sprinkle with parsley before serving.

Cook's know-how

Oxtail stew needs long, slow cooking to develop its rich brown gravy and to make the meat so soft that it falls off the bone. If possible, make the stew the day before serving; the excess fat can then be easily lifted from the surface of the cooled stew before reheating. If you have any leftover stew, thin it down with stock or water to make a tasty and nutritious soup.

PRESSED TONGUE

SERVES 10

2–2.5 kg (4–5 lb) salted ox tongue, trimmed
1 onion, quartered
1 bay leaf
1 tbsp gelatine powder
3 tbsp cold water
15 CM (6 IN) ROUND CAKE TIN OR STAINLESS STEEL SAUCEPAN

1 Put the ox tongue, onion, and bay leaf into a large saucepan, cover with cold water, and bring to a boil. Simmer very gently for 3–4 hours until tender. Test the water after 2 hours; if it is very salty, replace it with fresh water.

2 Lift the tongue out of the saucepan, reserving the cooking liquid, and leave to cool slightly. Remove and discard the skin, then cut the tongue in half lengthwise.

3 Sprinkle the gelatine over the measured water in a small bowl. Leave to stand for 3 minutes or until the gelatine is spongy. Put the bowl into a saucepan of gently simmering water and leave for 3 minutes or until the gelatine has dissolved.

4 Add 150 ml (¹/4 pint) of the cooking liquid to the gelatine and mix well.

5 Squash one half of the tongue, cut-side down, into the cake tin or saucepan, and put in the other half, cut-side up. Pour in the gelatine mixture, cover with a small plate, and weigh down with weights or heavy cans. Chill in the refrigerator overnight.

6 Dip the base of the tin or saucepan into a bowl of hot water, just long enough to melt the jelly slightly so that it comes away from the bottom. Serve the tongue chilled, and very thinly sliced.

LEMON ROAST VEAL
WITH SPINACH STUFFING

Loin of veal is a lean cut, so it has a tendency to be dry. Marinating for 2 days before roasting makes it more succulent. Loin of pork can be marinated and cooked in the same way.

SERVES 6–8

1.25 kg (2½ lb) boned veal roasting joint, such as loin

150 ml (¼ pint) dry white wine

150 ml (¼ pint) chicken stock

MARINADE

3 tbsp olive oil

grated zest and juice of 1 lemon

4 thyme sprigs

black pepper

STUFFING

30 g (1 oz) butter

1 shallot, finely chopped

2 streaky bacon rashers, rinds removed, finely chopped

175 g (6 oz) spinach leaves, coarsely shredded

grated zest of 1 lemon

60 g (2 oz) fresh brown breadcrumbs

salt and black pepper

1 small egg, lightly beaten

1 Combine the marinade ingredients. Turn the veal in the marinade, cover, and leave to marinate in the refrigerator for 2 days.

2 Make the stuffing: melt the butter, add the shallot and bacon, and cook for 5 minutes or until the shallot is softened. Stir in the spinach and cook for 1 minute. Remove from the heat, add the lemon zest and breadcrumbs, and season with salt and pepper. Mix well, then bind with the egg. Leave to cool completely.

3 Remove the veal from the marinade, reserving the marinade. Spread the stuffing over the veal and roll up (see box, right).

4 Weigh the veal, insert a meat thermometer, if using, into the middle of the meat, and place in a roasting tin. Pour the marinade around the meat. Roast in a preheated oven at 180°C (350°F, Gas 4) for 25 minutes per 500 g (1 lb), until the juices run clear or until the thermometer registers 80°C (175°F). Transfer to a platter, cover loosely with foil, and leave to stand in a warm place for 10 minutes.

5 Meanwhile, spoon the fat from the tin, and remove the thyme sprigs. Put the tin on the hob, add the wine and stock, and bring to a boil, stirring to dissolve the sediment from the bottom of the tin. Boil for 5 minutes or until thickened and reduced by about half.

6 Taste the gravy for seasoning, and pour into a warmed gravy boat. Carve the veal, and serve hot.

Rolling up the veal

Bring the 2 sides of the veal together, enclosing the stuffing. Tie fine string around the veal at regular intervals.

GRAVIES FOR MEAT

MUSHROOM GRAVY

Melt 30 g (1 oz) butter in a saucepan. Add 1 finely chopped shallot and cook for 2 minutes until softened. Add 250 g (8 oz) sliced mushrooms and cook gently for 5 minutes. Pour in 300 ml (½ pint) beef stock, and simmer for about 5 minutes. Add 1 tbsp chopped parsley, 1 tsp chopped fresh thyme, and salt and black pepper to taste.

ONION GRAVY

Heat 1 tbsp sunflower oil and 30 g (1 oz) butter in a saucepan. Add 1 sliced onion and cook for 5–7 minutes until golden. Add 1 tbsp plain flour and cook, stirring, for 1 minute. Add 300 ml (½ pint) chicken stock. Simmer for about 5 minutes. Add salt and pepper to taste.

RED WINE GRAVY

Melt 30 g (1 oz) butter in a saucepan. Add 1 sliced small onion and cook for 5 minutes or until beginning to brown. Add 1 tbsp plain flour and cook, stirring, for 1 minute. Add 100 ml (3½ fl oz) red wine and 300 ml (½ pint) beef stock. Simmer for about 5 minutes. Pour in any juices from the meat, and add salt and pepper to taste.

VEAL WITH TUNA MAYONNAISE

SERVES 8

1.5 kg (3 lb) boned and rolled veal roasting joint, such as loin
2 large rosemary sprigs
2 garlic cloves, cut into slivers
salt and black pepper
250 ml (8 fl oz) dry white wine

TUNA MAYONNAISE

1 x 200 g (7 oz) can tuna in oil, drained
2 tbsp lemon juice
1 garlic clove, crushed
2 tbsp capers
1 tsp chopped fresh thyme
dash of Tabasco sauce
125 ml (4 fl oz) olive oil
250 ml (8 fl oz) mayonnaise

TO GARNISH

black olives
1 red pepper, halved, seeded, and cut into strips
fresh basil

1 Make incisions in the veal and push 1 or 2 rosemary leaves and a sliver of garlic into each incision. Season, and rub with any remaining rosemary and garlic.

2 Place the veal in a large roasting tin and pour the wine around it. Cover with foil and roast in a preheated oven at 160°C (325°F, Gas 3) for 2–2¹/2 hours or until tender.

3 Remove the veal from the oven, and leave to cool completely in the cooking liquid. Remove any fat that solidifies on the surface. Slice the veal thinly and arrange the slices on a serving platter.

4 Make the tuna mayonnaise: purée the tuna, reserving a little for the garnish, with the lemon juice, garlic, capers, thyme, and Tabasco sauce in a food processor until smooth. Gradually blend in the oil, then add the mayonnaise, and season with salt and pepper. Pour over the veal. At this stage you can garnish and serve, or cover and refrigerate overnight to serve the next day.

5 To serve, garnish with the reserved tuna, the black olives, red pepper, and basil. Serve at room temperature (if refrigerated overnight, take it out for about 1 hour before serving).

VEAL CHOPS WITH MUSHROOMS & CREAM

SERVES 4

15 g (¹/2 oz) dried porcini mushrooms
250 ml (8 fl oz) warm water
2 tbsp plain flour
salt and black pepper
4 x 250 g (8 oz) veal loin chops
45 g (1¹/2 oz) butter
8 shallots, chopped
3 garlic cloves, crushed
250 g (8 oz) button mushrooms, thinly sliced
250 ml (8 fl oz) dry white wine
300 ml (¹/2 pint) single cream
1 tbsp chopped fresh tarragon, plus extra to garnish

1 Put the dried mushrooms into a bowl, pour over the warm water, and leave to soak for 30 minutes or until soft.

2 Sprinkle the flour on to a plate, and season with salt and pepper. Lightly coat the chops with the flour.

3 Melt half of the butter in a frying pan, add the veal chops, and cook for about 4 minutes on each side.

4 Remove the chops and keep warm. Melt the remaining butter in the pan, add the shallots and garlic, and cook gently, stirring occasionally, for a few minutes until softened.

5 Drain the dried mushrooms, reserving the soaking liquid. Add the dried and button mushrooms to the pan and cook for 3 minutes or until tender. Remove the shallots and mushrooms from the pan and keep warm.

6 Pour in the wine and boil until reduced to about 3 tbsp. Add the mushroom liquid and boil until reduced to about 125 ml (4 fl oz).

7 Stir in the cream and heat gently. Add the tarragon, and season with salt and pepper. Return the chops, shallots, and mushrooms to the pan and heat through gently. Transfer to serving plates, sprinkle with the extra chopped tarragon, and serve hot.

SALTIMBOCCA

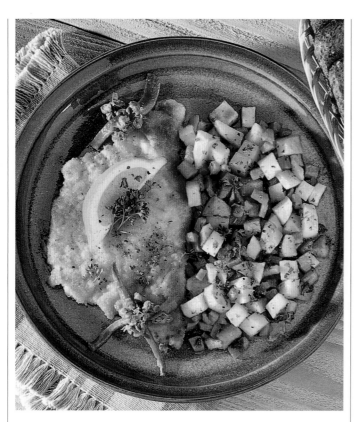

SERVES 4

4 x 60–90 g (2–3 oz) veal escalopes
8–12 fresh sage leaves
4 thin slices of Parma ham, trimmed of fat
2 tbsp plain flour
salt and black pepper
30 g (1 oz) butter
1 garlic clove, crushed
125 ml (4 fl oz) dry white wine
4 tbsp double cream

1 Put each veal escalope between 2 sheets of cling film and pound until 3 mm ($^1/8$ in) thick with a rolling pin.

2 Lay 2 or 3 sage leaves on each escalope, and press a slice of Parma ham firmly on top. Sprinkle the flour on to a plate and season with salt and pepper. Lightly coat both sides of the escalopes with the flour, shaking off any excess.

3 Melt half of the butter in a large frying pan until foaming. Add half of the escalopes and cook for 2 minutes on each side, sprinkling them with half of the garlic as they cook. Lift out and keep warm while you cook the remaining escalopes in the same way, with the remaining butter and garlic.

4 Pour the white wine into the empty pan and boil for a few minutes until it is reduced to about 2 tbsp.

5 Stir in the cream and heat gently, then taste for seasoning. Pour the sauce over the escalopes on warmed plates, and serve at once.

Healthy option

Omit the ham, wine, and cream. Before serving, squeeze the juice of 1 lemon over the veal, and sprinkle with 2 tbsp shredded fresh basil and salt and pepper to taste.

VEAL SCHNITZELS

SERVES 4

4 x 60–90 g (2–3 oz) veal escalopes
salt and black pepper
1 egg, beaten
125 g (4 oz) fresh white breadcrumbs
60 g (2 oz) butter
1 tbsp sunflower oil

TO SERVE

8 anchovy fillets, drained and halved lengthwise
2 tbsp coarsely chopped capers
lemon wedges
parsley

1 Put each veal escalope between 2 sheets of cling film and pound to a 3 mm ($^1/8$ in) thickness with a rolling pin. Season with salt and pepper.

2 Spread the beaten egg over a plate, and sprinkle the breadcrumbs over another plate. Dip each escalope into the beaten egg, then into the breadcrumbs, to coat evenly. Chill in the refrigerator for about 30 minutes.

3 Melt the butter with the oil in a large frying pan until foaming, add 2 of the escalopes, and cook for 2 minutes on each side until golden. Drain on paper towels and keep warm while cooking the remaining escalopes. Serve the veal escalopes hot, with anchovy fillets, capers, lemon wedges, and parsley.

Healthy option

Traditonal Austrian Wienerschnitzel is cooked in butter to give it a really good golden colour, but if you use a non-stick frying pan you can omit the butter and use 2 tbsp sunflower oil.

VEAL MARSALA

SERVES 4

4 x 60–90 g (2–3 oz) veal escalopes

1 tbsp plain flour

salt and black pepper

45 g (1 1/2 oz) butter

1 large onion, finely chopped

125 ml (4 fl oz) Marsala

125 ml (4 fl oz) chicken stock

chopped parsley to garnish

1 Put each veal escalope between 2 sheets of cling film and pound until 3 mm (1/8 in) thick with a rolling pin.

2 Season the flour with salt and pepper and use to lightly coat the escalopes.

3 Melt 30 g (1 oz) of the butter in a frying pan, and cook the escalopes, in batches if necessary, for 2 minutes on each side or until golden. Remove from the pan and keep hot.

4 Melt the remaining butter, add the onion, and cook gently for about 5 minutes until soft and lightly browned. Pour in the Marsala and boil, stirring, until reduced to 2 tbsp. Add the stock and boil until reduced to 90 ml (3 fl oz).

5 Return the escalopes to the pan, spoon over the sauce, and warm the escalopes through. Sprinkle with chopped parsley.

OSSO BUCO

Originally from Milan, the name of this Italian classic means "bone with a hole", as it is made from thick slices of veal shin that have the central bone in – they are called shanks by some butchers. For authenticity, serve with gremolata and a creamy risotto Milanese (page 356).

SERVES 6

30 g (1 oz) plain flour

salt and black pepper

6 veal shanks (bone-in), cut about 3.5–5 cm (1 1/2–2 in) thick

30 g (1 oz) butter

2 tbsp olive oil

2 onions, finely chopped

175 g (6 oz) carrots, finely chopped

2 celery stalks, finely chopped

2 garlic cloves, crushed

300 ml (1/2 pint) dry white wine

300 ml (1/2 pint) chicken stock

1 x 400 g (13 oz) can chopped tomatoes

2 tsp chopped fresh oregano or 1 tsp dried oregano

1 bay leaf

gremolata (see box, right) to serve

1 Put the flour into a large plastic bag and season with salt and pepper. Put the veal shanks into the bag and shake until all the meat is evenly coated with flour.

2 Melt the butter with the oil in a large flameproof casserole. When the butter is foaming, add the veal and cook in batches, for 10 minutes or until golden all over. Lift out and drain on paper towels. Lower the heat, add the onions, carrots, celery, and garlic, and cook for 5 minutes.

3 Pour in the wine and boil until reduced by half. Add the stock, tomatoes, oregano, and bay leaf, and bring to a boil. Return the veal to the casserole, bring back to a boil, cover, and cook in a preheated oven at 160°C (325°F, Gas 3) for 1 1/2–2 hours until very tender.

4 If the sauce in the casserole is too thin, lift out the veal and keep hot, then boil the sauce until reduced to a thicker consistency. Taste for seasoning. Sprinkle the gremolata over the veal just before serving.

Gremolata

Put 2 tbsp chopped parsley, the finely grated zest of 1 lemon, and 1 finely chopped garlic clove into a small bowl and stir to mix thoroughly.

Cook's know-how

In Italy the veal is sold with the marrow in the middle of the bone because it is a traditional custom to scoop it out of the bone after finishing the meat. It tastes really good spread on fresh crusty bread.

VEAL STEW WITH OLIVES & PEPPERS

SERVES 8

2 tbsp plain flour

salt and black pepper

1.5 kg (3 lb) stewing veal, cut into 3.5 cm (1 1/2 in) cubes

2–3 tbsp olive oil

2 garlic cloves, crushed

1 red, 1 green, and 1 yellow pepper, halved, seeded, and cut into strips

250 ml (8 fl oz) dry white wine

2 x 400 g (13 oz) cans chopped tomatoes

4 tbsp tomato purée

1 tsp dried rosemary

250 g (8 oz) pitted black olives

1 tbsp chopped fresh rosemary to garnish

1 tbsp chopped parsley to garnish

1 Put the flour into a plastic bag and season with salt and pepper. Toss the veal in the seasoned flour to coat lightly.

2 Heat the oil in a large flameproof casserole. Add the veal and sprinkle with half of the garlic, then cook for 5–7 minutes until browned all over. Lift out the veal and set aside.

3 Add the peppers and cook, stirring, for 3 minutes, until almost soft. Remove from the casserole and set aside.

4 Return the veal to the casserole, and add the wine, tomatoes, tomato purée, remaining garlic, and rosemary. Cover and simmer for 1 hour.

5 Return the peppers to the casserole and cook for a further 30 minutes or until the meat is very tender.

6 Stir the olives into the casserole and heat through. Serve hot, lightly sprinkled with rosemary and parsley.

LIVER & BACON WITH ONION SAUCE

SERVES 4

2 tbsp sunflower oil

1 large onion, thinly sliced

125 g (4 oz) streaky bacon rashers, rinds removed, cut into strips

500 g (1 lb) calf's liver, trimmed and cut into 1 cm (1/2 in) strips

2 tbsp plain flour

600 ml (1 pint) beef stock

3 tbsp tomato ketchup

dash of Worcestershire sauce

salt and black pepper

chopped fresh tarragon to garnish

1 Heat the oil in a large frying pan, add the onion and bacon, and cook gently, stirring occasionally, for a few minutes until the onion is soft and the bacon crisp. Add the liver and cook, stirring, for 2 minutes. Remove with a slotted spoon and keep warm.

2 Add the flour to the pan and cook, stirring, for 1 minute. Pour in the stock and bring to a boil, stirring until thickened.

3 Add the ketchup and Worcestershire sauce, and season with salt and pepper. Return the onion, bacon, and liver to the pan, cover, and simmer for 5 minutes. Sprinkle with tarragon before serving.

Cook's know-how

Lamb's liver can also be used in this recipe. Pig's liver is a less expensive alternative to calf's or lamb's liver but it has a stronger flavour. To make it less strong, soak it in milk for about 30 minutes.

LIVER STROGANOFF

Use 150 ml (1/4 pint) chicken stock instead of the beef stock and omit the ketchup and Worcestershire sauce. Stir in 150 ml (1/4 pint) soured cream.

CALF'S LIVER WITH SAGE

SERVES 4

2 tbsp plain flour

salt and black pepper

500 g (1 lb) calf's liver, sliced

60 g (2 oz) butter

1 tbsp sunflower oil

juice of 1 lemon

3 tbsp roughly chopped fresh sage

sage leaves and lemon slices to garnish

1 Sprinkle the flour on to a plate and season with salt and pepper. Coat the liver slices in the seasoned flour, shaking off any excess.

2 Melt half of the butter with the oil in a large frying pan. When the butter is foaming, add half of the liver slices and cook over a high heat for about 1 minute on each side until browned all over. Lift out with a slotted spoon and keep warm. Repeat with the remaining liver slices.

3 Melt the remaining butter in the pan, and add the lemon juice and sage, stirring to dissolve any sediment from the bottom of the pan. Pour the pan juices over the liver, garnish with sage leaves and lemon slices, and serve at once.

Cook's know-how

Overcooking liver will toughen it, so make sure that the butter and oil are really hot, then the liver will cook quickly.

CALF'S LIVER WITH APPLE

Halve and slice 1 eating apple and add to the pan with the lemon juice and sage. Cook, stirring, for 3 minutes, and serve with the liver.

CREAMED SWEETBREADS

SERVES 6

500 g (1 lb) calf's sweetbreads

2 tbsp lemon juice

1 small onion, chopped

a few parsley sprigs

1 bay leaf

salt and black pepper

45 g (1 1/2 oz) butter

45 g (1 1/2 oz) plain flour

300 ml (1/2 pint) milk

chopped parsley to garnish

1 Put the sweetbreads into a bowl, cover with cold water, add 1 tbsp of the lemon juice. Leave to soak for 2–3 hours.

2 Drain, rinse, and trim the sweetbreads (page 240).

3 Put the sweetbreads into a large saucepan with the onion, parsley, bay leaf, and a sprinkling of salt and pepper. Cover with cold water and bring slowly to a boil. Simmer gently for 5 minutes or until just tender, skimming off any scum as it rises to the surface.

4 Drain the sweetbreads, and reserve 300 ml (1/2 pint) of the cooking liquid. Cut the sweetbreads into bite-sized pieces.

5 Melt the butter in a saucepan, add the flour, and cook, stirring, for 1 minute. Remove the pan from the heat, and gradually blend in the milk and reserved cooking liquid. Bring to a boil, stirring constantly, and boil for 2–3 minutes until the mixture thickens. Add the remaining lemon juice and season with salt and pepper.

6 Add the sweetbreads to the sauce and simmer gently for about 5 minutes to warm through. Transfer to warmed plates and garnish with chopped parsley before serving.

270

ROAST LEG OF LAMB WITH RED WINE GRAVY

A rich gravy that incorporates all the flavoursome juices from the meat is traditonal with roast lamb. Red wine boosts the gravy's flavour, and you can add a spoonful of redcurrant jelly too, plus a squeeze of lemon juice and a dash of Worcestershire sauce if you like.

SAUCES FOR LAMB

MINT SAUCE

In a small bowl, combine 3 tbsp finely chopped fresh mint with 1–2 tbsp caster sugar, to taste. Add 3 tbsp white wine vinegar or cider vinegar and stir well to mix.

SERVES 4–6

2 kg (4 lb) leg of lamb

salt and black pepper

2 tbsp chopped fresh rosemary

1 tbsp plain flour

300 ml (½ pint) lamb or chicken stock

90 ml (3 fl oz) red wine

mint sauce (see recipe, far right) to serve

rosemary and thyme to garnish

1 Trim the skin and excess fat from the lamb. Score the fat (see box, right).

2 Insert a meat thermometer, if using, into the middle of the meat. Put the lamb, fat-side up, on a rack in a roasting tin, and rub with salt and pepper and the rosemary.

3 Roast the lamb in a preheated oven at 200°C (400°F, Gas 6) for 20 minutes. Lower the oven temperature to 180°C (350°F, Gas 4) and roast for 20 minutes per 500 g (1 lb) for medium-done meat, 25 minutes per 500 g (1 lb) for well-done meat, until the meat thermometer registers 75–80°C (170–175°F), and the fat is crisp and golden.

4 Remove the lamb, cover with foil, and leave to stand for 10 minutes.

5 Meanwhile, make the gravy: spoon all but 1 tbsp fat from the tin. Put the tin on the hob, add the flour, and cook, stirring, for 1 minute. Pour in the stock and wine, and bring to a boil, stirring to dissolve any sediment.

6 Simmer the gravy for about 3 minutes, season with salt and pepper, then strain if you like. Serve the gravy and mint sauce with the lamb, garnished with rosemary and thyme.

Scoring the fat

Score the fat in a criss-cross pattern using a small, sharp knife, making sure that only the fat is cut, and that the meat underneath remains completely untouched.

CUMBERLAND SAUCE

Put 4 tbsp redcurrant jelly into a small saucepan and heat gently until melted. Add 125 ml (4 fl oz) red wine and the grated zest of 1 orange. Bring to simmering point, and simmer, whisking constantly, for 5 minutes. Add the juices of 1 orange and ½ lemon and simmer for a further 5 minutes. Strain, then add salt and pepper. Serve hot.

TZATZIKI SAUCE

Put 150 g (5 oz) Greek yogurt, the grated zest and juice of 1 lemon, 1 crushed garlic clove, 1 tbsp chopped fresh mint, and salt and pepper into a small bowl. Mix well to combine, then taste for seasoning. Cover and chill until required.

GREEK ROAST LAMB

SERVES 6

2 kg (4 lb) leg of lamb

4 garlic cloves, cut into slivers

2 large rosemary sprigs, chopped

1 tbsp olive oil

salt and black pepper

chopped fresh rosemary to garnish

1 With a sharp knife, make small incisions in the lamb and insert a sliver of garlic into each incision.

2 Rub the lamb with the rosemary, olive oil, and salt and pepper, then put it in a roasting tin.

3 Roast in a preheated oven at 220°C (425°F, Gas 7) for 30 minutes or until the lamb is browned. Lower the oven temperature to 140°C (275°F, Gas 1), cover, and cook for a further 3 1/2 hours or until the lamb is very tender.

4 Cover the lamb with foil and leave to rest in a warm place for 10 minutes. Carve the lamb and serve hot, garnished with rosemary. Any cooking juices can be served with the meat, if you like.

SPINACH-STUFFED LAMB

The lamb in this recipe is distinctively flavoured with spinach, wine, and anchovies. Stuffed mushrooms are a perfect accompaniment.

SERVES 6–8

2 kg (4 lb) leg of lamb, boned but left whole (page 237)

150 ml (1/4 pint) dry white wine

4 canned anchovy fillets, chopped

about 150 ml (1/4 pint) lamb or chicken stock

salt and black pepper

stuffed mushrooms (page 383)

SPINACH STUFFING

30 g (1 oz) butter

3–4 garlic cloves, crushed

250 g (8 oz) spinach leaves, coarsely shredded

60 g (2 oz) fresh brown breadcrumbs

1 egg, beaten

1 Make the stuffing: melt the butter in a pan. Add the garlic and cook, stirring, for 2–3 minutes until soft. Stir in the spinach, season with salt and pepper, and cook for 1 minute. Add the breadcrumbs, cool, then mix in the egg.

2 Stuff the lamb (see box, right). Secure with fine skewers or thin string.

3 Put the lamb on a rack in a roasting tin and roast in a preheated oven at 200°C (400°F, Gas 6) for 15 minutes. Turn, insert a meat thermometer, if using, and cook for 15 minutes.

4 Drain the fat from the tin, then add the wine and anchovies. Cover the lamb loosely with foil, lower the oven temperature to 180°C (350°F, Gas 4), and cook for 1 1/2 hours or until the juices run slightly pink. The thermometer should register 75–80°C (170–175°F).

5 Remove the lamb from the tin. Leave to stand, covered with the foil, in a warm place for about 10 minutes.

6 Pour the cooking liquid into a measuring jug and make up to 300 ml (1/2 pint) with stock.

7 Return the cooking liquid to the tin. Bring to a boil, stirring to dissolve the sediment. Season, and strain into a warmed gravy boat. Serve the lamb with the stuffed mushrooms, and hand the gravy separately.

Stuffing the lamb

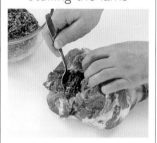

Season the cavity of the lamb with salt and pepper, then spoon in the cold spinach stuffing, packing it in tightly.

SHOULDER OF LAMB WITH LEMON & OLIVES

SERVES 6–8

2 kg (4 lb) shoulder of lamb, boned

2 garlic cloves, cut into slivers

150 ml (1/4 pint) dry white wine

150 ml (1/4 pint) lamb or chicken stock

LEMON & OLIVE STUFFING

1 tbsp olive oil

1 shallot, finely chopped

125 g (4 oz) fresh breadcrumbs

30 g (1 oz) pitted black olives, roughly chopped

finely grated zest of 1 lemon

1 tbsp chopped fresh thyme

1 tbsp chopped fresh rosemary

1 small egg, beaten

salt and black pepper

1 Make the stuffing: heat the olive oil in a small pan, add the shallot, and cook for about 5 minutes. Remove from the heat and add the breadcrumbs, olives, lemon zest, herbs, and egg. Season with salt and pepper, stir, and leave to cool.

2 Make incisions in the meat side of the lamb, insert the garlic slivers into them, then sprinkle with salt and pepper and spread with the stuffing. Roll up and secure with skewers, then weigh the lamb.

3 Put the lamb into a roasting tin and insert a meat thermometer, if using, into the middle of the meat. Pour over the wine and stock and cook in a preheated oven at 200°C (400°F, Gas 6) for 20–25 minutes. Lower the temperature to 180°C (350°F, Gas 4) and cook for 20 minutes per 500 g (1 lb) or until the juices run clear. The meat thermometer should register 75–80°C (170–175°F).

4 Remove the lamb, cover loosely with foil, and leave to stand for 10 minutes. Put the tin on the hob and spoon off any fat. Bring to a boil, and boil for 5 minutes, stirring to dissolve any sediment from the tin. Season, strain, and serve.

LEMON-GRILLED LAMB

SERVES 6–8

2 –2.5 kg (4–5 lb) leg of lamb, butterflied (page 237)

MARINADE

juice of 3 lemons

4 tbsp clear honey

3 large garlic cloves, quartered

2 tbsp coarse-grain mustard

1 Make the marinade: in a non-metallic dish, mix together the lemon juice, honey, garlic, and mustard. Turn the lamb in the marinade, cover, and leave to marinate in the refrigerator, turning the lamb occasionally, for 1–2 days.

2 Remove the lamb from the marinade. Strain and reserve the marinade. Cook the lamb under a hot grill, 15 cm (6 in) from the heat, basting from time to time with the marinade, for 20–25 minutes on each side.

3 Test the lamb: insert a skewer into the thickest part – the juices will run clear when it is cooked.

4 Leave the lamb to stand, covered with foil, in a warm place for 5–10 minutes. Spoon the fat from the grill pan, strain the juices into a gravy boat, and serve with the lamb.

Cook's know-how

Butterflied leg of lamb is a good cut for cooking on the barbecue as well as under the grill because the meat is thin enough to cook quickly without becoming too charred on the outside. The marinade in this recipe works equally well for lamb chops and cutlets, which can also be grilled or barbecued.

KEBABS ON THE BARBECUE

If you are having a barbecue party, threading the meat on skewers makes cooking, serving,
and eating really easy, so it is well worth the little extra time it takes to get them assembled.
You can choose from metal or bamboo skewers (see box below), as both are suitable for barbecuing.

BEEF & RED ONION

SERVES 4

500 g (1 lb) rump steak, cut into chunks

2 red onions, cut into wedges

salt and black pepper

olive oil for brushing

MARINADE

50 ml (2 fl oz) olive oil

50 ml (2 fl oz) port, sherry, or Marsala

2 tbsp Dijon mustard

1 Combine the marinade ingredients, add the beef, and stir well. Cover and leave to marinate in the refrigerator for at least 2 hours, turning the meat occasionally.

2 Thread the beef and onions on to skewers, season, and brush with olive oil. Barbecue for 2–3 minutes on each side for rare beef, 3–4 minutes for medium, and 4–5 minutes for well-done.

CURRIED LAMB

SERVES 4

500 g (1 lb) boneless loin or leg of lamb, trimmed and cut into chunks

lime wedges to serve

MARINADE

3 tbsp plain yogurt

juice of 1/2 lime

4 garlic cloves, crushed

3 tbsp chopped fresh coriander

1 tbsp chopped fresh mint

2 tsp curry powder

1 Combine the marinade ingredients in a large bowl. Stir in the lamb, cover, and marinate in the refrigerator for at least 2 hours, turning the meat occasionally.

2 Thread the lamb on to skewers. Barbecue for 4 minutes on each side for medium lamb, or 5 minutes for well-done, basting with the marinade a few times. Serve with lime wedges.

ORIENTAL PORK

SERVES 4

500 g (1 lb) pork fillet (tenderloin), cut into chunks

1 red pepper, halved, seeded, and cut into chunks

1 green pepper, halved, seeded, and cut into chunks

1 onion, cut into chunks

1/4 fresh pineapple, peeled and cut into chunks

MARINADE

90 ml (3 fl oz) sunflower oil

90 ml (3 fl oz) soy sauce

juice of 1 lime

3 garlic cloves, crushed

3 tbsp sugar

1/4 tsp ground ginger

1 Combine the marinade ingredients in a bowl. Add the pork, peppers, onion, and pineapple, and stir well. Cover and chill for at least 2 hours.

2 Thread the meat on to skewers, alternating with peppers, onions, and pineapple. Baste with any remaining marinade. Barbecue for 4–5 minutes on each side, basting, until the pork is cooked.

SAUSAGE & SESAME

SERVES 4

16 cocktail sausages

8 button mushrooms

8 cherry tomatoes

2 courgettes, each cut into 4 thick slices on the diagonal

salt and black pepper

olive oil, for brushing

about 2 tbsp mango chutney

about 2 tbsp toasted sesame seeds

1 Thread the sausages lengthwise on to skewers, putting 4 sausages on each skewer, then thread the vegetables on to 4 skewers, alternating the mushrooms, tomatoes, and courgettes. Season and brush with olive oil.

2 Barbecue for 4–5 minutes on each side, until cooked through. While the sausages are still hot, brush them with mango chutney and sprinkle with toasted sesame seeds.

SUCCESSFUL BARBECUES

Cooking over charcoal requires no special skills, but it helps to know
a few simple rules before you start.

Meat is best if it is marinated before being cooked over a barbecue. The basis of a marinade should be an oil to keep the food moist, an acid such as lemon or lime juice to help tenderize the meat, and herbs, spices, or other seasonings to add flavour.

Basting or brushing with the marinade while the meat is cooking will help keep it moist.

Light the barbecue well before you want to start cooking – the coals should have stopped glowing and be covered in grey ash or the food may singe and burn on the outside before it is cooked inside. It takes about 30 minutes to get to this stage.

If you are using bamboo skewers for kebabs, soak them in warm water for 30 minutes before use so that they don't burn.

TOP PLATTER: Beef & Red Onion (left) with Oriental Pork. BOTTOM PLATTER: Sausage & Sesame (top and middle); Curried Lamb

SHOULDER OF LAMB WITH GARLIC & HERBS

SERVES 6

2 kg (4 lb) shoulder of lamb, trimmed of excess fat

haricot bean cassoulet (page 381) to serve

HERB BUTTER

90 g (3 oz) butter, softened

2 garlic cloves, crushed

1 tbsp chopped fresh thyme

1 tbsp chopped fresh rosemary

1 tbsp chopped fresh mint

2 tbsp chopped parsley

salt and black pepper

GRAVY

1 tbsp plain flour

150 ml (1/4 pint) red wine

150 ml (1/4 pint) lamb or chicken stock

1 Make the herb butter: mix the butter, garlic, thyme, rosemary, mint, and parsley, and season with salt and pepper.

2 Slash the lamb at regular intervals with a sharp knife, then push the herb butter into the cuts. Rub any remaining butter over the lamb. Weigh the lamb.

3 Put the lamb on a rack in a roasting tin and insert a meat thermometer, if using, into the middle of the meat. Cook in a preheated oven at 200°C (400°F, Gas 6) for 30 minutes.

4 Lower the temperature to 180°C (350°F, Gas 4) and cook for 20 minutes per 500 g (1 lb). The thermometer should register 75–80°C (170–175°F).

5 Remove the lamb. Cover loosely with foil and leave to stand in a warm place for about 10 minutes.

6 Make the gravy: drain all but 1 tbsp of the fat from the tin. Set the tin on the hob, add the flour, and cook, stirring, for 1 minute. Pour in the wine and stock, bring to a boil, and simmer for 2–3 minutes. Taste for seasoning, and strain into a warmed gravy boat. Serve with the lamb and creamed haricot beans.

INDIAN SPICED LAMB

SERVES 6

1.5 kg (3 lb) shoulder or leg of lamb

1 tsp lemon juice

salt and black pepper

cashew nuts and chopped coriander to garnish

SPICED YOGURT MARINADE

4 garlic cloves, coarsely chopped

7 cm (3 in) piece of fresh root ginger, peeled and grated

2 tbsp clear honey

1 tbsp lemon juice

seeds of 5 cardamom pods

1 tsp ground cumin

1 tsp turmeric

1/4 tsp cayenne pepper

1 tsp salt

1/2 tsp ground cinnamon

1/4 tsp ground cloves (optional)

150 g (5 oz) Greek yogurt

1 Make the spiced yogurt marinade: purée the garlic, ginger, honey, lemon juice, cardamom, cumin, turmeric, cayenne, salt, cinnamon, cloves (if using), and yogurt in a blender or food processor.

2 Spread the mixture over the lamb (see box, right). Cover and leave to marinate in the refrigerator for at least 2 hours, or overnight.

3 Put the lamb on a rack in a roasting tin and cook in a preheated oven at 160°C (325°F, Gas 3) for 3 1/2 hours or until the meat is tender.

4 Remove the lamb and keep hot. Spoon the fat from the tin. Set the tin on the hob and stir in the lemon juice and enough water to make a sauce. Bring to a boil, stirring, and season with salt and pepper.

5 Cut the lamb from the bone, then cut the meat into chunks and mix with the sauce on the hob. Serve hot, garnished with cashew nuts and chopped coriander.

Coating the lamb

Make incisions in the lamb, then spread the marinade over the whole joint, making sure it goes into the incisions.

RACK OF LAMB WITH A WALNUT & HERB CRUST

Also called best end of neck, a rack of lamb usually has 6–8 bones, which are called cutlets. The bones should be scraped clean of all fat – this is called "French trimmed" by some butchers.

SERVES 4–6

2 prepared racks of lamb (page 238)

1 egg, beaten

WALNUT & HERB CRUST

30 g (1 oz) fresh wholemeal breadcrumbs

30 g (1 oz) parsley, chopped

2 tbsp coarsely chopped walnut pieces

2 large garlic cloves, crushed

finely grated zest of 1 lemon

1 tbsp walnut oil

salt and black pepper

WINE & GRAPE SAUCE

150 ml (¼ pint) dry white wine

150 ml (¼ pint) lamb or chicken stock

125 g (4 oz) seedless green grapes, halved

1 Brush the outsides of the racks of lamb with some of the beaten egg.

2 Prepare the walnut and herb crust: combine the breadcrumbs, parsley, walnuts, garlic, lemon zest, and oil, season with salt and pepper, and bind with the remaining egg. Chill for 30 minutes.

3 Coat the racks with the walnut and herb crust (see box, right), and put them crust-side up into a roasting tin. Cook in a preheated oven at 200°C (400°F, Gas 6) for 30 minutes.

4 Remove the lamb, cover with foil, and leave to stand in a warm place for 10 minutes. Meanwhile, make the sauce: spoon all but 1 tbsp of the fat from the roasting tin.

5 Set the tin on the hob, pour in the wine, and bring to a boil, stirring to dissolve any sediment from the bottom of the tin.

6 Add the stock and boil, stirring occasionally, for 2–3 minutes. Taste the sauce for seasoning, strain into a warmed sauce boat, and stir in the grapes. Serve with the lamb.

Coating the lamb

Press half of the walnut and herb crust mixture on to the meaty side of each rack of lamb, using a palette knife.

LAMB WITH MINT GLAZE

SERVES 4

8 best end lamb chops, well trimmed

MINT GLAZE

3 tbsp dry white wine

1 tbsp white wine vinegar

4 mint sprigs, leaves stripped and chopped

1 tbsp clear honey

1 tsp Dijon mustard

salt and black pepper

1 Make the mint glaze: combine the wine, vinegar, mint, honey, and mustard, and season with salt and pepper. Brush the glaze over the chops, and leave to marinate for about 30 minutes.

2 Place the chops over a barbecue or under a hot grill, 7 cm (3 in) from the heat, and cook, brushing often with the glaze, for 4–6 minutes on each side, until done to your liking.

LAMB WITH ORANGE GLAZE

Instead of the mint glaze, combine 3 tbsp orange juice with 1 tbsp each white wine vinegar, orange marmalade, and chopped fresh thyme, and 1 tsp Dijon mustard. Season with salt and pepper.

HERBED BUTTERFLY CHOPS

SERVES 4

4 butterfly lamb chops
1 tbsp olive oil
black pepper
4 rosemary sprigs
4 mint sprigs
4 thyme sprigs

1 Place the lamb chops on a grill rack and brush each one with half of the oil. Sprinkle with black pepper and scatter with the herb sprigs.

2 Place the chops under a hot grill, 10 cm (4 in) from the heat, and cook for 4–6 minutes. Remove from the heat, lift off the herbs, and turn the chops over. Brush the chops with the remaining oil, replace the herbs, and grill for 4–6 minutes until done to your liking. Serve hot.

Cook's know-how

Butterfly chops are double-sided, cut from a saddle of lamb, or double loin. They are also known as Barnsley chops.

LAMB CHOPS WITH MINTED HOLLANDAISE SAUCE

Instead of the traditional mint sauce, lamb chops are served here with a creamy hollandaise sauce flavoured with fresh mint. The sauce is easy to make, as long as you take care not to get the melted butter too hot.

SERVES 4

4 chump lamb chops
a little olive oil
salt and black pepper
minted hollandaise sauce to serve (see box, below)

1 Brush the chops on both sides with a little oil, and season with salt and pepper.

2 Put the chops under a hot grill, 10 cm (4 in) from the heat, and cook for 3–4 minutes on each side for medium-rare chops, slightly longer for well-done.

3 Arrange the lamb chops on warmed serving plates and serve at once with the warm minted hollandaise sauce.

LEMON & THYME HOLLANDAISE

Substitute 1 tsp finely grated lemon zest and 1 tbsp chopped fresh thyme leaves for the chopped mint.

Minted hollandaise sauce

Whisk together 2 tsp lemon juice, 2 tsp white wine vinegar, and 3 egg yolks at room temperature. Put over a pan of simmering water and whisk until thick. In another pan, gently melt 125 g (4 oz) unsalted butter (do not let it get too hot). Pour into a jug.

Pour the melted butter, a little at a time, into the egg-yolk mixture, whisking constantly until the sauce thickens. Remove from the heat, stir in 2 tbsp chopped fresh mint, and season with salt and pepper. Pour into a sauce boat and serve at once.

LANCASHIRE HOT POT

SERVES 4

2 tbsp sunflower oil

I kg (2 lb) middle neck lamb chops, trimmed

3 lamb's kidneys, trimmed (page 240) and halved

I kg (2 lb) potatoes, cut into 5 mm (1/4 in) slices

500 g (1 lb) carrots, sliced

2 large onions, chopped

I tsp caster sugar

salt and black pepper

I bay leaf

I rosemary sprig

a few parsley sprigs

600–750 ml (1–1 1/4 pints) lamb or chicken stock, or water

chopped parsley to garnish

1 Heat the oil in a flameproof casserole, add the lamb in batches, and brown over a medium heat for 5 minutes. Remove and set aside. Add the kidneys and cook for 3–5 minutes. Remove and set aside.

2 Add the potatoes, carrots, and onions, and cook for 5 minutes. Remove from the casserole.

3 Make layers of lamb chops, kidneys, and vegetables in the casserole, sprinkling with the sugar and a little salt and pepper, and putting the herbs in the middle.

4 Top with a neat layer of potatoes. Pour in enough stock or water to come up to the potato layer. Cover tightly and cook in a preheated oven at 160°C (325°F, Gas 3) for 2 hours or until the meat and vegetables are tender.

5 Remove the casserole lid, increase the oven temperature to 220°C (425°F, Gas 7), and cook for 20–30 minutes to brown the potato topping. Sprinkle with parsley before serving.

COUNTRY HOT POT

Omit the kidneys, and substitute 250 g (8 oz) swede for half of the carrots. Layer the meat and vegetables with 60 g (2 oz) pearl barley.

LAMB NOISETTES WITH ORANGE & HONEY

SERVES 4

8 lamb noisettes

2 lamb's kidneys, trimmed (page 240) and quartered (optional)

chopped fresh thyme and rosemary to garnish

MARINADE

grated zest and juice of I orange

4 tbsp clear honey

3 tbsp olive oil

2 garlic cloves, crushed

I tbsp chopped fresh thyme

I tbsp chopped fresh rosemary

salt and black pepper

1 Make the marinade: in a shallow, non-metallic dish, combine the orange zest and juice, honey, oil, garlic, thyme, and rosemary, and season with salt and pepper. Add the lamb noisettes to the marinade, turn them, then cover, and leave to marinate in the refrigerator overnight.

2 Lift the lamb noisettes out of the marinade, reserving the marinade. Place a piece of kidney, if using, in the middle of each lamb noisette.

3 Put under a hot grill, 10 cm (4 in) from the heat, and cook for 7 minutes on each side until the lamb is tender.

4 Meanwhile, strain the marinade into a small saucepan, bring to a boil, and simmer for a few minutes until it reaches a syrupy consistency. Taste for seasoning, spoon over the lamb noisettes, and garnish with thyme and rosemary.

Cook's know-how

Noisettes are taken from the loin of the lamb. The eye of meat is cut away, then rolled, tied, and cut into thick slices. It is an expensive cut but gives neat portions of tender, lean meat, with no waste.

IRISH STEW

SERVES 4

1 kg (2 lb) main-crop potatoes, cut into 5 mm (1/4 in) slices
2 large onions, sliced
1 kg (2 lb) middle neck lamb chops, trimmed
a few parsley stalks
1 thyme sprig
1 bay leaf
salt and black pepper
300–500 ml (10–16 fl oz) water
chopped parsley to garnish

1 Put half of the potatoes into a flameproof casserole, cover with half of the onions, then add the chops, parsley, thyme, and bay leaf, and season with salt and pepper. Add the remaining onions, then the remaining potatoes, seasoning each layer with salt and pepper.

2 Pour in enough water to half-fill the casserole, and then bring to a boil. Cover tightly and cook in a preheated oven at 160°C (325°F, Gas 3) for 2–2 1/2 hours until the lamb and potatoes are just tender.

3 Remove the lid, increase the oven temperature to 220°C (425°F, Gas 7), and cook for 20–30 minutes to brown the topping. Sprinkle with parsley before serving.

FRAGRANT LAMB KORMA

This aromatic lamb dish is enriched with yogurt instead of cream, which makes it healthier than a traditional korma. The fresh mint and paprika garnish adds to both flavour and presentation. For an authentic accompaniment, serve with spiced red lentils.

SERVES 6

5 cm (2 in) piece of fresh root ginger, peeled and grated
3 large garlic cloves, peeled
2 large green chillies, halved and seeded
60 g (2 oz) salted cashew nuts (optional)
2 tsp ground cumin
2 tsp ground cardamom
2 tsp turmeric
6 tbsp water
3 tbsp sunflower oil
1 kg (2 lb) lamb neck fillet, trimmed and cut into 4 cm (1 1/2 in) cubes
2 large onions, roughly chopped
300 ml (1/4 pint) full-fat Greek yogurt
salt and black pepper
about 1 tbsp lemon juice
fresh mint and paprika to garnish

1 Place the ginger, garlic, chillies, cashew nuts (if using), cumin, cardamom, turmeric, and measured water in a food processor or blender, and purée until smooth.

Cook's know-how

To make this recipe even more special, experiment with other spices. The traditional garam masala powder is usually sold ready mixed, and can include ground coriander, cinnamon, cloves, mace, bay leaves, and pepper, as well as the three spices used in the recipe here. For a subtly different flavour, try adding 1 tsp ground cinnamon next time you make this recipe, or any of the other garam masala spices mentioned above.

2 Heat 2 tbsp of the oil in a large flameproof casserole, and brown the lamb on all sides (you may need to do this in batches). Remove with a slotted spoon and set aside to drain on kitchen paper.

3 Heat the remaining oil in the same pan, and fry the onions over a high heat for 2–3 minutes. Return the lamb to the pan, add the puréed spice blend, and stir in the yogurt. Season with salt and pepper, cover, and simmer gently for about 1 1/2–2 hours until the lamb is tender.

4 Just before serving, add the lemon juice, and check the seasoning. Garnish with a sprinkling of mint and paprika, and serve hot.

BLANQUETTE OF LAMB

SERVES 6

1 kg (2 lb) boneless shoulder of lamb, trimmed and cut into chunks

1.25 litres (2 pints) water

8 button onions

2 large carrots, thickly sliced

2 bay leaves

juice of ½ lemon

salt and black pepper

250 g (8 oz) button mushrooms

45 g (1½ oz) butter

45 g (1½ oz) plain flour

150 ml (¼ pint) single cream

1 egg yolk

chopped parsley to garnish

1 Put the chunks of lamb into a large saucepan, cover with cold water, and bring to a boil. Drain, then rinse the meat thoroughly to remove the scum.

2 Return the meat to the saucepan and pour in the measured water. Add the button onions, carrots, bay leaves, and lemon juice, and season with salt and pepper. Bring to a boil, cover, and simmer gently for 1 hour.

3 Add the mushrooms and simmer for 30 minutes. Lift out the lamb and vegetables, reserving the liquid, and keep hot.

4 Melt the butter in a small pan. Add the flour and cook, stirring occasionally, for 1 minute. Gradually blend in the reserved cooking liquid, stirring constantly. Bring to a boil, stirring, then simmer until the sauce thickens.

5 In a bowl, whisk together the cream and egg yolk. Blend in 2 tbsp of the hot sauce. Take the saucepan off the heat, stir the cream mixture into the sauce, then reheat very gently. Taste for seasoning. Pour the sauce over the lamb and garnish with parsley before serving.

Healthy option

Substitute 1 x 400 g (13 oz) can chopped tomatoes and 300 ml (½ pint) dry white wine for the water. Cook the lamb as in the recipe here, but do not make the white sauce. This will not be a classic blanquette, but it will cut down on the fat content.

AROMATIC LAMB WITH LENTILS

SERVES 8

1.5 kg (3 lb) lamb neck fillet, trimmed and cut into chunks

2 tbsp olive oil

2 onions, chopped

125 g (4 oz) brown or green Puy lentils, rinsed

175 g (6 oz) ready-to-eat dried apricots

salt and black pepper

600 ml (1 pint) lamb or chicken stock

MARINADE

175 ml (6 fl oz) orange juice

2 tbsp olive oil

3 garlic cloves, crushed

1 tsp ground ginger

1 tsp ground coriander

½ tsp ground cinnamon

1 Make the marinade: in a large bowl, combine the orange juice, oil, garlic, ginger, coriander, and cinnamon.

2 Turn the chunks of lamb in the marinade, cover loosely, and then leave to marinate in the refrigerator overnight.

3 Remove the lamb from the marinade, reserving the marinade. Heat the olive oil in a large flameproof casserole, add the lamb in batches, and cook over a high heat for 5 minutes or until browned all over. Lift out the lamb chunks with a slotted spoon.

4 Lower the heat slightly, add the onions, and cook gently, stirring occasionally, for a few minutes until just soft but not coloured. Lift out of the casserole.

5 Make layers of lamb, onions, lentils, and apricots in the casserole, sprinkling each layer with salt and pepper. Pour in the stock and the reserved marinade and bring to a boil. Cover and cook in a preheated oven at 160°C (325°F, Gas 3) for 2 hours or until the meat is tender. Taste for seasoning before serving.

281

LAMB TAGINE

SERVES 8

¹/₄ tsp saffron threads
150 ml (¹/₄ pint) hot water
3 tbsp olive oil
1.5 kg (3 lb) boneless shoulder of lamb, well trimmed and cut into 2.5 cm (1 in) cubes
1 fennel bulb or 4 celery stalks, trimmed and sliced crosswise
2 green peppers, halved, seeded, and cut into strips
1 large onion, sliced
30 g (1 oz) plain flour
¹/₂ tsp ground ginger
450 ml (³/₄ pint) lamb or chicken stock
grated zest and juice of 1 orange
125 g (4 oz) ready-to-eat dried apricots
salt and black pepper
mint sprigs to garnish

1 Prepare the saffron (see box, right). Heat the oil in a flameproof casserole, add the lamb in batches, and cook over a high heat for 5 minutes or until browned. Lift out and drain on paper towels.

2 Lower the heat, add the fennel or celery, peppers, and onion, and cook gently, stirring, for 5 minutes.

3 Sprinkle the flour and ginger into the vegetables and cook, stirring occasionally, for 1 minute. Add the saffron liquid to the casserole, return the cubes of lamb, then add the stock and orange zest, and season with salt and pepper. Bring to a boil, cover, and cook in a preheated oven at 160°C (325°F, Gas 3) for 1 hour.

4 Add the orange juice and apricots and cook for about 30 minutes until the lamb is very tender. Taste for seasoning and garnish with mint sprigs before serving.

Preparing saffron

Put the saffron threads into a small bowl, add the measured hot water, and leave to soak for 10 minutes.

SPICED LAMB WITH COCONUT

SERVES 6

1 kg (2 lb) lamb neck fillet, trimmed and cut into 2.5 cm (1 in) cubes
30 g (1 oz) butter
1 tbsp sunflower oil
1 large Spanish onion, sliced
2 large garlic cloves, crushed
1 tbsp plain flour
1 x 400 g (13 oz) can chopped tomatoes
150 ml (¹/₄ pint) lamb or chicken stock
grated zest and juice of 1 lime
2 tbsp mango chutney
60 g (2 oz) creamed coconut, chopped
250 g (8 oz) Greek yogurt
coriander sprigs to garnish

SPICE MIX

2.5 cm (1 in) piece of fresh root ginger, peeled and grated
1 tbsp ground cumin
1 tbsp ground coriander
1 tbsp mild curry powder
salt and black pepper

1 Toss the meat in the ginger, cumin, coriander, and curry powder, and season with salt and pepper.

2 Melt the butter with the oil in a large flameproof casserole. When the butter is foaming, add the lamb in batches, and cook over a high heat for about 5 minutes until browned all over.

3 Lift out with a slotted spoon and set aside. Lower the heat, add the onion and garlic, and cook gently, stirring occasionally, for a few minutes until soft but not coloured.

4 Sprinkle in the flour and cook, stirring, for 1 minute. Add the tomatoes, stock, lime zest and juice, and chutney, and season with salt and pepper. Bring to a boil, stirring.

5 Return the lamb to the casserole, add the coconut, and bring back to a boil. Cover and cook in a preheated oven at 160°C (325°F, Gas 3) for 2 hours or until the lamb is tender.

6 Stir in the yogurt and taste for seasoning. Garnish with coriander sprigs before serving.

SHEPHERD'S PIE

SERVES 6

750 g (1 1/2 lb) minced lamb
125 g (4 oz) mushrooms, sliced
2 carrots, diced
1 large onion, chopped
1 garlic clove, crushed
30 g (1 oz) plain flour
150 ml (1/4 pint) beef stock
2 tbsp Worcestershire sauce
salt and black pepper
750 g (1 1/2 lb) potatoes
about 4 tbsp hot milk
30 g (1 oz) butter

1 Put the minced lamb into a large frying pan and heat gently until the fat runs. Increase the heat and cook, turning and mashing the meat, until it browns. Using a slotted spoon, lift the lamb out of the pan and spoon off the excess fat.

2 Add the mushrooms, carrots, onion, and garlic to the pan, and cook gently, stirring occasionally, for a few minutes until just beginning to soften.

3 Return the lamb to the frying pan. Sprinkle in the flour and cook, stirring, for about 1 minute.

4 Add the stock and the Worcestershire sauce, and season with salt and pepper. Bring to a boil, cover, and simmer gently for 30 minutes.

5 Meanwhile, cook the potatoes in boiling salted water for 15–20 minutes until tender. Drain. Add the milk and butter to the potatoes and mash until soft, then season with salt and pepper.

6 Taste the lamb mixture for seasoning. Turn into an ovenproof dish, then spread the potato on top. With a fork, score the potato in a decorative pattern. Cook in a preheated oven at 200°C (400°F, Gas 6) for about 20 minutes until the potato topping is golden and the meat mixture bubbling.

Cook's know-how

To make the pie more special, use half red wine and half beef stock.

LIGHT MOUSSAKA WITH FRESH MINT

SERVES 8

750 g (1 1/2 lb) lean minced lamb
2 large onions, roughly chopped
2 garlic cloves, crushed
2 tsp ground coriander
30 g (1 oz) plain flour
150 ml (1/4 pint) red wine
500 ml (16 fl oz) passata (sieved tomatoes
2 tbsp tomato purée
salt and black pepper
2 tbsp chopped fresh mint
2 large aubergines, thinly sliced
olive oil, for brushing
1 egg
200 ml (7 fl oz) full-fat Greek yogurt
60 g (2 oz) Parmesan cheese, grated
30 x 25 x 6 CM (12 x 10 x 2 1/2 IN) BAKING DISH

1 Put the lamb into a large frying pan and heat gently until the fat runs. Increase the heat and cook, stirring, until browned. Spoon off excess fat.

2 Add the onions and garlic and cook for 2–3 minutes until softened. Add the ground coriander and the flour and cook, stirring, for 1 minute.

3 Gradually blend in the wine, passata, and tomato purée, and season with salt and pepper. Bring to a boil, stirring, until thickened. Cover and simmer for 20–30 minutes, then add the fresh mint.

4 Line the rack of a grill pan with foil and place in the pan. Brush the aubergine slices with olive oil on both sides, and season with salt and pepper. Place the slices on the foil and cook under a hot grill, 10 cm (4 in) from the heat, for 5–6 minutes until golden brown on both sides.

5 Lightly beat the egg with the yogurt, and season with salt and pepper. Spoon the meat mixture into the oiled baking dish and level the top. Arrange the aubergine slices in an overlapping pattern over the meat. Pour over the yogurt mixture and spread to the edges so the aubergine is covered. Sprinkle with the cheese.

6 Bake in a preheated oven at 180°C (350°F, Gas 4) for about 45 minutes or until piping hot and golden.

KIDNEYS TURBIGO

SERVES 4

6 lamb's kidneys

60 g (2 oz) butter

250 g (8 oz) thin chipolata sausages

250 g (8 oz) button mushrooms

12 button onions, peeled, with roots left intact

1 tbsp plain flour

300 ml (1/2 pint) lamb or chicken stock

3 tbsp medium sherry

2 tsp tomato purée

1 bay leaf

salt and black pepper

2 tbsp chopped parsley to garnish

croûtes (page 49) to serve (optional)

1 Prepare the kidneys (page 214). Melt the butter in a large frying pan, add the kidneys, and cook, stirring, over a high heat for about 3 minutes until browned.

2 Lift the kidneys out and drain on paper towels. Add the sausages and cook for 3 minutes or until browned. Lift out and drain on paper towels.

3 Add the mushrooms and onions to the pan and cook for 3–5 minutes until browned.

4 Sprinkle in the flour and cook, stirring, for 1 minute. Add the stock, sherry, and tomato purée, and bring to a boil, stirring constantly. Add the bay leaf, and season with salt and pepper.

5 Slice the sausages thickly. Return to the pan with the kidneys, cover and simmer for 20–25 minutes until tender.

6 Spoon the kidney mixture on to a warmed platter, garnish with parsley, and serve with croûtes if you like.

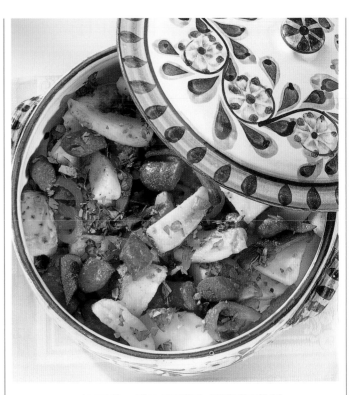

MERGUEZ WITH POTATOES & PEPPERS

SERVES 4

3 large potatoes, unpeeled

salt and black pepper

1 red pepper

1 green pepper

250 g (8 oz) merguez (spicy sausages), cut into bite-sized pieces

3 garlic cloves, crushed

1/2 tsp ground cumin

1–2 tbsp olive oil, more if needed

chopped fresh coriander to garnish

1 Put the potatoes into a large saucepan of boiling salted water and cook for 10 minutes. Drain and leave to cool.

2 Put the peppers under a hot grill, 10 cm (4 in) from the heat, and grill, turning as needed, for 10–12 minutes until charred and blistered. Put the peppers into a plastic bag, seal, and leave to cool.

3 Cut the peppers lengthwise into strips, removing and discarding the skins, cores, and seeds. Pat the peppers dry.

4 Cut the potatoes into wedges and put into a casserole with the peppers and merguez. Stir in the garlic, cumin, and 1 tbsp oil, and season with salt and pepper. Cook in a preheated oven at 190°C (375°F, Gas 5), turning occasionally, for 45 minutes or until the potatoes are tender and the sausages cooked through, adding a little more oil if the potatoes look dry.

5 Remove the casserole from the oven, and spoon off any excess fat. Garnish with coriander before serving.

BONED LOIN OF PORK WITH APRICOT STUFFING

Succulent boned loin of pork, with an apricot stuffing flavoured with lemon juice and lemon thyme, is served here with a white wine gravy. The crackling is cooked separately, in the top half of the oven, to ensure that it is deliciously crisp.

SERVES 8

1.5 kg (3 lb) boned loin of pork, skin removed and scored at 1 cm (1/2 in) intervals

sunflower oil for brushing

APRICOT STUFFING

30 g (1 oz) butter

1 small onion, finely chopped

90 g (3 oz) fresh brown breadcrumbs

90 g (3 oz) ready-to-eat dried apricots, coarsely chopped

1 tbsp chopped parsley

1 tbsp lemon juice

2 tsp chopped fresh lemon thyme

1 egg, beaten

salt and black pepper

GRAVY

1 tbsp plain flour

150 ml (1/4 pint) chicken stock

150 ml (1/4 pint) dry white wine

1 Make the stuffing: melt the butter in a saucepan and cook the onion gently until soft.

2 Remove from the heat and add the breadcrumbs, apricots, parsley, lemon juice, lemon thyme, and egg. Season with salt and pepper, mix well, and leave until cold.

3 Brush the scored side of the pork skin with a little oil, and sprinkle generously with salt and pepper. Place the skin on a rack in a roasting tin.

4 Remove as much fat as possible from the pork, especially on the top where the skin has been removed. Season the meat well, then stuff and roll (see box, below right).

5 Place the pork skin in the top of a preheated oven at 180°C (350°F, Gas 4). Put the pork into another roasting tin, brush with oil, and season generously. Insert a meat thermometer, if using, into the middle of the loin, and cook the pork in the oven for 2 hours or until the thermometer registers 80°C (175°F).

6 Transfer the pork to a carving board, cover with foil, and leave to stand for 10 minutes. If the crackling is not really crisp, increase the oven temperature to 200°C (400°F, Gas 6) and let it continue to cook while making the gravy.

7 Put the roasting tin on the hob and spoon off all but 1 tbsp of the fat. Sprinkle in the flour, and cook, stirring to dissolve any sediment from the bottom of the tin, for 1 minute. Pour in the stock and wine, and bring to a boil, stirring constantly. Simmer for 3 minutes. Season to taste and strain into a gravy boat. Serve with the pork.

Stuffing and rolling a loin of pork

Open out the loin of pork and spread the stuffing over the meat.

Roll the pork around the stuffing and tie at intervals with fine string, or use skewers.

SAUCES FOR PORK

APRICOT SAUCE

Melt 30 g (1 oz) butter, and cook 1 thinly sliced small onion until soft. Add 125 g (4 oz) chopped ready-to-eat dried apricots, 150 ml (1/4 pint) each chicken stock and dry white wine, and 1/4 tsp ground cinnamon. Season with salt and pepper, and simmer for about 20 minutes until pulpy.

APPLE SAUCE

Peel, core, and slice 500 g (1 lb) cooking apples and put into a saucepan with the finely grated zest of 1 lemon and 2–3 tbsp water. Cover tightly and cook gently for about 10 minutes until soft. Stir in 30 g (1 oz) caster sugar. Beat the sauce until smooth, then stir in 15 g (1/2 oz) butter if you like.

SWEET & SOUR SAUCE

Finely slice 1 onion, 1 leek, and 2 celery stalks. Cut 2 carrots into matchstick-thin strips. Heat 2 tbsp sunflower oil in a pan and cook the vegetables for 3 minutes or until softened. Blend 2 tbsp tomato ketchup, 1 tbsp soy sauce, 1 tbsp white wine vinegar, 4 tsp cornflour, and 2 tsp caster sugar, then blend in 300 ml (1/2 pint) water. Add to the pan and bring to a boil, stirring until thickened.

285

MARINATED LOIN OF PORK WITH PINEAPPLE

SERVES 8

1.5 kg (3 lb) boned loin of pork, skin removed

grilled pineapple rings and parsley sprigs to serve

MARINADE

250 ml (8 fl oz) pineapple juice

2 tbsp maple syrup

2 tbsp soy sauce

2 garlic cloves, crushed

2 tbsp chopped fresh thyme

1 tsp ground coriander

1 Make the marinade: in a large non-metallic bowl, combine the pineapple juice, maple syrup, soy sauce, garlic, thyme, and coriander. Add the pork, cover, and marinate in the refrigerator, turning occasionally, for 8 hours.

2 Remove the pork from the marinade, reserving the marinade. Put the pork flat, fat-side up, in a small roasting tin. Insert a meat thermometer, if using, into the middle of the pork. Cover loosely with foil and cook in a preheated oven at 220°C (425°F, Gas 7) for 1 hour.

3 Remove the foil and pour the marinade over the pork. Return to the oven and cook for 20–30 minutes or until the marinade has darkened and the juices run clear when the meat is pierced with a fine skewer. The meat thermometer should register 80°C (175°F).

4 Transfer the pork to a carving board, cover with foil, and leave to stand for 10 minutes. Strain the cooking juices and remove the fat (see box, below), then reheat. Serve the pork sliced, with the juices poured over, garnished with pineapple and parsley.

Removing the fat

Skim the layer of fat from the surface of the juices, using a skimmer or spoon.

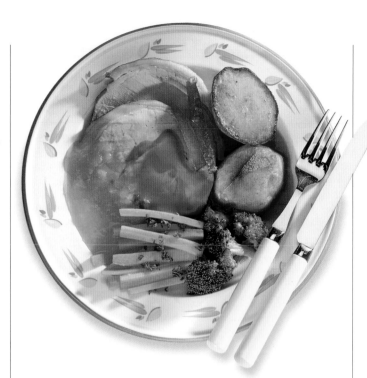

ROAST LEG OF PORK

SERVES 6–8

2 kg (4 lb) leg of pork, skin removed and scored at 1 cm (1/2 in) intervals

sunflower oil for brushing

salt and black pepper

1 carrot, thickly sliced

1 onion, thickly sliced

1 tbsp plain flour

300 ml (1/2 pint) chicken stock

apple sauce to serve (page 285)

1 Brush the scored side of the pork skin with a little oil, and sprinkle generously with salt and black pepper. Place on a rack in a small roasting tin.

2 Remove as much fat as possible from the pork, especially on top where the skin has been removed. Put the pork into another roasting tin, and arrange the carrot and onion around it. Brush the meat with a little oil, season well, and insert a meat thermometer, if using, into the middle of the pork.

3 Put both roasting tins in a preheated oven at 180°C (350°F, Gas 4), with the pork skin at the top.

4 Roast for 2 1/2 hours or until the thermometer registers 80°C (175°F). Transfer the pork to a carving board, cover with foil, and leave to stand for 10 minutes. If the crackling is not really crisp, increase the oven temperature to 200°C (400°F, Gas 6) and let it continue to cook while making the gravy.

5 Put the roasting tin on the hob. Remove the carrot and onion and spoon off all but 1 tbsp of the fat from the tin.

6 Add the flour and cook, stirring to dissolve any sediment from the bottom of the tin, for 1 minute. Pour in the stock and bring to a boil. Simmer for 3 minutes, then season, and strain into a gravy boat. Serve the pork with the gravy and apple sauce.

Cook's know-how

The high oven temperature needed for crisp crackling can make meat tough and dry. Removing the skin and cooking it separately, above the pork, avoids this problem.

MADEIRA PORK WITH PAPRIKA

SERVES 4

30 g (1 oz) butter

2 tbsp sunflower oil

750 g (1½ lb) pork fillet (tenderloin), trimmed and cut diagonally into 1 cm (½ in) slices

1 onion, chopped

1 large red pepper, halved, seeded, and cut into strips

1 tbsp paprika

1 tbsp plain flour

300 ml (½ pint) chicken stock

75 ml (2½ fl oz) Madeira

175 g (6 oz) button mushrooms

1 tsp tomato purée

150 ml (¼ pint) single cream

salt and black pepper

1 Melt the butter with the oil in a large frying pan. When the butter is foaming, add the pork slices, in batches if necessary, and cook over a high heat for about 3 minutes until just beginning to brown. Lift out with a slotted spoon and drain on paper towels.

2 Add the onion and red pepper and cook, stirring, for 2 minutes. Add the paprika and flour, and cook, stirring, for 1 minute. Remove the pan from the heat and blend in the stock. Return to the heat and add the Madeira, mushrooms, and tomato purée. Simmer for 2–3 minutes.

3 Return the pork to the pan and season with salt and pepper. Cover and simmer very gently for 20 minutes or until the pork is tender. Stir in the cream, taste for seasoning, and heat through gently. Serve hot.

Healthy option

The cream makes the sauce both look and taste rich, but it can be omitted and the sauce will still be good. Pork fillet (tenderloin) is an excellent cut of meat to use if you are trying to cut down on fat because it is very lean and yet tender and succulent.

BACON-WRAPPED PORK IN VERMOUTH SAUCE

SERVES 6

2 pork fillets (tenderloins), about 375 g (12 oz) each, trimmed

2 tbsp Dijon mustard

salt and black pepper

375 g (12 oz) streaky bacon rashers, rinds removed

VERMOUTH SAUCE

30 g (1 oz) butter

1 tbsp olive oil

1 shallot, finely chopped

1 tbsp plain flour

200 ml (7 fl oz) chicken stock

90 ml (3 fl oz) dry vermouth

125 g (4 oz) button or chestnut mushrooms, sliced

1 Spread the pork fillets with the mustard and season with salt and pepper. Stretch the bacon rashers with the back of a knife and wrap around the fillets (see box, right).

2 Place the fillets in a roasting tin and cook in a preheated oven at 220°C (425°F, Gas 7), turning the fillets halfway through cooking, for 30–35 minutes until the juices from the pork run clear and the bacon is crisp and golden.

3 Meanwhile, make the sauce: melt the butter with the oil in a small pan. When the butter is foaming, add the shallot, and cook gently until softened.

4 Add the flour and cook, stirring, for 1 minute. Gradually blend in the stock and vermouth. Bring to a boil, add the mushrooms, and simmer for 15 minutes.

5 Transfer the pork to a warmed platter. Spoon off the fat from the roasting tin and strain the juices into the sauce. Heat through and taste for seasoning. Serve with the pork.

Wrapping pork fillets

Overlap half of the bacon rashers on a work surface. Lay 1 pork fillet across the bacon and plait the rashers around the meat. Secure with a fine skewer. Repeat with the second pork fillet.

GRILLED PORK CHOPS WITH MANGO SAUCE

SERVES 4

4 pork loin chops, on the bone

sunflower oil for brushing

salt and black pepper

1 ripe mango

flat-leaf parsley to garnish

MANGO SAUCE

1 ripe mango

150 ml (1/4 pint) chicken stock

1 tbsp mango chutney

1 Cut through the fat at regular intervals on the edge of each pork chop (this will help prevent the chops from curling up during cooking).

2 Brush the chops on each side with oil and sprinkle with black pepper. Put under a hot grill, 10 cm (4 in) from the heat, and grill for 6 minutes on each side or until cooked through (timing depends on size of chops).

3 Meanwhile, make the mango sauce: peel, stone, and cube the mango (page 466), then purée in a food processor until smooth.

4 Put into a small saucepan with the stock, mango chutney, and salt and pepper. Bring to a boil and simmer for about 3 minutes until heated through. Taste for seasoning.

5 Peel the remaining mango and cut it into 2 pieces lengthwise, slightly off-centre to miss the stone. Cut the flesh from around the stone. Slice the flesh into thin strips

6 Arrange the mango strips on the chops, garnish with flat-leaf parsley, and serve with the mango sauce.

PORK WITH CHILLI & COCONUT

SERVES 6

750 g (1 1/2 lb) pork fillet (tenderloin), trimmed and cut into 5 mm (1/4 in) strips

2 tbsp sunflower oil

8 spring onions, cut into 2.5 cm (1 in) pieces

1 large red pepper, halved, seeded, and cut into thin strips

1 x 400 g (13 oz) can chopped tomatoes

60 g (2 oz) creamed coconut, coarsely chopped

4 tbsp water

2 tbsp chopped fresh coriander

1 tbsp lemon juice

salt and black pepper

coriander sprigs to garnish

SPICE MIX

2.5 cm (1 in) piece of fresh root ginger, peeled and grated

2 fresh red chillies, halved, seeded, and finely chopped

1 garlic clove, crushed

1 tbsp mild curry powder

1 Make the spice mix: in a bowl, combine the ginger, chillies, garlic, and curry powder, and season with salt and pepper. Turn the pork in the mix, cover, and leave to marinate in the refrigerator for 2 hours.

2 Heat a wok or large frying pan, add the oil, and heat until hot. Add the strips of pork in batches, and stir-fry over a high heat for 5 minutes or until browned all over.

3 Add the spring onions and stir-fry for 1 minute. Add the red pepper and stir-fry for 1 minute, then add the tomatoes, coconut, and measured water. Bring to a boil, cover, and simmer very gently for 15 minutes or until the pork is tender.

4 Add the chopped coriander, lemon juice, and salt and pepper to taste. Garnish with coriander sprigs before serving.

PORK CHOPS WITH SPINACH & MUSHROOM STUFFING

Tender pork loin chops are topped with a spinach and chestnut mushroom stuffing mixture, and finished off under the grill with Gruyère cheese. A wedge of the stuffing accompanies each chop as a delicious extra.

SERVES 6

6 lean pork loin chops, on the bone

olive oil for brushing

SPINACH AND MUSHROOM STUFFING

1 tbsp olive oil

1 large onion, chopped

150 g (5 oz) chestnut mushrooms, roughly chopped

250 g (8 oz) baby spinach leaves, shredded

90 g (3 oz) fresh breadcrumbs

salt and black pepper

about 90 g (3 oz) Gruyère cheese, cut into 6 thin slices

1 Make the stuffing: heat the oil in a large frying pan, add the onion, cover, and cook gently for about 15 minutes or until soft.

2 Uncover the pan, increase the heat, and add the mushrooms. Stir-fry for 2–3 minutes, then add the spinach and stir-fry until it has just wilted. Add the breadcrumbs, season with salt and pepper, and stir well. Leave to cool.

3 Brush the chops on each side with oil, and season well. Put under a hot grill, 10 cm (4 in) from the heat, and grill for 7–8 minutes each side or until cooked through and golden brown.

4 Spoon 1 tablespoon of the stuffing mixture on top of each chop, and top with a slice of cheese. Grill for 3–4 minutes until the cheese has melted.

5 Meanwhile, heat a little oil in a small non-stick frying pan. Put the remaining stuffing into the pan, then press down and level with a wooden spoon so that the stuffing forms a thick pancake.

6 Fry the stuffing for about 5 minutes until the underside is brown and crisp. Transfer the pan to the grill for 2–3 minutes to brown the top. Turn upside down onto a plate, and slice into 6 wedges. Serve a wedge of stuffing with each chop.

PORK CHOPS WITH ORANGES

SERVES 6

6 boneless pork loin chops

3 tbsp coarse-grain mustard

125 g (4 oz) demerara sugar

3 small oranges

90 ml (3 fl oz) orange juice

salt and black pepper

1 Spread both sides of each pork chop with the mustard, and sprinkle one side with half of the demerara sugar. Arrange the chops, sugared-side down, in a single layer in a shallow ovenproof dish.

2 With a sharp knife, carefully peel the oranges, removing all the pith. Cut the oranges into thin slices.

3 Cover the chops with the orange slices. Pour the orange juice over the top, season with salt and pepper, and sprinkle with the remaining sugar.

4 Cook, uncovered, in a preheated oven at 200°C (400°F, Gas 6) for about 35 minutes, basting the chops occasionally, until cooked through. Serve hot.

PORK STEAKS WITH MIXED PEPPERCORNS

SERVES 4

4 lean boneless pork steaks

salt

3–4 tbsp mixed or black
  peppercorns

30 g (1 oz) butter

350 ml (12 fl oz) dry white wine

350 ml (12 fl oz) chicken stock

175 ml (6 fl oz) double cream

1 Season the steaks on each side with salt. Coarsely crush the peppercorns, spread them on a plate, and press the steaks into them to encrust the surface of the meat. Turn the steaks over and repeat on the other side. Cover and set aside for about 30 minutes, if you have the time.

2 Melt the butter in a large frying pan, add the steaks, and cook over a medium heat for 5 minutes on each side or until the meat is just cooked through but still juicy. Lift the steaks out, and keep hot.

3 Pour the wine into the pan and boil until it has reduced by half, stirring to mix in the peppercorns and the sediment from the bottom of the pan.

4 Pour in the stock and cook for 5 minutes. Strain the sauce to remove the peppercorns, then return to the pan and boil for 3 minutes or until the sauce is reduced but not too thick.

5 Add the cream and cook, stirring, over a high heat until the sauce is reduced and thickened. Return the pork steaks to the pan, heat through, and serve at once.

SWEET & SOUR CHINESE SPARE RIBS

SERVES 4

1.25 kg (2¹/₂ lb) pork spare ribs

salt and black pepper

spring onions to garnish (optional)

SWEET & SOUR SAUCE

2.5 cm (1 in) piece of fresh root
  ginger, peeled and grated

2 garlic cloves, crushed

2 tbsp soy sauce

2 tbsp rice wine or dry sherry

2 tbsp hoisin sauce

2 tbsp tomato purée

1 tbsp sesame oil (optional)

1 tbsp caster sugar

1 Lay the ribs in 1 layer in a roasting tin, season with salt and pepper, and cook in a preheated oven at 140°C (275°F, Gas 1) for 1¹/₂ hours.

2 Make the sauce: combine all the ingredients in a small pan and heat gently.

3 Spoon the sauce over the ribs, turning them to coat. Increase the oven temperature to 180°C (350°F, Gas 4), and cook for 25–30 minutes. Serve hot, garnished with spring onions if you like.

SPICY SPARE RIBS

Add 1 tbsp brown sugar, ¹/₂ tsp grated nutmeg, and ¹/₄ tsp each ground cloves and ground cinnamon to the sauce.

Cook's know-how

Spare ribs are excellent for a barbecue, but they are best partially cooked first or they will burn on the outside before the meat is properly cooked inside. Cook them in the oven as in step 1 and coat with the sweet and sour sauce, then cook over hot charcoal for 15 minutes on each side.

WILTSHIRE PORK CASSEROLE

SERVES 8

2 tbsp sunflower oil
1.5 kg (3 lb) shoulder of pork, trimmed and cut into 3.5 cm (1 1/2 in) cubes
40 g (1 1/2 oz) plain flour
450 ml (3/4 pint) chicken stock
4 tbsp white wine vinegar
3 tbsp clear honey
2 tbsp soy sauce
250 g (8 oz) large mushrooms, quartered
250 g (8 oz) ready-to-eat pitted prunes
salt and black pepper
chopped parsley to garnish

1 Heat the oil in a large flameproof casserole. Add the pork in batches and cook over a medium to high heat for 5 minutes or until golden brown all over.

2 Return all of the meat to the casserole, sprinkle in the flour, and cook, stirring, for 1 minute.

3 Stir in the chicken stock, white wine vinegar, honey, and soy sauce, season with of salt and pepper, and bring to a boil. Cover and cook in a preheated oven at 160°C (325°F, Gas 3) for 2 hours.

4 Stir the mushrooms and prunes into the casserole and cook for 1 hour or until the pork is tender. Taste for seasoning and garnish with parsley before serving.

BOSTON PORK & BEAN CASSEROLE

Add 2 tbsp tomato purée with the stock and substitute 1 × 400 g (13 oz) can haricot beans for the mushrooms and prunes.

Healthy option

Use lean pork fillet (tenderloin) instead of shoulder, which can be fatty, and reduce the cooking time to 50–60 minutes in the oven in step 3.

AFELIA

SERVES 4

750 g (1 1/2 lb) boneless spare rib pork chops, cut into 3.5 cm (1 1/2 in) cubes
90 ml (3 fl oz) olive oil
1 large onion, chopped
3 garlic cloves, crushed
250 ml (8 fl oz) beef or chicken stock
250 ml (8 fl oz) red wine
1/2 tsp cumin seeds

MARINADE

250 ml (8 fl oz) red wine
2 tbsp crushed coriander seeds
1/2 tsp ground cinnamon
salt and black pepper

1 Make the marinade: in a large bowl, combine the red wine, coriander seeds, and cinnamon, and season with salt and pepper. Toss the pork in the marinade, cover, and leave to marinate in the refrigerator overnight.

2 Remove the pork from the marinade, reserving the marinade. Pat the pork dry with paper towels.

3 Heat the oil in a large frying pan, add the onion and garlic, and cook gently, stirring occasionally, for a few minutes until soft but not coloured.

4 Add the pork and cook over a medium to high heat for 5 minutes or until golden brown all over. Discard any excess fat. Pour in the reserved marinade, the stock, and wine, and bring to a boil. Simmer for 1 hour or until the meat is tender.

5 Remove the meat with a slotted spoon and transfer to a shallow ovenproof dish into which it just fits in 1 layer. Skim any fat from the sauce, then strain to remove the coriander seeds. Pour the sauce over the meat, sprinkle with cumin seeds and salt, and cook in a preheated oven at 200°C (400°F, Gas 6) for 40 minutes or until crisp and browned.

Healthy option

If you cook the pork in a non-stick frying pan, you can reduce the amount of oil to 1–2 tbsp.

DANISH MEATBALLS

SERVES 4–6

500 g (1 lb) minced pork
1 small onion, very finely chopped
30 g (1 oz) plain flour, plus extra for coating
1 tsp chopped fresh thyme
1/4 tsp paprika
1 egg, beaten
salt and black pepper
a little milk
30 g (1 oz) butter
1 tbsp sunflower oil
Greek yogurt or soured cream to serve
chopped fresh thyme to garnish

TOMATO SAUCE

30 g (1 oz) butter
30 g (1 oz) plain flour
450 ml (3/4 pint) chicken stock
1 x 400 g (13 oz) can chopped tomatoes
1 tbsp tomato purée
1 garlic clove, crushed
1 bay leaf

1 Mix the pork, onion, flour, thyme, paprika, and egg. Season, and add enough milk to give a soft, not sticky, texture.

2 Shape the mixture into 20 ovals, using 2 dessertspoons or your hands. Roll lightly in flour, then chill in the refrigerator.

3 Make the tomato sauce: melt the butter in a pan, sprinkle in the flour, and cook, stirring, for 1 minute.

4 Blend in the stock, then add the tomatoes, tomato purée, garlic, and bay leaf, and season with salt and pepper. Bring to a boil, stirring until thickened. Cover and simmer for 20–25 minutes.

5 Meanwhile, melt the butter with the oil in a flameproof casserole. Cook the meatballs in batches, for 5 minutes or until browned all over. Lift out and drain on paper towels.

6 Pour the fat out of the casserole. Return the meatballs, add the sauce, and bring to a boil. Cover and cook in a preheated oven at 180°C (350°F, Gas 4) for 30 minutes. Spoon over a little yogurt or soured cream and garnish with thyme. Serve hot.

PASTICCIO

SERVES 6

1 tbsp sunflower oil
500 g (1 lb) minced pork or beef
2 onions, chopped
3 garlic cloves, crushed
1 x 400 g (13 oz) can chopped tomatoes
90 g (3 oz) tomato purée
90 ml (3 fl oz) red wine
2 bay leaves
1 tsp sugar
1 tsp dried oregano
1/2 tsp ground cinnamon (optional)
250 g (8 oz) short-cut macaroni
salt and black pepper

CHEESE SAUCE

30 g (1 oz) butter
30 g (1 oz) plain flour
300 ml (1/2 pint) milk
175 g (6 oz) mature Cheddar cheese, grated
1 egg yolk
1 tsp Dijon mustard

1 Heat the sunflower oil in a large frying pan, add the meat, onions, and garlic, and cook over a medium heat for 5 minutes or until lightly browned.

2 Add the tomatoes, tomato purée, and wine. Bring to a boil and simmer for 15 minutes.

3 Add the bay leaves, sugar, oregano, and cinnamon (if using), and season with salt and pepper. Simmer gently for about 10 minutes or until the sauce is thickened.

4 Meanwhile, cook the macaroni in boiling salted water for 8–10 minutes until just tender. Drain and set aside.

5 Make the cheese sauce: melt the butter in a saucepan, sprinkle in the flour, and cook, stirring, for 1 minute. Remove from the heat and gradually blend in the milk. Bring to a boil, stirring constantly, until the mixture thickens. Simmer for 2–3 minutes. Remove from the heat and stir in the cheese, egg yolk, and mustard, and season with salt and pepper.

6 Spoon half of the meat mixture into an ovenproof dish and add half of the macaroni. Cover with the remaining meat mixture, then top with the remaining macaroni and the cheese sauce.

7 Bake the pasticcio in a preheated oven at 180°C (350°F, Gas 4) for 40 minutes or until the topping is golden.

MUSTARD-GLAZED HAM

Gammon tastes best when it is cooked on the bone, especially if it is home-baked. Here, gammon slowly steam-roasts in its own juices, spiked with cider, and it is coated with a tangy glaze. Watercress and orange slices are the perfect finishing touch. Once gammon is cooked it is properly called ham.

SERVES 16–20

4–5 kg (8–10 lb) smoked gammon

400 ml (14 fl oz) cider or apple juice

3 tbsp English mustard

90 g (3 oz) demerara sugar

LEMON MUSTARD SAUCE

4 tbsp olive oil

juice of 1 lemon

1 tbsp caster sugar

2 tsp coarse-grain mustard

salt and black pepper

150 ml (¼ pint) crème fraîche

1 Put the gammon into a large container, cover with cold water, and leave to soak for at least 12 hours.

2 Drain and rinse the gammon. Arrange 2 pieces of foil, long enough to cover the gammon, across a large roasting tin.

3 Pour the cider into the foil. Stand a wire rack on the foil and stand the gammon on the rack. Insert a meat thermometer, if using, into the thickest part of the meat.

4 Wrap the foil loosely over the gammon, leaving plenty of space for air to circulate. Place the gammon just below the middle of a preheated oven and cook at 160°C (325°F, Gas 3) for 20 minutes per 500 g (1 lb). The meat thermometer should register 75°C (170°F). Remove the ham from the oven and leave to cool for a few minutes.

5 Increase the oven temperature to 230°C (450°F, Gas 8). Transfer the ham to a board, drain the cooking juices from the foil, and discard. Glaze the gammon with the mustard and sugar (see box, right).

6 Return the ham to the rack in the roasting tin. Cover any lean parts with foil, return to the oven, and cook, turning the roasting tin if necessary, for 15–20 minutes until the glaze is golden brown all over.

7 Meanwhile, make the lemon mustard sauce: put the olive oil, lemon juice, caster sugar, and mustard into a screw-top jar, season with salt and pepper, and shake vigorously to mix the ingredients together.

8 Put the crème fraîche into a bowl and stir in the lemon and mustard mixture. Taste for seasoning and leave to chill in the refrigerator until needed.

9 Carve the ham into slices and serve either warm or cold, with the lemon mustard sauce.

Glazing ham

Cut away the skin with a sharp knife, leaving behind a thin layer of fat. Discard the skin.

Score the fat all over in a diamond pattern, so that the glaze penetrates the fat.

Spread a generous layer of mustard over the fat, using a palette knife or your hands.

Press the demerara sugar on to the layer of mustard, making sure it is evenly coated all over.

BOSTON BAKED BEANS

SERVES 6–8

375 g (12 oz) dried haricot beans

60 g (2 oz) dark muscovado sugar

2 tbsp tomato purée

2 tsp black treacle

2 tsp golden syrup

2 tsp mustard powder

2 tsp salt

black pepper

250 g (8 oz) piece of streaky bacon, cut into 2.5 cm (1 in) cubes

3 onions, quartered

600 ml (1 pint) water

1 Put the haricot beans into a large bowl, cover with plenty of cold water, and leave to soak overnight.

2 Drain the beans, and rinse under cold running water. Put the beans into a saucepan, cover with cold water, and bring to a boil. Boil rapidly for 10 minutes, then partially cover the pan and simmer for 30 minutes. Drain and set aside.

3 Put the sugar, tomato purée, black treacle, golden syrup, and mustard into a large flameproof casserole. Season with salt and pepper and heat gently, stirring constantly.

4 Add the bacon and onions to the casserole with the drained beans and measured water. Bring to a boil, cover tightly, and cook in a preheated oven at 140°C (275°F, Gas 1), stirring occasionally, for 4½–5 hours. Taste for seasoning before serving.

Healthy option

Boston baked beans traditionally contain belly pork or bacon, which makes the dish quite high in fat. Without the pork or bacon, the beans make a tasty vegetarian main course that is much lower in fat, and if you serve it with crusty bread and a leafy green salad it makes a well-balanced, nutritious meal.

FARMER'S BACON BAKE

SERVES 6–8

1 x 750 g (1½ lb) bacon joint

a few parsley stalks

6 black peppercorns

1 bay leaf

4 potatoes, cut into large chunks

4 carrots, thickly sliced

4 celery stalks, thickly sliced

chopped parsley to garnish

CHEESE SAUCE

45 g (1½ oz) butter

45 g (1½ oz) plain flour

200 ml (7 fl oz) milk

90 g (3 oz) mature Cheddar cheese, grated

salt and black pepper

1 Put the bacon joint into a large pan, cover with cold water, and bring to a boil. Drain, rinse, and cover with fresh cold water. Add the parsley stalks, peppercorns, and bay leaf, and bring to a boil. Cover and simmer very gently for 45 minutes.

2 Add the potatoes, carrots, and celery and bring back to a boil. Cover and simmer very gently for 20 minutes or until the meat and vegetables are tender. Drain, reserving the cooking liquid, and allow the bacon to cool slightly.

3 Remove the rind and fat from the bacon, cut the meat into bite-sized pieces, and place in a shallow baking dish with the vegetables. Keep hot.

4 Make the cheese sauce: melt the butter in a saucepan, sprinkle in the flour, and cook, stirring, for 1 minute. Remove from the heat and gradually blend in the milk and 250 ml (8 fl oz) of the reserved cooking liquid. Bring to a boil, stirring constantly until the mixture thickens. Simmer for 2–3 minutes. Add three-quarters of the cheese, and season with salt and pepper.

5 Pour the sauce over the meat and vegetables and sprinkle with the remaining cheese. Bake in a preheated oven at 180°C (350°F, Gas 4) for 30 minutes or until the cheese topping is bubbling. Garnish with chopped parsley before serving.

SAUSAGE CASSOULET

Cassoulet is a hearty dish from Languedoc in the south-west of France.
This is a simple and satisfying version. The types of meat used in more traditional recipes
may include duck, goose, or lamb.

SERVES 8

375 g (12 oz) dried haricot beans

2 tbsp olive oil

500 g (1 lb) coarse pork sausages, such as Toulouse

250 g (8 oz) piece of smoked bacon, cut into strips

2 large onions, sliced

250 g (8 oz) piece of garlic sausage, cut into 2.5 cm (1 in) chunks

2 x 400 g (13 oz) cans chopped tomatoes

300 ml (½ pint) chicken stock

150 ml (¼ pint) dry white wine

2 tbsp tomato purée

2 garlic cloves, crushed

1 bouquet garni

salt and black pepper

125–175 g (4–6 oz) fresh white breadcrumbs

chopped parsley to garnish

1 Put the haricot beans into a large bowl, cover with plenty of cold water, and leave to soak overnight.

2 Drain the beans, and rinse under cold running water. Put the beans into a saucepan, cover with fresh cold water, and bring to a boil. Boil rapidly for 10 minutes, then simmer for 30 minutes or until just tender. Drain.

3 Heat the olive oil in a large flameproof casserole, add the sausages and bacon, and cook for 5 minutes or until browned all over. Lift out and drain on paper towels. Thickly slice the sausages.

4 Pour off all but 1 tbsp of the fat from the casserole. Add the onions and cook gently, stirring occasionally, for a few minutes until soft but not coloured.

5 Return the bacon and sausages to the casserole, add the beans, the garlic sausage, tomatoes, stock, wine, tomato purée, garlic, and bouquet garni. Season with salt and pepper and bring to a boil.

6 Cover and cook in a preheated oven at 160°C (325°F, Gas 3) for 1 hour, then sprinkle the breadcrumbs over the top and continue cooking, uncovered, for 30 minutes or until the topping is golden brown. Garnish with chopped parsley before serving.

SAUSAGE BAKE

SERVES 6

1 tbsp sunflower oil

1 kg (2 lb) coarse-cut pork sausages

500 g (1 lb) leeks, thickly sliced

750 g (1½ lb) potatoes, cut into 5 mm (¼ in) slices

90 g (3 oz) red lentils

salt and black pepper

2 bay leaves

2 cloves

1 garlic clove, crushed

900 ml (1½ pints) chicken stock

chopped parsley to garnish

1 Heat the oil in a large flameproof casserole and brown the sausages. Lift out, then cut into thick slices.

2 Layer the leeks, potatoes, sausages, and lentils in the casserole, adding seasoning and placing the bay leaves, cloves, and garlic among the layers. Top with a layer of potatoes.

3 Pour in the stock and bring to a boil. Cover tightly and cook in a preheated oven at 160°C (325°F, Gas 3) for 2½ hours, checking the liquid level occasionally.

4 Remove the lid, increase the oven temperature to 200°C (400°F, Gas 6), and cook for 20–25 minutes until the potato is browned. Garnish with parsley and serve hot.

TOAD IN THE HOLE WITH ONION SAUCE

SERVES 4

400 g (13 oz) pork sausagemeat

1 leek, finely chopped

2 tbsp chopped fresh sage or 1 tbsp dried sage

1 tbsp chopped parsley

3 tbsp sunflower oil

3 onions, chopped

2 tbsp plain flour

300 ml (1/2 pint) milk

250 ml (8 fl oz) chicken stock

chopped parsley to garnish

BATTER

125 g (4 oz) self-raising flour

3 eggs, beaten

300 ml (1/2 pint) milk

1 tbsp chopped parsley

salt and black pepper

1 Make the batter: sift the flour into a bowl. Make a well in the middle and add the eggs and a little milk. Blend to a smooth paste, then gradually whisk in the remaining milk until the batter has the pouring consistency of cream.

2 Add the chopped parsley, season with salt and pepper, and whisk again.

3 In another bowl, combine the sausagemeat, leek, sage, and parsley, and season with salt and pepper. Shape into 12 balls and set aside.

4 Heat the oil in a saucepan, add the onions, and cook for a few minutes until soft but not coloured. Transfer one-third of the onions to 4 small ovenproof dishes or 1 large dish. Set aside the remainder.

5 Add the sausage balls to the dishes and bake in a preheated oven at 220°C (425°F, Gas 7) for about 10 minutes until brown.

6 Add the batter mixture, and return at once to the oven. Bake for 20–25 minutes until the batter is risen and golden.

7 Meanwhile, add the plain flour to the onions in the pan and cook, stirring, for 1 minute. Remove from the heat and gradually blend in the milk and stock. Bring to a boil, stirring constantly, and simmer for 2–3 minutes until the mixture thickens. Serve the toad in the hole hot, sprinkled with parsley, with the sauce handed separately.

SAUSAGE & LENTIL CASSEROLE

SERVES 6

300 g (10 oz) brown or green Puy lentils

2 bay leaves

2 tbsp sunflower oil

2 large onions, chopped

1 large potato, chopped

1 celery stalk, diced

1 carrot, diced

2 ripe tomatoes, diced

2 tbsp plain flour

250 ml (8 fl oz) chicken or vegetable stock

2–3 tbsp chopped parsley

1 tbsp chopped fresh sage or 1 1/2 tsp dried sage

salt and black pepper

500 g (1 lb) herby pork sausages

chopped parsley to garnish

1 Put the lentils and bay leaves into a saucepan, cover with water, and bring to a boil. Cover, simmer for 30 minutes or until the lentils are just tender, then drain.

2 Heat the oil in a large saucepan, add the onions, and cook gently, stirring occasionally, until softened.

3 Add the potato, celery, carrot, and tomatoes, and cook for 10 minutes or until the onions are browned and the other vegetables are softened. Using a slotted spoon, lift out the vegetables and set aside.

4 Sprinkle the flour into the pan and cook, stirring, for 1 minute. Remove the pan from the heat and gradually blend in the stock. Bring to a boil, stirring constantly, and simmer for 2–3 minutes until the sauce thickens.

5 Add the lentils to the sauce with the vegetables, parsley, and sage. Season with salt and pepper, mix well, and turn into a large ovenproof casserole.

6 Arrange the sausages on top and cook in a preheated oven at 190°C (375°F, Gas 5) for about 30 minutes until the sausages are browned all over and cooked through. Garnish with chopped parsley before serving.

7

VEGETARIAN DISHES

UNDER 30 MINUTES

BARBECUE

HALLOUMI & VEGETABLE KEBABS
Cubes of halloumi cheese, cherry tomatoes, baguette slices, and red pepper threaded on to skewers, then briefly marinated, and grilled.

SERVES 4 722 calories per serving
Takes 25 minutes   Page 321

RED BEAN & TOMATO CURRY
Rich and spicy: red kidney beans cooked with tomatoes, garlic, chilli, ginger, curry powder, turmeric, coriander, and cayenne.

SERVES 4 218 calories per serving
Takes 20 minutes   Page 320

VEGETABLE STIR-FRY WITH TOFU
Tofu marinated in soy sauce and sherry, stir-fried with carrots, ginger, mushrooms, bean sprouts, chicory, and spring onions.

SERVES 4 335 calories per serving
Takes 15 minutes, plus marinating   Page 322

30–60 MINUTES

COUSCOUS WITH ROASTED PEPPERS
Tasty and simple to make: couscous with chick peas, courgettes, carrots, and spices. Topped with peppers and almonds.

SERVES 4–6 418–279 calories per serving
Takes 45 minutes   Page 315

HIGH FIBRE

FELAFEL WITH SESAME YOGURT SAUCE
Chick pea, spring onion, herb, and spice patties, cooked until golden. Served with a creamy sauce.

SERVES 6 326 calories per serving
Takes 20 minutes, plus standing   Page 321

SPINACH & RICOTTA SAMOSAS
Light and crispy: spinach combined with ricotta cheese, onion, and nutmeg, and baked in cases of filo pastry until golden.

MAKES 4 307 calories per serving
Takes 40 minutes   Page 317

LOW FAT

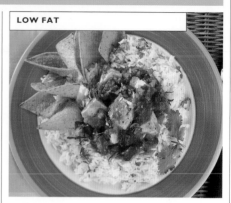

MEXICAN CHILLI WITH TOFU
Bite-sized pieces of tofu cooked with red kidney beans and tomato sauce seasoned with garlic, chilli, paprika, cumin, and oregano.

SERVES 6 257 calories per serving
Takes 35 minutes   Page 322

CARROT ROULADE
Fresh and creamy: carrot mixed with garlic, red pepper, tomatoes, and eggs, baked, then rolled around a cheese and cucumber filling.

SERVES 6–8 483–363 calories per serving
Takes 30 minutes, plus chilling   Page 327

FAMILY CHOICE

VEGETARIAN BURGERS
Butter beans with mushrooms, leeks, garlic, and chilli. Shaped into burgers, and served with crunchy dressed lettuce.

SERVES 6 134 calories per serving
Takes 30 minutes, plus chilling   Page 323

HIGH FIBRE

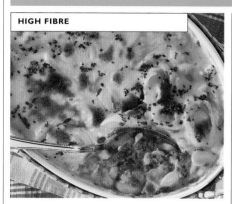

MIXED BEAN BAKE

Aduki and butter beans simmered with mushrooms, tomatoes, and parsley. Topped with leeks and a cheese sauce.

SERVES 6 376 calories per serving
Takes 60 minutes   Page 305

SPINACH ROULADE

Combined spinach, butter, and eggs, briefly baked, sprinkled with Parmesan, and rolled with a crème fraîche and mushroom filling.

SERVES 6–8 250–187 calories per serving
Takes 30 minutes, plus chilling   Page 327

ITALIAN CLASSIC

AUBERGINE PARMIGIANA

Rich and tangy: aubergine slices layered with garlic- and basil-flavoured tomato sauce, and mozzarella and Parmesan cheeses.

SERVES 6 516 calories per serving
Takes 1¼ hours, plus standing   Page 308

ITALIAN STUFFED COURGETTES

Baked courgettes with a delicious tomato and basil stuffing. Topped with capers and Fontina cheese.

SERVES 4 437 calories per serving
Takes 50 minutes   Page 310

RED LENTIL & COCONUT CURRY

Lentils cooked with coconut and seasoned with ginger, chilli, garlic, and turmeric. Topped with mustard-seed butter.

SERVES 6 481 calories per serving
Takes 40 minutes   Page 320

BARBECUE

POLENTA WITH GRILLED VEGETABLES

Barbecued strips of polenta served with marinated and barbecued courgettes, fennel, tomatoes, and red onion.

SERVES 6 319 calories per serving
Takes 45 minutes, plus marinating   Page 314

ROAST VEGETABLES NIÇOISE

Rich and aromatic: black olives, courgettes, tomatoes, red onion, and garlic, sprinkled with capers, herbes de Provence, and pepper, and baked.

SERVES 4 237 calories per serving
Takes 60 minute   Page 304

Garnished with shredded fresh basil. It is delicious served hot or cold with croûtons or toasted baguette.

GLAMORGAN SAUSAGES

Caerphilly and goat's cheeses combined with breadcrumbs, leek, walnuts, sage, lemon zest, mustard, and eggs, and fried until crisp.

SERVES 4 526 calories per serving
Takes 35 minutes, plus chilling   Page 323

OVER 60 MINUTES

MUSHROOM GOUGERE

Savoury choux pastry with a filling of mixed mushrooms, flavoured with tarragon, and baked until golden brown.

SERVES 4 558 calories per serving

Takes 1½ hours, plus chilling · Page 316

SPINACH GNOCCHI WITH TOMATO SAUCE

Dumplings of spinach, ricotta and Parmesan cheeses, and eggs, served with tomato sauce.

SERVES 4 738 calories per serving

Takes 1¼ hours, plus chilling · Page 314

ECONOMICAL

COUNTRY VEGETABLE PIES

Carrots and parsnips baked with onion, garlic, and parsley sauce. Topped with mashed potato for a nourishing meal.

SERVES 6 428 calories per serving

Takes 1¼ hours · Page 305

HIGH FIBRE

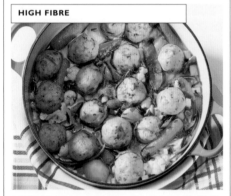

VEGETABLE & BARLEY CASSEROLE

Pearl barley, shallots, carrots, parsnips, courgettes, mangetout, and cauliflower, cooked with stock. Topped with dumplings.

SERVES 6 339 calories per serving

Takes 1¼ hours · Page 315

POTATO, CELERIAC, & PARMESAN GRATIN

Potatoes and celeriac baked with cream and ricotta cheese, breadcrumbs and Parmesan.

SERVES 6 451 calories per serving

Takes 1¾ hours · Page 308

CHESTNUT LOAF

Chestnuts baked with potatoes and celery, flavoured with garlic, parsley, soy sauce, and tomato purée. Served with spicy tomato salsa.

SERVES 6 226 calories per serving

Takes 1¼ hours · Page 326

PICNIC FARE

TOMATO & OLIVE TART

Poppyseed pastry base baked with a topping of onions, tomatoes, tomato purée, basil, garlic, vignotte cheese, and black olives.

SERVES 8 377 calories per serving

Takes 60 minutes, plus chilling · Page 316

STUFFED RED PEPPERS

Baked peppers with a nourishing stuffing of button mushrooms, onion, rice, red lentils, stock, pine nuts, and parsley.

SERVES 4 622 calories per serving

Takes 1½ hours · Page 309

CHEESE-TOPPED BAKED AUBERGINES

Aubergines spiked with garlic slivers dipped in herbs and olive oil. Topped with Gorgonzola and Cheddar cheeses.

SERVES 4 447 calories per serving

Takes 1¼ hours · Page 309

OVER 60 MINUTES

MUSHROOM LASAGNE

Lasagne layered with mushroom and tomato sauce, spinach balls, béchamel sauce, and grated Cheddar cheese, then baked.

SERVES 6 684 calories per serving

Takes 1¼ hours · Page 311

DAIRY-FREE LASAGNE

Tomato sauce layered with lasagne, lightly browned aubergine slices, and spinach, topped with courgettes, and baked.

SERVES 4–6 364–243 calories per serving

Takes 60 minutes, plus standing · Page 311

DINNER PARTY

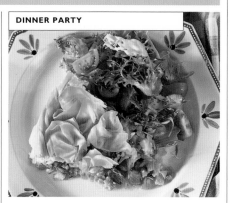

SPICED AUBERGINES WITH FILO CRUST

Diced aubergine, onions, Caerphilly cheese, lentils, red peppers, spices, and oregano, in filo pastry.

SERVES 6 569 calories per serving

Takes 1¼ hours, plus standing · Page 317

HIGH PROTEIN

CHRISTMAS NUT LOAF

Brown rice blended with ceps, mushrooms, carrots, parsley, and rosemary, and baked in a loaf tin with walnuts, Brazil nuts, pine nuts, and Cheddar cheese.

SERVES 6–8 600–450 calories per serving

Takes 2½ hours, plus soaking · Page 326

Garnished with rosemary sprigs, served in slices, and accompanied by cranberry sauce.

FAMILY CHOICE

CHEESE & VEGETABLE PIE

A variety of vegetables mixed with parsley and marjoram, in a Cheddar cheese and mustard sauce. Topped with cheese pastry.

SERVES 6 406 calories per serving

Takes 1½ hours, plus chilling · Page 304

WINTER VEGETABLE TERRINE

Three colourful layers of puréed carrot, celeriac, and broccoli, baked and served in slices.

SERVES 4–6 142–95 calories per serving

Takes 1¾ hours, plus chilling · Page 328

DINNER PARTY

BAKED MARROW WITH COUSCOUS

Marrow slices filled with a mixture of steamed couscous, mushrooms, lemon, spring onions, yogurt, mint, and olives, then baked.

SERVES 4 247 calories per serving

Takes 1¼ hours · Page 310

SUMMER VEGETABLE TERRINE

Aubergine and red and yellow peppers layered with a soft cheese mixture, wrapped in spinach leaves, and baked.

SERVES 8 194 calories per serving

Takes 2¼ hours, plus chilling · Page 328

VEGETARIAN KNOW-HOW

THERE ARE TWO BASIC types of vegetarian diet. A vegan diet is the strictest – vegans do not eat any meat, poultry, fish, eggs, or dairy products – while a vegetarian diet excludes meat, poultry, and fish, but may include eggs and dairy products. In addition, there is the "demi-vegetarian" diet, which can include fish and even poultry. With such a great variety of foods from which to choose, vegetarian diets, based largely on complex carbohydrates, pulses, vegetables, fruits, nuts, and seeds, can be imaginative and nutritious.

MAINTAINING A BALANCED DIET

Fish, meat, poultry, dairy products, and eggs are high-quality protein foods – they contain all the essential dietary amino acids (the building blocks of protein) that the body needs. Many vegetarians replace fish, meat, and poultry with eggs, cheese, and other dairy products, but this is not the ideal solution as many dairy foods are high in saturated fats and calories.

A healthy alternative in a vegetarian diet is to focus on protein-rich pulses, nuts, and seeds. The protein these foods offer does not contain all 8 of the essential amino acids (with the exception of that from soya beans, which is "complete"), but it is easy to enhance their nutritional value – simply eat them with bread, pasta, and rice or other grains. Examples of vegetarian protein combinations drawn from cuisines around the world are beans or dhal (lentils) and rice, hummus and pitta bread, or a mixed nut, lentil, and vegetable salad.

Another dietary interaction that vegetarians should be aware of is that between iron and vitamin C. The form of iron found in meat is easily absorbed by the body, whereas the iron in vegetables, nuts, grains, pulses, and eggs needs a helping hand. This is provided by vitamin C, which enhances iron uptake. So when planning meals, include vitamin C-rich foods such as fresh fruit (in particular citrus, berries, and kiwi fruit) and vegetables (peppers, tomatoes, broccoli, mange-tout, and cabbages are all good sources).

TOFU

Tofu is a high-protein food manufactured from soya beans. It is low in fat and calories, so can make a healthy basis for many vegetarian dishes. It is very bland (unless it is smoked), but easily absorbs flavours from marinades and sauces. Silken tofu has a soft, creamy texture: use it in sauces, dips, and puddings. Firm tofu, which has a texture similar to feta cheese, can be stir-fried, grilled, or casseroled. Other vegetarian meat substitutes include TVP (textured vegetable protein), which is also made from soya beans, and Quorn.

A gelatine substitute

Gelatine is a natural protein found in the bones, skin, and connective tissues of animals. Commercial powdered gelatine is derived from pig skin, and is thus unacceptable in a vegetarian diet. The most common substitutes are agar-agar (or kanten) and carrageen (or Irish moss), both of which are derived from seaweeds. They have stronger setting properties than gelatine, so less is needed. Follow the packet instructions for amounts to use.

VEGETABLE STOCK

Add any vegetable trimmings you have (celery tops or tomato skins, for example), or vary the ingredients to emphasize the flavour of the dish in which you want to use the stock.

1 Coarsely chop 2 onions, 1 leek, 3 celery stalks, and 2–3 carrots. Put into a large saucepan or stockpot and add 1 large bouquet garni, plus 1 crushed garlic clove, if wished.

2 Add 1.25 litres (2 pints) water and bring to a boil. Skim off any scum that rises to the surface, then lower the heat and simmer for 30 minutes.

3 Strain the stock through a sieve. If not using immediately, leave to cool, then cover and store in the refrigerator for up to 5 days or in the freezer for up to 1 month.

COOKING PULSES

Pulses are the dried, edible seeds of the legume family – beans, peas, and lentils. Stored in a cool, dark place, they will keep for up to 6 months. They're easy to prepare, but if you want to save time you can use canned pulses, which are already cooked.

1 Put the pulses into a large bowl and cover with plenty of cold water. Leave to soak for the recommended time (see below). Drain and rinse in cold water.

2 Put into a saucepan and add cold water – about twice their volume. Bring to a boil and fast boil for 10–15 minutes. Cover and simmer until tender (see below).

Pulses know-how

Pulses are usually soaked for at least 8 hours, but you can speed up the process: boil for 3 minutes, then cover and soak for 1–2 hours.

Add salt towards the end of cooking: if it is added at the beginning, it could toughen the skins of the pulse.

Pulses double in size and weight when cooked, so if a recipe calls for 250 g (8 oz) cooked pulses, you will need 125 g (4 oz) dried weight.

Adding bicarbonate of soda to the cooking water can adversely affect the nutritional value of pulses.

WARNING

Most pulses contain toxins that we cannot digest, and these can cause symptoms of severe food poisoning. To destroy the toxins, boil the pulses rapidly for 10–15 minutes at the start of cooking, then reduce the heat to carry on cooking at a simmer. Chick peas, lentils, and split peas do not need this fast boil.

SOAKING & COOKING TIMES OF PULSES

Cooking times depend on the variety of pulse and whether it is recently dried or has been stored a long time and thus is very dry. The cooking times given below are therefore only a guide.

Pulse	Soaking	Cooking
Aduki beans	8–12 hours	45 minutes
Black-eyed beans	8–12 hours	1 hour
Butter beans	8–12 hours	1–1 1/2 hours
Chick peas	8–12 hours	2 hours
Flageolet beans	8–12 hours	1–1 1/2 hours
Haricot beans	8–12 hours	1–1 1/2 hours
Red lentils	not required	20–30 minutes
Green lentils	not required	30–45 minutes
Mung beans (whole)	8–12 hours	45 minutes
Red kidney beans	8–12 hours	1 3/4 hours
Soya beans	10–12 hours	2 1/2–4 hours
Split peas	not required	2 hours

GRAINS

Whole grains are first-class sources of carbohydrate, fibre, vitamins, and minerals.

Bulgur wheat
Also known as burghul wheat, this is made from steamed, dried, and crushed wheat kernels. It cooks very quickly, or can just be soaked and used in salads. Cracked wheat is similar, but is not pre-cooked and so takes longer to cook than bulgur wheat.

Couscous
Made from semolina, the wheat flour also used for pasta, couscous only needs to be soaked to allow the grains to swell and soften. For extra flavour, steam the couscous over a vegetable stew in a colander set over a large pot.

Pearl barley
The nutty flavour and chewy texture of this grain is delicious in vegetable soups and stews. The starch in the grain acts as a thickener too.

Polenta
Made from ground maize or corn, and also known as cornmeal, polenta is added to simmering water and stirred constantly until it is very thick. Instant polenta takes only about 8 minutes to cook. Serve warm, or leave to cool and set, then slice and grill.

Millet
Available as flakes or whole grains, millet has a delicate, slightly nutty flavour. Add a small handful to soups to thicken them.

Oats
Oatflakes, also called rolled oats, are the basis of porridge and muesli. Fine oatmeal can be used to make biscuits, bread, and oatcakes – and to thicken soups; coarser varieties can be cooked into porridge.

Quinoa
A tiny grain from South America with a slightly sweet taste, quinoa can be used like brown rice and other whole grains. Rinse it well before cooking.

ROAST VEGETABLES NIÇOISE

SERVES 4

750 g (1 1/2 lb) courgettes, sliced

1 large red onion, thinly sliced

3 garlic cloves, crushed

4 tbsp olive oil, more if needed

125 g (4 oz) black olives, pitted

2 tsp dried mixed herbs

1 tbsp capers

black pepper

250 g (8 oz) cherry tomatoes, halved

1 tbsp shredded fresh basil

1 Put the courgettes, red onion, and garlic in an ovenproof dish, drizzle with 4 tbsp oil, and toss to mix.

2 Arrange the black olives on top of the vegetables, then sprinkle with the herbs and capers, and plenty of pepper.

3 Roast in a preheated oven at 190°C (375°F, Gas 5) for 25 minutes, then add the tomatoes and roast for a further 20 minutes, checking occasionally to see if the surface is getting too dry. If it is, drizzle a little more olive oil over the vegetables.

4 Sprinkle the dish with the shredded fresh basil. Serve hot or cold.

CHEESE & VEGETABLE PIE

SERVES 6

30 g (1 oz) butter

1 onion, chopped

2 carrots, sliced

500 g (1 lb) courgettes, sliced

2 large tomatoes, chopped

125 g (4 oz) mushrooms, sliced

2 tbsp chopped parsley

1/2 tsp dried marjoram or oregano

salt and black pepper

CHEESE SAUCE

30 g (1 oz) butter

30 g (1 oz) plain flour

300 ml (1/2 pint) milk

60 g (2 oz) mature Cheddar cheese, grated

1 tsp English mustard

pinch of cayenne pepper

CHEESE PASTRY

125 g (4 oz) plain flour

60 g (2 oz) butter

60 g (2 oz) mature Cheddar cheese, grated

1 small egg, beaten

1 Make the cheese pastry: sift the flour into a bowl. Add the butter and rub in lightly until the mixture resembles fine breadcrumbs. Stir in the cheese, then bind to a soft but not sticky dough with 1 tbsp of the beaten egg and 1 tbsp cold water. Chill for 30 minutes.

2 Melt the butter in a large pan, add the onion, and cook gently for 3–5 minutes until softened. Add the carrots and cook for about 5 minutes.

3 Add the courgettes, tomatoes, mushrooms, and herbs, and season with salt and pepper. Cook over a low heat, stirring occasionally, for 10–15 minutes until softened. Remove from the heat.

4 Make the cheese sauce: melt the butter in a saucepan, add the flour, and cook, stirring, for 1 minute. Remove from the heat and gradually blend in the milk.

5 Bring to a boil, stirring until the mixture thickens. Simmer for 2–3 minutes, then stir in the cheese, mustard, and cayenne, and season with salt and pepper. Stir the vegetables into the sauce, remove from the heat, and leave to cool.

6 Roll out the pastry on a floured work surface. Invert a pie dish on to the pastry and cut around the edge. Reserve the trimmings.

7 Transfer the vegetable and sauce mixture to the pie dish and top with the pastry. Crimp the edges with a fork and make a hole in the top of the pastry to allow steam to escape.

8 Decorate the pie with the pastry trimmings, attaching them with beaten egg. Brush the pastry all over with the remaining beaten egg. Bake in a preheated oven at 200°C (400°F, Gas 6) for 30 minutes or until the pastry is crisp and golden all over.

COUNTRY VEGETABLE PIES

SERVES 6

8 carrots, diced

8 parsnips, diced

300 ml (1/2 pint) vegetable stock

2 tbsp olive oil

1 onion, chopped

1 head of garlic, separated into cloves and peeled

750 g (1 1/2 lb) potatoes, diced

salt and black pepper

4 tbsp hot milk

45 g (1 1/2 oz) butter

paprika to garnish

PARSLEY SAUCE

45 g (1 1/2 oz) butter

45 g (1 1/2 oz) plain flour

150 ml (1/4 pint) milk

4 tbsp chopped parsley

1 Blanch the carrots and parsnips in the stock for 1 minute. Drain, reserving the stock. Put the oil into an ovenproof dish, add the vegetables and half of the garlic, and stir well. Roast in a preheated oven at 200°C (400°F, Gas 6) for 30 minutes.

2 Meanwhile, cook the potatoes and the remaining garlic in boiling salted water for 15–20 minutes until tender. Drain, return to the pan, and add the hot milk and 30 g (1 oz) of the butter. Mash, and season with salt and pepper.

3 Remove the roasted vegetables with a slotted spoon, divide among 6 small ovenproof dishes, and season well.

4 Make the parsley sauce: melt the butter in a small pan, add the flour, and cook, stirring, for 1 minute. Remove from the heat and blend in the milk and reserved stock. Bring to a boil, stirring, until thick. Simmer for 2–3 minutes, then stir in the parsley and season with salt and pepper.

5 Pour the sauce over the vegetables, top with the potato, and dot with the remaining butter. Bake for 20 minutes. Serve hot, with paprika sprinkled on top.

MIXED BEAN BAKE

SERVES 6

2 tbsp olive oil

3 large leeks, trimmed and sliced

1 garlic clove, crushed

250 g (8 oz) mushrooms, sliced

1 x 400 g (13 oz) can aduki or red kidney beans, drained and rinsed

1 x 400 g (13 oz) can butter beans, drained and rinsed

1 x 400 g (13 oz) can chopped tomatoes

3 tbsp tomato purée

4 tbsp chopped parsley

salt and black pepper

CHEESE SAUCE

30 g (1 oz) butter

30 g (1 oz) plain flour

300 ml (1/2 pint) milk

1 egg, beaten

125 g (4 oz) Cheddar cheese, grated

1 Heat the olive oil in a large saucepan. Add the leeks and cook gently, stirring, for a few minutes until softened but not coloured. Lift out with a slotted spoon and set aside.

2 Add the garlic and mushrooms and cook, stirring occasionally, for about 5 minutes. Add the canned beans, tomatoes, tomato purée, and 3 tbsp of the parsley. Season with salt and pepper. Bring to a boil, cover, and simmer very gently for about 20 minutes.

3 Meanwhile, make the cheese sauce: melt the butter in a small saucepan, add the flour, and cook, stirring, for 1 minute. Remove the pan from the heat and gradually blend in the milk. Bring to a boil, stirring constantly until the mixture thickens. Simmer for 2–3 minutes, then leave to cool slightly. Stir in the egg and cheese, and season with salt and black pepper.

4 Transfer the bean mixture to an ovenproof dish and arrange the leeks on top. Pour the cheese sauce over the leeks, and bake in a preheated oven at 190°C (375°F, Gas 5) for 30 minutes or until the top is golden. Serve hot, sprinkled with the remaining parsley.

VEGETABLE CASSEROLES

Delicious, satisfying casseroles can be made from fresh vegetables whatever the season, particularly when herbs, spices, and flavourings are carefully chosen to complement their flavours. These recipes make hearty main courses, served with either hot crusty bread or boiled or steamed rice.

ROASTED VEGETABLE MEDLEY

SERVES 4

175 g (6 oz) small new potatoes, scrubbed and halved

8 baby carrots, scrubbed and trimmed

2 red onions, cut into wedges

2 garlic cloves, sliced

salt and black pepper

about 2 tbsp olive oil

a few rosemary sprigs

250 g (8 oz) cherry tomatoes

125 g (4 oz) French beans

1 small cauliflower, broken into florets

1 x 400 g (13 oz) can butter beans, drained

2 tbsp balsamic vinegar

2 tbsp coarse-grain mustard

a handful of chopped fresh herbs (eg parsley, chives, basil, chervil)

1 Put the potatoes, carrots, onions and garlic in a roasting tin. Season and add the olive oil, then turn to coat. Tuck in the rosemary sprigs, and roast in a preheated oven at 190°C (375°F, Gas 5) for 40–45 minutes or until the vegetables are tender, stirring in the tomatoes about 15–20 minutes before the end.

2 Meanwhile, cook the French beans and cauliflower in boiling salted water for 4 minutes. Drain and set aside.

3 Mix the roasted vegetables with the French beans, cauliflower, and butter beans, then gently mix in the balsamic vinegar, mustard, and herbs. Serve hot.

MUSHROOM STROGANOFF

SERVES 4

20 g (3/4 oz) dried mushrooms (porcini)

2 tbsp olive oil

1 onion, chopped

1 garlic clove, crushed

500 g (1 lb) chestnut mushrooms

2 red peppers, halved, seeded, and sliced

2 tsp paprika

salt and black pepper

30 g (1 oz) cornflour

300 ml (1/2 pint) cold vegetable stock

1 x 400 g (13 oz) can artichoke hearts, drained

2 tbsp dry white or red wine

1 tbsp tomato purée

low-fat crème fraîche or plain yogurt to serve

1 Soak the dried mushrooms in 150 ml (1/4 pint) warm water for 20 minutes, then drain and reserve the soaking water.

2 Heat the oil in a flameproof casserole, add the onion and garlic, and cook for 3–5 minutes until softened.

3 Add the mushrooms, peppers, and paprika, and season with salt and pepper. Cook, stirring, for 5 minutes. Mix the cornflour and stock, add to the pan with the artichokes, wine, mushroom water, and tomato purée and bring to a boil. Simmer gently for 10–15 minutes. Taste for seasoning. Serve hot, with crème fraîche or yogurt.

SPICY PUMPKIN CASSEROLE

SERVES 4

2 tbsp olive oil

2 onions, cut into wedges

2 potatoes, cut into 2.5 cm (1 in) cubes

2 parsnips, cut into 2.5 cm (1 in) cubes

500 g (1 lb) pumpkin, peeled and cut into 2.5 cm (1 in) cubes

1–2 tbsp curry paste

375 ml (13 fl oz) vegetable stock

salt and black pepper

chopped fresh coriander to garnish

1 Heat the olive oil in a flameproof casserole. Add the onions and cook gently for 3–5 minutes or until softened.

2 Add the vegetable cubes, curry paste, and stock. Season and bring to a boil. Cover and simmer, stirring, for 20 minutes.

3 Remove the vegetables with a slotted spoon and transfer to a warmed serving dish. Bring the sauce to a boil and boil until reduced and thickened. Spoon the sauce over the vegetables, garnish with coriander, and serve hot.

CLOCKWISE FROM TOP: Spicy Pumpkin Casserole, Mushroom Stroganoff, Roasted Vegetable Medley.

ROASTED VEGETABLE GRATIN

Transfer the vegetables to an ovenproof dish. Sprinkle with 90 g (3 oz) grated Cheddar cheese mixed with 60 g (2 oz) fresh breadcrumbs. Return to the oven for about 10–15 minutes until golden.

MUSHROOM VOL-AU-VENT

When cooking the mushrooms, increase the heat to reduce and thicken the sauce. Warm through a ready made large vol-au-vent shell, and fill with the hot Mushroom Stroganoff.

SPICY PUMPKIN IN A PIE

Cool the vegetables and sauce, transfer to a pie dish, and top with ready rolled pastry. Bake at 190°C (375°F, Gas 5) for 15 minutes or until the pastry is cooked and the filling is hot.

POTATO, CELERIAC, & PARMESAN GRATIN

SERVES 6

60 g (2 oz) butter, plus extra for greasing
1 onion, sliced
2 garlic cloves, crushed
1 kg (2 lb) floury potatoes, thinly sliced
375 g (12 oz) celeriac, peeled and thinly sliced
300 ml (1/2 pint) single cream
150 ml (1/4 pint) milk
250 g (8 oz) ricotta cheese
3 tbsp snipped fresh chives
salt and black pepper
2 tbsp fresh breadcrumbs
3 tbsp grated Parmesan cheese, plus extra for serving

1 Melt the butter in a frying pan, add the sliced onion and crushed garlic, and cook gently, stirring occasionally, for 3–5 minutes until softened but not coloured. Lightly butter a large gratin dish.

2 Arrange the potatoes, celeriac, and the onion mixture in layers in the prepared gratin dish, finishing with a neat layer of potatoes.

3 In a large bowl, combine the cream, milk, ricotta cheese, and chives, and season with salt and pepper. Beat well together, then pour over the vegetables.

4 In a small bowl, combine the breadcrumbs and 3 tbsp grated Parmesan cheese, and then sprinkle evenly over the potatoes.

5 Bake in a preheated oven at 180°C (350°F, Gas 4) for about 1 hour or until the potatoes and celeriac are tender and the top is golden brown.

6 Serve the gratin hot, sprinkled with extra grated Parmesan cheese.

AUBERGINE PARMIGIANA

SERVES 6

1.5 kg (3 lb) aubergines
2 eggs, lightly beaten
60 g (2 oz) plain flour
3 tbsp olive oil, more if needed
2 onions, chopped
3 x 400 g (13 oz) cans chopped tomatoes, drained
1 x 140 g (4 3/4 oz) can tomato purée
2 garlic cloves, crushed
2 tbsp chopped fresh basil
1/4 tsp caster sugar
salt and black pepper
300–375 g (10–12 oz) mozzarella cheese, sliced
125 g (4 oz) Parmesan cheese, grated

1 Cut the aubergines into 1 cm (1/2 in) slices. Dip into the beaten eggs, then into the flour, shaking off any excess.

2 Heat 1 tbsp olive oil in a large frying pan, add the aubergine slices in batches, and cook for 3–4 minutes on each side until golden, adding more oil between batches if necessary. Lift out with a slotted spoon and drain on paper towels.

3 Heat another tablespoon of olive oil in a saucepan, add the onions, and cook gently until soft. Stir in the tomatoes, tomato purée, garlic, and basil. Bring to a boil, then simmer for 10–15 minutes until thickened. Add the sugar and season with salt and pepper.

4 Spoon some of the tomato mixture into a shallow ovenproof dish and cover with a layer of aubergine slices, then with a layer each of mozzarella and Parmesan. Continue layering, finishing with tomato mixture, mozzarella, and Parmesan.

5 Bake in a preheated oven at 190°C (375°F, Gas 5) for 15–20 minutes until the cheese is lightly browned.

Healthy option

For a lighter version of this dish, omit the egg and flour coating for the aubergines in step 1. In step 2, lightly brush the slices with olive oil, and grill or chargrill them until golden brown on each side.

STUFFED RED PEPPERS

SERVES 4

8 small red peppers

4 tbsp water

STUFFING

4 tbsp olive oil

1 large onion, finely chopped

1 garlic clove, crushed

175 g (6 oz) button mushrooms, chopped

250 g (8 oz) long grain rice

90 g (3 oz) red lentils

450 ml (¾ pint) vegetable stock

salt and black pepper

60 g (2 oz) pine nuts, toasted

4 tbsp chopped parsley

fresh coriander to garnish

1 Slice the tops off the red peppers and reserve. Cut out and discard the cores, seeds, and white ribs, and set the peppers aside.

2 Make the stuffing: heat the oil in a pan. Add the onion and garlic and cook gently, stirring occasionally, for 3–5 minutes until soft but not coloured. Add the mushrooms and cook for 10 minutes.

3 Add the rice and lentils and stir to coat in the oil. Pour in the stock, season with salt and pepper, and bring to a boil. Cover and simmer very gently for 15–20 minutes until the rice is tender and the liquid has been absorbed. Stir in the pine nuts and parsley, then taste for seasoning.

4 Divide the stuffing among the peppers, stand them upright in a casserole dish that just contains them, and replace the tops.

5 Pour the measured water into the bottom of the casserole, cover, and bake in a preheated oven at 180°C (350°F, Gas 4) for about 40 minutes until the peppers are tender. Serve at once, garnished with coriander.

Healthy note

Using a non-stick pan in step 2 will enable you to halve the amount of oil to 1 or 2 tbsp, and cutting out the pine nuts will reduce the fat content even further.

CHEESE-TOPPED BAKED AUBERGINES

SERVES 4

3 tbsp chopped parsley

2 tbsp chopped fresh basil

2 tbsp olive oil

1 tsp salt

4 medium aubergines

6 garlic cloves, cut into thin slivers

175 g (6 oz) Gorgonzola or Danish blue cheese, crumbled

175 g (6 oz) Cheddar or mozzarella cheese, grated

1 In a small bowl, combine the parsley, half of the basil, the olive oil, and salt.

2 Prepare the aubergines (see box, right). Put the aubergines into an ovenproof dish and bake in a preheated oven at 180°C (350°F, Gas 4) for 40–50 minutes until they are very tender and soft to the touch.

3 Remove the aubergines from the oven, sprinkle with the Gorgonzola and Cheddar cheeses, and bake for 5 minutes or until the cheese is melted. Serve at once, sprinkled with the remaining basil.

Preparing the aubergines

Cut diagonal slits one-third of the way into each aubergine. Stuff the garlic slivers and then the chopped herb mixture into each slit.

Healthy note

To reduce the fat content of these stuffed aubergines, use half the amount of Gorgonzola or Danish blue cheese and half the amount of Cheddar or mozzarella. You could even use reduced-fat or low-fat Cheddar or mozzarella to lower the fat content further – the strong flavours of the garlic and herbs will compensate for the lack of fat.

ITALIAN STUFFED COURGETTES

SERVES 4

4 large courgettes
30 g (1 oz) butter
2 tbsp olive oil, plus extra for greasing
1 small onion, finely chopped
4 ripe tomatoes, finely chopped
4 tbsp chopped fresh basil
salt and black pepper
2 tbsp capers, drained and coarsely chopped
250 g (8 oz) Fontina cheese, grated

1 Cut the courgettes in half lengthwise. Scoop out the flesh and chop finely.

2 Melt the butter with 1 tbsp of the olive oil in a saucepan.

3 When the butter is foaming, add the onion and cook gently, stirring occasionally, for 3–5 minutes until softened but not coloured.

4 Add the courgette flesh, tomatoes, and basil, and season with salt and pepper. Cook, stirring, for 5 minutes.

5 Brush the insides of the courgette shells with the remaining oil and arrange in a lightly oiled shallow ovenproof dish. Bake the shells in a preheated oven at 180°C (350°F, Gas 4) for 5–10 minutes.

6 Divide half of the tomato mixture among the courgette shells. Cover with the chopped capers and a thin layer of cheese. Spoon over the remaining tomato mixture and top with the remaining cheese. Return to the oven and bake for 10–15 minutes until the cheese topping is bubbling.

BAKED MARROW WITH COUSCOUS

SERVES 4

250 g (8 oz) couscous
150 ml (¼ pint) hot vegetable stock
1 kg (2 lb) marrow
salt and black pepper
butter for greasing
1 tbsp olive oil
1 shallot, finely chopped
125 g (4 oz) button mushrooms, sliced
grated zest and juice of ½ lemon
2 spring onions, finely chopped
4 tbsp Greek yogurt
1 tbsp chopped fresh mint
12 pitted green olives, chopped
chopped parsley to garnish
tomato sauce (page 314) to serve

1 Put the couscous into a bowl and pour in the hot stock. Stir well, and leave to stand for about 10 minutes.

2 Peel the marrow, cut it crosswise into 5 cm (2 in) slices, and scoop out and discard the seeds from each slice. Blanch the slices in boiling salted water for 2 minutes, then drain and arrange in a single layer in a lightly buttered ovenproof dish.

3 Heat the oil in a saucepan and cook the shallot gently for 2–3 minutes until softened. Add the mushrooms, lemon zest and juice, season with salt and pepper, and cook for about 8 minutes or until tender.

4 Drain the mushroom mixture and stir into the couscous. Add the spring onions, yogurt, mint, olives, and salt and pepper to taste.

5 Spoon the mixture over the marrow slices. Cover with foil and bake in a preheated oven at 190°C (375°F, Gas 5) for 20–25 minutes. Garnish with parsley and serve hot, with the tomato sauce.

310

MUSHROOM LASAGNE

SERVES 6

2 tbsp olive oil

1 large onion, finely chopped

500 g (1 lb) mushrooms, sliced

2 large garlic cloves, crushed

30 g (1 oz) plain flour

2 x 400 g (13 oz) cans chopped tomatoes

1 tbsp chopped fresh basil

1 tsp caster sugar

salt and black pepper

500 g (1 lb) frozen whole leaf spinach, thawed and drained

White sauce (page 385), made with 90 g (3 oz) each butter and plain flour, 900 ml (1½ pints) milk, and 1 tsp Dijon mustard

300 g (10 oz) mature Cheddar cheese, grated

150 g (5 oz) pre-cooked lasagne sheets

1 Heat the oil in a saucepan, add the onion, mushrooms and garlic and cook for 10 minutes or until soft. Sprinkle in the flour and cook, stirring, for 1 minute.

2 Add the tomatoes, basil, and sugar, and season with salt and pepper. Cover and simmer for 20 minutes.

3 Season the spinach with salt and pepper. Taking 1 teaspoonful at a time, shape it loosely into 24 balls.

4 Spoon one-third of the mushroom mixture into a large ovenproof dish, and place 8 of the spinach balls on top. Cover with one-third of the white sauce and one-third of the cheese. Arrange half of the lasagne on top. Repeat the layers, finishing with cheese.

5 Bake in a preheated oven at 190°C (375°F, Gas 5) for 35 minutes or until the pasta is tender. Serve hot.

Healthy option

This is a luxury lasagne for a special occasion. For everyday, halve the amount of white sauce and cheese.

DAIRY-FREE LASAGNE

SERVES 4–6

2–3 tbsp olive oil, more if needed

2 courgettes, sliced

salt and black pepper

1 aubergine, cut into 5 mm (¼ in) slices

2 onions, chopped

1 red pepper, halved, seeded, and diced

2 garlic cloves, crushed

2 x 400 g (13 oz) cans chopped tomatoes

1 x 140 g (4¾ oz) can tomato purée

¼ tsp caster sugar

3 tbsp chopped fresh basil

150 g (5 oz) pre-cooked lasagne sheets

250 g (8 oz) frozen chopped spinach, thawed, drained, and seasoned well

1 Heat 1 tbsp olive oil in a large non-stick frying pan, add the courgettes, and cook for 3 minutes. Turn into a bowl, and sprinkle with salt.

2 Heat another tablespoon of oil in the pan, and cook the aubergine slices for about 3–5 minutes on each side until golden. Remove and set aside.

3 Add the onions, red pepper, and garlic to the pan, with more oil if needed, and soften gently for 3–5 minutes. Add the tomatoes, tomato purée, and sugar and bring to a boil. Simmer for 10 minutes until thickened, stir in the basil, and season with salt and pepper.

4 Spoon one-third of the tomato sauce into a large ovenproof dish and cover with one-third of the lasagne. Add the aubergine, then half of the remaining tomato sauce. Add half of the remaining lasagne, then the spinach. Add the remaining lasagne and tomato sauce, and finish with an overlapping layer of courgettes.

5 Bake in a preheated oven at 190°C (375°F, Gas 5) for 35 minutes or until the pasta is tender and the top is golden.

VEGETARIAN BAKES

It is often hard to find inspiration for vegetarian main meals, especially when you are entertaining meat eaters at the same time. These special "two-in-one" recipes are the perfect answer – the vegetarians in your party will love have something cooked especially for them, while the meat eaters will enjoy a spoonful or two alongside their own main course.

MAJORCAN TUMBET CASSEROLE

SERVES 6

625 g (1¼ lb) baby new potatoes

500 g (1 lb) courgettes, thickly sliced

500 g (1 lb) Spanish onions, thickly sliced

500 g (1 lb) tomatoes, halved

3 fat garlic cloves, peeled and left whole

olive oil

salt and black pepper

3 tsp chopped fresh rosemary

400 ml (14 fl oz) passata (sieved tomatoes)

Tabasco sauce

3 fresh thyme sprigs, plus extra to garnish

1.8 LITRE (3 PINT) OVENPROOF DISH, ABOUT 20 × 28 × 5 CM (8 × 11 × 2 IN)

1 Boil the potatoes in salted water for about 15–20 minutes until not quite done. Drain and leave until cool enough to handle, then peel and cut in half.

2 Toss the courgettes, onions, tomatoes, and garlic cloves in a couple of tablespoons of olive oil and season well. Arrange cut-side down on a large baking sheet or in a shallow roasting tin. Roast in a preheated oven at 220°C (425°F, Gas 7) for about 30–40 minutes, turning once, until the vegetables are charred and soft.

3 Pick out the garlic, squash it with the back of a knife, and return it to the other vegetables. Layer the vegetables in an ovenproof dish – first the potatoes with some seasoning and rosemary, about 6 tbsp passata, and a good dash of Tabasco, then the onions, tomatoes, and courgettes with seasoning, rosemary, passata, and Tabasco as before. Push 3 sprigs of thyme in near the top.

4 Bake in a preheated oven at 200°C (400°F, Gas 6) for about 15–20 minutes, or at 170°C (325°F, Gas 3) for 30–40 minutes, until hot and bubbling. Before serving, replace the cooked thyme with fresh thyme. Good served with Vegetarian Burgers (see page 323).

KILKERRY PIE

SERVES 6

90 g (3 oz) butter

500 g (1 lb) leeks, trimmed and thickly sliced

60 g (2 oz) plain flour

300 ml (½ pint) apple juice

300 ml (½ pint) milk

1 tsp coarse-grain mustard

salt and black pepper

4 hard-boiled eggs, roughly chopped

150 g (5 oz) mature Cheddar cheese, grated

500 g (1 lb) potatoes, cut into 5 mm (¼ in) slices (not peeled)

5 sheets of filo pastry, each about 25 × 38 cm (10 × 15 in)

SHALLOW OVENPROOF DISH, ABOUT 25 CM (10 INS) SQUARE

1 Melt 60 g (2 oz) of the butter in a large frying pan, and cook the leeks for about 8–10 minutes until softened. Stir in the flour and cook for 1 minute, then gradually add the apple juice and milk, stirring constantly until boiling. It may look slightly curdled at this stage, but don't worry, it will come together. Reduce the heat, and simmer gently for 2–3 minutes. Add the mustard and season well.

2 Remove the sauce from the heat and stir in the roughly chopped eggs and the cheese. Now cook the potatoes in boiling salted water for 4–5 minutes until just tender. Drain, and mix into the sauce, then season, and pour into the dish.

3 Melt the remaining butter. Brush one of the filo sheets with butter and put it over the mixture in the dish, scrunching up the edges to fit. Repeat with the remaining filo sheets, scrunching up the last sheet before putting it on top of the pie. You can leave the pie for up to 6 hours at this stage, then bake it when you need it.

4 Bake in a preheated oven at 200°C (400°F, Gas 6) for 30–40 minutes until the filo is crisp and golden and the pie is hot right through.

TUSCAN CANNELLONI

SERVES 4

8 sheets of fresh lasagne, or dried lasagne cooked according to packet instructions

500 g (1 lb) passata (sieved tomatoes) or ready made fresh tomato and basil pasta sauce

2–3 tbsp grated fresh Parmesan cheese

a small handful of chopped fresh basil

FILLING

a little olive oil

2 shallots, finely chopped

1 garlic clove, crushed

2 × 300 g (10 oz) cans cannellini beans, drained

60 g (2 oz) sun-blushed or sun-dried tomatoes, snipped into pieces

150 g (5 oz) Dolcelatte cheese, roughly chopped

2 heaped tbsp chopped fresh basil

salt and black pepper

SHALLOW OVENPROOF DISH, ABOUT 28 × 20 CM (11 × 8 IN)

1 Make the filling: heat the oil in a small pan, and cook the shallots and garlic until soft. Allow to cool. Crush the beans with a fork so that most are mashed but a few still retain some shape, then mix them with the shallots and garlic, tomatoes, Dolcelatte, and basil. Season well, taste, and add more seasoning if necessary.

2 Lay the lasagne sheets flat, divide the filling between them, and roll up from the short ends to enclose the filling. Put the cannelloni seam-side down into an oiled or buttered ovenproof dish – they should fit snugly. Season, then pour over the passata or pasta sauce.

3 Cover and cook at 190°C (375°F, Gas 5) for 45–50 minutes until the pasta is cooked and the filling piping hot. (If pre-cooked pasta was used, bake for 25–30 minutes.) Scatter the Parmesan and basil over the top before serving.

CLOCKWISE FROM TOP RIGHT: Tuscan Cannelloni, Kilkerry Pie, Majorcan Tumbet Casserole.

SPINACH GNOCCHI WITH TOMATO SAUCE

SERVES 4

1 kg (2 lb) spinach
375 g (12 oz) ricotta cheese
3 eggs
4 tbsp grated Parmesan cheese
pinch of grated nutmeg
salt and black pepper
60–75 g (2–2¹/₂ oz) plain flour

TOMATO SAUCE

30 g (1 oz) butter
1 small onion, chopped
1 small carrot, chopped
30 g (1 oz) plain flour
1 x 400 g (13 oz) can chopped tomatoes
300 ml (¹/₂ pint) vegetable stock
1 bay leaf
1 tsp caster sugar

TO SERVE

125 g (4 oz) butter
grated Parmesan cheese and Parmesan shavings

1 Wash the spinach and put into a saucepan with only the water remaining on the leaves. Cook over a gentle heat until just wilted. Drain the spinach throughly, squeezing to remove any excess water.

2 Put the spinach, ricotta, eggs, Parmesan, and nutmeg into a food processor, season with salt and pepper and purée until smooth. Turn into a bowl and gradually add flour until the mixture just holds its shape.

3 Using 2 dessertspoons, form the mixture into 20 oval shapes. Cover and chill in the refrigerator for 1 hour.

4 Make the tomato sauce: melt the butter in a pan, add the onion and carrot, and cook for 10 minutes or until softened. Sprinkle in the flour and cook, stirring, for 1 minute. Add the tomatoes, stock, bay leaf, and sugar, season with salt and pepper, and bring to a boil. Cover and simmer for 30 minutes. Purée in a food processor until smooth. Keep hot.

5 Cook the gnocchi in batches in boiling salted water for about 5 minutes or until they float to the surface. Lift out and keep hot. Melt the butter and pour over the gnocchi. Serve the gnocchi hot, with the tomato sauce, grated Parmesan, and Parmesan shavings.

POLENTA WITH GRILLED VEGETABLES

SERVES 6

175 g (6 oz) polenta
150 ml (¼ pint) cold water
600 ml (1 pint) boiling salted water
30 g (1 oz) butter
2 courgettes, halved and thickly sliced lengthwise
2 tomatoes, cored and sliced
1 fennel bulb, trimmed and quartered lengthwise
1 red onion, thickly sliced
melted butter for brushing

MARINADE

4 tbsp olive oil
2 tbsp red wine vinegar
3 garlic cloves, chopped
2–3 tbsp chopped parsley
salt and black pepper

1 Put the polenta into a saucepan, cover with the measured cold water, and leave to stand for 5 minutes.

2 Add the boiling salted water to the pan, return to a boil, and stir for 10–15 minutes, until smooth and thickened.

3 Sprinkle a baking tray with water. Stir the butter into the polenta, then spread the mixture over the tray in a 1 cm (¹/₂ in) layer. Leave to cool.

4 Combine the marinade ingredients in a bowl. Add the courgettes, tomatoes, fennel, and onion. Cover and marinate in the refrigerator for 30 minutes.

5 Lift the vegetables out of the marinade and cook over a hot barbecue for 2–3 minutes on each side. Cut the polenta into strips and cook over a hot barbecue, brushing with melted butter, for 1–2 minutes on each side until golden. Serve hot.

Cook's know-how

Instead of barbecuing the polenta and vegetables, you can cook them on a ridged cast-iron chargrill pan, or under a preheated grill, for the same length of time.

VEGETABLE & BARLEY CASSEROLE

SERVES 6

60 g (2 oz) butter
125 g (4 oz) shallots or small onions, halved
1.25 litres (2 pints) vegetable stock
250 g (8 oz) baby carrots
250 g (8 oz) baby parsnips
60 g (2 oz) pearl barley
1 bay leaf
2 courgettes, sliced
1 small cauliflower, separated into florets
125 g (4 oz) mangetout
1 tbsp chopped fresh mixed herbs

DUMPLINGS

125 g (4 oz) self-raising flour
60 g (2 oz) shredded vegetable suet
1 tbsp chopped fresh mixed herbs
salt and black pepper

1 Make the dumplings: sift the flour into a bowl, add the suet and herbs, and season with salt and pepper. Add enough water to make a soft, not sticky, dough. Shape into 16–18 balls. Cover and set aside.

2 Melt the butter in a large flameproof casserole. When the butter is foaming, add the shallots and cook gently, stirring occasionally, for 3–5 minutes until soft but not coloured.

3 Add the stock, carrots, parsnips, pearl barley, and bay leaf, and bring to a boil. Cover and bake in a preheated oven at 190°C (375°F, Gas 5) for about 30 minutes.

4 Remove the casserole from the oven, and stir in the courgettes, cauliflower, mangetout, and herbs. Season with salt and pepper.

5 Arrange the dumplings on top of the casserole, cover, and return to the oven for 20 minutes or until the dumplings are cooked. Discard the bay leaf before serving.

COUSCOUS WITH ROASTED PEPPERS

SERVES 4–6

1 large red pepper
1 large yellow pepper
175 g (6 oz) couscous
600 ml (1 pint) hot vegetable stock
2 tbsp olive oil
60 g (2 oz) blanched almonds
2 courgettes, sliced
1 large red onion, chopped
1 large carrot, thinly sliced
1–2 garlic cloves, crushed
1 x 400 g (13 oz) can chick peas, drained and rinsed
1 tsp ground cumin
1/2 tsp curry powder
1/4–1/2 tsp crushed dried red chillies
salt and black pepper
chopped coriander to garnish

1 Cook the peppers under a hot grill, 10 cm (4 in) from the heat, for 10 minutes or until charred. Seal in a plastic bag and leave to cool.

2 Put the couscous into a bowl and stir in the hot stock. Cover and leave to stand for 10 minutes.

3 Meanwhile, heat the oil in a large frying pan, add the almonds, and cook gently, stirring, for 3 minutes or until lightly browned. Lift out with a slotted spoon and drain on paper towels.

4 Add the courgettes, onion, carrot, and garlic to the pan, and cook, stirring, for about 5 minutes.

5 Stir in the chick peas, cumin, curry powder, and crushed chillies, and cook, stirring occasionally, for a further 5 minutes. Stir in the couscous, and cook for 3–4 minutes until heated through. Season to taste.

6 Remove the skins, cores, and seeds from the grilled peppers, and cut the flesh into thin strips.

7 Divide the couscous among warmed serving plates and arrange the pepper strips on top. Serve at once, sprinkled with the almonds and chopped coriander.

TOMATO & OLIVE TART

SERVES 8

3 tbsp olive oil

2 large onions, coarsely chopped

3 garlic cloves, crushed

1 x 400 g (13 oz) can chopped tomatoes

1 x 140 g (4¾ oz) can tomato purée

2 tsp chopped fresh basil

1 tsp caster sugar

125 g (4 oz) vignotte or mozzarella cheese, grated

90 g (3 oz) pitted black olives

shredded fresh basil to garnish

POPPYSEED BASE

250 g (8 oz) plain flour

125 g (4 oz) butter

90 g (3 oz) poppyseeds

1 tbsp light muscovado sugar

salt and black pepper

about 4 tbsp cold water

1 Make the base: put the flour, butter, poppyseeds, and sugar in a food processor, season with salt and pepper, and pulse until the mixture resembles fine breadcrumbs.

2 Add the water and process until the mixture forms a ball. Turn out and knead lightly, then roll out to a 30 cm (12 in) round on a baking sheet and pinch the edge to form a rim. Prick the base all over with a fork and chill for 30 minutes.

3 Heat the oil in a pan, add the onions and garlic, and cook gently for 3–5 minutes until soft. Add the tomatoes, tomato purée, basil, and sugar. Season and bring to a boil. Boil for 5–7 minutes until thick. Leave to cool slightly.

4 Bake the poppyseed base in a preheated oven at 220°C (425°F, Gas 7) for 15 minutes. Spread the tomato mixture over the base, sprinkle with the cheese and olives, and bake for 15–20 minutes. Serve hot or cold, sprinkled with basil.

Cook's know-how

If you are short of time, use ready made shortcrust pastry instead of the poppyseed base. You will need a 500 g (1 lb) packet.

MUSHROOM GOUGERE

SERVES 4

60 g (2 oz) butter

375 g (12 oz) mixed mushrooms, such as oyster, shiitake, and button, sliced

60 g (2 oz) plain flour

450 ml (¾ pint) milk

1 tsp chopped fresh tarragon

tarragon leaves to garnish

CHOUX PASTRY

125 g (4 oz) plain flour

salt and black pepper

300 ml (½ pint) water

60 g (2 oz) butter, plus extra for greasing

4 eggs, beaten

1 Make the choux pastry: sift the flour with a pinch of salt. Put the measured water and butter into a saucepan and bring to a boil.

2 Remove from the heat and add the flour. Beat well until the mixture is smooth and glossy and leaves the side of the pan clean. Leave to cool slightly.

3 Beat the eggs into the flour mixture until smooth and glossy. Make the gougère (see box, right). Cover and chill while preparing the filling.

4 Melt the butter in a large saucepan, add the mushrooms, and cook gently for 3–4 minutes. Lift out with a slotted spoon and set aside. Sprinkle in the flour and cook, stirring, for 1 minute. Remove from the heat and gradually blend in the milk. Bring to a boil, stirring until thickened. Simmer for 2–3 minutes.

5 Return the mushrooms to the pan, add the tarragon, and season with salt and pepper. Pour into the middle of the choux ring and bake in a preheated oven at 220°C (425°F, Gas 7) for 35–40 minutes until well risen and golden. Garnish with tarragon, and serve hot.

Making the gougère

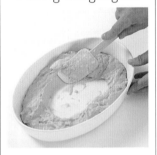

Butter a large shallow ovenproof dish, and lightly press the choux pastry around the edge with a spatula.

SPINACH & RICOTTA SAMOSAS

SERVES 4

4 sheets of filo pastry

60 g (2 oz) melted butter, plus extra for greasing

FILLING

30 g (1 oz) butter

1 small onion, finely chopped

300 g (10 oz) spinach, shredded

125 g (4 oz) ricotta cheese

pinch of grated nutmeg

salt and black pepper

tomato sauce (page 314) to serve

1 Make the filling: melt the butter in a saucepan, add the onion, and cook gently for 3–5 minutes until softened.

2 Add the spinach to the onion and cook for 1–2 minutes. Leave to cool. Add the ricotta and nutmeg, season with salt and pepper, and mix well. Divide into 8 portions.

3 Lightly butter a baking tray. Cut each sheet of filo pastry lengthwise into 2 long strips. Brush 1 strip with melted butter, covering the remaining strips with a damp tea towel. Fill and fold the parcels (see box, right).

4 Bake in a preheated oven at 200°C (400°F, Gas 6) for 20 minutes or until the pastry is crisp and golden. Serve with the tomato sauce.

Filling and folding the parcels

Spoon 1 portion of filling on to a corner of the filo strip. Fold over opposite corner to form a triangle.

Fold the filled triangle until you reach the end of the strip. Brush with melted butter and put on to the baking tray. Butter, fill, and fold the remaining filo strips

SPICED AUBERGINES WITH FILO CRUST

SERVES 6

2 tbsp olive oil

2 large onions, chopped

2 tbsp mild curry paste

2 aubergines, cut into 1 cm (½ in) dice

2 red peppers, halved, seeded, and diced

salt and black pepper

175 g (6 oz) red lentils

250 g (8 oz) Caerphilly cheese, diced

300 g (10 oz) filo pastry

60 g (2 oz) melted butter

26 CM (10½ IN) SPRINGFORM CAKE TIN

1 Heat the oil in a large saucepan or deep frying pan. Cook the onions over a low heat, stirring occasionally, for 3–5 minutes until softened. Stir in the curry paste, and cook for 2 minutes.

2 Add the aubergines and the red peppers and cook for 10–15 minutes until soft. Season with salt and pepper and leave to cool.

3 Meanwhile, put the lentils into a pan, cover with water, and bring to a boil. Simmer for 15 minutes or until just soft. Drain and cool.

4 Stir the lentils and diced cheese into the aubergine mixture. Taste for seasoning.

5 Using two-thirds of the filo, line the bottom and side of the cake tin, brushing each sheet with melted butter, and letting them overhang the rim of the tin. Spoon in the aubergine mixture and fold the filo over the top. Brush the remaining filo with butter, crumple, and arrange on top.

6 Bake in a preheated oven at 190°C (375°F, Gas 5) for 40 minutes or until the pastry is golden. Serve hot.

Cook's know-how

If you are short of time, omit the filo. Spread the aubergine, pepper, and lentil mixture in a baking dish and grate the cheese over the top.

VEGETARIAN CURRIES

The cuisine of India, with its use of aromatic spices to enhance the flavour of vegetables
and pulses, is one in which vegetarians can find a wide range of dishes to enjoy.
The tradition of eating a selection of small dishes, accompanied by rice and breads,
makes for well-balanced, nutritious meals.

NIRAMISH

SERVES 6

2 tbsp sunflower oil

3 tbsp curry paste

1/2 tsp chilli powder

2.5 cm (1 in) piece of fresh root ginger, peeled and grated

1 large onion, chopped

2 garlic cloves, crushed

3 tbsp mango chutney

1 small cauliflower, cut into florets

2 potatoes, cut into chunks

2 large carrots, sliced

2 red peppers, halved, seeded, and cut into chunks

1 x 400 g (13 oz) can chopped tomatoes

1 x 400 g (13 oz) can coconut milk

250 g (8 oz) green beans, chopped into short lengths

salt and black pepper

juice of 1 lime

fresh coriander leaves to garnish

1 Heat the oil in a large saucepan, add the curry paste and chilli powder, and cook, stirring constantly, for 1 minute. Add the ginger, onion, garlic, and mango chutney, and cook, stirring, for 3–5 minutes until the onion is softened but not coloured.

2 Add the cauliflower, potatoes, and carrots to the pan, and stir well to coat in the spices. Cook, stirring occasionally, for 5 minutes.

3 Add the red peppers, tomatoes, and coconut milk to the pan and bring to a boil, then add the beans and season with salt and pepper. Stir well.

4 Cover and simmer gently for 25–30 minutes or until all the vegetables are tender. Stir in the lime juice and taste for seasoning. Serve hot, garnished with coriander leaves.

SAG ALOO

SERVES 6

500 g (1 lb) new potatoes

salt

2 tbsp sunflower oil

1 tsp mustard seeds

1 tsp cumin seeds

2 onions, sliced

3 garlic cloves, chopped

2.5 cm (1 in) piece of fresh root ginger, peeled and grated

1 small fresh green chilli, halved, seeded, and finely chopped

2 tsp ground coriander

1/2 tsp turmeric

250 ml (8 fl oz) water

500 g (1 lb) fresh baby leaf spinach

2 tbsp lime or lemon juice

plain yogurt to serve

1 Cook the potatoes in a saucepan of boiling salted water for 10 minutes. Drain and leave to cool. Cut into bite-sized pieces and set aside.

2 Heat the oil in a large, heavy frying pan. Add the mustard and cumin seeds and cook, stirring, for a few seconds until they pop. Add the onions, garlic, ginger, and chilli and cook for about 5 minutes until soft.

3 Add 1 tsp salt, the ground coriander, and the turmeric Cook, stirring, for 1 minute. Add the potatoes and turn to coat in the spices, then pour in the water and bring to a boil. Cover and cook over a gentle heat for 15 minutes or until the potatoes are tender.

4 Remove the lid and stir in the spinach. Increase the heat and cook, stirring occasionally, for about 10 minutes or until the spinach wilts right down into the sauce. Stir in the lime or lemon juice and taste for seasoning. Serve hot, with yogurt.

DHAL

SERVES 4–6

225 g (8 oz) green lentils

1 bay leaf

2 tbsp vegetable oil

1 large carrot, chopped

1 large green pepper, halved, seeded, and chopped

1 large onion, chopped

1 garlic clove, crushed

1 cm (1/2 in) piece of fresh root ginger, peeled and finely grated

1/2 tsp each ground cinnamon, cumin, and coriander

1 x 400 g (13 oz) can chopped tomatoes

salt and black pepper

1 Rinse and drain the lentils, put them into a large saucepan, and pour in enough cold water to cover. Bring to a boil and add the bay leaf, then cover and simmer for 30 minutes or until the lentils are tender. Drain and remove the bay leaf.

2 Heat the oil in the saucepan, add the vegetables, garlic, and ginger, and fry for 10 minutes, stirring occasionally. Add the lentils, ground spices, and tomatoes and cook gently for 10 minutes or until the carrot is soft.

3 Purée the mixture in 3 batches in a blender or food processor. Do not purée for longer than about 30 seconds for each batch because the dhal should not be too smooth – it should retain some of the texture of the lentils. Reheat in the rinsed-out pan, and add salt and pepper to taste.

ACCOMPANIMENTS

- tomato and coriander relish
- yogurt and cucumber raita
- grated carrot salad
- mango chutney
- poppadoms
- basmati rice
- naan bread

CLOCKWISE FROM TOP RIGHT: Yogurt and cucumber raita, Niramish, Sag Aloo, Dhal.

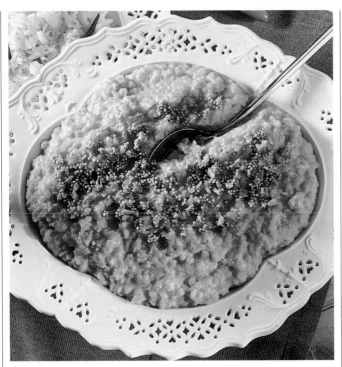

RED BEAN & TOMATO CURRY

SERVES 4

2 tbsp sunflower oil
1 large onion, sliced
3 garlic cloves, crushed
1–2 fresh green chillies, halved, seeded, and sliced
2.5 cm (1 in) piece of fresh root ginger, peeled and grated
1 tbsp Madras or other hot curry powder
salt
1 x 400 g (13 oz) can chopped tomatoes
2 x 400 g (13 oz) cans red kidney beans, drained and rinsed
1 tbsp lemon juice
fresh coriander leaves to garnish

1 Heat the oil in a large frying pan, add the onion, garlic, chillies, and ginger, and cook, stirring occasionally, for a few minutes until all the aromas are released, and the onion is softened but not coloured.

2 Add the curry powder and season with salt, then cook, stirring, for 2 minutes.

3 Add the tomatoes with most of their juice and cook for about 3 minutes. Add the beans and cook for a further 5 minutes or until the beans are warmed through and the sauce is thickened. Add the lemon juice and serve hot, garnished with coriander.

RED LENTIL & COCONUT CURRY

SERVES 6

300 g (10 oz) red lentils
900 ml (1½ pints) water
2.5 cm (1 in) piece of fresh root ginger, peeled and grated
1½ fresh green chillies, halved, seeded, and finely chopped
4 garlic cloves
90 g (3 oz) creamed coconut, grated
½ tsp turmeric
1 tbsp lemon juice
salt
30 g (1 oz) butter
4 tsp black mustard seeds

1 Put the lentils into a pan and add the water. Bring to a boil and simmer for about 20 minutes or until tender.

2 Using a pestle and mortar, crush the fresh root ginger, two-thirds of the chillies, and 2 of the garlic cloves until smooth. Add to the lentils.

3 Add the creamed coconut, turmeric, lemon juice, and a pinch of salt. Cook gently, stirring, until the coconut dissolves, then increase the heat and cook for 5 minutes or until any excess liquid has evaporated. Taste for seasoning.

4 Crush the remaining garlic and set aside. Melt the butter in a frying pan and add the mustard seeds. As soon as they begin to pop, remove the frying pan from the heat and stir in the crushed garlic and the remaining chopped chilli.

5 Transfer the lentil mixture to a warmed serving dish, top with the garlic, chilli, and mustard seeds. Serve hot.

Cook's know-how

To save time grating a block of creamed coconut, use a carton of coconut cream (either full-fat or reduced-fat). This can be poured straight into the lentils in step 3.

FELAFEL WITH SESAME YOGURT SAUCE

SERVES 6

1 x 400 g (13 oz) can chick peas, drained and rinsed

6 spring onions, chopped

30 g (1 oz) fresh white bread

1 egg

grated zest and juice of 1/2 lemon

1 garlic clove, roughly chopped

2 tbsp roughly chopped fresh coriander

2 tbsp roughly chopped parsley

1 tbsp tahini paste

1 tsp ground coriander

1 tsp ground cumin

1/2 tsp ground cinnamon

pinch of cayenne pepper

salt and black pepper

sunflower oil for shallow-frying

chopped fresh coriander to garnish

warmed mini pitta breads to serve

SESAME YOGURT SAUCE

4 tbsp plain yogurt

2 tbsp olive oil

1 tbsp lemon juice

1 tbsp tahini paste

1 Put the chick peas into a food processor, add the onions, bread, egg, lemon zest and juice, garlic, coriander, parsley, tahini, ground coriander, cumin, cinnamon, and cayenne pepper, and season with salt and pepper. Purée until smooth.

2 Turn into a bowl, cover, and leave to stand for at least 30 minutes.

3 Meanwhile, make the sesame yogurt sauce: in a bowl, combine the yogurt, oil, lemon juice, tahini, and salt and pepper to taste.

4 With dampened hands, shape the felafel mixture into balls about the size of a walnut, then flatten them into patties.

5 Pour enough oil into a non-stick frying pan to just cover the base, and heat until hot. Shallow-fry the felafel in batches for 2–3 minutes on each side until golden. Lift out and drain on paper towels. Garnish with coriander and serve warm, with mini pitta breads and sesame yogurt sauce.

HALLOUMI & VEGETABLE KEBABS

SERVES 4

1 small baguette

250 g (8 oz) halloumi cheese

1 large red pepper, halved and seeded

150 ml (1/4 pint) olive oil, plus extra for greasing

16 large cherry tomatoes

grated zest and juice of 1 lemon

1 garlic clove, crushed

2 tbsp chopped fresh basil

1 tbsp snipped fresh chives

salt and black pepper

8 METAL SKEWERS

1 Cut the bread into 8 thick slices and cut each slice in half. Cut the halloumi into 16 cubes and cut the red pepper into 8 pieces.

2 Oil the skewers and thread alternately with the tomatoes, bread, cheese, and red pepper. Place in a shallow flameproof dish.

3 Mix the oil, lemon zest and juice, garlic, and herbs, and season with salt and pepper. Drizzle over the kebabs.

4 Cook the kebabs under a hot grill, 10 cm (4 in) from the heat, turning once and basting with the marinade, for 3–4 minutes until the cheese is lightly browned.

Cook's know-how

Halloumi is a semi-hard Greek cheese which is usually made from ewe's milk. It is best eaten hot, straight from the grill, as it becomes rubbery when it cools down.

TOFU & VEGETABLE KEBABS

Substitute smoked tofu for the halloumi cheese, and 8 button mushrooms for the red pepper.

VEGETABLE STIR-FRY WITH TOFU

SERVES 4

250 g (8 oz) firm tofu, cut into bite-sized pieces

2 tbsp sesame oil

1 tbsp sunflower oil

1 head of chicory, halved lengthwise

4 carrots, thinly sliced diagonally

5 cm (2 in) piece of fresh root ginger, peeled and grated

250 g (8 oz) shiitake mushrooms, sliced

8 spring onions, sliced into 2.5 cm (1 in) pieces

250 g (8 oz) bean sprouts

3 tbsp toasted sesame seeds

MARINADE

3 tbsp soy sauce

3 tbsp dry sherry

1 garlic clove, crushed

salt and black pepper

1 Make the marinade: in a bowl, combine the soy sauce, sherry, and garlic, and season with salt and pepper. Turn the tofu in the marinade, cover, and leave to marinate at room temperature for at least 15 minutes.

2 Drain the tofu, reserving the marinade. Heat the sesame and sunflower oils in a wok or large frying pan, add the tofu, and carefully stir-fry over a high heat for 2–3 minutes, being careful not to break up the tofu. Remove from the wok with a slotted spoon and drain on paper towels.

3 Separate the chicory halves into leaves. Add the carrots and ginger to the wok and stir-fry for about 2 minutes. Add the mushrooms and spring onions and stir-fry for a further 2 minutes, then add the bean sprouts and chicory leaves and stir-fry for 1 minute.

4 Return the tofu to the wok, pour the reserved marinade over the top, and boil quickly until almost all of the marinade has evaporated and the tofu has warmed through. Generously sprinkle with the toasted sesame seeds, taste for seasoning, and serve at once.

MEXICAN CHILLI WITH TOFU

SERVES 6

3 onions, chopped

3 garlic cloves, roughly chopped

1 fresh green chilli, halved, seeded, and roughly chopped

2 tsp paprika

1 tbsp mild chilli powder

4 tbsp sunflower oil

1 x 400 g (13 oz) can chopped tomatoes, drained and juice reserved

500 ml (16 fl oz) hot vegetable stock

625 g (1 1/4 lb) firm tofu, cut into bite-sized pieces

1 x 400 g (13 oz) can red kidney beans, drained

salt and black pepper

chopped fresh coriander to garnish

1 Put the onions, garlic, green chilli, and spices into a food processor and process until fairly chunky.

2 Heat the oil in a large frying pan. Add the onion mixture and cook for a few minutes, stirring occasionally, until softened and fragrant.

3 Add the tomatoes to the pan and cook, stirring occasionally, until reduced and thickened. Pour in the stock and cook for 5–10 minutes more until thickened again.

4 Add the tofu, kidney beans, and the reserved tomato juice, and cook, spooning the sauce over the tofu pieces, for 5–8 minutes until heated through. Do not stir the tofu as it may break up. Season, and serve hot, sprinkled with coriander.

Cook's know-how

Reducing a sauce involves cooking it over a high heat to allow the moisture to evaporate and the flavours to become concentrated.

322

VEGETARIAN BURGERS

SERVES 6

15 g (1/2 oz) butter

125 g (4 oz) chestnut mushrooms, finely chopped

1 small leek, finely chopped

1 small green chilli, halved, seeded, and finely chopped

1 tsp sugar

1 garlic clove, crushed

2 x 400 g (13 oz) cans butter beans or cannellini beans (or use one of each), drained and rinsed

salt and black pepper

plain flour for coating

4 tbsp olive or sunflower oil

DRESSED LETTUCE

4 tbsp reduced-calorie mayonnaise

2 tbsp Dijon mustard

dash of lemon juice

1/2 small iceberg lettuce, finely shredded

1 small onion, thinly sliced

1 Melt the butter in a frying pan, add the mushrooms and leek, and cook over a high heat for 2–3 minutes until fairly soft. Add the chilli, sugar, and garlic, and stir fry for 2–3 minutes. Add the beans and cook, stirring, for 1 minute.

2 Remove from the heat, season well, and mash with a potato masher until the beans are broken into a rough mixture with no large lumps. Shape into 6 burgers.

3 Spinkle some flour on to a plate and season with salt and pepper. Coat both sides of each burger in flour.

4 Heat the oil in a frying pan, add the burgers, and cook for about 3–4 minutes on each side until golden brown and heated right through.

5 Make the dressed lettuce: combine the mayonnaise, mustard, and lemon juice. Stir in the lettuce and onion. Serve with the burgers.

GLAMORGAN SAUSAGES

SERVES 4

150 g (5 oz) fresh white breadcrumbs

125 g (4 oz) Caerphilly or Cheddar cheese, grated

1 small leek, finely chopped

30 g (1 oz) walnuts, finely chopped

2 tbsp chopped fresh sage or parsley

1 tsp grated lemon zest

1 tsp mustard powder

60 g (2 oz) Welsh goat's cheese, coarsely chopped

2 eggs

1 tbsp milk

salt and black pepper

plain flour for coating

2 tbsp sunflower oil

fresh sage or parsley to garnish

1 In a bowl, combine the breadcrumbs, cheese, leek, walnuts, sage or parsley, lemon zest, and mustard. Blend the goat's cheese into the mixture.

2 Separate 1 egg, reserving the white and adding the yolk to the remaining egg. Beat the egg and yolk into the cheese mixture with the milk, and season with salt and pepper.

3 Divide the mixture into 8 pieces and roll into sausages about 7 cm (3 in) long. Cover and chill for about 1 hour to allow the flavours to develop.

4 Sprinkle some flour on to a plate and season with salt and pepper. Brush the sausages with the reserved egg white, then dip into the seasoned flour until lightly coated all over. Shake off any excess flour.

5 Heat the oil in a frying pan, add the sausages, and cook over a medium heat, turning occasionally, for 8–10 minutes until golden. Drain on paper towels, and serve hot, garnished with sage or parsley.

GOAT'S CHEESE NUGGETS

Cut the goat's cheese into 16 cubes. Combine the breadcrumbs with the other ingredients as above. Mould the mixture around the goat's cheese cubes, forming small balls. Chill, then coat and cook as in steps 4 and 5.

ORIENTAL VEGETARIAN DISHES

Vegetarians fare better in the East than they do in the West because vegetarianism has been popular there for so much longer than here, and there are so many more dishes to choose from. These recipes from Thailand, Japan and China are just a small sample to inspire you.

THAI CURRY

SERVES 4

1 tbsp sunflower or sesame oil

1 fresh green chilli, halved, seeded, and finely chopped

2.5 cm (1 in) piece of fresh root ginger, peeled and grated

1 tbsp Thai green curry paste

1 large cauliflower, cut into bite-sized florets

375 g (12 oz) fine green beans, halved

1 x 400 g (13 oz) can coconut milk

150 ml (¼ pint) vegetable stock

1 fresh lemon grass stalk, bruised by bashing with a rolling pin

salt and black pepper

1 x 200 g (7 oz) can water chestnuts

3 tbsp chopped fresh coriander, to garnish

boiled or steamed Thai jasmine rice, to serve

1 Heat the oil in a wok or large non-stick frying pan and stir-fry the chilli and ginger for 2 minutes. Add the curry paste and stir-fry for a further minute.

2 Add the cauliflower and beans and stir to evenly coat the vegetables in the spices. Pour in the coconut milk and stock, then add the lemon grass and seasoning. Bring to a boil and simmer gently for about 20–30 minutes until the beans and cauliflower are just cooked (take care not to overcook them). Add the water chestnuts for the last 5 minutes. Remove and discard the lemon grass, scatter over the coriander and serve with rice.

JAPANESE NOODLE SOUP

SERVES 6

1.5 litres (2⅓ pints) miso soup (3 sachets)

1 tsp five-spice paste or 1 tsp five-spice powder mixed to a paste with a little water

300 g (10 oz) udon noodles (made from wheat flour)

250 g (8 oz) tofu, cut into 1 cm (½ in) cubes

3 spring onions, trimmed and shredded

1 Make up the miso soup, bring to a boil and add the five-spice paste. Simmer for 5 minutes, then add the noodles and simmer for 2 minutes, gently separating them with chopsticks or a fork.

2 Add the tofu and heat through for 1 minute. Ladle into soup dishes and scatter over the shredded spring onions before serving.

FIRECRACKER STIR-FRY

SERVES 4

250 g (8 oz) pak choi

2–3 tbsp sunflower or sesame oil

250 g (8 oz) sugarsnap peas, trimmed

1 red pepper, halved, seeded, and cut into strips

1 yellow pepper, halved, seeded, and cut into strips

2–3 hot fresh red chillies, halved, seeded, and sliced

300 g (10 oz) shiitake mushrooms, sliced

2–3 tbsp soy sauce

salt and black pepper

boiled or steamed long grain rice, to serve

1 Cut the leafy tops off the pak choi, shred the leaves coarsely, and reserve. Slice the stems in half, or into quarters if they are large.

2 Heat the oil in a wok or large frying pan. Add the peas, peppers and chilli and stir-fry over a high heat for about 3–4 minutes. Add the mushrooms and pak choi stems and continue to stir-fry for another 2–3 minutes.

3 When the vegetables are just about tender, add the shredded pak choi leaves with a dash of soy sauce. Taste and add salt and pepper if needed, plus more soy sauce if you like. Serve immediately, with rice.

PEKING TOFU
WITH PLUM SAUCE

SERVES 6

sunflower oil, for frying

250 g (8 oz) tofu, cut into 1.5 cm (just over ½ in) cubes

18 Chinese pancakes (ready made or see page 212)

6 spring onions, trimmed and cut into matchsticks

¼ cucumber, peeled, seeded, and cut into matchsticks

PLUM SAUCE

250 g (8 oz) dark red plums, halved and stoned

1 small cooking apple, peeled, cored, and sliced

1 fresh red chilli, halved, seeded, and finely chopped

90 g (3 oz) caster sugar

50 ml (2 fl oz) white wine vinegar

1 Make the plum sauce. Put the plums, apple, chilli, sugar, vinegar, and 25 ml (1 fl oz) water into a pan. Heat gently to dissolve the sugar, then bring to a boil. Partially cover and simmer gently for about 30–40 minutes until the fruits have cooked down and only a little liquid remains. Remove from the heat and allow to cool.

2 Pour enough oil into a non-stick frying pan to cover the base. Heat until hot, then fry the tofu for 3–4 minutes until golden brown all over, turning carefully. Remove and drain on kitchen paper.

3 To serve, spread a pancake with a little plum sauce, top with a little crispy fried tofu, spring onions, and cucumber and roll up to eat.

CLOCKWISE FROM TOP: Thai Curry with jasmine rice, Firecracker Stir-fry with long-grain rice, Japanese Noodle Soup, Peking Tofu with Plum Sauce.

CHESTNUT LOAF

SERVES 6

250 g (8 oz) frozen chestnuts, thawed

I tbsp olive oil, plus extra for greasing

I onion, coarsely chopped

2 celery stalks, chopped

2 garlic cloves, crushed

250 g (8 oz) potatoes, boiled and mashed

125 g (4 oz) fresh wholemeal breadcrumbs

I egg, beaten

2 tbsp chopped parsley

I tbsp soy sauce

I tbsp tomato purée

salt and black pepper

red pepper strips and watercress sprigs to garnish

spicy tomato salsa (see box, right) to serve

I KG (2 LB) LOAF TIN

1 Coarsely chop half of the chestnuts, and finely chop the remainder.

2 Heat the oil in a pan, add the onion, celery, and garlic, and cook, stirring, for 3–5 minutes until soft. Remove from the heat.

3 Stir in the chestnuts, potatoes, breadcrumbs, egg, parsley, soy sauce, and tomato purée, and season with salt and pepper.

4 Spoon the mixture into the greased loaf tin, and level the top. Cover with foil and cook in a preheated oven at 180°C (350°F, Gas 4) for 1 hour or until firm. Turn out, cut into slices, and garnish. Serve hot or cold, with the spicy tomato salsa.

Spicy tomato salsa

Dice 8 large tomatoes, and put into a bowl. Stir in 2 chopped spring onions, I seeded and finely chopped fresh green chilli, the zest and juice of 2 limes, 3 tbsp chopped fresh coriander, and I tsp caster sugar. Season with salt and pepper, and chill.

CHRISTMAS NUT LOAF

SERVES 6–8

75 g (2½ oz) brown rice

salt and black pepper

15 g (½ oz) dried ceps

30 g (1 oz) butter

2 carrots, grated

I small onion, finely chopped

I garlic clove, crushed

250 g (8 oz) button mushrooms, chopped

2 tbsp chopped parsley

I tbsp chopped fresh rosemary

125 g (4 oz) walnuts, toasted and chopped

125 g (4 oz) Brazil nuts, toasted and chopped

60 g (2 oz) pine nuts, toasted

175 g (6 oz) Cheddar cheese, grated

I egg, beaten

sunflower oil for greasing

rosemary sprigs to garnish

cranberry sauce (page 202) to serve

I KG (2 LB) LOAF TIN

1 Cook the rice in boiling salted water for 30–35 minutes until tender.

2 Meanwhile, soak the ceps in a bowl of warm water for about 20–30 minutes.

3 Drain the rice when it is ready. Drain the ceps, pat dry, and chop finely.

4 Melt the butter in a frying pan, add the carrots, onion, and garlic, and cook gently, stirring occasionally, for 5 minutes. Stir in the chopped mushrooms, rice, ceps, parsley, and rosemary, and cook until softened.

5 Purée the mixture in a food processor. Stir in the walnuts, Brazil nuts, pine nuts, cheese, and egg. Season with salt and pepper.

6 Lightly grease the loaf tin, spoon in the mixture, and level the top. Cover with foil and bake in a preheated oven at 190°C (375°F, Gas 5) for 1½ hours or until firm. Turn out, cut into slices, and garnish. Serve hot, with cranberry sauce.

SPINACH ROULADE

SERVES 6–8

560 g (1 lb 2 oz) spinach

30 g (1 oz) butter, plus extra for greasing

4 eggs, separated

¼ tsp grated nutmeg

1 tbsp finely grated Parmesan cheese

FILLING

15 g (½ oz) butter

250 g (8 oz) button mushrooms, sliced

juice of ½ lemon

salt and black pepper

200 ml (7 fl oz) crème fraîche

2 tbsp chopped parsley

33 × 23 CM (13 × 9 IN) SWISS ROLL TIN

1 Make the filling: melt the butter in a pan, add the mushrooms and lemon juice, and season with salt and pepper. Cook for 3 minutes until just softened, then leave to cool.

2 Wash the spinach and put into a pan with only the water remaining on the leaves. Cook over a gentle heat for 1–2 minutes until the spinach has just wilted. Drain well, and squeeze out the excess water.

3 Butter the tin and line with baking parchment. Butter the parchment.

4 Coarsely chop the spinach, turn into a large bowl, and beat in the butter, egg yolks, and nutmeg. Season with salt and pepper. In another bowl, whisk the egg whites until firm but not dry, then fold gently into the spinach mixture.

5 Pour the spinach mixture into the Swiss roll tin and bake in a preheated oven at 220°C (425°F, Gas 7) for 10–12 minutes until firm.

6 Sprinkle the Parmesan cheese on to a sheet of baking parchment. Turn the roulade out on to the cheese, leave to cool for 5–10 minutes, then peel off the lining paper. Trim the edges of the roulade.

7 Drain the mushrooms, reserving some of the cooking liquid. Put them into a bowl, add the crème fraîche, parsley, and season to taste. Add a little of the reserved liquid if too thick. Spread the filling over the roulade, leaving a 2.5 cm (1 in) border. Roll up from one long side. Cover and chill for 30 minutes. Cut into slices to serve.

CARROT ROULADE

SERVES 6–8

125 g (4 oz) butter, plus extra for greasing

1 large garlic clove, crushed

½ red pepper, halved, seeded, and finely chopped

1 × 200 g (7 oz) can tomatoes

750 g (1½ lb) carrots, grated

6 eggs, separated

FILLING

1 cucumber, seeded and diced

salt and black pepper

125 g (4 oz) goat's cheese

125 g (4 oz) full-fat soft cheese

3 spring onions, thinly sliced

1 large garlic clove, crushed

2–3 tbsp finely chopped parsley

milk if needed

33 × 23 CM (13 × 9 IN) SWISS ROLL TIN

1 Put the diced cucumber into a colander, sprinkle with salt, and leave to stand for 20 minutes.

2 Butter the tin and line with baking parchment. Butter the parchment.

3 Melt the butter, add half of the garlic, the red pepper, and tomatoes, and cook gently for 5 minutes.

4 Add the carrots and cook gently for 2 minutes or until soft. Turn the carrot mixture into a large bowl and beat in the egg yolks. Season with salt and pepper. In another bowl, whisk the egg whites until firm but not dry, then fold into the carrot mixture.

5 Pour the carrot mixture into the Swiss roll tin and bake in a preheated oven at 200°C (400°F, Gas 6) for 10 minutes or until golden. Cover and leave to cool.

6 Make the filling: rinse the cucumber and pat dry with paper towels. Turn into a bowl and combine with the goat's cheese, soft cheese, spring onions, garlic, parsley, and black pepper to taste. If the mixture is very thick, stir in 1–2 tbsp milk.

7 Turn the roulade out on to a sheet of baking parchment and peel off the lining paper. Trim the edges. Spread the filling over the roulade, leaving a 2.5 cm (1 in) border on each side. Roll up the roulade from one long side, using the baking parchment for support. Cover and chill for 30 minutes. Cut into slices to serve.

SUMMER VEGETABLE TERRINE

SERVES 8

12–16 large spinach leaves

salt and black pepper

1 aubergine, sliced lengthwise

1 tbsp olive oil, plus extra for greasing

2 large red peppers, halved, seeded, and halved

1 large yellow pepper, halved, seeded, and halved

500 g (1 lb) low-fat soft cheese

2 eggs, lightly beaten

4 tbsp single cream

30 g (1 oz) Parmesan cheese, grated

2 tbsp ready made pesto

1 KG (2 LB) LOAF TIN OR TERRINE

Lining the loaf tin

Oil the loaf tin and line with the spinach leaves, letting 5 cm (2 in) overhang the sides.

1 Blanch the spinach in boiling salted water for 30 seconds. Drain, rinse in cold water, and pat dry. Line the loaf tin (see box, right).

2 Brush the aubergine with the oil, and cook under a hot grill for 6–8 minutes on each side. Roast and peel the peppers (page 388). Cut the pepper halves into strips.

3 Combine the soft cheese, eggs, cream, grated Parmesan, and pesto. Season with salt and pepper.

4 Cover the base of the tin with some of the cheese. Layer in half of the red peppers and half of the aubergine slices, spreading cheese between each layer, then layer in the yellow pepper and repeat the layers of aubergine and red pepper, spreading the cheese between them as before. Finish with the remaining cheese. Fold over the spinach leaves.

5 Tightly cover the tin with oiled foil. Put the tin into a roasting tin and pour in boiling water to come halfway up the sides. Cook in a preheated oven at 180°C (350°F, Gas 4) for 1½ hours or until firm. Remove from the water, cool, then chill thoroughly. Slice and serve.

WINTER VEGETABLE TERRINE

SERVES 4–6

375 g (12 oz) carrots, coarsely chopped

2.5 cm (1 in) piece of fresh root ginger, peeled and grated

salt and black pepper

375 g (12 oz) celeriac, peeled and coarsely chopped

375 g (12 oz) broccoli

sunflower oil for greasing

3 eggs

1 KG (2 LB) LOAF TIN OR TERRINE

1 Cook the carrots with the ginger in boiling salted water for 10–15 minutes until the carrots are just tender. Cook the celeriac in boiling salted water for 8–10 minutes until tender.

2 Cut the stalks off the broccoli and cook them in boiling salted water for 8–10 minutes until almost tender, then add the broccoli florets and cook for 1 minute longer.

3 Drain all of the vegetables separately and rinse in cold water. Line the base of the oiled loaf tin with greaseproof paper.

4 Put the broccoli in a food processor, add 1 egg, and season with salt and pepper. Purée until smooth, then turn the mixture into the loaf tin and level the surface.

5 Put the celeriac in the food processor, add another egg, and season with salt and pepper, then purée until smooth. Spread over the broccoli mixture and level the surface.

6 Purée the carrots and ginger with the remaining egg and salt and pepper in the food processor until smooth. Spread over the celeriac and level the surface.

7 Tightly cover the tin with oiled foil. Put the tin into a roasting tin and pour in boiling water to come halfway up the sides. Cook in a preheated oven at 180°C (350°F, Gas 4) for 1 hour or until firm.

8 Remove from the water, and leave to cool in the loaf tin. Chill thoroughly in the refrigerator. Turn out the terrine, and cut into slices to serve.

8

PASTA & RICE

UNDER 30 MINUTES

PENNE WITH SPINACH & STILTON

Pasta quills with mushrooms, cream, and garlic, mixed with spinach, Stilton cheese, and lemon juice.

SERVES 4 976 calories per serving
Takes 15 minutes   Page 339

PASTA ALLA MARINARA

Pasta bows combined with squid, scallops, prawns, button mushrooms, white wine, onion, and parsley. Enriched with cream.

SERVES 6 531 calories per serving
Takes 15 minutes   Page 337

SPAGHETTI ALLA CARBONARA

Crisp-cooked strips of bacon mixed with garlic, eggs, and Parmesan cheese, then tossed with spaghetti and single cream.

SERVES 4 906 calories per serving
Takes 20 minutes   Page 344

DINNER PARTY

PASTA SHELLS WITH SCALLOPS

Scallops simmered with lemon juice, onion, peppercorns, and bay leaf. Served with a creamy mushroom sauce and pasta shells.

SERVES 4 753 calories per serving
Takes 25 minutes   Page 338

TAGLIATELLE WITH VEGETABLE RIBBONS

Fine ribbons of courgette and carrot cooked with tagliatelle. Mixed with pesto sauce.

SERVES 6 294 calories per serving
Takes 25 minutes   Page 339

CHINESE CLASSIC

EGG-FRIED RICE

Delicious and simple: long grain rice boiled then stir-fried with bacon, peas, eggs, and bean sprouts. Sprinkled with spring onions.

SERVES 4 441 calories per serving
Takes 25 minutes   Page 360

PENNE WITH ASPARAGUS

Bite-sized pieces of asparagus and pasta quills in a light, aromatic mixture of olive oil, garlic, basil, and goat's cheese.

SERVES 6 462 calories per serving
Takes 20 minutes   Page 342

TORTELLINI WITH PEAS & BACON

Rich and creamy: petits pois and diced bacon combined with double cream, salt, black pepper, and a pinch of grated nutmeg. This delicious sauce is tossed with tortellini, and servings are sprinkled generously with grated Parmesan cheese.

SERVES 6 643 calories per serving
Takes 25 minutes   Page 343

30–60 MINUTES

STIR-FRIED CHINESE NOODLES

Egg noodles stir-fried with mangetout, bean sprouts, shiitake mushrooms, garlic, and ginger, served sprinkled with spring onions.

SERVES 4 476 calories per serving

Takes 20 minutes, plus soaking   Page 343

CARIBBEAN RICE & PEAS

Traditional West Indian dish: rice cooked with kidney beans, stock, spring onions, bacon, garlic, tomatoes, herbs, and spices.

SERVES 4–6 435–290 calories per serving

Takes 35 minutes   Page 351

RISI E BISI

Risotto rice cooked with peas, stock, and Parma ham. Flavoured with garlic, onion, Parmesan cheese, and parsley.

SERVES 6 390 calories per serving

Takes 40 minutes   Page 354

SUMMER RISOTTO AL VERDE

Risotto rice cooked with stock and garlic, mixed with cream, blue cheese, pesto, and pine nuts. Served sprinkled with basil.

SERVES 4 734 calories per serving

Takes 35 minutes   Page 357

KEDGEREE

Anglo-Indian breakfast dish: long grain rice baked with smoked haddock, hard-boiled eggs, cream, and lemon juice. Mixed with parsley.

SERVES 4 470 calories per serving

Takes 45 minutes   Page 357

TAGLIATELLE WITH PRAWNS

Ribbon pasta served with a sauce of button mushrooms, tomatoes, prawns, and crème fraîche, garnished with parsley.

SERVES 4 734 calories per serving

Takes 35 minutes   Page 338

SAVOURY RICE

Long grain rice simmered with tomatoes, stock, sweetcorn, onion, carrot, and peas, and flavoured with garlic.

SERVES 4 356 calories per serving

Takes 30 minutes   Page 351

PASTA SPIRALS WITH HERBY MEATBALLS

Minced turkey or chicken, breadcrumbs, Parmesan cheese, parsley, and thyme in a tomato basil sauce.

SERVES 8 384 calories per serving

Takes 35 minutes   Page 345

PERSIAN PILAF

Rice cooked with cumin and cardamom seeds, cinnamon, cloves, and bay leaves. Combined with pistachio nuts and raisins.

SERVES 4 426 calories per serving

Takes 40 minutes   Page 355

30–60 MINUTES

SPAGHETTI ALLE VONGOLE

Fresh clams cooked in tomatoes and wine, and seasoned with onion, garlic, chilli powder, and parsley. Served with spaghetti.

SERVES 4 626 calories per serving
Takes 40 minutes   Page 337

VEGETARIAN

WILD RICE GRATIN

Basmati and wild rice baked with broccoli, garlic, onions, soured cream, mozzarella and Parmesan cheeses, and rosemary.

SERVES 6 446 calories per serving
Takes 60 minutes   Page 354

FETTUCCINE PRIMAVERA

Asparagus, broccoli, courgette, pepper, garlic, tomatoes, petits pois, and cream mixed with fettuccine. Served with basil and Parmesan.

SERVES 4 831 calories per serving
Takes 35 minutes   Page 344

ITALIAN CLASSIC

RISOTTO MILANESE

Rice cooked with stock and onion, flavoured with saffron, and mixed with Parmesan cheese. Served with Parmesan shavings.

SERVES 6 403 calories per serving
Takes 45 minutes   Page 356

PORTUGUESE RICE WITH TUNA

Nourishing meal: brown rice simmered with stock, bacon, and onion. Combined with fresh tuna, pimientos, and olives.

SERVES 4 603 calories per serving
Takes 45 minutes   Page 355

HIGH PROTEIN

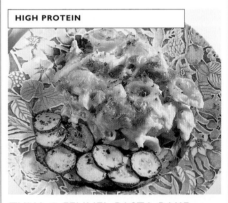

TUNA & FENNEL PASTA BAKE

Fresh and aromatic: fennel and onion baked with white sauce, pasta shells, tuna, eggs, and Cheddar cheese.

SERVES 6 512 calories per serving
Takes 45 minutes   Page 348

SPAGHETTI ALL' AMATRICIANA

Diced bacon cooked with tomatoes, garlic, red and green peppers, fresh chilli, and herbs, then tossed with spaghetti.

SERVES 6 431 calories per serving
Takes 40 minutes   Page 342

CHICKEN LIVER RISOTTO

Wild and risotto rice cooked with stock and bacon. Combined with chicken livers, mushrooms, and sun-dried tomatoes.

SERVES 4–6 619–413 calories per serving
Takes 40 minutes   Page 356

VEGETARIAN

FUSILLI ALLA NAPOLETANA

Broccoli, shiitake mushrooms, red pepper, courgettes, and mustard-flavoured white sauce baked with pasta twists.

SERVES 4 713 calories per serving
Takes 55 minutes   Page 348

OVER 60 MINUTES

THREE-CHEESE MACARONI

Macaroni baked with a sauce flavoured with smoked and mature Cheddar, and light mozzarella cheeses, topped with breadcrumbs.

SERVES 6–8 581–436 calories per serving

Takes 1 hour 5 minutes   Page 349

CLASSIC LASAGNE

Pasta layered with minced beef, simmered with stock, tomatoes, celery, white sauce, and Cheddar and Parmesan cheeses.

SERVES 8 641 calories per serving

Takes 1½ hours, plus simmering   Page 350

CANNELLONI WITH RICOTTA & SPINACH

Cannelloni tubes filled with spinach and ricotta cheese, and topped with tomato sauce.

SERVES 6 462 calories per serving

Takes 40 minutes, plus simmering   Page 350

FISHERMAN'S LASAGNE

Pasta layered with haddock, prawns, courgettes, and parsley sauce. Sprinkled with Cheddar and Parmesan cheeses.

SERVES 8 477 calories per serving

Takes 1¼ hours   Page 349

SPAGHETTI BOLOGNESE

Traditional Italian dish: spaghetti served with a sauce of minced beef simmered with celery, garlic, tomato, and redcurrant jelly.

SERVES 4 904 calories per serving

Takes 15 minutes, plus simmering   Page 345

PAELLA

Chicken and rice are cooked in the oven with bacon, stock, tomatoes, onion, peppers, peas, and saffron. Mussels and prawns are stirred in and cooked gently on top of the stove, then the dish is served garnished with jumbo prawns, lemon wedges, olives, and parsley.

SERVES 6 718 calories per serving

Takes 1¼ hours   Page 360

PASTA & RICE KNOW-HOW

BOTH PASTA AND RICE are natural convenience foods: they are so quick to cook and they do not need any elaborate preparation. They are also endlessly versatile, working well with almost every ingredient imaginable to make starters, soups, main dishes, side dishes, salads, snacks, and even a few desserts.

Pasta and rice are very nutritious, being high in starchy carbohydrates, and in their wholegrain forms also offering vitamins, minerals, and fibre. As long as rich ingredients such as butter, cream, and cheese, are kept to a minimum, pasta and rice dishes can be very low in fat and calories.

BUYING & STORING

Pasta is available both fresh and dried as well as vacuum-packed, in a huge variety of shapes, both plain and stuffed. The best commercial dried pasta is made from durum wheat. Egg is sometimes added to dried pasta, while the fresh pasta sold in packets in supermarkets is most often enriched with eggs. Pasta is also coloured and flavoured – with spinach or tomato, for example. Fresh pasta is convenient because it cooks quickly, but its texture is not necessarily as good as some dried pasta. A good Italian brand of dried pasta, made from 100% durum wheat (*semola di grano duro*), is often of superior quality.

Dried pasta, in a tightly closed packet, will keep almost indefinitely in the storecupboard (up to 2 years); fresh pasta must be refrigerated and can only be kept for 2–3 days (check the use-by date). For longer storage, freeze it (see below).

Rice is another good storecupboard stand-by. As long as it is stored in an airtight container in a cool, dry, dark place, it will keep for up to a year. But make sure that the container is tightly closed to prevent moisture or insects from getting in.

Store any leftover cooked pasta or rice in a tightly closed container in the refrigerator. Use pasta within 2 days. Rice should be eaten on the day it is cooked as it is susceptible to toxins that cause food poisoning.

MICROWAVING

There is no advantage to cooking pasta in a microwave because it takes just as long as conventional cooking. However, many pasta sauces can be microwaved quickly and successfully, dishes containing layered or filled pasta cook really well in the microwave, and it is also an excellent way to reheat cooked pasta (be careful not to overcook it). The microwave is excellent for cooking rice, plain or turned into a pilaf or risotto, and the liquid does not have to be brought to a boil before the rice is added. Risotto turns out as tender and creamy as one made by the classic method that involves constant stirring, and yet it can be left totally unattended in the microwave.

FREEZING

Fresh uncooked pasta can be frozen for up to 3 months and then cooked from frozen. Layered or filled pasta dishes such as cannelloni, lasagne, and macaroni cheese freeze very well and can also be stored for up to 3 months. Put them in foil or other freezerproof containers that can go straight from the freezer into the oven.

There is no advantage to freezing cooked rice as it takes a long time to thaw – longer than it would take to cook a fresh batch.

It is not advisable to freeze pasta and rice in soups and other dishes that contain a lot of liquid because the pasta and rice become mushy when thawed. Instead, add when reheating the soup or casserole.

ORIENTAL NOODLES

Oriental noodles are made from a variety of flours. The most popular types are available in supermarkets and delicatessens; others can be found in Chinese or Japanese shops.

Wheat noodles
The most common of Oriental noodles, these are made from wheat flour usually enriched with egg. They are available both flat and round and in a variety of widths.

Cellophane noodles
Sometimes referred to as transparent noodles or bean thread noodles, these are very fine and white. They are made from ground mung beans.

Rice noodles
Rice vermicelli are long, thin, white strands made from rice flour. Sold dried or fresh in bundles, they are used in soups and are also deep-fried.

Rice sticks
Made from the same dough as rice noodles, rice sticks are broad ribbons. They are usually served in a broth or sauce.

Soba
These thin, brownish Japanese noodles are made from buckwheat flour. They are often served with a dipping sauce.

Udon
Made from white wheat flour, these are also from Japan.

Noodles know-how

Store Oriental noodles in the same way as pasta.

•

Most Oriental noodles need only be soaked or briefly cooked in boiling water before being added to soups and broths, vegetable dishes and stir-fries.

PASTA SHAPES

Of the many pasta shapes available there are some that are traditionally served with certain sauces – spaghetti with bolognese sauce, for example. But you can mix and match as you wish.

Long, thin varieties
Capelli d'angelo or angel hair, vermicelli, spaghettini, spaghetti, and bucatini are best served with a thin oily sauce that clings without making the strands stick together.

Long flat ribbons
Pasta such as linguine, fettuccine, and tagliatelle is usually served with a creamy sauce such as *alfredo*.

Tubular pasta
Macaroni, penne (quills), and rigatoni are best with rich sauces that will run inside their tubes.

Interesting shapes
There is a vast range of small pasta shapes, and more are being created every day. The most common include ditali (thimbles), fusilli (spirals), conchiglie (shells),

farfalle (bows), gnocchi (fluted shells), lumache (snails), orecchiette (ears), and radiatori (grills). Sauce them like tubular pasta.

Soup pasta
Very small pasta shapes, such as conchigliette, ditalini, farfallette and orzo, are used in soup.

Filled pastas
Agnolotti, capelletti, ravioli, and tortellini are some of the shapes stuffed with ground meats or mixtures such as spinach and ricotta, and served with a simple sauce.

Sheet pasta
Flat sheets of lasagne are layered with sauce and baked. Fresh lasagne, and cooked dried lasagne, can be rolled around a filling to make cannelloni.

PRE-COOKED LASAGNE

The sheets of dried lasagne that are labelled "pre-cooked" or "no pre-cooking required" are a great boon to the busy, time-stretched cook because they can be taken straight from the packet and layered with the other ingredients. However, this lasagne needs to absorb liquid during cooking, so if you are using it in a recipe that calls for fresh pasta or for ordinary dried lasagne, increase the quantity of sauce and make it thinner and runnier. Or briefly soak the sheets in a dish of hot water for about 5 minutes to moisten and soften them before layering in the baking dish.

Coloured & flavoured pasta

Not only does pasta come in a vast range of shapes, you can also choose from a variety of colours and flavours. Green is the most common colour, and is derived from spinach. Other colours include red, from tomato purée, pink, coloured with beetroot, yellow, from saffron, and even black pasta, coloured with squid ink. These colourings affect the taste very little. Flavoured pasta usually has ingredients such as herbs, garlic, or black pepper added to the dough. Serve with a complementary sauce.

COOKING PASTA

There is one golden rule when cooking pasta: use plenty of water and salt – at least 2 litres (3½ pints) water and 2 tsp salt for every 250 g (8 oz) of pasta.

1 Bring the salted water to a boil. Add the pasta and stir to separate. If cooking spaghetti, let the ends soften before stirring. Return the water to a boil as quickly as possible. Reduce the heat so that the water is bubbling briskly and cook, uncovered.

2 When the pasta is al dente (see box, below), immediately tip it into a large colander, and shake to drain the pasta thoroughly.

3 Return the pasta to the pan or transfer to a warmed bowl. Toss with olive oil or butter, add plenty of ground black pepper and chopped fresh herbs, if liked, and serve immediately.

Pasta know-how

To test pasta, lift out a piece and bite it – it should be tender but still a little firm. The Italians call this al dente, literally "to the tooth".

If you are going to use cooked pasta in a baked dish, undercook it slightly before mixing it with sauce. This will help prevent it from being overcooked when it comes out of the oven.

COOKING TIMES & QUANTITIES

These times can only be a guide because they depend on the freshness of fresh pasta and the age of dried pasta, as well as shape and thickness. Start timing as soon as the water returns to a boil, and for fresh pasta, start testing three-quarters of the way through the suggested cooking time. If using dried pasta, start testing as soon as the minimum time given on the packet is reached. Fresh, store-bought pasta takes 2–4 minutes, 7–10 minutes if filled. Most dried pastas cook in 8–12 minutes (less for fine pasta such as capelli d'angelo and vermicelli).

In Italy, pasta is usually eaten as a first course. Use 500 g (1 lb) fresh or dried pasta (uncooked weight) to serve 6 people as a first course and 4 people as a main dish. If the dish has a rich sauce or filling it will stretch even further. As an accompaniment to another dish, this amount would serve 6–8 people.

COOKING WITH RICE

The length of the rice grain determines how it should be cooked and used. Short grain rice is almost round in shape and very starchy. It is best cooked by absorption, so that it remains moist and sticky, and used for puddings, risottos, paella, stir-fried rice, and croquettes. The grains of long grain rice are separate, dry, and fluffy after cooking so it can be boiled and then used in pilafs, salads, and other savoury dishes.

White rice has been milled to remove the husk, bran, and germ, whereas for brown rice only the tough outer husk has been removed, leaving the nutritious bran layer. This gives it its distinctive colour and nutty flavour.

COOKING RICE BY ABSORPTION

Cook the rice very gently in simmering salted water. Use 2 parts water to 1 part rice.

1 Bring the salted water to a boil and add the rice. Return to a boil and stir once. Cover, reduce the heat, and cook gently until the water is absorbed.

2 Remove the pan from the heat and leave to stand, covered, for at least 5 minutes. Fluff up the rice with chopsticks or a fork just before serving.

BOILING RICE

Long grain rice should be rinsed well before and after boiling, to remove starch that would cause stickiness.

1 Put the rice into a large bowl of cold water. Swirl it around with your fingertips until the water becomes milky. Drain and repeat until the water stays clear. Drain again. Bring a large pan of salted water to a boil and add the rice.

2 Bring the water back to a boil. Reduce the heat so that the water is simmering quite vigorously. Cook until the rice is just tender. Drain well and rinse with boiling water to remove any excess starch.

COOKING RISOTTO RICE

An authentic risotto requires constant attention as the hot liquid (usually stock) must be stirred into the rice very gradually. This basic technique can be varied in many ways by adding shellfish, mushrooms, herbs, ham, and so on.

1 Heat butter or oil in a large saucepan and soften the onion, garlic, or other flavourings as specified in the recipe.

2 Add the rice and stir to coat the grains with the fat (this will keep them separate during cooking). Cook, stirring, for 1–2 minutes or until the rice grains look translucent.

3 Add a ladleful, about 150 ml (1/4 pint), of the hot stock. Cook until absorbed. Add another ladleful and cook until absorbed.

4 Continue adding stock, stirring, for 25–30 minutes. When the rice is tender but still firm to the bite, you have added enough stock.

RICE VARIETIES

There are many varieties of rice, each with a distinct flavour and aroma. Here are the most common.

Camargue red
Similar to brown rice in texture, flavour, and cooking time.

Basmati
Available in brown or white varieties. Used mainly in Indian dishes. Cook for 10–15 minutes.

Brown
Has a slightly chewy texture with a mild nutty flavour. Cook for 30–35 minutes.

Easy-cook
Part-cooked so the grains stay separate. Cook for 10–12 minutes.

Long grain
Mild in flavour. The most widely used type of white rice. Cook for 12–15 minutes.

Short grain
Italian short grain (eg arborio, carnaroli) is used for risotto; Spanish paella rice is similar but less creamy (the best is said to come from Valencia). Short grain rice is also used for rice pudding. Cook for 20–25 minutes.

Wild
Not a true rice, but an aquatic grass from North America. Cook for 35–40 minutes.

PASTA ALLA MARINARA

SERVES 6

500 g (1 lb) pasta bows

salt and black pepper

2 tbsp olive oil

1 large onion, finely chopped

1 large garlic clove, crushed

125 ml (4 fl oz) dry white wine

125 g (4 oz) squid, cut into strips or rings

60 g (2 oz) button mushrooms, sliced

125 g (4 oz) scallops, halved

125 g (4 oz) cooked peeled prawns

150 ml (¼ pint) double cream

4 tbsp chopped parsley

1 Cook the pasta bows in a large saucepan of boiling salted water for 8–10 minutes until just tender.

2 Meanwhile, heat the oil in a large pan, add the onion and garlic, and cook gently, stirring occasionally, for 3–5 minutes until softened but not coloured.

3 Pour in the white wine and boil to reduce the liquid in the saucepan to about 2 tbsp, stirring constantly. Add the squid and cook for 1 minute, then add the mushrooms and scallops, and cook, stirring, for a further 2 minutes. Add the prawns, cream, and half of the parsley, and heat through.

4 Drain the pasta bows thoroughly, and add to the seafood mixture, stirring well to combine. Season with salt and black pepper, and serve at once, garnished with the remaining chopped parsley.

Healthy option

Seafood and cream are a classic combination for a pasta sauce, but you may prefer a slightly less rich alternative. In fact, you can omit the cream altogether and use a few tablespoons of the pasta cooking water instead. Italian cooks often use this technique.

SPAGHETTI ALLE VONGOLE

SERVES 4

about 3 dozen fresh clams in their shells, cleaned (page 124)

2 tbsp olive oil, plus extra for tossing

1 onion, chopped

1 garlic clove, crushed

¼ tsp chilli powder

1 x 400 g (13 oz) can chopped tomatoes

4 tbsp dry white wine

salt and black pepper

500 g (1 lb) spaghetti

2 tbsp chopped parsley

1 Holding each clam in a tea towel, insert a thin knife blade between the shells and twist the knife to open the shells. Reserve 4 clams for garnish. Remove the remaining clams from their shells, cut them into bite-sized pieces, and set aside with any juices.

2 Heat the olive oil in a large pan, add the onion and garlic, and cook gently, stirring occasionally, for 3–5 minutes until softened but not coloured. Add the chilli powder and cook gently, stirring, for 1 minute.

3 Add the tomatoes and wine, season with salt and pepper, and bring to a boil. Simmer, uncovered, for about 15 minutes or until the mixture has thickened.

4 Meanwhile, cook the spaghetti in a large saucepan of boiling salted water for 8–10 minutes until just tender. Drain, then toss the spaghetti in a little olive oil to prevent sticking. Transfer to warmed serving bowls.

5 Add the parsley, and the clams and their juices to the tomato mixture, and cook for 2 minutes. Do not cook longer or the clams will toughen.

6 Taste for seasoning, then spoon the sauce over the spaghetti. Serve at once, garnished with the reserved clams in their shells.

Cook's know-how

Live clams should be tightly closed in their shells. If any are open, give them a sharp tap on the work surface, then discard any that do not close.

TAGLIATELLE WITH PRAWNS

SERVES 4

2 tbsp olive oil

1 large onion, chopped

1 garlic clove, crushed

375 g (12 oz) button mushrooms, halved

500 g (1 lb) tomatoes, chopped into small pieces, cores removed

salt and black pepper

500 g (1 lb) tagliatelle

375 g (12 oz) cooked peeled prawns

125 ml (4 fl oz) crème fraîche

4 tbsp chopped parsley to garnish

1 Heat the oil in a large pan, add the onion and garlic, and cook gently, stirring, for 3–5 minutes until softened but not coloured. Add the mushrooms and cook over a high heat, stirring, for about 5 minutes.

2 Add the tomatoes, season with salt and pepper, and simmer gently, uncovered, for about 20 minutes or until the mixture has thickened.

3 Meanwhile, cook the tagliatelle in a large saucepan of boiling salted water for 8–10 minutes until just tender.

4 Add the prawns and crème fraîche to the tomato mixture and cook gently for about 2 minutes until the prawns are heated through. Taste for seasoning.

5 Drain the tagliatelle thoroughly and pile on to warmed serving plates. Spoon the prawn mixture on top, sprinkle with parsley, and serve at once.

PASTA WITH SMOKED SALMON & PRAWNS

Substitute 125 g (4 oz) smoked salmon, cut into bite-sized pieces, for 125 g (4 oz) of the prawns. Add the smoked salmon after the prawns have been heated through in step 4.

PASTA SHELLS WITH SCALLOPS

SERVES 4

8 large scallops, each cut into 3 slices

75 ml (2½ fl oz) water

juice of 1 lemon

1 slice of onion

6 black peppercorns

1 small bay leaf

500 g (1 lb) pasta shells

15 g (½ oz) butter

chopped parsley and lemon slices to garnish

SAUCE

45 g (1½ oz) butter

125 g (4 oz) button mushrooms, sliced

30 g (1 oz) plain flour

150 ml (¼ pint) double cream or crème fraîche

1 tbsp tomato purée

salt and black pepper

1 Put the scallops into a pan with the measured water, half the lemon juice, the onion, peppercorns, and bay leaf.

2 Bring to a gentle simmer, cover, and poach very gently for 2–3 minutes or until the scallops are opaque.

3 Remove the scallops with a slotted spoon, strain the liquid, and reserve.

4 Make the sauce: melt the butter in a saucepan, add the mushrooms, and cook gently, stirring occasionally, for 2 minutes. Sprinkle in the flour and cook, stirring, for 1 minute. Remove from the heat and blend in the strained poaching liquid. Cook, stirring, for 1 minute until thickened.

5 Add the cream and tomato purée and bring to a boil, stirring constantly until the mixture thickens. Simmer for 2 minutes, then add salt and pepper to taste.

6 Cook the pasta shells in a large saucepan of boiling salted water for 8–10 minutes or until tender. Drain, then toss with the butter and the remaining lemon juice. Add the scallops to the sauce, and heat through very gently.

7 Pile the pasta on warmed serving plates, and spoon the sauce on top. Serve at once, garnished with the parsley and lemon slices.

TAGLIATELLE WITH VEGETABLE RIBBONS

SERVES 4

375 g (12 oz) courgettes

250 g (8 oz) carrots, peeled

salt

375 g (12 oz) fresh tagliatelle

scant 1 tbsp olive oil

1 garlic clove, crushed

200 ml (7 fl oz) half-fat crème fraîche

2 tbsp pesto (page 388) or use ready made

60 g (2 oz) dolcelatte cheese

chopped parsley to garnish

1 Thinly slice the courgettes and carrots into wide, thin ribbons (page 369).

2 Bring a large pan of salted water to a boil, add the tagliatelle, courgettes, and carrots, and cook for 3 minutes. Drain and refresh under cold running water.

3 Heat the oil in a large frying pan, add the garlic, and stir-fry for about 1 minute.

4 Add the crème fraîche and pesto, then crumble in the cheese. Simmer and stir the sauce for 2–3 minutes, then add the tagliatelle and vegetables. Mix gently, turn into a warmed serving dish, and sprinkle with chopped parsley. Serve immediately

Cook's know-how

Dolcelatte is a mild and creamy blue cheese from Italy. For a change you could use gorgonzola, another Italian blue cheese which has a stronger, saltier flavour. The French Roquefort could also be used.

PENNE WITH SPINACH & STILTON

SERVES 4

500 g (1 lb) penne

salt and black pepper

45 g (1 1/2 oz) butter

2 large garlic cloves, crushed

250 g (8 oz) chestnut mushrooms, sliced

300 ml (1/2 pint) double cream

1 egg, lightly beaten (optional)

90 g (3 oz) spinach, coarsely shredded

90 g (3 oz) blue Stilton cheese, crumbled

juice of 1/2 lemon

pinch of grated nutmeg

1 Cook the pasta quills in boiling salted water for 8–10 minutes until just tender.

2 Meanwhile, melt the butter in a large pan, add the garlic, and cook, stirring, for 1 minute. Add the mushrooms and cook, stirring occasionally, for 2 minutes. Stir in the cream and boil for 2–3 minutes until the mixture reaches a coating consistency.

3 Drain the pasta, add to the mushroom and cream mixture with the egg (if using), stir well, and heat through. Add the spinach, Stilton cheese, lemon juice, nutmeg, and pepper to taste, and stir well to coat the pasta. Serve at once.

Cook's know-how

Adding an egg to the sauce makes it richer and creamier, but you can omit it if you prefer a lighter consistency.

PENNE WITH BROCCOLI & STILTON

Substitute 125 g (4 oz) small broccoli florets for the spinach. Cook in boiling salted water for 3–4 minutes or until just tender. Add to the pasta with the cheese, lemon juice, nutmeg, and pepper, omitting the egg. Stir well, and serve at once.

EASY PASTA SUPPER DISHES

Pasta is so popular with most people that you can never have enough recipes for tasty dishes to make with it. These three make delicious everyday meals, and are equally good for informal entertaining. All you need to accompany them is a tossed green salad and some good bread.

FUSILLI WITH DOUBLE TOMATOES

SERVES 4

375 g (12 oz) fusilli tricolore

250 g (8 oz) asparagus tips, cut into 5 cm (2 in) lengths

3 tbsp olive oil

2 garlic cloves, crushed

90 g (3 oz) chestnut mushrooms, sliced

500 g (1 lb) ripe cherry tomatoes, halved

60 g (2 oz) sun-blushed or sun-dried tomatoes, each piece snipped into three

salt and black pepper

TO SERVE

30 g (1 oz) pine nuts, toasted

a small handful of fresh basil leaves, shredded

1 Cook the pasta in boiling salted water according to packet instructions until just tender, adding the asparagus 2 minutes before the end of cooking. Drain the pasta and asparagus together and refresh under cold running water. Drain well.

2 Heat the oil in a large frying pan, add the garlic and mushrooms, and fry over a high heat for a couple of minutes. Add both kinds of tomatoes and continue to stir-fry over a high heat until they are just heated through. Season well.

3 Quickly toss the pasta and asparagus through the tomato mixture in the pan until everything is hot, then scatter over the pine nuts and basil. Serve at once.

Healthy note

Tomatoes contain beneficial amounts of vitamins C and E. More importantly, they are a rich source of lycopene, a powerful antioxidant that can help to protect the body from harmful free radical damage. Lycopene is most easily absorbed from tomatoes that have been heat processed in some way; a little oil helps absorption, too. Cherry tomatoes are also especially rich in antioxidants. All these ingredients make this recipe a perfect addition to a healthy diet.

RED HOT RAGU

SERVES 6

375 g (12 oz) rigatoni or other tubular pasta

60 g (2 oz) Parmesan cheese, coarsely grated

3 tbsp chopped parsley, or 175 g (6 oz) young spinach leaves, shredded

SAUCE

500 g (1 lb) good-quality pork sausages with herbs

a little olive oil

3 garlic cloves, crushed

2 small red chillies, halved, cored, and finely chopped

2 x 400 g (13 oz) cans chopped tomatoes

1 large onion, finely chopped

1 good tbsp sun-dried tomato purée

1 tbsp chopped fresh basil

1/2–1 tsp caster or granulated sugar, to taste

salt and black pepper

1 Make the sauce. Cut long slits in each sausage and remove the skins. Heat a little oil in a non-stick frying pan and add the garlic and sausagemeat. Fry over a medium heat for about 4–5 minutes, breaking the meat up with a wooden spatula until it is brown, with a minced pork consistency. Stir in the remaining sauce ingredients. Bring to a boil, cover, and simmer gently for 40–50 minutes or until the sausagemeat is cooked. Check the seasoning.

2 Meanwhile, cook the pasta in boiling salted water according to packet instructions until just tender.

3 Drain the pasta and mix it into the sauce in the pan with half the Parmesan, then check the seasoning again. Scatter the parsley and remaining Parmesan over individual servings.

NOTE: If using spinach, stir it into the bubbling sauce and cook for a couple of minutes until it wilts before adding the pasta and half the Parmesan.

RIGATONI WITH MUSHROOMS AND ROCKET

SERVES 6

375 g (12 oz) rigatoni or other tubular pasta

150 ml (5 fl oz) dry white wine

1 small onion, finely chopped

500 g (1 lb) mixed wild or cultivated mushrooms, such as shiitake, oyster, ceps, coarsely sliced

salt and black pepper

6 tbsp whipping cream

4 tbsp good-quality pesto (ready made or see page 388)

60 g (2 oz) rocket leaves

coarsely grated Parmesan cheese, to serve

1 Cook the pasta in boiling salted water according to packet instructions until just tender.

2 Meanwhile, pour the wine into a large frying pan, add the onion and cook over a low heat until the onion has softened, about 10–15 minutes. Add the mushrooms and stir over a high heat for a few minutes until the mushrooms are cooked and the liquid has reduced (there should be about 2 tablespoons left). Season with salt and pepper, add the cream and pesto, and stir to mix.

3 Drain the pasta and add to the mushroom mixture in the pan. Check the seasoning. At the last moment, stir in the rocket leaves and allow to wilt for about 2 minutes. Serve immediately, scattered with Parmesan.

NOTE: The warm, peppery, pungent taste of rocket is one people love or hate. If you love it and you're making your own pesto for this dish, try substituting rocket for basil in the pesto recipe on page 388.

CLOCKWISE FROM TOP: Red Hot Ragù, Rigatoni with Mushrooms & Rocket, Fusilli with Double Tomatoes.

PENNE WITH ASPARAGUS

SERVES 6

125 g (4 oz) goat's cheese, cut into small pieces

3 tbsp olive oil

3 garlic cloves, crushed

3 tbsp shredded fresh basil

500 g (1 lb) penne or spaghetti

salt and black pepper

500 g (1 lb) asparagus

1 In a small bowl, combine the goat's cheese, olive oil, garlic, and shredded fresh basil.

2 Cook the pasta in a large saucepan of boiling salted water for 8–10 minutes until just tender.

3 Meanwhile, trim any woody ends from the asparagus and peel the spears if they are not young. Cut the asparagus into bite-sized pieces and cook in boiling salted water for about 3 minutes until just tender.

4 Drain the pasta thoroughly, add the goat's cheese mixture, and toss together. Drain the asparagus and add to the pasta mixture. Toss lightly together, season with salt and black pepper, and serve at once.

SPAGHETTI ALL' AMATRICIANA

A speciality of Amatrice, near Rome, this tomato-based sauce is spiked with chilli and garlic, and richly flavoured with diced bacon and roast peppers.

SERVES 6

1 red pepper

1 green pepper

4 tbsp olive oil

5 unsmoked bacon or pancetta rashers, any rinds removed, diced

1/2–1 fresh green chilli, halved, seeded, and thinly sliced

3 garlic cloves, crushed

2 ripe tomatoes, finely chopped

2 tbsp chopped flat-leaf parsley

salt and black pepper

500 g (1 lb) spaghetti

shavings of Parmesan cheese to serve

1 Halve the red and green peppers, and remove the cores and seeds. Roast and peel the peppers (page 388). Cut the flesh into thin strips.

2 Heat the oil in a frying pan, add the bacon, and cook over a high heat for 5 minutes or until crisp. Add the roasted pepper strips and the chilli, and cook for 2 minutes. Stir in the garlic and cook for about 1 minute.

3 Add the tomatoes and parsley and cook for 3 minutes or until thickened. Remove from the heat and season with salt and pepper.

4 Cook the spaghetti in a large saucepan of boiling salted water for 8–10 minutes until just tender.

5 Drain the spaghetti thoroughly. Add the sauce and toss with the spaghetti. Serve at once, topped with Parmesan cheese shavings.

SPAGHETTI ALL' ARRABBIATA

Melt 30 g (1 oz) butter with 2 tbsp olive oil in a frying pan, add 3 crushed garlic cloves and 1/2–1 tsp crushed dried red chillies (chilli flakes), and cook gently. Drain 1 x 400 g (13 oz) can chopped tomatoes, stir the tomatoes into the pan, and bring slowly to a boil. Simmer until reduced and thickened, add 1/4 tsp dried oregano, and season with salt and black pepper. Toss with the spaghetti, and serve at once.

STIR-FRIED CHINESE NOODLES

SERVES 4

5 dried shiitake mushrooms

250 ml (8 fl oz) hot vegetable stock

375 g (12 oz) Chinese egg noodles

salt

about 2 tsp soy sauce

1 tbsp sunflower oil

250 g (8 oz) mangetout

3 garlic cloves, crushed

5 mm (1/4 in) piece of fresh root ginger, peeled and grated

1/4 tsp sugar (optional)

125 g (4 oz) bean sprouts

about 1/2 tsp crushed dried red chillies (chilli flakes)

TO SERVE

3 spring onions, sliced

2 tsp sesame oil

1 tbsp chopped fresh coriander

1 Put the mushrooms into a bowl, pour over the hot vegetable stock, and leave to soak for about 30 minutes.

2 Drain the mushrooms, reserving the liquid. Squeeze the mushrooms dry, then cut into thin strips.

3 Cook the noodles in a large saucepan of boiling salted water for 3 minutes or according to packet instructions. Drain the noodles, toss with soy sauce to taste, and set aside.

4 Heat the sunflower oil in a wok or large frying pan, add the mushrooms, mangetout, garlic, and ginger, and stir-fry for 2 minutes. Add the sugar, if using, bean sprouts, crushed chillies to taste, and 3 tbsp of the reserved mushroom soaking liquid. Stir-fry for 2 minutes.

5 Add the egg noodles and stir-fry for 2 minutes or until heated through. Serve at once, sprinkled with the spring onions, sesame oil, and coriander.

TORTELLINI WITH PEAS & BACON

SERVES 6

500 g (1 lb) tortellini

salt and black pepper

1 tbsp sunflower oil

250 g (8 oz) bacon or pancetta rashers, any rinds removed, diced

175 g (6 oz) frozen petits pois

300 ml (1/2 pint) double cream

grated Parmesan cheese to serve

1 Cook the tortellini in boiling salted water for about 10–12 minutes, or according to packet instructions, until tender.

2 Meanwhile, heat the oil in a frying pan, add the bacon, and cook over a high heat, stirring, for 3 minutes or until crisp.

3 Cook the petits pois in boiling salted water for about 2 minutes until just tender. Drain.

4 Drain the tortellini thoroughly and return to the saucepan. Add the bacon, petits pois, cream, and nutmeg, and season with salt and pepper. Heat gently for 1–2 minutes to warm through. Serve at once, sprinkled with grated Parmesan cheese.

Healthy option

Use just 150 ml (1/4 pint) low-fat crème fraîche instead of the double cream. Then do what the Italians do – splash a few ladlefuls of the pasta water into the sauce and stir vigorously to make enough sauce to coat the pasta.

FETTUCCINE PRIMAVERA

SERVES 4

125 g (4 oz) asparagus, trimmed and cut into bite-sized pieces

125 g (4 oz) broccoli florets

1 courgette, sliced

salt and black pepper

3 tbsp olive oil

1/2 red and 1/2 yellow pepper, halved, seeded, and diced

3 garlic cloves, crushed

1 x 200 g (7 oz) can chopped tomatoes

90 g (3 oz) frozen petits pois

125 ml (4 fl oz) double cream

500 g (1 lb) fettuccine

4 tbsp shredded fresh basil

90 g (3 oz) Parmesan cheese, grated, to serve

1 Cook the asparagus, broccoli, and courgette in boiling salted water for 3 minutes or until just tender. Drain, rinse under cold running water, and set aside.

2 Heat the oil in a large, deep frying pan, add the peppers and garlic, and cook, stirring, for 4 minutes or until the peppers are softened.

3 Add the tomatoes and the petits pois, and cook for 5 minutes or until the liquid in the pan is reduced by half.

4 Add the asparagus, broccoli, and courgette, stir in the cream, and boil for 1–2 minutes to reduce the liquid and concentrate the flavour. Add salt and pepper to taste, and remove from the heat.

5 Cook the fettuccine in a large saucepan of boiling salted water for 8–10 minutes until just tender.

6 Drain the fettuccine thoroughly, add to the sauce, and toss over a high heat. Stir in the shredded basil and serve at once, sprinkled with Parmesan cheese.

Healthy option

For a lighter, less creamy, version of this classic dish, use 1 x 400 g (13 oz) can chopped tomatoes and omit the cream. Instead of sprinkling with Parmesan to serve, sprinkle with more shredded fresh basil.

SPAGHETTI ALLA CARBONARA

SERVES 4

500 g (1 lb) spaghetti

salt and black pepper

175 g (6 oz) diced pancetta or streaky bacon, any rinds removed

1 garlic clove, crushed

4 eggs

125 g (4 oz) Parmesan cheese, grated

150 ml (1/4 pint) single cream

chopped parsley to garnish

1 Cook the spaghetti in a large saucepan of boiling salted water for 8–10 minutes until just tender.

2 Meanwhile, put the pancetta or bacon into a frying pan and heat gently for 7 minutes until the fat runs. Increase the heat and add the garlic. Cook for 2–3 minutes or until the bacon is crisp.

3 Break the eggs into a bowl. Add the bacon and garlic mixture, using a slotted spoon. Add the Parmesan cheese, season generously with salt and pepper, and whisk until well blended.

4 Drain the spaghetti and return to the hot pan. Stir in the bacon and egg mixture and toss quickly until the egg just begins to set. Stir in the cream and heat gently. Serve at once, sprinkled with parsley.

Cook's know-how

It is best to buy a whole piece of Parmesan cheese and grate the quantity you need for a given dish. Ready grated Parmesan in packets is less economical and lacks the flavour of freshly grated Parmesan.

SPAGHETTI ALFREDO

Heat 150 ml (1/4 pint) double cream with 30 g (1 oz) butter until the mixture has thickened. Set aside. Cook the pasta, drain, then add to the cream mixture. Add 90 ml (3 fl oz) more cream, 90 g (3 oz) Parmesan cheese, a pinch of grated nutmeg, and season with salt and pepper. Heat gently until thickened, and serve.

PASTA SPIRALS WITH HERBY MEATBALLS

SERVES 8

500 g (1 lb) pasta spirals (fusilli)

shredded fresh basil to garnish

TOMATO BASIL SAUCE

1 tbsp olive oil

1 onion, coarsely chopped

2 garlic cloves, crushed

2 x 400 g (13 oz) cans chopped tomatoes

1 tsp caster sugar

salt and black pepper

MEATBALLS

500 g (1 lb) minced turkey or chicken

2 tbsp chopped parsley

1 tsp chopped fresh thyme

60 g (2 oz) Parmesan cheese, grated

60 g (2 oz) fresh breadcrumbs

1 egg, beaten

a little olive oil, for frying

1 Make the tomato basil sauce: heat the oil in a deep frying pan, add the onion and garlic, and cook gently, stirring occasionally, for 3–4 minutes.

2 Add the tomatoes and sugar, season with salt and pepper, and stir well. Simmer, uncovered, for about 20 minutes, stirring occasionally, until the onion is soft and the sauce reduced.

3 Make the meatballs: in a large bowl, combine the minced turkey or chicken, parsley, thyme, Parmesan cheese, breadcrumbs, and egg, then season with salt and pepper. With dampened hands, shape the mixture into balls about the size of large walnuts.

4 Heat a little oil in a large frying pan, add the meatballs, and cook for about 8 minutes until browned and cooked through. Lift out with a slotted spoon and drain on paper towels. Add to the tomato sauce and heat gently for about 5 minutes.

5 Meanwhile, cook the pasta in a large pan of boiling salted water for 8–10 minutes until tender. Drain thoroughly, and top with the meatballs and sauce. Serve at once, garnished with shredded basil.

SPAGHETTI BOLOGNESE

SERVES 4

3 tbsp olive oil

500 g (1 lb) minced beef

1 large onion, finely chopped

2 celery stalks, sliced

1 tbsp plain flour

2 garlic cloves, crushed

90 g (3 oz) tomato purée

150 ml (¼ pint) beef stock

150 ml (¼ pint) red wine

1 x 400 g (13 oz) can chopped tomatoes

1 tbsp redcurrant jelly

salt and black pepper

500 g (1 lb) spaghetti

grated Parmesan cheese to serve

1 Heat 2 tbsp of the oil in a saucepan. Add the minced beef, onion, and celery, and cook, stirring, for 5 minutes or until the beef is browned. Add the flour, garlic, and tomato purée, and cook, stirring, for about 1 minute.

2 Pour in the stock and wine. Add the tomatoes and redcurrant jelly, season with salt and pepper, and bring to a boil. Cook, stirring, until the mixture has thickened.

3 Lower the heat, partially cover the pan, and simmer very gently, stirring occasionally, for about 1 hour.

4 Meanwhile, cook the spaghetti in boiling salted water for 8–10 minutes until just tender. Drain thoroughly.

5 Return the spaghetti to the saucepan, add the remaining oil, and toss gently to coat.

6 Divide the spaghetti among warmed serving plates and ladle some of the sauce on top of each serving. Sprinkle with a little Parmesan cheese and hand the remainder separately.

RAVIOLI

Ravioli is one of the easiest of home-made pastas to prepare because it does not need a pasta machine – simply roll out the dough by hand, then fill with a savoury stuffing. Home-made ravioli is so delicious that it needs only a simple accompaniment of melted butter and freshly grated Parmesan.

BASIC PASTA DOUGH

SERVES 3

300 g (10 oz) "00" flour or strong plain white flour

3 eggs

1 tsp salt

1 tbsp olive oil

1 Sift the flour into a mound on a work surface. Make a well in the middle of the flour and add the eggs, salt, and oil. Using your fingertips, gradually draw the flour into the egg mixture until a sticky ball of dough is formed.

2 Knead the dough on a floured work surface for 10 minutes or until the pasta dough is smooth and no longer sticks to the work surface.

3 Shape the dough into a ball, put into an oiled plastic bag, and leave to rest at room temperature for about 30 minutes.

4 Roll out the dough very thinly on a lightly floured work surface into a 37 cm (15 in) square. Leave the pasta uncovered for about 20 minutes to dry out slightly. Cut the pasta in half, fill, and cook the ravioli (see box, right).

CRAB & PRAWN

90 g (3 oz) cooked white crabmeat, flaked

90 g (3 oz) cooked peeled prawns, chopped

60 g (2 oz) full-fat soft cheese

1 spring onion, very finely chopped

salt and black pepper

coriander sauce (page 339) to serve

1 Combine the crabmeat and prawns with the cheese and spring onion, and season with salt and pepper.

2 Fill and cook the ravioli (see box, right). Toss in coriander sauce and serve at once.

CLOCKWISE FROM TOP: Chicken & Prosciutto with tomato basil sauce, Cheese & Spinach with grated Parmesan, Crab & Prawn with coriander sauce.

CHICKEN & PROSCIUTTO

15 g (½ oz) butter

90 g (3 oz) cooked chicken, minced

75 g (2½ oz) prosciutto, finely chopped

1 tbsp fresh white breadcrumbs

1 tbsp chopped fresh flat-leaf parsley

2 tsp each water and tomato purée

salt and black pepper

1 egg

TO SERVE

tomato basil sauce (page 345)

basil sprigs

1 Melt the butter in a saucepan. Add the chicken and fry for 5 minutes. Stir in the remaining ingredients.

2 Fill and cook the ravioli (see box, below). Toss in the tomato basil sauce, and serve at once, garnished with basil sprigs.

RICOTTA & SPINACH

125 g (4 oz) ricotta cheese

60 g (2 oz) Parmesan cheese, grated

1 egg, beaten

¼ tsp grated nutmeg

250 g (8 oz) spinach leaves, cooked, squeezed dry, and chopped

salt and black pepper

30 g (1 oz) butter to serve

1 Beat together the ricotta, half of the Parmesan, the egg, nutmeg, and spinach. Season with salt and pepper.

2 Fill and cook the ravioli (see box, below). Serve with butter, the remaining Parmesan, and black pepper.

Filling and cooking the ravioli

1 Place 18 spoonfuls of filling at regular intervals on to one half of the pasta. Lightly brush the pasta between the filling with water.

2 Roll the remaining pasta around a rolling pin and unroll over the filling. Press the pasta around the edges and the spoofuls of filling.

3 With a knife, pastry wheel, or pastry cutter, cut into round or square ravioli. Leave for about 30 minutes, turning once, until dried out.

4 Add a little oil to a large saucepan of boiling salted water, add the ravioli, and cook for 4–5 minutes until just tender. Serve immediately.

TUNA & FENNEL PASTA BAKE

SERVES 6

250 g (8 oz) pasta shells (conchiglie)

salt and black pepper

1 tbsp sunflower oil

1 fennel bulb, trimmed and finely sliced

1 onion, finely sliced

60 g (2 oz) butter

60 g (2 oz) plain flour

600 ml (1 pint) milk

1 x 200 g (7 oz) can tuna in brine, drained and flaked

3 hard-boiled eggs, coarsely chopped

125 g (4 oz) mature Cheddar cheese, grated

2 tbsp chopped parsley to garnish

1 Cook the pasta shells in boiling salted water for 8–10 minutes until just tender. Drain thoroughly and set aside.

2 Heat the sunflower oil in a large frying pan, add the fennel and onion, and cook for 3–5 minutes until softened but not coloured. Set aside.

3 Melt the butter in a large saucepan, sprinkle in the flour, and cook, stirring, for 1 minute. Remove from the heat and gradually blend in the milk. Bring to a boil, stirring until the mixture thickens. Simmer for 2–3 minutes.

4 Stir in the pasta, the fennel and onion, tuna, eggs, and cheese. Season with salt and pepper, then turn the mixture into a shallow ovenproof dish.

5 Bake in a preheated oven at 200°C (400°F, Gas 6) for about 30 minutes or until heated through and golden brown on top. Serve hot, sprinkled with chopped parsley.

Healthy option

To reduce fat, boil the fennel and onion with the pasta, make half the quantity of sauce in step 3, and make up the volume with pasta cooking water. You could also omit the eggs and halve the amount of cheese.

FUSILLI ALLA NAPOLETANA

SERVES 4

250 g (8 oz) pasta spirals (fusilli)

salt and black pepper

250 g (8 oz) broccoli

15 g (1/2 oz) butter

1 tbsp olive oil

1 large onion, chopped

2 large garlic cloves, crushed

150 g (5 oz) shiitake mushrooms, coarsely chopped

1 red pepper, halved, seeded, and sliced

250 g (8 oz) courgettes, sliced

75 g (3 oz) Cheddar cheese, grated

SAUCE

60 g (2 oz) butter

60 g (2 oz) plain flour

600 ml (1 pint) milk

1 tsp Dijon mustard

1 Cook the pasta in a large pan of boiling salted water for 8–10 minutes until just tender. Drain thoroughly.

2 Cook the broccoli stalks in boiling salted water for 3 minutes, then add the florets, and cook for 2 minutes longer. Drain and rinse in cold water.

3 Melt the butter with the oil in a large frying pan. Add the onion and garlic and cook gently, stirring occasionally, for 3–5 minutes, until softened.

4 Add the mushrooms, red pepper, and courgette slices, and cook, stirring occasionally, for 3 minutes. Remove from the heat and stir in the broccoli.

5 Make the sauce: melt the butter in a large saucepan, sprinkle in the flour and cook, stirring, for 1 minute. Remove from the heat and gradually blend in the milk. Bring to a boil, stirring constantly until thickened. Simmer for 2–3 minutes. Add the mustard, and season with salt and pepper.

6 Remove the sauce from the heat, add the vegetables and pasta, and stir well to coat.

7 Divide the mixture among 4 individual gratin dishes, sprinkle with the Cheddar cheese, and bake in a preheated oven at 200°C (400°F, Gas 6) for 20–25 minutes until golden. Serve hot.

Healthy option

For a lighter, and quicker, version of this baked pasta dish, make it without the sauce in step 5 and simply toss the hot vegetables with the freshly cooked pasta, moistening with a few spoonfuls of the pasta cooking water or 1–2 tbsp olive oil if you prefer. Serve at once.

FISHERMAN'S LASAGNE

SERVES 8

625 g (1¼ lb) haddock fillet

1 slice of onion

1 bay leaf

4 black peppercorns

300 ml (½ pint) dry white wine

250 g (8 oz) cooked peeled prawns

30 g (1 oz) butter

500 g (1 lb) courgettes, thickly sliced

1 garlic clove, crushed

175 g (6 oz) pre-cooked lasagne sheets

60 g (2 oz) Cheddar cheese, grated

2 tbsp grated Parmesan cheese

SAUCE

90 g (3 oz) butter

90 g (3 oz) plain flour

300 ml (½ pint) single cream

3 tbsp chopped parsley

1 tbsp chopped fresh dill

salt and black pepper

1 Put the haddock into a large pan with the onion, bay leaf, peppercorns, and wine. Add enough water to cover, bring to a boil, and simmer for 5 minutes or until the fish is just cooked.

2 Lift out the fish, remove the skin and bones, and flake the flesh. Mix with the prawns. strain the liquid, and make up to 900 ml (1½ pints) with water. Set aside.

3 Melt the butter in a saucepan, add the courgettes and garlic, and cook for 3 minutes until beginning to soften.

4 Make the sauce: melt the butter in a saucepan, sprinkle in the flour, and cook, stirring, for 1 minute. Remove the pan from the heat, and gradually blend in the reserved cooking liquid. Bring to a boil, stirring until thickened. Simmer for 2–3 minutes. Stir in the cream, parsley, dill, and salt and pepper to taste.

5 Spoon one-third of the fish mixture into a shallow ovenproof dish, top with one-third of the courgettes, and pour over one-third of the sauce. Arrange half of the lasagne in a single layer. Repeat the layers, finishing with sauce.

6 Sprinkle with the cheeses and bake in a preheated oven at 200°C (400°F, Gas 6) for 40 minutes or until golden.

THREE-CHEESE MACARONI

SERVES 6–8

375 g (12 oz) short-cut macaroni

salt and black pepper

45 g (1½ oz) butter, plus extra for greasing

45 g (1½ oz) plain flour

900 ml (1½ pints) milk

2 tsp Dijon mustard

175 g (6 oz) smoked Cheddar cheese, grated

60 g (2 oz) light mozzarella cheese, grated

90 g (3 oz) mature Cheddar cheese, grated

60 g (2 oz) fresh white breadcrumbs

1 Cook the macaroni in boiling salted water for 8–10 minutes until just tender. Drain and set aside.

2 Melt the butter in a large saucepan. Add the flour and cook, stirring, for 1 minute. Remove the pan from the heat and gradually blend in the milk. Bring to a boil, stirring constantly until the mixture thickens. Simmer for about 5 minutes, stirring.

3 Stir in the mustard, smoked Cheddar and mozzarella cheeses, 60 g (2 oz) of the mature Cheddar cheese, and the cooked macaroni. Season with salt and pepper.

4 Lightly butter a large shallow ovenproof dish and spoon in the macaroni mixture. Sprinkle with the breadcrumbs and the remaining Cheddar cheese and bake in a preheated oven at 200°C (400°F, Gas 6) for about 15–20 minutes until golden and bubbling.

CHEESE & LEEK MACARONI

Omit the mozzarella cheese. Melt 30 g (1 oz) butter in a saucepan, add 2–3 trimmed and finely sliced leeks, and cook gently for 3–5 minutes until softened. Add the leeks to the sauce with the two Cheddar cheeses and the cooked and drained macaroni.

CANNELLONI WITH RICOTTA & SPINACH

SERVES 6

butter for greasing

18 pre-cooked cannelloni tubes

30 g (1 oz) Parmesan cheese, grated

TOMATO SAUCE

1 tbsp olive oil

2 celery stalks, chopped

1 small onion, chopped

1 carrot, chopped

1 garlic clove, crushed

300 ml (1/2 pint) chicken or vegetable stock

2 x 400 g (13 oz) cans chopped tomatoes

2 tbsp tomato purée

salt and black pepper

60 g (2 oz) sun-dried tomatoes in oil, drained and chopped

FILLING

2 tbsp olive oil

1 small onion, chopped

1 garlic clove, crushed

500 g (1 lb) spinach, chopped

500 g (1 lb) ricotta cheese

1/4 tsp grated nutmeg

1 Make the tomato sauce: heat the oil in a saucepan, add the celery, onion, carrot, and garlic, and cook gently for 3–5 minutes until softened. Stir in the stock, tomatoes, and tomato purée, season with salt and pepper, and bring to a boil. Cover and simmer, stirring occasionally, for 30 minutes.

2 Meanwhile, make the filling: heat the oil in a large pan, add the onion and garlic, and cook for 3–5 minutes until softened. Add the spinach and cook over a high heat for 1–2 minutes. Cool slightly, add the ricotta and nutmeg, and season with salt and pepper.

3 Purée the tomato sauce in a food processor, then stir in the sun-dried tomatoes.

4 Grease an ovenproof dish. Spoon the spinach filling into the cannelloni. Arrange in the dish, cover with the sauce, and sprinkle with Parmesan. Bake in a preheated oven at 200°C (400°F, Gas 6) for 30 minutes. Serve hot.

CLASSIC LASAGNE

SERVES 8

125 g (4 oz) mature Cheddar cheese, grated

30 g (1 oz) Parmesan cheese, grated

175 g (6 oz) pre-cooked lasagne sheets

chopped parsley to garnish

MEAT SAUCE

2 tbsp olive oil

1 kg (2 lb) minced beef

45 g (1 1/2 oz) plain flour

300 ml (1/2 pint) beef stock

1 x 400 g (13 oz) can chopped tomatoes

6 celery stalks, sliced

2 onions, chopped

2 large garlic cloves, crushed

4 tbsp tomato purée

1 tsp sugar

salt and black pepper

WHITE SAUCE

60 g (2 oz) butter

45 g (1 1/2 oz) plain flour

600 ml (1 pint) milk

1 tsp Dijon mustard

1/4 tsp grated nutmeg

1 Make the meat sauce: heat the oil in a saucepan, add the beef, and cook, stirring, until browned.

2 Sprinkle in the flour and stir for 1 minute, then add the stock, tomatoes, celery, onions, garlic, tomato purée, and sugar. Season with salt and pepper and bring to a boil. Cover and simmer for 1 hour.

3 Meanwhile, make the white sauce: melt the butter in a saucepan, sprinkle in the flour and cook, stirring, for 1 minute. Remove from the heat and gradually blend in the milk. Bring to a boil, stirring until the mixture thickens. Simmer for 2–3 minutes. Stir in the mustard and nutmeg, and season with salt and pepper.

4 Spoon one-third of the meat sauce into a large shallow ovenproof dish, cover with one-third of the white sauce, and one-third of the Cheddar and Parmesan cheeses. Arrange half of the lasagne in a single layer. Repeat the layers, finishing with the Cheddar and Parmesan cheeses.

5 Bake in a preheated oven at 190°C (375°F, Gas 5) for 45–60 minutes until the pasta is tender and the topping is a golden brown colour. Serve at once, sprinkled with parsley.

CARIBBEAN RICE & PEAS

SERVES 4–6

2 tbsp olive oil
8 spring onions, sliced
3 smoked bacon rashers, rinds removed, diced
2 garlic cloves, crushed
250 g (8 oz) long grain rice
1 x 200 g (7 oz) can tomatoes
3 tbsp chopped parsley
2 bay leaves
1 small green chilli, halved, seeded, and thinly sliced
1/2 tsp turmeric
1/2 tsp cumin seeds
1/2 tsp dried thyme
1 x 400 g (13 oz) can red kidney beans or black-eyed beans, drained and rinsed
375 ml (13 fl oz) chicken stock
1 lime, cut into wedges, to serve

1 Heat the oil in a pan, add the spring onions and bacon, and cook for about 5 minutes or until the bacon is crisp. Add the garlic and cook for 2 minutes.

2 Add the rice and stir to coat the grains in the oil. Add the tomatoes with their juice, 2 tbsp of the parsley, the bay leaves, chilli, turmeric, cumin, and thyme, and cook for 2 minutes.

3 Add the beans and stock and bring to a boil. Cover and cook over a low heat for 15 minutes until the rice is tender and the liquid has been absorbed.

4 Sprinkle with remaining parsley, and serve at once, with lime wedges.

Cook's know-how

Don't be misled by the name of this dish – there are no peas in it, but this is not a mistake. In the Caribbean the dish is traditionally made with small round beans, which are known as pigeon peas, hence the name of the dish. Red kidney beans make a good substitute when pigeon peas are not available.

SAVOURY RICE

SERVES 4

2 tbsp olive oil
1 onion, chopped
1 carrot, diced
200 g (7 oz) long grain rice
250 g (8 oz) tomatoes, finely chopped
500 ml (16 fl oz) hot chicken or vegetable stock
150 g (5 oz) sweetcorn kernels
90 g (3 oz) frozen peas
2 tbsp tomato purée
salt and black pepper
1 garlic clove, crushed
chopped parsley to garnish

1 Heat the oil in a frying pan, add the onion and carrot, and cook gently, stirring, for 3–5 minutes until the onion is softened but not coloured.

2 Add the rice, and stir to coat the grains in the oil. Add the tomatoes and stock.

3 Add the sweetcorn, peas, and tomato purée, and bring to a boil. Simmer, stirring occasionally, for 12–15 minutes or until the rice is tender and the liquid has been absorbed.

4 Add salt and pepper to taste, and stir in the garlic. Serve at once, sprinkled with parsley.

Cook's know-how

Savoury rice is a delicious accompaniment to simple grilled or roasted foods, or it can make a tasty vegetarian meal on its own, to serve two people. For extra flavour just before serving, add a little chopped fresh coriander, finely chopped spring onions or raw red onion, or a sprinkling of crushed dried red chillies or Tabasco sauce. If you have any leftovers, spoon into hot chicken or vegetable soup to make them go further.

ORIENTAL NOODLE DISHES

There is such a wide range of oriental noodles that it is often difficult to know which to choose and how to cook them. In fact there is no mystery about them, and they are as quick and easy to deal with as Italian pasta. These three simple recipes will give you confidence to cook with them.

SINGAPORE NOODLES

SERVES 6

250 g (8 oz) rice noodles

2 tbsp sunflower oil

375 g (12 oz) pork fillet or tenderloin, cut into thin strips

1 tsp crushed dried red chillies (chilli flakes)

90 g (3 oz) shiitake mushrooms, sliced

200 g (7 oz) pak choi, coarsely chopped, keeping white and green parts separate

2 tbsp mild curry powder

2 tbsp soy sauce

2 tbsp oyster sauce

juice of 1/2 lime

4 tbsp coconut cream

chopped fresh coriander to garnish

1 Cook the noodles according to packet instructions. Drain, refresh under cold running water, and set aside.

2 Heat 1 tbsp oil in a large wok or non-stick frying pan and stir-fry the pork over a high heat for about 2 minutes until brown and cooked through. Remove from the pan with a slotted spoon and set aside.

3 Heat the remaining oil in the pan. Add the chilli flakes, mushrooms, and the white parts of the pak choi, and stir-fry for 1–2 minutes. Add the curry powder, soy, oyster sauce, lime juice, and coconut cream, and stir-fry for a further few minutes.

4 Add the green parts of the pak choi, then return the pork and noodles to the pan. Stir-fry for a few minutes until piping hot, then scatter over the coriander.

Cook's know-how

For a vegetarian version of Singapore Noodles, omit the pork and substitute the same weight of firm tofu, cut into strips. Add the tofu with the pak choi in step 3, omit the oyster sauce, and replace it with an extra tablespooon or two of soy sauce if you like.

SZECHUAN NOODLES WITH WATER CHESTNUTS

SERVES 6

375 g (12 oz) medium egg noodles

1 tbsp olive oil

250 g (8 oz) minced pork

2.5 cm (1 in) piece of fresh root ginger, peeled and finely grated

2 garlic cloves, crushed

2 spring onions, trimmed and sliced on the diagonal, keeping white and green parts separate

1 red pepper, halved, seeded, and finely sliced

3 tbsp soy sauce, or more to taste

3 tbsp black bean sauce

2 tsp caster or granulated sugar

90 g (3 oz) bean sprouts

1 x 220 g (7 1/2 oz) can water chestnuts, drained and halved

salt and black pepper

1 Cook the noodles according to packet instructions. Drain, refresh under cold running water, and set aside.

2 Heat the oil in a wok or large non-stick frying pan and stir-fry the pork for about 2 minutes until brown. Add the ginger, garlic, white parts of the spring onions, and the red pepper, and stir-fry for a few minutes more.

3 Stir in the 3 tbsp soy sauce, the black bean sauce, sugar, and 5 tbsp water, and boil for few minutes. Add the bean sprouts and water chestnuts, and return the noodles to the pan, then toss over a high heat for about 2 minutes until everything is hot. Check the seasoning, and add more soy sauce if you like. Serve immediately, with the green spring onions scattered on top.

PAD THAI WITH TIGER PRAWNS

SERVES 6

250 g (8 oz) thick rice noodles

2 tbsp olive oil

2 skinless, boneless chicken breasts (about 125 g/4 oz each), cut into thin strips

1 small fresh red chilli, halved, seeded and finely chopped

2.5 cm (1 in) piece of fresh root ginger, peeled and finely grated

2.5 cm (1 in) piece of fresh lemongrass from the lower part of the stalk, very finely chopped

125 g (4 oz) peeled raw tiger prawns

90 g (3 oz) oyster mushrooms, thinly sliced

125 g (4 oz) sugarsnap peas, trimmed and sliced on the diagonal

3 tbsp soy sauce

2 tbsp lime juice

1 tbsp fish sauce

salt and black pepper

TO SERVE

30 g (1 oz) salted or unsalted peanuts, coarsely chopped

a handful of fresh coriander, chopped

1 Cook the noodles according to packet instructions. Drain, refresh under cold running water, and set aside.

2 Heat 1 tbsp of the oil in a wok or large non-stick frying pan, and stir-fry the chicken over a high heat for 2 minutes or until golden brown and cooked through. Remove with a slotted spoon and set aside.

3 Heat the remaining oil in the pan, add the chilli, ginger, lemongrass, prawns, mushrooms, and peas and stir-fry for 1 minute. Add the soy, lime juice and fish sauce and season with salt and pepper. Return the noodles and chicken to the pan and stir-fry until the prawns are pink and everything is piping hot, 2–3 minutes. Serve hot, scattered with peanuts and coriander.

CLOCKWISE FROM TOP RIGHT: Singapore Noodles, Pad Thai with Tiger Prawns, Szechuan Noodles with Water Chestnuts.

WILD RICE GRATIN

SERVES 6

375 g (12 oz) mixed basmati and wild rice

salt and black pepper

250–375 g (8–12 oz) broccoli

15 g (½ oz) butter

2 onions, chopped

3 garlic cloves, crushed

125 ml (4 fl oz) soured cream or crème fraîche

125 g (4 oz) mozzarella cheese, grated

60 g (2 oz) Parmesan cheese, grated

1 tbsp chopped fresh rosemary

1 Cook the rice in boiling salted water for about 35 minutes, or according to packet instructions. Drain thoroughly and rinse with cold water. Drain again.

2 Meanwhile, cut the stalks off the broccoli and cook them in boiling salted water for 8–10 minutes until almost tender, then add the florets, and cook for 2 minutes longer. Drain and rinse in cold water. Drain again and set aside.

3 Melt the butter in a frying pan, add the onions, and cook gently, stirring occasionally, for 3–5 minutes until softened. Add the garlic, and cook, stirring occasionally, for 3–5 minutes until the onions are lightly browned.

4 Coarsely chop the broccoli, then stir into the rice with the onion and garlic mixture, soured cream, three-quarters of the mozzarella and Parmesan cheeses, and the rosemary. Season with salt and pepper.

5 Turn the mixture into an ovenproof dish and sprinkle with the remaining mozzarella and Parmesan cheeses. Bake in a preheated oven at 180°C (350°F, Gas 4) for about 20 minutes until the cheese has melted. Serve hot.

Healthy option

Reduce the fat content by using low-fat crème fraîche instead of soured cream, reduced-fat mozzarella, and just 2 tbsp grated Parmesan.

RISI E BISI

SERVES 6

60 g (2 oz) butter

1 onion, finely chopped

60 g (2 oz) Parma ham, diced, or 90 g (3 oz) unsmoked lean bacon rashers, rinds removed, diced

2 garlic cloves, crushed

300 g (10 oz) risotto rice

300 g (10 oz) frozen peas

salt and black pepper

1 litre (1¾ pints) hot chicken or vegetable stock

60 g (2 oz) Parmesan cheese, grated, and 2 tbsp chopped parsley to garnish

1 Melt the butter in a large pan. When it is foaming, add the onion, Parma ham, and garlic, and cook gently, stirring occasionally, for 3–5 minutes until the onion is soft but not coloured.

2 Add the rice and stir to coat in the butter. Add the frozen peas and seasoning.

3 Pour in half of the stock and cook, stirring constantly, over a low heat until it is absorbed. Add a little more stock and cook, stirring, until it has been absorbed.

4 Continue adding the stock in this way until the rice is just tender and the mixture is thick and creamy. It should take about 25 minutes.

5 Serve hot, sprinkled with the grated Parmesan cheese and chopped parsley.

Healthy option

This is a classic Venetian rice dish, traditionally served with more liquid than a risotto. If you want to cut down on the fat content, use just 1 slice of Parma ham, trimmed of all fat, and omit the Parmesan garnish. You can omit the ham altogether, but even a small amount will give the dish an authentic flavour.

PORTUGUESE RICE WITH TUNA

SERVES 4

3 streaky bacon rashers, rinds removed, cut into strips

3 tbsp olive oil

1 small onion, thinly sliced

250 g (8 oz) long grain brown rice

600 ml (1 pint) hot chicken stock

salt and black pepper

375 g (12 oz) fresh tuna, cut into chunks

1 x 400 g (13 oz) can pimientos, drained and cut into strips

16 black olives

dill sprigs and lemon slices to garnish

1 Put the bacon into a large, heavy saucepan and heat until it begins to sizzle. Add the olive oil and onion, and cook gently, stirring occasionally, for 3–5 minutes until soft but not coloured. Add the rice and stir to coat the grains in the oil.

2 Pour the stock into the pan, season with salt and pepper, and bring to a boil. Cover and simmer for 25–30 minutes.

3 Add the tuna, pimientos, and olives, and cook for 5 minutes or until all the liquid has been absorbed and the rice and tuna are tender. Season, garnish with dill sprigs and lemon slices, and serve at once.

PORTUGUESE RICE WITH CANNED TUNA

Substitute 2 x 200 g (7 oz) cans tuna in brine for the fresh tuna. Drain the tuna well, and flake it roughly with a fork.

Cook's know-how

If you prefer, use a 300 g (10 oz) jar roasted peppers instead of the pimientos.

PERSIAN PILAF

SERVES 4

1 small cinnamon stick

2 tsp cumin seeds

6 black peppercorns

seeds of 4 cardamom pods, crushed

3 cloves

2 tbsp sunflower oil

1 small onion, chopped

1 tsp turmeric

250 g (8 oz) long grain rice

1.25 litres (2 pints) hot vegetable or chicken stock

2 bay leaves, torn into pieces

salt and black pepper

60 g (2 oz) shelled pistachio nuts, coarsely chopped

30 g (1 oz) raisins

fresh coriander to garnish

1 Heat a heavy pan and add the cinnamon stick, cumin seeds, peppercorns, cardamom seeds, and cloves.

2 Dry-fry the spices over a medium heat for 2–3 minutes until they begin to release their aromas.

3 Add the oil to the pan and, when it is hot, add the onion and turmeric. Cook gently, stirring occasionally, for about 10 minutes until the onion is softened.

4 Add the rice and stir to coat the grains in the oil. Slowly pour in the hot stock, add the bay leaves, season with salt and pepper, and bring to a boil. Lower the heat, cover, and cook very gently for about 10 minutes without lifting the lid.

5 Remove the saucepan from the heat and leave to stand, still covered, for about 5 minutes.

6 Add the pistachio nuts and raisins to the pilaf, and fork them in gently to fluff up the rice. Garnish with fresh coriander, and serve at once.

CHICKEN LIVER RISOTTO

SERVES 4–6

75 g (2½ oz) butter

1 tbsp sunflower oil

125 g (4 oz) smoked bacon rashers, rinds removed, diced

1 onion, chopped

1 garlic clove, crushed

175 g (6 oz) risotto rice

60 g (2 oz) wild rice

600 ml (1 pint) hot chicken stock

250 g (8 oz) chicken livers, sliced

125 g (4 oz) wild mushrooms (see box, below right), sliced

60 g (2 oz) sun-dried tomatoes in oil, drained and chopped

salt and black pepper

30 g (1 oz) Parmesan cheese, grated

1 tbsp chopped fresh rosemary

1 Melt 60 g (2 oz) of the butter with the oil in a large frying pan. When the butter is foaming, add the bacon, onion, and garlic, and cook gently, stirring occasionally, for 3–5 minutes until the onion is soft but not coloured.

2 Add the risotto rice and wild rice, stirring to coat the grains in the oil, then pour in the hot chicken stock. Cover and simmer for 25 minutes.

3 Meanwhile, melt the remaining butter in a saucepan. Add the chicken livers, and cook, stirring, for 2–3 minutes until a rich brown colour. Add the mushrooms, and cook, stirring occasionally, for 5–7 minutes.

4 Stir the chicken livers into the rice. Add the sun-dried tomatoes, season with salt and pepper, and cook for 5 minutes or until all the liquid has been absorbed. Serve hot, garnished with Parmesan and rosemary.

Cook's know-how

Wild mushrooms add a special touch to this risotto. Chanterelles, ceps, and morels are all suitable, or you can use cultivated chestnut mushrooms instead, if you prefer their flavour.

RISOTTO MILANESE

SERVES 6

90 g (3 oz) butter

1 onion, chopped

375 g (12 oz) risotto rice

1.25 litres (2 pints) hot vegetable or chicken stock

a few pinches of saffron strands

salt and black pepper

60 g (2 oz) Parmesan cheese, grated

Parmesan shavings to serve

1 Melt 30 g (1 oz) of the butter in a large saucepan, add the chopped onion, and cook gently, stirring occasionally, for 3–5 minutes until softened but not coloured.

2 Add the rice, stirring to coat the grains in the butter, and cook for 1 minute. Add a ladleful of hot stock to the pan, and cook gently, stirring constantly, until all the stock has been absorbed.

3 Sprinkle in the saffron strands and season with salt and pepper. Continue to add the stock, a ladleful at a time, stirring constantly, until the risotto is thick and creamy and the rice tender. This will take 20–25 minutes.

4 Stir in the remaining butter and the Parmesan cheese, and season to taste with salt and pepper. Serve at once, topped with Parmesan shavings.

Cook's know-how

Risotto milanese is the traditional accompaniment to Osso buco (page 242), but you can serve it with any other dish of meat or poultry, or as a first course on its own. In the past, it was traditionally cooked with the marrow from the veal shanks used for the osso buco, but nowadays the finished risotto is sometimes topped with a few spoonfuls of the juices from a veal roast to give it a more traditional and authentic flavour. If you want to reduce the fat content in this recipe, omit the butter in step 4.

KEDGEREE

SERVES 4

175 g (6 oz) long grain rice
1/4 tsp turmeric
375 g (12 oz) smoked haddock fillet
2 hard-boiled eggs
60 g (2 oz) butter, plus extra for greasing
juice of 1/2 lemon
150 ml (1/4 pint) single cream
salt
cayenne pepper
2 tbsp finely chopped parsley

1 Simmer the rice and turmeric, covered, in boiling salted water for 12–15 minutes until tender. Rinse with boiling water, drain, and keep warm.

2 Meanwhile, put the haddock, skin-side down, in a frying pan, cover with cold water, and poach for 8–10 minutes.

3 Cut 1 egg lengthwise into quarters and reserve for garnish. Coarsely chop the second egg.

4 Drain the haddock, remove the skin and bones, then flake the fish. Put the fish into a large bowl, add the rice, chopped egg, butter, lemon juice, and cream, and season with salt and cayenne pepper. Stir gently to mix.

5 Butter an ovenproof dish, add the kedgeree, and bake in a preheated oven at 180°C (350°F, Gas 4), stirring occasionally, for 10–15 minutes.

6 To serve, stir in the parsley and garnish with the reserved egg quarters.

Cook's know-how

Some smoked haddock is dyed bright yellow, so look out for smoked haddock that is pale in colour and labelled "undyed" if you want to avoid artificial colourings.

RISOTTO AL VERDE

SERVES 4

15 g (1/2 oz) butter
3 garlic cloves, crushed
250 g (8 oz) risotto rice
1 litre (1 3/4 pints) hot vegetable stock
175 ml (6 fl oz) single cream
90 g (3 oz) blue cheese, crumbled
4 tbsp ready made pesto
90 g (3 oz) Parmesan cheese, grated
4 tbsp pine nuts, lightly toasted
4 tbsp shredded fresh basil

1 Melt the butter in a large saucepan. When it is foaming, add the garlic and cook gently for 1 minute.

2 Add the risotto rice, stirring to coat the grains in the butter, and cook for 2 minutes. Add a ladleful of the hot vegetable stock, and cook gently, stirring constantly, until the stock has been absorbed. Continue to add the stock, a ladleful at a time, and cook for 20–25 minutes or until the rice is just tender.

3 Add the cream, and cook gently, stirring, until it has been absorbed. Stir in the blue cheese, then the pesto, Parmesan, and pine nuts. Garnish with shredded fresh basil, and serve.

CHICKEN & MUSHROOM RISOTTO

Add 125 g (4 oz) sliced mushrooms to the saucepan with the garlic in step 1 and cook for 3–5 minutes until the mushrooms are soft. Substitute chicken stock for the vegetable stock, omit the blue cheese and pesto, then add 250 g (8 oz) cooked diced chicken with the cream in step 3.

ASPARAGUS RISOTTO

Add 1 finely chopped onion to the pan with the garlic in step 1, and cook for 3–5 minutes until soft. Omit the blue cheese and pesto, and add 375 g (12 oz) trimmed and chopped asparagus in step 2, about 5 minutes before the end of the cooking time.

NASI GORENG

The name of this Indonesian recipe simply means fried rice. Prepared with a variety of ingredients, it is one of the best known Indonesian dishes, and one of the easiest to make. Traditional garnishes such as crushed peanuts, fried eggs and omelette strips give contrasting flavours and textures to the dish.

CHICKEN NASI GORENG

SERVES 6

375 g (12 oz) long grain rice

salt and black pepper

90 ml (3 fl oz) olive oil

6 streaky bacon rashers, chopped

2 large onions, chopped

3 garlic cloves, crushed

1/4 tsp chilli powder

2 tsp mild curry powder

2 cooked chicken breasts, skinned and cubed

90 ml (3 fl oz) soy sauce

6 spring onions, chopped

60 g (2 oz) cooked peeled prawns

60 g (2 oz) almonds, halved, and toasted (page 186)

TO GARNISH

coriander sprigs

6 fried eggs (optional)

prawn crackers

1 Cook the rice in boiling salted water for 12–15 minutes until tender. Drain, rinse with boiling water, drain again, and set aside.

2 Heat 1 tbsp of the oil in a large frying pan or wok, add the bacon, and cook for 3–5 minutes until browned. Add the remaining oil, the onions, and garlic, and cook over a gentle heat for 3–5 minutes until the onions are soft but not coloured.

3 Add the chilli and curry powders and cook, stirring, for 1 minute or until fragrant. Add the chicken and cook for 5–6 minutes until just beginning to brown.

4 Add the soy sauce and half of the rice and stir well. Add the remaining rice, and season with salt and pepper. Cook over a gentle heat, stirring, for 7–8 minutes until the rice is heated through. Stir in the spring onions, prawns, and almonds, and heat through.

5 Serve hot, garnished with coriander sprigs, and fried eggs if you like. Serve prawn crackers in a separate bowl.

VEGETARIAN NASI GORENG

SERVES 6

375 g (12 oz) long grain rice

salt

2 tbsp tamarind paste (optional)

2 tbsp vegetable oil

1 red pepper, halved, seeded, and thinly sliced

1 large onion, chopped

3 garlic cloves, crushed

1 cm (1/2 in) piece of fresh root ginger, peeled and grated

2 tsp curry powder

1/4 tsp each crushed dried red chillies (chilli flakes) and turmeric

1/2 small hard white cabbage, thinly sliced

1 x 200 g (7 oz) can chopped tomatoes

3 tbsp soy sauce

TO GARNISH

3 tomatoes, cut into strips

1/2 cucumber, cut into strips

omelette strips (see right)

1 Cook the rice in boiling salted water for 12–15 minutes until tender. Drain, rinse with boiling water, and drain again. Stir in the tamarind paste (if using) and set aside.

2 Heat 1 tbsp of the oil in a large frying pan or wok, add the red pepper and onion, and cook for 3–5 minutes until softened. Add the garlic, ginger, curry powder, crushed chillies, and turmeric, and cook gently, stirring, for 1 minute.

3 Add the cabbage and cook for 3–5 minutes. Add the tomatoes and cook for 2–3 minutes. Remove from the pan.

4 Heat the remaining oil in the pan, add the rice, and cook gently until lightly browned. Return the vegetables to the pan. Add the soy sauce and heat gently to warm through.

5 Serve hot, garnished with tomato, cucumber, and omelette strips.

QUICK NASI GORENG

SERVES 6

375 g (12 oz) long grain rice

2 tbsp vegetable oil

1 onion, chopped

1/2 tsp paprika

1 tsp ground ginger

125 g (4 oz) button mushrooms, sliced

60 g (2 oz) bean sprouts

1 tsp soy sauce

125 g (4 oz) cooked peeled prawns

2 spring onions, finely sliced

chopped coriander to garnish

1 Cook the rice in boiling salted water, for 12–15 minutes until tender. Drain, rinse with boiling water, drain again, and set aside.

2 Heat 1 tbsp of the oil in a frying pan or wok, add the onion, and cook for 3–5 minutes until soft. Add the paprika and ginger, and cook over a low heat for 1 minute. Add the mushrooms and bean sprouts and cook for 2–3 minutes until softened. Remove from the pan.

3 Heat the remaining oil in the pan, add the rice, and cook over a gentle heat, stirring, for 7–8 minutes to warm through. Stir in the soy sauce. Return the vegetables to the pan and add the prawns and onions. Serve hot, garnished with coriander.

OMELETTE GARNISH

Whisk 2 eggs with plenty of salt and pepper. Melt 30 g (1 oz) butter in an omelette pan or small frying pan. Add the eggs to the pan and cook until set. Slide the omelette out of the pan and roll it up, then leave to cool before slicing across into fine strips.

CLOCKWISE FROM TOP: Chicken Nasi Goreng, Vegetarian Nasi Goreng, Quick Nasi Goreng.

EGG-FRIED RICE

SERVES 4

250 g (8 oz) long grain rice

salt and black pepper

3 tbsp sunflower oil

60 g (2 oz) bacon rashers, rinds removed, diced

125 g (4 oz) frozen peas

2 eggs, beaten

125 g (4 oz) bean sprouts

6 spring onions, sliced

1 Cook the rice in boiling salted water for 12–15 minutes until tender. Drain.

2 Heat the oil in a wok or large frying pan, add the bacon, and cook over a high heat, stirring, for 2 minutes. Add the rice and peas and cook, stirring, for 5 minutes.

3 Add the eggs and bean sprouts, and stir-fry for 2 minutes until the eggs have just set. Taste for seasoning, sprinkle with the sliced spring onions, and serve at once.

SPECIAL EGG-FRIED RICE

Add 125 g (4 oz) cooked peeled prawns when you add the rice and peas in step 2, and sprinkle with 60 g (2 oz) toasted cashew nuts just before serving.

PAELLA

SERVES 6

3 tbsp olive oil

6 chicken thighs

250 g (8 oz) smoked bacon, rind removed, cut into strips

1 large onion, chopped

1 litre (1 3/4 pints) chicken stock

250 g (8 oz) tomatoes, chopped

2 garlic cloves, crushed

a few pinches of saffron threads, soaked in a little hot water

500 g (1 lb) short grain rice

1 red and 1 green pepper, halved, seeded, and sliced

125 g (4 oz) frozen peas

salt and black pepper

500 g (1 lb) mussels, cleaned (page 124)

125 g (4 oz) cooked peeled prawns

TO FINISH

12 black olives, pitted

6 large cooked prawns, unpeeled

lemon wedges

2 tbsp chopped parsley

1 Heat the oil in a paella pan or a large, deep frying pan or sauté pan. Add the chicken and cook over a medium heat for 10 minutes until browned all over. Add the bacon and onion and cook for 5 minutes.

2 Stir in the stock, tomatoes, garlic, and the saffron with its soaking liquid, and bring to a boil. Add the rice, red and green peppers, and peas, and season with salt and pepper. Cover and bake in a preheated oven at 180°C (350°F, Gas 4) for 35–40 minutes until the rice is nearly tender and the stock has been absorbed.

3 Meanwhile, put the mussels into a large pan with about 1 cm (1/2 in) water. Cover tightly, and cook, shaking the pan occasionally, for 5 minutes or until the shells open. Drain the mussels, and throw away any which have not opened: do not try to force them open.

4 Stir the peeled prawns into the paella, cover, and cook gently on the hob for about 5 minutes. Taste for seasoning. Arrange the mussels around the pan, and the olives, large prawns, and lemon wedges on top. Serve hot, sprinkled with parsley.

Healthy option

If you remove the skin from the chicken before cooking this will considerably reduce the fat content of the paella.

9

VEGETABLES
& SALADS

UNDER 30 MINUTES

CUCUMBER SALAD
Light and summery: thin cucumber slices in a vinaigrette dressing of white wine vinegar and sunflower oil, sprinkled with dill.

SERVES 4–6 75–50 calories per serving
Takes 10 minutes   Page 393

GARLIC SPRING GREENS
Light and nutritious: spring greens cut into thin strips, then blanched and stir-fried with olive oil and garlic.

SERVES 6 103 calories per serving
Takes 15 minutes   Page 379

WALDORF SALAD
Fruity salad: celery and apple flavoured with lemon and coated with mayonnaise. Mixed with pieces of walnut.

SERVES 4 469 calories per serving
Takes 15 minutes, plus chilling   Page 390

GREEK SALAD
Tomato wedges with cucumber, green pepper, feta cheese, and olives. Flavoured with olive oil, lemon, and oregano.

SERVES 4–6 503–335 calories per serving
Takes 10 minutes   Page 393

MIXED VEGETABLE STIR-FRY
Sliced courgette stir-fried with yellow pepper and a variety of mushrooms. Flavoured with lemon juice, and sprinkled with almonds.

SERVES 4 155 calories per serving
Takes 10 minutes   Page 384

CELERIAC REMOULADE
Matchstick-thin strips of celeriac tossed with yogurt and mayonnaise dressing flavoured with capers and mustard.

SERVES 4–6 100–66 calories per serving
Takes 15 minutes   Page 391

MIXED LEAF SALAD
Crisp lettuce, lamb's lettuce, watercress, and rocket leaves tossed with vinaigrette dressing, and sprinkled with herbs.

SERVES 4–6 117–78 calories per serving
Takes 10 minutes   Page 389

RED SALAD BOWL
Bite-sized pieces of radicchio and oak leaf and lollo rosso lettuces mixed with onion, grapes, and balsamic vinegar dressing.

SERVES 4–6 387–258 calories per serving
Takes 15 minutes   Page 389

CARROT JULIENNE SALAD
Matchstick-thin strips of carrot briefly cooked, then coated in a dressing of olive oil, white wine vinegar, garlic, and parsley.

SERVES 4–6 79–53 calories per serving
Takes 20 minutes   Page 391

UNDER 30 MINUTES

CABBAGE & MIXED PEPPER STIR-FRY

Crunchy and nourishing: shredded white cabbage stir-fried with onion, celery, red and yellow peppers, and mushrooms.

SERVES 6–8 128–96 calories per serving
Takes 15 minutes   Page 379

ITALIAN CLASSIC

TRICOLORE SALAD

Thinly sliced beefsteak tomatoes arranged with slices of mozzarella cheese and avocado, and drizzled with olive oil.

SERVES 4 509 calories per serving
Takes 20 minutes   Page 392

OKRA WITH CHILLI

Hot and spicy: okra, onion, garlic, and fresh red chilli, stir-fried until just tender but still slightly crisp.

SERVES 4 152 calories per serving
Takes 15 minutes   Page 384

LOW CALORIE

SWEET & SOUR BEETROOT

Juicy and well-flavoured: diced beetroot cooked with onions, garlic, lemon juice, and mint. Served warm or cold.

SERVES 4 242 calories per serving
Takes 20 minutes   Page 378

CHIPPED POTATOES

Popular accompaniment or snack: potatoes, cut into sticks, then deep fried until crispy and brown.

SERVES 6 281 calories per serving
Takes 20 minutes, plus soaking   Page 374

CRUNCHY ORIENTAL SALAD

Iceberg lettuce, bean sprouts, spring onions, and green pepper tossed with ginger dressing, and sprinkled with sesame seeds.

SERVES 6 141 calories per serving
Takes 10 minutes, plus soaking   Page 389

CREAMED SPINACH

Creamy and nutritious: lightly cooked spinach mixed with crème fraîche, Parmesan cheese, chives, and nutmeg, then grilled.

SERVES 4 250 calories per serving
Takes 20 minutes   Page 378

AROMATIC BRUSSELS SPROUTS

Tender and tangy: Brussels sprouts simmered, then tossed with mustard-seed butter, and flavoured with lemon juice.

SERVES 6–8 125–94 calories per serving
Takes 15 minutes   Page 379

CAESAR SALAD

Pieces of cos lettuce tossed with olive oil, lemon juice, and hard-boiled egg quarters. Mixed with croûtons and Parmesan cheese.

SERVES 4 421 calories per serving
Takes 20 minutes   Page 390

UNDER 30 MINUTES

AVOCADO SALAD
Fresh and tangy: avocado with orange, pine nuts, and mixed salad leaves, tossed with orange and walnut oil dressing.

SERVES 6   240 calories per serving

Takes 20 minutes   Page 392

CELERY & LEEK STIR-FRY
Fresh and summery: sliced young leeks cooked with sliced celery, mixed with chives, and garnished with cashew nuts.

SERVES 6   235 calories per serving

Takes 20 minutes   Page 382

SUMMER PEAS & BEANS
Shelled peas cooked with French beans, then combined with cooked young broad beans, butter, and mint.

SERVES 6–8   107–80 calories per serving

Takes 20 minutes   Page 381

SALADE NIÇOISE
Lettuce, French beans, and cucumber topped with tomatoes, eggs, tuna, anchovies, olives, and a garlic and mustard dressing.

SERVES 4   530 calories per serving

Takes 25 minutes   Page 396

GLAZED CARROTS & TURNIPS
Strips of carrot and whole baby turnips glazed with chicken stock, butter, and sugar. Flavoured with fresh mint and parsley.

SERVES 4   115 calories per serving

Takes 20 minutes   Page 378

HIGH PROTEIN

YANKEE SUCCOTASH
Hearty and wholesome: sweetcorn kernels simmered with cream, borlotti beans, bacon, and onion. Flavoured with chives.

SERVES 6   491 calories per serving

Takes 25 minutes   Page 382

SPINACH & BACON SALAD
Pieces of spinach and crispy bacon lightly tossed with vinaigrette or blue cheese dressing, and topped with croûtons.

SERVES 6   436 calories per serving

Takes 25 minutes   Page 389

HIGH FIBRE

FRENCH-STYLE PEAS
Light and summery: sweetened shelled peas simmered with shredded lettuce, chopped spring onions, butter, and parsley.

SERVES 4–6   237–158 calories per serving

Takes 25 minutes   Page 381

STUFFED MUSHROOMS
Tasty and healthy: mushrooms stuffed with chopped mushroom stalks, carrots, courgettes, and parsley, then baked.

SERVES 6   91 calories per serving

Takes 25 minutes   Page 383

30–60 MINUTES

PEPPERATA SALAD
Courgette slices tossed with roasted peppers, watercress, and vinaigrette dressing.

SERVES 4–6 310–207 calories per serving

Takes 20 minutes, plus cooling   Page 388

GOLDEN ROASTED PUMPKIN
Chunks of pumpkin sprinkled with a mixture of oil, balsamic vinegar, garlic, thyme, and paprika. Baked until tender.

SERVES 6–8 93–70 calories per serving

Takes 30 minutes   Page 384

WILD RICE SALAD
Wild and long grain rice in a dressing of oils, vinegar, and mustard. Mixed with French beans, mushrooms, parsley, and walnuts.

SERVES 4–6 554–369 calories per serving

Takes 30 minutes   Page 397

HERBED ROASTED TOMATOES
Cherry tomatoes baked until lightly browned and tender. Dotted with butter combined with herbs, garlic, and lemon juice.

SERVES 4 106 calories per serving

Takes 35 minutes   Page 384

DINNER PARTY

GINGER PARSNIPS
Matchstick-thin strips of parsnip lightly cooked with ginger, covered with crème fraîche, then baked until tender.

SERVES 8 249 calories per serving

Takes 30 minutes   Page 378

TOMATO & COURGETTE BAKE
Light and delicious: layers of sliced courgette and tomato baked in a white sauce flavoured with nutmeg.

SERVES 4–6 238–159 calories per serving

Takes 40 minutes   Page 385

SPICED YAMS
Chunky and spicy: cubed yams cooked with tomatoes, garlic, and cinnamon. Spiked with chilli powder and paprika.

SERVES 4 381 calories per serving

Takes 30 minutes   Page 377

ASPARAGUS WITH PARMESAN
Asparagus marinated in olive oil, wine, vinegar, and garlic. Rolled in Parmesan cheese, and baked with marinade.

SERVES 4 215 calories per serving

Takes 35 minutes, plus marinating   Page 383

PASTA SALAD WITH PEPPERS
Cooked pasta bows combined with diced red and green peppers and spring onions. Coated in mayonnaise.

SERVES 4–6 556–370 calories per serving

Takes 20 minutes, plus chilling   Page 398

30–60 MINUTES

SWEET & SOUR RED CABBAGE

Shredded red cabbage cooked with bacon, apple, sugar, red wine, vinegar, sultanas, caraway seeds, cinnamon, and nutmeg.

SERVES 8 225 calories per serving

Takes 55 minutes   Page 380

FRENCH CLASSIC

POMMES ANNA

Thinly sliced potatoes, layered in a frying pan, dotted with butter, and seasoned with salt and pepper, then cooked until tender.

SERVES 6 205 calories per serving

Takes 55 minutes   Page 375

COUSCOUS SALAD

Couscous cooked with sultanas and ginger. Mixed with chilli oil, raspberry vinegar, tomatoes, onion, spring onions, and mint.

SERVES 4–6 420–280 calories per serving

Takes 20 minutes, plus cooling   Page 397

GARLIC CREAMED POTATOES

Hearty and satisfying: boiled potato, mashed, then mixed with roasted garlic, warm milk, and butter. Sprinkled with chives.

SERVES 6 227 calories per serving

Takes 45 minutes   Page 375

CAULIFLOWER & BROCCOLI LAYERS

Florets of cauliflower and broccoli layered in rings, and moulded in a basin. Topped with almonds and breadcrumbs.

SERVES 4–6 341–227 calories per serving

Takes 35 minutes   Page 380

FAMILY CHOICE

RICE SALAD

Long grain rice in a dressing flavoured with mustard and garlic. Mixed with peas, red pepper, sweetcorn, and coriander.

SERVES 4–6 517–345 calories per serving

Takes 25 minutes, plus cooling   Page 397

DINNER PARTY

ITALIAN FENNEL

Quartered fennel bulbs lightly cooked until tender, topped with mozzarella cheese, and baked until golden.

SERVES 8 108 calories per serving

Takes 30 minutes   Page 383

GLAZED SHALLOTS

Whole shallots simmered in water, butter, caster sugar, and thyme until glazed and golden brown.

SERVES 6 150 calories per serving

Takes 30 minutes   Page 382

TABBOULEH

Fresh and herby: bulgur wheat mixed with vinaigrette dressing, lemon juice, tomatoes, spring onions, parsley, and mint.

SERVES 4 276 calories per serving

Takes 10 minutes, plus standing   Page 397

OVER 60 MINUTES

TOMATO & BASIL SALAD
Assortment of tomatoes and chunks of yellow pepper dressed in oil and balsamic vinegar. Sprinkled with basil.

SERVES 4–6 146–97 calories per serving
Takes 10 minutes, plus standing   Page 393

LOW CALORIE

TOMATO & ONION SALAD
Thinly sliced tomatoes and mild onion dressed in olive oil, red wine vinegar, and caster sugar. Sprinkled with snipped chives.

SERVES 6 166 calories per serving
Takes 15 minutes, plus chilling   Page 393

AUBERGINE WITH FRESH PESTO
Mediterranean flavours: slices of aubergine grilled until lightly browned, cooled, then spread with pesto, and sprinkled with basil.

SERVES 4 499 calories per serving
Takes 20 minutes, plus standing   Page 388

POTATO, APPLE, & CELERY SALAD
Hearty salad: pieces of boiled potato tossed with vinaigrette dressing, mixed with apple, celery, onion, and mayonnaise.

SERVES 6 332 calories per serving
Takes 30 minutes, plus chilling   Page 391

THREE-BEAN SALAD
French beans, chick peas, and red kidney beans combined with olives in a Greek yogurt dressing, flavoured with vinegar and mustard.

SERVES 4 315 calories per serving
Takes 15 minutes, plus standing   Page 396

TRADITIONAL

CRUNCHY COLESLAW
Shredded white cabbage tossed with onion, celery, carrot, sultanas, vinaigrette dressing, mustard, and mayonnaise.

SERVES 8 245 calories per serving
Takes 15 minutes, plus chilling   Page 390

PASTA & MACKEREL SALAD
Pasta shells tossed with courgettes, French beans, orange segments, mackerel, walnuts, and a dressing of oils and orange juice.

SERVES 4–6 965–643 calories per serving
Takes 30 minutes, plus chilling   Page 398

POTATO SALAD
Tender new potatoes and onion coated in vinaigrette dressing, then mixed with chives and mayonnaise.

SERVES 8 357 calories per serving
Takes 30 minutes, plus chilling   Page 392

MUSHROOM SALAD
Mushrooms cooked with coriander, then dressed in yogurt flavoured with mustard and garlic. Chilled, and mixed with celery.

SERVES 6 102 calories per serving
Takes 15 minutes, plus chilling   Page 392

OVER 60 MINUTES

SWISS ROSTI

Grated potatoes seasoned with pepper, and shaped into a cake. Lightly cooked in butter until golden.

SERVES 8 230 calories per serving
Takes 45 minutes, plus chilling   Page 373

POTATOES LYONNAISE

Mouthwateringly delicious: thickly sliced potatoes layered with onion. Baked until the potatoes are tender.

SERVES 6 246 calories per serving
Takes 1³/4 hours   Page 374

LOW FAT

RATATOUILLE

Slices of aubergine, courgette, and red pepper cooked with tomatoes. Flavoured with onion, garlic, and basil.

SERVES 4–6 236–157 calories per serving
Takes 1¹/2 hours, plus standing   Page 385

TRADITIONAL

ROAST POTATOES

Classic accompaniment to roast meat or poultry: briefly simmered pieces of potato roasted in a little fat until crisp and golden.

SERVES 6 192 calories per serving
Takes 1¹/4 hours   Page 374

SWEET POTATOES WITH GINGER BUTTER

Baked sweet potatoes, flavoured with soy sauce, and served with ginger and garlic butter.

SERVES 4 381 calories per serving
Takes 1 hour 5 minutes   Page 377

SPINACH & CHEESE BAKED POTATOES

Hearty and healthy: baked potatoes scooped out and mixed with spinach, onion, and ricotta cheese.

SERVES 4–8 146–291 calories per serving
Takes 1³/4 hours   Page 376

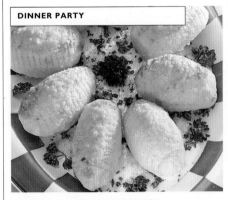

DINNER PARTY

HASSELBACK POTATOES

Simple to make: whole potatoes sliced almost through at intervals. Brushed with butter, sprinkled with Parmesan, and baked.

SERVES 8 183 calories per serving
Takes 1 hour 5 minutes   Page 376

HARICOT BEAN CASSOULET

Hearty dish: haricot beans simmered with carrot, onion, and herbs. Thickened with puréed beans and garnished with chopped parsley.

SERVES 6 167 calories per serving
Takes 1¹/2 hours, plus soaking   Page 381

FRENCH CLASSIC

GRATIN DAUPHINOIS

Rich and creamy: thinly sliced potato layered with cream, garlic, and grated Gruyère cheese, then baked until golden.

SERVES 8 279 calories per serving
Takes 1³/4 hours   Page 373

VEGETABLES & SALADS KNOW-HOW

ON EVERY SHOPPING TRIP there seem to be more new vegetables to try – strangely shaped squashes and roots like kohlrabi, tomatoes and peppers of all colours, exotic mushrooms, Chinese cabbages, and salad greens such as wild rocket, mizuna, and red chard – as well as different varieties of familiar vegetables like potatoes, each suitable for particular cooking methods. Imported produce adds to the bounty of our own seasonal vegetables. And for added convenience, chilled ready-prepared vegetables and salads are widely available. This wonderful variety enables a cook to be innovative, creating nutritious, appetizing dishes with minimum effort.

BUYING AND STORING

When choosing vegetables and salad leaves, look for the freshest available. Their colour should be bright and their texture firm and crisp. Any vegetables that are bruised or show signs of age – those that are discoloured, shrivelled, or flabby – are past their best. In general, small, young vegetables are more tender than large, older ones, although very small baby vegetables can be quite tasteless.

Some vegetables, including onions, garlic, roots such as potatoes, parsnips and swede, and pumpkin, can be stored in a cool, dark, well-ventilated place. More perishable vegetables, such as peas, sweetcorn, celery, salad leaves, spinach, and ripe tomatoes, should be chilled. Keep them in the special salad drawer in the refrigerator, unwrapping them or piercing their bags to prevent moisture build-up.

Many vegetables can be prepared ahead of time and kept in sealed plastic bags in the fridge. The exceptions to this are vegetables such as celeriac and Jerusalem artichokes that discolour when cut and exposed to the air. Salad leaves can also be prepared in advance, but do not dress until ready to serve or they will wilt.

NUTRITION

A healthy, well-balanced diet should include plenty of vegetables, because they supply essential vitamins, minerals, fibre, and disease-fighting compounds. And vegetables are low in calories and fat. To get the maximum benefit from the vegetables you eat:
• choose the freshest produce
• keep it in the fridge, or in a cool, dark place, and do not store for too long
• prepare as close to cooking or eating as possible
• leave on the peel or skin as it provides fibre, and nutrients are often concentrated just under the skin
• rinse thoroughly but don't soak before cooking, particularly if the vegetable is peeled or cut
• cut large pieces if boiling or steaming
• use the cooking liquid in a sauce or soup

CUTTING VEGETABLES

Keep pieces to a unifom size and shape to ensure they cook evenly.

Julienne
Cut into 5 mm (1/4 in) slices. Stack the slices then cut into sticks, 5 mm (1/4 in) thick.

Dice
Cut into 1 cm (1/2 in) strips, then cut across the strips to form neat dice.

Ribbons
Using a vegetable peeler, carefully shave off thin, wide ribbons.

MICROWAVING

The microwave is ideal for cooking small quantities of vegetables: little water is used so they retain their nutrients as well as colours and flavours. Cut vegetables into uniform pieces, or pierce skins of those that are left whole. Arrange them so that the tender parts are in the centre of the dish, to prevent overcooking. Add salt when serving. Keep the dish tightly covered during cooking, and turn or stir once or twice if necessary.

FREEZING

Most vegetables freeze very well, whether plain, in a sauce, or in a prepared dish. The exceptions are potatoes and watery vegetables like cucumber and tomatoes. Vegetables that are to be frozen plain should be very fresh. Before freezing blanch them in boiling water, then cool quickly in iced water; this will set the fresh colour. Vegetables can be kept in the freezer for 6–12 months, and can be cooked directly from frozen.

PREPARING VEGETABLES

Knowing the most efficient way to prepare vegetables will save you time and effort in the kitchen.
For most tasks, a chopping board and a sharp chef's knife, small knife, or vegetable peeler are all you'll need.
Here's how the professionals deal with more unusual vegetables.

Dicing fresh chillies

1 Cut the chilli in half lengthwise. Remove the stalk and core and scrape out the fleshy white ribs and seeds.

2 Set the chilli cut-side up and cut into thin strips. Hold the strips together and cut across to make dice. (See know-how box below.)

Preparing peppers

1 Cut around the stalk and the core. Twist and pull them out in one piece.

2 Cut the pepper in half. Scrape out the fleshy white ribs and the seeds.

Chopping fresh root ginger

1 With a small knife, peel off the skin. Slice the ginger across the fibrous grain.

2 Set the flat of a knife on top of the slices and crush. Chop the crushed slices.

Preparing asparagus

Cut off any woody ends from the asparagus and make the spears uniform in length. If you like, peel them: using a vegetable peeler, and working down towards the end of the spear, shave off the tough layer of skin from all sides.

Chopping garlic

1 Set the flat side of a knife on top of the clove and crush it lightly. Peel off the skin.

2 With a sharp chef's knife, chop the crushed garlic clove finely.

Preparing avocado

Cut the avocado in half lengthwise around the stone and twist the 2 halves to separate them. Remove the stone. If the avocado is to be mashed, the flesh can simply be scooped out of the skin with a teaspoon. To serve in slices, lightly score the skin into 2 or 3 strips, then peel off the strips of skin and slice the flesh.

Preparing vegetables know-how

The juices produced by fresh chillies can burn the skin, so it's best to wear rubber gloves when cutting them and to avoid touching your eyes or lips.

•

The more finely you chop garlic, the stronger the flavour. Garlic crushed in a press will have the strongest flavour of all.

•

Avocados discolour quickly, so brush cut surfaces with lemon juice, and use as soon as possible. Other vegetables that discolour when cut and exposed to the air include globe artichokes, celeriac and Jerusalem artichokes.

COOKING VEGETABLES

Choose the right cooking method to bring out the best in vegetables and create exciting accompaniments or main dishes. If cooking a variety of vegetables at the same time, remember that some take longer to cook than others, so you may have to add them in stages.

Baking
Potatoes, sweet potatoes, aubergines, and pumpkin are all delicious baked. Prick the skins of whole vegetables or, if cut, moisten cut surfaces with oil or butter. Push a skewer through the centres of large vegetables to conduct heat and speed up cooking time.

Chargrilling
Many types of quick-cooking vegetables can be cooked on a chargrill, as well as under a grill or on a barbecue. Halve the vegetables or cut into thick slices. Brush with oil and chargrill, turning at least once, until tender. For extra flavour, marinate vegetables first (page 386).

Braising
Carrots, celery, and other root vegetables are ideal for braising. Put the vegetables into a heavy pan or flameproof casserole, add a small amount of water or stock, and bring to the boil. Cover tightly and cook over a gentle heat until just tender. Boil to evaporate the liquid or drain.

Sautéing
Vegetables can be sautéed in oil or a mixture of oil and butter (butter alone burns if it becomes too hot). Cook the vegetables over a high heat, stirring and turning constantly, until they start to brown. Reduce the heat and continue cooking, stirring occasionally, until tender.

Roasting
Cut any root vegetables into large chunks and parboil them. Drain well. Put olive oil or duck fat into a roasting tin and heat in a preheated 180°C (350°F, Gas 4) oven. Add the vegetables to the tin and turn to coat with the fat. Roast, turning occasionally, until well browned.

Boiling
Drop vegetables (both greens and roots) into a large pan of boiling salted water and bring back to the boil as quickly as possible. Simmer until just tender, then drain. To stop further cooking and set the colour of green vegetables, rinse briefly under cold running water.

Deep-frying
Most vegetables (except roots like potatoes) need a protective coating such as batter before being deep-fried. Heat oil in a deep-fat fryer to the required temperature. Add the vegetables in batches and fry until golden, bringing the oil back to the required temperature between each batch. Drain on paper towels.

Stir-frying
Cut the vegetables into small, even-sized pieces. Heat a little oil in a wok. When it is hot, add the vegetables, starting with those that need the longest cooking time. Keep the heat high, and toss and stir the vegetables constantly. Cook for just a few minutes until the vegetables are tender but still crisp.

Steaming
This method is ideal for delicate vegetables such as cauliflower, broccoli, and asparagus. Bring water to the boil in a steamer base. Put the vegetables in a single layer on the rack, cover, and steam until just tender. If you don't have a steamer, use a large saucepan with a steamer basket, or a wok and a bamboo steamer.

MAYONNAISE

This always useful sauce is the base for many others – add crushed garlic and you have aioli – and for salad dressings. It can be made by hand, with a balloon whisk, or more quickly in a food processor or blender. For a lighter result use 1 whole egg rather than 2 egg yolks, and sunflower oil alone.

Traditional mayonnaise

1 Put a bowl on a tea towel to steady it. Add 2 egg yolks, 1 tsp Dijon mustard, and salt and pepper to taste, and beat together with a balloon whisk until the egg yolks have thickened slightly.

2 Whisk in 150 ml (1/4 pint) olive or sunflower oil, or a mixture of the two, just a drop at a time at first, whisking until the mixture is thick. Stir in 2 tsp white wine vinegar or lemon juice. Check the seasoning, adding sugar to taste if liked. Serve at once, or chill. This makes 200 ml (7 fl oz).

Food processor mayonnaise

1 Put 2 whole eggs, 2 tsp Dijon mustard, and salt and pepper to taste in the bowl of a food processor or blender. Process briefly to combine.

2 With the blades turning, slowly add 300 ml (1/2 pint) olive or sunflower oil, or a mixture of the two. Finish as for traditional mayonnaise above.

SALAD DRESSINGS

Most salad dressings can be made in a matter of seconds – for vinaigrette the ingredients only need to be shaken together in a screw-topped jar, and the basic mixture can be endlessly varied. Other dressings are simply made by whisking flavourings into a creamy mixture based on mayonnaise.

Vinaigrette dressing

Put 6 tbsp olive oil, 2 tbsp white wine vinegar, 1 tbsp lemon juice, 1 tbsp Dijon mustard, 1/4 tsp caster sugar, and salt and pepper to taste into a screw-topped jar. Shake until combined. This makes 150 ml (1/4 pint).

Blue cheese dressing

Put 150 ml (1/4 pint) each of mayonnaise and soured cream into a bowl with 90 g (3 oz) mashed blue cheese, 1 tsp white wine vinegar, 1 crushed garlic clove, and black pepper to taste. Whisk until smooth.

Nutty vinaigrette
Use red wine vinegar instead of the white wine vinegar and lemon juice in the recipe above, and replace 2 tbsp of the olive oil with walnut or hazelnut oil.

Herb vinaigrette
Add 2 tbsp chopped fresh herbs (eg dill, tarragon, chervil, or flat-leaf parsley) to the vinaigrette just before serving.

Green mayonnaise dressing
Put 50 g (2 oz) each watercress sprigs and flat-leaf parsley in a blender or food processor with 4 chopped spring onions and 1 garlic clove. Process until finely chopped. Whisk into a mixture of 150 ml (1/4 pint) each mayonnaise and soured cream or Greek-style yogurt.

Easy coleslaw dressing
Whisk 5 tbsp cider vinegar and 1 tbsp caster sugar into 150 ml (1/4 pint) mayonnaise. Season with salt and pepper to taste. If liked stir in a pinch of caraway seeds.

Salad dressings know-how

If mayonnaise curdles, add 1 tbsp hot water and beat well, or start again with fresh egg yolks and oil and slowly add the curdled mixture once the eggs and oil thicken.

•

For best results have the eggs for mayonnaise at room temperature.

•

Keep mayonnaise, tightly covered, in the refrigerator for no more than 1–2 days (remember that it contains raw eggs).

•

Vinaigrette dressing can be kept in its screw-topped jar in the fridge for up to 1 week. Shake well before serving.

GRATIN DAUPHINOIS

SERVES 8

butter for greasing

150 ml (¼ pint) single cream

150 ml (¼ pint) double cream

1 large garlic clove, crushed

1 kg (2 lb) main-crop potatoes

salt and black pepper

125 g (4 oz) Gruyère cheese, grated

1 Lightly butter a shallow gratin dish. Put the single and double creams into a bowl, add the garlic, and stir to mix.

2 Thinly slice the potatoes, preferably with the slicing disc of a food processor.

3 Prepare the gratin dauphinois (see box, right).

4 Bake in a preheated oven at 160°C (325°F, Gas 3) for 1½ hours or until the potatoes are tender and the topping is golden brown. Serve at once.

Preparing the gratin dauphinois

Arrange a layer of potatoes, slightly overlapping, in the bottom of the gratin dish. Season with salt and pepper.

Pour a little of the cream mixture over the potatoes, then sprinkle with grated cheese. Continue layering the potatoes, cream, and cheese, and adding salt and pepper, then finish with a layer of cheese.

SWISS ROSTI

SERVES 8

1.5 kg (3 lb) large baking potatoes, scrubbed

black pepper

60 g (2 oz) butter

2 tbsp sunflower oil

fresh thyme to garnish

1 Cook the potatoes in boiling salted water for about 10 minutes until just tender. Drain the potatoes thoroughly, leave to cool, then peel. Cover and chill for about 4 hours.

2 Coarsely grate the potatoes into a large bowl, season with pepper, and stir carefully to mix.

3 Melt 30 g (1 oz) of the butter with 1 tbsp of the oil in a frying pan, add the grated potato, and flatten into a cake with a fish slice. Cook over a low heat for about 15 minutes until the base is crisp and golden brown. Turn on to a large buttered plate.

4 Melt the remaining butter and oil in the frying pan, slide in the potato cake, and cook for 5–10 minutes to brown the second side. Turn out on to a warmed platter, garnish, and serve cut into wedges.

CELERIAC ROSTI

Substitute 750 g (1½ lb) celeriac for half of the potato. Before boiling in step 1, peel the celeriac, and toss in lemon juice to prevent discoloration.

ONION ROSTI

Heat 1 tbsp sunflower oil in a frying pan, add 1 large chopped onion, and cook for 3–5 minutes until softened but not coloured. Fork the onion into the grated potato in step 2, before seasoning with pepper

POTATOES LYONNAISE

SERVES 6

90 g (3 oz) butter, plus extra for greasing

1 large onion, sliced

1 kg (2 lb) floury potatoes, thickly sliced

salt and black pepper

chopped parsley to garnish

1 Lightly butter a gratin dish. Melt the butter in a frying pan, add the onion, and cook gently, stirring occasionally, for 3–5 minutes until the onions are softened but not coloured.

2 Layer the potatoes and onion in the gratin dish, seasoning each layer with salt and pepper, and finishing with a neat layer of potatoes.

3 Pour any butter left in the frying pan over the potatoes. Bake in a preheated oven at 190°C (375°F, Gas 5) for 1–1½ hours until the potatoes are tender. Garnish with parsley, and serve hot.

CHIPPED POTATOES

SERVES 6

750 g (1½ lb) floury potatoes

sunflower oil for deep-frying

salt

DEEP-FAT FRYER

1 Cut the potatoes into 5 x 1 cm (2 x ½ in) sticks, put into a bowl of cold water, and leave to soak for 5–10 minutes.

2 Heat the oil in a deep-fat fryer to 160°C (325°F). Dry the chips thoroughly, then lower them into the deep-fat fryer, in batches if necessary, and deep-fry for 5–6 minutes until soft and very pale golden.

3 Lift the basket out of the fryer. Increase the temperature of the oil to 190°C (375°F). Carefully return the basket of chips to the fryer and deep-fry for 3–4 minutes until crisp and golden brown. Lift out the basket and drain the chips on paper towels. Sprinkle with salt, and serve hot.

FRENCH FRIES

Cut the potatoes into 5 cm x 5 mm (2 x ¼ in) sticks and leave to soak as directed. Heat the oil as directed and deep-fry the sticks for 4–5 minutes. Lift out of the fryer, increase the heat as directed, return and deep-fry the sticks for 1–2 minutes. Sprinkle with salt, and serve at once.

> ### Cook's know-how
>
> Good chips should be crisp and golden on the outside and soft and tender in the middle. The secret is to cook the potatoes first in medium-hot oil until tender, then lift them out, increase the temperature of the oil, and cook the chips quickly to brown and crisp the outsides. Drain well on paper towels before serving.

ROAST POTATOES

SERVES 6

1 kg (2 lb) floury potatoes, cut into even-sized pieces

3 tbsp goose or duck fat, or sunflower oil

salt

1 Put the potatoes into a large saucepan, cover with cold water, and bring to a boil. Simmer for 1 minute, then drain thoroughly.

2 Return the potatoes to the saucepan and shake over a gentle heat to roughen the surfaces and dry the potatoes thoroughly.

3 Put the fat into a roasting tin, heat until very hot, then add the potatoes, turning to coat them in the fat. Roast the potatoes in a preheated oven at 220°C (425°F, Gas 7), turning and basting occasionally, for 45–60 minutes until tender, crisp, and golden. Sprinkle with salt, and serve at once.

> ### Cook's know-how
>
> Roughening the outside of blanched potatoes before roasting helps make them them really crisp. If you like, you can also score them roughly with a fork.

POMMES ANNA

SERVES 6

750 g (1 1/2 lb) floury potatoes

90 g (3 oz) butter, plus extra for greasing

salt and black pepper

1 Slice the potatoes very thinly, preferably with the slicing disc of a food processor.

2 Generously butter the base and sides of an ovenproof frying pan. Layer the potatoes in the frying pan, seasoning each layer with salt and pepper, and dotting with the butter.

3 Cover the pan tightly with buttered foil and the lid, and cook over a medium heat for about 15 minutes or until the base of the potato cake is light golden brown.

4 Transfer the pan to a preheated oven and cook at 190°C (375°F, Gas 5) for 30 minutes or until the potato cake is tender.

5 Invert a warmed serving platter over the pan, and turn out the potato cake so that the crisp layer is on the top. Serve at once, cut into wedges.

Cook's know-how

Arrange the potatoes in the frying pan as soon as they have been sliced. Don't leave them to soak in water or the starch in them will leach out and they will not hold together to make the cake.

INDIVIDUAL POMMES ANNA

Layer the sliced potatoes in well-buttered individual patty tins, seasoning the layers and dotting with butter as in step 2. Omit the cooking on the hob in step 3, and bake, uncovered, in the hottest part of a preheated oven at 220°C (425°F, Gas 7) for 30–35 minutes or until the potatoes are tender and golden brown.

GARLIC CREAMED POTATOES

SERVES 4

750 g (1 1/2 lb) floury potatoes, cut into large chunks

4 garlic cloves, unpeeled

salt and black pepper

about 150 ml (1/4 pint) milk

60 g (2 oz) butter

2 tbsp snipped fresh chives

1 Cook the potatoes and whole garlic cloves in boiling salted water for 20–30 minutes until tender. Drain thoroughly, and peel the skins off the garlic cloves.

2 Return the potatoes to the saucepan and toss over a gentle heat for a few seconds to dry thoroughly, shaking the saucepan so that the potatoes do not burn.

3 Mash the potatoes and garlic together, or work through a sieve for a finer purée, then push them to one side of the pan.

4 Pour the milk into the saucepan and heat until almost boiling. Beat the milk into the potatoes and garlic with the butter, and salt and pepper to taste. Sprinkle with chives, and serve hot.

HERB & CHEESE CREAMED POTATOES

Omit the garlic, and add 2 tbsp chopped parsley and 60 g (2 oz) finely grated Cheddar cheese when you beat in the milk.

CREAMED POTATOES WITH SWEDE

Omit the garlic and fresh chives. Substitute 250 g (8 oz) swede, cut into small chunks, for 250 g (8 oz) of the potatoes, and add a pinch of grated nutmeg just before serving.

HASSELBACK POTATOES

SERVES 8

8 large floury potatoes

60 g (2 oz) butter, melted, plus
    extra for greasing

salt and black pepper

4 tbsp grated Parmesan cheese

parsley to garnish

1 Peel the potatoes, then slice them (see box, right).

2 Put the potatoes into a buttered roasting tin and brush with the melted butter, separating the slices slightly so a little of the butter goes between them. Season with salt and pepper.

3 Bake in a preheated oven at 220°C (425°F, Gas 7) for 45 minutes, then sprinkle with the Parmesan cheese and return to the oven for 10–15 minutes or until the potatoes are tender.

4 Transfer to a warmed serving platter, garnish with parsley, and serve at once.

Slicing the potatoes

Cut a thin slice off one side of each potato, and place the potato cut-side down on a board. Make vertical cuts, three-quarters of the way through, at 5 mm (1/4 in) intervals.

Cook's know-how

To make it easier to slice the potatoes, push a skewer lengthwise through the lower part of each potato, and slice as far down as the skewer. Remove the skewer before cooking.

SPINACH & CHEESE BAKED POTATOES

SERVES 4–8

4 baking potatoes, scrubbed

250 g (8 oz) spinach

1 tbsp olive oil

1 small onion, finely chopped

125 g (4 oz) ricotta cheese

1/4 tsp grated nutmeg

salt and black pepper

1 Prick the potatoes all over with a fork. Bake in a preheated oven at 220°C (425°F, Gas 7) for 1–1 1/4 hours until tender.

2 Meanwhile, wash the spinach and put it into a saucepan with only the water remaining on the leaves. Cook over a gentle heat for 1–2 minutes until the spinach has just wilted. Drain thoroughly, squeezing to remove excess water. Chop the spinach finely.

3 Heat the olive oil in a small saucepan, add the onion, and cook gently, stirring occasionally, for 3–5 minutes until softened but not coloured.

4 Cut the potatoes in half lengthwise, scoop out the flesh and turn it into a bowl. Add the spinach, onion, any oil left in the pan, the ricotta cheese, and nutmeg. Season with salt and pepper, and mix thoroughly. Fill the potato skins with the mixture, return to the oven at the same temperature as before, and cook for 20 minutes or until piping hot. Serve hot.

SPRING ONION & HUMMUS BAKED POTATOES

Bake the potatoes, cut in half lengthwise, and scoop out the flesh. Mix with 4 finely chopped spring onions, 150 g (5 oz) hummus, and season with salt and pepper. Fill the potato skins and bake as in step 4.

SPICED YAMS

SWEET POTATOES WITH GINGER BUTTER

SERVES 4

4 sweet potatoes, scrubbed

60 g (2 oz) sesame seeds

soy sauce to taste

GINGER BUTTER

45 g (1 1/2 oz) butter, softened

1 garlic clove, crushed

1 cm (1/2 in) piece of fresh root ginger, peeled and grated

1 Lightly prick the skins of the sweet potatoes with a fork. Bake in a preheated oven at 180°C (350°F, Gas 4) for 1 hour or until tender.

2 Meanwhile, make the ginger butter: put the butter into a small bowl and blend in the garlic and grated ginger.

3 Put the sesame seeds into a frying pan and toss over a low heat for 2–3 minutes until golden brown. Remove from the frying pan. Lightly crush about half of the sesame seeds to release more of their fragrance. Set aside.

4 Cut the sweet potatoes into wedges and arrange on a serving plate with the ginger butter. Sprinkle with soy sauce and sesame seeds, and serve at once.

Healthy note

Sesame seeds contain phytic acid, which can inhibit certain cancers, especially cancer of the colon. Dry-frying the seeds not only enhances their flavour, it also destroys unwanted phytochemicals.

SERVES 4

45 g (1 1/2 oz) butter

2 garlic cloves, crushed

2 yams, total weight 1 kg (2 lb), trimmed but unpeeled, cubed

1 tsp mild chilli powder

1/4 tsp paprika

1/4 tsp ground cinnamon

1 x 200 (7 oz) can chopped tomatoes

salt

plain yogurt and chopped parsley to serve

1 Melt the butter in a large pan. When it is foaming, add the garlic, and cook gently, stirring occasionally, for 1–2 minutes until soft but not coloured.

2 Add the yams to the pan and toss over a medium to high heat for 1–2 minutes.

3 Stir in the chilli powder, paprika, and cinnamon, then add the tomatoes, and cook the mixture over a medium heat for 1–2 minutes.

4 Season with salt, cover, and simmer for 15–20 minutes until the yams are tender. Turn the yams occasionally with a palette knife, but do not stir or they will break up. Serve hot, topped with yogurt and parsley.

Cook's know-how

Yams and sweet potatoes are often confused, but they are not the same. Yams are a hard, starchy vegetable that comes in many different sizes, shapes, and colours, whereas sweet potatoes are softer and torpedo-shaped, with orange or yellow flesh. Sweet potatoes are rich in vitamins A and C (both antioxidants), whereas yams are not.

GINGER PARSNIPS

SERVES 8

1 kg (2 lb) parsnips, cut into matchstick-thin strips

salt and black pepper

60 g (2 oz) butter

2.5 cm (1 in) piece of fresh root ginger, peeled and grated

300 ml (1/2 pint) crème fraîche

1 Blanch the parsnips in a large saucepan of boiling salted water for 2 minutes. Drain the parsnips.

2 Melt the butter in the saucepan. Add the ginger and cook gently, stirring, for 2–3 minutes. Add the parsnips, tossing to coat in the butter. Season with salt and pepper, then turn the mixture into a large, shallow ovenproof dish.

3 Pour the crème fraîche over the parsnip mixture and bake in a preheated oven at 190°C (375°F, Gas 5) for 10–15 minutes until tender. Serve hot.

GLAZED CARROTS & TURNIPS

SERVES 4

375 g (12 oz) carrots, cut into 5 cm (2 in) strips

375 g (12 oz) baby turnips

300 ml (1/2 pint) chicken stock

30 g (1 oz) butter

1 tsp caster sugar

salt and black pepper

1 tbsp mixed chopped fresh mint and parsley

1 Put the vegetables into a pan with the stock, butter, and sugar. Season with salt and pepper, and bring to a boil. Cover and cook for about 10 minutes until the vegetables are almost tender.

2 Remove the lid and boil rapidly until the liquid in the pan has evaporated and formed a glaze on the vegetables. Stir in the herbs, and serve hot.

CREAMED SPINACH

SERVES 4

750 g (1 1/2 lb) fresh spinach

45 g (1 1/2 oz) butter

125 ml (4 fl oz) crème fraîche

1/4 tsp grated nutmeg

salt and black pepper

1–2 tbsp grated Parmesan cheese

1 Cut any coarse outer leaves and stalks off the spinach and discard, then wash the spinach thoroughly in plenty of cold water.

2 Melt the butter in a saucepan, add the spinach, and stir until it has absorbed the butter.

3 Add half of the crème fraîche, season with the nutmeg and salt and pepper, and heat through.

4 Transfer to a shallow flameproof dish, pour the remaining crème fraîche on top, and sprinkle with grated Parmesan. Put under a hot grill for a few minutes until lightly browned. Serve hot.

SWEET & SOUR BEETROOT

SERVES 4

3 tbsp olive oil

2 onions, chopped

2 garlic cloves, crushed

30 g (1 oz) caster sugar

4 cooked beetroot, diced

juice of 1 lemon

2 tsp chopped fresh mint

salt and black pepper

fresh mint to garnish

1 Heat the olive oil in a large saucepan, add the onions and garlic, and cook gently, stirring occasionally, for 3–5 minutes until the onions are softened but not coloured.

2 Stir in the sugar, beetroot, half of the lemon juice, and the mint. Cook gently, stirring, for 10 minutes. Taste for seasoning, adding salt and pepper, and more lemon juice if needed.

3 Serve warm or cold, garnished with fresh mint.

GARLIC SPRING GREENS

SERVES 6

1 kg (2 lb) spring greens, tough stalks removed
salt
2 tbsp olive oil
3 garlic cloves, coarsely chopped

1 Roll up the spring greens, a few leaves at a time, and cut across into thin strips. Blanch in boiling salted water for 2 minutes.

2 Drain and rinse in iced water to cool. Drain thoroughly, squeezing to remove excess water.

3 Heat the olive oil in a large saucepan, add the garlic, and cook gently for 1 minute or until lightly browned. Add the spring greens, toss to coat thoroughly in the garlic and oil, and cook for 2–3 minutes until the spring greens are heated through.

4 Season with salt to taste. Serve hot or cold.

AROMATIC BRUSSEL SPROUTS

SERVES 6–8

1 kg (2 lb) Brussels sprouts
salt and black pepper
45 g (1 1/2 oz) butter
2 tsp mustard seeds
1 tbsp lemon juice

1 Cut a cross in the base of each sprout, and simmer the sprouts in boiling salted water for 5–10 minutes until just tender. Drain.

2 Melt the butter in a large saucepan, add the mustard seeds, cover, and cook over a low heat for 1–2 minutes until the mustard seeds have stopped popping and the butter is lightly browned. Do not let the butter burn.

3 Add the sprouts to the pan, tossing to heat them through and coat them in the mustard-seed butter. Add the lemon juice, season with salt and pepper, and serve at once.

CABBAGE & MIXED PEPPER STIR-FRY

SERVES 6–8

2–3 tbsp olive oil
1 large onion, finely sliced
6 celery stalks, sliced diagonally
2 red peppers, halved, seeded, and cut into thin strips
1 yellow pepper, halved, seeded, and cut into thin strips
175 g (6 oz) mushrooms, quartered
salt and black pepper
1 small white cabbage, finely shredded

1 Heat 1 tbsp olive oil in a wok or large frying pan, add the sliced onion, and stir-fry over a high heat for about 2 minutes until beginning to brown.

2 Add the sliced celery and stir-fry for about 1 minute, then lower the heat and stir-fry for 2 minutes.

3 Add another tablespoon of olive oil to the wok. When it is hot, add the peppers and mushrooms, season with salt and pepper, and stir-fry for 3 minutes.

4 Add the cabbage, with the remaining oil if needed, and stir-fry for 2 minutes or until tender-crisp. Taste for seasoning.

SAVOY CABBAGE STIR-FRY

Heat 1 tbsp sunflower oil in a wok and stir-fry 1 finely sliced large onion, and 2 crushed garlic cloves for a few minutes. Add a further 1 tbsp sunflower oil, then 1 shredded small Savoy cabbage, and stir-fry for 2 minutes. Sprinkle with 2 tbsp soy sauce and 1 tsp sesame oil.

Cook's know-how

This is a good vegetable dish to serve when entertaining. Prepare and stir-fry the vegetables up to the end of step 3. The final cooking of the cabbage can be done just before serving.

CAULIFLOWER & BROCCOLI LAYERS

SERVES 6

500 g (1 lb) broccoli florets

500 g (1 lb) cauliflower florets

salt and black pepper

60 g (2 oz) butter, plus extra for greasing

60 g (2 oz) flaked almonds

4 tbsp fresh white breadcrumbs

1 garlic clove, crushed

1 LITRE (1³/4 PINT) BOWL

1 Cook the broccoli and cauliflower in boiling salted water for 10 minutes or until just tender. Drain.

2 Butter the bowl and layer the cauliflower and broccoli (see box, right).

3 Cover the bowl with a small plate and press down lightly to mould the vegetables. Leave in a warm place for 5 minutes.

4 Melt the remaining butter in a frying pan. Add the almonds, breadcrumbs, and garlic, and cook, stirring, for 3–5 minutes until golden. Season with salt and pepper.

5 Invert the bowl on to a warmed platter. Serve with the almond mixture on top.

Layering the vegetables

Arrange a layer of cauliflower florets, stalk-sides up, in the bottom of the bowl.

Place a ring of outward-facing broccoli florets, then of cauliflower florets on top. Continue layering alternately. Tightly pack the middle of the bowl with the remaining florets.

SWEET & SOUR RED CABBAGE

SERVES 8

1 tbsp sunflower oil

4 streaky bacon rashers, rinds removed, diced

125 g (4 oz) light soft brown sugar

2 onions, chopped

1 red cabbage, weighing about 1 kg (2 lb), shredded

1 tart apple, cored and diced

250 ml (8 fl oz) red wine

4 tbsp red wine vinegar

60 g (2 oz) sultanas

2 tsp caraway seeds

¹/4 tsp ground cinnamon

pinch of grated nutmeg (optional)

salt and black pepper

1 Heat the sunflower oil in a large saucepan, add the diced bacon, and cook for about 5 minutes until crisp and browned.

2 Stir in 90 g (3 oz) of the sugar and cook gently, stirring constantly, for 1–2 minutes, taking care that it does not burn.

3 Add the onions, cabbage, and apple, and cook, stirring occasionally, for about 5 minutes.

4 Pour in the wine and half of the wine vinegar, then add the sultanas, caraway seeds, cinnamon, and nutmeg (if using). Season with salt and pepper. Cover and cook over a low heat for 30 minutes or until the cabbage is tender but still firm. If there is too much liquid, uncover, and boil rapidly until the liquid evaporates completely.

5 Stir in the remaining sugar and wine vinegar, heat through, and taste for seasoning. Serve hot.

VEGETARIAN RED CABBAGE WITH CHESTNUTS

Omit the bacon. Add 125 g (4 oz) coarsely chopped peeled chestnuts in step 3, with the onions, cabbage, and diced apple.

HARICOT BEAN CASSOULET

SERVES 6

250 g (8 oz) dried haricot beans
30 g (1 oz) butter
1 small carrot, finely chopped
1 small onion, finely chopped
1 bouquet garni or a bunch of fresh mixed herbs
salt and black pepper
2 tbsp chopped parsley

1 Put the beans into a large bowl, cover with cold water, then leave to soak for at least 8 hours.

2 Drain the beans. Rinse under cold water and drain again. Put the beans into a saucepan and cover with cold water. Bring to a boil and boil rapidly for 10 minutes. Drain.

3 Melt the butter in a heavy saucepan, add the carrot and onion, and cook, stirring, for 3–4 minutes until beginning to soften.

4 Add the beans and bouquet garni or fresh herbs, and pour in enough cold water to cover the beans generously. Bring to a boil, cover, and simmer gently for 1 hour or until the beans are soft but not breaking up.

5 Drain the bean mixture, reserving the cooking liquid. Discard the bouquet garni or herbs. Purée one-third of the bean mixture in a food processor.

6 Stir the purée back into the unpuréed bean mixture in the pan, adding a little of the reserved cooking liquid to make a sauce-like consistency. Season with salt and pepper. Reheat gently and serve hot, sprinkled with chopped parsley,

FRENCH-STYLE PEAS

SERVES 4–6

1 small round lettuce, shredded
6 spring onions, chopped
60 g (2 oz) butter
1 tbsp chopped parsley
1 tsp caster sugar
500 g (1 lb) shelled fresh peas (they must be young)
4 tbsp water
salt and black pepper

1 Line the bottom of a saucepan with the lettuce. Add the spring onions, butter, parsley, and sugar, and top with the peas. Add the water, season with salt and pepper, and bring to a boil.

2 Simmer gently, uncovered, for 15–20 minutes until the liquid has evaporated and the peas are tender. Taste for seasoning and serve hot.

SUMMER PEAS & BEANS

SERVES 6–8

250 g (8 oz) shelled fresh broad beans (they must be young)
salt and black pepper
250 g (8 oz) shelled peas (they must be young)
250 g (8 oz) French beans, halved
30 g (1 oz) butter
2 tbsp chopped fresh mint
fresh mint to garnish

1 Cook the broad beans in a saucepan of boiling salted water for a few minutes until just tender. Add the peas and French beans and cook for another 5–10 minutes or until tender (the timing depends on their freshness).

2 Drain all the vegetables, and return to the pan. Add the butter and mint and stir until the butter melts. Taste for seasoning, and serve hot, garnished with fresh mint.

GLAZED SHALLOTS

SERVES 6

750 g (1½ lb) small shallots or pickling onions
90 g (3 oz) butter
1 tbsp caster sugar
1 tbsp chopped fresh thyme
salt and black pepper
chopped parsley to garnish

1 Place the shallots in a single layer in a large frying pan and cover with cold water.

2 Add the butter, sugar, and thyme, and season with salt and pepper. Cover and bring to a boil. Uncover, and simmer gently for 10–15 minutes until the shallots are golden and the liquid almost evaporated. Shake the pan vigorously at intervals, to prevent the shallots sticking.

3 Garnish the shallots with parsley, and serve hot.

CELERY & LEEK STIR-FRY

SERVES 6

30 g (1 oz) butter
2 tbsp olive oil
500 g (1 lb) young leeks, trimmed and thinly sliced
12 celery stalks, thinly sliced diagonally
salt and black pepper
2 tbsp snipped fresh chives
125 g (4 oz) salted cashew nuts to garnish

1 Melt the butter with the olive oil in a wok or large frying pan.

2 When the butter is foaming, add the leeks, and cook over a high heat, stirring occasionally, for 5 minutes.

3 Add the celery, and cook for 3–5 minutes. Add salt and pepper, then stir in the snipped fresh chives. Garnish with the salted cashew nuts, and serve at once.

Healthy note

Celery is a good source of potassium, and is known to help prevent and reduce high blood pressure.

YANKEE SUCCOTASH

SERVES 6

2 tbsp sunflower oil
1 large onion, chopped
8 thick streaky bacon rashers, rinds removed, diced
500 g (1 lb) sweetcorn kernels
250 ml (8 fl oz) single cream
1 x 400 g (13 oz) can beans, such as borlotti or broad beans, drained
salt
Tabasco sauce
3–4 tbsp snipped fresh chives
fresh chives to garnish

1 Heat the sunflower oil in a large frying pan, add the onion and bacon, and cook gently, stirring occasionally, for 7 minutes or until lightly browned.

2 Stir in the sweetcorn and cream and simmer for 2 minutes. Purée 3–4 tbsp of the sweetcorn mixture in a food processor until quite smooth, then stir back into the frying pan.

3 Add the beans and return to a boil. Simmer, stirring occasionally, for 5–10 minutes until the mixture is thickened.

4 Add salt and Tabasco sauce to taste, and stir in the snipped chives. Serve at once, garnished with chives.

Healthy option

Succotash is a native Indian dish traditionally made rich with bacon and cream, but you can omit these two ingredients from this recipe and use vegetable stock instead of the cream.

382

STUFFED MUSHROOMS

SERVES 6

250 g (8 oz) cup mushrooms

60 g (2 oz) butter

125 g (4 oz) carrots, diced small

125 g (4 oz) courgettes, diced small

1 tbsp chopped parsley

salt and black pepper

1 Remove the stalks from the mushrooms and chop the stalks finely.

2 Melt the butter in a frying pan. When it is foaming, add the mushroom stalks, carrots, and courgettes, and cook, stirring, for 1 minute. Add the parsley and season with salt and pepper.

3 Put the mushroom cups in a single layer in a shallow ovenproof dish. Fill with the vegetable mixture.

4 Cook in a preheated oven at 180°C (350°F, Gas 4) for 15 minutes. Serve hot.

GARLIC-STUFFED MUSHROOMS

Substitute 60 g (2 oz) fresh white breadcrumbs and 4 crushed garlic cloves for the carrots and courgettes.

ITALIAN FENNEL

SERVES 8

4 fennel bulbs, trimmed and quartered lengthwise

salt and black pepper

butter for greasing

250 g (8 oz) mozzarella cheese, grated

chopped parsley to garnish

1 Cook the fennel in boiling salted water for 3–5 minutes until just tender. Drain thoroughly.

2 Butter a shallow ovenproof dish. Add the fennel and season with salt and pepper. Sprinkle the grated mozzarella cheese on top.

3 Bake in a preheated oven at 200°C (400°F, Gas 6) for 15–20 minutes until the cheese topping is golden and bubbling. Sprinkle with chopped parsley, and serve hot.

ASPARAGUS WITH PARMESAN

SERVES 4

625 g (1 1/4 lb) asparagus

90 g (3 oz) Parmesan cheese, grated

lemon wedges and flat-leaf parsley sprigs to garnish

MARINADE

2 tbsp olive oil

2 tsp white wine vinegar

3 garlic cloves, crushed

salt and black pepper

1 Trim the woody ends from the asparagus.

2 Make the marinade: in a shallow dish, combine the oil, vinegar, garlic, a pinch of salt, and plenty of pepper.

3 Roll the asparagus in the marinade, cover, and leave to marinate for 15 minutes.

4 Sprinkle the Parmesan on to a plate. Roll the asparagus in the Parmesan, then arrange in a single layer in a large ovenproof dish.

5 Pour any remaining marinade over the asparagus, and roast in a preheated oven at 200°C (400°F, Gas 6) for 10–15 minutes until lightly browned and sizzling hot. Garnish with the lemon wedges and parsley sprigs, and serve hot.

Cook's know-how

To save time, you can omit the marinating and cook the asparagus on a ridged cast-iron chargrill pan. The charred stripes from the pan will boost the flavour of the asparagus and make it look attractive too.

HERBED ROASTED TOMATOES

SERVES 4

500 g (1 lb) cherry tomatoes

fresh herb sprig to garnish

HERB BUTTER

45 g (1½ oz) butter, softened

2 tbsp chopped fresh herbs (eg coriander, basil, flat-leaf parsley)

1 garlic clove, crushed

½ tsp lemon juice

salt and black pepper

1 Arrange the tomatoes in a single layer in an ovenproof dish. Roast in a preheated oven at 230°C (450°F, Gas 8) for 15–20 minutes until the tomatoes are tender but still retain their shape.

2 Meanwhile, make the herb butter: put the butter into a small bowl and beat in the herbs, garlic, and lemon juice. Season with salt and pepper. Garnish and serve hot, dotted with the herb butter.

GOLDEN ROASTED PUMPKIN

SERVES 6–8

1 kg (2 lb) piece of pumpkin, skinned, seeded, and cut into large chunks

2–3 tbsp olive oil

1 tsp balsamic or red wine vinegar

3 garlic cloves, crushed

1 tsp chopped fresh thyme

1 tsp paprika

salt and black pepper

fresh thyme to garnish

1 Put the pumpkin chunks on a baking tray. Mix the oil, vinegar, garlic, thyme, and paprika, season with salt and pepper, and pour over the pumpkin.

2 Roast in a preheated oven at 190°C (375°F, Gas 5) for 15–20 minutes until the pumpkin is tender and lightly browned on top. Garnish with thyme, and serve at once. If preferred, leave to cool and serve with a vinaigrette dressing (page 372).

OKRA WITH CHILLI

SERVES 4–6

3 tbsp sunflower oil

1 small onion, sliced

1 garlic clove, crushed

500 g (1 lb) okra, trimmed

1 large fresh red chilli, halved, seeded, and diced

salt and black pepper

1 Heat the oil in a wok or large frying pan, add the onion, and stir-fry over a high heat for 3 minutes or until golden. Add the garlic and stir-fry for 1 minute.

2 Add the okra and chilli and stir-fry over a high heat for 5–10 minutes until the okra is tender, but still retains some crispness. Add salt and pepper to taste. Serve hot.

Cook's know-how

Because of its shape, okra is sometimes known as ladies' fingers. Trim the ends carefully so that the sticky juices and seeds are not exposed and released.

MIXED VEGETABLE STIR-FRY

SERVES 4

1 tbsp olive oil

250 g (8 oz) courgettes, sliced thinly on the diagonal

1 yellow pepper, halved, seeded, and thinly sliced

250 g (8 oz) mixed mushrooms, sliced

salt and black pepper

1 tbsp lemon juice

60 g (2 oz) flaked almonds, toasted

1 Heat the olive oil in a wok or large frying pan, add the courgettes, and stir-fry for 3–4 minutes until the courgettes are just beginning to colour.

2 Add the yellow pepper and mushrooms and stir-fry for 2 minutes. Add salt and pepper, stir in the lemon juice, and leave the mixture to bubble for about 1 minute. Sprinkle with the toasted flaked almonds, and serve hot.

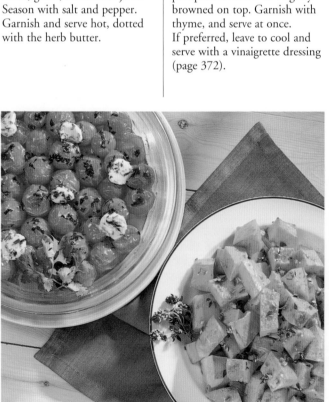

TOMATO & COURGETTE BAKE

SERVES 4–6

2 courgettes, sliced
salt and black pepper
3 large juicy ripe tomatoes, sliced
snipped fresh chives to garnish

WHITE SAUCE

30 g (1 oz) butter
30 g (1 oz) plain flour
300 ml (½ pint) milk
¼ tsp grated nutmeg

1 Arrange half of the courgette slices in the bottom of a shallow ovenproof dish. Season with a little salt and pepper.

2 Arrange half of the tomato slices in a layer on top of the courgettes. Season again.

3 Layer the remaining courgette and tomato slices in the dish, sprinkling them with salt and pepper.

4 Make the white sauce: melt the butter in a small saucepan. Sprinkle in the flour, and cook, stirring, for 1 minute. Remove from the heat and gradually blend in the milk. Bring to a boil, stirring, until the mixture thickens. Simmer for 2–3 minutes. Add the nutmeg, and season with salt and pepper.

5 Pour the white sauce over the vegetables. Cook in a preheated oven at 190°C (375°F, Gas 5) for 15–20 minutes until the vegetables are just cooked. Sprinkle with snipped chives, and serve hot.

Healthy option

Instead of the white sauce, layer the tomatoes and courgettes with 1 x 150 g (5 oz) packet half-fat mozzarella cheese, drained and thinly sliced, and lots of chopped fresh basil.

RATATOUILLE

SERVES 4–6

4 tbsp olive oil
1 large onion, sliced
1 large garlic clove, crushed
1 large aubergine, cut into 1 cm (½ in) slices
4 courgettes, sliced
6 juicy ripe tomatoes, sliced
1 large red pepper, halved, seeded, and sliced
1 tsp caster sugar
salt and black pepper
1 tbsp chopped fresh basil to garnish

1 Heat the olive oil in a large frying pan, add the onion and garlic, and cook gently, stirring occasionally, for 3–5 minutes until softened.

2 Add the aubergine slices, cover, and simmer gently for 20 minutes.

3 Add the courgettes, tomatoes, red pepper, and sugar. Season with salt and pepper. Cover and cook gently, stirring occasionally, for 30 minutes or until the vegetables are soft.

4 Taste for seasoning and serve hot or cold, sprinkled with the chopped fresh basil.

Cook's know-how

Ratatouille is a summer dish from Provence in the south of France. You can make it at other times of the year, but if you cannot get good ripe, juicy tomatoes you will get a better flavour if you use 1 x 400 g (13 oz) can chopped tomatoes instead of fresh. Some recipes for ratatouille include coriander seeds. If you like their flavour, add ¼ tsp crushed seeds in step 1 when softening the onion and garlic, and sprinkle some chopped fresh coriander over at the end, instead of the basil.

CHARGRILLED VEGETABLE PLATTER

Vegetables are delicious chargrilled – their flesh is tender and smoky in flavour. Serve them hot as a side dish with roast meat, poultry, or grilled fish, or cold as an unusual salad with picnics and barbecues. Experiment with different vegetables, oils, and marinades to suit your taste.

SERVES 4

4 baby aubergines

salt and black pepper

4 baby courgettes

1 red pepper

1 yellow pepper

1 large red onion

500 g (1 lb) asparagus

4 large mushrooms

175 g (6 oz) pattypan squash

olive oil for brushing

8–10 WOODEN COCKTAIL STICKS

1 Prepare the vegetables. Trim the aubergines, cut in half lengthwise, and score a criss-cross pattern on the cut surfaces.

2 Cut the courgettes in half lengthwise. Cut the red peppers in half lengthwise and cut out the fleshy ribs and seeds. Peel the red onioin and cut lengthwise into 4-6 wedges. Trim the woody ends from the asparagus and cut the spears to an even length.

3 Gently wipe the mushrooms with damp paper towels and remove the stalks. Trim the squash if necessary.

4 Place the asparagus spears side by side in groups of 3 or 4 (depending on thickness). Gently push a cocktail stick through the asparagus, about 1 cm (1/2 in) from the tips, until they are all skewered. Insert a second cocktail stick at the bases of the spears. Repeat for the remaining groups of asparagus spears.

5 Brush all of the vegetables generously with olive oil and season with salt and pepper to taste.

6 Place a batch at a time over a hot barbecue or on a preheated ridged griddle pan, and cook for 10–15 minutes, turning occasionally, until the vegetables are lightly charred. Keep each batch warm while you cook the remaining vegetables.

Cook's know-how

If you are using a ridged chargrill pan, either non-stick or cast iron, it is important to preheat it empty first, before laying the food on the ridges. Never oil the pan before preheating, as this will cause it to smoke. The secret is to oil the food, not the pan, and put the food in once the pan is good and hot. Press down hard on the food to help mark the ridges, and avoid moving the food in the pan as this will prevent the ridges from charring.

ADDING EXTRA FLAVOUR

If you are cooking the vegetables over a barbecue, lay some woody herbs such as thyme or rosemary over the rack before you put the vegetables on. Another way of injecting flavour into the vegetables is to soak them in a well-flavoured marinade for about an hour before cooking – you can leave them overnight if this suits you better.

HERB & GARLIC MARINADE

Put 250 ml (8 fl oz) olive oil, 2 finely chopped garlic cloves, 1 tbsp chopped fresh rosemary, oregano, or thyme, and salt and pepper to taste into a bowl and whisk to mix thoroughly.

HONEY & MUSTARD MARINADE

Put 250 ml (8 fl oz) sunflower oil, 2 tbsp soy sauce, 1 tbsp clear honey, 2 tsp Dijon mustard, and salt and pepper to taste into a small bowl and whisk to mix.

FLAVOURED OILS

Flavoured oils are easy to make and add an individual touch.
One of these flavoured oils can be used to baste the vegetables during chargrilling instead of the olive oil in the recipe above.

Thai perfumed oil
Lightly bruise 2–3 sprigs coriander and 3 x 5 cm (2 in) pieces fresh lemon grass. Put the coriander, lemon grass, and 2 dried chillies into a clean jar or bottle. Pour in 500 ml (16 fl oz) groundnut oil or corn oil and seal the bottle. Leave in a cool, dark place for 2 weeks, remove the coriander and lemon grass, and use to baste as directed.

Paprika oil
Spoon 2 tbsp paprika into a clean jar or bottle. Pour in 500 ml (16 fl oz) extra-virgin olive oil and seal the bottle. Leave in a cool, dark place, shaking the bottle from time to time, for 1 week. Line a funnel with a double layer of muslin and then strain the oil into another bottle. Use the oil to baste as directed.

Mixed herb oil
Lightly bruise 1 rosemary sprig and 1 thyme sprig. Put the herbs, 1 bay leaf, and 6 black peppercorns into a clean jar or bottle. Pour in 500 ml (16 fl oz) extra-virgin olive oil and seal the bottle. Leave in a cool, dark place for about 2 weeks. Use to baste as directed.

PEPPERATA SALAD

SERVES 4–6

2 courgettes, sliced lengthwise

1 tbsp olive oil

2 red peppers

2 yellow peppers

150 g (5 oz) watercress

vinaigrette dressing (page 372)

1 Brush the courgette slices on both sides with the olive oil, and cook under a hot grill, about 10 cm (4 in) from the heat, for 1–2 minutes on each side until golden. Leave to cool.

2 Halve the peppers lengthwise and remove the cores and seeds. Roast and peel the peppers (see box, right). Cut the flesh into chunks. Cut the courgette slices crosswise.

3 Put the watercress into a large serving bowl. Mix in the peppers and courgettes, pour over the dressing, and toss to coat. Serve at once.

Roasting and peeling peppers

Cook the pepper halves, cut-side down, under a hot grill, 10 cm (4 in) from the heat, until the skin is black and blistered. Seal in a plastic bag and leave to cool. Peel off the skin, using your fingers.

Healthy note

Red peppers are an excellent source of vitamin C and carotenes, which are linked to reduced risk of heart disease and strokes, and many forms of cancer.

AUBERGINE WITH FRESH PESTO

SERVES 4

1 large aubergine

75 ml (2¹/2 fl oz) olive oil, plus extra for greasing

2–3 tsp balsamic or wine vinegar

fresh pesto (see box, below)

shredded fresh basil to garnish

Healthy option

To cut down on the oil content in this dish, brush the aubergines with as little oil as possible, then use only half the amount of pesto and thin it down with hot water.

1 Cut the aubergine crosswise into thin slices and arrange in a single layer on a lightly oiled baking tray. Brush the slices with one-quarter of the oil, place under a hot grill, 7 cm (3 in) from the heat, and grill for 5 minutes or until lightly browned. Turn, brush with one-third of the remaining oil, and grill 5 minutes more.

2 Sprinkle the remaining oil and the vinegar over the aubergine slices. Leave to cool. Spread pesto over one side of each slice, garnish with fresh basil, and serve at room temperature.

Fresh pesto

Purée 60 g (2 oz) grated Parmesan cheese, 1 garlic clove, 60 g (2 oz) pine nuts, 60 g (2 oz) fresh basil leaves, and salt and pepper to taste in a food processor until almost smooth.

Add 4 tbsp olive oil gradually, with the blades turning, scraping the side of the bowl occasionally with a rubber spatula to ensure that all of the mixture is incorporated.

CRUNCHY ORIENTAL SALAD

SERVES 6

| 1 iceberg or romaine lettuce |
| 175 g (6 oz) bean sprouts |
| 6 spring onions, thinly sliced on the diagonal |
| 1 green pepper, halved, seeded, and thinly sliced |
| 2 tbsp toasted sesame seeds |

DRESSING

| 3 tbsp sunflower or olive oil |
| 1 tsp sesame oil |
| 1 tbsp white wine vinegar |
| 1 garlic clove, crushed |
| 1 cm (1/2 in) piece of fresh root ginger, peeled and grated |
| 1/2 tsp caster sugar, or to taste |
| salt and black pepper |

1 Tear the lettuce leaves into bite-sized pieces. Put the lettuce, bean sprouts, spring onions, and pepper into a salad bowl and mix together.

2 Make the dressing: combine the oils, vinegar, garlic, and ginger, and season to taste with sugar, salt, and pepper.

3 Toss the salad with the dressing, sprinkle with the sesame seeds, and serve.

SPINACH & BACON SALAD

SERVES 6

| 500 g (1 lb) baby spinach leaves, all stalks removed |
| 3 large slices of thick-cut white bread, crusts removed |
| 4 tbsp sunflower oil |
| 1 garlic clove, crushed |
| 12 streaky bacon rashers, rinds removed, cut into strips |
| 4–5 tbsp vinaigrette or blue cheese dressing (page 372) |
| salt and black pepper |

1 Tear the spinach leaves into large pieces and put them into a salad bowl.

2 Make the croûtons: cut the bread into small cubes. Heat the sunflower oil in a frying pan, add the garlic, and cook for 1 minute. Add the bread cubes and cook, stirring, for 1–2 minutes until golden and crisp. Lift out the croûtons and drain on paper towels.

3 Add the bacon to the pan and fry for 5 minutes or until crisp. Lift out and drain on paper towels.

4 Sprinkle the bacon over the spinach. Spoon the dressing over the salad, season with salt and pepper, and toss gently. Scatter the croûtons over the salad, and serve at once.

MIXED LEAF SALAD

SERVES 4–6

| 1 crisp lettuce, such as iceberg or romaine |
| 1 bunch of watercress, tough stalks removed |
| 60 g (2 oz) lamb's lettuce |
| 60 g (2 oz) rocket |
| about 4 tbsp vinaigrette dressing (page 372) |
| 1 tbsp snipped fresh chives |

1 Tear the lettuce leaves into bite-sized pieces and put them into a large salad bowl. Add the watercress, lamb's lettuce, and rocket, and mix together.

2 Pour the dressing over the salad and toss gently. Sprinkle with the chives, and serve at once.

Cook's know-how

When making a leafy salad, do not drown the leaves in dressing – there should be just enough to cling to the leaves. Add the dressing just before serving so the leaves stay crisp, and toss gently until each leaf is lightly and evenly coated.

RED SALAD BOWL

SERVES 4–6

| 1 small head of radicchio |
| 1 small oak leaf lettuce |
| 1 small lollo rosso lettuce |
| 1 small red onion, thinly sliced |
| 125 g (4 oz) seedless red grapes |

DRESSING

| 150 ml (1/4 pint) olive oil |
| 3 tbsp balsamic vinegar |
| 1 garlic clove, crushed (optional) |
| 1/2 tsp caster sugar, or to taste |
| salt and black pepper |

1 Tear the radicchio leaves and the oak leaf and lollo rosso lettuce leaves into bite-sized pieces. Put them into a large salad bowl and mix together, then add the onion and grapes.

2 Make the dressing: combine the oil, vinegar, and garlic, if using, with sugar, salt, and pepper to taste.

3 Pour just enough dressing over the salad to cling to the leaves, toss gently, and serve at once.

CAESAR SALAD

SERVES 4

1 cos or romaine lettuce

4 tbsp olive oil

2 tbsp lemon juice

salt and black pepper

2 hard-boiled eggs

30 g (1 oz) Parmesan cheese, coarsely grated

CROUTONS

3 large slices of thick-cut white bread, crusts removed

4 tbsp olive oil

1 garlic clove, crushed

1 Make the croûtons: cut the bread into small cubes. Heat the olive oil in a frying pan, add the garlic, and cook for 1 minute. Add the bread cubes and cook, stirring, for 1–2 minutes until crisp. Lift out and drain on paper towels.

2 Tear the lettuce leaves into bite-sized pieces and put them into a salad bowl. Whisk the olive oil and lemon juice, season with salt and pepper, and toss with the leaves.

3 Cut the hard-boiled eggs into quarters, and add to the salad. Add the croûtons and Parmesan cheese and toss gently. Serve at once.

CAESAR SALAD WITH ANCHOVIES

Coarsely chop 6 canned anchovy fillets and add to the salad with the hard-boiled eggs in step 3.

Cook's know-how

If you prefer a lighter salad, you can toast the bread to make the croûtons rather than frying it in oil.
For a sophisticated change, use 4 hard-boiled quails' eggs, halved, instead of hens' eggs.

WALDORF SALAD

SERVES 4

500 g (1 lb) crisp red-skinned apples, cored and diced

juice of 1/2 lemon

4 celery stalks, thickly sliced

150 ml (1/4 pint) mayonnaise (page 372)

salt and black pepper

90 g (3 oz) walnut pieces, coarsely chopped

chopped parsley to garnish

1 Put the diced apples into a bowl, pour the lemon juice over the top, and stir to coat thoroughly to prevent discoloration. Transfer to a salad bowl and add the celery.

2 Spoon the mayonnaise over the salad, season with salt and pepper, and toss gently to mix. Cover and chill until required. Stir in the walnut pieces and garnish with chopped parsley just before serving.

CRUNCHY COLESLAW

SERVES 8

1 white cabbage, weighing about 750 g (1 1/2 lb)

150 ml (1/4 pint) vinaigrette dressing (page 372)

1 small onion, finely chopped

1 tsp Dijon mustard

salt and black pepper

3 celery stalks, thinly sliced

2 carrots, grated

60 g (2 oz) sultanas

75–90 ml (2 1/2–3 fl oz) mayonnaise (page 372)

1 Cut the cabbage into quarters lengthwise and cut out the core. Shred the cabbage finely, using either a sharp knife or the slicing blade of a food processor.

2 Put the cabbage into a large bowl, add the vinaigrette, onion, and Dijon mustard, and season with salt and pepper. Toss to mix thoroughly. Cover the bowl tightly, and leave to chill for about 8 hours.

3 Add the celery, carrots, and sultanas, and toss to mix thoroughly. Stir in the mayonnaise. Cover and chill until ready to serve. Toss the coleslaw well and taste for seasoning before serving.

POTATO, APPLE, & CELERY SALAD

SERVES 6

750 g (1 1/2 lb) new potatoes, scrubbed

salt and black pepper

75 ml (2 1/2 fl oz) vinaigrette dressing (page 372)

6 celery stalks, sliced

1 small red onion, very finely sliced

2 red-skinned apples, such as Red Delicious or Spartan, cored and diced

125 ml (4 fl oz) mayonnaise (page 372)

2 tbsp snipped fresh chives to garnish

1 Put the potatoes into a large saucepan of boiling salted water and simmer gently for 10–15 minutes until just tender. Drain, leave to cool, then cut the potatoes in half.

2 Put the potatoes into a large salad bowl, add the vinaigrette dressing, and toss gently while the potatoes are still warm. Leave to cool.

3 Add the celery, onion, and apples to the cold potatoes. Mix gently until all the ingredients are thoroughly coated with dressing, then season with salt and pepper. Cover and chill for at least 1 hour.

4 Gently stir in the mayonnaise, taste for seasoning, then sprinkle with the chives, and serve at once.

CELERIAC REMOULADE

SERVES 4–6

500 g (1 lb) celeriac

juice of 1 lemon

1 tsp sliced gherkins and 2 tbsp chopped parsley to garnish

DRESSING

150 ml (1/4 pint) plain yogurt

2 tbsp mayonnaise (page 372)

1 tsp finely chopped capers

1/2 tsp Dijon mustard

salt and black pepper

1 Make the dressing: combine the yogurt, mayonnaise, capers, and Dijon mustard, and season with salt and pepper.

2 Peel the celeriac, cut into matchstick-thin strips, and place in a bowl of cold water. Add the lemon juice and toss to prevent discoloration.

3 Drain the celeriac and transfer to a salad bowl. Pour over the dressing and toss gently to mix. Garnish with the gherkins and chopped parsley, and serve at once.

CARROT JULIENNE SALAD

SERVES 4–6

5 carrots

salt and black pepper

DRESSING

1 tbsp olive oil

1 tsp white wine vinegar

1 garlic clove, crushed

1 tsp chopped parsley

lemon and fresh chives to garnish

1 Cut the carrots into matchstick strips. Blanch in a saucepan of salted boiling water for 2–3 minutes. Drain, refresh under cold running water, and drain again.

2 Make the dressing: combine the oil, white wine vinegar, garlic, and parsley, and season with salt and pepper.

3 Put the carrots into a salad bowl, pour over the dressing, and toss to coat evenly. Leave to cool. Garnish with lemon and chives before serving.

POTATO SALAD

SERVES 8

1 kg (2 lb) new potatoes, scrubbed
salt and black pepper
1 small mild onion, very finely chopped
4 tbsp vinaigrette dressing (page 372)
250 ml (8 fl oz) mayonnaise (page 372), or less if preferred
2 tbsp snipped fresh chives, plus extra to garnish

1 Put the potatoes into a large saucepan of boiling salted water and simmer for 15–20 minutes until tender. Drain the potatoes thoroughly. Cut them into even-sized pieces.

2 Put the potatoes into a large salad bowl and add the chopped onion.

3 While the potatoes are still quite warm, spoon the vinaigrette dressing over them and then toss gently to mix all the ingredients thoroughly.

4 Add the mayonnaise and the chives, and mix together gently. Add salt and pepper to taste, cover, and chill for about 30 minutes (the salad is best served not too cold). Garnish with extra chives before serving.

MUSHROOM SALAD

SERVES 6

3 tbsp sunflower oil
1/2 tsp ground coriander
750 g (1 1/2 lb) button mushrooms
salt and black pepper
4 celery stalks, thinly sliced
shredded fresh basil to garnish

DRESSING

150 ml (1/4 pint) plain yogurt
1 tbsp lemon juice
1 tbsp white wine vinegar
1 tsp Dijon mustard
1 garlic clove, crushed

1 Heat the oil in a frying pan, add the ground coriander, and cook gently, stirring, for 1 minute. Add the mushrooms, season lightly, and cook over a high heat, stirring, for 5 minutes. Lift out with a slotted spoon. Leave to cool.

2 Make the dressing: combine the yogurt, lemon juice, vinegar, Dijon mustard, garlic, and salt and pepper to taste. Pour the dressing over the mushrooms, and toss to mix. Cover and chill for 8 hours. Stir in the celery and garnish with basil before serving.

AVOCADO SALAD

SERVES 6

60 g (2 oz) pine nuts
250 g (8 oz) mixed salad leaves
2 oranges
2 avocados

DRESSING

finely grated zest of 1 orange
3 tbsp orange juice
1 tbsp walnut oil
1–2 tsp caster sugar
salt and black pepper

1 Spread the pine nuts on a baking tray, and toast under a hot grill for 2 minutes.

2 Put the salad leaves into a large salad bowl. Peel the oranges, removing the rind and pith, and separate into segments (page 466).

3 Halve, stone, and peel the avocados (page 370). Slice lengthwise and mix with the orange segments and pine nuts.

4 Whisk together the dressing ingredients, and pour over the salad. Toss gently and serve.

TRICOLORE SALAD

SERVES 4

4 beefsteak or slicing tomatoes
salt and black pepper
250 g (8 oz) mozzarella cheese
2 avocados
2 tbsp lemon juice
3–4 tbsp extra virgin olive oil
basil sprigs to garnish

1 Slice the tomatoes thinly, put into a bowl, and sprinkle with salt and pepper. Thinly slice the mozzarella.

2 Cut the avocados in half lengthwise. Twist to loosen the halves and pull them apart. Remove the stones (page 370), score and peel off the skin, then cut the halves crosswise.

3 Cut the avocado quarters into slices lengthwise, then sprinkle with lemon juice to prevent discoloration.

4 Arrange the tomato, mozzarella, and avocado slices attractively on a platter. Drizzle with the extra virgin olive oil and garnish with basil sprigs before serving.

TOMATO & ONION SALAD

SERVES 6

750 g (1 1/2 lb) ripe but firm tomatoes, thinly sliced

1 mild onion, cut into thin rings

1 tbsp snipped fresh chives

DRESSING

90 ml (3 fl oz) extra virgin olive oil

2 tbsp red wine vinegar

1/4 tsp caster sugar

salt and black pepper

1 Overlap the tomato slices in circles of diminishing size in a large shallow dish. Arrange the onion rings on top.

2 Make the dressing: combine the olive oil, red wine vinegar, and caster sugar, and add salt and pepper to taste.

3 Spoon the dressing over the tomatoes and onions, cover, and leave to chill for about 2 hours. Sprinkle with the snipped chives before serving.

TOMATO & BASIL SALAD

SERVES 4–6

2 beefsteak or slicing tomatoes

4 ripe salad tomatoes

125 g (4 oz) cherry tomatoes

1 yellow pepper, cored, deseeded, and cut into chunks

2 tbsp shredded fresh basil

DRESSING

3 tbsp extra virgin olive oil

2 tsp balsamic vinegar

1/4 tsp caster sugar

salt and black pepper

1 Make the dressing: combine the olive oil, vinegar, sugar, and salt and pepper to taste.

2 Cut the tomatoes in half lengthwise, cut out the core, and cut each half into 4 wedges. Thickly slice the salad tomatoes. Halve the cherry tomatoes.

3 Put all the tomatoes and the yellow pepper into a salad bowl, and sprinkle with the dressing. Cover and leave to stand for 1 hour to let the flavours mingle. Sprinkle with the basil just before serving.

CUCUMBER SALAD

SERVES 4–6

1 cucumber, peeled and cut in half lengthwise

1 tbsp chopped fresh dill

DRESSING

2 tbsp hot water

2 tbsp white wine vinegar

1 tbsp sunflower oil

2 tbsp caster sugar

salt and black pepper

1 Scoop out the cucumber seeds. Cut the flesh crosswise into thin slices, and arrange in a serving dish.

2 Make the dressing: whisk together the water, wine vinegar, oil, sugar, and salt and pepper to taste.

3 Pour the dressing over the cucumber and sprinkle with the dill before serving.

Serving suggestion

This Danish-style salad goes well with both grilled or baked fresh fish and smoked fish.

GREEK SALAD

SERVES 4–6

4 beefsteak or slicing tomatoes

1 cucumber, sliced

250 g (8 oz) feta cheese, diced

24 black olives, pitted

125 ml (4 fl oz) extra virgin olive oil

4 tbsp lemon juice

salt and black pepper

2 tbsp chopped fresh oregano or flat-leaf parsley

1 Halve the tomatoes lengthwise, cut out the cores, and cut each half into 4 wedges.

2 Put the tomatoes into a large salad bowl, and add the cucumber, feta cheese, and olives.

3 Spoon over the olive oil and lemon juice, and add salt and black pepper to taste (do not use too much salt as feta is a salty cheese), then toss gently to mix.

4 Sprinkle the salad with the oregano or parsley before serving.

FRESH & LIGHT SALADS

Some of the most interesting salads are made from vegetables, pulses, and grains rather than leaves.
They have more flavour and texture, and they can be served as a meal in their own right.
These four recipes are light, healthy, and low in fat.

PUY LENTIL SALAD

SERVES 6

250 g (8 oz) Puy lentils, rinsed

3 tbsp olive oil

2 tbsp balsamic vinegar

salt and black pepper

1 bunch of spring onions, trimmed and finely sliced

3 tbsp chopped fresh flat-leaf parsley

1 Pour the lentils into a medium saucepan, cover with plenty of cold water, and bring to a boil. Reduce the heat, cover, and simmer for 15 minutes or until the lentils are tender.

2 Drain the lentils well, tip into a serving bowl, and add the olive oil and vinegar, and plenty of seasoning (warm lentils absorb the flavours of dressing better than cold lentils). Leave to cool, then mix in the spring onions and chopped parsley just before serving.

TABBOULEH

SERVES 4

125 g (4 oz) bulgur wheat

3 tbsp extra virgin olive oil

juice of 2 lemons

salt and black pepper

¼ bunch spring onions, finely sliced

½ cucumber, peeled, seeded, and finely diced

6 tbsp chopped fresh mint

6 tbsp chopped fresh flat-leaf parsley

1 Soak the bulgur wheat in boiling water for 30 minutes. Drain well, tip into a serving bowl, and add the olive oil, lemon juice, and plenty of seasoning. Do this immediately while the wheat is still warm so that it absorbs the maximum flavour.

2 Add the spring onions, cucumber, and freshly chopped herbs to the bowl. Stir well and check the seasoning. Chill before serving.

ITALIAN PESTO SALAD

SERVES 4-6

375 g (12 oz) broccoli, cut into bite-sized florets

375 g (12 oz) cauliflower, cut into bite-sized florets

about 12 black olives, pitted

PESTO

30 g (1 oz) fresh basil

1 garlic clove

1 tbsp pine nuts

30 g (1 oz) Parmesan cheese, grated

salt and black pepper

5 tbsp extra virgin olive oil

1 Make the pesto: put the basil, garlic, pine nuts, Parmesan and seasoning into a small food processor and process until the basil is finely chopped. With the machine running, add the oil in a fine stream until the paste is creamy. Check the seasoning.

2 Blanch the broccoli and cauliflower florets in boiling salted water for about 2 minutes (they should retain plenty of bite, so take care not to overcook them). Drain and refresh under cold running water. Drain again, then toss with the pesto. Scatter with the olives and chill before serving.

Healthy note

Broccoli and cauliflower are both cruciferous vegetables (the name crucifer comes from the cross shape of their 4-petalled flowers), known to be excellent nutrition boosters. They are rich in the antioxidants vitamin C, vitamin E, and carotenes, which can help guard against heart disease and strokes, and they have a strong link to a lower risk of cancer. Crucifers are also rich in folate and iron, minerals that help prevent and correct anaemia, and in potassium, a mineral that helps avoid and regulate high blood pressure.

HERB SALAD WITH ORANGE & MUSTARD DRESSING

SERVES 4-6

125 g (4 oz) fine asparagus

salt and black pepper

½ romaine lettuce

60 g (2 oz) lamb's lettuce

60 g (2 oz) rocket

1 small bunch of flat-leaf parsley, stalks removed

60 g (2 oz) pine nuts, toasted

60 g (2 oz) sun-blushed or sun-dried tomatoes, snipped into small pieces

DRESSING

1 orange

2 tbsp olive oil

1 tsp maple syrup

1 tsp wholegrain mustard

1 Trim the asparagus and cut into 2.5 cm (1 in) lengths. Cook in boiling salted water for about 3 minutes until just tender. Drain and refresh under cold running water.

2 Break the romaine lettuce into manageable pieces and mix with the lamb's lettuce, rocket, and parsley leaves in a salad bowl. Add the asparagus, pine nuts, and tomatoes, and toss gently.

3 Remove the zest of the orange with a zester and add the strips to the salad. Squeeze the juice from half of the orange to give about 3 tbsp, then mix with the remaining dressing ingredients and seasoning to taste. Toss the salad with the dressing just before serving.

CLOCKWISE FROM TOP: Herb Salad with Orange & Mustard Dressing, Puy Lentil Salad, Tabbouleh, Italian Pesto Salad.

SALADE NIÇOISE

SERVES 4

250 g (8 oz) French beans, cut in half crosswise

salt and black pepper

2 hard-boiled eggs

I cos or romaine lettuce

¹/₂ cucumber, sliced

4 tomatoes, quartered

I x 200 g (7 oz) can tuna, drained

I small mild onion, very thinly sliced

I x 50 g (1³/₄ oz) can anchovy fillets, drained

12 pitted black olives

chopped parsley to garnish

DRESSING

150 ml (¹/₄ pint) olive oil

3 tbsp white wine vinegar

I garlic clove, crushed

¹/₂ tsp Dijon mustard

1 Cook the French beans in boiling salted water for 4–5 minutes until just tender. Drain, rinse under cold running water, and drain again.

2 Peel the shells from the eggs, and cut the eggs into wedges lengthwise.

3 Make the dressing: combine the oil, vinegar, garlic, and mustard, and season with salt and pepper.

4 Tear the lettuce leaves into pieces and place on a large serving plate. Arrange the cucumber and beans on top of the lettuce.

5 Arrange the tomatoes and eggs on the serving plate. Coarsely flake the tuna with a fork and place in the middle. Arrange the onion, anchovy fillets, and olives over the tuna. Pour over the dressing, garnish with parsley, and serve at once.

THREE-BEAN SALAD

SERVES 4

250 g (8 oz) French beans, cut in half crosswise

salt and black pepper

I x 400 g (13 oz) can chick peas, drained and rinsed

I x 400 g (13 oz) can red kidney beans, drained and rinsed

10 pitted black olives, halved

chopped parsley to garnish

DRESSING

4 tbsp Greek yogurt

3 tbsp olive oil

3 tbsp red wine vinegar

2 tsp Dijon mustard

¹/₄ tsp caster sugar, or to taste

1 Cook the French beans in boiling salted water for 4–5 minutes until just tender. Drain, rinse under cold running water, and drain again.

2 Make the dressing: combine the Greek yogurt, oil, red wine vinegar, and mustard, and season with sugar, salt, and pepper to taste.

3 Put the chick peas, red kidney beans, and French beans into a large bowl. Pour the dressing over the beans and stir gently to mix. Cover and leave to stand for 1 hour. Add the olives, sprinkle with the chopped parsley, and serve at once.

THREE-BEAN SALAD WITH BACON

Substitute 250 g (8 oz) shelled and skinned broad beans for the chick peas, and omit the olives. Cut 60 g (2 oz) streaky bacon rashers into strips, and dry-fry until crisp and golden. Sprinkle over the salad just before serving.

BULGUR WHEAT SALAD

SERVES 4

175 g (6 oz) bulgur wheat

4–5 tbsp vinaigrette dressing (page 372)

juice of 1 lemon

3 tomatoes, diced

4 spring onions, chopped

3 tbsp chopped parsley

3 tbsp chopped fresh mint

salt and black pepper

parsley sprigs to garnish

1 Put the bulgur wheat into a large bowl, cover with cold water, and leave to stand for 30 minutes.

2 Drain the bulgur wheat, pressing out as much of the liquid as possible. Transfer to a salad bowl, and mix in the vinaigrette dressing, lemon juice, tomatoes, spring onions, parsley, and mint. Season with salt and pepper, toss well, and garnish with parsley. Serve at room temperature.

COUSCOUS SALAD

SERVES 4–6

1/2 tsp crushed dried red chillies

90 ml (3 fl oz) olive oil

250 g (8 oz) couscous

500 ml (16 fl oz) boiling water

3–4 tbsp sultanas

5 cm (2 in) piece of fresh root ginger, peeled and grated

salt and black pepper

3–4 tbsp white wine vinegar

5 ripe tomatoes, diced

1 onion, chopped

3 spring onions, thinly sliced

2 tbsp chopped fresh mint

mint sprigs to garnish

1 Combine the chillies and olive oil, and set aside.

2 Put the couscous into a bowl, stir in the measured water, sultanas, ginger, and a good pinch of salt. Cover and leave to stand for 10 minutes.

3 Stir in the chilli oil, vinegar, tomatoes, onion, spring onions, and mint. Season with salt and pepper to taste, and garnish with mint sprigs before serving.

WILD RICE SALAD

SERVES 4–6

250 g (8 oz) mixed long grain and wild rice

salt and black pepper

175 g (6 oz) French beans, cut in half crosswise

2 tbsp chopped parsley

60 g (2 oz) button mushrooms, thinly sliced

60 g (2 oz) walnut pieces

DRESSING

4 tbsp sunflower oil

2 tbsp walnut oil

2 tbsp white wine vinegar

1 tsp Dijon mustard

1 Cook the rice in boiling salted water for 15 minutes, or according to packet instructions, until just tender. Drain, rinse in boiling water, and drain again. Transfer to a large bowl.

2 Cook the beans in boiling salted water for 4–5 minutes until just tender. Drain, rinse in cold water, and drain again.

3 Make the dressing: combine the oils, vinegar, mustard, and salt and pepper to taste. Pour over the rice while still warm, stir, and leave to cool.

4 Add the beans, parsley, mushrooms, and walnuts to the rice. Stir before serving.

RICE SALAD

SERVES 4–6

250 g (8 oz) long grain rice

salt and black pepper

125 g (4 oz) frozen peas

125 g (4 oz) frozen sweetcorn kernels

1 red pepper, halved, seeded, and diced

2 tbsp chopped fresh coriander

DRESSING

90 ml (3 fl oz) olive oil

3 tbsp white wine vinegar

1 tsp Dijon mustard

1 garlic clove, crushed

1 Cook the rice in boiling salted water for 12–15 minutes until just tender, adding the peas and sweetcorn for the last 3 minutes. Drain, rinse in boiling water, and drain again. Transfer to a bowl.

2 Make the dressing: combine the olive oil, wine vinegar, mustard, and garlic, and season with salt and pepper. Pour over the rice while still warm, stir gently, and leave to cool.

3 Add the red pepper, and coriander to the rice, and stir to combine. Serve at once.

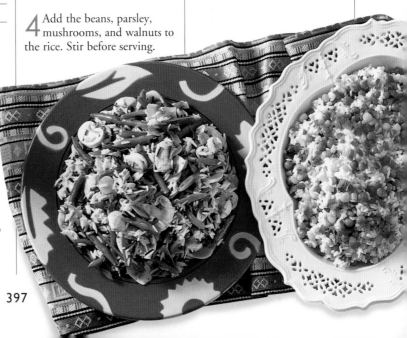

PASTA & MACKEREL SALAD

SERVES 4–6

500 g (1 lb) pasta shells

salt and black pepper

2 courgettes, sliced

125 g (4 oz) French beans, cut in half crosswise

2 oranges

375 g (12 oz) peppered smoked mackerel fillets

30 g (1 oz) walnut pieces

DRESSING

juice of 1 orange

2 tbsp sunflower oil

1 tbsp walnut oil

2 tbsp chopped parsley

1 Cook the pasta shells in a large saucepan of boiling salted water for 8–10 minutes until just tender. Drain, rinse under cold running water, and drain again.

2 Cook the courgettes and French beans in another pan of boiling salted water for 4–5 minutes until tender. Drain, rinse, and drain again.

3 Peel and segment the oranges (page 466) and set aside. Remove the skin and any bones from the mackerel, then flake the flesh into large pieces.

4 Make the dressing: combine the orange juice, sunflower and walnut oils, and parsley, and season with salt and pepper.

5 Put the pasta, courgettes, French beans, orange segments, flaked mackerel, and walnut pieces into a large salad bowl. Add the dressing and toss gently so that the fish does not break up. Leave to chill in the refrigerator for at least 30 minutes before serving.

Cook's know-how

Smoked trout can be used instead of mackerel – it is less rich, and milder in flavour. If you see smoked eel at the fishmonger or supermarket, this would be another good choice.

PASTA SALAD WITH PEPPERS

SERVES 4–6

500 g (1 lb) pasta bows

salt and black pepper

1 red pepper, halved, seeded, and diced

1 green pepper, halved, seeded, and diced

3 spring onions, sliced diagonally

4 tbsp mayonnaise (page 372)

spring onion tops, sliced, to garnish

1 Cook the pasta bows in a large saucepan of boiling salted water for 8–10 minutes until just tender.

2 Drain, rinse under cold running water, and drain again. Leave to cool.

3 Put the pasta, peppers, and spring onions into a salad bowl, and season with salt and pepper. Add the mayonnaise, stir well to coat all the ingredients evenly, then chill for 30 minutes. Garnish with spring onions before serving.

PASTA SALAD WITH MANGETOUT & SESAME SEEDS

Substitute 125 g (4oz) blanched mangetout for the red and green peppers. Omit the mayonnaise. Mix together 2 tbsp white wine vinegar, 1 tbsp sunflower oil, and 1 tsp sesame oil, and pour over the salad. Taste for seasoning. Substitute 2 tbsp toasted sesame seeds for the spring onion garnish, and serve at once.

Healthy option

If you prefer not to use mayonnaise for the dressing, use 2 tbsp olive oil whisked with the juice of 1 lemon, 1 tsp Dijon mustard, and a good handful of roughly chopped herbs. Fresh basil, dill, parsley, chervil, and chives can all be used, on their own or mixed together.

10

YEAST COOKERY

OVER 60 MINUTES

FOCACCIA

Italian classic: flat pizza-like bread flavoured with olive oil and fresh rosemary. Sprinkled with coarse sea salt.

MAKES I LARGE LOAF 2989 calories per loaf

Takes 35 minutes, plus rising   Page 411

TRADITIONAL

HOT CROSS BUNS

Slightly sweet spiced buns studded with currants and mixed peel, decorated with pastry crosses, and baked until golden.

MAKES 12 279 calories each

Takes 35 minutes, plus rising   Page 422

DINNER ROLLS

A simple dough shaped into rolls and baked until golden. Served warm or cool and spread with butter.

MAKES 18 95 calories each

Takes 40 minutes, plus rising   Page 407

BRIOCHES

Classic and rich: an egg- and butter- enriched dough baked until dark golden brown in characteristic fluted moulds.

MAKES 12 149 calories each

Takes 35 minutes, plus rising   Page 416

WHOLEMEAL COUNTRY LOAF

Hearty and flavourful: a close-textured loaf made from wholemeal flour, shaped into a crown, and baked until golden.

MAKES I LARGE LOAF 2975 calories per loaf

Takes 50 minutes, plus rising   Page 408

CINNAMON ROLLS

Breakfast treat: a plain dough enriched with egg, kneaded with cinnamon and raisins, rolled into spirals, baked, and glazed.

MAKES 16 450 calories each

Takes 60 minutes, plus rising   Page 422

FAMILY CHOICE

BATH BUNS

Sweetened rich dough with sultanas and mixed peel. Shaped into buns, topped with crushed sugar, and baked until golden.

MAKES 18 196 calories each

Takes 40 minutes, plus rising   Page 421

DINNER PARTY

MILK ROLLS

Attractive rolls in a variety of shapes: knots, twists, and rosettes. Decorated with poppyseeds and sesame seeds, and baked until golden.

MAKES 18 188 calories each

Takes 50 minutes, plus rising   Page 407

CROISSANTS

Classic French breakfast roll: made rich and flaky with butter. Shaped into crescents, glazed, and baked until golden.

MAKES 12 352 calories each

Takes 55 minutes, plus chilling   Page 415

OVER 60 MINUTES

CRUMPETS

Golden and fresh from the griddle: a simple batter cooked until light and tender. Served warm spread with butter.

MAKES 20 73 calories each
Takes 50 minutes, plus rising   Page 420

DEVON FLAT BAPS

Soft-crusted rolls made slightly sweet with the addition of honey. Dusted with flour and baked until golden.

MAKES 16 135 calories each
Takes 45 minutes, plus rising   Page 406

CHEESE & HERB BREAD

Hearty and flavourful: Cheddar and Parmesan cheeses, chopped parsley, and mustard flavour this crisp-crusted bread.

MAKES 1 MEDIUM LOAF 2707 calories per loaf
Takes 55 minutes, plus rising   Page 410

CALZONE

A delicious and aromatic mixture of Mediterranean ingredients wrapped in pizza dough and baked until golden.

MAKES 4 637 calories each
Takes 35 minutes, plus rising   Page 414

SPICY DEEP-PAN PIZZA

Thick, crisp-crusted pizza covered with tomatoes, pepperoni sausage, mozzarella, and Parmesan cheeses. Spiked with green chillies.

MAKES 1 LARGE PIZZA 3596 calories
Takes 35 minutes, plus rising   Page 414

JAM DOUGHNUTS

Old-fashioned favourite: doughnuts filled with raspberry jam, deep-fried, and sprinkled with cinnamon and sugar.

MAKES 16 269 calories each
Takes 40 minutes, plus rising   Page 417

WALNUT BREAD

Hearty and rustic: a coarse-textured loaf studded with chopped walnuts and parsley. Slashed in a criss-cross pattern, dusted with flour, then baked until golden brown. This bread is the classic accompaniment to a traditional ploughman's lunch.

MAKES 2 SMALL LOAVES 1657 calories per loaf
Takes 55 minutes, plus rising   Page 409

FARMHOUSE LOAF

Simple to make: white flour loaf dusted with flour and baked until well risen and golden. It has a large and tender crumb.

MAKES 1 LARGE LOAF 2790 per loaf
Takes 50 minutes, plus rising   Page 406

OVER 60 MINUTES

CHELSEA BUNS

A plain dough rolled with a filling of sultanas, currants, orange zest, and mixed spices. Sliced, baked, and glazed with honey.

MAKES 12 298 calories each
Takes 60 minutes, plus rising   Page 421

CHALLAH

Tender and golden: an egg-enriched dough, shaped into a plait, and baked until golden. Excellent toasted or used to make French toast.

MAKES 2 SMALL LOAVES 1144 calories per loaf
Takes 60 minutes, plus rising   Page 416

OLIVE & SUN-DRIED TOMATO BREADS

The flavours of Provence: pungent olives and sun-dried tomatoes are kneaded into a dough darkened with buckwheat flour.

MAKES 2 SMALL LOAVES 1139 calories per loaf
Takes 60 minutes, plus rising   Page 410

POTATO BREAD

Old-fashioned favourite: mashed potato and butter enrich this simple bread. Makes 2 hearty, coarse-textured loaves.

MAKES 2 SMALL LOAVES 1002 calories per loaf
Takes 60 minutes, plus rising   Page 409

SOURDOUGH RYE BREAD

Sourdough starter gives a slightly tangy flavour to this hearty loaf. Studded with caraway seeds.

MAKES 2 LARGE LOAVES 3329 calories per loaf
Takes 1 hour 5 minutes, plus rising   Page 411

LARDY CAKE

Traditional English cake made tender and crisp with lard and studded with mixed fruit. Baked until dark golden brown.

MAKES 1 LARGE LOAF 8186 calories per loaf
Takes 1 hour 5 minutes, plus rising   Page 417

TRADITIONAL

GRIDDLED ENGLISH MUFFINS

Savoury quick bread: wholemeal flour is used to make these muffins. Cooked on a hot griddle. Served spread with butter and jam.

MAKES ABOUT 12 158 calories each
Takes 60 minutes, plus rising   Page 420

HIGH FIBRE

MULTI-GRAIN LOAF

A nutritious, coarse-textured wholemeal and white flour loaf studded with a combination of wheat flakes, linseed and sunflower seeds. The loaves are lightly brushed with milk, generously sprinkled with wheat flakes, and baked until golden brown.

MAKES 2 SMALL LOAVES 1495 calories per loaf
Takes 60 minutes, plus rising   Page 408

YEAST COOKERY KNOW-HOW

THE PLEASURE of baking bread is legendary. From making and kneading the dough to slicing a freshly baked loaf, the experience is a thoroughly satisfying one that cooks the world over have shared for centuries. Indeed, yeast cookery is perhaps the most popular of all kitchen crafts.

From this rich history comes a wide variety of recipes, both sweet and savoury, many of which are easily made; others are more time-consuming to prepare. Crumpets and hot cross buns, Danish pastries and croissants, wholemeal bread and crispy, thin-crusted pizzas are all equally delicious.

Successful home baking

The quantity of liquid given in a recipe can only be a guide because the absorbency of flour can vary. The quantity of liquid that flour can absorb depends on temperature and humidity, how much hard wheat the flour contains (proportions vary from one brand to another) and whether it is wholemeal or white.

•

Dough can be kneaded in a food processor or an electric mixer fitted with a dough hook, as well as by hand.

•

Dough rises quickest in a warm environment. A slow rise, such as in the fridge overnight, gives bread more flavour.

•

To test if dough has risen sufficiently, push in a finger; when withdrawn, an indentation should remain in the dough.

BREAD MACHINES

Although keen bakers maintain that bread made in a machine can never be as good to eat as a loaf made by hand, bread machines are increasingly popular, perhaps because they mean you can enjoy a freshly baked loaf at any time. Pop in the ingredients and the machine will mix, knead, raise, knock up, and bake for you. Just be sure to follow the manufacturer's recipes and instructions.

FREEZING

It is a good idea to halve or quarter loaves before freezing so you can take out what you need. Pack in moisture-proof wrapping and seal well. Most loaves can be frozen for up to 4 months; if enriched with milk or fruit, storage time is 3 months. Thaw, still wrapped, at room temperature. Bread with a crust, such as baguette, does not freeze well as the crust lifts off.

YEAST COOKERY INGREDIENTS

There is a large range of flours to choose from, each with its own unique texture and flavour.
The different types of yeast, on the other hand, vary simply in their method of preparation.

Flour
The best flours to use for yeast doughs are those labelled "strong". These are milled from hard wheat with a high gluten content and produce a good open-textured bread. Ordinary plain flour, which contains a higher proportion of soft wheat, can be used for yeast doughs, but the result will be a more close-textured and crumbly loaf.

The flour most commonly used for bread-making is white wheat flour. Other wheat flours include wholemeal flour, also called whole wheat, which is milled from the entire wheat kernel, including the bran and germ; brown or wheatmeal flour, which contains more of the bran and wheat germ than white flour; and granary flour, which is brown flour with malted wheat flakes and cracked and whole wheat grains added.

Other grains and cereals, such as barley, buckwheat, maize (corn), millet, oats, and rye, are milled into flour for bread-making. Soya beans are also ground into a flour-like powder. Most of these flours are low in gluten, or contain no gluten at all, so they are normally combined with wheat flour to prevent the bread from being too dense.

Fresh yeast
This form of yeast, which looks like creamy-grey putty, is perishable and so needs to be refrigerated (keep it in an airtight container for up to 4–5 days). You will find it at a bakery where they bake on the premises or at a healthfood shop. Fresh yeast should be almost odourless, with only a slightly yeasty smell, and it should break apart cleanly. It needs to be blended with warm liquid and "fed" with sugar,

then left to become frothy before mixing with flour. To substitute fresh yeast for dried yeast, use double the weight, ie 15 g (1/2 oz) fresh yeast for 7 g (1/4 oz) dried.

Dried yeast
Fast-action dried yeast (also known as easy-blend) is added directly to flour with other dry ingredients. Ordinary dried yeast needs to be blended with warm liquid and a little sugar before mixing with flour. After 5 minutes or so, the yeast should dissolve and the mixture should be foamy. If this is not the result, discard the yeast and start again. Dried yeast will keep for up to 6 months in a cool place.

Lukewarm water (40–43°C/105–110°F) should be used to blend and dissolve both fresh and ordinary dried yeast. If the water is too hot it will kill the yeast.

MAKING A YEAST DOUGH

Making bread is not difficult, nor does it take up a lot of time – the most lengthy parts of the procedure, the rising and baking, are done by the bread itself. Here are the basic techniques, using fast-action dried yeast.

1 Sift the flour into a large bowl, and then mix in the yeast and any other dry ingredients. Make a well in the middle and pour in almost all of the measured liquid (the precise amount is difficult to gauge).

2 Using your fingers, mix the liquid ingredients together, then gradually incorporate the flour. Mix thoroughly until a soft, quite sticky dough is formed, adding the remaining liquid if it is needed.

3 Turn the dough on to a lightly floured work surface and knead: fold it over towards you, then push it down and away with the heel of your hand. Turn the dough, fold it, and push it away again. Continue kneading for 5–10 minutes until the dough is elastic and smooth. Doughs made with strong wheat flour take longer to knead than those made with soft flour.

4 Shape the dough into a ball. Put the dough into a lightly oiled bowl and turn to coat it all over with oil. Cover with oiled cling film or a damp tea towel and leave to rise in a warm, draught-free place such as an airing cupboard (or in a cool place for a longer time).

5 When the dough has doubled in size, turn it on to a lightly floured work surface and knock out the air by punching the dough gently. Knead the dough vigorously for 2–3 minutes until smooth and elastic.

6 Shape the dough as directed. Cover loosely with cling film or a dry tea towel and leave in a warm, draught-free place to rise until doubled in size again. Bake according to the recipe.

BUTTER SHAPES

When you are entertaining, butter looks much better if it is shaped rather than just being left in a block. These shapes can be prepared in advance, tray frozen, and packed in freezer bags, then thawed when needed. If you like, flavour the butter with herbs, garlic, or mustard to serve with savoury breads, and spices, honey, or sugar for sweet breads.

Discs

Use butter at room temperature. Beat it with a wooden spoon until it is soft, then beat in any flavourings. Spoon on to a sheet of greaseproof paper and spread into a rough sausage, then roll in the paper until it forms a neat sausage shape. Wrap the butter tightly in the greaseproof paper and twist the ends to secure. Chill in the refrigerator until firm. Unwrap and slice the butter across into thin discs. Use immediately or keep chilled; or freeze until required.

Curls

Use a well-chilled block of butter. Warm a butter curler in hot water, then dry it. Pull the curler lengthwise along the surface of the block, to shave off curls. Use the butter curls immediately, or keep them in iced water in the refrigerator until required.

GLAZES & TOPPINGS

Breads and rolls can be glazed before or after baking to add flavour and, depending on the glaze, to make the crust soft or shiny and crisp. Apply the glaze thinly, using a pastry brush. Here are a few suggestions for different glazes:
- water (before baking) for a crisp crust
- milk or cream (before baking) for a soft crust
- egg or egg yolk beaten with a pinch of salt (before baking) for a shiny, crisp crust
- butter (after baking) for a shiny crust
- sugar and water (after baking) for a shiny crust.

Toppings such as wheat or barley flakes, woody herbs such as rosemary, sunflower or sesame seeds, poppyseeds, grated cheese, chopped nuts, and coarse sea salt can be sprinkled over glazed breads and rolls before baking. Sweetened breads are often sprinkled with sugar or a spice and sugar mixture after cooking.

TESTING LOAVES

At the end of cooking, bread should be well risen, firm, and golden brown. To test if it is thoroughly cooked, tip out of the tin or lift off the baking tray and tap the base. The bread should have a hollow, drum-like sound. If it does not sound hollow, return it to the oven to bake for a further 5 minutes, then remove it and test again.

SHAPING LOAVES

Because of the elastic quality of dough, it can very easily be formed into a variety of different shapes. Here are some of the more traditional ones.

Cottage loaf

Cut off one-third of the dough. Roll each piece into a ball and put the small ball on top of the large ball. Push a forefinger through the middle all the way to the base.

Tin loaf

Shape the dough into a cylinder a little longer than the tin, then tuck the ends under so the shape will just fit the tin. Place the dough in the tin, with the joins underneath.

Round loaf

Roll the dough into a ball, then pull up the sides of the ball to the middle, to make a tight, round ball. Turn the ball over and put on a baking tray.

Plaited loaf

Divide the dough into 3 and and roll each piece into a strand. Place them side by side and pinch together at one end. Plait the strands, pinching them together at the other end to secure.

Crown loaf

Divide the dough into 9 even-sized pieces and shape each into a ball. Place 8 balls around the side of a deep cake tin, then place one ball in the middle to form a crown. The balls will rise to fill the tin.

FARMHOUSE LOAF

MAKES I LARGE LOAF

750 g (1 1/2 lb) strong white flour, plus extra for dusting

30 g (1 oz) butter or margarine

2 tsp salt

1 x 7 g (1/4 oz) sachet fast-action dried yeast

about 450 ml (3/4 pint) lukewarm water

sunflower oil for greasing

1 KG (2 LB) LOAF TIN

1 Put the flour into a bowl, rub in the butter with the fingertips until the mixture resembles breadcrumbs, then stir in the salt and yeast, and make a well in the middle. Add enough water to mix to a soft dough that is quite sticky.

2 Knead the dough on a lightly floured surface until smooth and elastic. Shape into a round and place in a lightly oiled large bowl.

3 Cover the bowl with oiled cling film and leave to rise in a warm place for 1–1 1/2 hours or until the dough has doubled in size.

4 Turn out the dough on to a lightly floured surface and knock back with your fists. Knead vigorously for 2–3 minutes until the dough is smooth and elastic.

5 Lightly oil the loaf tin. Shape the dough to fit the tin, tucking the ends under to give a smooth top, and place in the tin. Cover loosely with oiled cling film and leave to rise in a warm place for 30 minutes or until the dough reaches the top of the tin.

6 Lightly dust the top of the loaf with flour and bake in a preheated oven at 230°C (450°F, Gas 8) for 30–35 minutes until golden. Turn the loaf out and tap the base: it should sound hollow if it is cooked. Leave the loaf to cool on a wire rack.

DEVON FLAT BAPS

MAKES 16

500 g (1 lb) strong white flour, plus extra for dusting

45 g (1 1/2 oz) butter

1 tsp salt

1 x 7 g (1/4 oz) sachet fast-action dried yeast

about 150 ml (1/4 pint) very hot water

about 150 ml (1/4 pint) milk

1 tsp clear honey

sunflower oil for greasing

1 Put the flour into a large bowl. Add the butter and rub in with the fingertips until the mixture resembles fine breadcrumbs. Stir in the salt and yeast, and make a well in the middle. Mix the water, milk, and honey together, and add to the flour until a soft, quite sticky, dough is formed.

2 Knead the dough on a lightly floured surface until smooth and elastic. Shape into a round and place in a lightly oiled large bowl. Cover with oiled cling film and leave to rise in a warm place for 1–1 1/2 hours or until doubled in size.

3 Turn out the dough on to a lightly floured surface and knock back with your fists. Knead for 2–3 minutes until the dough is smooth and elastic.

4 Lightly oil 2 baking trays. Divide the dough into 16 even-sized pieces. Knead and roll into rounds and place well apart on the baking trays. With the heel of your hand, flatten each round so that it measures 7 cm (3 in) across.

5 Cover loosely with oiled cling film and leave to rise in a warm place for about 30 minutes or until the dough has doubled in size.

6 Lightly flour the baps and bake in a preheated oven at 200°C (400°F, Gas 6) for 15–20 minutes until golden. Leave to cool on a wire rack.

Cook's know-how

If you are short of time, just mix and shape these baps, omitting the first rise step 2 and giving them just one rise in step 5. The texture of the bread will not be quite as light, but it will still be good.

MILK ROLLS

MAKES 18

750 g (1 1/2 lb) strong white flour, plus extra for dusting

60 g (2 oz) butter or white vegetable fat

2 tsp salt

1 x 7 g (1/4 oz) sachet fast-action dried yeast

about 450 ml (3/4 pint) lukewarm milk

sunflower oil for greasing

1 egg, beaten

poppyseeds and sesame seeds for sprinkling

1 Put the flour into a large bowl, rub in the butter, then stir in the salt and yeast. Make a well in the middle and add enough milk to mix to a soft, quite sticky, dough.

2 Knead the dough on a lightly floured surface until smooth and elastic. Shape into a round and place in a lightly oiled large bowl. Cover with oiled cling film and leave to rise in a warm place for 1–1 1/2 hours or until doubled in size.

3 Turn out the dough on to a lightly floured surface and knock back with your fists. Knead for 2–3 minutes until smooth and elastic.

4 Divide the dough into 18 even-sized pieces and shape into balls, folding the sides to the middles to form tight round balls, or shape as required (see box, right).

5 Lightly oil 2 or 3 baking trays. Arrange the rolls on the baking trays, leaving enough room between them for the dough to expand, cover loosely with oiled cling film, and leave to rise in a warm place for 15–20 minutes or until doubled in size.

6 Brush the rolls with the beaten egg to glaze and sprinkle with poppyseeds and sesame seeds. Bake in a preheated oven at 230°C (450°F, Gas 8) for about 15 minutes until golden. Leave to cool on a wire rack.

Shaping milk rolls

Form each piece of dough into a long rope and tie into a single knot.

Roll each piece of dough into a thin strand. Fold in half and twist together, sealing the ends well to form a twist. Shape each piece of dough into a ball or an oval. Snip tops with scissors.

DINNER ROLLS

MAKES 18

500 g (1 lb) strong white flour

1 tsp salt

1 x 7 g (1/4 oz) sachet fast-action dried yeast

about 350 ml (12 fl oz) lukewarm water

sunflower oil for greasing

1 Put the flour into a large bowl, then stir in the salt and yeast. Make a well in the middle and pour in enough water to make a soft, quite sticky, dough.

2 Knead the dough on a lightly floured surface until smooth and elastic. Shape into a round and place in a lightly oiled large bowl. Cover with oiled cling film and leave to rise in a warm place for 1–1 1/2 hours or until doubled in size.

3 Lightly oil 2 or 3 baking trays. Divide the dough into 18 pieces. Shape into balls, folding the sides to the middles to form round balls. Arrange on the trays, leaving room for expansion. Cover loosely with oiled cling film and leave to rise in a warm place for 20 minutes or until doubled in size.

4 Bake in a preheated oven at 190°C (375°F, Gas 5) for 20 minutes or until golden. Leave to cool on a wire rack.

WHOLEMEAL COUNTRY LOAF

MAKES I LARGE LOAF

750 g (1½ lb) strong wholemeal flour, plus extra for dusting

30 g (1 oz) butter or margarine

1 tbsp caster sugar

2 tsp salt

1 x 7 g (¼ oz) sachet fast-action dried yeast

about 450 ml (¾ pint) lukewarm water

sunflower oil for greasing

milk for glazing

cracked wheat for sprinkling

20 CM (8 IN) ROUND CAKE TIN

1 Put the flour into a large bowl. Rub in the butter with the fingertips, then stir in the sugar, salt, and yeast. Make a well in the middle and add enough water to mix to a soft, quite sticky, dough.

2 Knead the dough on a lightly floured surface until smooth and elastic, then shape into a round.

3 Place the dough in a lightly oiled large bowl, cover with oiled cling film, and leave to rise in a warm place for 1–1½ hours or until the dough has doubled in size.

4 Turn out the dough on to a lightly floured surface and knock back with your fists. Knead for 2–3 minutes until smooth.

5 Shape the dough into a round and put it into the lightly oiled cake tin. Flatten with your hand, then mark into 8 wedges with a knife. Cover loosely with oiled cling film and leave to rise in a warm place for 1–1½ hours or until doubled in size.

6 Brush the loaf with milk and sprinkle with cracked wheat. Bake in a preheated oven at 230°C (450°F, Gas 8) for 20–25 minutes. Tap the base to see if the loaf is cooked: it should sound hollow. Leave to cool on a wire rack.

MULTI-GRAIN LOAF

MAKES 2 SMALL LOAVES

150 g (5 oz) wheat flakes

45 g (1½ oz) linseed

300 ml (½ pint) boiling water

500 g (1 lb) strong white flour, plus extra for dusting

125 g (4 oz) strong wholemeal flour

60 g (2 oz) sunflower seeds

20 g (¾ oz) salt

1 x 7 g (¼ oz) sachet fast-action dried yeast

about 350 ml (12 fl oz) lukewarm water

sunflower oil for greasing

milk for glazing

wheat flakes to decorate

2 x 500 G (1 LB) LOAF TINS

1 Put the wheat flakes and linseed into a large bowl, pour the boiling water over, and stir. Cover and set aside for 30 minutes or until the water has been absorbed.

2 Stir the flours, sunflower seeds, salt, and yeast into the wheat-flake mixture. Make a well in the middle and add enough water to mix to a soft, quite sticky, dough.

3 Knead the dough on a lightly floured surface until smooth and elastic. Shape into a round and place in a lightly oiled large bowl. Cover with oiled cling film and leave to rise in a warm place for 1–1½ hours or until doubled in size.

4 Turn out the dough on to a floured surface and knock back with your fists. Knead for 2–3 minutes until smooth and elastic once again.

5 Oil the tins. Divide the dough in half, and shape into oblongs, tucking the ends under to give smooth tops. Place in the tins. Alternatively, shape into 2 rounds and place on oiled baking trays. Cover loosely with oiled cling film and leave to rise in a warm place for 20–30 minutes.

6 Brush the loaves with milk to glaze and sprinkle with wheat flakes. Bake in a preheated oven at 230°C (450°F, Gas 8) for 10 minutes; reduce the oven temperature to 200°C (400°F, Gas 6), and bake for 20–25 minutes. Tap the bases to see if the loaves are cooked: they should sound hollow. Leave to cool on a rack.

POTATO BREAD

MAKES 2 SMALL LOAVES

500 g (1 lb) strong white flour, plus extra for dusting
1 tsp salt
15 g (¹/2 oz) butter
1 x 7 g (¹/4 oz) sachet fast-action dried yeast
250 g (8 oz) cold mashed potato
about 250 ml (8 fl oz) lukewarm water
sunflower oil for greasing
2 x 500 G (1 LB) LOAF TINS

1 Put the flour and salt into a large bowl, rub in the butter, then stir in the yeast. Add the potato, rubbing it loosely into the flour. Make a well in the middle of the ingredients and add enough water to mix to a soft, quite sticky, dough.

2 Knead the dough on a floured surface until smooth and elastic, then shape into a round. Place in a lightly oiled large bowl, cover with oiled cling film, and leave to rise in a warm place for 1 hour or until doubled in size.

3 Turn out the dough on to a lightly floured surface and knock back with your fists. Knead until smooth and elastic.

4 Lightly oil the loaf tins. Divide the dough in half, and shape to fit the tins, tucking the ends underneath. Place in the tins. Cover loosely with oiled cling film and leave in a warm place to rise for 30 minutes or until the dough reaches the tops of the tins.

5 Bake in a preheated oven at 230°C (450°F, Gas 8) for 10 minutes; reduce the oven temperature to 200°C (400°F, Gas 6), and bake for 20–25 minutes until golden. Tap the bases of the loaves to see if they are cooked: they should sound hollow. Serve warm or cold.

Cook's know-how

Always add the measured liquid gradually when making dough. Recipes cannot specify exact amounts because flours vary in how much liquid they will absorb.

WALNUT BREAD

MAKES 2 SMALL LOAVES

650 g (1 lb 5 oz) strong white flour, plus extra for dusting
2 tsp salt
30 g (1 oz) butter or margarine
125 g (4 oz) walnut pieces, coarsely chopped
2 tbsp chopped parsley
1 x 7 g (¹/4 oz) sachet fast-action dried yeast
about 400 ml (14 fl oz) lukewarm water
sunflower oil for greasing

1 Put the flour and salt into a large bowl. Rub in the butter, then stir in the walnuts, parsley, and yeast. Make a well in the middle and add enough water to mix to a soft, quite sticky, dough.

2 Knead the dough on a lightly floured surface until smooth and elastic. Shape into a round and place in a lightly oiled large bowl. Cover loosely with oiled cling film and leave in a warm place for 1–1¹/2 hours or until doubled in size.

3 Lightly oil 2 baking trays. Knock back the dough with your fists, then knead for 2–3 minutes until smooth and elastic.

4 Divide the dough in half, shape each half into a round, and then place on a baking tray.

5 Cover the rounds loosely with oiled cling film, and leave to rise in a warm place for 20–30 minutes.

6 Dust each loaf with flour, slash the tops in a criss-cross pattern, and bake in a preheated oven at 220°C (425°F, Gas 7) for about 10 minutes; reduce the oven temperature to 190°C (375°F, Gas 5), and bake for 20 minutes or until the bread is golden brown.

7 Tap the bases to see if the loaves are cooked: they should sound hollow. Best eaten while still warm.

409

CHEESE & HERB BREAD

MAKES I MEDIUM LOAF

500 g (1 lb) strong white flour, plus extra for dusting

90 g (3 oz) mature Cheddar cheese, grated

30 g (1 oz) Parmesan cheese, grated

2 tsp mustard powder

2 tbsp chopped parsley

1 1/2 tsp salt

1 x 7 g (1/4 oz) sachet fast-action dried yeast

about 350 ml (12 fl oz) lukewarm milk

sunflower oil for greasing

beaten egg for glazing

2 tbsp grated Cheddar cheese for sprinkling

1 Put the flour into a large bowl and stir in the cheeses, mustard powder, parsley, salt, and yeast, mixing thoroughly. Make a well in the middle and add enough milk to mix to a soft, quite sticky, dough.

2 Knead the dough on a lightly floured surface until smooth and elastic.

3 Shape the dough into a round and place in a lightly oiled bowl. Cover with oiled cling film, and leave to rise in a warm place for 1–1 1/2 hours or until doubled in size.

4 Turn the dough on to a floured surface and knock back. Knead for 2–3 minutes until smooth and elastic.

5 Lightly flour a baking tray. Shape the dough into a 15 cm (6 in) round and place on the baking tray. Cover loosely with oiled cling film and leave to rise in a warm place for 20–30 minutes.

6 Brush with the egg to glaze, cut a shallow cross in the top, and sprinkle with the grated Cheddar cheese. Bake in a preheated oven at 230°C (450°F, Gas 8) for 10 minutes; reduce the oven temperature to 200°C (400°F, Gas 6), and bake for 20 minutes, covering the loaf loosely with foil halfway through baking if it is browning too much. Leave to cool on a wire rack.

OLIVE & SUN-DRIED TOMATO BREADS

MAKES 2 SMALL LOAVES

400 g (13 oz) strong white flour

60 g (2 oz) buckwheat flour

I tsp salt

I x 7 g (1/4 oz) sachet fast-action dried yeast

black pepper

about 300 ml (1/2 pint) lukewarm water

I tbsp olive oil, plus extra for greasing

125 g (4 oz) pitted black olives, coarsely chopped

125 g (4 oz) sun-dried tomatoes in oil, drained and chopped

I tbsp chopped parsley

I tbsp chopped fresh basil

I tbsp coarse sea salt

1 Put the flours into a large bowl. Stir in the salt and yeast and season with black pepper. Make a well in the middle. Pour in the water and oil and mix to a soft but not sticky dough.

2 Knead until smooth and elastic, shape into a round, and place in a lightly oiled large bowl. Cover with oiled cling film, and leave to rise in a warm place for 1–1 1/2 hours or until doubled in size.

3 Lightly oil a baking tray. Knock back the dough, then knead for 2–3 minutes. Divide the dough into 2 pieces. Roll out each piece until about 23 x 25 cm (9 x 10 ins). Spread one of the pieces with the olives and the other with the sun-dried tomatoes, parsley, and basil.

4 Roll up each piece of dough from one long end and place, seam-side down, on the tray. Make 4–5 diagonal slashes on the top of each loaf, cover loosely with oiled cling film, and leave to rise in a warm place for 20–30 minutes.

5 Brush the top of each loaf with water and lightly sprinkle with sea salt. Bake in a preheated oven at 230°C (450°F, Gas 8) for 15 minutes; reduce the oven temperature to 190°C (375°F, Gas 5), and bake for a further 15 minutes or until golden.

6 Tap the bases to see if the loaves are cooked: they should sound hollow. Leave to cool on a wire rack.

SOURDOUGH RYE BREAD

A satisfying and tasty country bread from Eastern Europe, this rye bread is not difficult to make but, because the starter has to be left to ferment for a couple of days, it does require a little forward planning.

MAKES 2 LARGE LOAVES

1.5 kg (3 lb) strong white flour, plus extra for sprinkling

1 x 7 g (1/4 oz) sachet fast-action dried yeast

250 ml (8 fl oz) lukewarm water

3 tbsp caraway seeds (optional)

1 tbsp salt

sunflower oil for greasing

polenta for sprinkling

SOURDOUGH STARTER

250 g (8 oz) strong white flour

1 tsp fast-action dried yeast

250 ml (8 fl oz) lukewarm water

SPONGE

200 g (7 oz) rye flour

250 ml (8 fl oz) lukewarm water

1 Make the sourdough starter: put the flour into a large bowl and stir in the yeast. Make a well in the middle, pour in the lukewarm water, and mix together.

2 Cover tightly and leave at room temperature for 2 days. Alternatively, leave the starter in the refrigerator for up to 1 week.

3 Make the sponge: put the rye flour into a large bowl, add the sourdough starter and the lukewarm water, and stir to mix. Cover tightly and leave at room temperature for 8 hours or chill in the refrigerator for up to 2 days.

4 Put the flour into a bowl, add the sponge mixture, yeast, lukewarm water, caraway seeds, if using, and salt, and mix to a soft and slightly sticky dough.

5 Turn the dough into a large ungreased bowl, sprinkle the top with flour, cover loosely with oiled cling film, and leave to rise in a warm place for 2 hours or until doubled in size.

6 Lightly sprinkle 2 baking trays with polenta. Turn out the dough on to a lightly floured surface and knock back with your fists. Knead for 3–4 minutes until smooth and elastic. Halve the dough and form into 2 rounds. Score the tops with a sharp knife.

7 Place on the baking trays, cover loosely with oiled cling film, and leave to rise in a warm place for 45 minutes or until doubled in size.

8 Place the loaves in a preheated oven at 220°C (425°F, Gas 7). Fill a roasting tin with boiling water and place at the bottom of the oven. Bake the loaves for about 35 minutes until they are lightly browned. Tap the bases to see if the loaves are cooked: they should sound hollow. Leave to cool on wire racks.

FOCACCIA

MAKES 1 LARGE LOAF

750 g (1 1/2 lb) strong white flour, plus extra for dusting

1 x 7 g (1/4 oz) sachet fast-action dried yeast

3–4 tbsp chopped fresh rosemary

3 tbsp olive oil, plus extra for greasing

about 450 ml (3/4 pint) lukewarm water

2 tsp coarse sea salt

1 Put the flour into a bowl, and add the yeast and rosemary. Make a well in the middle, add the oil and enough water to make a soft but not sticky dough. Knead the dough until smooth and elastic, then shape into a round.

2 Place the dough in a lightly oiled large bowl, cover loosely with oiled cling film, and leave to rise in a warm place for about 1 hour or until the dough has doubled in size.

3 Turn out the dough on to a lightly floured surface and knock back with your fists. Knead for 2–3 minutes until smooth. Roll out the dough to a round 5 cm (2 in) thick. Cover loosely with oiled cling film and leave in a warm place for 1 hour or until doubled in size.

4 Brush with olive oil and sprinkle with sea salt. Bake in a preheated oven at 190°C (375°F, Gas 5) for 20 minutes until golden. Best eaten warm.

THIN-CRUST PIZZAS

Tomatoes, cheese, herbs, and olive oil are just a few characteristic pizza toppings, but there are endless combinations. Pizza bases can be bought ready-made, but if you follow the steps illustrated below it is easy to make them at home.

NAPOLETANA

MAKES 1 LARGE PIZZA

1 x 400 g (13 oz) can chopped tomatoes, drained
1 pizza base (see box, below)
1 x 60 g (2 oz) can anchovy fillets, drained
125 g (4 oz) mozzarella cheese, chopped
2 tbsp olive oil

Spread the tomatoes over the pizza base. Halve the anchovies and arrange on top with the remaining ingredients.

TUNA & CAPER

MAKES 1 LARGE PIZZA

1 x 400 g (13 oz) can chopped tomatoes, drained
1 pizza base (see box, below)
1 x 200 g (7 oz) can tuna, drained
2 tbsp capers
125 g (4 oz) mozzarella cheese, chopped
1 tsp dried oregano
2 tbsp olive oil

Spread the tomatoes over the pizza base. Top with the remaining ingredients.

FOUR SEASONS

MAKES 1 LARGE PIZZA

1 x 400 g (13 oz) can chopped tomatoes, drained
1 pizza base (see box, below)
salt and black pepper
60 g (2 oz) thinly sliced salami
1/2 tsp dried oregano
60 g (2 oz) small button mushrooms, sliced
30 g (1 oz) mozzarella cheese, chopped
30 g (1 oz) anchovy fillets, drained
12 pitted black olives
2–3 pieces of bottled red peppers (in oil), thinly sliced
2 tbsp olive oil
grated Parmesan and fresh basil leaves to finish

1 Spread the tomatoes over the pizza base and season to taste.

2 Put salami and oregano on one quarter of the pizza, the mushrooms and mozzarella on a second quarter, the anchovies and olives on a third, the peppers on the fourth. Lightly sprinkle with olive oil. Sprinkle with Parmesan and basil after baking.

MINI PIZZAS

MAKES 12

1 x 400 g (13 oz) can chopped tomatoes, drained
1 quantity pizza dough (see box, below), shaped into 12 x 7 cm (3 in) rounds
salt and black pepper
2 tbsp olive oil

GOAT'S CHEESE TOPPING

8 sun-dried tomatoes in oil, diced
6 pitted black olives, diced
2 garlic cloves, crushed
60 g (2 oz) goat's cheese, diced

PARMA HAM TOPPING

2 thin slices of Parma ham, diced
6 artichoke hearts in oil, drained and sliced

Spread the tomatoes over the rounds and season. Top half with the sun-dried tomatoes, olives, garlic, and goat's cheese, and half with the Parma ham and artichokes. Sprinkle with the oil.

CLOCKWISE FROM TOP: Mini Pizzas, Four Seasons, Tuna & Caper, Napoletana.

MAKING THE THIN-CRUST PIZZA BASE

1 Sift 250 g (8 oz) strong white flour on to a work surface and add a heaped 1/2 tsp fast-action dried yeast and 1/2 tsp salt. Make a well in the middle and add about 150 ml (5 fl oz) lukewarm water and 1 tbsp olive oil. Draw in the flour with your fingertips or a pastry scraper and work to form a smooth dough.

2 Lightly oil a large bowl. Knead the dough for 10 minutes until smooth. Shape into a round and put in the bowl. Cover loosely with oiled cling film and leave in a warm place to rise for about 1 hour or until doubled in size. Turn out of the bowl and knead for 2–3 minutes on a lightly floured surface until smooth.

3 Roll and stretch the dough until it is about 35 cm (14 in) round and about 1 cm (1/2 in) thick. Make a rim around the edge. Put on a baking tray, add topping, and bake in a preheated oven at 220°C (425°F, Gas 7) for 20–30 minutes. Bake mini pizzas for only 12–15 minutes.

CALZONE

MAKES 4

125 g (4 oz) ricotta cheese

250 g (8 oz) tomatoes, chopped

60 g (2 oz) mozzarella cheese, chopped

2 garlic cloves, crushed

30 g (1 oz) pitted black olives, chopped

60 g (2 oz) mushrooms, sliced

1 green pepper, halved, seeded, and sliced

1/2 tsp dried oregano

salt and black pepper

beaten egg for sealing and glazing

DOUGH

500 g (1 lb) strong white flour

1 x 7 g (1/4 oz) sachet fast-action dried yeast

2 tbsp olive oil, plus extra for greasing

about 300 ml (1/2 pint) lukewarm water

1 Make the dough: mix the flour, yeast, 1/2 tsp salt, and 2 tbsp oil in a large bowl. Add enough water to mix to a soft, quite sticky, dough. Knead on a lightly floured surface for 5–10 minutes until smooth.

2 Shape into a round and place in a lightly oiled large bowl. Cover with oiled cling film, and leave to rise in a warm place for 1–1½ hours or until doubled in size.

3 Knock back the dough on a floured surface, and shape into four 20 cm (8 in) rounds. Combine the ricotta, tomatoes, mozzarella, garlic, olives, mushrooms, green pepper, and oregano. Season well and use to fill the calzone (see box, below).

4 Put on an oiled baking tray and bake in a preheated oven at 240°C (475°F, Gas 9) for 15 minutes.

Filling the calzone

Put one-quarter of the ricotta mixture on to half of each dough round.

Brush the edge of the dough with beaten egg and fold over to enclose the filling. Seal the the edges and crimp as shown, then brush the top with egg.

SPICY DEEP-PAN PIZZA

MAKES 1 LARGE PIZZA

125 g (4 oz) tomato purée

1 x 400 g (13 oz) can chopped tomatoes, drained

60 g (2 oz) pepperoni sausage, sliced

300 g (10 oz) mozzarella cheese, grated

60 g (2 oz) Parmesan cheese, grated

2 tbsp sliced pickled green chillies (from a can or jar)

DOUGH

500 g (1 lb) strong white flour

1 x 7 g (1/4 oz) sachet fast-action dried yeast

1/2 tsp salt

2 tbsp olive oil, plus extra for greasing

about 300 ml (1/2 pint) lukewarm water

DEEP DISH 35 CM (14 IN) ROUND PIZZA PAN

1 Make the dough: mix the flour, yeast, salt, and 2 tbsp oil in a large bowl. Add enough water to mix to a soft, quite sticky, dough. Knead on a lightly floured surface for 5–10 minutes until smooth and elastic.

2 Put into an oiled large bowl, turn to coat with the oil, cover with oiled cling film and leave to rise in a warm place for 1 hour or until doubled in size.

3 Lightly oil the pizza pan. Knock back the dough on a floured surface, roll out, and shape into a 35 cm (14 in) round. Put into the pan and shape the edge to form a rim.

4 Spread the tomato purée over the base. Top with the tomatoes and pepperoni. Sprinkle over the mozzarella, Parmesan, and green chillies.

5 Bake in a preheated oven at 240°C (475°F, Gas 9) for 10–15 minutes until the crust is golden and the cheese topping melted. Serve hot.

CROISSANTS

Croissant is the French word for crescent, the traditional shape for this classic breakfast roll. The dough for croissants is made with butter and milk, so they are rich enough to be served just as they are, but they are even more delicious served warm with butter and jam, or marmalade.

MAKES 12

500 g (1 lb) strong white flour

1/2 tsp salt

300 g (10 oz) butter, at room temperature

1 x 7 g (1/4 oz) sachet fast-action dried yeast

30 g (1 oz) caster sugar

about 150 ml (1/4 pint) milk

about 150 ml (1/4 pint) very hot water

sunflower oil for greasing

beaten egg for glazing

1 Put the flour and salt into a large bowl, add 60 g (2 oz) of the butter, and rub in with your fingertips until the mixture resembles fine breadcrumbs. Stir in the yeast and sugar.

2 Make a well in the middle of the dry ingredients. Mix the milk and water together, pour into the well, and mix with a wooden spoon until smooth.

3 Cover the bowl with oiled cling film and chill the dough for 2 hours.

4 Meanwhile, on a sheet of baking parchment, spread out the remaining butter into a 12 x 20 cm (5 x 8 in) rectangle. Cover with another sheet of baking parchment and chill.

5 Roll out the dough on a floured surface into an 18 x 35 cm (7 x 14 in) rectangle, and place the chilled butter on top so that it covers the top two-thirds of the rectangle.

6 Fold the bottom third of the dough over the middle third, and fold the top third, with the butter, over the top to form a neat parcel. Seal the edges with the edge of your hand. Wrap and chill for 30 minutes.

7 Roll out the dough parcel into an 18 x 35 cm (7 x 14 in) rectangle, fold into 3 as before, and seal the edges. Wrap and chill for a few hours until firm enough to roll and shape.

8 Shape the croissants (see box, right). Place on 2 baking trays and leave for about 30 minutes until almost doubled in size.

9 Lightly brush the croissants with the beaten egg and bake in a preheated oven at 220°C (425°F, gas 7) for 12–15 minutes until crisp and golden brown. Leave to cool slightly before serving.

CHOCOLATE CROISSANTS

Make the dough. Before rolling the triangles into sausage shapes, sprinkle them with 90 g (3 oz) plain chocolate chips.

Shaping the croissants

Roll out the dough into a 35 x 53 cm (14 x 21 in) rectangle, and cut into 12 triangles.

Roll each triangle into a sausage shape, starting from the long side and ending with the point of the triangle.

Bend the ends of each croissant to give the traditional shape.

Cook's know-how

Savoury croissants can easily be made by sprinkling the dough with a little grated cheese (Emmental, Gruyère, and Cheddar are best) and strips of cooked ham before rolling the triangles into sausage shapes.

CHALLAH

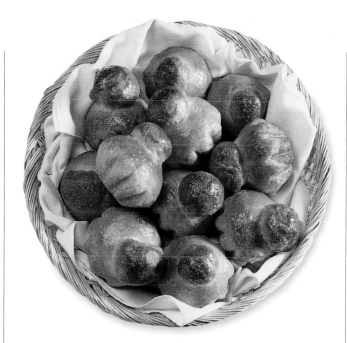

MAKES 2 SMALL LOAVES

500 g (1 lb) strong white flour, plus extra for dusting

1 tbsp caster sugar

2 tsp salt

1 x 7 g (¼ oz) sachet fast-action dried yeast

250 ml (8 fl oz) lukewarm water

2 eggs, beaten

2 tbsp sunflower oil, plus extra for greasing

beaten egg for glazing

poppyseeds for sprinkling

1 Put the flour, sugar, and salt into a bowl. Stir in the yeast. Make a well in the middle. Combine the water, eggs, and oil, and pour into the well. Mix to a soft dough.

2 Knead the dough on a lightly floured surface until firm and elastic. Shape into a round and place in a lightly oiled bowl. Cover with oiled cling film and leave to rise in a warm place for 1–1½ hours or until doubled in size.

3 Turn out the dough on to a lightly floured surface and knock back with your fists. Knead for 2–3 minutes until smooth and elastic. Divide the dough into 2 pieces.

4 Lightly oil a baking tray. Divide each piece of dough into 3 even-sized strands, and shape into a plait (page 404). Place on the baking tray, cover loosely with oiled cling film, and leave to rise in a warm place for 30 minutes or until doubled in size.

5 Brush the loaves with the beaten egg and sprinkle generously with poppyseeds. Bake in a preheated oven at 230°C (450°F, Gas 8) for 10 minutes; reduce the oven temperature to 200°C (400°F, Gas 6), and bake for 20 minutes, or until the loaves are a rich brown colour. Tap the bases to see if the loaves are cooked: they should sound hollow. Cool on a wire rack.

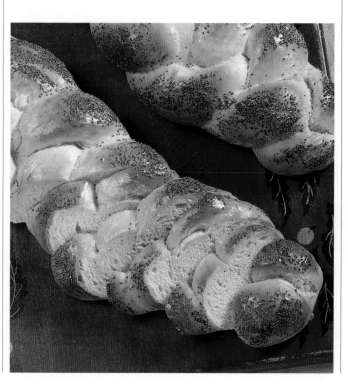

BRIOCHES

MAKES 12

275 g (9 oz) strong white flour, plus extra for dusting

30 g (1 oz) caster sugar

60 g (2 oz) butter

1 x 7 g (¼ oz) sachet fast-action dried yeast

2 eggs, beaten

about 3 tbsp lukewarm milk

sunflower oil for greasing

beaten egg for glazing

12 INDIVIDUAL BRIOCHE MOULDS

1 Sift the flour and sugar into a large bowl. Rub in the butter until the mixture resembles fine breadcrumbs, then stir in the yeast. Make a well in the middle, then pour in the eggs and enough milk to mix to a soft dough.

2 Knead the dough on a lightly floured surface until smooth and elastic. Shape into a round and place in a lightly oiled large bowl. Cover with oiled cling film and leave to rise in a warm place for 1–1½ hours or until doubled in size.

3 Turn out the dough on to a lightly floured surface and knock back with your fists. Knead the dough for 2–3 minutes until smooth.

4 Lightly oil the brioche moulds. Shape the brioches (see box, below).

5 Cover loosely with oiled cling film and leave to rise in a warm place for 20 minutes or until doubled in size.

6 Brush the brioches with a little beaten egg and bake in a preheated oven at 200°C (400°F, Gas 6) for 10–12 minutes until golden brown. Tap the bases to see if the brioches are cooked through: they should sound hollow. Leave to cool on a wire rack.

Shaping brioches

Divide the dough into 12 pieces, then cut one-quarter from each. Shape each piece into a ball. Place the large balls in the moulds, and press a hole in the middle of each. Place the small balls over the holes and press down to seal.

JAM DOUGHNUTS

MAKES 16

500 g (1 lb) strong white flour, plus extra for dusting
30 g (1 oz) butter or margarine
90 g (3 oz) caster sugar
1 x 7 g (¼ oz) sachet fast-action dried yeast
about 90 ml (3 fl oz) milk
about 90 ml (3 fl oz) very hot water
2 eggs, beaten
sunflower oil for greasing and deep-frying
150 g (5 oz) raspberry jam
125 g (4 oz) caster sugar
2 tsp ground cinnamon

1 Put the flour into a large bowl and rub in the butter with the fingertips until the mixture resembles fine breadcrumbs. Stir in the sugar and yeast, and make a well in the middle. Mix the milk and hot water together. Pour the eggs into the well and mix with the flour, adding enough milk and water to make a smooth dough.

2 Knead the dough on a lightly floured surface until smooth and elastic. Shape into a round and place in a lightly oiled large bowl.

3 Cover with oiled cling film and leave in a warm place for 1–1½ hours until doubled in size. Turn out on to a lightly floured surface, and knock back with your fists. Knead for 2–3 minutes until smooth.

4 Divide the dough into 16 pieces. Shape each one into a ball, then flatten slightly. Fill the doughnuts (see box, below). Place the doughnuts on oiled baking trays, cover with oiled cling film, and leave to rise in a warm place for 30 minutes.

5 Heat the oil in a deep-fat fryer to 160°C (325°F), and cook the doughnuts in batches for 5 minutes until golden. Drain, toss in sugar and cinnamon, and serve warm.

Filling the doughnuts

Place 1 tsp raspberry jam in the middle of each doughnut. Gather the edges over the jam and pinch firmly to seal.

LARDY CAKE

MAKES 1 LARGE LOAF

500 g (1 lb) strong white flour, plus extra for dusting
1 tsp salt
1 x 7 g (¼ oz) sachet fast-action dried yeast
15 g (½ oz) white vegetable fat
about 300 ml (½ pint) lukewarm water
sunflower oil for greasing

FILLING

90 g (3 oz) lard or white vegetable fat
60 g (2 oz) butter, plus extra for greasing
90 g (3 oz) currants
90 g (3 oz) sultanas
60 g (2 oz) chopped mixed candied peel
90 g (3 oz) light muscovado sugar

GLAZE

1 tbsp caster sugar
1 tbsp boiling water
23 x 30 CM (9 x 12 IN) ROASTING TIN

1 Mix the flour, salt, and yeast in a bowl. Rub in the fat. Make a well in the middle and pour in enough water to mix to a soft dough.

2 Knead on a lightly floured surface until smooth and elastic, place in a lightly oiled large bowl, and cover with oiled cling film. Leave to rise in a warm place, 1–1½ hours.

3 Turn out the dough on to a lightly floured surface and roll out to a rectangle about 5 mm (¼ in) thick. Dot with one-third each of the vegetable fat and butter. Sprinkle over one-third each of the dried fruit, mixed peel, and sugar.

4 Fold into three, folding the bottom third up and the top third down on top of it. Seal the edges to trap the air, then give the dough a quarter turn. Repeat the rolling and folding twice more, with the remaining fat, fruit, peel, and sugar.

5 Lightly butter the roasting tin. Roll out the dough to fit the tin, and lift it into the tin. Cover with oiled cling film and leave to rise in a warm place for about 30 minutes or until doubled in size.

6 Score the top of the dough in a criss-cross pattern, and bake in a preheated oven at 200°C (400°F, Gas 6) for about 30 minutes or until golden brown. Leave to cool in the tin for about 10 minutes.

7 Meanwhile, make the glaze: dissolve the caster sugar in the measured water. Brush the glaze on top of the warm cake and leave to cool.

DANISH PASTRIES

These melt-in-the-mouth, flaky pastries are quick and easy to make and are particularly good for breakfast. Vary the fillings, bake them ahead, and freeze. Warm the pastries, loosely covered with foil, in a low oven, and serve for a special breakfast or brunch.

MAKES 16

500 g (1 lb) strong white flour, plus extra for dusting
1/2 tsp salt
375 g (12 oz) butter, plus extra for greasing
1 x 7 g (1/4 oz) sachet fast-action dried yeast
60 g (2 oz) caster sugar
150 ml (1/4 pint) tepid milk
2 eggs, beaten
beaten egg to glaze

FILLING & TOPPING

250 g (8 oz) white almond paste
4 apricot halves, canned or fresh
about 2 tsp water
125 g (4 oz) icing sugar
60 g (2 oz) flaked almonds
60 g (2 oz) glacé cherries

1 Put the flour and salt into a bowl and rub in 60 g (2 oz) of the butter. Stir in the yeast and sugar. Make a well in the middle, add the lukewarm milk and eggs, and mix to a soft dough.

2 Turn out the dough on to a floured surface and knead for 10 minutes or until smooth. Shape into a round and place in an oiled bowl. Cover with oiled cling film and leave in a warm place to rise for 1 hour or until doubled in size.

3 Turn out the dough on to a lightly floured work surface and knead for 2–3 minutes until smooth. Roll out into a 20 x 35 cm (8 x 14 in) rectangle. Dot the top two-thirds of the dough with half of the remaining butter. Fold the bottom third up and the top third down to form a parcel. Seal the edges, then give the dough a quarter turn so the folded side is to the left.

4 Roll out the dough into a 20 x 35 cm (8 x 14 in) rectangle as before. Dot with the remaining butter, fold, and chill for 15 minutes. Roll, fold, and chill twice more.

5 Divide the dough into 4 pieces. Shape and fill the pastries (see box, below). Arrange on buttered baking trays and leave to rise in a warm place for 20 minutes. Brush with beaten egg and bake in a preheated oven at 220°C (425°F, Gas 7) for 15 minutes or until golden brown. Transfer to a wire rack.

6 Mix the water and icing sugar and spoon a little over each pastry while still warm. Decorate kites with flaked almonds and pinwheels with glacé cherries. Leave to cool.

CLOCKWISE FROM TOP: Pinwheels, Envelopes, Crescents, Kites.

SHAPING DANISH PASTRIES

Crescents

1 Roll out the dough into a 23 cm (9 in) round. Cut into quarters. Place a small roll of almond paste at the wide end of each piece.

2 Starting from the wide end, roll up each dough quarter loosely around the almond paste, then curve the ends to form a crescent.

Kites

1 Roll out the dough into a 20 cm (8 in) square. Cut into 4 squares. Make cuts around 2 corners of each square, 1 cm (1/2 in) in from the edge.

2 Place a round of almond paste in the middle of each square. Lift each cut corner and cross it over the almond paste to the opposite corner.

Pinwheels & Envelopes

For pinwheels: roll out dough and cut into 4 squares as for kites. Put almond paste in middle of each. Cut from the corners almost to the middle. Fold in alternate points.

For envelopes: roll out the dough, cut into 4, and fill as for pinwheels. Fold 2 opposite corners into the middle. Top with a half apricot, cut-side down.

CRUMPETS

MAKES 20

375 g (12 oz) strong white flour

1/2 tsp salt

1 x 7 g (1/4 oz) sachet fast-action dried yeast

about 250 ml (8 fl oz) milk

about 300 ml (1/2 pint) very hot water

sunflower oil for greasing

4 CRUMPET RINGS OR 4 x 7 CM (3 IN) PASTRY CUTTERS

1 Put the flour into a large bowl, stir in the salt and yeast, and make a well in the middle. Mix the milk and water together, pour in, and beat to form a smooth, thick batter.

2 Cover and leave in a warm place to rise for 1 hour or until the surface is bubbling.

3 Beat the batter mixture for 2 minutes, then pour into a jug. Lightly oil the crumpet rings or pastry cutters and oil a griddle or frying pan. Place the rings or cutters on the griddle and then leave for 1–2 minutes to heat through.

4 Pour 2 cm (3/4 in) of batter into each ring and cook for 5–7 minutes until the surface is dry and full of holes, and the crumpets are shrinking away from the sides of the rings.

5 Lift off the rings, turn the crumpets over, and cook for 1 minute until pale golden. Transfer the crumpets to a wire rack and leave to cool.

6 Repeat with the remaining batter, lightly greasing the griddle and rings between each batch. Serve warm.

GRIDDLED ENGLISH MUFFINS

MAKES ABOUT 12

500 g (1 lb) strong wholemeal flour, plus extra for dusting

1 tsp salt

1 x 7 g (1/4 oz) sachet fast-action dried yeast

about 250 ml (8 fl oz) milk

about 125 ml (4 fl oz) very hot water

sunflower oil for greasing

7 CM (3 IN) PASTRY CUTTER

1 Put the flour into a large bowl, stir in the salt and yeast, and make a well in the middle. Mix the milk and water together, pour in all at once, and mix to a soft dough.

2 Knead on a lightly floured surface until smooth and elastic, then shape into a round. Place the dough in a lightly oiled large bowl, cover with oiled cling film, and leave to rise in a warm place for 45–60 minutes until doubled in size.

3 Knock back the dough, then turn out on to a lightly floured surface and knead for 2–3 minutes until smooth and elastic.

4 Roll out the dough until 1 cm (1/2 in) thick. Using the cutter, cut into 12 rounds, re-rolling and kneading the dough as necessary.

5 Lightly dust 2 baking trays with flour, arrange the rounds on the trays, and cover loosely with oiled cling film. Leave to rise in a warm place for about 30 minutes or until doubled in size.

6 Lightly oil a griddle or frying pan, and cook the muffins over a medium heat, 3 or 4 at a time, for about 7 minutes on each side until golden and cooked through. Do not allow the griddle to get too hot or the outside of the muffins will burn before the inside is cooked.

CHELSEA BUNS

MAKES 12

500 g (1 lb) strong white flour

1 tsp salt

60 g (2 oz) butter

1 x 7 g (1/4 oz) sachet fast-action dried yeast

30 g (1 oz) caster sugar

about 200 ml (7 fl oz) lukewarm milk

1 large egg, beaten

sunflower oil for greasing

4 tbsp clear honey

FILLING

60 g (2 oz) butter

30 g (1 oz) light muscovado sugar

60 g (2 oz) sultanas

60 g (2 oz) currants

grated zest of 1 orange

1 tsp ground mixed spice

1 Put the flour into a large bowl and stir in the salt. Rub in the butter and yeast. Stir in the sugar. Make a well in the middle, pour in the milk and egg, and mix to a soft dough.

2 Knead the dough on a lightly floured surface until smooth and elastic, then shape into a round and place in a lightly oiled large bowl. Cover with oiled cling film and leave in a warm place for 1–1 1/2 hours or until doubled in size.

3 Make the filling: cream the butter with the muscovado sugar. In another bowl, combine the sultanas, currants, orange zest, and mixed spice.

4 Lightly oil an 18 x 28 cm (7 x 11 in) roasting tin. Turn out the dough on to a lightly floured surface, and knock back with your fists. Knead for 2–3 minutes until smooth.

5 Roll out into a 30 cm (12 in) square and dot with the butter mixture. Fold in half and roll out into a 30 cm (12 in) square. Sprinkle with the fruit mixture, then roll up.

6 Cut the roll into 12 pieces and arrange cut-side up in the roasting tin. Cover with oiled cling film. Leave in a warm place to rise for about 30 minutes or until the pieces are touching.

7 Bake in a preheated oven at 220°C (425°F, Gas 7) for 20–25 minutes, covering the buns loosely with foil after about15 minutes to prevent them from browning too much. Transfer to a wire rack.

8 Warm the honey in a small pan and brush over the buns to glaze. Pull the buns apart, and serve warm.

BATH BUNS

MAKES 18

500 g (1 lb) strong white flour

60 g (2 oz) caster sugar

1 tsp salt

1 x 7 g (1/4 oz) sachet fast-action dried yeast

about 150 ml (1/4 pint) lukewarm milk

60 g (2 oz) butter, melted and cooled slightly

1 egg and 2 egg yolks, beaten

150 g (5 oz) sultanas

90 g (3 oz) chopped mixed peel

sunflower oil for greasing

TOPPING

1 egg, beaten

30 g (1 oz) nibbed sugar or coarsely crushed sugar cubes

1 Put the flour and sugar into a large bowl and stir in the salt and yeast. Make a well in the middle and add the milk, butter, egg and egg yolks, sultanas, and mixed peel. Mix to a soft dough.

2 Knead the dough on a lightly floured surface until smooth and elastic.

3 Shape the dough into a round and place in an oiled bowl. Cover with oiled cling film and leave to rise in a warm place for 1–1 1/2 hours or until the dough has doubled in size.

4 Turn the dough on to a lightly floured surface and knock back. Knead the dough for 2–3 minutes until smooth and elastic.

5 Lightly oil 2 or 3 baking trays. Divide the dough into 18 pieces, shape into rolls, and place on the baking trays. Cover loosely with oiled cling film and leave to rise in a warm place for about 30 minutes or until doubled in size.

6 Brush the tops of the buns with the beaten egg and sprinkle with the sugar. Bake in a preheated oven at 190°C (375°F, Gas 5) for 15 minutes or until golden brown.

7 Tap the bases of the buns to see if they are cooked through: they should sound hollow. Leave to cool on a wire rack.

CINNAMON ROLLS

MAKES 16

1 kg (2 lb) plain flour	
60 g (2 oz) caster sugar	
1 x 7 g (¼ oz) sachet fast-action dried yeast	
1 tsp salt	
about 350 ml (12 fl oz) lukewarm milk	
2 eggs, lightly beaten	
30 g (1 oz) butter, melted	
250 g (8 oz) raisins	
1 tbsp ground cinnamon	
sunflower oil for greasing	
milk for glazing	

GLAZE

200 g (7 oz) icing sugar	
4 tbsp water	
1 tsp vanilla essence	

1 Sift the flour and 30 g (1 oz) of the sugar into a bowl, then stir in the yeast and salt. Make a well in the middle, pour in the milk, eggs, and butter, and stir to make a sticky dough.

2 Knead the dough on a lightly floured surface until smooth and elastic.

3 Knead in the raisins and half of the cinnamon, then divide the dough into 16 even-sized pieces. Shape each piece into a 20–25 cm (8–10 in) strand, then flatten.

4 Combine the remaining sugar and cinnamon, sprinkle the mixture over the strips of dough, then roll up tightly into spirals.

5 Lightly oil 2 baking trays. Arrange the rolls on the trays, cover loosely with oiled cling film, and leave to rise in a warm place for about 1 hour or until doubled in size.

6 Brush the rolls with milk to glaze, then bake them in a preheated oven at 190°C (375°F, Gas 5) for 30–40 minutes until lightly browned. Transfer the rolls to a rack.

7 Meanwhile, make the glaze: in a small bowl, combine the icing sugar, measured water, and vanilla essence. As soon as the cinnamon rolls come out of the oven, brush them with the glaze. Serve the rolls warm or cold.

HOT CROSS BUNS

MAKES 12

500 g (1 lb) strong white flour	
60 g (2 oz) caster sugar	
1 x 7 g (¼ oz) sachet fast-action dried yeast	
1 tsp salt	
1 tsp ground mixed spice	
1 tsp ground cinnamon	
½ tsp grated nutmeg	
about 150 ml (¼ pint) milk	
about 75 ml (2½ fl oz) very hot water	
60 g (2 oz) butter, melted and cooled slightly	
1 egg, beaten	
90 g (3 oz) currants	
60 g (2 oz) chopped mixed peel	
sunflower oil for greasing	
60 g (2 oz) shortcrust pastry	

GLAZE

2 tbsp caster sugar	
2 tbsp water	

1 Sift the flour into a large bowl, stir in the sugar, yeast, salt, mixed spice, cinnamon, and nutmeg, and make a well in the middle. Mix the milk and water together and add to bowl with the butter, egg, currants, and mixed peel. Mix to a soft dough.

2 Knead the dough on a lightly floured surface until smooth and elastic, then shape into a round.

3 Put into an oiled large bowl, cover with oiled cling film, and leave to rise in a warm place for 1–1½ hours or until doubled in size.

4 Knock back the dough with your fists, then turn on to a lightly floured surface and knead for 2–3 minutes until smooth and elastic. Divide the dough into 12 pieces and shape into round rolls.

5 Roll out the shortcrust pastry to 5 mm (¼ in) thickness, cut it into 24 narrow strips, and press 2 strips in the form of a cross on each bun. Secure with a little water.

6 Lightly oil 2 baking trays, arrange the buns on the trays, and cover with oiled cling film. Leave to rise in a warm place for 30 minutes or until doubled in size.

7 Bake the buns in a preheated oven at 220°C (425°F, Gas 7) for 15 minutes or until golden brown. Transfer the buns to a wire rack, and serve warm or cold.

11

PIES, TARTS, & HOT DESSERTS

UNDER 30 MINUTES

30–60 MINUTES

CHERRIES JUBILEE

Morello cherries simmered in sugar and flavoured with almond essence and brandy. Served with vanilla ice cream.

SERVES 4 162 calories per serving

Takes 20 minutes   Page 435

FRENCH PANCAKES

Small golden pancakes, baked, then folded over a filling of apricot jam, and sprinkled with caster sugar.

SERVES 4 378 calories per serving

Takes 35 minutes   Page 436

FAMILY CHOICE

MAGIC CHOCOLATE PUDDING

Irresistible light chocolate sponge flavoured with cocoa and vanilla essence, and baked in a chocolate sauce.

SERVES 4 361 calories per serving

Takes 45 minutes   Page 440

JAMAICAN BANANAS

Banana halves coated in a rich caramel and cinnamon sauce, spiked with rum. Served warm with vanilla ice cream.

SERVES 4 269 calories per serving

Takes 15 minutes   Page 434

TRADITIONAL

BAKED APPLES

Cooking apples filled with sugar and butter, then baked until soft and served hot with their juices spooned over.

SERVES 6 235 calories per serving

Takes 55 minutes   Page 433

APPLE BROWN BETTY

Layers of spiced apple slices and buttered breadcrumbs sprinkled with caster sugar, then baked until golden brown.

SERVES 6 284 calories per serving

Takes 55 minutes   Page 433

FRUIT FRITTERS

Bite-sized pieces of apple and banana coated in batter, and deep-fried until golden. Sprinkled with sugar and cinnamon.

SERVES 6 361 calories per serving

Takes 25 minutes   Page 435

FRENCH CLASSIC

CREPES SUZETTE

Delicious crêpes coated with a sweet orange sauce including brandy or orange liqueur, folded in quarters, and served hot.

SERVES 4 604 calories per serving

Takes 55 minutes   Page 436

PLUM CRUMBLE

Sweet and crunchy: juicy plums sprinkled with sugar and cinnamon, and baked beneath a golden brown topping.

SERVES 6 436 calories per serving

Takes 50 minutes   Page 434

OVER 60 MINUTES

MAGIC LEMON PUDDING

Fresh and tangy: a light lemony mixture separates during cooking into a sponge on top and a delicious lemon sauce underneath.

SERVES 4 295 calories per serving
Takes 1 hour 5 minutes
Page 437

APPLE CHARLOTTE

Slices of buttered bread covered with an apple and apricot jam mixture, and topped with a layer of bread triangles.

SERVES 6 428 calories per serving
Takes 1 hour 5 minutes
Page 432

DINNER PARTY

MILLE-FEUILLE

Melt-in-the-mouth puff pastry layered with whipped cream, jam, and crème pâtissière, and topped with glacé icing.

SERVES 6 486 calories per serving
Takes 45 minutes, plus chilling
Page 458

AMERICAN CLASSIC

KEY LIME PIE

Creamy, tangy lime-flavoured filling is set in a baked shortcrust pastry shell, then chilled and served decorated with lime slices.

SERVES 8 489 calories per serving
Takes 60 minutes, plus chilling
Page 454

PINEAPPLE UPSIDE-DOWN PUDDING

Pineapple rings and chopped apricots beneath a light and springy sponge topping, turned out and served "upside-down".

SERVES 8 375 calories per serving
Takes 1 hour 5 minutes
Page 437

EVE'S PUDDING

Warming and filling: sweetened sliced cooking apples, and lemon zest and juice, are topped with a golden sponge.

SERVES 6 414 calories per serving
Takes 1 hour 5 minutes
Page 432

BANOFFI PIE

Rich and creamy: crushed biscuit base with a caramel filling, topped with banana slices, whipped cream, and grated chocolate.

SERVES 6 653 calories per serving
Takes 20 minutes, plus chilling
Page 454

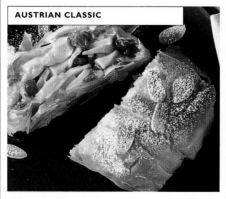

AUSTRIAN CLASSIC

APPLE STRUDEL

Sheets of filo pastry enclosing apples, lemon zest and juice, sugar, spices, and sultanas, and sprinkled with almonds.

SERVES 8 278 calories per serving
Takes 1¼ hours
Page 447

BANANA CUSTARD TART WITH BERRIES

Muesli pastry shell filled with layers of creamy custard and fruit, and covered with whipped cream.

SERVES 6–8 787–590 calories per serving
Takes 60 minutes, plus chilling
Page 455

OVER 60 MINUTES

QUEEN OF PUDDINGS

Old-fashioned favourite: smooth set creamy custard is flavoured with orange zest, spread with melted jam, and topped with meringue.

SERVES 6 386 calories per serving

Takes 60 minutes, plus standing   Page 441

AMERICAN CLASSIC

MISSISSIPPI MUD PIE

Popular American dessert: pastry shell with a sweetened chocolate and coffee filling, decorated with whipped cream.

SERVES 8–10 692–553 calories per serving

Takes 1¼ hours, plus chilling   Page 455

TREACLE TART

Rich and sweet: pastry shell filled with golden syrup, breadcrumbs, and lemon zest and juice. Served warm.

SERVES 8 386 calories per serving

Takes 60 minutes, plus chilling   Page 450

FAMILY CHOICE

STICKY TOFFEE PUDDING

Rich pudding flavoured with coffee essence, dates, and walnuts, and served with a deliciously sticky toffee sauce.

SERVES 8 690 calories per serving

Takes 1 hour 5 minutes   Page 440

HOT CHOCOLATE SOUFFLES

Light and airy: individual soufflés made from dark chocolate, baked until well risen and fluffy, then dusted with icing sugar.

SERVES 4 494 calories per serving

Takes 1¼ hours   Page 441

GREEK CLASSIC

BAKLAVA

Traditional Greek pastry: layers of buttered filo pastry and walnuts soaked in honey and lemon juice, and cut into squares.

MAKES 20 SQUARES 249 calories per serving

Takes 60 minutes, plus cooling   Page 458

BAKED APPLE DUMPLINGS

Cooking apples filled with sugar and cinnamon, enclosed in decorative pastry case, and baked until golden.

SERVES 4 781 calories per serving

Takes 60 minutes, plus chilling   Page 445

TRADITIONAL

LEMON MERINGUE PIE

Deliciously sweet: golden brown pastry with tangy lemon filling, topped with light and fluffy meringue.

SERVES 8–10 537–430 calories per serving

Takes 1¼ hours, plus chilling   Page 453

DOUBLE CRUST APPLE PIE

Family favourite: light and golden puff pastry encases tender apple slices in this traditional apple pie.

SERVES 6 432 calories per serving

Takes 60 minutes, plus cooling   Page 446

OVER 60 MINUTES

BAKEWELL TART
Traditional sweet dessert: pastry shell spread with jam, topped with an almond-flavoured sponge and a pastry lattice.

SERVES 6 560 calories per serving
Takes 1¼ hours, plus chilling   Page 451

TRADITIONAL

BREAD & BUTTER PUDDING
Slices of white bread thickly spread with butter, layered with dried fruit, lemon zest, and sugar, and baked in a custard.

SERVES 6 516 calories per serving
Takes 60 minutes, plus standing   Page 442

STRAWBERRY & RHUBARB PIE
Sweet strawberries and rhubarb are lightly spiced, and baked in a pastry shell with a lattice topping.

SERVES 6–8 371–278 calories per serving
Takes 1¼ hours, plus chilling   Page 445

DINNER PARTY

FRENCH APRICOT & ALMOND TART
French classic: apricots in lemon juice, on a bed of crème pâtissière in a pastry shell. Glazed with brandy and flaked almonds.

SERVES 10 398 calories per serving
Takes 45 minutes, plus chilling   Page 452

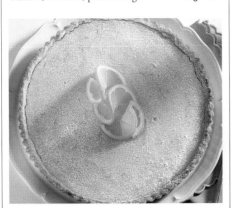

TARTE AU CITRON
Light and tangy: pastry shell with a cream and lemon filling, baked until set, and lightly dusted with icing sugar.

SERVES 10–12 572–476 calories per serving
Takes 1¼ hours, plus chilling   Page 453

FAMILY CHOICE

RICE PUDDING
Rich and creamy: pudding rice, milk, caster sugar, and lemon zest mixed together, then sprinkled with freshly grated nutmeg and dotted with small knobs of butter. Baked slowly in the oven until the top turns golden brown.

SERVES 4 210 calories per serving
Takes 2¾ hours, plus standing   Page 442

OVER 60 MINUTES

AMERICAN CLASSIC

PECAN PIE

Deliciously rich: pecan pie is an American classic originating from the Southern States of America. The buttery rich pecan kernels are toasted, then mixed with a lightly spiced syrup, and flavoured with brandy and vanilla essence.

SERVES 6–8 611–458 calories per serving
Takes 1 1/4 hours, plus chilling   Page 451

FRENCH APPLE TART

Apple chunks, jam, sugar, and lemon zest, puréed, and spooned into a pastry shell, and topped with apple slices and jam glaze.

SERVES 8–10 593–474 calories per serving
Takes 2 hours, plus chilling   Page 450

FAMILY CHOICE

TREACLE PUDDING

Wonderfully sweet and sticky: a simple, traditional steamed pudding, deliciously sweetened with golden syrup.

SERVES 4–6 619–413 calories per serving
Takes 3 1/4 hours   Page 444

TARTE TATIN

Rich and fruity: crisp pastry baked over caramel and apple slices, then turned out with the glazed apples on top.

SERVES 6 511 calories per serving
Takes 60 minutes, plus chilling   Page 447

MINCEMEAT & ALMOND TART

A pastry shell filled with mincemeat and topped with a light, creamy almond mixture, then baked until golden.

SERVES 8–10 856–685 calories per serving
Takes 60 minutes, plus chilling   Page 444

STEAMED JAM PUDDING

Traditional pudding: a temptingly light sponge mixture is steamed over jam. A firm family favourite.

SERVES 4–6 573–382 calories per serving
Takes 1 3/4 hours   Page 443

CHRISTMAS PUDDING

TRADITIONAL

Rich, dark and fruity traditional Christmas pudding: dried fruits are combined with nuts, and lemon zest and juice. Grated carrot ensures that the pudding stays deliciously moist. Once steamed, the pudding is liberally laced with rum.

SERVES 8–10 522–418 calories per serving
Takes 6 1/4 hours, plus storing   Page 443

PIES, TARTS, & HOT DESSERTS KNOW-HOW

PUDDINGS MAY no longer be a feature of every family meal, but few people can say that they don't enjoy something sweet from time to time, be it a traditional steamed pudding or comforting bread and butter pudding – one of the nation's favourites – or a glamorous golden pastry filled with fresh fruit or a rich custard. Hot pastry desserts can take very little time to make these days as bought pastry, especially the ready-rolled varieties, is so good. But if you have the time, and you enjoy it, then it's very satisfying to make your own, and you can try all the different types of pastry.

TYPES OF PASTRY

All pastries are based on a mixture of flour, fat, and a liquid to bind them. Plain white flour is usually used, although wholemeal or a mixture of the two gives a "nuttier" pastry. The liquid used for binding may be water, milk, or egg; the fat may be butter, margarine, lard, white vegetable fat, or a combination.

Shortcrust pastry

A blend of 2 parts flour, 1 part fat, and usually water, shortcrust pastry (page 430) is used for sweet and savoury pies and tarts.

Pâte sucrée

Bound with egg yolks, pâte sucrée (page 430) is richer than shortcrust pastry and is used for sweet tarts and tartlets. The classic method for mixing the dough is on a flat marble work surface.

Puff pastry

This light, flaky pastry is made by rolling and folding the dough many times to make paper-thin layers of dough and butter. Ready-made fresh or frozen pastry is very convenient, but not all brands are made with butter. Puff pastry is often used as a top crust for sweet and savoury pies, to wrap beef Wellington, and for mille-feuille.

Flaky pastry

This is a short-cut version of puff pastry. The rolling and folding process is repeated only a few times. It is used for pies and tarts.

Quick puff pastry

Like puff and flaky pastry, this is rolled and folded, but the butter is added all at once, in large cubes. Quick puff pastry can be used in the same ways as flaky pastry and for dishes normally made with puff pastry.

Filo & strudel pastry

These are similar types of pastry made from a pliable dough that is stretched and rolled until extremely thin. It is then rolled around a filling or layered with melted butter. Filo and strudel pastries are difficult to make at home, but ready-made varieties are available fresh and frozen. Common uses include strudel and baklava.

MICROWAVING

The microwave can be a helpful tool when preparing pies, tarts, and hot desserts. For baking pastry-based pies and tarts, however, there really is no substitute for the conventional oven.

The microwave is perfect for cooking fruit fillings for pies and tarts. The fruit remains plump and colourful. It can also be used to melt or soften butter and to heat liquids in which fruit is left to soak. Under careful watch, the microwave can be used to melt chocolate and to make caramel.

FREEZING

Most puddings freeze well, particularly baked sponge and steamed suet puddings (before or after cooking), bread and butter pudding (before cooking), crumbles (before or after cooking), and pancakes. Custard-based and milk puddings are not as successful because they tend to separate.

Pastry dough is an excellent freezer standby; thaw before rolling out. Unbaked pastry shells are ideal for last-minute desserts as they can be baked from frozen. It's not a good idea to freeze baked pastries.

QUICK PUFF PASTRY

Ideal for both sweet and savoury pies. These quantities make sufficient pastry for a 25 cm (10 in) double-crust pie.

1 Sift 250 g (8 oz) plain flour into a bowl. Add 90 g (3 oz) each of cubed butter and white vegetable fat, and stir to coat in flour. Add 150 ml (1/4 pint) cold water and, with a table knife, bind to a lumpy dough.

2 Roll out the dough into a rectangle 3 times as long as it is wide. Fold the bottom third up and the top third down. Press the edges with the side of your hand, to seal. Wrap and chill for 15 minutes, then place so the folded edges are to the sides.

3 Roll out the dough into a rectangle and fold as before. Turn the dough so the folded edges are to the sides again. Repeat the rolling, folding, and turning twice more. Wrap and chill for 30 minutes.

SHORTCRUST PASTRY

You can also make shortcrust in a food processor: pulse the flour with the fat until like breadcrumbs, then add the water and pulse again briefly (do this briefly or the pastry will be tough). Tip on to a floured surface and knead lightly to mix to a smooth dough. These quantities make sufficient pastry to line a 23–25 cm (9–10 in) flan dish, flan tin, or pie dish.

1 Sift 175 g (6 oz) plain flour into a bowl. Cut 90 g (3 oz) well-chilled butter, margarine, or other fat into small pieces and add to the bowl. Stir to coat the fat with flour.

2 Using your fingertips, quickly and lightly rub the fat into the flour, lifting the mixture to incorporate air, until it resembles fine breadcrumbs. Sprinkle over about 2 tbsp cold water and stir gently with a table knife to mix. If the mixture seems too dry to bind together, add a little more water.

3 Gather the mixture together and knead very briefly until smooth (handle the dough as little as possible or the pastry will be tough. If the dough feels at all sticky, add a little more flour. Shape into a ball, wrap, and chill for 30 minutes.

PATE SUCREE

This French sweet pastry is traditionally made on a marble surface. These quantities make sufficient pastry to line a 25 cm (10 in) flan dish, tin, or pie dish.

1 Sift 200 g (7 oz) plain flour on to a work surface. Make a well in the middle and add 90 g (3 oz) softened butter, 60 g (2 oz) caster sugar, and 3 egg yolks (for a less rich pastry, use just 1 egg yolk). With your fingertips blend together the butter, sugar, and egg yolks.

2 Using your fingertips, gradually work the sifted flour into the blended butter mixture until the mixture resembles coarse crumbs. If the mixture seems too sticky, work in a little more flour.

3 With your fingers or a pastry scraper, gather the dough into a ball, then knead briefly until it is smooth and pliable. Shape the dough into a ball again, wrap, and chill for 30 minutes or until it feels just firm.

MAKING A PASTRY SHELL

Careful handling of pastry dough should ensure it does not shrink or distort when baking.

1 Put the pastry dough on a floured work surface and flour the rolling pin. Roll out into a round, starting in the middle each time and lifting and turning the pastry round a quarter turn after each roll.

2 If lining a pie dish, roll out the pastry dough to a round 5 cm (2 in) larger than the top of the dish; a pastry lid should also be 5 cm (2 in) larger. Roll the pastry up loosely around the rolling pin, and unroll over the dish.

3 Gently ease the pastry into the dish, pressing it firmly and neatly into the bottom edge. Be very careful not to stretch the pastry. Carefully trim off the excess pastry with a table knife. If there are any holes, patch them with bits of pastry dough.

BAKING BLIND

A pastry shell may be partly baked before adding a filling, to help it stay crisp, or it may be fully baked if the filling itself does not need to be cooked. The shell is filled with baking beans to weigh down the pastry.

1 Prick the pastry shell all over with a fork. Line with a piece of foil or greaseproof paper, allowing it to come high above the rim so that it can be lifted out easily after baking.

2 Fill the shell with ceramic baking beans, dried pulses, or uncooked rice, and bake in a preheated oven at 190°C (375°F, Gas 5) for 10 minutes.

3 Remove the beans and foil. Return the shell to the oven and bake for 5 minutes (part-baked) or 15 minutes (fully baked). If the pastry rises during baking, gently press it down with your hand.

DECORATIVE EDGES

A simple way to give a decorative finish to a pie is to crimp the edge. Place the tips of the thumb and forefinger of one hand against the outside rim of the dish. With the forefinger of your other hand, gently push the pastry edge outwards between the thumb and finger, and pinch the pastry to make a rounded "V" shape. Repeat this action all around the pastry lid. Alternatively, push and pinch in the opposite direction, working from the outside of the edge inwards.

STEAMED PUDDINGS

Light sponges and rich suet mixtures can both be gently cooked by steaming. Be sure to make the seal tight so moisture cannot get inside. It is important to keep the water in the saucepan topped up, so boil some water ready to add to the pan when needed.

1 Turn the mixture into a greased, heatproof bowl. Layer a piece of greaseproof paper with a piece of foil and make a pleat across the middle, to allow for the pudding's expansion during cooking. Butter the paper.

2 Place the foil and paper, buttered-side down, over the top of the bowl. Secure by tying string tightly under the rim. Form a handle with another piece of string. Trim away excess paper and foil.

3 Put a trivet or upturned saucer or plate in the bottom of a saucepan and half fill with water. Bring to a simmer. Lower the bowl into the saucepan; add more boiling water to come halfway up the side of the bowl. Cover tightly and steam for the required time. Make sure that the water stays at simmering point and top up when necessary.

Decorating pies & tarts

Keep pastry trimmings to make small decorative shapes. Cut them freehand or use cutters. They can be fixed to the edge of a pastry shell or arranged on a lid. If the pastry has a glaze, attach the shapes with water, then apply the glaze all over the pie, brushing it on gently so the shapes are not disturbed.

•

A pastry lid can be brushed with a glaze before baking. A little milk or beaten egg will give a shiny finish, as will egg white alone – this is a good way to use up whites when the pastry is made with egg yolks. Sprinkle a pastry lid with sugar for a crisp, sweet glaze.

APPLE CHARLOTTE

SERVES 6

1 kg (2 lb) cooking apples, quartered, cored, peeled, and sliced

125 g (4 oz) caster sugar

3 tbsp water

2 tbsp apricot jam

125 g (4 oz) butter, softened, plus extra for greasing

12 slices of bread, crusts removed

15 CM (6 IN) SQUARE CAKE TIN

1 Put the apples, sugar, and measured water in a saucepan and cook over a medium heat for about 10–15 minutes until the apples are soft but still holding their shape. Stir in the apricot jam.

2 Spread the butter on one side of each slice of bread. Lightly butter the cake tin and assemble the pudding (see box, right).

3 Bake in a preheated oven at 200°C (400°F, Gas 6) for about 40 minutes until crisp and golden. Serve hot.

Assembling the charlotte

Use 8 of the bread slices to line the tin, cutting them into strips or squares as necessary, and placing them buttered-side down. Spoon in the apple mixture. Cut the remaining slices of bread into quarters diagonally. Arrange the quarters, buttered-side up, on top of the apple mixture.

EVE'S PUDDING

SERVES 6

butter for greasing

500 g (1 lb) cooking apples, quartered, cored, peeled, and sliced

90 g (3 oz) demerara sugar

grated zest and juice of 1 lemon

SPONGE TOPPING

125 g (4 oz) baking margarine, straight from the refrigerator

125 g (4 oz) caster sugar

2 eggs, beaten

125 g (4 oz) self-raising flour

1 tsp baking powder

1.25 LITRE (2 PINT) OVENPROOF DISH

1 Lightly butter the ovenproof dish and arrange the apples in the bottom. Sprinkle over the demerara sugar and the lemon zest and juice.

2 Make the sponge topping: put the margarine, sugar, eggs, flour, and baking powder in a large bowl, and beat until smooth and well blended. Spoon on top of the apple slices, and level the surface.

3 Bake in a preheated oven at 180°C (350°F, Gas 4) for about 45 minutes until the sponge topping is well risen, golden, and springy to the touch. Serve hot.

SPICED EVE'S PUDDING

Add 1 tsp ground cinnamon to the sponge topping, and 60 g (2 oz) raisins, 1 tsp ground cinnamon, and 1 tsp ground mixed spice to the apple mixture.

Cook's know-how

Instead of the demerara sugar on top of the apples, you can use apricot jam, with the grated zest and juice of an orange rather than the lemon. To make a Christmas Eve's Pudding, use mincemeat instead of the sugar or jam, or a mixture of chopped dried cranberries and apricots with 30 g (1 oz) demerara sugar and a splash of brandy, rum, or sherry.

APPLE BROWN BETTY

Easy to prepare from mainly storecupboard ingredients, this pudding is real comfort food, and it can be made with fruits other than apples if you prefer. Serve it with vanilla or yogurt ice cream, crème fraîche, or whipped cream.

SERVES 6

30–45 g (1–1½ oz) butter

175 g (6 oz) fresh breadcrumbs

1 kg (2 lb) cooking apples, quartered, cored, peeled, and thinly sliced

125 g (4 oz) caster sugar, plus extra for sprinkling

1 tbsp lemon juice

1–2 tsp ground cinnamon

DEEP 1.5–2 LITRE (2½–3½ PINT) OVENPROOF DISH

1 Melt the butter in a frying pan. Add the breadcrumbs and stir over a medium heat for 5 minutes or until the crumbs are crisp and golden. Remove from the heat.

2 Toss the apples with the caster sugar, lemon juice, and ground cinnamon.

3 Press one-quarter of the crisp breadcrumbs over the bottom of the dish. Cover with half of the apple mixture and sprinkle with a further one-quarter of the breadcrumbs.

4 Arrange the remaining apple mixture on top of the breadcrumbs, spoon over any juices, and cover with the remaining breadcrumbs. Sprinkle the top of the pudding lightly with caster sugar.

5 Cover the dish with foil. Bake in a preheated oven at 200°C (400°F, Gas 6) for about 20 minutes.

6 Remove the foil and continue baking for a further 20 minutes or until the apples are tender and the top is golden brown. Serve warm.

APPLE & CRANBERRY BROWN BETTY

Add 175 g (6 oz) fresh or thawed frozen cranberries to the apple mixture. Add a little more sugar if necessary.

PEACH MELBA BROWN BETTY

Substitute 3 peeled, stoned, and sliced peaches, and 250 g (8 oz) raspberries for the apples. Omit the lemon juice and cinnamon.

Cook's know-how

White or brown bread can be used for the breadcrumbs. Wholemeal gives a nutty flavour, and granary gives an interesting texture. For best results, the bread should be about 2 days old.

BAKED APPLES

SERVES 6

6 cooking apples

90 g (3 oz) light muscovado sugar

90 g (3 oz) butter, diced

3 tbsp water

1 Wipe the apples, and remove the cores using an apple corer. Make a shallow cut through the skin around the equator of each apple.

2 Put the apples into an ovenproof dish and fill their middles with the sugar and butter. Pour the water around the apples.

3 Bake in a preheated oven at 190°C (375°F, Gas 5) for 40–45 minutes until the apples are soft. Serve hot, spooning all the juices from the dish over the apples.

CITRUS BAKED APPLES

Add the finely grated zest of 1 orange or 1 lemon to the muscovado sugar.

BAKED APPLES WITH MINCEMEAT

Use 125 g (4 oz) mincemeat instead of the sugar and butter.

JAMAICAN BANANAS

SERVES 4

30–45 g (1–1 1/2 oz) unsalted butter

2–3 tbsp dark muscovado sugar

1/2 tsp ground cinnamon

60 ml (2 fl oz) dark rum

4 firm but ripe bananas, cut in half lengthwise

vanilla ice cream to serve

1 Put the butter and sugar into a large heavy frying pan, and heat gently until the butter has melted and sugar dissolved. Stir to blend together, then cook gently, stirring, for about 5 minutes.

2 Stir the cinnamon and rum into the caramel mixture, then add the banana halves. Cook for 3 minutes on each side until warmed through.

3 Transfer the bananas and hot sauce to serving plates. Serve at once, with scoops of vanilla ice cream.

Cook's know-how

If you want to serve these bananas to children, use the freshly squeezed juice of an orange instead of the rum, plus the grated orange zest if you think they will like it. In summer you could bake the bananas wrapped in foil on the barbecue and make the sauce separately.

PLUM CRUMBLE

SERVES 6

1 kg (2 lb) plums, halved and stoned

60 g (2 oz) light muscovado sugar

1 tsp ground cinnamon

CRUMBLE TOPPING

250 g (8 oz) self-raising wholemeal flour

90 g (3 oz) butter

150 g (5 oz) light muscovado sugar

1 Put the plums into a shallow ovenproof dish and sprinkle with the sugar and cinnamon.

2 Make the topping: put the flour into a bowl, and rub in the butter with the fingertips until the mixture resembles fine breadcrumbs. Stir in the sugar.

3 Sprinkle the topping evenly over the plums, without pressing it down, and bake in a preheated oven at 180°C (350°F, Gas 4) for 30–40 minutes until golden. Serve the crumble hot.

CRUNCHY APRICOT CRUMBLE

Substitute fresh apricots for the plums, and omit the cinnamon. Substitute porridge oats or muesli for half of the flour in the crumble topping, or use up to 125 g (4 oz) chopped toasted hazelnuts. You can also use half white and half wholemeal flour.

RHUBARB & GINGER CRUMBLE

Substitute 1 kg (2 lb) rhubarb, cut into 2.5 cm (1 in) pieces, for the plums. Put into a saucepan with the sugar, 2 tbsp water, and 1 tsp ground ginger instead of the cinnamon, and cook gently until the rhubarb is soft.

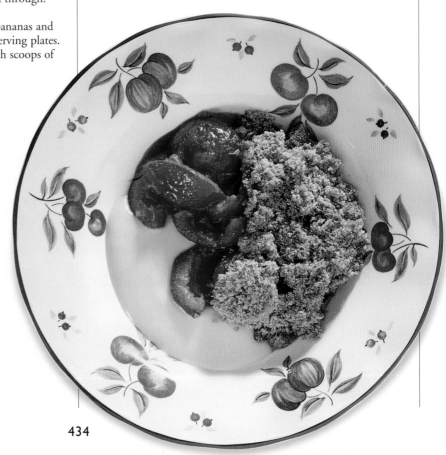

CHERRIES JUBILEE

SERVES 4

1 x 425 g (14 oz) jar or can Morello cherries in syrup
2–3 tbsp caster sugar
75 ml (2½ fl oz) brandy
a few drops of almond essence
vanilla ice cream to serve

FRESH CHERRIES JUBILEE

Replace the Morello cherries with 500 g (1 lb) fresh cherries. Pit the cherries and poach them in 250 ml (8 fl oz) red wine and 100 g (3½ oz) caster sugar until tender. Substitute the poaching liquid for the syrup.

1 Drain the cherries, reserving 125 ml (4 fl oz) of the syrup. Put the cherries into a saucepan with the measured syrup and the sugar.

2 Heat gently, stirring, until the sugar has dissolved, then bring to a boil. Simmer for about 5 minutes until the liquid has thickened and reduced by about half.

3 Pour the brandy over the cherries, and add the almond essence. Boil to evaporate the alcohol, then spoon the hot cherries and syrup over scoops of vanilla ice cream, and serve at once.

Cook's know-how

Instead of boiling the syrup until it is reduced in step 2, stir in 1 tsp cornflour mixed to a paste with a little cold water. Bring to a boil, stirring, until thickened.
The cherries and their sauce are very versatile – serve them with meringues and cream, or spooned over slices of meringue or chocolate roulade, or over scoops of vanilla or frozen yogurt ice cream.

FRUIT FRITTERS

SERVES 6

2 apples
3 bananas
juice of ½ lemon
sunflower oil for deep-frying
60 g (2 oz) caster sugar
1 tsp ground cinnamon
BATTER
125 g (4 oz) plain flour
1 tbsp icing sugar
1 egg, separated
150 ml (¼ pint) mixed milk and water

1 Quarter, core, and peel the apples. Cut the apples and bananas into bite-sized pieces. Toss the pieces in the lemon juice to prevent discoloration.

2 Make the batter: sift the flour and sugar into a bowl, and make a well. Add the egg yolk and a little of the milk mixture and whisk together. Whisk in half of the remaining milk mixture, drawing in the flour to form a smooth batter. Add the remaining milk.

3 Whisk the egg white in a separate clean bowl until stiff but not dry. Fold into the batter until evenly mixed.

4 Heat the oil in a deep-fat fryer to 190°C (375°F). Pat the fruit dry. Dip each piece of fruit into the batter, lower into the hot oil, and cook in batches for 3–4 minutes until golden and crisp. Drain on paper towels and keep warm while cooking the remainder.

5 Combine the caster sugar and cinnamon, sprinkle generously over the fritters, and serve at once.

Cook's know-how

For a light, crisp batter, the egg white should be whisked and folded in just before you are ready to cook the fritters – don't leave the batter to stand or it will lose its airy texture.

435

FRENCH PANCAKES

SERVES 4

60 g (2 oz) butter, softened, plus extra for greasing

60 g (2 oz) caster sugar

2 eggs, beaten

60 g (2 oz) self-raising flour

300 ml (1/2 pint) milk

apricot jam and caster sugar to serve

8-HOLE BUN TIN WITH 7 CM (3 IN) CUPS

1 Combine the butter and sugar in a bowl and cream together until soft. Beat in the eggs, a little at a time, then fold in the flour.

2 In a small saucepan, heat the milk to just below boiling point. Stir into the creamed mixture.

3 Lightly butter the bun tin cups, and divide the batter equally among them. Bake in a preheated oven at 190°C (375°F, Gas 5) for about 20 minutes until the pancakes are well risen and golden brown.

4 Slide the pancakes out of the cups, and serve with apricot jam and caster sugar. To eat, place a little jam in the middle of each pancake, fold in half, and sprinkle with sugar.

CREPES SUZETTE

SERVES 4

juice of 2 oranges

125 g (4 oz) unsalted butter

60 g (2 oz) caster sugar

3–4 tbsp orange liqueur or brandy

CREPES

125 g (4 oz) plain flour

1 egg

1 tbsp oil, plus extra for frying

300 ml (1/2 pint) milk

18–20 CM (7–8 IN) FRYING PAN

1 Make the crêpes: sift the flour into a bowl. Make a well in the middle. Mix together the egg, 1 tbsp oil, and the milk, and pour into well. Gradually beat in the flour, to make a fairly thin batter.

2 Heat a little oil in the frying pan, then wipe away the excess oil. Add 2–3 tbsp batter to the pan, tilting it to coat the bottom evenly. Cook for 45–60 seconds, then turn over, and cook the other side for about 30 seconds. Slide the crêpe out on to a warmed plate.

3 Repeat to make 7 more crêpes. Stack the crêpes on top of each other as soon as they are cooked (they will not stick together).

4 Make the orange sauce and add and fold the crêpes (see box, right). Heat to warm through.

Cook's know-how

In traditional French restaurants the crêpes are usually flambéed with orange liqueur or brandy at the table. At home this is not so practical, which is why the alcohol is simply heated with the other sauce ingredients in this recipe.

Making the sauce and folding the crêpes

Put the orange juice, butter, sugar, and liqueur or brandy into a large frying pan, and boil for 5 minutes until reduced. Place 1 crêpe in the pan, coat with sauce, fold in half, then in half again. Move to one side of the pan. Add another crêpe. Coat with the sauce, and fold as before. Repeat with the remaining crêpes.

MAGIC LEMON PUDDING

SERVES 4

60 g (2 oz) butter, softened, plus extra for greasing

grated zest and juice of 1 large lemon

90 g (3 oz) caster sugar

2 eggs, separated

30 g (1 oz) plain flour

175 ml (6 fl oz) milk

lemon or lime slices to decorate

SHALLOW **600** ML (1 PINT) OVENPROOF DISH

1 Put the butter, lemon zest, and sugar into a bowl and beat together until pale and fluffy.

2 Add the egg yolks, flour, and lemon juice, and stir to combine. Gradually stir in the milk until evenly mixed.

3 Whisk the egg whites until stiff but not dry. Gradually fold into the lemon mixture.

4 Lightly butter the ovenproof dish. Pour the lemon mixture into the dish, and put the dish into a roasting tin. Add enough hot water to the roasting tin to come almost to the rim of the dish. Bake in a preheated oven at 160°C (325°F, Gas 3) for 40 minutes or until the sponge feels springy. Serve hot, decorated with lemon or lime slices. Leftovers are good cold.

Cook's know-how

This "magic" pudding separates during cooking to form a sponge topping with a tangy lemon sauce beneath.

PINEAPPLE UPSIDE-DOWN PUDDING

SERVES 8

60 g (2 oz) butter, softened, plus extra for greasing

60 g (2 oz) light muscovado sugar

1 x 225 g (7½ oz) can pineapple rings in natural juice, drained, and juice reserved

4 ready-to-eat dried apricots, coarsely chopped

SPONGE

125 g (4 oz) butter, softened

125 g (4 oz) caster sugar

2 eggs, beaten

175 g (6 oz) self-raising flour

1 tsp baking powder

18 CM (7 IN) ROUND CAKE TIN

1 Lightly butter the tin and line the bottom with baking parchment. Cream together the butter and sugar and spread evenly over the baking parchment.

2 Arrange the pineapple rings on top of the butter and sugar mixture, and sprinkle the chopped dried apricots between the pineapple rings.

3 Make the sponge: put the butter, caster sugar, eggs, flour, and baking powder into a bowl with 2 tbsp of the reserved pineapple juice. Beat for 2 minutes or until smooth and well blended. Spoon the mixture on top of the pineapple rings and level the surface.

4 Bake in a preheated oven at 180°C (350°F, Gas 4) for about 45 minutes until the sponge is well risen and springy to the touch. Invert the sponge on to a warmed serving plate, and serve at once.

APRICOT UPSIDE-DOWN PUDDING

Substitute 1 x 400 g (13 oz) can apricot halves for the pineapple, and 2 tbsp chopped stem ginger for the dried apricots.

437

DESSERT FONDUES

We are all used to savoury fondues made with cheese or meat, but dessert fondues are less well known
This is a pity, because they are quick and easy to prepare and great fun to share at the end of an
informal meal. Offer a good selection of dippers for dunking and you can't go wrong.

DARK CHOCOLATE FONDUE

SERVES 6

200 g (7 oz) good-quality dark chocolate

30 g (1 oz) caster sugar

125 ml (4 fl oz) water

finely grated zest of 2 oranges (optional)

dippers of your choice (see box, below)

1 Break the chocolate into small pieces
and put them into a heatproof bowl. Sit
the bowl on top of a small saucepan of gently
simmering water, making sure the bottom
of the bowl does not touch the water or
the chocolate may get too hot and "seize"
into a ball. Heat very gently, stirring only
once or twice, until the chocolate has just
melted, then remove the pan from the
heat, keeping the bowl over the hot water.

2 Put the sugar into another saucepan,
pour in the measured water, and bring
to a boil. Simmer for 5 minutes, then
slowly stir this sugar syrup into the melted
chocolate and whisk until smooth. Stir in
the orange zest, if using.

3 Pour the chocolate fondue into a fondue
pot and place over a low flame to keep
warm. Serve with dippers of your choice.

WHITE CHOCOLATE FONDUE

SERVES 6

175 g (6 oz) good-quality white chocolate

150 ml (¼ pint) double cream

dippers of your choice (see box, below)

1 Roughly chop the chocolate and put
the pieces into a heatproof bowl. Sit the
bowl on top of a small saucepan of gently
simmering water, making sure the bottom
of the bowl does not touch the water or the
chocolate may get too hot and "seize" into
a ball. Heat very gently, stirring only once
or twice, until the chocolate has just
melted, then remove the bowl from the pan
and set aside.

2 Pour the cream into a heavy-based
saucepan and bring almost to boiling
point (you should see bubbles beginning to
break around the edge of the cream).
Slowly pour the hot cream onto the melted
chocolate, stirring gently.

3 Pour the chocolate fondue into a
fondue pot and place over a low flame
to keep warm. Serve with dippers of your
choice.

CHOCOLATE FUDGE FONDUE

SERVES 6

1 x 125 g (4 oz) bar caramel and fudge chocolate

90 g (3 oz) good-quality dark chocolate

125 g (4 oz) butter

60 g (2 oz) golden syrup

4 tbsp double cream

dippers of your choice (see box, below left)

1 Roughly chop the caramel and fudge
bar and the dark chocolate, and put the
pieces into a small saucepan. Cut the butter
into small cubes and drop them into the
pan, then pour in the golden syrup.

2 Cook the mixture over a very low heat,
stirring only once or twice, for 10–12
minutes. Remove from the heat and whisk
together until smooth, then whisk in the
cream.

3 Pour the chocolate fondue into a
fondue pot and place over a low flame
to keep warm. Serve with dippers of your
choice.

Cook's know-how

When a recipe calls for good-quality
chocolate, this means a chocolate with a
high cocoa solids content. This will be
given on the label, so always check before
you buy. A chocolate with over 50% cocoa
solids will be good, but for the very best
quality, look for one with around
70% cocoa solids.
White chocolate is not a true chocolate, so
it is important to check the label carefully –
to have a good 'chocolatey' flavour it must
contain cocoa solids amongst its
ingredients.

DIPPERS

Increase the fun of your fondue by offering as wide a choice as possible of
ingredients for dipping and dunking. You can be as creative as you like, but
bear in mind that the ingredients need to be speared on small forks so they
should not be too hard or crisp. Conversely, if the texture of the dippers is soft
and crumbly, they will drop into the pot and spoil the fondue. Here is a
selection of tried-and-tested dippers.

- Strawberries with hulls intact, either whole fruits or halved if large
- Cherries, still on their stalks if possible
- Banana slices (slightly under-ripe)
- Fig wedges
- Apricots and peaches, stoned and cut into quarters
- Kiwi fruits, cut lengthwise into eighths
- Pears, cut into chunky wedges and tossed in lemon juice

- Grapes, the large seedless variety
- Dried fruits, such as apricots, peaches, or mango
- Panettone cake, cut into cubes
- Brioche, cut into squares
- Long biscuits, such as Viennese fingers, langues de chats, or cigarettes russes

CLOCKWISE FROM TOP: Dippers, Dark Chocolate
Fondue, White Chocolate Fondue, Chocolate
Fudge Fondue.

MAGIC CHOCOLATE PUDDING

SERVES 4

60 g (2 oz) caster sugar

60 g (2 oz) fine semolina

30 g (1 oz) cocoa powder

1 tsp baking powder

30 g (1 oz) butter, melted, plus extra for greasing

2 eggs, beaten

2–3 drops of vanilla essence

icing sugar for dusting

SAUCE

90 g (3 oz) light muscovado sugar

2 tbsp cocoa powder

300 ml (1/2 pint) hot water

1 LITRE (13/4 PINT) OVENPROOF DISH

1 Mix together the sugar and semolina in a large bowl. Sift the cocoa powder and baking powder into the bowl, and mix thoroughly.

2 In a separate bowl, whisk together the melted butter, eggs, and vanilla essence with an electric whisk. Add this mixture to the dry ingredients and stir with a wooden spoon until well blended.

3 Lightly butter the ovenproof dish. Pour the mixture into the dish.

4 Make the sauce: mix together the muscovado sugar and cocoa powder, and gradually stir in the measured hot water. Pour the liquid over the pudding.

5 Bake the pudding in a preheated oven at 180°C (350°F, Gas 4) for 30 minutes or until the liquid has sunk to the bottom and the sponge is well risen and springy to the touch. Sprinkle with icing sugar, and serve at once.

NUTTY CHOCOLATE PUDDING

Add 60 g (2 oz) chopped pecan nuts or walnuts to the dry ingredients in step 1.

STICKY TOFFEE PUDDING

SERVES 8

90 g (3 oz) butter, softened, plus extra for greasing

150 g (5 oz) light muscovado sugar

2 eggs, beaten

1 tbsp coffee essence

175 g (6 oz) self-raising flour

1 tsp baking powder

175 g (6 oz) stoned dates, roughly chopped

90 g (3 oz) walnuts, roughly chopped

175 ml (6 fl oz) hot water

TOFFEE SAUCE

125 g (4 oz) butter

175 g (6 oz) light muscovado sugar

6 tbsp double cream

60 g (2 oz) walnuts, roughly chopped

DEEP 18 CM (7 IN) SQUARE CAKE TIN

1 Butter the cake tin and line the bottom with baking parchment.

2 Put the butter, sugar, eggs, coffee essence, flour, and baking powder into a large bowl. Beat well until smooth and thoroughly blended.

3 Stir in the dates and walnuts, and then the measured hot water. Pour the mixture into the tin.

4 Bake in a preheated oven at 180°C (350°F, Gas 4) for 45–50 minutes until the pudding is well risen, browned on top, and springy to the touch.

5 About 10 minutes before the pudding is ready, make the toffee sauce: put the butter and sugar into a small saucepan, and heat gently, stirring, until the butter has melted and the sugar dissolved. Stir in the cream and walnuts and heat gently to warm through.

6 Cut the pudding into 8 even-sized squares, and transfer to serving plates. Spoon over the toffee sauce, and serve at once.

Cook's know-how

Serve the toffee sauce with other hot or cold desserts, such as steamed puddings or ice cream.

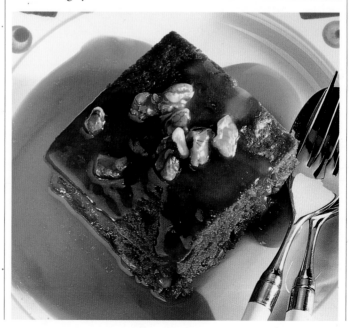

QUEEN OF PUDDINGS

SERVES 6

4 egg yolks

600 ml (1 pint) milk

30 g (1 oz) butter, plus extra for greasing

60 g (2 oz) caster sugar

grated zest of 1 orange

90 g (3 oz) fresh white breadcrumbs

3 tbsp strawberry or raspberry jam

MERINGUE TOPPING

4 egg whites

175 g (6 oz) caster sugar

SHALLOW 1.25 LITRE (2 PINT) OVENPROOF DISH

1 In a large bowl, lightly beat the egg yolks. Set aside. Heat the milk in a small saucepan until bubbles appear around the edge. Add the butter, sugar, and orange zest, and heat gently until the butter has melted and the sugar dissolved.

2 Lightly butter the ovenproof dish and set aside. Gradually add the hot milk mixture to the egg yolks, whisking all the time.

3 Stir in the breadcrumbs, then pour into the ovenproof dish. Leave to stand for 15 minutes.

4 Bake the pudding in a preheated oven at 180°C (350°F, Gas 4) for about 30 minutes until just set. Remove from the oven and set aside.

5 Warm the jam in a small saucepan until melted. Spread the warmed jam evenly over the surface of the pudding.

6 Make the meringue topping: whisk the egg whites until stiff but not dry. With an electric mixer, whisk in the caster sugar, 1 tsp at a time, keeping the mixer at full speed.

7 Spoon the meringue on top of the pudding, spreading it to the edge and pulling it up to form peaks.

8 Return the pudding to the oven and bake for a further 10–15 minutes until the top of the meringue is crisp and golden brown. Serve at once.

HOT CHOCOLATE SOUFFLES

SERVES 4

125 g (4 oz) plain chocolate

2 tbsp water

300 ml (1/2 pint) milk

45 g (1 1/2 oz) butter, plus extra for greasing

45 g (1 1/2 oz) plain flour

2–3 drops of vanilla essence

60 g (2 oz) caster sugar

4 egg yolks

5 egg whites

sifted icing sugar for dusting

4 x 300 ML (1/2 PINT) SOUFFLÉ DISHES

1 Break the chocolate into pieces, and put into a small saucepan with the meaured water and a few tablespoons of the milk. Heat gently, stirring, until the chocolate has melted. Add the remaining milk, stirring to blend.

2 Melt the butter in a pan, add the flour, and cook, stirring, for 1 minute. Remove from the heat, and gradually add the chocolate and milk mixture. Bring to a boil, stirring, until the sauce has thickened. Stir in the vanilla essence and caster sugar, and leave to cool.

3 Beat the egg yolks into the cooled chocolate mixture. Lightly butter the individual soufflé dishes and set aside.

4 Whisk the egg whites until stiff but not dry. Stir 1 large spoonful of the egg whites into the chocolate mixture, then carefully fold in the remainder. Divide the mixture between the 4 soufflé dishes.

5 Place on a hot baking tray and bake in a preheated oven at 190°C (375°F, Gas 5) for 40–45 minutes until the soufflés are well risen and firm. Dust with sifted icing sugar. Serve the soufflés at once.

Cook's know-how

If you prefer, you can make 1 large soufflé instead of individual soufflés. Simply use 1 x 1.25 litre (2 pint) soufflé dish and bake in the oven for 45–50 minutes. Another alternative is to make 8 small soufflés, ideal for a dinner party after a rich main course. If you use 8 x 150 ml (1/4 pint) dishes they will take about 20–30 minutes to bake in the oven.

BREAD & BUTTER PUDDING

SERVES 6

12 thin slices of white bread, crusts removed
about 125 g (4 oz) butter, softened, plus extra for greasing
175 g (6 oz) mixed dried fruit
grated zest of 2 lemons
125 g (4 oz) demerara sugar
600 ml (1 pint) milk
2 eggs
1.7 LITRE (3 PINT) OVENPROOF DISH

1 Spread one side of each slice of bread with a thick layer of butter. Cut each slice of bread in half diagonally. Lightly butter the ovenproof dish and arrange 12 of the triangles, buttered-side down, in the bottom of the dish.

2 Sprinkle over half of the dried fruit, lemon zest, and sugar. Top with the remaining bread, buttered-side up. Sprinkle over the remaining fruit, lemon zest, and sugar.

3 Beat together the milk and eggs, and strain over the bread. Leave for 1 hour so that the bread can absorb some of the liquid.

4 Bake in a preheated oven at 180°C (350°F, Gas 4) for about 40 minutes until the bread slices on the top of the pudding are a golden brown colour and crisp, and the custard mixture has set completely. Serve at once.

BREAD & BUTTER PUDDING WITH MARMALADE

Spread 6 of the slices of bread with thick-cut marmalade after spreading all of them with the butter. Halve the slices, and arrange the buttered ones buttered-side down in the dish. Sprinkle with the dried fruit, lemon zest, and sugar, then arrange the remaining triangles, marmalade-side up, on top.

BREAD & BUTTER PUDDING WITH APRICOTS

Add 60 g (2 oz) roughly chopped ready-to-eat dried apricots to the dried fruit.

RICE PUDDING

SERVES 4

15 g (1/2 oz) butter, plus extra for buttering the dish
60 g (2 oz) short-grain (pudding) rice
600 ml (1 pint) milk
30 g (1 oz) caster sugar
1 strip of lemon zest
1/4 tsp grated nutmeg
900 ML (1 1/2 PINT) OVENPROOF DISH

1 Lightly butter the ovenproof dish. Rinse the rice under cold running water and drain well.

2 Put the rice into the dish and stir in the milk. Leave for about 30 minutes to allow the rice to soften.

3 Add the caster sugar and lemon zest to the rice mixture, and stir to mix. Sprinkle the surface of the milk with freshly grated nutmeg and dot with small knobs of butter.

4 Bake in a preheated oven at 150°C (300°F, Gas 2) for 2–2 1/2 hours until the skin of the pudding is brown. Serve at once.

Cook's know-how

Pudding rice has short, rounded grains which absorb the milk to give a rich, creamy consistency. For the creamiest pudding, use full-fat milk.

CHILLED RICE WITH PEARS

Let the pudding cool, then lift off the skin. Chill the pudding and serve in glass dishes, topped with slices of poached fresh or canned pears, topped with melted strawberry jam.

CHRISTMAS PUDDING

This is a rich, dark pudding, laden with dried fruit, spices, and alcohol – the traditional way to finish the festive meal. A delicious cold alternative is the Iced Christmas Pudding on page 493.

SERVES 8–10

90 g (3 oz) self-raising flour

125 g (4 oz) shredded vegetable suet or grated chilled butter

30 g (1 oz) blanched almonds, shredded

125 g (4 oz) carrot, grated

250 g (8 oz) raisins

125 g (4 oz) currants

125 g (4 oz) sultanas

125 g (4 oz) fresh breadcrumbs

1/4 tsp grated nutmeg

60 g (2 oz) mixed candied peel, chopped

90 g (3 oz) light muscovado sugar

grated zest and juice of 1 lemon

2 eggs, beaten

butter for greasing

75 ml (2 1/2 fl oz) dark rum or brandy

brandy butter to serve

1.25 LITRE (2 PINT) PUDDING BOWL

1 In a large bowl, combine the flour, suet or butter, almonds, carrot, raisins, currants, sultanas, breadcrumbs, nutmeg, candied peel, sugar, and lemon zest. Add the lemon juice and eggs, and stir until well combined.

2 Lightly butter the pudding bowl. Spoon in the pudding mixture and level the surface.

3 Cover with buttered greaseproof paper, then foil, both pleated in the middle. Secure the paper and foil in place by tying string under the rim of the bowl (page 431).

4 Put the bowl into a steamer or saucepan of simmering water, making sure the water comes halfway up the side of the bowl. Cover and steam, topping up with boiling water as needed, for about 6 hours.

5 Remove the bowl from the steamer or pan and leave to cool. Remove the paper and foil covering. Make a few holes in the pudding with a fine skewer, and pour in the rum or brandy.

6 Cover the pudding with fresh greaseproof paper and foil. Store in a cool place for up to 3 months.

7 To reheat for serving, steam the pudding for 2–3 hours. Serve at once, with brandy butter.

Brandy butter

Make your own brandy butter by creaming together 250 g (8 oz) each of unsalted butter and caster sugar or icing sugar, and 90 ml (3 fl oz) brandy. The brandy butter can be frozen for up to 3 months.

STEAMED JAM PUDDING

SERVES 4–6

125 g (4 oz) soft butter or margarine, plus extra for greasing

3 tbsp jam

125 g (4 oz) caster sugar

2 eggs, beaten

175 g (6 oz) self-raising flour

1 tsp baking powder

about 1 tbsp milk

1.25 LITRE (2 PINT) PUDDING BOWL

1 Lightly grease the pudding bowl, and spoon the jam into the bottom.

2 Put the butter or margarine, sugar, eggs, flour, and baking powder into a large bowl, and beat until smooth and thoroughly blended. Add enough milk to give a dropping consistency.

3 Spoon the mixture into the pudding bowl, and smooth the surface. Cover with greased greaseproof paper and foil, both pleated in the middle. Secure with string (page 431).

4 Put the bowl into a steamer or saucepan of simmering water, making sure the water comes halfway up the side of the bowl. Cover and steam, topping up with boiling water as needed, for about 1 1/2 hours. Turn the pudding out on to a warmed plate, and serve hot.

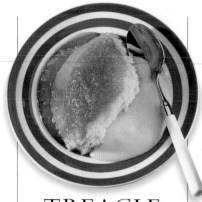

TREACLE PUDDING

SERVES 4–6

butter for greasing

90 ml (3 fl oz) golden syrup

125 g (4 oz) self-raising flour

125 g (4 oz) shredded vegetable suet or grated chilled butter

125 g (4 oz) fresh white breadcrumbs

60 g (2 oz) caster sugar

about 125 ml (4 fl oz) milk

900 ML (1½ PINT) PUDDING BOWL

1 Lightly butter the bowl and spoon the golden syrup into the bottom.

2 Put the flour, suet or butter, breadcrumbs, and sugar into a bowl and stir to combine. Stir in enough milk to give a dropping consistency. Spoon into the bowl on top of the syrup.

3 Cover the bowl with buttered baking parchment and foil, both pleated in the middle. Secure by tying string under the rim of the bowl (page 431).

4 Put the bowl into a steamer or saucepan of simmering water, making sure the water comes halfway up the side of the bowl if using a saucepan. Cover and steam, topping up with boiling water as needed, for about 3 hours. Turn out the pudding, and serve.

MINCEMEAT & ALMOND TART

This is a rich dessert, ideal for a Christmas dinner party or lunch. For an everyday pudding you could use a little less mincemeat and add some stewed apple, which will give a lighter texture and flavour.

SERVES 8–10

175 g (6 oz) butter, softened

175 g (6 oz) caster sugar

4 eggs

175 g (6 oz) ground almonds

1 tsp almond essence

about 8 tbsp good-quality mincemeat

PASTRY

250 g (8 oz) plain flour

125 g (4 oz) chilled butter, cut into cubes

60 g (2 oz) caster sugar

1 egg, beaten

TOPPING

175 g (6 oz) icing sugar, sifted

juice of ½ lemon

1–2 tbsp water

60 g (2 oz) flaked almonds

DEEP 28 CM (11 IN) LOOSE-BOTTOMED FLUTED FLAN TIN

1 Make the pastry: put the flour into a large bowl. Add the butter and rub in with the fingertips until the mixture resembles fine breadcrumbs. Stir in the sugar, then mix in the egg to bind to a soft, pliable dough. Wrap the dough in cling film and chill for about 30 minutes.

2 Roll out the dough on a lightly floured surface and use to line the tin. Prick the bottom with a fork. Cover and chill while preparing the filling.

3 Put the butter and sugar into a large bowl and cream together until pale and fluffy. Add the eggs one at a time, beating well after each addition, then mix in the ground almonds and almond essence.

4 Spread the mincemeat evenly over the bottom of the pastry shell. Pour the almond mixture over the mincemeat.

5 Bake in a preheated oven at 190°C (375°F, Gas 5) for about 40 minutes until the filling is golden and firm to the touch. Cover loosely with foil if it is browning too much.

6 Meanwhile, make the topping: stir together the icing sugar, lemon juice, and enough water to make a thin glacé icing. Spread evenly over the tart, then sprinkle with the almonds.

7 Return to the oven for 5 minutes or until the icing is shiny and the almonds lightly coloured. Serve warm or cold.

STRAWBERRY & RHUBARB PIE

SERVES 6–8

150 g (5 oz) caster sugar, plus extra for sprinkling

45 g (1¹/₂ oz) cornflour

750 g (1¹/₂ lb) rhubarb, cut into 1 cm (¹/₂ in) slices

1 cinnamon stick, halved

375 g (12 oz) strawberries, hulled and halved

SHORTCRUST PASTRY

175 g (6 oz) plain flour

90 g (3 oz) chilled butter, cut into cubes

about 2 tbsp cold water

23 CM (9 IN) FLAN DISH OR TIN

1 Make the pastry: put the flour into a large bowl, add the butter, and rub in with the fingertips until the mixture resembles fine breadcrumbs. Add enough water to bind to a soft, but not sticky dough. Wrap the pastry in cling film and leave to chill in the refrigerator for about 30 minutes.

2 Meanwhile, combine the sugar with the cornflour and toss with the rhubarb, cinnamon, and strawberries. Leave to soak for 15–20 minutes.

3 On a lightly floured surface, divide the dough in half and roll out one half into a thin round to line the bottom and sides of the flan dish.

4 Put the soaked fruit into the pastry shell, removing the cinnamon.

5 Roll out the second half of pastry to the same size as the first round. Cut a 1 cm (¹/₂ in) strip from around the edge of the pastry.

6 Cut the remaining pastry into 1 cm (¹/₂ in) strips and arrange in a lattice on top of the pie. Brush the ends with water and attach the long strip around the rim of the pie. Sprinkle with 1–2 tbsp sugar.

7 Bake in a preheated oven at 220°C (425°F, Gas 7) for 10 minutes; reduce the oven temperature to 180°C (350°F, Gas 4), and bake for a further 30–40 minutes until the fruit is just cooked, and the pastry golden. Serve warm or cold.

BAKED APPLE DUMPLINGS

SERVES 4

4 cooking apples, peeled and cored

60 g (2 oz) demerara sugar

¹/₂ tsp ground cinnamon

milk for glazing

SHORTCRUST PASTRY

375 g (12 oz) plain flour

90 g (3 oz) chilled butter, cut into cubes, plus extra for greasing

90 g (3 oz) chilled white vegetable fat, cut into cubes

3–4 tbsp cold water

1 Make the pastry: put the flour into a large bowl. Add the butter and white vegetable fat, and rub in with the fingertips until the mixture resembles fine breadcrumbs. Mix in enough water to make a soft, pliable dough. Wrap the dough in cling film and chill for about 30 minutes.

2 Divide the dough into 4 pieces. Roll out each piece on a lightly floured surface and cut into an 18 cm (7 in) round. Reserve the trimmings. Put an apple in the centre of each round and make 4 dumplings (see box, above right).

Making the apple dumplings

Fill the apples with the demerara sugar and cinnamon. Draw up a pastry round to enclose each apple, sealing the joins with a little water. Place, with the joins underneath, on a baking tray.

3 Cut leaf shapes from the pastry trimmings, and use to decorate the tops of the dumplings, attaching them with a little water. Make a hole in the top of each dumpling, and lightly brush all over with milk.

4 Bake in a preheated oven at 200°C (400°F, Gas 6) for 35–40 minutes until the pastry is golden and the apples tender. Serve hot.

SWEET WHITE SAUCE

Blend 1 tbsp cornflour with 1 tbsp caster sugar, and a little milk taken from 300 ml (½ pint). Bring the remaining milk to a boil and stir into the cornflour mixture. Return to the saucepan and heat gently, stirring, until thickened. If preferred, add flavourings such as grated orange zest, brandy, rum, or vanilla essence to the sauce. Serve warm.

POURING CUSTARD

Blend together 3 eggs, 30 g (1 oz) caster sugar, and 1 tsp cornflour. Heat 600 ml (1 pint) milk to just below boiling and stir into the egg mixture. Return to the pan and heat gently, stirring, until thickened. Strain into a cold bowl to prevent further cooking, and serve warm or cold.

SABAYON SAUCE

Put 4 egg yolks, 60 g (2 oz) caster sugar, and 150 ml (¼ pint) dry white wine into a bowl over a saucepan of gently simmering water. Whisk for 5–8 minutes or until the mixture is frothy and thick. Remove from the heat and whisk in the grated zest of 1 orange. Serve at once or, to serve cool, continue whisking the mixture until cool.

DOUBLE CRUST APPLE PIE

For a successful double crust pie, the pastry underneath should be properly cooked and not soggy. Putting the dish on a hot baking tray at the start of baking is the key.

SERVES 6

500 g (1 lb) cooking apples, preferably Bramley's, quartered, cored, peeled, and sliced

250 g (8 oz) Cox's apples, quartered, cored, peeled, and sliced

about 30 g (1 oz) caster sugar, plus extra for sprinkling

2 tbsp water

rough puff pastry (page 430)

milk for glazing

24 CM (9½ IN) PIE DISH

1 Put the apples into a large pan and add the sugar and water. Cover and cook gently, stirring, for about 10 minutes until the apples are soft and fluffy. Taste for sweetness and add more sugar if necessary. Turn into a bowl and leave the apples to cool.

2 Divide the pastry into 2 portions, 1 portion slightly larger than the other. Roll out the larger portion on a lightly floured surface and use to line the pie dish.

3 Spoon the apple filling on to the pastry shell, spreading it almost to the edge and then doming it in the middle.

4 Roll out the remaining pastry. Brush the edge of the pastry shell with a little water, then lay the pastry lid over the apple filling. Trim the edge, then crimp to seal. Make a small hole in the pastry lid to allow the steam to escape.

5 Use the pastry trimmings to make leaves to decorate the pie, attaching them with milk. Brush the pastry lid with milk and sprinkle with sugar.

6 Put a baking tray in the oven and preheat the oven to 220°C (425°F, Gas 7). Put the pie dish on the hot baking tray (this helps ensure a crisp pastry base) and bake for 25–30 minutes until the pastry is golden.

DUTCH APPLE PIE

When cooking the apples, substitute light muscovado sugar for the caster sugar, and add 90 g (3 oz) raisins, ½ tsp ground cinnamon, and ½ tsp ground mixed spice to the apple filling.

ST CLEMENT'S APPLE PIE

When cooking the apples, add the grated zest and juice of 1 large lemon, and 3 tbsp fine-cut orange marmalade to the apples.

TARTE TATIN

SERVES 6

90 g (3 oz) butter

90 g (3 oz) demerara sugar

1 kg (2 lb) Cox's apples or similar firm eating apples

grated zest and juice of 1 lemon

PASTRY

175 g (6 oz) plain flour

125 g (4 oz) chilled butter, cut into cubes

30 g (1 oz) icing sugar

1 egg yolk

about 1 tbsp cold water

SHALLOW 23 CM (9 IN) ROUND CAKE TIN

1 Make the pastry: put the flour into a large bowl and add the butter. Rub in until the mixture resembles fine breadcrumbs. Stir in the icing sugar, then mix in the egg yolk and enough water to make a soft, but not sticky, dough. Wrap and chill for 30 minutes.

2 Put the butter and sugar into a pan and heat very gently until the sugar dissolves. Increase the heat and cook gently for 4–5 minutes until the mixture turns dark golden brown and is thick, but pourable. Pour evenly over the bottom of the tin.

3 Peel, core, and slice the apples. Toss them with the lemon zest and juice. Arrange in the cake tin (see box, below).

4 Roll out the pastry on a lightly floured surface into a round slightly larger than the tin. Lay the pastry over the apples, tucking the excess down the side of the tin.

5 Bake in a preheated oven at 200°C (400°F, Gas 6) for 25–30 minutes until the pastry is crisp and golden. Invert a serving plate on top of the tin, turn the tin and plate over, and lift the tin to reveal the caramelized apples. Serve warm or cold.

Arranging the apples in the cake tin

Arrange a single layer of the best apple slices in a circular pattern on top of the caramel mixture. Cover evenly with the remaining apple slices.

APPLE STRUDEL

SERVES 8

four 25 x 45 cm (10 x 18 in) sheets of filo pastry

60 g (2 oz) butter, melted

30 g (1 oz) fresh white breadcrumbs

15 g (1/2 oz) flaked almonds

icing sugar for dusting

FILLING

750 g (1 1/2 lb) cooking apples, quartered, cored, peeled, and sliced

grated zest and juice of 1 lemon

3 tbsp light muscovado sugar

1/2 tsp ground mixed spice

1/2 tsp ground cinnamon

125 g (4 oz) sultanas

60 g (2 oz) blanched almonds, roughly chopped

1 Make the filling: mix together the apples, lemon zest and juice, sugar, mixed spice, cinnamon, sultanas, and almonds.

2 Lightly brush 1 sheet of filo pastry with melted butter. Cover with the remaining sheets, brushing each with butter. Add the filling and finish the strudel (see box, right).

3 Brush the strudel with melted butter and sprinkle with the almonds. Bake in a preheated oven at 190°C (375°F, Gas 5) for 40–45 minutes until the pastry is crisp and golden. Dust with icing sugar. Serve warm or cold.

Finishing the strudel

Sprinkle the breadcrumbs over the pastry. Spoon the apple mixture along the middle of the pastry.

Fold the pastry to enclose the filling, turn over on to a baking tray, and bend into a horseshoe shape.

THE APPLE COLLECTION

Apples have a natural affinity with pastry, and they are the best of fruits to cook with. In these three recipes, pastry is used in different ways to show the apples off to their best advantage – and to make the fruit go further. When you are feeling indulgent, serve with custard, cream, or vanilla ice cream.

APPLE TARTE AU CITRON

SERVES 10

4 eggs

250 g (8 oz) caster sugar

finely grated zest and juice of 2 lemons

125 g (4 oz) butter, melted

2 large cooking apples, eg Bramley's, quartered, cored, and peeled – about 350 g (12 oz) prepared weight

2 red eating apples, quartered, cored, and thinly sliced (leave the red skin on)

about 30 g (1 oz) demerara sugar

PASTRY

250 g (8 oz) plain flour

30 g (1 oz) icing sugar

125 g (4 oz) butter, cubed

1 egg, beaten

1 Make the pastry: sift the flour and icing sugar into a bowl and rub in the cubes of butter until the mixture resembles breadcrumbs. Stir in the egg and bring together to form a dough. (If making the pastry in a food processor, process the flour, butter, and icing sugar until like breadcrumbs, pour in the beaten egg, and pulse until the dough forms a ball.) Form the pastry into a smooth ball, put inside a plastic bag, and chill in the refrigerator for at least 30 minutes.

2 Roll out the chilled dough on a lightly floured surface and use to line a deep 25 cm (10 in) loose-bottomed flan tin. Chill again for 30 minutes.

3 Prepare the filling: beat the eggs, caster sugar, and lemon zest and juice in a bowl. Stir in the warm melted butter, then coarsely grate the cooking apples directly into mixture and mix well.

4 Spread the runny lemon mixture in the chilled pastry case. Level the surface with the back of a spoon and arrange the red-skinned apples around the outside edge.

5 Bake on a hot baking sheet in a preheated oven at 200°C (400°F, Gas 6) for about 40–50 minutes or until the centre feels firm to the touch and the apples are tinged brown.

CLASSIC APPLE CRUMBLE

SERVES 6

900 g (2 lb) cooking apples, eg Bramley's

175 g (6 oz) granulated sugar

finely grated zest of 1 lemon

6 tbsp water

TOPPING

175 g (6 oz) plain flour

90 g (3 oz) butter

60 g (2 oz) demerara sugar

1 Quarter, peel, and core the apples, then slice them fairly thinly. Toss the slices in the sugar, lemon zest, and water. Put in a shallow 20 cm (8 in) ovenproof dish.

2 Make the topping: put the flour in a bowl and rub in the butter until the mixture resembles fine breadcrumbs, then stir in the sugar.

3 Sprinkle the topping evenly over the apple mixture in the dish and bake in a preheated oven at 180°C (350°F, Gas 4) for 40–45 minutes until golden brown and bubbling.

> ### Cook's know-how
>
> For a crunchier topping on the Classic Apple Crumble, use 125 g (4 oz) wholemeal flour and 60 g (2 oz) porridge oats or muesli instead of the plain flour.
>
> To sweeten cooking apples, especially windfall apples that are not at their best, use apricot jam instead of some – or all – of the sugar. Apricot jam gives a gentle sweetness, and it improves the texture of the apples, especially if you are using them for a purée or a pie.

BLACKBERRY & APPLE COBBLER

SERVES 4

2 cooking apples, eg Bramley's

500 g (1 lb) blackberries

60 g (2 oz) caster sugar

finely grated zest and juice of 1 lemon

COBBLER TOPPING

250 g (8 oz) self-raising flour

60 g (2 oz) butter, cubed

90 g (3 oz) caster sugar

90 ml (3 fl oz) milk, plus extra for glazing

5 CM (2 IN) ROUND FLUTED BISCUIT CUTTER

1 Quarter, peel, and core the apples, then cut into large slices, about 1 cm (1/2 in) thick.

2 Put the apples into a saucepan with the blackberries, sugar, and lemon zest and juice. Cover and simmer gently for 10–15 minutes until the apple pieces are tender but not broken up.

3 Meanwhile, make the cobbler topping: put the flour into a bowl, add the cubes of butter, and rub in with the fingertips until the mixture resembles fine breadcrumbs. Stir in the sugar, add the milk, and mix to form a soft dough.

4 Roll out the dough on a lightly floured surface until 1 cm (1/2 in) thick. Cut out as many shapes as you can with the biscuit cutter, then re-roll the trimmings and cut out more. If you do not have a biscuit cutter, stamp out rounds with the rim of a glass or coffee mug.

5 Transfer the fruit to an ovenproof dish, arrange the pastry shapes on top and brush with milk to glaze.

6 Bake in a preheated oven at 220°C (425°F, Gas 7) for 15–20 minutes until the cobbler topping is golden.

CLOCKWISE FROM TOP RIGHT: Classic Apple Crumble, Apple Tarte au Citron, Blackberry & Apple Cobbler.

TREACLE TART

SERVES 8

375 g (12 oz) golden syrup

about 200 g (7 oz) fresh white or brown breadcrumbs

grated zest and juice of 1 large lemon

PASTRY

175 g (6 oz) plain flour

90 g (3 oz) chilled butter, cut into cubes

about 2 tbsp cold water

25 CM (10 IN) LOOSE-BOTTOMED FLUTED FLAN TIN

1 Make the pastry: put the flour into a large bowl, add the butter, and rub in with the fingertips until the mixture resembles fine breadcrumbs. Mix in enough water to make a soft pliable dough.

2 Wrap the dough in cling film and leave to chill in the refrigerator for about 30 minutes.

3 Roll out the dough on a lightly floured surface and use to line the flan tin.

4 Gently heat the golden syrup in a saucepan until melted, and stir in the breadcrumbs and lemon zest and juice. Pour into the pastry shell.

5 Bake in a preheated oven at 200°C (400°F, Gas 6) for 10 minutes; reduce the oven temperature to 180°C (350°F, Gas 4), and bake for a further 30 minutes or until the pastry is golden and the filling firm.

6 Leave to cool in the tin for a few minutes. Serve warm, cut into slices.

Cook's know-how

To weigh the golden syrup, put the pan on the scales set to zero and pour in the syrup from the can.

FRENCH APPLE TART

SERVES 8–10

90 g (3 oz) butter

1.5 kg (3 lb) cooking apples, quartered, cored, and cut into chunks

3 tbsp water

6 tbsp apricot jam

125 g (4 oz) caster sugar

grated zest of 1 large lemon

APPLE TOPPING & GLAZE

375 g (12 oz) eating apples, quartered, cored, peeled, and sliced

juice of 1 lemon

1 tbsp caster sugar

6 tbsp apricot jam

PASTRY

250 g (8 oz) plain flour

125 g (4 oz) chilled butter, cubed

125 g (4 oz) caster sugar

4 egg yolks

28 CM (11 IN) LOOSE-BOTTOMED FLUTED FLAN TIN

BAKING BEANS

1 Make the pastry: put the flour into a bowl and rub in the butter until the mixture resembles fine breadcrumbs. Stir in the sugar, then the egg yolks and a little cold water, if needed, to make a soft dough. Wrap and chill for 30 minutes.

2 Melt the butter in a large saucepan, and add the cooking apples and water. Cover and cook very gently for 20–25 minutes until the apples are soft.

3 Rub the apples through a nylon sieve into a clean pan. Add the jam, sugar, and lemon zest. Cook over a high heat for 15–20 minutes, stirring constantly, until all the liquid has evaporated and the apple purée is thick. Leave to cool.

4 Roll out the pastry on a lightly floured surface and use to line the flan tin. Bake blind (page 431) in a preheated oven at 190°C (375°F, Gas 5) for 10–15 minutes. Remove the beans and foil and bake for another 5 minutes. Cool.

5 Spoon the apple purée into the shell. Arrange the apple slices on top, brush with lemon juice, and sprinkle with caster sugar. Return to the oven and bake for 30–35 minutes until the apples are tender and their edges lightly browned.

6 Heat the jam, work through a sieve, then brush over the apples. Serve warm or cold.

450

BAKEWELL TART

SERVES 6

125 g (4 oz) butter

125 g (4 oz) caster sugar

I egg, lightly beaten

125 g (4 oz) ground rice or semolina

1/2 tsp almond essence

2 tbsp raspberry jam

icing sugar for sprinkling

PASTRY

175 g (6 oz) plain flour

45 g (1 1/2 oz) chilled butter, cut into cubes

45 g (1 1/2 oz) chilled white vegetable fat, cut into cubes

about 2 tbsp cold water

milk for glazing

19 CM (7 1/2 IN) LOOSE-BOTTOMED FLUTED FLAN TIN

1 Make the pastry: put the flour into a large bowl. Rub in the butter and vegetable fat until the mixture resembles fine breadcrumbs. Mix in enough water to make a soft, pliable dough. Wrap in cling film and chill for 30 minutes.

2 Roll out the pastry on a lightly floured work surface and use to line the flan tin. Reserve the trimmings.

3 Melt the butter in a saucepan, stir in the caster sugar, and cook for about 1 minute. Remove from the heat, leave to cool a little, then gradually stir in the egg, ground rice or semolina, and almond essence.

4 Spread the jam evenly over the bottom of the pastry shell, and pour the almond mixture on top.

5 Roll out the reserved pastry trimmings, and cut into thin strips, long enough to fit across the tart. Arrange the strips on top of the almond filling to form a lattice, attaching them to the edge of the pastry shell with a little milk.

6 Bake in a preheated oven at 200°C (400°F, Gas 6) for 45–50 minutes until the filling is well risen and golden and springs back when lightly pressed with a finger. If the pastry is browning too much, cover the tart loosely with foil.

7 Remove the tart from the oven. Sprinkle with icing sugar and serve the tart warm or cold.

PECAN PIE

SERVES 6–8

150 g (5 oz) pecan halves

30 g (1 oz) unsalted butter

60 g (2 oz) light muscovado sugar

30 g (1 oz) caster sugar

125 ml (4 fl oz) golden syrup

3 tbsp brandy

I tsp vanilla essence

2 tbsp single cream

1/4 tsp ground cinnamon

pinch of grated nutmeg

I large egg, lightly beaten

2 egg yolks

PASTRY

175 g (6 oz) plain flour

90 g (3 oz) chilled butter, cubed

about 2 tbsp cold water

I egg white, lightly beaten

23 CM (9 IN) LOOSE-BOTTOMED FLUTED FLAN TIN

BAKING BEANS

1 Make the pastry: put the flour into a bowl, add the butter, and rub in with the fingertips until the mixture resembles fine breadcrumbs. Add enough water to make a soft dough. Leave to chill for about 30 minutes.

2 Roll out the pastry on a lightly floured work surface and line the flan tin. Bake blind (page 431) in a preheated oven at 180°C (350°F, Gas 4) for 10 minutes.

3 Remove the beans and foil, lightly brush the pastry shell with egg white, and return to the oven for 1–2 minutes.

4 Meanwhile, toast the pecans in a preheated oven at 180°C (350°F, Gas 4), turning occasionally, for 10–15 minutes. Reserve a few pecan halves and coarsely chop the remainder.

5 Put the butter into a heavy saucepan and cook over a gentle heat until it turns golden brown. Add the sugars and golden syrup, and heat gently until the sugars dissolve. Add the brandy, bring to a boil, and cook for 5 minutes.

6 Remove from the heat and stir in the vanilla essence, cream, cinnamon, and nutmeg.

7 Whisk together the egg and egg yolks. Whisk a little hot syrup into the eggs. Add half of the syrup, little by little, then add the remainder. Leave to cool.

8 Arrange the chopped pecans and pecan halves in the pastry shell. Pour the syrup and egg mixture over them. Bake in a preheated oven at 180°C (350°F, Gas 4) for about 40 minutes until golden brown and set. Leave to cool before serving.

FRENCH APRICOT & ALMOND TART

So often the star of French pâtisserie, this golden fruit tart is easy enough to make at home. Fresh apricots really make it special, but if they are not available, canned apricots can be used instead.

SERVES 10

crème pâtissière (see box, right)

TOPPING

1 kg (2 lb) fresh apricots, halved and stoned

juice of 1 lemon

125 ml (4 fl oz) water

75 g (2½ oz) caster sugar

1 tsp arrowroot

1 tbsp brandy

30 g (1 oz) toasted flaked almonds

PASTRY

250 g (8 oz) plain flour

125 g (4 oz) chilled butter, cubed

60 g (2 oz) caster sugar

1 egg, beaten

28 CM (11 IN) LOOSE-BOTTOMED FLUTED FLAN TIN

BAKING BEANS

1 Sift the flour into a large bowl. Add the butter and rub in until the mixture resembles fine breadcrumbs.

2 Stir in the sugar, then mix in the egg to make a soft, pliable dough. Wrap in cling film and chill for 30 minutes.

3 Roll out the pastry on a lightly floured surface and use to line the flan tin. Bake blind (page 431) in a preheated oven at 200°C (400°F, Gas 6) for 10 minutes until the pastry shell is beginning to brown at the edge. Remove the beans and foil and bake for another 5–10 minutes. Leave to cool.

4 Put the apricots, cut-side down, in a shallow pan with the lemon juice, measured water, and sugar. Cover tightly and bring to a boil. Lower the heat and simmer gently for 3 minutes or until just soft.

5 Remove the apricots with a slotted spoon, reserving the juices. Drain on paper towels, and leave to cool.

6 Remove the pastry shell from the flan tin and put on a serving plate. Spread the crème pâtissière over the pastry shell, and smooth the surface.

7 Arrange the apricots, cut-side down, on the crème pâtissière. Combine the arrowroot and brandy in a small bowl and stir in the reserved apricot juices.

8 Return the mixture to the pan and bring to a boil, stirring until thick. Add the toasted flaked almonds.

9 Spoon the glaze over the apricots, making sure they are evenly coated. (Add a little water to the glaze if it is too thick.) Leave to stand until the glaze has cooled and set. Serve the tart cold.

Crème pâtissière

Put 3 eggs, 90 g (3 oz) vanilla sugar, and 60 g (2 oz) plain flour into a large bowl, add a little milk taken from 400 ml (14 fl oz), and mix until smooth. Pour the remaining milk into a heavy saucepan and bring almost to a boil. Pour on to the egg mixture, whisking well.

Rinse out the saucepan to remove any milk residue. Return the egg mixture to the pan, and cook over a gentle heat, stirring continuously, until thickened.

Pour into a bowl and cover with cling film, gently pressing it over the surface of the custard to prevent a skin from forming. Leave to cool.

LEMON MERINGUE PIE

SERVES 8–10

grated zest and juice of 4 large lemons
90 g (3 oz) cornflour
600 ml (1 pint) water
4 egg yolks
175 g (6 oz) caster sugar

MERINGUE

5 egg whites
250 g (8 oz) caster sugar

PASTRY

250 g (8 oz) plain flour
30 g (1 oz) icing sugar
125 g (4 oz) chilled butter, cut into cubes
1 egg yolk
2 tbsp cold water
25 CM (10 IN) LOOSE-BOTTOMED FLUTED FLAN TIN
BAKING BEANS

1 Make the pastry: sift the flour and icing sugar into a large bowl. Add the butter and rub in with the fingertips until the mixture resembles fine breadcrumbs.

2 Mix in the egg yolk and enough cold water to make a soft, pliable dough. Wrap the dough in cling film and chill in the refrigerator for about 30 minutes.

3 Roll out the dough on a lightly floured surface and use to line the flan tin. Bake blind (page 431) in a preheated oven at 200°C (400°F, Gas 6) for 10 minutes.

4 Remove the baking beans and foil and bake the pastry shell for 5 minutes or until the base has dried out. Remove from the oven and reduce the temperature to 150°C (300°F, Gas 2).

5 Mix the lemon zest and juice with the cornflour. Bring the water to a boil, then stir into the lemon mixture. Return to the pan and bring back to a boil, stirring, until the mixture thickens. Remove from heat.

6 Leave to cool slightly, then stir in the egg yolks and sugar. Return to a low heat and cook, stirring, until just simmering. Pour into the pastry shell.

7 Whisk the egg whites until stiff but not dry. Whisk in the sugar 1 tsp at a time. Pile on top of the filling and spread over evenly. Bake for 45 minutes or until crisp and brown. Serve the pie warm or cold.

TARTE AU CITRON

SERVES 10–12

9 eggs
300 ml (1/2 pint) double cream
grated zest and juice of 5 large lemons
375 g (12 oz) caster sugar
icing sugar for dusting
lemon twists to decorate

PASTRY

250 g (8 oz) plain flour
125 g (4 oz) chilled butter, cut into cubes
60 g (2 oz) caster sugar
1 egg
28 CM (11 IN) LOOSE-BOTTOMED FLUTED FLAN TIN
BAKING BEANS

1 Make the pastry: put the flour into a large bowl. Add the butter and rub in with the fingertips until the mixture resembles fine breadcrumbs.

2 Stir in the caster sugar, then bind together with the egg to make a soft, pliable dough. Wrap in cling film and chill for 30 minutes.

3 Roll out the dough on a lightly floured surface and use to line the flan tin. Bake blind (page 431) in a preheated oven at 200°C (400°F, Gas 6) for 10 minutes.

4 Remove the baking beans and foil and bake the pastry shell for 5 minutes or until the base has dried out. Remove from the oven and reduce the oven temperature to 180°C (350°F, Gas 4).

5 Beat the eggs in a bowl and add the cream, lemon zest and juice, and caster sugar. Stir until smooth, and pour into the pastry shell.

6 Bake for 35–40 minutes until the lemon filling has set. Cover the tart loosely with foil if the pastry begins to brown too much.

7 Leave the tart to cool a little, then dust with icing sugar. Decorate with lemon twists, and serve warm or at room temperature.

KEY LIME PIE

SERVES 8

300 ml (1/2 pint) double cream

1 x 400 g (13 oz) can sweetened condensed milk

grated zest and juice of 1 lime

lime slices to decorate

PASTRY

175 g (6 oz) plain flour

90 g (3 oz) chilled butter, cut into cubes

about 2 tbsp cold water

23 CM (9 IN) LOOSE-BOTTOMED FLUTED FLAN TIN

BAKING BEANS

1 Make the pastry: put the flour into a large bowl, add the butter, and rub in until the mixture resembles fine breadcrumbs. Add enough cold water to make a soft pliable dough.

2 Wrap the dough in cling film or foil and chill in the refrigerator for 30 minutes.

3 Roll out the dough on a lightly floured surface and use to line the flan tin.

4 Bake the pastry shell blind (page 395) in a preheated oven at 200°C (400°F, Gas 6) for about 10 minutes. Remove the baking beans and foil and return the shell to the oven for 5 minutes. Cool slightly.

5 Whip the cream to soft peaks in a large bowl and mix together with the condensed milk. Slowly stir in the lime zest and juice until the mixture thickens.

6 Pour the mixture into the shell and smooth the top, or create a pattern with a palette knife. Chill in the refrigerator for at least 2 hours or until the filling is set firm.

7 Serve the pie chilled, decorated with lime slices.

BANOFFI PIE

SERVES 6

90 g (3 oz) butter

1 x 400 g (13 oz) can sweetened condensed milk

2 bananas, peeled and sliced

150 ml (1/4 pint) double cream, lightly whipped

30 g (1 oz) plain chocolate, grated, to decorate

BISCUIT CRUST

60 g (2 oz) butter

150 g (5 oz) ginger biscuits, crushed

18 CM (7 IN) LOOSE-BOTTOMED FLUTED FLAN TIN

1 Make the biscuit crust (see box, right).

2 Melt the butter in a small saucepan over a low heat. Stir until the butter has melted.

3 Add the condensed milk to the pan, and heat gently, stirring constantly, until the mixture is a pale caramel colour, about 10 minutes. The butter may separate from the condensed milk, but the mixture will be smooth when cooled slightly.

4 Pour the mixture into the biscuit crust and leave to cool. Chill until the caramel filling is set.

5 Arrange the banana slices evenly over the caramel filling. Top with the whipped cream, and decorate with the grated chocolate. Serve chilled.

Making the biscuit crust

Melt the butter in a saucepan, add the crushed biscuits, and stir well to combine. Press on to the bottom and side of the flan tin. Chill until set.

MISSISSIPPI MUD PIE

SERVES 8–10

200 g (7 oz) plain chocolate

125 g (4 oz) butter

1 tbsp coffee essence

3 eggs

150 ml (¼ pint) single cream

175 g (6 oz) dark muscovado sugar

150 ml (¼ pint) whipping cream to decorate

PASTRY

250 g (8 oz) plain flour

125 g (4 oz) chilled butter, cut into cubes

about 2–3 tbsp cold water

25 CM (10 IN) LOOSE-BOTTOMED FLUTED FLAN TIN

BAKING BEANS

1 Make the pastry: put the flour into a large bowl. Add the butter and rub in until the mixture resembles fine breadcrumbs. Add enough cold water to make a soft pliable dough.

2 Wrap the dough and chill for 30 minutes.

3 Roll out the dough on a lightly floured surface and use to line the flan tin.

4 Bake the pastry shell blind (page 431) in a preheated oven at 200°C (400°F, Gas 6) for about 10 minutes until the pastry edge begins to brown.

5 Remove the baking beans and foil and bake for a further 5 minutes or until the base has dried out. Remove the pastry shell from the oven, and reduce the oven temperature to 190°C (375°F, Gas 5).

6 Break the chocolate into pieces, and place in a heavy pan with the butter and coffee essence. Heat gently, stirring occasionally, until the chocolate and butter have melted. Remove from the heat. Leave the mixture to cool slightly.

7 Beat the eggs, then add to the saucepan with the cream and sugar. Stir thoroughly to mix.

8 Pour the filling into the pastry shell. Bake for 30–35 minutes until the filling has set. Leave to cool.

9 Pipe whipped cream rosettes around the edge of the pie before serving.

BANANA CUSTARD TART WITH BERRIES

SERVES 6–8

200 g (7 oz) sugar

3 tbsp cornflour

1 tbsp plain flour

pinch of salt

2 egg yolks, lightly beaten

175 ml (6 fl oz) milk

175 ml (6 fl oz) double cream

1 tsp vanilla essence

2 ripe bananas, peeled and sliced

125 g (4 oz) raspberries

250 ml (8 fl oz) whipping or double cream, chilled

2 tbsp caster sugar

PASTRY

175 g (6 oz) plain flour

90 g (3 oz) chilled butter, cubed

3 tbsp muesli

about 2–3 tbsp cold water

23 CM (9 IN) LOOSE-BOTTOMED FLUTED FLAN TIN

BAKING BEANS

1 Make the pastry: put the flour into a bowl, add the butter, and rub in with the fingertips until it resembles fine breadcrumbs. Mix in the muesli. Add enough cold water to make a soft pliable dough. Chill for 30 minutes.

2 Roll out the pastry on a lightly floured work surface and use to line the tin (patch it with your fingers if the dough breaks).

3 Bake the pastry shell blind (page 431) in a preheated oven at 200°C (400°F, Gas 6) for 10 minutes. Remove the beans and foil and bake for a further 10–15 minutes.

4 Combine the sugar, cornflour, flour, and salt. Mix together the egg yolks, milk, and cream, and whisk into the cornflour mixture.

5 Cook over a medium heat, stirring constantly, until the mixture boils and thickens. If the egg begins to curdle or stick, lower the heat. Remove from the heat, stir in the vanilla essence, and leave to cool.

6 Spread half of the custard over the pastry shell and arrange the fruit on top, reserving some berries for decoration. Spread with the remaining custard. Chill until serving time.

7 Before serving, whip the cream with the caster sugar until it forms stiff peaks. Spread over the pie, and decorate with the reserved berries.

FRUIT TARTLETS

A mouth-watering combination of crisp golden pastry, creamy filling, and refreshing fruits always makes a special treat, whether served as a dessert or as part of a teatime spread. For convenience, use the same pastry and filling, but vary the toppings for a stunning display.

RASPBERRY TARTLETS

MAKES 16

250 g (8 oz) mascarpone
2 tbsp caster sugar
350 g (12 oz) raspberries
3 tbsp redcurrant jelly
1–2 tsp lemon juice to taste

PASTRY

250 g (8 oz) plain flour
125 g (4 oz) chilled butter, cut into cubes
2 tbsp caster sugar
3–4 tbsp cold water
7 CM (3 IN) PASTRY CUTTER
16 X 6 CM (2½ IN) ROUND TARTLET TINS

1 Make the pastry: put the flour into a bowl, add the butter, and rub in with the fingertips until the mixture resembles fine breadcrumbs. Stir in the sugar, then add enough cold water to bind to a soft pliable dough. Wrap and chill for at least 30 minutes.

2 On a lightly floured surface, roll out the pastry thinly. Using the pastry cutter, cut out 16 rounds.

3 Gently press the rounds into the tartlet tins. Prick all over with a fork and bake in a preheated oven at 190°C (375°F, Gas 5) for 12–15 minutes until golden. Leave in the tins for 10 minutes, then remove and transfer to a wire rack. Leave to cool completely.

4 Beat together the mascarpone and sugar and spoon into the pastry shells. Top with the raspberries, pressing them gently into the filling.

5 Melt the jelly with lemon juice to taste in a small pan, then spoon over the fruits. Leave to set before serving.

BLUEBERRY PUFFS

MAKES 8

500 g (1 lb) ready-made puff pastry
beaten egg
100 g (4 oz) blueberries
150 ml (5 fl oz) double or whipping cream
1 tbsp caster sugar
1 ripe nectarine or peach, stoned and sliced
icing sugar for dusting

1 Roll out the pastry until 5 mm (¼ in) thick on a lightly floured surface. Cut into strips 7 cm (3 in) wide, then cut the strips diagonally into 8 diamond shapes.

2 With a sharp knife, score each pastry diamond 1 cm (½ in) from the edge, taking care not to cut all the way through. Place on a dampened baking tray and glaze with beaten egg.

3 Bake in a preheated oven at 230°C (450°F, Gas 8) for 10–15 minutes until golden. Transfer to a wire rack. Remove the pastry centres, reserving them for lids if desired. Leave to cool.

4 Divide half of the blueberries among the pastry shells. Whip the cream and sugar and divide among the shells. Top with nectarine or peach slices, and the remaining blueberries. Dust the pastry lids with icing sugar, replace, and serve.

TROPICAL TARTLETS

MAKES 10

about 600 ml (1 pint) ready-made thick custard
1 x 200 g (7 oz) can mandarin oranges in natural juice, well drained
1 x 200 g (7 oz) can apricot halves in natural juice, well drained and cut into pieces
about 3 tbsp apricot jam
about 60 g (2 oz) toasted flaked almonds

ALMOND PASTRY

60 g (2 oz) ground almonds
125 g (4 oz) plain flour
2 tbsp caster sugar
90 g (3 oz) chilled butter, cut into cubes
about 3 tbsp cold water
10 X 7 CM (3 IN) ROUND TARTLET TINS OR BOAT-SHAPED TINS (BARQUETTE MOULDS)

1 Make the pastry: combine the almonds, flour, and sugar in a bowl. Add the butter and rub in with the fingertips until the mixture resembles fine breadcrumbs. Add enough cold water to make a soft pliable dough. Wrap and chill for 1 hour.

2 Put the pastry on a floured surface and flatten slightly. Place a large sheet of baking parchment on top and roll out the pastry, beneath the parchment, until about 3 mm (⅛ in) thick. Line the tartlet tins with pastry and chill for 2 hours.

3 Prick the pastry all over and bake in a preheated oven at 190°C (375°F, Gas 5) for 10 minutes. Leave the shells to cool in the tins for 10 minutes. Remove and transfer to a wire rack. Leave to cool.

4 Spoon custard into each shell, then top with the mandarin oranges and apricots. Melt the jam in a small pan, sieve, then spoon over the fruit. Sprinkle with the almonds and leave to set before serving.

CLOCKWISE FROM TOP: Raspberry Tartlets, Blueberry Puffs, Tropical Tartlets.

MILLE-FEUILLE

SERVES 6

250 g (8 oz) puff pastry, thawed if frozen

3 tbsp raspberry jam

150 ml (¼ pint) double or whipping cream, whipped

CREME PATISSIERE

2 eggs, beaten

60 g (2 oz) vanilla sugar

30 g (1 oz) plain flour

300 ml (½ pint) milk

ICING

125 g (4 oz) icing sugar

about 1 tbsp water

1 Make the crème pâtissière (page 452), using the quantities listed above.

2 Roll out the pastry on a floured surface to make a thin, 28 x 33 cm (11 x 13 in) rectangle. Lay it over a dampened baking tray.

3 Prick the pastry with a fork. Bake in a preheated oven at 220°C (425°F, Gas 7) for 10–15 minutes until the pastry is crisp and a deep brown colour.

4 Remove from the oven and leave to cool. Reduce the oven temperature to 180°C (350°F, Gas 4).

5 Trim the edges of the pastry to a rectangle, then cut into 3 equal rectangles, 10 cm (4 in) wide. Crush the pastry trimmings and set aside.

6 Mix the icing sugar and enough water to make a smooth glacé icing. Spread over 1 of the rectangles, and place on a baking tray.

7 Bake for 2 minutes or until the icing has just set and has a slight sheen. Leave to cool.

8 Place a second pastry rectangle on a serving plate. Spread evenly with the jam and then the whipped cream. Set the third rectangle on top and cover with the crème pâtissière.

9 Top with the iced pastry rectangle. Decorate the long edges of the rectangle with thin rows of crushed pastry trimmings.

10 Chill the mille-feuille in the refrigerator until ready to serve.

Cook's know-how

If you are short of time, use ready rolled puff pastry and a carton of ready made thick custard.

BAKLAVA

MAKES 20 SQUARES

250 g (8 oz) walnut pieces, finely chopped

60 g (2 oz) light muscovado sugar

1 tsp ground cinnamon

175 g (6 oz) butter, melted, plus extra for greasing

24 sheets of filo pastry, weighing about 500 g (1 lb)

90 ml (3 fl oz) clear honey

2 tbsp lemon juice

SHALLOW 18 x 23 CM (7 x 9 IN) RECTANGULAR CAKE TIN

1 Mix together the walnuts, sugar, and cinnamon.

2 Lightly butter the cake tin and lay 1 sheet of filo pastry in the bottom of the tin, allowing the pastry to come up the sides. (If necessary, cut the sheets in half to fit in the tin.) Brush the pastry with a little melted butter.

3 Repeat with 5 more filo sheets, layering and brushing each one with the butter. Sprinkle with one-third of the nut mixture.

4 Repeat this process twice, using 6 more sheets of filo pastry each time, brushing each sheet with butter and sprinkling the nut mixture over each sixth sheet. Finish with 6 buttered sheets of filo pastry, and lightly brush the top with melted butter.

5 Trim the edges of the filo, then, using a sharp knife, cut about halfway through the pastry layers to make 20 squares.

6 Bake in a preheated oven at 220°C (425°F, Gas 7) for 15 minutes, then reduce the oven temperature to 180°C (350°F, Gas 4) and bake for 10–15 minutes until the pastry is crisp and golden brown. Remove the baklava from the oven.

7 Heat the honey and lemon juice in a heavy saucepan until the honey has melted. Spoon over the hot baklava. Leave to cool in the tin for 1–2 hours. Cut into the marked squares, and serve the baklava at room temperature.

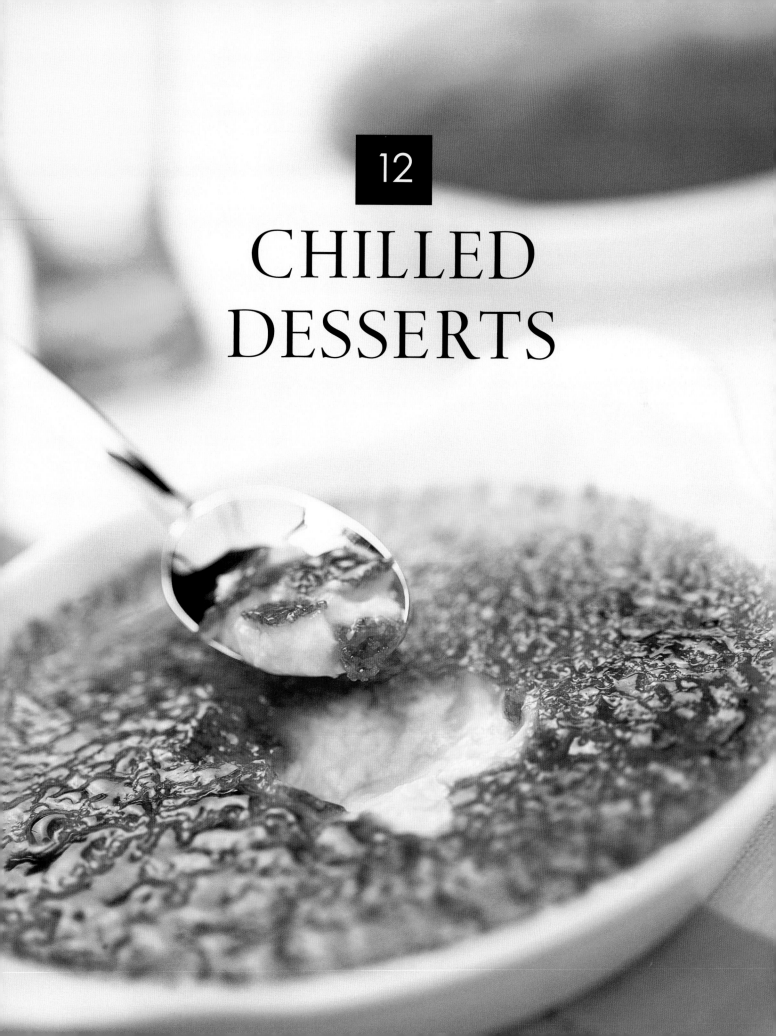

12
CHILLED DESSERTS

UNDER 30 MINUTES

SCOTCH MIST
Rich double cream whipped with whisky and crushed meringues, chilled, and sprinkled with toasted flaked almonds.

SERVES 6 446 calories per serving

Takes 10 minutes, plus chilling   Page 474

ITALIAN CLASSIC

ZABAGLIONE
Light dessert: egg yolks, sugar, and Marsala whisked until creamy, and served with boudoir biscuits.

SERVES 6 114 calories per serving

Takes 20 minutes   Page 485

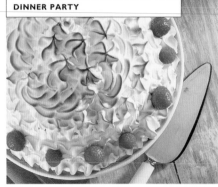

PEACH MELBA
Deliciously ripe peaches and raspberries, topped with a large scoop of vanilla ice cream and a sweet raspberry sauce.

SERVES 4 273 calories per serving

Takes 15 minutes   Page 492

30–60 MINUTES

DINNER PARTY

BAKED ALASKA
Impressive dessert: sponge case filled with layers of raspberries, strawberries, or other summer fruits, topped with ice cream and meringue, and browned.

SERVES 8 256 calories per serving

Takes 30 minutes   Page 493

GOOSEBERRY FOOL
Fresh gooseberries are lightly cooked with fragrant elderflowers until soft, mixed with whipped cream, and decorated with lime zest.

SERVES 6 396 calories per serving

Takes 30 minutes, plus chilling   Page 469

TRADITIONAL

LEMON SYLLABUB
Lemon zest and juice, whipped double cream, sweet white wine, and whisked egg whites, folded together, and topped with lemon zest.

SERVES 4 470 calories per serving

Takes 20 minutes, plus standing   Page 473

OVER 60 MINUTES

HELEN'S PUDDING
Easy and delicious: chocolate and coffee flavoured breadcrumbs are layered with whipped cream, and sprinkled with chocolate.

SERVES 6 510 calories per serving

Takes 15 minutes, plus chilling   Page 486

LOW CALORIE

WINTER FRUIT SALAD
Light and refreshing: a variety of fruit including pink grapefruit, oranges, green grapes, pears, and bananas coated in syrup.

SERVES 6 173 calories per serving

Takes 25 minutes, plus chilling   Page 468

POTS AU CHOCOLAT
Rich and smooth: chocolate, coffee, butter, egg yolks, and vanilla essence mixed with egg whites and decorated with whipped cream.

SERVES 6 324 calories per serving

Takes 15 minutes, plus chilling   Page 484

FROZEN LEMON FLUMMERY

Whipped double cream, lemon zest and juice, caster sugar, and milk, frozen, and decorated with strips of lemon zest.

SERVES 4 391 calories per serving

Takes 20 minutes, plus freezing   Page 494

CHOCOLATE & BRANDY MOUSSE

Smooth and delicious: an egg and whipped cream mousse flavoured with chocolate and brandy. Topped with cream and chocolate.

SERVES 6 585 calories per serving

Takes 45 minutes, plus chilling   Page 487

OLD ENGLISH TRIFLE

Family favourite: sponges layered with peaches or pears, crisp biscuits, custard, and whipped cream. Decorated with toasted almonds.

SERVES 8 401 calories per serving

Takes 35 minutes, plus chilling   Page 468

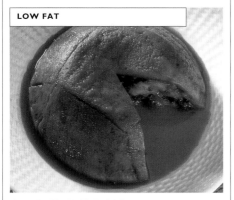

LOW FAT

SUMMER PUDDING

Ripe and juicy strawberries, redcurrants, blackcurrants, cherries, and raspberries wrapped in juice-soaked bread.

SERVES 6 240 calories per serving

Takes 35 minutes, plus chilling   Page 469

FAMILY CHOICE

QUICK VANILLA ICE CREAM

Plain and simple: fresh eggs and double cream flavoured with vanilla, whisked until light and creamy, and frozen.

SERVES 4–6 799–533 calories per serving

Takes 20 minutes, plus freezing   Page 489

CHOCOLATE CHIP CHEESECAKE

Rich and delicious: a crunchy muesli base is topped with a creamy mixture enriched with both melted chocolate and chocolate chips. The cheesecake is decorated with piped rosettes of whipped cream and chocolate caraque for a luscious finish.

SERVES 8 628 calories per serving

Takes 50 minutes, plus chilling   Page 484

OVER 60 MINUTES

PAVLOVA WITH PINEAPPLE & GINGER

Crisp meringue case filled with whipped double
cream and ginger, and topped with pineapple rings
and strips of ginger.

SERVES 6–8 504–378 calories per serving
Takes 2¹/2 hours, plus cooling   Page 474

TIRAMISU

Traditional Italian dessert: a sponge base layered
with creamy mascarpone cheese flavoured with
brandy, chocolate, and coffee.

SERVES 8 508 calories per serving
Takes 45 minutes, plus chilling   Page 487

FRENCH CLASSIC

CREME BRULEE

Simple and delicious: egg and cream custard baked
until tender, finished with crisp, caramelized sugar
on top.

SERVES 6 302 calories per serving
Takes 45 minutes, plus chilling   Page 488

MANGO & LIME MOUSSE

Light and refreshing: mangoes and tangy lime zest
and juice mixed with whipped cream. Decorated
with lime slices and cream.

SERVES 6 354 calories per serving
Takes 40 minutes, plus chilling   Page 472

CHOCOLATE ROULADE

Rich and creamy: a chocolate-flavoured sponge
with a deliciously rich cream and chocolate filling.

SERVES 6 677 calories per serving
Takes 60 minutes, plus cooling   Page 485

ICED CHRISTMAS PUDDING

Easy and delicious: dried fruit, apricots, cherries,
and brandy combined with custard and whipped
cream, and frozen.

SERVES 8 437 calories per serving
Takes 20 minutes, plus freezing   Page 493

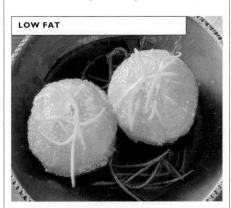

LOW FAT

CARAMELIZED ORANGES

Quick and easy: oranges caramelized and served in
their own juices, and decorated with strips of
orange zest.

SERVES 4 388 calories per serving
Takes 30 minutes, plus chilling   Page 472

CHILLED LEMON SOUFFLE

Light and fluffy: refreshing, smooth dessert with a
citrus tang, decorated with whipped cream and
toasted almonds.

SERVES 4 883 calories per serving
Takes 40 minutes, plus chilling   Page 473

FLOATING ISLANDS

Fluffy oval-shaped meringues are served floating on
a smooth and creamy vanilla custard. Decorated
with almonds.

SERVES 4 412 calories per serving
Takes 40 minutes, plus cooling   Page 479

OVER 60 MINUTES

AUSTRIAN CHEESECAKE
Smooth and creamy: curd cheese, butter, egg, almonds, and semolina folded with sultanas and lightened with egg whites.

SERVES 8 331 calories per serving
Takes 50 minutes, plus cooling   Page 481

DINNER PARTY

CHOCOLATE LAYERED TERRINE
Two chocolate and brandy mousse-like layers sandwiched with white chocolate. Decorated with whipped cream and chocolate shavings.

SERVES 8–10 641–513 calories per serving
Takes 45 minutes, plus chilling   Page 486

TROPICAL FRUIT CHEESECAKE
Crunchy coconut biscuit base topped with a creamy mango mixture, and decorated with tropical fruits.

SERVES 10 396 calories per serving
Takes 1¼ hours   Page 481

FRENCH CLASSIC

CREME CARAMEL
Easy and delicious: velvety vanilla-flavoured custard coated with a tempting golden brown caramel sauce.

SERVES 6 255 calories per serving
Takes 60 minutes, plus chilling   Page 488

CHERRY CHEESECAKE
Black cherries flavoured with Kirsch top a slightly sweet and creamy cheese filling with a crisp biscuit base.

SERVES 8 530 calories per serving
Takes 60 minutes, plus chilling   Page 479

FAMILY CHOICE

RICH VANILLA ICE CREAM
Creamy and irresistible: rich egg custard mixed with double cream, flavoured with vanilla essence, churned, and then frozen. A delicious and versatile recipe every cook should know. Colourful strawberry fans highlight each serving.

SERVES 4–6 577–385 calories per serving
Takes 30 minutes, plus freezing   Page 492

463

OVER 60 MINUTES

MANGO & PASSION FRUIT MERINGUE

Two light and crunchy meringue rounds are sandwiched together with cream, mango slices, strawberries, and passion fruit.

SERVES 6 503 calories per serving
Takes 1½ hours, plus cooling   Page 475

ITALIAN CLASSIC

CASSATA

Layers of ice cream, rum-soaked fruit, and sorbet are frozen to make this traditional Italian dessert.

SERVES 8 364 calories per serving
Takes 30 minutes, plus freezing   Page 494

MARBLED RASPBERRY CHEESECAKE

Crunchy base of walnuts and oats is topped with a creamy raspberry and cheese filling. Decorated with whipped cream.

SERVES 10 439 calories per serving
Takes 45 minutes, plus chilling   Page 480

PREPARE AHEAD

CHOCOLATE & MERINGUE BOMBE

Delicious layers of vanilla and chocolate ice cream with a surprise centre of whipped cream and meringue.

SERVES 8 413 calories per serving
Takes 45 minutes, plus freezing   Page 489

DINNER PARTY

HAZELNUT MERINGUE GATEAU

Toasted hazelnuts add a rich flavour to meringue rounds, which are sandwiched with cream and served with raspberry sauce.

SERVES 8 429 calories per serving
Takes 1¼ hours   Page 478

STRAWBERRY MERINGUE ROULADE

A light meringue layer scattered with flaked almonds, spread with whipped double cream and strawberries, and rolled into a roulade. Chilled, then lightly dusted with icing sugar before serving. A perfect and attractive end to a special dinner.

SERVES 8 349 calories per serving
Takes 55 minutes, plus chilling   Page 475

CHILLED DESSERTS KNOW-HOW

CHILLED DESSERTS can be made well in advance so are great for dinner parties. Fruit salads and fools, trifles, creamy mousses and light chilled soufflés, meringue baskets, gateaux, rich cheesecakes, layered terrines, ice creams, and sorbets – all can be kept in the refrigerator or freezer, to be served when you're ready.

WHISKING EGG WHITES

A balloon whisk is the classic tool for whisking egg whites, but an electric mixer saves time and effort. Ensure all your equipment is clean, dry, and grease-free, and that the egg whites are at room temperature.

Whisk the whites as forcefully as possible (on maximum speed if using an electric mixer) right from the start. When they look like a cloud, add any sugar little by little. The mixture will get stiffer and stiffer as you add sugar and whisk.

FREEZING

Many completed desserts, as well as ingredients and accompaniments for desserts, can be stored in the freezer. Freeze chocolate, caramel, or fruit sauces; thaw at room temperature, or reheat from frozen if serving warm. Tray freeze piped rosettes of cream, then pack in a freezer bag; pack chocolate decorations in rigid containers. Both can be used frozen – they will thaw in minutes. Freeze citrus zest, and thaw, unwrapped, at room temperature. Tray freeze baked meringue shells, gateau layers, and cheesecake; unwrap and thaw in the refrigerator. Crème caramel can be frozen uncooked in the mould and baked from frozen, allowing extra time.

Egg safety

Some of the chilled desserts in this book, such as mousses and soufflés, contain uncooked eggs. Because of the risk of salmonella poisoning, it is usually recommended that those in vulnerable groups should not eat raw or undercooked eggs (see also page 32).

DISSOLVING GELATINE

Gelatine is a flavourless setting agent used in chilled desserts such as fruit jellies. It is most commonly available as a powder, in sachets. Leaf gelatine can also be used (4 sheets in place of 1 sachet): soften in cold water for 5 minutes, then drain and melt in the hot dessert mixture, whisking well.

1 Put the given quantity of cold water or other liquid into a small heatproof bowl and sprinkle the given quantity of gelatine over the surface. Leave to soak for about 10 minutes until the gelatine has absorbed the liquid and become spongy.

2 Put the bowl of gelatine into a pan of hot water and heat until the gelatine has dissolved and is clear. Use a metal spoon to check that there are no granules left. Use the gelatine at the same temperature as the mixture it is setting.

PREPARING A SOUFFLE DISH

To give a chilled soufflé the appearance of having risen above the rim of the dish, it is set with a raised collar.

Cut out a piece of foil or greaseproof paper 5 cm (2 in) longer than the circumference of the dish and wide enough to stand 5 cm (2 in) above it when folded. Fold in half. Wrap around the dish and secure with tape or string. Remove before serving.

FOLDING EGG WHITES

To retain as much air as possible, egg whites should be folded gently and quickly into a mixture.

Mix a spoonful of the whites into the heavy mixture to lighten it. Using a rubber spatula or metal spoon, fold in the remaining whites using a "figure of eight" motion, cutting straight through the mixture, then turning it over until well blended.

PREPARING CITRUS FRUITS

When taking the zest from citrus fruits (even if they are unwaxed), first scrub the fruit with hot soapy water, rinse well, and dry.

Grating
Hold the grater on a plate. Rub the fruit over the medium grid of the grater, removing just the zest and leaving behind the bitter white pith. Use a pastry brush to remove all the zest from the grater.

Paring
Use a vegetable peeler or small knife to pare off strips of zest, trying not to take any of the white pith with the zest. Cut the pieces of zest lengthwise into very fine strips or "julienne".

Zesting
For speedy removal of zest in tiny strips, use a citrus zester or a flat ultra-sharp grater.

Peeling
Use a small sharp knife. Cut off a slice of peel across the top and the base, cutting through to the flesh. Set the fruit upright on a chopping board and cut away the peel from top to bottom, following the curve of the fruit and cutting away the white pith as well.

Segmenting
Hold the peeled fruit over a bowl to catch the juice. With a sharp knife, cut down one side of a segment, cutting it from the dividing membrane. Cut away from the membrane on the other side, and remove the segment. Continue all around the fruit.

Citrus tips

To get the maximum juice from citrus fruits, first roll the fruit gently on a work surface, pressing lightly. Or heat in the microwave, on HIGH (100% power) for 30 seconds, just until the fruit feels warm.

If a recipe includes citrus zest, add it immediately after grating or zesting, preferably to any sugar in the recipe. Then the zest won't discolour or dry out, and all the flavoursome oils from the zest will be absorbed by the sugar.

PREPARING A PINEAPPLE

When peeling pineapple, cut away the skin in strips, taking out all the "eyes". If there are any left after peeling, cut them out with the tip of a knife.

Wedges or cubes

1 Cut off the green crown, then cut a slice from the base. Set the pineapple upright on a chopping board and slice away strips of skin, cutting from top to bottom.

2 To remove the core, cut the pineapple into quarters lengthwise. Cut the central core from each quarter. Cut the quarters into wedges or cubes as required.

Rings

Do not cut the pineapple lengthwise, but cut crosswise into 1 cm (½ in) slices. Stamp out the central core from each slice using a biscuit or pastry cutter.

PREPARING MANGOES

Mangoes have a large, flat central stone and the flesh clings to it tightly. There are 2 methods of preparation, depending on how the flesh is to be used.

Slicing
For flesh to be used sliced or puréed, cut the flesh from each side of the stone with a sharp knife. Also cut the flesh from the edges of the stone. Then peel and slice or purée.

Dicing

1 Cut the unpeeled flesh away from each side of the stone. With a sharp knife, score the flesh in a criss-cross pattern, cutting just to the skin but not through it.

2 Press in the middle of the skin to open out the cubes of flesh, then cut them away from the skin with a sharp knife.

DECORATING WITH CHOCOLATE

Chocolate decorations can transform a dessert, and you don't have to reserve them for desserts made only from chocolate – fruit fools and mousses can also benefit from a contrasting finishing touch.

Grating chocolate

Use chilled chocolate and hold it firmly in a piece of greaseproof paper. Hold the grater on a sheet of greaseproof paper and rub the chocolate over the large grid of the grater.

Chocolate curls

Have the chocolate at room temperature, and use a vegetable peeler to shave off long curls on to a sheet of greaseproof paper. Lift the paper to tip the curls on to the dessert.

Chocolate caraque

1 Spread a smooth, thin layer of melted chocolate, about 1.5 mm (1/16 in) thick, on to a cool work surface (preferably marble), and leave to cool until nearly set.

2 Using a long, sharp knife held at an angle, push across the chocolate with a slight sawing action, to shave it into "caraque" curls. Use a cocktail stick to pick up the caraque.

MELTING CHOCOLATE

Care is needed when melting chocolate, especially white chocolate. Don't allow it to overheat or come into contact with any steam as this could cause it to scorch or harden.

Chop the chocolate and put it into a heatproof bowl set over a pan of hot, not boiling, water. The base of the bowl should not be touching the water. Heat gently, without stirring, until the chocolate becomes soft. Remove from the heat, but leave the bowl over the water. Stir until the chocolate is very smooth and creamy.

DECORATING WITH CREAM

Piped whipped cream adds a professional touch to desserts and cakes, and with a little practice and some confidence this is not difficult to do. A star-shaped nozzle is the most useful.

1 Drop the nozzle into the piping bag, then tuck the lower half of the piping bag into the nozzle, to prevent the cream from leaking out when filling the bag.

2 Hold the bag in one hand, folding the top of the bag over your hand. Spoon in the whipped cream.

3 When the bag is full, twist the top until there is no air left. Pipe the cream as desired, gently squeezing the twisted end to force out the cream in a steady stream.

Rosette
Hold the bag upright, just above the surface of the cake. Squeeze gently, moving the bag in a small circle. Stop squeezing and lift the nozzle away.

Swirl
Hold the bag upright, just above the surface of the cake. Squeeze the bag and pipe the cream in a steady stream, guiding the nozzle in an "S" shape.

Rope
Hold the bag at a 45° angle. Pipe a short length of cream to 1 side. Pipe another length of cream to the opposite side, overlapping the first one.

OLD ENGLISH TRIFLE

SERVES 8

1 x 400 g (13 oz) can peach or pear halves

6 trifle sponges

4 tbsp red fruit jam

60 g (2 oz) ratafia biscuits or macaroons

75 ml (2½ fl oz) sherry

3 egg yolks

30 g (1 oz) caster sugar

1 tsp cornflour

300 ml (½ pint) milk

300 ml (½ pint) double or whipping cream

30 g (1 oz) flaked almonds, toasted, to decorate

1 Drain and slice the fruit, reserving the juice.

2 Cut the trifle sponges in half horizontally and sandwich the halves together with the jam.

3 Line the bottom of a glass serving bowl with the trifle sponges, and arrange the fruit and biscuits on top. Drizzle over the sherry and reserved fruit juice, and leave to soak while you make the custard.

4 In a bowl, mix together the egg yolks, sugar, and cornflour. Warm the milk in a heavy saucepan, then pour it into the egg yolk mixture, stirring constantly. Return the mixture to the pan and cook over a low heat, stirring constantly, until the custard thickens. Leave the custard to cool slightly.

5 Pour the custard over the sponges, fruit, and biscuits in the glass bowl. Cover the surface of the custard with a sheet of cling film, to prevent a skin from forming, and chill until set, preferably overnight (to let the flavours mingle).

6 Whip the cream until thick and spread over the custard. Scatter the almonds over the top to decorate. Serve chilled.

APRICOT & GINGER TRIFLE

Use 1 x 400 g (13 oz) can apricot halves. Sandwich the sponges with apricot jam and sprinkle with 1 piece of stem ginger in syrup, chopped, instead of the almonds.

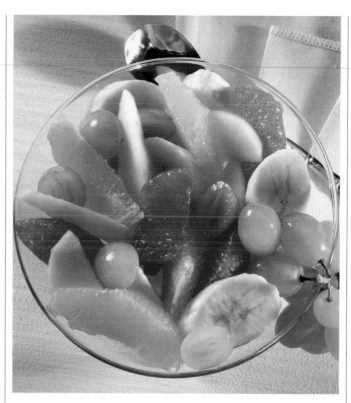

WINTER FRUIT SALAD

SERVES 6

60 g (2 oz) caster sugar

90 ml (3 fl oz) water

pared zest of ½ lemon

2 pink grapefruit

2 oranges

250 g (8 oz) seedless green grapes, halved

2 ripe pears, peeled, cored, and sliced

2 bananas, sliced

1 Put the sugar and measured water into a saucepan and heat gently until the sugar has dissolved. Add the lemon zest and bring the syrup to a boil. Boil for 1 minute, then strain into a serving bowl. Leave to cool.

2 Using a sharp serrated knife, cut the peel and pith from each grapefruit and orange. Remove the segments by cutting between each membrane. Add the segments to the bowl.

3 Add the grapes, pears, and bananas to the serving bowl and gently mix to coat all of the fruit in the sugar syrup.

4 Cover and chill the fruit salad for up to 1 hour before serving.

SUMMER BERRY SALAD

Cut 750 g (1½ lb) strawberries in half, then mix them with 250 g (8 oz) raspberries and 250 g (8 oz) blueberries. Sift 3 tbsp icing sugar over the fruit, and pour the juice of 2 oranges on top. Stir gently, cover, and chill for 1 hour.

Cook's know-how

If you are short of time you can just sprinkle the fruit with caster sugar to taste rather than making a sugar syrup. To prevent the pears and bananas from discolouring when sliced and exposed to the air, toss the pieces in lemon juice.

SUMMER PUDDING

This classic English summer-time treat is very easy to make, and not at all high in calories. For a perfect, evenly coloured result, reserve half of the cooking juices and pour them over any pale patches of bread after unmoulding the pudding.

SERVES 6

8 slices of stale medium-sliced white bread, crusts removed

875 g (1¾ lb) mixed summer fruits such as strawberries, redcurrants, blackcurrants, cherries, and raspberries

150 g (5 oz) caster sugar

75 ml (2½ fl oz) water

2 tbsp framboise or crème de cassis liqueur

crème fraîche or Greek yogurt to serve

1.25 LITRE (2 PINT) PUDDING BOWL

1 Set 2 slices of bread aside for the top of the pudding, then use the remaining slices to line the bowl (see box, right).

2 Hull and halve the strawberries if large, strip the currants from their stalks, and pit the cherries.

3 Place the redcurrants, blackcurrants, and cherries in a saucepan with the sugar and measured water. Heat gently until the juices begin to run. Stir until the sugar has dissolved, and cook until all of the fruit is just tender.

4 Remove from the heat and add the strawberries, raspberries, and liqueur.

5 Spoon the fruit and half of the juice into the lined bowl, reserving the remaining juice. Cover the top of the fruit with the reserved bread slices.

6 Stand the bowl in a shallow dish to catch any juices that may overflow, then put a saucer on top of the bread lid. Place a kitchen weight (or a can of food) on top of the saucer. Leave to chill for 8 hours.

7 Remove the weight and saucer and invert the pudding on to a serving plate. Spoon the reserved juices over the top, paying particular attention to any pale areas, and serve with either crème fraîche or Greek yogurt.

Lining the pudding bowl

Put a slice of bread in the bottom of the bowl, cutting it to fit if necessary, then use the remainder to line the sides. The slices should fit snugly together.

GOOSEBERRY FOOL

SERVES 6

500 g (1 lb) gooseberries, topped and tailed

1 tbsp water

60 g (2 oz) butter

2 elderflower heads (optional)

sugar to taste

300 ml (½ pint) double cream, whipped until thick

strips of blanched lime zest to decorate

1 Put the gooseberries into a pan with the measured water, butter, and elderflowers, if using. Cover and cook gently for 5–10 minutes until the gooseberries are soft.

2 Beat with a wooden spoon until smooth, and add sugar to taste. Leave to cool.

3 Fold mixture into cream. Turn into serving glasses and chill for 30 minutes. Decorate with lime zest.

RHUBARB & ORANGE FOOL

Substitute 500 g (1 lb) chopped rhubarb for the gooseberries and omit the elderflowers. Cook the rhubarb until soft with sugar to taste and the finely grated zest and juice of 1 large orange.

RED FRUIT DESSERTS

There is nothing more stunning than a dessert made with red fruits. The colour speaks for itself, so there is very little you have to do – the less the better. Ring the changes with different fruits as they come into season. There are no hard-and-fast rules.

PORT & CLARET JELLY

SERVES 8

8 sheets of leaf gelatine (about 25 g/scant 1 oz)

250 g (8 oz) caster or granulated sugar

450 ml (¾ pint) water

2 tbsp redcurrant jelly

1 cinnamon stick

450 ml (¾ pint) claret

300 ml (½ pint) ruby port

TO SERVE

small seasonal red fruits, eg raspberries, cherries, redcurrants, wild strawberries

cream (optional)

1.5 LITRE (2⅓ PINT) JELLY MOULD OR 8 WINE GLASSES

1 Put the sheets of gelatine in a medium bowl and cover with cold water. Leave to soak for about 5 minutes until softened.

2 Meanwhile, put the sugar into a large saucepan, pour in the measured water, and add the redcurrant jelly. Heat gently until the sugar and jelly have dissolved, then add the cinnamon stick, claret, and port. Bring to a boil, bubble for 1 minute, then remove the pan from the heat.

3 Pour the wine through a sieve lined with a double layer of muslin (or a J-cloth) into a bowl. Lift the gelatine out of the water, squeeze it, then add to the wine and stir until the gelatine has dissolved. Cool a little, pour into a mould or glasses, and leave until completely cold. Cover, and chill until set, at least 4 hours. Serve with seasonal fruits, and cream if you like.

Cook's know-how

If you want to use powdered gelatine instead of gelatine leaves, for the Port & Claret Jelly you will need to sprinkle 2 tbsp gelatine powder over 6 tbsp cold water in a small bowl, and for the Cranberry & Vodka Sparkle you will need to sprinkle 1½ tsp gelatine powder 1½ tbsp cold water. Leave to sponge for 10 minutes before stirring into the hot liquid.

RASPBERRY PASSION

SERVES 6

3 ripe passion fruit

500 g (1 lb) plain yogurt

200 ml (7 fl oz) half-fat crème fraîche

375 g (12 oz) raspberries

90 g (3 oz) light muscovado sugar

6 x 300 ML (½ PINT) STEMMED GLASSES

1 Using a teaspoon, scoop the seeds and flesh from the passion fruit into a bowl, and mix with the yogurt and crème fraîche.

2 Put an equal quantity of raspberries in each glass, then fill with the crème fraîche mixture. Cover and refrigerate for up to 8 hours.

3 An hour or so before serving, sprinkle with sugar and return to the refrigerator until ready to serve.

CRANBERRY & VODKA SPARKLE

SERVES 4

2 sheets of leaf gelatine

175 ml (6 fl oz) cranberry juice

125 ml (4 fl oz) vodka

squeeze of lime juice

dainty red fruits (eg raspberries, cherries, redcurrants, wild strawberries) to serve

4 x 100 ML (3½ FL OZ) GLASSES

1 Put the sheets of gelatine into a medium bowl and cover with cold water. Leave to soak for about 5 minutes until softened.

2 Heat the cranberry juice in a pan. Lift the gelatine out of the water, squeeze it, then add to the cranberry juice and stir until the gelatine has dissolved. Cool slightly, then add the vodka and lime juice. Cool completely, then pour into glasses, cover and chill until set, about 6 hours. Serve topped with dainty red fruits.

JUBILEE TRIFLE

SERVES 6

8 trifle sponges

about 7 tbsp black cherry jam

1 x 420 g (13½ oz) can pear quarters in natural juice, drained and juice reserved

1 x 420 g (13½ oz) can red cherries, drained and juice reserved

4 tbsp kirsch or other cherry liqueur

500 ml (18 fl oz) custard (ready made or see page 446 and use double the amount of cornflour)

150 ml (¼ pint) whipping cream

6 INDIVIDUAL GLASS DISHES, OR A 1.5 LITRE (2⅓ PINT) SHALLOW GLASS DISH, ABOUT 20 CM (8 IN) IN DIAMETER

1 Split the trifle sponges in half, spread generously with about 4 tbsp jam, and sandwich together again. Place four in the bottom of 6 individual glass dishes, cutting them to fit.

2 Chop each pear quarter into small pieces, and put some of the pieces around the edges of the dishes, and some in between the sponges. Dot with the cherries.

3 Mix the 5 tbsp of the pear juice with the kirsch, and pour half of it over the sponges. Arrange the last four sponges in the dishes, again cutting them to fit, then pour over the remaining juice and kirsch. Leave for a few minutes, then gently squash flat with the back of a spoon. Pour over the custard, level gently, and chill for 1 hour.

4 Lightly whip the cream – it should still be soft and floppy – and spread over the custard. Cover and chill for at least 4 hours (or up to 24 hours).

5 To serve, warm 3 tbsp cherry jam in a small pan with 2 tbsp of the reserved cherry juice until the jam has dissolved. Leave to cool, then sieve to remove any lumps, and drizzle over the trifles.

CLOCKWISE FROM TOP LEFT: Port & Claret Jelly, Raspberry Passion, Cranberry & Vodka Sparkle, Jubilee Trifle.

CARAMELIZED ORANGES

SERVES 4

250 g (8 oz) granulated sugar

150 ml (1/4 pint) cold water

150 ml (1/4 pint) lukewarm water

3 tbsp orange liqueur

8 thin-skinned oranges

1 Put the sugar and measured cold water into a heavy pan and heat gently until the sugar dissolves.

2 When all the sugar has dissolved, bring to a boil and boil steadily until a rich brown colour. (If the caramel is too light in colour it will be very sweet, but be careful not to let it burn.)

3 Protect your hand by covering it with a cloth, and remove the pan from the heat. Pour the measured lukewarm water into the caramel.

4 Return the pan to the heat and stir to melt the caramel. Pour the caramel into a heatproof serving dish. Leave to cool for 30 minutes. Stir in the orange liqueur.

5 Pare the zest from 1 of the oranges, using a vegetable peeler. Cut the zest into very thin strips (page 466). Cook for 1 minute in boiling water, drain, rinse thoroughly under cold running water, and set aside.

6 Using a sharp knife, remove the peel and pith from each orange, catching any juice to add to the caramel in the dish. Cut each orange into slices crosswise, then reassemble the oranges, holding the slices together with cocktail sticks.

7 Place the oranges in the dish of caramel and spoon the caramel over them. Scatter the strips of orange zest over the top. Chill for about 30 minutes. Remove the cocktail sticks before transferring the oranges to individual bowls to serve.

MANGO & LIME MOUSSE

SERVES 6

2 large ripe mangoes

grated zest and juice of 2 limes

15 g (1/2 oz) powdered gelatine

3 eggs, plus 1 egg yolk

45 g (1 1/2 oz) caster sugar

150 ml (1/4 pint) double or whipping cream, whipped until thick

DECORATION

150 ml (1/4 pint) double or whipping cream, whipped until thick

1 lime, thinly sliced

1 Slice the mango flesh away from the stones (page 466). Peel the flesh, then purée in a blender or food processor. Add the lime zest to the purée.

2 Put the lime juice into a small bowl, sprinkle the gelatine over the top, and leave for 10 minutes until it becomes spongy.

3 Stand the bowl in a pan of hot water and heat until the gelatine has dissolved.

4 Combine the eggs, egg yolk, and sugar in a large bowl and whisk vigorously for about 10 minutes until the mixture is pale and very thick. Gradually add the mango purée, whisking between each addition to keep the mixture thick.

5 Fold the whipped cream into the mango mixture. Add the dissolved gelatine in a steady stream, stirring gently to mix. Pour the mixture into a glass serving bowl and chill until set.

6 To decorate, pipe rosettes of whipped cream (page 467) on top of the mousse. Cut the lime slices in half, place 2 slices between each rosette of cream, and serve chilled.

LEMON SYLLABUB

SERVES 4

150 ml (¹/4 pint) dessert wine or sweet white wine

2 large lemons

90 g (3 oz) caster sugar

300 ml (¹/2 pint) double cream

2 egg whites

1 Put the wine into a bowl with the grated zest and juice of 1 of the lemons, and the sugar. Stir to mix, then leave to stand for about 15 minutes, stirring occasionally, until the sugar has dissolved.

2 Meanwhile, remove the zest from the remaining lemon in long, very thin strips. Blanch the strips in a small saucepan of boiling water for 1 minute. Drain, rinse under cold running water, and pat dry.

3 In a medium bowl, whip the cream until it just holds its shape. Add the wine mixture very slowly, whisking well between each addition to ensure that the mixture remains thick.

4 In a separate bowl, whisk the egg whites until stiff but not dry. Carefully fold into the cream and wine mixture. Spoon into 4 tall syllabub glasses. Decorate the top of each syllabub with a strip of lemon zest, and serve at once.

Cook's know-how

For a less rich syllabub, use half whipped double cream and half Greek yogurt. Do not use whipping cream instead of double cream because it will not be heavy enough to hold the weight of the wine. Serve with shortbread biscuits, if you like.

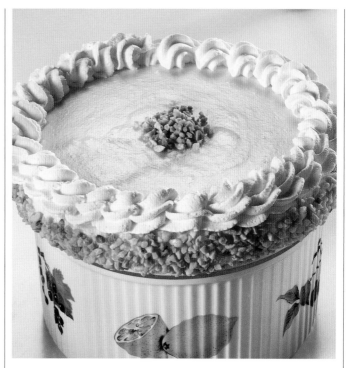

CHILLED LEMON SOUFFLE

SERVES 4

3 tbsp cold water

15 g (¹/2 oz) powdered gelatine

3 large eggs, separated

250 g (8 oz) caster sugar

grated zest and juice of 3 lemons

300 ml (¹/2 pint) double or whipping cream, whipped until thick

DECORATION

30 g (1 oz) nibbed almonds, lightly toasted

150 ml (¹/4 pint) double or whipping cream, whipped until stiff

1 LITRE (1³/4 PINT) SOUFFLÉ DISH

1 Prepare the soufflé dish: tie a band of double thickness greaseproof paper or foil around the outside so that it stands about 5 cm (2 in) above the top of the dish (page 465).

2 Put the water into a small bowl and sprinkle the gelatine over the top. Leave for about 10 minutes until it becomes spongy. Stand in a pan of hot water and heat until dissolved.

3 Put the egg yolks and sugar into a heatproof bowl and put over a pan of gently simmering water. Do not let the bottom of the bowl touch the water. Using an electric hand-held mixer, whisk together. Add the lemon zest and juice and whisk at full speed until the mixture is pale and thick.

4 Fold the whipped cream into the lemon mixture, then fold in the dissolved gelatine.

5 In a separate large bowl, whisk the egg whites until stiff but not dry. Fold into the lemon mixture, and carefully pour into the prepared soufflé dish. Level the surface, then chill for about 4 hours until set.

6 Carefully remove the paper collar. Decorate the outside edge of the soufflé with the lightly toasted almonds and sprinkle some in the middle. Pipe the cream (page 467) around the edge of the soufflé, and serve chilled.

SCOTCH MIST

SERVES 6

450 ml (3/4 pint) double or whipping cream

4 tbsp whisky

90 g (3 oz) meringues, coarsely crushed

30 g (1 oz) flaked almonds, toasted

1 Whip the cream with the whisky until it just holds its shape. Fold in the crushed meringues.

2 Spoon the mixture into 6 glass serving bowls, cover, and chill for about 20 minutes or until firm.

3 Scatter the toasted flaked almonds over the desserts just before serving.

ETON MESS

Substitute 4 tbsp brandy for the whisky, and add 500 g (1 lb) chopped strawberries to the cream mixture. Decorate with strawberry halves and mint leaves instead of the almonds.

PAVLOVA WITH PINEAPPLE & GINGER

Pavlova meringue is crisp on the outside, soft and slightly chewy like marshmallows inside. This pineapple and ginger topping is good in winter, but if you want to make a summer pavlova, use sweetened fresh red berries instead – and omit the ginger.

SERVES 6–8

4 egg whites

250 g (8 oz) caster sugar

1 1/2 tsp cornflour

1 1/2 tsp white wine vinegar

TOPPING

375 ml (13 fl oz) double or whipping cream

60 g (2 oz) stem ginger in syrup, cut into matchstick-thin strips

1 x 400 g (13 oz) can pineapple rings, drained

1 Preheat the oven to 160°C (325°F, Gas 3). Mark a 23 cm (9 in) circle on a sheet of non-stick baking parchment, turn the paper over, and line a baking tray.

2 Whisk the egg whites until stiff, then add the sugar, 1 tsp at a time, whisking the mixture constantly.

3 Blend the cornflour and vinegar and whisk into the egg white mixture.

4 Spread the mixture inside the circle on the baking parchment, building the sides up so that they are higher than the middle. Place in the oven, then immediately reduce the heat to 150°C (300°F, Gas 2).

5 Bake the meringue for 1 hour or until firm to the touch. Turn off the oven and leave the meringue inside for another hour.

6 Peel the lining paper from the meringue, and transfer the meringue to a serving plate. Leave to cool.

7 Before serving, whip the cream until stiff, and stir in half of the stem ginger strips. Spoon the mixture into the middle of the meringue. Top with the pineapple rings and the remaining stem ginger strips.

Cook's know-how

Keep the oven door closed when you leave the meringue to dry out, but if you have a fan-assisted oven, you should leave the door slightly open. The meringue base can be made a day in advance and kept in an airtight container in a cool place until needed. Add the cream and fruit topping just before serving.

MANGO & PASSION FRUIT MERINGUE

SERVES 6

4 egg whites

250 g (8 oz) caster sugar

FILLING

1 ripe mango

1 passion fruit

300 ml (½ pint) whipping cream, whipped until thick

125 g (4 oz) strawberries, sliced

DECORATION

150 ml (¼ pint) double or whipping cream, whipped until stiff

a few strawberries

1 Mark 2 x 20 cm (8 in) circles on 2 sheets of non-stick baking parchment, turn the paper over, and use to line 2 baking trays.

2 Whisk the egg whites with a hand-held electric mixer until stiff but not dry. Add the sugar, 1 tsp at a time, and continue to whisk until all the sugar has been incorporated and the mixture is stiff and glossy.

3 Pipe the meringue, in concentric circles, inside the marked circles on the paper-lined baking trays.

4 Bake the meringue rounds in a preheated oven at 140°C (275°F, Gas 1) for 1–1¼ hours until crisp and dry. Leave to cool, then carefully peel off the paper.

5 Dice the mango very fine (page 466). Halve the passion fruit and scoop out the pulp.

6 Spread the whipped cream over 1 of the meringue rounds. Arrange the mango, passion fruit pulp, and strawberries on top, and cover with the remaining meringue round.

7 Decorate with piped rosettes of whipped cream (page 467), strawberry slices, and a whole strawberry.

PEACH MERINGUE

Substitute 2 peeled and sliced peaches for the mango, and 125 g (4 oz) raspberries for the strawberries. Decorate the top of the peach meringue with a few whole raspberries.

STRAWBERRY MERINGUE ROULADE

SERVES 8

sunflower oil for greasing

4 egg whites

250 g (8 oz) caster sugar

45 g (1½ oz) flaked almonds

icing sugar for dusting

FILLING

300 ml (½ pint) double or whipping cream, whipped until thick

250 g (8 oz) strawberries, quartered

23 x 33 CM (9 x 13 IN) SWISS ROLL TIN

1 Lightly oil the Swiss roll tin and line with a sheet of baking parchment.

2 Whisk the egg whites until stiff but not dry. Add the sugar, 1 tsp at a time, and continue to whisk, until all the sugar has been incorporated and the mixture is stiff and glossy.

3 Spoon the meringue into the lined tin and tilt to level the surface. Sprinkle over the flaked almonds.

4 Bake near the top of a preheated oven at 200°C (400°F, Gas 6) for about 8 minutes until the top is golden brown.

5 Reduce the oven temperature to 160°C (325°F, Gas 3), and continue baking for 10 minutes or until the meringue is firm to the touch.

6 Remove the meringue from the oven and turn out on to a sheet of baking parchment. Peel the lining paper from the base and leave the meringue to cool for 10 minutes.

7 Spread the whipped cream evenly over the meringue, and scatter the strawberries over the cream.

8 Roll up the meringue from a long side, using the lining paper to help lift it. Wrap the roulade in baking parchment and leave to chill in the refrigerator for about 30 minutes. Lightly dust with sifted icing sugar before serving.

MERINGUES

Meringues are very quick and easy to prepare, and they can be made weeks in advance and kept in the freezer, so they are ideal for impromptu entertaining and special occasions of all kinds. The picture shows Mocha Meringue Mille-Feuilles (top left), Chocolate Meringue Shells (top right), and Fresh Fruit Baskets (below).

FRESH FRUIT BASKETS

MAKES 8

| 1 quantity basic meringue (see below right) |
| 250 ml (8 fl oz) double cream |
| berries and mint sprigs (optional) to decorate |

RASPBERRY SAUCE

| 250 g (8 oz) fresh or frozen raspberries |
| 2 tbsp icing sugar |
| a squeeze of lemon juice, to taste |

1 Make the raspberry sauce: purée the raspberries in a blender or food processor, then push the purée through a sieve with a spoon into a bowl (discard the seeds in the sieve). Stir in the sugar and lemon juice to taste. Chill in the refrigerator until ready to use.

2 Pipe 8 meringue baskets (see box, below). Bake in a preheated oven at 120°C (250°F, Gas ¹/2) for 1–1¹/2 hours until firm. Leave to cool.

3 Whip the cream until it forms stiff peaks. Fill the baskets with the cream, top with berries, and decorate with mint sprigs if you like. Serve with the chilled raspberry sauce.

MOCHA MERINGUE MILLE-FEUILLES

MAKES 6

| 1 quantity basic meringue (below right) |
| 125 g (4 oz) slivered almonds |
| icing sugar for dusting |

COFFEE CHANTILLY CREAM

| 250 ml (8 fl oz) double cream |
| 1 tsp instant coffee, dissolved in 1 tbsp water |
| 2–3 tbsp caster sugar |

1 Spoon 18 mounds of meringue on to non-stick baking parchment, then spread them flat with a palette knife until they are very thin and about 7.5 cm (3 in) in diameter. Sprinkle over the almonds. Bake in a preheated oven at 120°C (250°F, Gas ¹/2) for 1–1¹/2 hours until firm. Cool.

2 Make the coffee Chantilly cream: whip the cream until it forms soft peaks. Add the coffee and sugar to the cream and whip until stiff peaks form.

3 Sandwich the meringue discs together in threes, with the coffee Chantilly cream in between. Dust with a little icing sugar before serving.

CHOCOLATE MERINGUE SHELLS

MAKES 12

| 1 quantity basic meringue (below) |
| 60 g (2 oz) plain chocolate, chopped |

CHOCOLATE GANACHE

| 125 g (4 oz) plain chocolate, chopped |
| 125 ml (4 fl oz) double cream |

1 Pipe 24 shells (see box, below left). Bake in a preheated oven at 120°C (250°F, Gas ¹/2) for 1–1¹/2 hours until firm. Leave to cool. Put the chocolate into a heatproof bowl over a pan of hot water and heat until melted. Drizzle over the meringues and leave to set.

2 Make the ganache: put the chopped chocolate and the cream into a heavy-based saucepan and heat gently, stirring occasionally, until the chocolate has melted.

3 Remove the pan from the heat and whisk the ganache for about 5 minutes until the mixture is fluffy and cooled. Sandwich the meringues together with the chocolate ganache.

BASIC MERINGUE

| 4 egg whites |
| 250 g (8 oz) caster sugar |

1 Whisk the egg whites in a scrupulously clean large bowl, with an electric hand mixer on maximum speed, until the whites are stiff and look like clouds.

2 Keeping the mixer on maximum speed, add the caster sugar a teaspoon at a time and continue whisking until the mixture is stiff and shiny.

3 Pipe, spoon, or spread the meringue as preferred and bake as in the recipes above. All ovens vary, so baking times cannot be exact. You will know the meringues are cooked when they can be lifted easily from the parchment.

PIPING MERINGUE SHAPES

Baskets

Mark 8 x 10 cm (4 in) circles on non-stick baking parchment; turn over. Spoon the meringue into a piping bag fitted with a medium star nozzle, and pipe inside the circles, building up the sides to form baskets.

Shells

Spoon the meringue into a piping bag fitted with a medium star nozzle. Pipe 24 even-sized shells, about 5 cm (2 in) in diameter at the base, on to non-stick baking parchment .

SAUCES FOR DESSERTS

HOT CHOCOLATE SAUCE

Heat 175 g (6 oz) plain chocolate, broken into pieces, 2 tsp instant coffee granules, 125 ml (4 fl oz) hot water, and 90 g (3 oz) caster sugar in a pan until the chocolate has melted. Serve hot.

CHOCOLATE MARSHMALLOW SAUCE

Heat 60 g (2 oz) chopped plain chocolate, 100 g (3 1/2 oz) marshmallows, 75 ml (2 1/2 fl oz) double cream, and 75 ml (2 1/2 fl oz) honey in a pan until the chocolate and marshmallows have melted. Serve hot.

BUTTERSCOTCH SAUCE

Heat 60 g (2 oz) butter, 150 g (5 oz) light muscovado sugar, and 150 g (5 oz) golden syrup in a pan until melted. Remove from the heat and add 150 ml (1/4 pint) double cream and a few drops of vanilla essence, stirring until smooth. Serve hot.

PEACH SAUCE

Put 1 x 400 g (13 oz) can peaches and their juice into a food processor or blender with 1/4 tsp almond essence. Work to a smooth purée. Serve chilled.

HAZELNUT MERINGUE GATEAU

Crisp meringues made with toasted hazelnuts are sandwiched with a whipped cream filling. The attractive decoration is easy to create: piped rosettes of cream are topped with hazelnuts and raspberries, and the gâteau is accompanied by a raspberry sauce.

SERVES 8

125 g (4 oz) shelled hazelnuts
4 egg whites
275 g (9 oz) caster sugar
1/2 tsp white wine vinegar
300 ml (1/2 pint) whipping cream, whipped until thick
icing sugar for dusting

RASPBERRY SAUCE

250 g (8 oz) raspberries
about 4 tbsp icing sugar, sifted

1 Mark 2 x 20 cm (8 in) circles on 2 sheets of non-stick baking parchment. Turn the paper over and use to line 2 baking trays.

2 Spread the hazelnuts on another baking tray and toast in a preheated oven at 190°C (375°F, Gas 5) for about 10 minutes. Remove from the oven, then turn the temperature down to 160°C (325°F, Gas 3).

3 Tip the hazelnuts on to a clean tea towel and rub together inside the towel to remove the skins. Reserve 8 whole nuts for decoration and grind the remaining nuts in a food processor.

4 Whisk the egg whites until stiff but not dry (if using an electric mixer turn it to high speed). Add the caster sugar, 1 tsp at a time, and continue to whisk, still at high speed, until all of the caster sugar has been incorporated and the mixture is stiff and glossy.

5 Whisk in the white wine vinegar, then fold in the ground hazelnuts.

6 Divide the hazelnut meringue mixture equally between the baking trays, spreading it out evenly within the marked circles.

7 Bake in the oven for about 30 minutes until the top of each meringue round is crisp and a pale beige colour. The insides of the meringues should still be soft like marshmallow.

8 Lift the meringue rounds off the baking trays and peel the lining paper from the bases. Leave to cool on a wire rack.

9 Make the raspberry sauce: reserve 8 whole raspberries for decoration, and put the remainder in a food processor. Blend until smooth, then push through a sieve to remove the seeds. Gradually whisk in icing sugar to taste.

10 Use two-thirds of the whipped cream to sandwich the meringue rounds together. Sift icing sugar on top and decorate with rosettes (page 467) of the remaining whipped cream. Top the rosettes with the reserved whole hazelnuts and raspberries. Serve with the raspberry sauce.

Cook's know-how

This kind of puréed fruit sauce is known as a coulis. It is a useful sauce to have in your repertoire because it gives a professional look to desserts, especially when individual slices are served on plates.

FLOATING ISLANDS

SERVES 4

butter for greasing

3 eggs, separated

30 g (1 oz) vanilla sugar

1 tsp cornflour

600 ml (1 pint) milk

175 g (6 oz) caster sugar

30 g (1 oz) flaked almonds, toasted

1 Butter 4 individual serving dishes. Line a baking tray with a sheet of baking parchment.

2 In a large bowl, mix together the egg yolks, vanilla sugar, and cornflour. In a heavy saucepan, bring the milk to a boil. Add the boiling milk to the egg-yolk mixture, stirring constantly, then pour the mixture back into the pan.

3 Return to the heat and cook gently, stirring constantly, until the froth disappears and the custard is thickened. Pour the custard into the buttered dishes, and leave to cool.

4 Whisk the egg whites until stiff but not dry. Add the caster sugar, 1 tsp at a time, and continue to whisk until all the sugar has been incorporated and the mixture is stiff and glossy.

5 Shape the meringue into 8 ovals by scooping it up between 2 tablespoons. Place the ovals on the baking tray.

6 Cook in a preheated oven at 160°C (325°F, Gas 3) for 20 minutes until the meringues are set and no longer sticky. Leave to cool, then arrange on top of the custard. Sprinkle with almonds before serving.

Cook's know-how

This classic dessert is called îles flottantes in French, although you may also see it described as oeufs à la neige, or "snow eggs". They are one and the same thing. You can buy vanilla sugar, or make it yourself (page 488).

CHERRY CHEESECAKE

SERVES 8

375 g (12 oz) full-fat soft cheese

125 g (4 oz) caster sugar

2 eggs, beaten

a few drops of vanilla essence

1 tbsp lemon juice

BISCUIT SHELL

175 g (6 oz) digestive biscuits, crushed

90 g (3 oz) butter, melted

2 tbsp demerara sugar

TOPPING

1 tsp arrowroot

1 x 400 g (13 oz) can pitted black cherries

1 tbsp kirsch

23 CM (9 IN) SPRINGFORM CAKE TIN

1 Make the biscuit shell: mix together the crushed biscuits, melted butter, and sugar, and press evenly over the bottom and up the side of the cake tin.

2 Put the soft cheese into a bowl and beat until smooth. Add the caster sugar and beat until well blended. Add the eggs, vanilla essence, and lemon juice. Mix until smooth and creamy.

3 Pour the filling into the biscuit shell. Bake in a preheated oven at 180°C (350°F, Gas 4) for 25–30 minutes until just set. Leave to cool completely, then transfer to the refrigerator and leave to chill.

4 Make the topping: dissolve the arrowroot in a little of the cherry juice. Put the cherries and their juice into a small pan and add the arrowroot mixture with the kirsch. Bring to a boil, stirring, until thick. Leave to cool completely.

5 Spoon the cherries on top of the cheese filling. Chill. Use a knife to loosen the side of the cheesecake from the tin, then remove the cheesecake. Serve chilled.

Cook's know-how

Cheesecakes freeze well, but should always be frozen without the topping. Thaw in the refrigerator, then decorate. Fruit toppings may be prepared at the same time and frozen separately. Thaw and add to the cheesecake just before serving.

MARBLED RASPBERRY CHEESECAKE

The crunchy base of this cheesecake, made with crushed oat biscuits and walnuts, provides a delicious
contrast to the creamy filling, marbled with streaks of fresh raspberry purée. It is a delicate cheesecake,
so for best results be sure to chill it well before slicing and serving.

SERVES 10

3 tbsp cold water

15 g (1/2 oz) powdered gelatine

500 g (1 lb) raspberries

4 tbsp framboise (raspberry liqueur)

250 g (8 oz) full-fat soft cheese, at
room temperature

150 ml (1/4 pint) soured cream

2 eggs, separated

125 g (4 oz) caster sugar

BISCUIT BASE

125 g (4 oz) sweet oat or digestive
biscuits, coarsely crushed

60 g (2 oz) butter, melted

30 g (1 oz) demerara sugar

45 g (1 1/2 oz) walnuts, chopped

DECORATION

150 ml (1/4 pint) whipping cream,
whipped until stiff

a few raspberries

mint sprigs

23 CM (9 IN) LOOSE-BOTTOMED OR
SPRINGFORM CAKE TIN

1 Make the biscuit base: mix together the biscuits, butter, demerara sugar, and walnuts and press evenly over the bottom of the tin.

2 Put the measured water into a heatproof bowl, sprinkle the gelatine over the top, and leave for about 10 minutes until spongy.

3 Meanwhile, purée the raspberries in a food processor, then push them through a sieve to remove the seeds. Stir in the liqueur. Set aside.

4 Put the soft cheese into a large bowl, and beat until soft and smooth. Add the soured cream and egg yolks, and beat until well blended.

5 Stand the bowl of gelatine in a saucepan of hot water and heat gently until it dissolves. Stir into the cheese mixture.

6 Make the filling (see box, right).

7 Use a knife to loosen the side of the cheesecake from the tin, then remove the cheesecake. Slide on to a serving plate. Pipe whipped cream (page 467) around the edge and decorate with raspberries and mint sprigs.

Cook's know-how

To achieve an attractive
marbled effect, fold in the
raspberry purée lightly but
thoroughly, so that it forms
thin streaks. If there are large
areas of raspberry purée, they
will not set with the rest of
the mixture.

Making the filling

Whisk the egg whites until stiff but not dry. Add the caster sugar, 1 tsp at a time, and keep whisking until all the sugar is incorporated and the meringue mixture is stiff and glossy.

Turn the cheese mixture into the meringue and fold together, blending well. Leave the mixture to thicken slightly.

Fold in the raspberry purée, swirling it in just enough to give an attractive marbled effect.

Pour the mixture carefully on to the biscuit base and chill until set.

AUSTRIAN CHEESECAKE

SERVES 8

90 g (3 oz) butter, at room temperature, plus extra for greasing

150 g (5 oz) caster sugar

300 g (10 oz) curd cheese

2 eggs, separated

60 g (2 oz) ground almonds

2 tbsp semolina

grated zest and juice of 1 large lemon

60 g (2 oz) sultanas

icing sugar for dusting

20 CM (8 IN) LOOSE-BOTTOMED OR SPRINGFORM CAKE TIN

1 Lightly butter the tin and line the bottom with a round of baking parchment.

2 Beat the butter with the sugar and curd cheese until light and creamy. Beat in the egg yolks, then stir in the almonds, semolina, and lemon zest and juice. Leave to stand for 10 minutes, then fold in the sultanas.

3 In a separate bowl, whisk the egg whites until stiff but not dry. Carefully fold into the cheese mixture.

4 Turn into the prepared tin and level the surface. Bake in a preheated oven at 190°C (375°F, Gas 5) for 30–35 minutes until browned and firm to the touch. Turn off the oven and leave the cheesecake inside to cool for about 1 hour. Chill before serving.

5 Use a knife to loosen the side of the cheesecake from the tin, then remove the cheesecake. Slide on to a serving plate, and dust with sifted icing sugar (see below).

Cook's know-how

For a decorative pattern on top of the cheesecake, place a doily on top, dust with icing sugar, then carefully lift off the doily.

TROPICAL FRUIT CHEESECAKE

SERVES 10

2 ripe mangoes

150 ml (¹/4 pint) mango and apple fruit juice

15 g (¹/2 oz) powdered gelatine

250 g (8 oz) full-fat soft cheese, at room temperature

125 g (4 oz) caster sugar

2 eggs, separated

150 ml (¹/4 pint) whipping cream, whipped until thick

BISCUIT BASE

125 g (4 oz) coconut or digestive biscuits, crushed

60 g (2 oz) butter, melted

30 g (1 oz) demerara sugar

DECORATION

2 kiwi fruit, peeled and sliced

1 x 250 g (8 oz) can pineapple pieces in natural juice, drained

23 CM (9 IN) LOOSE-BOTTOMED OR SPRINGFORM CAKE TIN

1 Make the biscuit base: mix together the biscuits, melted butter, and sugar, and press over the bottom of the tin.

2 Slice the mango flesh away from the stones (page 466). Peel, then purée in a food processor.

3 Pour the fruit juice into a heatproof bowl, and sprinkle the gelatine over the top. Leave for about 10 minutes until it becomes spongy. Stand the bowl in a small pan of hot water, and heat gently until the gelatine has dissolved.

4 In a large bowl, beat the soft cheese until smooth and creamy. Beat in half of the caster sugar, the egg yolks, and the mango purée. Gradually beat in the gelatine mixture.

5 In a separate bowl, whisk the egg whites until stiff but not dry. Whisk in the remaining sugar, 1 tsp at a time, and continue to whisk at high speed until the sugar is incorporated and the mixture is stiff and glossy.

6 Fold the whipped cream into the cheese and mango mixture, then fold in the egg whites. Pour on to the biscuit base and chill until set.

7 Use a knife to loosen the side of the cheesecake, then remove from the tin. Slide on to a serving plate. Decorate the top with slices of kiwi fruit and pieces of pineapple before serving.

FRUIT SALADS

A fruit salad is welcome at the end of any meal any time of year, whether it is a simple family supper or a special occasion. All of these fruit salads can be made well in advance and served just as they are, or with cream or ice cream, crème fraîche or yogurt.

TROPICAL ISLAND FRUIT SALAD

SERVES 6

1 small ripe pineapple

1 ripe charentais or cantaloupe melon

1 ripe mango

250 g (8 oz) seedless black grapes

150 ml (¼ pint) pineapple and coconut juice or pineapple juice

125 g (4 oz) physalis (cape gooseberries)

2 ripe guavas, preferably pink-fleshed

2 Asian (nashi) pears

1 Cut the top and bottom off the pineapple. Remove the skin with a sharp knife, then cut out the brown eyes. Cut the pineapple lengthwise into 4 and remove and discard the hard inner core. Cut the flesh into chunks and put into a large glass serving bowl.

2 Cut the melon into quarters, remove and discard the seeds with a spoon. Cut each melon quarter in half, remove the skin with a sharp knife, and cut the flesh into chunks. Add to the pineapple.

3 Peel the mango, cut either side of the large flat stone, and neatly cut the mango flesh into pieces. Add to the bowl with the grapes. Pour over the fruit juice, cover, and chill in the refrigerator for about 4 hours, or overnight.

4 Peel back the paper lanterns on the physalis. Remove the fruits from about half of the physalis, wipe gently with kitchen paper, and add to the bowl.

5 Peel the guavas, halve the fruits, and remove the seeds. Cut the flesh into neat pieces and add to the bowl. Peel and quarter the pears, remove the cores, and slice the flesh neatly into the bowl.

6 Stir the fruits gently together, making sure the pear is submerged in juice or it will discolour. Cover and chill in the refrigerator for about 1 hour. Serve chilled, decorated with the remaining physalis.

SPICED FRUIT SALAD

SERVES 4–6

500 g (1 lb) mixed no-need-to-soak dried fruits, eg pears, peaches, mango, prunes, pineapple, figs, apple

about 900 ml (1½ pints) apple juice

2–3 star anise, to taste

1 vanilla pod

75 g (2½ oz) dried cranberries

75 g (2½ oz) dried cherries

1 Put the mixed fruits into a saucepan with 900 ml (1½ pints) apple juice, the star anise, and vanilla pod. Bring to a boil and simmer gently for about 15 minutes.

2 Add the dried cranberries and cherries to the pan and continue cooking for about 15 minutes, adding more apple juice (or water) if necessary. Serve hot or cold.

ORANGE PASSION SALAD

SERVES 6

8 thin-skinned oranges

juice of 1 small lime

2 ripe papayas (pawpaws)

3 ripe passion fruit

1 Remove the thin orange skin from 2 of the oranges with a zester and set the strips of zest aside. Peel all the oranges and remove all the skin and pith. Slice into rounds and remove any pips.

2 Put the orange slices into a fairly shallow glass bowl with any juice from the oranges and the lime juice.

3 Halve the papayas lengthwise and scoop out the seeds. Peel the halves, cut crosswise into fairly thick slices, and add to the bowl. Cut the passion fruit in half crosswise and scoop the juice and pips over the fruit in the bowl. Top the salad with the orange zest, cover, and chill in the refrigerator for at least 2 hours. Stir before serving – there is no need for sugar.

FRUITS OF THE FOREST SALAD

SERVES 6–8

250 g (8 oz) fresh cranberries

60 g (2 oz) caster sugar

250 g (8 oz) strawberries, hulled and halved if large

125 g (4 oz) blueberries

250 g (8 oz) raspberries

250 g (8 oz) blackberries

250 g (8 oz) loganberries, or increase the amount of the other berries if loganberries are unavailable

2–3 tbsp balsamic vinegar

1 tsp green peppercorns in brine or oil, rinsed and lightly crushed

1 Put the cranberries into a stainless steel pan with 5 tbsp water. Cook gently for about 5–10 minutes or until the cranberries pop and are just soft. Remove from the heat, stir in the sugar, and leave until the sugar has dissolved and the mixture has cooled slightly (do not add the sugar at the beginning or it will make the cranberry skins tough).

2 Put the remaining fruit into a serving bowl, add the cooled cranberries and juice, and mix gently together.

3 Add the balsamic vinegar and green peppercorns and mix gently. Cover and chill in the refrigerator for at least 4 hours (or overnight) to allow to juices to develop and the flavours to mellow.

CLOCKWISE FROM TOP RIGHT: Spiced Fruit Salad, Orange Passion Salad, Tropical Island Fruit Salad, Fruits of the Forest Salad.

POTS AU CHOCOLAT

SERVES 6

175 g (6 oz) plain dark chocolate, broken into pieces

3 tbsp strong black coffee

15 g (½ oz) butter

a few drops of vanilla essence

3 eggs, separated

150 ml (¼ pint) double cream, whipped until stiff, to decorate

1 Put the chocolate pieces into a saucepan with the strong black coffee. Heat gently, stirring, until the chocolate melts.

2 Leave the chocolate mixture to cool slightly, then add the butter, vanilla essence, and egg yolks and stir until well blended.

3 Whisk the egg whites until stiff but not dry. Fold gently but thoroughly into the chocolate mixture.

4 Pour the mixture into 6 small custard pots, ramekins, or other serving dishes, and leave to chill for about 8 hours.

5 Decorate each pot of chocolate with a piped rosette of whipped cream (page 467) before serving.

CHOCOLATE CHIP CHEESECAKE

This delicious dessert, with its crunchy muesli base and rich chocolate filling, is ideal for parties. It can be prepared up to a month in advance and frozen in foil. Thaw, wrapped, in the refrigerator for 8 hours, then decorate.

SERVES 8

125 g (4 oz) plain dark chocolate, broken into pieces

3 tbsp cold water

15 g (½ oz) powdered gelatine

250 g (8 oz) full-fat soft cheese

2 eggs, separated

60 g (2 oz) caster sugar

150 ml (¼ pint) soured cream

30 g (1 oz) plain dark chocolate chips, coarsely chopped

BASE

125 g (4 oz) muesli

90 g (3 oz) butter, melted

30 g (1 oz) demerara sugar

DECORATION

300 ml (½ pint) whipping cream, whipped until stiff

chocolate curls or caraque (page 467)

20 CM (8 IN) LOOSE-BOTTOMED OR SPRINGFORM CAKE TIN

1 Make the base: mix together the muesli, melted butter, and sugar, and press evenly over the bottom of the tin. Chill.

2 Meanwhile, put the chocolate into a small heatproof bowl over a pan of hot water. Heat gently to melt the chocolate, stirring occasionally. Leave to cool.

3 Put the measured water into a heatproof bowl and sprinkle the gelatine over the top. Leave for 10 minutes until spongy. Stand the bowl in a pan of hot water and heat gently until the gelatine has dissolved.

4 Beat the cheese until smooth. Add the egg yolks and sugar and beat until blended. Stir in the soured cream, melted chocolate, chocolate chips, and gelatine. Mix well.

5 In a separate bowl, whisk the egg whites until stiff but not dry. Fold carefully into the chocolate mixture until evenly mixed. Pour on to the muesli base and chill until set.

6 Use a knife to loosen the side of the cheesecake from the tin, then remove the cheesecake. Slide on to a serving plate. Pipe rosettes of whipped cream (page 467) on top and decorate with chocolate curls or caraque.

Cook's know-how

Chocolate chips are convenient, but if you don't have any to hand, simply chop up a bar of chocolate.

CHOCOLATE ROULADE

This impressive dessert is made from a chocolate soufflé mixture which is baked and cooled, then rolled around a cream and chocolate filling. Use a long serrated knife to cut the roulade, and dip it in hot water before cutting each slice.

SERVES 6

sunflower oil for greasing

175 g (6 oz) plain dark chocolate, broken into pieces

6 large eggs, separated

175 g (6 oz) caster sugar

icing sugar for dusting

FILLING

90 g (3 oz) plain dark chocolate, broken into pieces

300 ml (1/2 pint) double or whipping cream, whipped until thick

23 x 33 CM (9 x 13 IN) SWISS ROLL TIN

1 Lightly grease the tin with sunflower oil and line with baking parchment.

2 Put the chocolate into a small heatproof bowl over a pan of hot water and heat gently, stirring occasionally, to melt the chocolate. Cool.

3 Combine the egg yolks and sugar in a large bowl and whisk together until light and creamy. Add the cooled chocolate and stir to blend evenly.

4 In a separate bowl, whisk the egg whites until stiff but not dry. Carefully fold into the chocolate mixture.

5 Turn the chocolate mixture into the tin, tilting the tin so that the mixture spreads evenly into the corners. Bake in a preheated oven at 180°C (350°F, Gas 4) for 20 minutes or until firm to the touch.

6 Remove the tin from the oven. Place a clean, dry tea towel on top of the cake and on top of this lay another tea towel that has been soaked in cold water and well wrung out. Leave the cake covered, in a cool place, for 8 hours.

7 Make the filling: put the chocolate into a heatproof bowl over a pan of hot water and heat gently, stirring occasionally, to melt the chocolate. Cool.

8 Remove the tea towels from the cake, and turn it out on to a sheet of baking parchment that has been liberally sprinkled with sifted icing sugar. Peel the lining paper from the cake.

9 Spread the melted chocolate over the cake, then spread the whipped cream evenly over the top.

10 Roll up the cake from a long edge, using the sugared paper to help lift the cake and roll it forward.

11 Dust the roulade with more sifted icing sugar before serving.

ZABAGLIONE

SERVES 6

4 egg yolks

75 g (2 1/2 oz) caster sugar

125 ml (4 fl oz) Marsala

savoiardi (Italian sponge fingers) or boudoir biscuits to serve

1 Whisk the egg yolks and sugar in a heatproof bowl until light and foamy. Add the Marsala, and whisk to blend.

2 Put the bowl over a pan of simmering water, making sure it does not touch the water. Heat gently, whisking the mixture until it becomes thick and creamy and stands in soft peaks.

3 Remove from the heat and whisk until cool. Pour into glass dishes and serve at once, with savoiardi.

Cook's know-how

Zabaglione is traditionally served warm, poured straight from the bowl into glass dishes as soon as it has thickened. This can be difficult if you are entertaining guests, which is why it is served cool in this recipe. Don't skimp on the whisking in step 3 or the mixture may separate.

HELEN'S PUDDING

SERVES 6

125 g (4 oz) fresh brown breadcrumbs

90 g (3 oz) demerara sugar

75 g (2¹/2 oz) drinking chocolate powder

2 tbsp instant coffee

300 ml (¹/2 pint) double cream

150 ml (¹/4 pint) single cream

60 g (2 oz) plain dark chocolate, grated

1 In a bowl, mix together the breadcrumbs, sugar, drinking chocolate, and coffee granules. In another bowl, whip the creams together until they form soft peaks.

2 Spoon half of the cream into 6 glass serving dishes. Cover with the breadcrumb mixture and then with the remaining cream. Chill for at least 6 hours, or overnight for best results.

3 Sprinkle generously with the grated chocolate just before serving.

Cook's know-how

To make grating chocolate easy, chill it well in the refrigerator before you grate it, and use the largest holes on the grater.

CHOCOLATE TERRINE

This rich and creamy dessert is ideal for a dinner party or weekend treat. A layer of white chocolate and double cream is sandwiched between layers of dark chocolate and double cream made heady with brandy.

SERVES 8–10

DARK CHOCOLATE LAYERS

250 g (8 oz) plain dark chocolate

2 tbsp brandy

2 eggs

375 ml (13 fl oz) double cream

WHITE CHOCOLATE LAYER

90 g (3 oz) white chocolate

1 egg

150 ml (¹/4 pint) double cream

DECORATION

150 ml (¹/4 pint) double or whipping cream, whipped, grated chocolate, and mint sprigs to decorate

1 KG (2 LB) LOAF TIN

1 Make the dark chocolate layers: break the dark chocolate into pieces and place in a heatproof bowl with the brandy over a pan of hot water. Heat gently to melt, then leave to cool.

2 Line the loaf tin with cling film. Set aside.

3 Put the eggs into a heatproof bowl over a pan of hot water. Whisk until the eggs are thick and mousse-like, and leave a trail when the whisk is lifted. Remove from the heat and whisk until the bowl is completely cold.

4 Whip the cream until it just holds its shape. Fold the whisked eggs into the cooled chocolate mixture, then fold in the cream.

5 Pour half of the dark chocolate mixture into the prepared tin, then place in the freezer for about 15 minutes until firm. Reserve the remaining dark chocolate mixture.

6 Meanwhile, make the white chocolate mixture in the same way as the dark chocolate mixture.

7 Pour the white chocolate mixture on top of the firm layer in the tin, and freeze for 15 minutes.

8 Spoon the reserved dark chocolate mixture on top of the white chocolate layer and freeze for about 30 minutes until it is firm enough to slice.

9 Invert the tin on to a serving plate, and remove the cling film. Decorate the terrine with piped rosettes of whipped cream (page 467), grated chocolate, and mint sprigs. Slice thinly to serve.

Healthy option

To make this chocolate terrine slightly less rich and calorific, use Greek yogurt in place of one-third of the double cream. Omit the cream and chocolate decoration, and dust with cocoa powder instead.

CHOCOLATE & BRANDY MOUSSE

SERVES 6

250 g (8 oz) plain dark chocolate, broken into pieces
3 tbsp brandy
3 tbsp cold water
15 g (¹/2 oz) powdered gelatine
4 eggs, plus 2 egg yolks
90 g (3 oz) caster sugar
150 ml (¹/4 pint) whipping cream, whipped until thick

DECORATION

150 ml (¹/4 pint) double or whipping cream, whipped until stiff
chocolate curls or caraque (page 467) to decorate

1 Put the chocolate into a heatproof bowl with the brandy over a pan of hot water. Heat gently until melted. Leave to cool.

2 Put the cold water into a heatproof bowl and sprinkle the gelatine over the top. Leave for about 10 minutes until spongy. Stand the bowl in a pan of hot water and heat gently until dissolved.

3 Combine the eggs, egg yolks, and sugar in a large heatproof bowl, and put over a saucepan of simmering water. Whisk with a hand-held electric mixer until the egg mixture is very thick and mousse-like. Whisk in the dissolved gelatine.

4 Fold the whipped cream into the cooled chocolate, then fold into the egg mixture. Carefully pour into a glass serving bowl, cover, and leave in the refrigerator until set.

5 Decorate with piped rosettes of cream and chocolate curls or caraque (page 467). Serve the mousse chilled.

Cook's know-how

Buy a good-quality plain dark chocolate. For the best flavour, look for a brand with at least 70% cocoa solids.

TIRAMISU

SERVES 8

1 heaped tsp instant coffee granules
125 ml (4 fl oz) boiling water
3 tbsp brandy
2 eggs
65 g (2¹/2 oz) caster sugar
250 g (8 oz) mascarpone cheese
300 ml (¹/2 pint) double cream, whipped until thick
1 packet trifle sponges
60 g (2 oz) plain dark chocolate, coarsely grated
30 g (1 oz) white chocolate, coarsely grated, to decorate

1 Dissolve the coffee in the measured boiling water and mix with the brandy.

2 Combine the eggs and caster sugar in a large bowl and whisk together until thick and light, and the mixture leaves a trail on the surface.

3 Put the mascarpone into a bowl and stir in a little of the egg mixture. Fold in the rest, then fold in the cream.

4 Cut the trifle sponges horizontally in half. Layer the tiramisu (see box, below) with half the sponges, half the coffee and brandy mixture, half the mascarpone mixture, and half the plain chocolate.

5 Repeat the layers with the remaining ingredients, decorating the top with the grated white chocolate and the remaining grated plain chocolate. Cover and chill for at least 4 hours before serving.

Layering the tiramisu

Line the bottom of a large glass serving bowl with half of the sponge pieces. Drizzle half of the coffee and brandy mixture over the sponges.

CREME CARAMEL

SERVES 6

175 g (6 oz) granulated sugar

150 ml (¼ pint) water

4 eggs

30 g (1 oz) vanilla sugar (see box, below right)

600 ml (1 pint) milk

6 SMALL RAMEKINS

1 Combine the sugar and water in a saucepan and heat gently until all the sugar has dissolved. Bring to a boil, and cook without stirring, until golden. Pour into the ramekins.

2 Whisk the eggs and vanilla sugar in a bowl. Heat the milk until just warm, then pour into the egg mixture, stirring well. Strain into the ramekins.

3 Put the ramekins in a roasting tin and add enough hot water to come halfway up the sides of the ramekins. Bake in a preheated oven at 160°C (325°F, Gas 3) for about 40 minutes until just set and firm to the touch but not solid. Cool, then chill for 8 hours.

4 Turn out on to individual plates to serve.

Cook's know-how

You can buy sachets of vanilla sugar or make your own by pushing a halved vanilla pod into a jar of caster sugar – after a few days the sugar will smell and taste of vanilla. If you don't have vanilla sugar, use caster sugar and 1½ tsp vanilla essence.

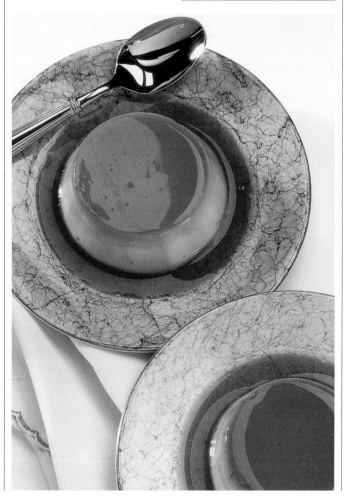

CREME BRULEE

SERVES 6

butter for greasing

4 egg yolks

30 g (1 oz) vanilla sugar (see box, above left)

600 ml (1 pint) single cream

60 g (2 oz) demerara sugar

6 SMALL RAMEKINS OR SHALLOW CREME BRULEE DISHES

1 Lightly butter the ramekins or crème brûlée dishes.

2 In a large bowl, beat the egg yolks with the vanilla sugar. Heat the cream to just below boiling point, then slowly pour into the egg-yolk mixture, stirring all the time.

3 Carefully pour the custard into the ramekins or dishes. Set in a roasting tin and add enough hot water to come halfway up the sides of the ramekins or dishes.

4 Bake in a preheated oven at 160°C (325°F, Gas 3) for about 25 minutes, or until just set and firm to the touch. Leave to cool.

5 Sprinkle the demerara sugar evenly over the top of the set custard. Place under a very hot grill until the sugar melts and caramelizes to a rich golden brown colour.

6 Chill the crème brûlées for no more than 2 hours before serving.

Cook's know-how

The caramel topping should be hard and crisp; don't chill crème brûlée for too long, or the caramel will begin to soften. To reach the rich and creamy custard beneath, crack the hard caramel with the edge of a spoon.

QUICK VANILLA ICE CREAM

SERVES 4–6

6 eggs, separated

175 g (6 oz) vanilla sugar (see box, opposite page far left) or 175 g (6 oz) caster sugar and 1 tsp vanilla essence

450 ml (3/4 pint) double cream, whipped until thick

1 Whisk the egg whites (at high speed if using an electric mixer) until stiff but not dry. Add the sugar, 1 tsp at a time, and continue whisking until the sugar has been incorporated and the egg-white mixture is very stiff and glossy.

2 Put the egg yolks into a separate bowl and whisk at high speed with an electric mixer until the mixture is blended thoroughly.

3 Gently fold the whipped cream and egg yolks into the egg-white mixture. Turn into a large shallow freezerproof container, cover, and leave the mixture to freeze for 8 hours.

4 Transfer the ice cream to the refrigerator for about 10 minutes before serving so that it softens slightly.

CAPPUCCINO ICE CREAM

Substitute caster sugar for the vanilla sugar, and add 3 tbsp each coffee essence and brandy when folding the mixtures in step 3.

LEMON ICE CREAM

Substitute caster sugar for the vanilla sugar, and add the finely grated zest and juice of 3 large lemons when folding the mixtures in step 3.

STRAWBERRY ICE CREAM

Substitute caster sugar for the vanilla sugar. Purée 375 g (12 oz) strawberries and add when folding the mixtures in step 3.

CHOCOLATE & MERINGUE BOMBE

SERVES 8

600 ml (1 pint) vanilla ice cream

600 ml (1 pint) chocolate ice cream

150 ml (1/4 pint) whipping cream

1 tbsp brandy

125 g (4 oz) meringues, coarsely crushed

1.5 LITRE (2 1/2 PINT) BOMBE MOULD OR PUDDING BOWL

1 Chill the bombe mould in the refrigerator. Layer the mould with the chocolate and vanilla ice creams (see box, right).

2 Whip the cream with the brandy until it just holds its shape. Gently fold in the crushed meringues. Use the cream mixture to fill the cavity in the mould. Cover and freeze overnight.

3 Dip the mould into cold water and invert the chocolate and meringue bombe on to a large serving plate. Slice and serve.

Filling the mould

Allow the vanilla ice cream to soften at room temperature for about 20 minutes. Spread it over the base and up the side of the mould. Chill in the freezer until solid.

Soften the chocolate ice cream, then spread it evenly over the vanilla ice cream to make a hollow inner layer. Return to the freezer until solid.

SORBETS

Light and refreshing, sorbets are the perfect ending to a rich meal. Flavoured with fresh fruits and made from a basic mixture of sugar, water, and egg white, they're also low in fat. Decorate each sorbet with its key ingredient or with an ingredient complementary in flavour.

LIME

SERVES 6–8

250 g (8 oz) granulated sugar

600 ml (1 pint) water

finely grated zest and juice of 6 limes

2 egg whites

strips of lime zest to decorate

1 Put the sugar and measured water into a saucepan and heat gently until the sugar dissolves. Bring to a boil and boil for 2 minutes. Remove from the heat, add the lime zest, and leave to cool completely. Stir in the lime juice.

2 Strain the lime syrup into a shallow freezerproof container and freeze for about 2 hours until just mushy. Turn the mixture into a bowl and whisk gently to break down any large crystals.

3 Whisk the egg whites until stiff but not dry, then fold into the lime mixture. Return to the freezer, and freeze until firm. Transfer the sorbet to the refrigerator to soften for about 30 minutes before serving, and top with strips of lime zest.

APRICOT

SERVES 6–8

90 g (3 oz) granulated sugar

300 ml (1/2 pint) water

juice of 1 lemon

750 g (1 1/2 lb) apricots, halved and stoned

2 egg whites

1 Put the sugar, measured water, and lemon juice into a saucepan and heat gently until the sugar has dissolved. Bring to a boil, add the apricots, and simmer for 15 minutes or until very tender. Cool.

2 Peel and slice a few apricots for decoration, and set aside. Press the remainder through a sieve. Mix with the syrup in a freezerproof container, then follow steps 2 and 3 of Lime Sorbet (above). Decorate with the sliced apricots before serving.

PEAR & GINGER

SERVES 6–8

90 g (3 oz) granulated sugar

300 ml (1/2 pint) water

1 tbsp lemon juice

750 g (1 1/2 lb) pears, peeled and cored

1 piece of stem ginger in syrup, finely chopped

2 egg whites

strips of stem ginger to decorate

1 Put the sugar, measured water, and lemon juice into a saucepan and heat gently until the sugar dissolves. Bring to a boil, add the pears, and poach gently, basting with the sugar syrup from time to time, for 20–25 minutes until the pears are tender. Cool, then purée in a food processor.

2 Add the chopped stem ginger to the pear purée. Pour the pear mixture into a freezerproof container, then follow steps 2 and 3 of Lime Sorbet (left). Decorate with stem ginger before serving.

RASPBERRY

SERVES 6–8

500 g (1 lb) raspberries

175 g (6 oz) granulated sugar

600 ml (1 pint) water

juice of 1 orange

3 egg whites

raspberries and mint sprigs to decorate

1 Purée the raspberries in a food processor, then push through a sieve to remove the seeds. Put the sugar and measured water into a saucepan and heat gently until the sugar dissolves. Bring to a boil, then boil for 5 minutes. Pour into a bowl and cool.

2 Stir in raspberry purée and orange juice. Pour into a freezerproof container, then follow steps 2 and 3 of Lime Sorbet (left). Decorate with raspberries and mint sprigs before serving.

GRANITAS

Italian granitas are similar to sorbets but even easier to make: they are simply flavoured ice crystals.

COFFEE

Put 60 g (2 oz) caster sugar and 4 tbsp instant coffee granules into a pan with 750 ml (1 1/4 pints) water and bring to a boil. Simmer for about 5 minutes. Leave to cool, then pour into a freezerproof container. Freeze, stirring occasionally, for 5 hours.

LEMON

Put 200 g (7 oz) caster sugar into a saucepan, add 500 ml (16 fl oz) water, and bring to a boil. Simmer for 5 minutes. Leave to cool. Add 2 tsp finely grated lemon zest and the juice of 4 lemons to the sugar syrup. Pour into a freezerproof container and freeze, stirring occasionally, for 5 hours.

WATERMELON

Remove and discard the rind and seeds from 1 kg (2 lb) watermelon. Purée the flesh in a food processor. Pour into a freezerproof container and mix in 30 g (1 oz) icing sugar and 1 1/2 tsp lemon juice. Freeze, stirring occasionally, for 5 hours.

CLOCKWISE FROM TOP RIGHT: Lime, Raspberry, Pear & Ginger, and Apricot Sorbets.

PEACH MELBA

SERVES 4

4 ripe peaches, peeled, stoned, and sliced

8 scoops of vanilla ice cream

mint sprigs to decorate

MELBA SAUCE

375 g (12 oz) raspberries

about 4 tbsp icing sugar

1 Make the Melba sauce (see box, below).

2 Arrange the peach slices in 4 glass serving dishes. Top each with 2 scoops of ice cream and some sauce. Decorate with mint sprigs and the remaining raspberries.

Making Melba sauce

Purée 250 g (8 oz) of the raspberries. Push through a sieve to remove the seeds.

Sift the icing sugar over the purée and stir in.

RICH VANILLA ICE CREAM

Home-made ice cream tastes better than commercially made ice cream, and it keeps for up to a month in the freezer. If you have an electric ice-cream maker, you will get a smoother result.

SERVES 4–6

4 egg yolks

125 g (4 oz) caster sugar

300 ml (1/2 pint) milk

300 ml (1/2 pint) double cream

1 1/2 tsp vanilla essence

strawberries to decorate

1 Put the egg yolks and sugar into a bowl and whisk until light in colour.

2 Heat the milk in a heavy pan to just below boiling point. Add a little of the hot milk to the egg-yolk mixture and stir to blend, then pour in the remaining milk.

3 Pour back into the pan and heat gently, stirring, until the froth disappears and the mixture coats the back of a spoon. Do not boil.

4 Leave the custard to cool, then stir in the cream and vanilla essence.

5 Pour into a container and freeze for 3 hours. Tip into a bowl and mash to break down the ice crystals. Return to container. Freeze for 2 hours. Mash and freeze for another 2 hours. Remove from the freezer 30 minutes before serving, and decorate.

CHOCOLATE ICE CREAM

In step 2, heat the milk with 125 g (4 oz) chopped dark chocolate. Let it melt before adding to the egg-yolk mixture.

CHOCOLATE CHIP ICE CREAM

In step 2, heat the milk with 125 g (4 oz) chopped white chocolate. Let it melt before adding to the egg-yolk mixture. Stir 60 g (2 oz) dark chocolate chips into the custard with the cream in step 4.

BANANA & HONEY ICE CREAM

Mash 500 g (1 lb) bananas with 3 tbsp lemon juice and 2 tbsp honey. Add to the custard with the cream in step 4.

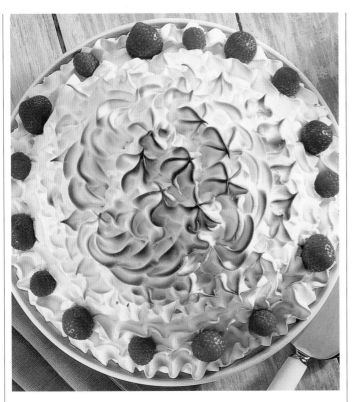

BAKED ALASKA

SERVES 8

1 x 20 cm (8 in) sponge flan case
250 g (8 oz) raspberries, sliced strawberries, or other summer fruits
450 ml (3/4 pint) vanilla ice cream
2 egg whites
125 g (4 oz) caster sugar
whole berries to decorate

1 Put the sponge flan case into a shallow ovenproof serving dish. Arrange the fruits in the case.

2 Put the ice cream on top of the fruits and put in the freezer to keep the ice cream frozen while making the meringue.

3 Whisk the egg whites (an electric mixer can be used) until stiff but not dry.

4 Add the caster sugar, 1 tsp at a time, and continue to whisk until the sugar has been incorporated and the meringue mixture is stiff and glossy.

5 Pipe or spoon the meringue over the ice cream, covering it completely.

6 Bake immediately in a preheated oven at 230°C (450°F, Gas 8) for 3–4 minutes until the meringue is tinged with brown. Serve at once, decorated with raspberries and strawberries.

Cook's know-how

A block of firm ice cream is needed for this recipe – do not use soft-scoop ice cream. Make sure the ice cream is completely covered by the egg white, which stops the ice cream melting.

ICED CHRISTMAS PUDDING

SERVES 8

175 g (6 oz) mixed dried fruit
60 g (2 oz) ready-to-eat dried apricots, chopped
60 g (2 oz) glacé cherries, halved
3 tbsp brandy
3 eggs
125 g (4 oz) caster sugar
450 ml (3/4 pint) milk
450 ml (3/4 pint) double cream
150 ml (1/4 pint) single cream
1.75 LITRE (3 PINT) PUDDING BOWL

1 Combine the dried fruit, apricots, glacé cherries, and brandy. Cover and leave to soak for 8 hours.

2 In a large bowl, whisk together the eggs and sugar. Heat the milk in a heavy saucepan to just below boiling point. Pour into the egg mixture, stirring.

3 Pour back into the pan. Cook gently, stirring with a wooden spoon, until the froth disappears and the mixture thickens. Do not boil. Remove from the heat and leave to cool.

4 Whip 300 ml (1/2 pint) double cream and the single cream together until they are just beginning to hold their shape. Fold into the custard with the fruit and brandy mixture.

5 Turn into a shallow freezerproof container and freeze for 2 hours or until beginning to set but still slightly soft.

6 Remove the pudding from the freezer and mix well to distribute the fruit evenly. Spoon into the pudding bowl, cover, and return to the freezer. Freeze for 3 hours or until firm.

7 Remove from the freezer about 20 minutes before serving to soften. Turn out on to a serving plate, and spoon the remaining cream, lightly whipped, on top. Slice and serve at once.

CASSATA

SERVES 8

30 g (1 oz) candied angelica, rinsed, dried, and chopped

30 g (1 oz) glacé cherries, rinsed, dried, and chopped

30 g (1 oz) chopped mixed candied peel

2 tbsp dark rum

600 ml (1 pint) raspberry sorbet

150 ml (¼ pint) double cream, whipped until thick

600 ml (1 pint) vanilla ice cream

900 ML (1 ½ PINT) TERRINE

1 Chill the terrine. Put the angelica, glacé cherries, and candied peel in a bowl.

2 Add the rum and stir well, then leave to soak while preparing the ice-cream layers.

3 Allow the sorbet to soften, then spread it evenly over the bottom of the chilled terrine. Chill in the freezer until solid.

4 Fold the fruit and rum mixture into the whipped cream. Spoon into the terrine and level the surface. Return to the freezer until firm.

5 Allow the vanilla ice cream to soften, then spread it evenly over the fruit layer. Cover and freeze for 8 hours.

6 To turn out, dip the terrine into warm water and invert the cassata on to a large serving plate. Slice, and serve at once.

Cook's know-how

This is not a true cassata, but a layered ice-cream "sandwich" that has borrowed its name. A true Sicilian cassata is a bombe of liqueur-soaked sponge cake filled with ricotta cheese studded with candied fruits and grated chocolate. It is often served at wedding feasts and other celebrations.

FROZEN LEMON FLUMMERY

SERVES 4

150 ml (¼ pint) double cream

finely grated zest and juice of 1 large lemon

175 g (6 oz) caster sugar

300 ml (½ pint) milk

thinly pared zest of 1 lemon, cut into strips, to decorate

1 Whip the cream until it forms soft peaks. Add the lemon zest and juice, caster sugar, and milk, and mix until evenly blended.

2 Pour into a shallow freezerproof container, cover, and freeze for at least 6 hours or until firm.

3 Cut the mixture into chunks, then transfer to a food processor and work until smooth and creamy. Pour into 4 individual freezerproof dishes and freeze for about 8 hours.

4 Blanch the strips of lemon zest in a pan of boiling water for 1 minute only. Drain, rinse, and pat dry.

5 Decorate the flummery with the strips of lemon zest and serve.

FROZEN ORANGE FLUMMERY

Substitute the finely grated zest and juice of 1 orange for the lemon, and reduce the caster sugar to 125 g (4 oz). Decorate with blanched strips of orange zest.

13
CAKES & TEABREADS

30–60 MINUTES

OVER 60 MINUTES

ECONOMICAL

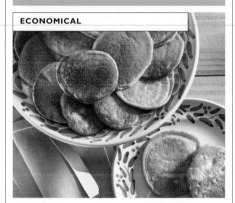

WHOLEMEAL DROP SCONES

Family favourite: a simple batter made with wholemeal flour for nutty flavour. Spooned on to a hot griddle and served with syrup.

MAKES 20 55 calories each

Takes 30 minutes   Page 519

BRANDY SNAPS

A delicate batter flavoured with ground ginger and lemon juice, baked until golden, and rolled before crisp.

MAKES 15 107 calories each

Takes 40 minutes, plus cooling   Page 521

FRENCH CLASSIC

ALMOND TUILES

Crisp and delicate: a sweet, almond-flavoured batter baked until golden brown, then shaped into curves before crisp.

MAKES 30 45 calories each

Takes 30 minutes, plus cooling   Page 520

TRADITIONAL

VICTORIA SANDWICH CAKE

Two light and golden layers of sponge sandwiched with jam, and sprinkled generously with caster sugar.

CUTS INTO 8 SLICES 386 calories each

Takes 35 minutes, plus cooling   Page 510

CORNBREAD

An American favourite: a simple, slightly sweet batter made from polenta. Baked until golden and served warm.

MAKES 9 SQUARES 230 calories each

Takes 40 minutes, plus cooling   Page 516

FAMILY CHOICE

DEVON SCONES

An English teatime favourite: a simple dough makes featherweight scones. Serve spread with butter and jam.

MAKES 12 133 calories each

Takes 30 minutes, plus cooling   Page 518

FORK BISCUITS

Plain and simple: a butter-enriched dough, imprinted with a fork pattern and baked until crisp and golden.

MAKES 32 104 calories each

Takes 30 minutes, plus cooling   Page 521

FRIDGE COOKIES

Crisp and sweet: a walnut-studded dough, shaped into a roll, cut into thin slices, and baked until golden. Very easy to make.

MAKES 50 59 calories each

Takes 35 minutes, plus chilling   Page 524

MINCEMEAT BUNS

Rich and fruity: a miniature and quick version of mince pies. Baked in individual cake cases.

MAKES 32 137 calories each

Takes 40 minutes, plus cooling   Page 512

OVER 60 MINUTES

SWISS ROLL

An old favourite: a light golden sponge spread generously with a layer of raspberry jam, rolled up, and decorated with sugar.

CUTS INTO 8 SLICES 195 calories each
Takes 45 minutes, plus cooling   Page 507

VIENNESE FINGERS

Pretty and delicious: a rich butter dough piped into fingers, baked until golden brown, and each end dipped in chocolate.

MAKES 12 215 calories each
Takes 30 minutes, plus cooling   Page 520

PINWHEEL BISCUITS

Attractive and easy: vanilla and coffee doughs rolled together, cut into thin slices, and baked.

MAKES 18 98 calories each
Takes 45 minutes, plus chilling   Page 524

COCONUT MACAROONS

Almonds and coconut flavour these macaroons. Crisp and golden on the outside and deliciously tender on the inside.

MAKES 26 116 calories each
Takes 40 minutes, plus cooling   Page 520

POTATO FARLS

An old-fashioned treat: a biscuit dough made with mashed potatoes and baked until crisp. Simple and delicious.

MAKES 12 113 calories each
Takes 40 minutes, plus cooling   Page 519

FAMILY CHOICE

FLAPJACKS

Rich, chewy, and very easy to make: an oat-studded batter is spread into a roasting tin, baked, and cut into fingers.

MAKES 24 102 calories each
Takes 45 minutes, plus cooling   Page 524

GINGER SNAPS

Crisp and spicy: ginger and cinnamon spice a dough enriched with butter and baked until dark golden brown.

MAKES 15 81 calories each
Takes 30 minutes, plus cooling   Page 521

WIMBLEDON CAKE

Two layers of golden sponge filled with freshly whipped cream, sweet and juicy strawberries, and tropical passion fruit.

CUTS INTO 8 SLICES 260 calories each
Takes 60 minutes, plus cooling   Page 507

ECONOMICAL

WELSH CAKES

Old-fashioned griddle cakes studded with currants and flavoured with mixed spice. Served hot from the pan or left to cool slightly.

MAKES 12 204 calories each
Takes 30 minutes, plus cooling   Page 518

OVER 60 MINUTES

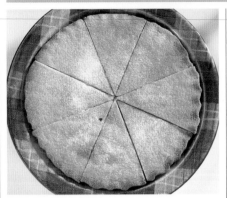

SHORTBREAD

Highland classic: a dough made rich with butter, baked until golden, and sprinkled with sugar.

MAKES 8 WEDGES 233 calories each

Takes 55 minutes, plus cooling   Page 516

AMERICAN CLASSIC

DEVIL'S FOOD CAKE

Layers of moist, rich chocolate sponge spread with a sweet, fluffy white American icing. Perfect for family gatherings.

CUTS INTO 12 SLICES 513 calories each

Takes 60 minutes, plus cooling   Page 504

CARROT CAKE

American favourite: moist cake with chopped walnuts, mashed banana, and grated carrot. Cream cheese icing is spread on top.

CUTS INTO 10 SQUARES 412 calories each

Takes 1¼ hours, plus cooling   Page 503

MARBLED COFFEE RING CAKE

Two batters, one coffee flavoured and one plain, swirled together, baked, and topped with coffee icing and white chocolate.

CUTS INTO 12 SLICES 471 calories each

Takes 1¼ hours   Page 505

IRISH SODA BREAD

A traditional bread made light and tasty with buttermilk. Scored and baked until golden brown.

CUTS INTO 8 WEDGES 227 calories each

Takes 45 minutes, plus cooling   Page 519

TRADITIONAL

GINGERBREAD

Moist and tasty: a batter made dark and delicious with treacle and spices. Best when baked ahead.

MAKES 15 SQUARES 349 calories each

Takes 1¼ hours, plus cooling   Page 516

ICED LIME TRAYBAKE

Light and delicious: a lime-flavoured cake batter baked in a rectangular tin, topped with tangy lime icing, and cut into squares.

MAKES 12 SQUARES 340 calories each

Takes 50 minutes, plus cooling   Page 510

CHOCOLATE & ORANGE MOUSSE CAKE

Two layers of delicate chocolate sponge filled with chocolate and orange flavoured mousse.

CUTS INTO 12 SLICES 417 calories each

Takes 1¼ hours, plus chilling   Page 506

WHITE CHOCOLATE GATEAU

Rich and attractive: delicious whipped cream hides a cocoa-flavoured sponge. Perfect for special occasions.

CUTS INTO 14 SLICES 391 calories each

Takes 1¼ hours, plus cooling   Page 505

OVER 60 MINUTES

FRUITY BANANA BREAD

A hearty loaf made from a spiced fruit batter. Perfect use for ripe bananas. Serve sliced and spread with butter.

CUTS INTO 12 SLICES 334 calories each

Takes 1½ hours, plus cooling   Page 513

PICNIC FARE

COURGETTE LOAF

American favourite: courgettes baked until sweet and tender in a deliciously spiced and walnut-studded batter.

CUTS INTO 12 SLICES 331 calories each

Takes 1½ hours, plus cooling   Page 503

DATE & WALNUT LOAF

Sweet dates and crunchy walnuts are baked in a lightly sweetened batter. Delicious sliced and spread with butter.

CUTS INTO 12 SLICES 269 calories each

Takes 1¾ hours, plus cooling   Page 517

BATTENBURG CAKE

Classic cake made from chocolate and vanilla batters wrapped with almond paste.

CUTS INTO 8 SLICES 425 calories each

Takes 60 minutes, plus cooling   Page 511

BARA BRITH

A deliciously tender loaf studded with tea-soaked dried fruit. Serve sliced and spread with butter.

CUTS INTO 12 SLICES 257 calories each

Takes 2 hours, plus soaking   Page 517

TRADITIONAL

SIMNEL CAKE

Moist and tender fruit cake, brushed with apricot jam, topped with almond paste, and decorated with balls of almond paste.

CUTS INTO 12 SLICES 494 calories each

Takes 2¾ hours, plus cooling   Page 512

FAMILY CHOICE

DUNDEE CAKE

Rich and fruity: sultanas, currants, raisins, cherries, and lemon, baked in a batter until golden, and decorated with almonds.

CUTS INTO 12 SLICES 384 calories each

Takes 1¾ hours, plus cooling   Page 513

HEAVENLY CHOCOLATE CAKE

A rich chocolate and almond sponge cut in half, filled and covered with fudge icing, and decorated with white chocolate curls.

CUTS INTO 8 SLICES 615 calories each

Takes 1½ hours, plus cooling   Page 504

RICH FRUIT CAKE

Classic: raisins, sultanas, glacé cherries, spices, and brandy flavour this moist cake. Best when baked ahead.

CUTS INTO 10 SLICES 570 calories each

Takes 2–2¼ hours, plus cooling   Page 511

CAKES & TEABREADS KNOW-HOW

CAKE-MAKING is often seen as the test of a cook's skills, but there are lots of cakes and teabreads, as well as scones, biscuits, cookies, and American-style muffins that are really quite simple to make and just as delicious as more elaborate creations. If you are a beginner, just remember to follow recipes carefully, and make sure your weighing and measuring is accurate. Use the right equipment and tins, and take the time to prepare cakes properly, and you'll achieve perfect results every time. You'll find that once you've gained confidence, you'll be able to experiment with more difficult recipes.

STORING

Most cakes are best eaten freshly made, particularly sponge cakes that don't contain fat, but if you do want to keep a cake, be sure to store it in an airtight container. Put the cake on the upturned lid of the cake tin, then put the tin over the top. This makes it easy to remove the cake from the tin. Fruit cakes and cakes made by the melting method, such as gingerbread, will improve with keeping (store in an airtight tin). Wrap fruit cake in greaseproof paper and then overwrap in foil. Don't put foil directly in contact with a fruit cake as the acid in the fruit may react with the foil. Any cake that has a filling or icing of whipped cream, butter-icing, or soft-cheese should be kept in the refrigerator. Scones, American-style muffins, and most teabreads are best eaten freshly made.

Most biscuits can be stored in an airtight tin for a few days; if they soften, crisp them up in a warm oven. Allow cakes and biscuits to cool completely on a wire rack before putting them into a tin. Do not store cakes and biscuits together as the moisture from the cake will soften the biscuits.

MICROWAVING

Microwave-baked cakes and biscuits can be disappointingly pale in colour and gluey in texture. Instead, in baking the microwave comes into its own when used as an accessory to the conventional oven. Here are good things to use it for:
• Melting chocolate: break chocolate into small pieces, put into a bowl, and cook on LOW for 3–5 minutes until melted and shiny; stir halfway.
• Melting crystallized honey or syrup: heat on HIGH for 1–2 minutes. If kept in the jar, take off the lid.
• Softening hardened, set sugar: cook on HIGH for 30–40 seconds.
• Skinning and toasting hazelnuts: place them on paper towels and cook on HIGH for 30 seconds, then remove skins. Cook until golden.

FREEZING

If baked goods are not eaten immediately freezing is a good way to keep them fresh. Cakes, teabreads, biscuits, American-style muffins, and scones all freeze well.

Wrap plain cakes, fruit cakes and teabreads in foil or freezer wrap. If a cake has been iced or decorated, tray freeze it, then place in a rigid container or freezer bag. Fruit cakes can be stored for up to 12 months; un-iced cakes for 4–6 months; iced cakes for 2–3 months. Unwrap decorated cakes before thawing, but leave other cakes in their wrapping.

Biscuits, muffins, and scones can be stored for 6 months. Interleave biscuits with foil or freezer wrap to keep them separate. Thaw biscuits and muffins at room temperature. Scones can be successfully reheated or toasted from frozen.

BAKING INGREDIENTS

In baking it is important to use the ingredients specified in a recipe. Choose the best quality available.

Butter and other fats
In simple cakes, biscuits, and teabreads, where flavour is important, always use butter. In other cakes, margarine is acceptable. For all-in-one mixtures soft margarine is best as it is made up of 80% fat and blends easily. Low-fat spreads are not suitable for baking because of their high water content, so check before you buy. If oil is called for, use a mild, light one such as sunflower oil or sweeter corn oil.

Flour
Both plain and self-raising flours are used in baking, either white or wholemeal. Self-raising flour includes a raising agent (usually a mixture of bicarbonate of soda and cream of tartar), so if you want to substitute plain flour, add 2 tsp baking powder to each 250 g (8 oz) flour.

Raising agents
Baking powder and bicarbonate of soda are used to raise cakes, teabreads, and biscuits. When a mixture contains baking powder, or self-raising flour, be sure to bake without delay, while the chemicals are still active.

Sugar
For most mixtures, it is essential to use a sugar that dissolves easily, such as caster sugar or soft, fine muscovado sugar. Granulated sugar can be used in rubbed-in mixtures. Coarse demerara sugar is fine for melted mixtures and is ideal for sprinkling on the top of cakes, as is icing sugar. Other sweeteners used in baking include golden syrup, honey, molasses, and malt extract, as well as concentrated fruit purée or juice.

Eggs
Eggs at room temperature are more easily aerated than cold eggs taken straight from the refrigerator. Cold eggs can also cause some cake mixtures to curdle.

BAKING BISCUITS

When arranging biscuits on prepared baking sheets, leave enough space between them to allow for spreading, if necessary. As biscuits cook quickly, they can easily be baked in batches if you don't have enough baking sheets.

At the end of the baking time, many biscuits will still feel a little soft in the middle: they will continue to bake on the hot sheet after being removed from the oven. If the recipe directs, leave them to firm up for 1–2 minutes before transferring to a wire rack. Avoid letting biscuits cool completely on the sheet or they may stick.

PREPARING CAKE TINS

Lightly greasing the tin ensures a cake will turn out easily. Some recipes also call for the tin to be floured or lined with greaseproof paper or baking parchment.

Greasing and flouring

Use melted or softened butter or margarine, or oil, according to the recipe. Brush over the bottom and side of the tin using a pastry brush or paper towels. If flouring, add a spoonful of flour and tilt the tin to coat it with a thin layer. Tip out any excess flour.

Lining

1 Set the cake tin on a sheet of greaseproof paper or parchment and mark around the base with a pencil or the tip of a knife.

2 Cut out the shape, cutting just inside the line, then press smoothly over the bottom of the tin. Lightly grease if directed in the recipe.

ALL-IN-ONE CAKES

Be sure to use a soft margarine for this quick, simple technique.

Put all the ingredients into a large bowl and beat together with a hand-held electric mixer until combined. You can also mix in a food processor or by hand.

WHISKED CAKES

Light, fatless sponges are raised by air whisked into eggs. Use a hand-held electric mixer or a large, table-top mixer. If using a hand-held mixer, set it at high speed.

1 Whisk the eggs, or egg yolks, with the sugar until the mixture is light, pale, and thick enough to leave a trail on the surface when the beaters are lifted out.

2 Gently fold in the flour and any other ingredients. If the eggs have been separated, the whisked egg whites should be folded into the mixture last of all.

CREAMED CAKES

The creaming method is used for both cakes and biscuits. A wooden spoon, rubber spatula, or electric mixer are all suitable. Be sure to soften the butter or margarine first.

1 Cream the fat and sugar together until the mixture is pale in colour and fluffy in texture. Keep scraping the side of the bowl with a spoon or spatula to incorporate all of the mixture.

2 Lightly beat the eggs. Gradually add the eggs to the creamed mixture, beating well between each addition. If the mixture curdles, which will result in a dense-textured cake, beat in a spoonful of the flour.

3 Sift over the flour and any other dry ingredients. Using a wooden spoon, gently fold in the flour until well combined. Any liquid ingredients should also be added at this stage.

BAKING, TESTING, & COOLING CAKES

Before baking cakes, teabreads, and biscuits, be sure to preheat the oven to the correct temperature. If you need to, adjust the position of the shelves before you turn on the oven.

1 As soon as the mixture is prepared, turn it into the tin and level the surface. Tap the tin on the work surface to break any large air bubbles. Transfer immediately to the oven.

2 When cooked, a cake will shrink slightly from the side of the tin. To test, lightly press the middle with a fingertip; the cake should spring back. Rich cakes should feel firm to the touch.

3 Set the cake tin on a wire rack and leave to cool for about 10 minutes. Run a knife around the side of the cake to free it from the tin.

4 Hold a wire rack over the top of the tin, then invert the rack and tin so that the cake falls on to the rack. Carefully lift the tin away from the cake.

5 Peel off the lining paper. With a light-textured cake, turn it over again so the base is on the rack; this will prevent the rack marking the top.

6 To cut the cake in half, steady it by setting one hand gently on top. Cut the cake horizontally, using a gentle sawing action.

Baking know-how

Be sure to use the correct size tin, as stated in the recipe. To check the dimensions of a cake tin, measure inside the top rim. To work out the depth, measure from the bottom to the top rim on the inside of the tin. To check the capacity of a tin, measure how much water is needed to fill it to the brim.

•

Bake for the minimum time given in the recipe before opening the oven door. If the door is opened too soon it may cause some cakes to deflate.

•

If a cake looks as though it is browning too quickly, cover the top loosely with foil.

•

If baking several cake layers, stagger them on the oven shelves so one is not directly beneath another.

•

When measuring ingredients with a spoon, don't hold the spoon directly over the bowl or you may accidentally add too much.

TESTING FRUIT CAKES

For fruit cakes and fruited teabreads, insert a metal skewer or long wooden cocktail stick into the middle: the skewer or stick should come out clean, without any moist crumbs sticking to it.

FILLING & ICING CAKES

There are many simple ways to fill or decorate cakes. Whipped cream, jam, or chocolate spread make quick and easy fillings. Butter-icing can be made in a variety of flavours, to complement the flavour of the cake.

Chocolate butter-icing
In a bowl, soften 150 g (5 oz) butter. Add 30 g (1 oz) cocoa powder and 250 g (8 oz) sifted icing sugar, and beat together until smooth. Add a little milk if necessary to give a spreading consistency. For a citrus icing, omit the cocoa powder and add finely grated orange or lemon zest.

Spreading icing
Only ice a cake when it has cooled completely. Use a large palette knife and spread the icing with long, smooth strokes over the top and side of the cake. Dip the palette knife in warm water if the icing sticks to it.

COURGETTE LOAF

CUTS INTO 12 SLICES

250 g (8 oz) courgettes
2 eggs
125 ml (4 fl oz) sunflower oil, plus extra for greasing
250 g (8 oz) caster sugar
1/4 tsp vanilla essence (optional)
375 g (12 oz) self-raising flour
1 tsp ground cinnamon
1/2 tsp salt
60 g (2 oz) walnut pieces, coarsely chopped
1 KG (2 LB) LOAF TIN

1 Coarsely grate the courgettes, put them into a sieve, and leave for about 30 minutes to drain.

2 Beat the eggs until light and foamy. Add the sunflower oil, sugar, vanilla essence (if using), and courgettes and mix lightly until combined.

3 Sift the flour, cinnamon, and salt into a large bowl. Make a well in the middle, pour in the courgette mixture, and stir to mix thoroughly. Stir in the chopped walnuts.

4 Pour the mixture into the greased loaf tin and bake in a preheated oven at 180°C (350°F, Gas 4) for about 50 minutes until firm. Turn out and cool.

Cook's know-how

For best results, the courgettes should be thoroughly drained. Press into the sieve with your hand or the back of a spoon to extract the excess juices.

CARROT CAKE

CUTS INTO 10 SQUARES

150 ml (1/4 pint) sunflower oil, plus extra for greasing
250 g (8 oz) wholemeal self-raising flour
2 tsp baking powder
150 g (5 oz) light muscovado sugar
60 g (2 oz) walnuts, coarsely chopped
125 g (4 oz) carrots, grated
2 ripe bananas, mashed
2 eggs
1 tbsp milk

TOPPING

250 g (8 oz) low-fat soft cheese, at room temperature
2 tsp clear honey
1 tsp lemon juice
chopped walnuts to decorate
18 CM (7 IN) SQUARE CAKE TIN

1 Lightly grease the cake tin and line the bottom with baking parchment.

2 Combine all the cake ingredients in a large bowl. Mix well until thoroughly blended. Turn into the prepared cake tin and level the surface.

3 Bake in a preheated oven at 180°C (350°F, Gas 4) for about 50 minutes until the cake is well risen, firm to the touch, and beginning to shrink away from the sides of the tin.

4 Leave the cake to cool in the tin for a few minutes. Turn out on to a wire rack, peel off the lining paper, and leave to cool completely.

5 Make the topping: mix together the cheese, honey, and lemon juice. Spread on top of the cake and sprinkle the walnuts over the top. Store the cake in the refrigerator until ready to serve.

Healthy option

A full-fat cream cheese frosting is the traditional topping for carrot cake, but here a low-fat soft cheese is suggested, and it tastes equally good. If you prefer not to have frosting at all, spread clear honey on top of the cake while it is hot from the oven, and sprinkle with chopped walnuts.

HEAVENLY CHOCOLATE CAKE

CUTS INTO 8 SLICES

125 g (4 oz) butter, plus extra for greasing

200 g (7 oz) plain dark chocolate, broken into pieces

2 tbsp water

3 eggs, separated

125 g (4 oz) caster sugar

90 g (3 oz) self-raising flour

60 g (2 oz) ground almonds

FUDGE ICING

60 g (2 oz) butter

30 g (1 oz) cocoa powder

3 tbsp milk

250 g (8 oz) icing sugar, sifted

white chocolate curls (page 467) to decorate

DEEP 20 CM (8 IN) CAKE TIN

1 Lightly butter the tin and line the bottom with baking parchment.

2 Put the chocolate into a heatproof bowl with the butter and water. Put the bowl over a pan of hot water and heat gently, stirring, until the mixture has melted. Cool.

3 Combine the egg yolks and caster sugar in a large bowl and whisk together with an electric whisk until fluffy and very light in colour. Stir in the cooled chocolate mixture. Carefully fold in the flour and ground almonds.

4 In a separate bowl, whisk the egg whites until stiff but not dry. Fold into the sponge mixture, gently but thoroughly. Pour the mixture into the prepared tin. Bake in a preheated oven at 180°C (350°F, Gas 4) for 50 minutes or until well risen and firm to the touch.

5 Leave the cake to cool in the tin for a few minutes, turn out on to a wire rack, and peel off the lining paper. Cool completely. Make the fudge icing: melt the butter in a pan, add the cocoa powder, and cook, stirring, for 1 minute. Stir in the milk and icing sugar. Beat well until smooth. Leave to cool until thickened.

6 Split the cake in half horizontally and sandwich the layers together with half of the fudge icing. With a palette knife, spread the remaining icing over the top and sides of the cake. Decorate with white chocolate curls.

DEVIL'S FOOD CAKE

CUTS INTO 12 SLICES

175 g (6 oz) soft butter or margarine, plus extra for greasing

90 g (3 oz) plain dark chocolate, broken into pieces

175 ml (6 fl oz) hot water

300 g (10 oz) light muscovado sugar

3 eggs, beaten

300 g (10 oz) plain flour

1½ tsp bicarbonate of soda

1½ tsp baking powder

1 tsp vanilla essence

150 ml (¼ pint) soured cream

AMERICAN FROSTING

400 g (13 oz) caster sugar

2 egg whites

4 tbsp hot water

pinch of cream of tartar

3 x 20 CM (8 IN) SANDWICH CAKE TINS

1 Grease the tins with butter and line the bottoms with baking parchment.

2 Put the chocolate into a pan with the water. Heat gently, stirring, until the chocolate melts. Cool.

3 Combine the butter and sugar in a bowl and beat until light and fluffy. Gradually add the eggs, beating well.

4 Stir in the melted chocolate. Sift together the flour, bicarbonate of soda, and baking powder. Fold into the chocolate mixture until evenly blended, then fold in the vanilla essence and soured cream.

5 Divide the mixture evenly among the prepared tins. Bake in a preheated oven at 190°C (375°F, Gas 5) for about 25 minutes until well risen, springy to the touch, and just shrinking away from the sides of the tins.

6 Turn out the cakes on to a wire rack, peel off the lining paper, and leave to cool.

7 Make the American frosting: combine all the ingredients in a heatproof bowl. Set the bowl over a pan of hot water and whisk with an electric mixer for 12 minutes or until the mixture is white, thick, and stands in peaks.

8 Use half of the American frosting to sandwich the layers together, then spread the remainder over the top and side of the cake, swirling it decoratively and pulling it into peaks with the flat of a small palette knife.

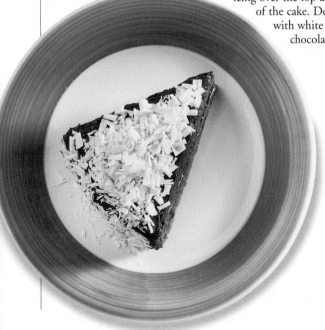

MARBLED COFFEE RING CAKE

CUTS INTO 12 SLICES

250 g (8 oz) soft butter, plus extra for greasing

250 g (8 oz) caster sugar

4 eggs

250 g (8 oz) self-raising flour

2 tsp baking powder

2 tsp instant coffee

1 tbsp hot water

30 g (1 oz) white chocolate

ICING

60 g (2 oz) butter, softened

3 tbsp milk

2 tbsp instant coffee

250 g (8 oz) icing sugar, sifted

1.75 LITRE (2¾ PINT) RING MOULD

1 Lightly grease the ring mould with butter.

2 Combine the butter, sugar, eggs, flour, and baking powder in a large bowl. Beat until smooth.

3 Put half of the mixture into another bowl. Dissolve the instant coffee in the measured hot water and stir into one half of the cake mixture.

4 Drop tablespoonfuls of the plain mixture into the ring mould, then tablespoonfuls of the coffee mixture on top of the plain mixture. Marble by swirling together with a skewer.

5 Bake in a preheated oven at 180°C (350°F, Gas 4) for 40 minutes or until well risen and firm to the touch. Leave to cool for a few minutes, then turn out on to a wire rack set over a tray, and cool completely.

6 Make the icing: combine the butter, milk, and coffee in a pan and heat, stirring, until smooth. Remove from the heat and beat in the icing sugar until smooth and glossy.

7 Leave to cool, then pour over the cake, spreading it over the sides to cover completely. Leave to set.

8 Melt the white chocolate in a heatproof bowl over a pan of hot water. Cool slightly, then spoon into a plastic bag. Snip off a corner of the bag and drizzle the chocolate over the cake. Leave to set.

WHITE CHOCOLATE GATEAU

CUTS INTO 14 SLICES

90 g (3 oz) butter, melted and cooled slightly, plus extra for greasing

6 large eggs

175 g (6 oz) caster sugar

125 g (4 oz) self-raising flour

30 g (1 oz) cocoa powder

2 tbsp cornflour

FILLING AND TOPPING

300 ml (½ pint) double or whipping cream, whipped until thick

white chocolate curls (optional – page 467)

DEEP 23 CM (9 IN) ROUND CAKE TIN

1 Lightly butter the cake tin and line the bottom of the tin with baking parchment.

2 Put the eggs and sugar into a large bowl and whisk together with an electric mixer on high speed until the mixture is pale and thick enough to leave a trail on itself when the whisk is lifted out.

3 Sift together the flour, cocoa powder, and cornflour, and fold half into the egg mixture. Pour half of the cooled butter around the edge; fold in gently.

4 Repeat with the remaining flour mixture and butter, folding gently.

5 Turn the mixture into the prepared cake tin and tilt the tin to level the surface. Bake in a preheated oven at 180°C (350°F, Gas 4) for 35–40 minutes until the sponge is well risen and firm to the touch. Turn out on to a rack, peel off the lining, and cool.

6 Cut the cake in half horizontally and sandwich the layers together with half of the whipped cream. Cover the cake with a thin layer of cream, then pipe the remainder around the top and bottom edges.

7 Press the chocolate curls over the top and side of the cake, if preferred.

505

CHOCOLATE & ORANGE MOUSSE CAKE

This cake is made of chocolate sponge layers sandwiched together with a deliciously fluffy chocolate and orange mousse. When making the mousse, do not overwhisk the egg whites; when they just flop over at the tip they are ready to fold into the chocolate mixture.

CUTS INTO 12 SLICES

butter for greasing

4 eggs

125 g (4 oz) caster sugar

90 g (3 oz) self-raising flour

30 g (1 oz) cocoa powder

MOUSSE

175 g (6 oz) plain dark chocolate, broken into pieces

grated zest and juice of 1 orange

1 tsp powdered gelatine

2 eggs, separated

300 ml (½ pint) double cream, whipped until thick

DECORATION

300 ml (½ pint) double or whipping cream, whipped until thick

strips of orange zest, blanched

DEEP 23 CM (9 IN) SPRINGFORM CAKE TIN

1 Lightly butter the tin and line the bottom with baking parchment. Make the sponge (see box, right).

2 Bake the sponge in a preheated oven at 180°C (350°F, Gas 4) for 40–45 minutes until the sponge is well risen and beginning to shrink away from the sides of the tin. Turn out on to a wire rack, peel off the lining paper, and leave to cool.

3 Cut the cake in half horizontally. Put one half back into the clean tin.

4 Make the mousse: put the chocolate into a heatproof bowl set over a pan of hot water. Heat gently, stirring occasionally, until the chocolate has melted. Leave to cool slightly.

5 Strain the orange juice into a small heatproof bowl and sprinkle over the gelatine. Leave for 3 minutes or until spongy, then stand the bowl in a saucepan of gently simmering water for 3 minutes or until the gelatine has dissolved.

6 Stir the egg yolks and orange zest into the cooled chocolate. Slowly stir in the dissolved gelatine, then fold in the whipped cream. In a separate bowl, whisk the egg whites until stiff but not dry, then gently fold into the chocolate mixture until well blended.

7 Pour the mousse on top of the cake layer in the tin. Put the remaining cake layer on top. Cover and chill in the refrigerator until the mousse filling is set.

8 Remove the side of the tin and slide the cake on to a serving plate. Decorate with cream and orange zest.

Making the sponge

Combine the eggs and sugar in a large bowl and whisk with an electric mixer at high speed until the mixture is pale and thick enough to leave a trail on itself when the whisk is lifted out.

Sift the flour and cocoa powder over the surface.

Fold in the flour and cocoa until blended.

Turn the mixture into the prepared tin and tilt to level the surface.

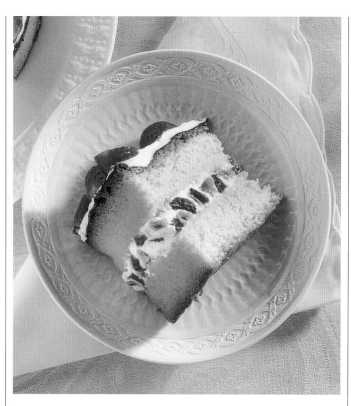

WIMBLEDON CAKE

CUTS INTO 8 SLICES

butter for greasing

3 eggs

90 g (3 oz) caster sugar

90 g (3 oz) self-raising flour

FILLING AND TOPPING

300 ml (½ pint) whipping cream, whipped until thick

125 g (4 oz) strawberries, sliced

1 passion fruit, halved

strawberries, halved, to decorate

2 x 18 CM (7 IN) SANDWICH CAKE TINS

1 Lightly butter the cake tins, line the bottoms with baking parchment, then butter the parchment.

2 Put the eggs and sugar into a large bowl. Whisk with an electric mixer at high speed until the mixture is pale and thick enough to leave a trail when the whisk is lifted out.

3 Sift in half of the flour and fold in gently. Repeat with the remaining flour.

4 Divide the mixture between the tins. Tilt to spread the mixture evenly.

5 Bake in a preheated oven at 190°C (375°F, Gas 5) for 20–25 minutes until well risen, golden, and beginning to shrink away from the sides of the tins. Turn out on to a wire rack, peel off the lining paper, and leave to cool.

6 Spread half of the whipped cream over 1 of the sponges. Top with the sliced strawberries and passion fruit pulp. Put the other sponge on top and press down gently.

7 Spread the remaining cream on top of the cake, smoothing it neatly with a palette knife. Decorate with strawberry halves.

SWISS ROLL

CUTS INTO 8 SLICES

butter for greasing

4 large eggs

125 g (4 oz) caster sugar, plus extra for sprinkling

125 g (4 oz) self-raising flour

icing sugar for sprinkling

FILLING

about 4 tbsp raspberry jam

23 x 33 CM (9 x 13 IN) SWISS ROLL TIN

1 Lightly butter the Swiss roll tin, line with baking parchment, then lightly butter the parchment.

2 Put the eggs and sugar into a large bowl. Whisk together with an electric mixer at high speed until the mixture is pale and thick enough to leave a trail when the whisk is lifted out.

3 Sift the flour into the egg mixture and fold in gently but thoroughly.

4 Turn the mixture into the prepared tin and tilt to spread the mixture evenly, particularly into the corners.

5 Bake in a preheated oven at 220°C (425°F, Gas 7) for 10 minutes or until the sponge is golden and starting to shrink away from the side of the tin.

6 Invert the sponge on to a large piece of baking parchment which has been liberally sprinkled with caster sugar. Peel off the lining paper and trim the edges of the sponge with a sharp knife.

7 Roll up the sponge and the baking parchment together, from one of the short ends. Leave to stand for 2–3 minutes.

8 Unroll the sponge, and remove the baking parchment. Spread the sponge with warmed jam and roll up again. Wrap tightly in baking parchment and leave to cool. Unwrap, dust with icing sugar, and serve in slices.

SMALL CHOCOLATE CAKES

All chocolate cakes are irresistible, but these chocolate brownies, cup cakes, and muffins look twice as tempting as a large cake, and they're quicker and easier to make too. The muffins are at their very best eaten warm, and the cup cakes will keep fresh for a day or two. Brownies will last longer, and will even improve with keeping for a day or so, stored in an airtight container.

BEST-EVER BROWNIES

MAKES 24

375 g (12 oz) plain chocolate, broken into pieces

250 g (8 oz) baking margarine

2 tsp instant coffee

2 tbsp hot water

2 eggs

250 g (8 oz) caster sugar

1 tsp vanilla essence

90 g (3 oz) self-raising flour

175 g (6 oz) walnut pieces

250 g (8 oz) plain chocolate chips

1 Grease a 30 x 23 cm (12 x 9 in) roasting tin, line the base with greaseproof paper, and grease the paper.

2 Put the chocolate and margarine in a bowl and sit the bowl on top of a small saucepan of gently simmering water. Melt the chocolate slowly, then remove the bowl from the pan and let the chocolate cool.

3 Put the coffee in another bowl, pour in the hot water, and stir to dissolve. Add the eggs, sugar, and vanilla essence. Gradually beat in the chocolate mixture. Fold in the flour and walnuts, then the chocolate chips.

4 Pour the mixture into the prepared tin and bake in a preheated oven at 190°C (375°F, Gas 5) for about 40–45 minutes or until firm to the touch. Don't overcook – the crust should be dull and crisp, but the middle may still be gooey. Leave to cool in the tin, then cut into 24 pieces.

Cook's know-how

For brownies to be good they must not be overcooked. The secret is to take them out of the oven just before you think they are done – the middle should be soft and squidgy, not set firm. Do not worry if there is a dip in the middle and a crack on top, this is how it should be, and you will find the mixture firms up on cooling.

CHOCOLATE CUP CAKES

MAKES 24

40 g (1½ oz) cocoa powder

about 4 tbsp boiling water

3 eggs

175 g (6 oz) baking margarine

175 g (6 oz) caster sugar

115 g (4½ oz) self-raising flour

1 rounded tsp baking powder

ICING

60 g (2 oz) butter

30 g (1 oz) cocoa powder

about 3 tbsp milk

250 g (8 oz) icing sugar

2 x 12-HOLE MUFFIN TINS AND 24 PAPER CASES

1 Line two 12-hole muffin tins with paper cases. Sift the cocoa powder into a bowl, pour in the boiling water, and mix into a thick paste. Add the remaining cake ingredients and mix with an electric hand whisk (or beat well with a wooden spoon).

2 Divide the mixture equally between the 24 paper cases. Bake in a preheated oven at 200°C (400°F, Gas 6) for about 10 minutes until well risen and springy to the touch. Cool in the cases on a wire rack.

3 Make the icing. Melt the butter, then pour it into a bowl. Sift in the cocoa powder and stir to mix. Stir in the milk and then sift in the icing sugar a little at a time to make a glossy, spreadable icing. Spread the icing over the cakes and leave to set before serving.

DOUBLE-CHOCOLATE MUFFINS

MAKES 12

2 eggs, lightly beaten

125 g (4 oz) plain yogurt

125 ml (4 fl oz) strong brewed coffee

125 ml (4 fl oz) milk

250 g (8 oz) self-raising flour, sifted

250 g (8 oz) caster sugar

75 g (2½ oz) cocoa powder

pinch of salt

100 g (3½ oz) plain chocolate chips

melted butter for greasing

12-HOLE MUFFIN TIN

1 Combine the eggs, yogurt, coffee, and milk in a large bowl.

2 Sift together the flour, sugar, cocoa powder, and salt, and stir into the milk mixture. Mix well. Stir in the chocolate chips.

3 Butter each cup of the muffin tin, then spoon in the muffin mixture, filling the cups almost to the tops.

4 Bake the muffins in a preheated oven at 200°C (400°F, Gas 6) for about 10 minutes; reduce the oven temperature to 180°C (350°F, Gas 4), and continue to bake for about 15 minutes until the muffins are golden and firm. Serve warm.

CLOCKWISE FROM TOP LEFT: Double-chocolate Muffins, Best-ever Brownies, Chocolate Cup Cakes.

VICTORIA SANDWICH CAKE

CUTS INTO 8 SLICES

175 g (6 oz) soft butter or margarine, plus extra for greasing

175 g (6 oz) caster sugar

3 eggs

175 g (6 oz) self-raising flour

1 1/2 tsp baking powder

FILLING

4 tbsp raspberry or strawberry jam

caster sugar for sprinkling

2 x 18 cm (7 in) sandwich tins

1 Lightly grease the tins and line the bottoms with baking parchment.

2 Combine all the cake ingredients in a large bowl. Beat well for about 2 minutes until smooth.

3 Divide the mixture between the prepared tins and level the surfaces. Bake in a preheated oven at 180°C (350°F, Gas 4) for about 25 minutes or until the cakes are well risen, golden, and springy to the touch.

4 Turn out on to a wire rack, peel off the lining paper, and leave to cool.

5 Sandwich the 2 cakes together with jam and sprinkle the top of the cake with caster sugar.

LEMON SANDWICH CAKE

Add the finely grated zest of 1 lemon to the cake ingredients before beating. Sandwich the cakes together with lemon curd and 150 ml (1/4 pint) whipping cream, whipped until thick. Dust with sifted icing sugar.

Cook's know-how

For a special occasion, sandwich the cakes together with low-fat soft cheese or mascarpone, sweetened with caster sugar to taste and beaten until light and fluffy with the pulp and seeds of 2 passionfruit. Dust the top of the cake with caster sugar or sifted icing sugar.

ICED LIME TRAYBAKE

MAKES 12 SQUARES

175 g (6 oz) soft butter or margarine, plus extra for greasing

175 g (6 oz) caster sugar

250 g (8 oz) self-raising flour

1 1/2 tsp baking powder

3 eggs

3 tbsp milk

finely grated zest of 2 limes

ICING

250 g (8 oz) icing sugar

juice of 2 limes

23 x 30 cm (9 x 12 in) cake tin

1 Lightly grease the tin and line the bottom with baking parchment.

2 Combine all the cake ingredients in a large bowl and beat well for about 2 minutes or until smooth and thoroughly blended.

3 Turn into the prepared tin and level the surface. Bake in a preheated oven at 180°C (350°F, Gas 4) for 35–40 minutes until the cake is well risen, springy to the touch, and beginning to shrink away from the sides of the cake tin.

4 Leave to cool slightly in the tin, then turn out on to a wire rack, peel off the lining paper, and cool.

5 Make the icing: sift the icing sugar into a bowl. Mix in enough of the lime juice to give a runny consistency. Pour over the cooled cake, spreading carefully with a palette knife, and leave to set. When cold, cut into squares and serve.

CHOCOLATE & MINT TRAYBAKE

Mix 4 tbsp cocoa powder with 4 tbsp hot water and leave to cool. Add to the basic cake ingredients with 4 tbsp chopped fresh mint. For the icing, break 250 g (8 oz) plain dark chocolate into pieces and put into a heatproof bowl with 90 g (3 oz) butter and 4 tbsp hot water. Put the bowl over a saucepan of hot water and heat gently until the chocolate has melted. Beat together until smooth and shiny, then spread over the top of the cooled cake.

BATTENBURG CAKE

CUTS INTO 8 SLICES

125 g (4 oz) soft butter or margarine, plus extra for greasing

125 g (4 oz) caster sugar

2 large eggs

60 g (2 oz) ground rice

125 g (4 oz) self-raising flour

1/2 tsp baking powder

a few drops of vanilla essence

1 1/2 tsp cocoa powder

3 tbsp apricot jam

250 g (8 oz) almond paste

SHALLOW 18 CM (7 IN) SQUARE CAKE TIN

1 Lightly grease the cake tin with butter. Line the bottom of the tin with baking parchment.

2 Beat the butter, sugar, eggs, ground rice, flour, baking powder, and vanilla essence in a large bowl for 2 minutes or until the mixture is smooth and evenly combined.

3 Spoon half of the mixture into one half of the prepared tin. Dissolve the cocoa in a little hot water to make a thick paste and add to the remaining cake mixture in the bowl. Mix well, then spoon into the other half of the tin.

4 Bake the mixture in a preheated oven at 160°C (325°F, Gas 3) for 35 minutes or until the cake is well risen and springy to the touch. Turn out on to a wire rack, peel off the lining paper, and cool.

5 Trim the edges of the cake. Cut it into 4 equal strips down the length of the 2 colours.

6 Warm the apricot jam in a small saucepan. Stack the cake strips, alternating the colours to give a chequerboard effect and sticking them together with the apricot jam.

7 Roll out the almond paste into an oblong that is the same length as the cake and wide enough to wrap around it. Put the cake on top, then brush with jam. Wrap the paste around the cake (see box, below).

8 Score the top with a criss-cross pattern and crimp the edges with your fingertips to make a decorative effect.

Wrapping the cake

Wrap the almond paste around the cake, pressing it on gently and making the join in 1 corner. Turn to hide the join.

RICH FRUIT CAKE

CUTS INTO 10 SLICES

250 g (8 oz) soft butter or margarine, plus extra for greasing

250 g (8 oz) light muscovado sugar

4 eggs

250 g (8 oz) self-raising flour

250 g (8 oz) raisins

250 g (8 oz) sultanas

125 g (4 oz) glacé cherries, halved and rinsed

1/2 tsp ground mixed spice

1 tbsp brandy

DEEP 20 CM (8 IN) ROUND CAKE TIN

1 Lightly grease the tin and line the bottom with greaseproof paper.

2 Combine all the ingredients in a large bowl and mix well until combined. Turn the mixture into the prepared cake tin and level the surface.

3 Bake in a preheated oven at 140°C (275°F, Gas 1) for 2–2 1/4 hours. Cover the top of the cake with foil after about 1 hour to prevent the top becoming too brown.

4 When cooked, the cake should be firm to the touch and a fine skewer inserted in the middle of the cake should come out clean. Leave the cake to cool in the tin before turning out. Store in an airtight container.

MINCEMEAT BUNS

MAKES 32

375 g (12 oz) mincemeat

250 g (8 oz) currants

2 eggs

150 g (5 oz) caster sugar

150 g (5 oz) soft butter or margarine

250 g (8 oz) self-raising flour

32 PAPER CAKE CASES

1 Combine all the ingredients in a large bowl and beat well for about 2 minutes.

2 Divide the cake mixture evenly among the paper cases, putting them into bun tins if preferred.

3 Bake in a preheated oven at 160°C (325°F, Gas 3) for 25–30 minutes until golden and springy to the touch. Transfer the cases to a wire rack and leave to cool.

Cook's know-how

Mincemeat is traditionally made with beef suet. If you want a vegetarian version, use vegetable suet or grated chilled butter. Home-made mincemeat is best, but you can improve on commercial ones by adding finely chopped nuts, angelica, dried apricots, peaches, or pears.

SIMNEL CAKE

This is now a traditional Easter cake, but originally it was given by girls to their mothers on Mothering Sunday. The almond paste balls represent the 11 disciples of Christ, excluding Judas Iscariot.

CUTS INTO 12 SLICES

175 g (6 oz) soft butter or margarine, plus extra for greasing

175 g (6 oz) light muscovado sugar

3 eggs

175 g (6 oz) self-raising flour

175 g (6 oz) sultanas

90 g (3 oz) currants

90 g (3 oz) glacé cherries, quartered, rinsed, and dried

30 g (1 oz) candied peel, roughly chopped

grated zest of 1 large lemon

1 tsp ground mixed spice

FILLING AND DECORATION

500 g (1 lb) almond paste

2 tbsp apricot jam

1 egg white

DEEP 18 CM (7 IN) ROUND LOOSE-BOTTOMED CAKE TIN

1 Roll out one-third of the almond paste. Using the base of the cake tin as a guide, cut out an 18 cm (7 in) round.

2 Grease the cake tin and line the bottom and side with greaseproof paper.

3 Combine all the cake ingredients in a bowl. Beat well until thoroughly blended. Spoon half of the cake mixture into the prepared tin and smooth the surface. Top with the round of almond paste.

4 Spoon the remaining cake mixture on top and level the surface.

5 Bake in a preheated oven at 150°C (300°F, Gas 2) for 2¼ hours or until golden brown and firm to the touch.

6 Cover the top of the cake with greaseproof paper if it is browning too quickly. Leave to cool for 10 minutes, then remove from the tin, and leave to cool completely.

7 Warm the jam and use to brush the top of the cake.

8 To decorate the cake, roll out half of the remaining almond paste and use the tin to cut out an 18 cm (7 in) round. Put on top of the jam and crimp the edges. Roll the remaining almond paste into 11 even-sized balls. Place around the edge of the cake, attaching them with egg white.

9 Brush the tops of the balls and the almond paste with egg white. Place under a hot grill for 1–2 minutes, until the balls are golden.

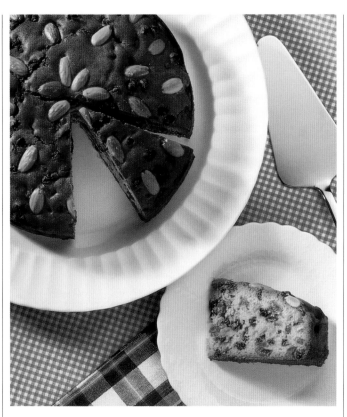

FRUITY BANANA BREAD

CUTS INTO 12 SLICES

125 g (4 oz) butter or margarine, plus extra for greasing

250 g (8 oz) self-raising flour

175 g (6 oz) caster sugar

125 g (4 oz) sultanas

60 g (2 oz) walnuts, roughly chopped

125 g (4 oz) glacé cherries, quartered, rinsed, and dried

2 large eggs, beaten

500 g (1 lb) bananas, weight with peel, peeled and mashed

1 KG (2 LB) LOAF TIN

1 Grease the loaf tin and line the bottom with greaseproof paper.

2 Put the flour into a bowl, add the butter, and rub in with the fingertips until the mixture resembles fine breadcrumbs. Mix in the caster sugar, sultanas, chopped walnuts, and glacé cherries.

3 Add the eggs and mashed bananas and beat the mixture until well blended. Spoon into the prepared tin.

4 Bake in a preheated oven at 160°C (325°F, Gas 3) for about 1 1/4 hours until well risen and firm to the touch. A fine skewer inserted into the middle of the loaf should come out clean.

5 Leave the loaf to cool slightly in the tin, then turn out on to a wire rack, and peel off the lining paper. Leave the loaf to cool completely before slicing and serving.

Cook's know-how

If you like, you can add some grated lemon zest or 1 tsp ground mixed spice to the mixture, for extra flavouring.

DUNDEE CAKE

CUTS INTO 12 SLICES

150 g (5 oz) butter, at room temperature, plus extra for greasing

150 g (5 oz) light muscovado sugar

3 eggs

250 g (8 oz) plain flour

1 tsp baking powder

175 g (6 oz) sultanas

90 g (3 oz) currants

90 g (3 oz) raisins

60 g (2 oz) glacé cherries, quartered, rinsed, and dried

60 g (2 oz) chopped mixed candied peel

2 tbsp ground almonds

grated zest of 1 large lemon

60 g (2 oz) whole almonds, blanched and halved, to decorate

DEEP 20 CM (8 IN) ROUND LOOSE-BOTTOMED CAKE TIN

1 Lightly butter the cake tin and line the bottom with greaseproof paper.

2 Combine the butter, sugar, eggs, flour, and baking powder in a bowl and beat for 2 minutes or until well blended. Stir in the fruit, mixed peel, ground almonds, and lemon zest.

3 Spoon the mixture into the prepared tin. Level the surface and arrange the halved almonds neatly in concentric circles on top.

4 Bake in a preheated oven at 160°C (325°F, Gas 3) for 1 1/2 hours or until well risen, golden, and firm to the touch. A fine skewer inserted into the middle of the cake should come out clean. Cover the cake with foil halfway through baking if it is browning too quickly.

5 Leave the cake to cool in the tin for a few minutes, then turn out on to a wire rack and leave to cool completely. Store in an airtight container for about 1 week before eating.

CHRISTMAS CAKES

One of the focal points of Christmas is a specially decorated cake. As rich fruit cake is usually eaten over a period of days, the decoration should be as attractive and long-lasting as possible. The picture shows two different presentation ideas – Candied Fruit Cake (above) and Snow White Cake (below). Each is easy to adapt according to available ingredients and personal taste.

RICH FRUIT CAKE

CUTS INTO ABOUT 30 SLICES

425 g (14 oz) currants

250 g (8 oz) sultanas

250 g (8 oz) raisins

300 g (10 oz) glacé cherries, quartered, rinsed, and dried

150 g (5 oz) ready-to-eat dried apricots, snipped into small pieces

75 g (2½ oz) mixed candied peel, roughly chopped

4 tbsp brandy, plus extra for soaking

300 g (10 oz) plain flour

1 tsp ground mixed spice

½ tsp grated nutmeg

300 g (10 oz) soft butter, plus extra for greasing

300 g (10 oz) dark muscovado sugar

5 eggs

60 g (2 oz) whole unblanched almonds, roughly chopped

1 tbsp black treacle

finely grated zest of 1 large lemon

finely grated zest of 1 large orange

DEEP 23 CM (9 IN) ROUND OR 20 CM (8 IN) SQUARE CAKE TIN

1 Combine the fruit and candied peel in a large bowl. Add the brandy, and stir to mix well. Cover and leave overnight.

2 Put the remaining ingredients into a large bowl and beat well with an electric mixer until thoroughly blended. Stir in the soaked fruits and any liquid.

3 Grease the cake tin with margarine, line the bottom and sides with a double layer of greaseproof paper, and grease the paper. Spoon the mixture into the prepared tin. Level the surface and cover the top of the cake with greaseproof paper.

4 Bake in a preheated oven at 140°C (275°F, Gas 1) for 4¾–5 hours until firm to the touch and a skewer inserted into the middle of the cake comes out clean. Leave the cake to cool in the tin.

5 When the cake has cooled, pierce it in several places with a fine skewer and pour over a little brandy. Remove the cake from the tin, but leave the lining paper on. Wrap the cake in more greaseproof paper, then overwrap with foil. Store the cake in a cool place for up to 3 months, to mature, unwrapping and spooning over more brandy (1–2 tbsp) occasionally.

6 Decorate the cake with glacé fruit, almond paste, or ready-to-use icing (see box, right). Tie a ribbon around the cake, if wished.

CAKE DECORATIONS

Whichever cake you choose, you need to melt and sieve about 90 g (3 oz) apricot jam before you apply any of the decorations or icing. The jam prevents the cake from drying out and suppresses any crumbs.

CANDIED FRUIT CAKE

This looks most dramatic if it is made in a square tin. Brush the jam over the top of the cake and then arrange nuts and whole or sliced candied fruits and peel in a decorative pattern while the jam is still warm and sticky. Glaze with more jam and leave until set firmly in place before tying a ribbon around the sides of the cake.

SNOW WHITE CAKE

Brush the jam over the top and sides of the cake. Roll out the marzipan and use it to cover the cake completely, then smooth it in place with your hands and trim off any excess. Let the marzipan dry out for a few days before covering with royal icing. Use a palette knife to rough up the icing into peaks, immediately after you have spread it all over the cake. If you are using bought decorations for the top of the cake (here, silver dragees and fresh cranberries), you need to gently press them in before the icing sets hard.

MARZIPAN (ALMOND PASTE)

MAKES ENOUGH FOR A 23 CM (9 IN) ROUND OR 20 CM (8 IN) SQUARE CAKE

250 g (8 oz) ground almonds

250 g (8 oz) caster sugar

250 g (8 oz) icing sugar, sifted

6 drops of almond essence

about 4 egg yolks, or about 2 whole eggs

1 Mix the ground almonds in a bowl with the two different types of sugar until evenly combined. Lightly beat together the essence and egg yolks or whole eggs. Add almost all of this mixture to the dry ingredients and mix together until a stiff paste forms; it is best to do this with your hands. Add the remaining egg if needed so that the mixtures comes together well.

2 Dust a flat surface lightly with icing sugar, turn out the mixture onto it, and knead with your hands to make a stiff paste. Take care not to over-knead or the paste will be oily. Wrap in cling film and store in the refrigerator until required.

ROYAL ICING

MAKES ENOUGH FOR A 23 CM (9 IN) ROUND OR 20 CM (8 IN) SQUARE CAKE

2 egg whites

500 g (1 lb) icing sugar, sifted

4 tsp lemon juice

1 Whisk the egg whites in a large bowl lightly with a fork until bubbles begin to form on the surface. Add about half the icing sugar and all of the lemon juice and beat well with a wooden spoon for about 10 minutes until brilliant white.

2 Gradually stir in the remaining icing sugar until the consistency is just right for spreading or piping. If not using immediately, keep the bowl covered with a damp cloth to prevent the icing drying out.

CORNBREAD

MAKES 9 SQUARES

sunflower oil for greasing
175 g (6 oz) polenta or fine yellow cornmeal
125 g (4 oz) plain flour
2–3 tbsp brown sugar
2 tsp baking powder
I tsp salt
300 ml (1/2 pint) lukewarm milk
2 eggs, lightly beaten
60 g (2 oz) butter, melted and cooled slightly
18 CM (7 IN) SQUARE CAKE TIN

1 Lightly oil the cake tin. Put the polenta, flour, sugar, baking powder, and salt into a large bowl and make a well in the middle. Pour in the milk, eggs, and butter, and beat the ingredients to form a batter.

2 Pour the mixture into the cake tin and bake in a preheated oven at 200°C (400°F, Gas 6) for 25–30 minutes until golden. Leave to cool, then cut into squares.

SHORTBREAD

MAKES 8 WEDGES

125 g (4 oz) plain flour
60 g (2 oz) ground rice
125 g (4 oz) butter, plus extra for greasing
60 g (2 oz) caster sugar, plus extra for sprinkling

1 Mix the flour with the ground rice in a bowl. Add the butter and rub in with the fingertips. Stir in the sugar. Knead the mixture lightly until it forms a smooth dough.

2 Lightly butter a baking tray. Roll out the dough on a lightly floured work surface into an 18 cm (7 in) round. Lift on to the baking tray. Crimp the edges to decorate, prick all over with a fork, and mark into 8 wedges with a sharp knife. Chill until firm.

3 Bake in a preheated oven at 160°C (325°F, Gas 3) for 35 minutes or until a pale golden brown colour. Mark the wedges again and sprinkle the shortbread with sugar.

4 Allow the shortbread to cool on the baking tray for about 5 minutes, then lift off carefully with a palette knife and transfer to a wire rack to cool completely. Cut into wedges to serve.

GINGERBREAD

MAKES 15 SQUARES

250 g (8 oz) butter or margarine, plus extra for greasing
250 g (8 oz) dark muscovado sugar
250 g (8 oz) black treacle
375 g (12 oz) plain flour
5 tsp ground ginger
2 tsp ground cinnamon
2 eggs, beaten
3 pieces of stem ginger in syrup, drained and roughly chopped
300 ml (1/2 pint) milk
2 tsp bicarbonate of soda
23 × 30 CM (9 × 12 IN) CAKE TIN

1 Lightly grease the tin and line the bottom with greaseproof paper.

2 Heat the butter, sugar, and treacle in a pan, stirring, until smooth. Cool slightly.

3 Sift in the flour and ground spices. Stir well, then beat in the eggs and stem ginger.

4 Warm the milk in a small heavy saucepan, and add the bicarbonate of soda. Pour into the gingerbread mixture and stir gently until thoroughly blended.

5 Pour the mixture into the prepared tin. Bake in a preheated oven at 160°C (325°F, Gas 3) for about 1 hour until well risen and springy to the touch.

6 Leave to cool in the tin for a few minutes, then turn out on to a wire rack, and peel off the paper. Leave to cool completely, then store in an airtight container for 2–3 days (it improves with keeping). Cut into squares to serve.

BARA BRITH

CUTS INTO 12 SLICES

375 g (12 oz) mixed dried fruit
250 g (8 oz) light muscovado sugar
300 ml (1/2 pint) strong hot tea, strained
butter for greasing
300 g (10 oz) self-raising flour
1 egg, beaten
1 KG (2 LB) LOAF TIN

1 Combine the dried fruit, sugar, and hot tea in a large bowl. Stir the mixture, then cover and leave to steep for at least 8 hours.

2 Lightly butter the loaf tin and line the bottom with greaseproof paper. Stir the flour and egg into the dried fruit and tea mixture, mixing thoroughly. Turn the mixture into the loaf tin and level the surface.

3 Bake in a preheated oven at 150°C (300°F, Gas 2) for 1 1/2–1 3/4 hours until well risen and firm to the touch. A fine skewer inserted into the middle should come out clean.

4 Leave to cool in the tin for about 10 minutes, then turn out on to a wire rack, and peel off the lining paper. Leave to cool completely. Serve sliced, and buttered if wished.

Cook's know-how

Mixed dried fruit is steeped in strong tea so that it is moist and well plumped up by the time the bara brith is mixed.

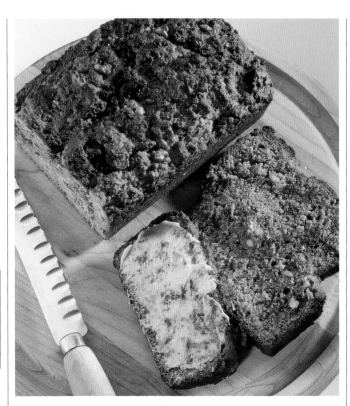

DATE & WALNUT LOAF

CUTS INTO 12 SLICES

90 g (3 oz) soft butter or margarine, plus extra for greasing
250 g (8 oz) dates, stoned and roughly chopped
150 ml (1/4 pint) boiling water
90 g (3 oz) caster sugar
1 egg
250 g (8 oz) self-raising flour
1 tsp baking powder
90 g (3 oz) walnuts, roughly chopped
1 KG (2 LB) LOAF TIN

1 Lightly grease the loaf tin with butter and line with greaseproof paper.

2 Put the dates into a bowl, pour over the measured boiling water, and leave for about 15 minutes.

3 Combine the butter, sugar, egg, flour, and baking powder in a large bowl and beat until well blended. Add the walnuts and dates, plus the soaking liquid, and stir to mix.

4 Spoon into the prepared loaf tin and bake in a preheated oven at 180°C (350°F, Gas 4) for 1 1/4–1 1/2 hours until well risen and firm to the touch. A fine skewer inserted into the middle of the loaf should come out clean.

5 Leave to cool in the loaf tin for a few minutes, then turn out on to a wire rack, and peel off the lining paper. Leave to cool completely. Serve sliced and buttered, if wished.

CHERRY & BANANA LOAF

Omit the dates and walnuts, and add 125 g (4 oz) quartered glacé cherries and 2 mashed large ripe bananas in step 3.

DEVON SCONES

MAKES 12

60 g (2 oz) butter, plus extra for greasing

250 g (8 oz) self-raising flour

2 tsp baking powder

30 g (1 oz) caster sugar

1 egg

about 150 ml (1/4 pint) milk, plus extra for glazing

butter and jam to serve

5 CM (2 IN) PASTRY CUTTER

1 Lightly butter a large baking tray.

2 Sift the flour and baking powder into a bowl. Rub in the butter with the fingertips until the mixture resembles fine breadcrumbs. Stir in the sugar.

3 Break the egg into a measuring jug and make up to 150 ml (1/4 pint) with milk. Beat lightly to mix. Add to the bowl and mix to a soft dough.

4 Lightly knead the dough until smooth. Roll out until 1 cm (1/2 in) thick, cut into rounds with the pastry cutter, and put on the baking tray. Brush with milk.

5 Bake in a preheated oven at 220°C (425°F, Gas 7) for about 10 minutes until risen and golden. Cool on a wire rack. Serve on the day of making, if possible, with butter and jam.

CHEESE SCONES

Omit the sugar, and add 125 g (4 oz) grated mature Cheddar cheese and 1/2 tsp mustard powder to the dry ingredients before mixing in the egg and milk. Roll out the dough into a 15 cm (6 in) round and cut it into wedges. Brush with milk and sprinkle with finely grated cheese. Bake as directed.

WELSH CAKES

MAKES 12

250 g (8 oz) self-raising flour

1 tsp baking powder

125 g (4 oz) butter

90 g (3 oz) caster sugar

90 g (3 oz) currants

1/2 tsp ground mixed spice

1 egg, beaten

about 2 tbsp milk

sunflower oil for greasing

7 CM (3 IN) PASTRY CUTTER

Cook's know-how

If preferred, serve the Welsh cakes hot, lightly sprinkled with sugar, straight from the griddle or frying pan.

1 Sift the flour and baking powder into a large bowl. Add the butter and rub in with the fingertips until the mixture resembles fine breadcrumbs.

2 Add the sugar, currants, and mixed spice, and stir to mix. Add the egg and enough milk to form a soft, but not sticky, dough.

3 On a lightly floured work surface, roll out the dough to a thickness of 5 mm (1/4 in). Cut into rounds with pastry cutter.

4 Heat a flat griddle or a heavy frying pan and grease with a little oil. Cook the Welsh cakes on the hot griddle or pan over a low heat for about 3 minutes on each side until cooked through and golden brown.

5 Leave to cool on a wire rack. Serve on the day of making, if possible.

IRISH SODA BREAD

CUTS INTO 8 WEDGES

500 g (1 lb) plain white flour, plus extra for dusting

1 tsp bicarbonate of soda

1 tsp salt

300 ml (½ pint) buttermilk, or half milk and half plain yogurt

90 ml (3 fl oz) lukewarm water

sunflower oil for greasing

1 Sift the flour, bicarbonate of soda, and salt into a large bowl. Pour in the buttermilk, or milk and yogurt, and the measured water. Mix with a wooden spoon or your hands to form a very soft dough.

2 Lightly oil a baking tray. Turn out the dough on to a lightly floured work surface and shape into a round measuring 18 cm (7 in) in diameter.

3 Place the loaf on the prepared baking tray and cut a deep cross in the top.

4 Bake in a preheated oven at 200°C (400°F, Gas 6) for 30 minutes. Turn the bread over and bake for a further 10 minutes or until the loaf sounds hollow when tapped on the base. Cool on a wire rack. Serve on the day of making.

POTATO FARLS

MAKES 12

175 g (6 oz) plain flour

1 tbsp baking powder

60 g (2 oz) butter, plus extra for greasing

45 g (1½ oz) caster sugar

125 g (4 oz) freshly boiled and mashed potato

3 tbsp milk

1 Sift the flour and baking powder into a bowl. Rub in the butter until the mixture resembles fine breadcrumbs. Stir in the sugar and mashed potato. Add enough milk to bind to a soft, but not sticky, dough.

2 Turn out the dough on to a floured surface and knead lightly until blended. Roll out until 1 cm (½ in) thick and cut into rectangles or triangles.

3 Place the farls on a buttered baking tray and bake in a preheated oven at 220°C (425°F, Gas 7) for 12–15 minutes until risen and golden. Leave to cool on a wire rack. Serve on the day of making.

WHOLEMEAL DROP SCONES

MAKES 20

175 g (6 oz) wholemeal self-raising flour

1 tsp baking powder

45 g (1½ oz) caster sugar

1 large egg

200 ml (7 fl oz) milk

sunflower oil for greasing

golden syrup or butter and jam to serve

1 Combine the flour, baking powder, and sugar in a bowl, and stir to mix. Make a well in the middle of the dry ingredients and add the egg and half of the milk. Beat well to make a smooth, thick batter.

2 Add enough milk to give the batter the consistency of thick cream.

3 Heat a flat griddle or heavy frying pan and grease with oil. Drop spoonfuls of batter on to the hot griddle or pan, spacing them well apart. When bubbles rise to the surface, turn scones over and cook until golden.

4 As each batch is cooked, wrap the scones in a clean tea towel to keep them soft. Serve warm, with syrup or butter and jam.

PLAIN DROP SCONES

Substitute plain self-raising flour for the wholemeal self-raising flour, and use a little less milk.

Cook's know-how

Drop scones are also known as Scotch pancakes. They freeze well if you have any left over. Interleave with freezer wrap or greaseproof paper and freeze for up to 6 months. Warm them through on the griddle before serving.

ALMOND TUILES

MAKES 30

2 egg whites

125 g (4 oz) caster sugar

60 g (2 oz) plain flour

1/2 tsp vanilla essence

60 g (2 oz) butter, melted and cooled

30 g (1 oz) flaked almonds

1 Line a baking tray with baking parchment. Put the egg whites into a bowl and beat in the sugar until frothy. Stir in the flour and vanilla essence, then add the melted butter.

2 Put 6 teaspoonfuls of the mixture on to the baking tray, spacing them well apart to allow for spreading. Flatten each with a fork.

3 Sprinkle with the almonds. Bake in a preheated oven at 180°C (350°F, Gas 4) for about 6 minutes until golden brown around the edges but still pale in the middle.

4 Allow the biscuits to cool on the baking tray for a few seconds, then lift off with a fish slice and gently lay them over a greased rolling pin to give the traditional curved shape.

5 Allow the biscuits to set, then lift off on to a wire rack and leave to cool.

6 Cook and shape the remaining mixture in batches, cooking one batch while another is setting on the rolling pin.

Cook's know-how

These dainty, crisp biscuits take their name from the French word for roof tiles, which is tuiles (in France the tiles on rooves are often curved). If you are short of time, omit the shaping in step 4, and just leave them to cool flat on the wire rack.

VIENNESE FINGERS

MAKES 12

175 g (6 oz) butter, plus extra for greasing

60 g (2 oz) caster sugar

175 g (6 oz) self-raising flour

90 g (3 oz) plain dark chocolate, broken into pieces

1 Lightly butter 2 baking trays. Combine the butter and sugar in a bowl and cream together until pale and fluffy. Stir in the flour and beat until well combined.

2 Spoon the mixture into a piping bag with a medium star nozzle. Pipe into 7 cm (3 in) lengths on the baking trays. Bake in a preheated oven at 160°C (325°F, Gas 3) for about 20 minutes until golden. Cool on a wire rack.

3 Put the chocolate into a heatproof bowl. Set the bowl over a pan of hot water and heat gently until the chocolate has melted. Dip both ends of each biscuit into the chocolate. Leave to set on the wire rack.

COCONUT MACAROONS

MAKES 26

3 egg whites

175 g (6 oz) icing sugar

175 g (6 oz) ground almonds

a few drops of almond essence

175 g (6 oz) desiccated coconut

about 13 whole almonds, blanched and halved

1 Line 2 baking trays with baking parchment.

2 Whisk the egg whites thoroughly until stiff but not dry. Sift in the icing sugar and fold it in gently. Fold in the ground almonds, almond essence, and desiccated coconut.

3 Put teaspoonfuls of the coconut mixture on to the baking trays. Top each with an almond half.

4 Bake in a preheated oven at 150°C (300°F, Gas 2) for about 25 minutes until golden brown and crisp on the outside and soft in the middle.

5 Leave the macaroons to cool on a wire rack. Best served on the day of making.

BRANDY SNAPS

MAKES 15

90 g (3 oz) butter

90 g (3 oz) demerara sugar

90 g (3 oz) golden syrup

90 g (3 oz) plain flour

3/4 tsp ground ginger

3/4 tsp lemon juice

1 Line a baking tray with baking parchment.

2 Combine the butter, sugar, and syrup in a saucepan and heat gently until the ingredients have melted and dissolved. Cool slightly, then sift in the flour and ginger. Add the lemon juice and stir well.

3 Place 3–4 teaspoonfuls of the mixture on the baking tray, leaving plenty of room for the biscuits to spread out.

4 Bake in a preheated oven at 160°C (325°F, Gas 3) for about 8 minutes until the mixture spreads out to form large, thin, dark golden rounds. While the biscuits are baking, oil the handles of 4 wooden spoons.

5 Remove the biscuits from the oven and leave for 1–2 minutes to firm slightly.

6 Lift a biscuit from the paper using a fish slice or palette knife, turn the biscuit over so that the rough side is on the outside, and wrap around an oiled wooden spoon handle. Repeat with the remaining biscuits. Transfer to a wire rack and cool until firm. Slip from the spoon handles.

7 Continue baking, shaping, and cooling the remaining mixture in batches.

GINGER SNAPS

MAKES 15

60 g (2 oz) butter, plus extra for greasing

90 g (3 oz) golden syrup

125 g (4 oz) self-raising flour

2 tsp ground ginger

1 tsp ground cinnamon

1/2 tsp bicarbonate of soda

1 tbsp caster sugar

1 Lightly grease 2 baking trays with butter.

2 Combine the butter and golden syrup in a small saucepan and heat gently until melted. Leave the mixture to cool slightly.

3 Sift the flour, spices, and bicarbonate of soda into a bowl, and stir in the sugar. Add the cooled syrup mixture, and stir to mix to a soft but not sticky dough.

4 Roll the dough into balls about the size of walnuts and place well apart on the baking trays. Flatten the dough balls slightly with the heel of your hand.

5 Bake in a preheated oven at 190°C (375°F, Gas 5) for about 15 minutes. Leave the biscuits to cool on the baking trays for a few minutes, then transfer them to a wire rack and leave to cool completely.

FORK BISCUITS

MAKES 32

250 g (8 oz) butter, at room temperature, plus extra for greasing

125 g (4 oz) caster sugar

300 g (10 oz) self-raising flour

1 Lightly grease 2 baking trays with butter.

2 Put the butter into a large bowl and beat with a wooden spoon to soften it. Gradually beat in the caster sugar, then stir in the flour. Use your hands to gather the mixture together into a soft but not sticky dough.

3 Roll the dough into balls about the size of walnuts and place well apart on the baking trays. Dip a fork into cold water and press on top of each ball to flatten it and imprint the fork pattern.

4 Bake in batches in a preheated oven at 180°C (350°F, Gas 4) for 15–20 minutes until the biscuits are a very pale golden colour. Transfer the biscuits from the baking tray to a wire rack and leave to cool completely.

CHOUX PASTRIES

Quite unlike any other pastry, choux is a thick paste that can be piped into any shape you like. Once baked, the light-as-air pastry literally melts in the mouth when it's packed with a creamy filling and topped with icing. These three classic recipes are all-time favourites.

COFFEE ECLAIRS

MAKES 10–12

butter for greasing

1 quantity choux pastry (see box, below)

1 egg, beaten

300 ml (1/2 pint) whipping cream, whipped

COFFEE ICING

1 tsp instant coffee

15 g (1/2 oz) butter

2 tbsp water

90 g (3 oz) icing sugar

1 Butter a baking tray and sprinkle with water. Spoon the choux into a piping bag fitted with a 1 cm (1/2 in) plain nozzle, pipe into 7 cm (3 in) lengths and brush with beaten egg. Bake in a preheated oven at 220°C (425°F, Gas 7) for 10 minutes, then bake at 190°C (375°F, Gas 5) for 20 minutes. Split in half and cool on a rack.

2 Spoon the whipped cream into the bottom halves of the éclairs.

3 Make the icing: put the coffee, butter, and water in a bowl over a pan of water. Heat gently until the butter melts. Remove from the heat and beat in the icing sugar. Dip the top half of each eclair in the icing, then place on top of the cream. Leave the icing to cool before serving.

CHOCOLATE PROFITEROLES

MAKES 12

butter for greasing

1 quantity choux pastry (see box, below)

1 egg, beaten

300 ml (1/2 pint) whipping cream, whipped

WICKED CHOCOLATE ICING

150 g (5 oz) plain chocolate, chopped

150 ml (1/4 pint) double cream

1 Butter a baking tray and sprinkle with water. Put 12 tablespoonfuls of choux on the tray and brush with beaten egg. Bake in a preheated oven at 220°C (425°F, Gas 7) for 10 minutes, then bake at 190°C (375°F, Gas 5) for 20 minutes. Split each profiterole in half and cool on a rack.

2 Make the wicked chocolate icing: gently melt the chocolate with the double cream in a bowl over a pan of simmering water, stirring until smooth and shiny (take care not to let it get too hot).

3 Sandwich the profiteroles together with the whipped cream, place on individual plates, and drizzle with the chocolate icing.

RELIGIEUSES

MAKES 10

butter for greasing

1 quantity choux pastry (see box, below)

1 egg, beaten

300 ml (1/2 pint) whipping cream, whipped

1 quantity warm Wicked Chocolate Icing (left)

1 Butter a baking tray and sprinkle with water. Spoon the choux into a piping bag fitted with a 1 cm (1/2 in) plain nozzle, pipe 10 small and 10 slightly larger balls, and brush with beaten egg. Bake in a preheated oven at 220°C (425°F, Gas 7) for 10 minutes, then bake at 190°C (375°F, Gas 5) for 20 minutes. Split one side of each bun and cool on a rack.

2 Reserve about 3 tbsp of the whipped cream. Fill the balls with the remaining whipped cream, spooning it in the sides.

3 Dip the tops of a large and small ball in icing. Fit a piping bag with a 1 cm (1/2 in) star nozzle and pipe the reserved cream on top of the large ball. Gently press the small ball on top of the cream, with the icing facing up. Repeat with the other balls.

CLOCKWISE FROM TOP LEFT: **Coffee Eclairs, Religieuses, Chocolate Profiteroles.**

BASIC CHOUX PASTRY

1 Put 60 g (2 oz) butter, cut into cubes, into a heavy saucepan with 150 ml (1/4 pint) water and heat until the butter melts. Bring to a boil.

2 Remove from the heat and add 75 g (2 1/2 oz) sifted plain flour and a pinch of salt, if preferred. Stir vigorously until the mixture forms a soft ball.

3 Leave to cool slightly, then gradually add 2 lightly beaten eggs, beating well between each addition, to form a smooth, shiny paste.

FLAPJACKS

MAKES 24

125 g (4 oz) butter, plus extra for greasing

90 g (3 oz) golden syrup

90 g (3 oz) light muscovado sugar

250 g (8 oz) rolled oats

ROASTING TIN OR SHALLOW CAKE TIN, ABOUT 20 X 30 CM (8 X 12 INS)

1 Lightly butter the roasting tin or cake tin.

2 Combine the butter, syrup, and sugar in a saucepan and heat gently until the ingredients have melted and dissolved. Stir in the oats and mix well.

3 Spoon into the prepared tin and smooth the surface with a palette knife. Bake in a preheated oven at 180°C (350°F, Gas 4) for about 30 minutes.

4 Leave to cool in the tin for about 5 minutes, then mark into 24 fingers. Leave to cool completely, then cut and remove from the tin.

FRIDGE COOKIES

MAKES 50

250 g (8 oz) plain flour

1 tsp baking powder

125 g (4 oz) butter, plus extra for greasing

175 g (6 oz) caster sugar

60 g (2 oz) walnuts, finely chopped

1 egg, beaten

1 tsp vanilla essence

1 Sift the flour and baking powder into a bowl. Rub in the butter with the fingertips until the mixture resembles breadcrumbs. Mix in the sugar and walnuts. Add the beaten egg and vanilla essence, and stir to form a smooth dough.

2 Shape the dough into a cylinder about 5 cm (2 in) in diameter. Wrap in foil, roll to give smooth sides, and refrigerate for about 8 hours.

3 Lightly butter several baking trays. Cut the cylinder into thin slices and place the biscuits on the baking trays. Bake in a preheated oven at 190°C (375°F, Gas 5) for 10–12 minutes until golden.

PINWHEEL BISCUITS

MAKES 18

VANILLA DOUGH

60 g (2 oz) butter, at room temperature

30 g (1 oz) caster sugar

90 g (3 oz) plain flour

a few drops of vanilla essence

about 1 tbsp water

COFFEE DOUGH

60 g (2 oz) butter, at room temperature

30 g (1 oz) caster sugar

90 g (3 oz) plain flour

1 tbsp coffee essence

milk for brushing

1 Combine the ingredients for the vanilla dough in a bowl and mix well, adding just enough water to bind. Knead lightly, then wrap and chill for at least 2 hours until very firm.

2 Mix the ingredients for the coffee dough, using the coffee essence to bind. Wrap and chill for at least 2 hours until very firm.

3 On a lightly floured work surface, roll out each dough to a rectangle about 18 x 25 cm (7 x 10 in).

4 Brush the coffee dough with a little milk, then place the vanilla dough on top. Roll up together like a Swiss roll, starting at a narrow end.

5 Wrap the roll tightly in foil and leave to chill in the refrigerator for about 30 minutes or until firm.

6 Lightly grease 1–2 baking trays. Cut the dough roll into about 18 thin slices and place them well apart on the baking trays.

7 Bake in a preheated oven at 180°C (350°F, Gas 4) for about 20 minutes until the vanilla dough is a very pale golden colour.

8 Leave the biscuits to cool on the baking trays for a few minutes, then lift off on to a wire rack and leave to cool completely.

Cook's know-how

If the doughs become too soft and difficult to roll out, put each piece of dough between sheets of greaseproof paper before rolling.

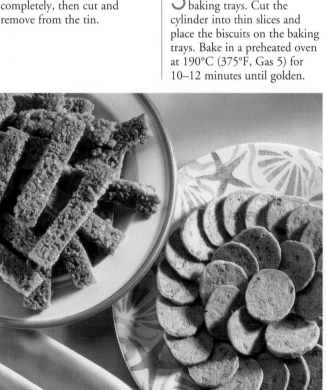

COOK'S NOTES

All the recipes in this book have been carefully tested to ensure that they produce successful results. When selecting a dish, shopping for ingredients, and making a recipe at home, bear in mind the following essential points.

- Use either all metric or all imperial measurements. Metric and imperial measurements are not interchangeable, so never combine the two.
- Tablespoons are 15 ml, and teaspoons are 5 ml. Spoon measurements are always level unless otherwise stated.
- Eggs are medium unless otherwise stated.
- To replace fresh herbs with dried, substitute 1 teaspoon dried herbs for 1 tablespoon chopped fresh herbs.
- Always preheat the oven before the food goes in to ensure successful results. Recipes in this book have been tested (where appropriate) in a preheated oven.

- No two ovens are alike, so temperatures and cooking times may need to be adjusted to suit your oven. For fan-assisted ovens, lower the temperature according to the manufacturer's instructions.
- When a dish is cooked in the oven, always use the middle shelf unless otherwise stated.
- Calorie counts are approximate and given for guidance only.
- Serving suggestions and accompaniments given with the recipes are optional, for guidance only, and are not included in the calorie counts.

CONVERSION TABLES

LINEAR MEASURES

METRIC	IMPERIAL
5 mm	¼ in
1 cm	½ in
2.5 cm	1 in
5 cm	2 in
7 cm	3 in
10 cm	4 in
12 cm	5 in
15 cm	6 in
18 cm	7 in
20 cm	8 in
23 cm	9 in
25 cm	10 in
28 cm	11 in
30 cm	12 in

VOLUME

METRIC	IMPERIAL
125 ml	4 fl oz
150 ml	¼ pint
175 ml	6 fl oz
250 ml	8 fl oz
300 ml	½ pint
350 ml	12 fl oz
400 ml	14 fl oz
450 ml	¾ pint
500 ml	16 fl oz
550 ml	18 fl oz
600 ml	1 pint
750 ml	1¼ pints
900 ml	1½ pints
1 litre	1¾ pints

WEIGHT

METRIC	IMPERIAL
15 g	½ oz
30 g	1 oz
60 g	2 oz
90 g	3 oz
125 g	4 oz
175 g	6 oz
250 g	8 oz
300 g	10 oz
375 g	12 oz
400 g	13 oz
425 g	14 oz
500 g	1 lb
750 g	1½ lb
1 kg	2 lb

OVEN TEMPERATURES

CELSIUS	FAHRENHEIT	GAS	DESCRIPTION
110°	225°	¼	Cool
120°	250°	½	Cool
140°	275°	1	Very slow
150°	300°	2	Very slow
160°	325°	3	Slow
180°	350°	4	Moderate
190°	375°	5	Moderate
200°	400°	6	Moderately hot
220°	425°	7	Hot
230°	450°	8	Hot
240°	475°	9	Very hot

INDEX

P

538

RECIPE NOTES

PAGE NO	RECIPE NAME	COMMENTS

PAGE NO	RECIPE NAME	COMMENTS

ACKNOWLEDGMENTS

AUTHOR'S ACKNOWLEDGMENTS
For the first edition, I would like to thank Fiona Oyston for her expertise in writing and testing recipes, and for all her hard work helping me produce the book. I would also like to thank managing editor Gillian Roberts for help in preparing the second edition.

PUBLISHER'S ACKNOWLEDGMENTS
The first (1995) edition of this book was created by Carroll & Brown Limited for Dorling Kindersley. Thanks to the following people for their help:
Editorial consultant Jeni Wright
Project editor Vicky Hanson
Editors Jo-Anne Cox, Stella Vayne, Anne Crane, Sophie Lankenau, Trish Shine
Cookery consultants Valerie Cipollone & Anne Hildyard
Art editors Louise Cameron & Gary Edgar-Hyde
Designers Alan Watt, Karen Sawyer, Lucy De Rosa
Photography David Murray & Jules Selmes
Assisted by Nick Allen & Sid Sideris
Production Wendy Rogers & Amanda Mackie
Food preparation Eric Treuille, Annie Nichols, Cara Hobday, Sandra Baddeley, Elaine Ngan
Assisted by Maddalena Bastianelli Sarah Lowman
Additional recipes/Contributors Marlena Spieler, Sue Ashworth, Louise Pickford, Cara Hobday, Norma MacMillan, Anne Gains
Nutritional consultant Anne Sheasby

The second (2003) edition of this book was created by Dorling Kindersley. Thanks to the following people for their help:
Editorial contributor Norma MacMillan
Editorial assistance Hugh Thompson
DK Picture Library Claire Bowers & Charlotte Oster
DK India Dipali Singh (project editor), Kajori Aikat (editor), Romi Chakraborty (project designer), Rashmi Battoo (designer), Narender Kumar, Rajesh Chibber, Nain Singh Rawat (all DTP), Ira Pande (managing editor), Aparna Sharma (managing art editor)
Nutritional consultant Wendy Doyle
Index Helen Smith
Loan of props Villeroy & Boch (+44 (0) 20 8871 0011), Thomas Goode & Co. (+44 (0) 20 7499 2823), Chomett (+44 (0) 20 8877 7000)

All images © Dorling Kindersley
Discover more at www.dkimages.com
DK Images is part of the Pearson Asset Library